Lecture Notes in Computer Science 13450

More information about this series at https://link.springer.com/bookseries/558

Isabel Hilliger · Pedro J. Muñoz-Merino ·
Tinne De Laet · Alejandro Ortega-Arranz ·
Tracie Farrell (Eds.)

Educating for a New Future: Making Sense of Technology-Enhanced Learning Adoption

17th European Conference
on Technology Enhanced Learning, EC-TEL 2022
Toulouse, France, September 12–16, 2022
Proceedings

Springer

Editors
Isabel Hilliger
Pontificia Universidad Católica de Chile
Santiago, Chile

Pedro J. Muñoz-Merino
Universidad Carlos III de Madrid
Madrid, Spain

Tinne De Laet
KU Leuven
Leuven, Belgium

Alejandro Ortega-Arranz
Universidad de Valladolid
Valladolid, Spain

Tracie Farrell
The Open University
Milton Keynes, UK

ISSN 0302-9743 ISSN 1611-3349 (electronic)
Lecture Notes in Computer Science
ISBN 978-3-031-16289-3 ISBN 978-3-031-16290-9 (eBook)
https://doi.org/10.1007/978-3-031-16290-9

This Springer imprint is published by the registered company Springer Nature Switzerland AG
The registered company address is: Gewerbestrasse 11, 6330 Cham, Switzerland

Preface

Welcome to the proceedings of the 17th European Conference on Technology Enhanced Learning (EC-TEL 2022) - one of the flagship events of the European Association of Technology Enhanced Learning (EATEL). Due to the restrictions imposed by the COVID-19 pandemic, EC-TEL 2020 and 2021 were held in an online format. However, EC-TEL 2022 was able to be held in person in Tolouse, France, and was hosted by the Institut de Recherche en Informatique de Toulouse during September 12–16, 2022.

In addition to the restrictions of hosting EC-TEL 2022 as an in-person event, the COVID-19 pandemic generated further challenges concerning technology-enhanced learning. In order to avoid the spread of the virus, many educational institutions rapidly shifted to remote learning activities. This derived to an intensive use of educational technologies without necessarily having the required capacities. Still, best practices and lessons learned can be captured by looking back to what happened during that period of time. In this context, researchers and practitioners who are involved in the design and implementation of technology enhanced learning (TEL) not only have the responsibility of understanding the consequences of the pandemic in terms of TEL adoption, but also the opportunity to evaluate and improve the learning processes at an institutional level.

In this context, the conference topic for EC-TEL 2022 was "Educating for a new future: Making sense of technology-enhanced learning adoption". In the past two decades, many educational technologies emerged and evolved along with the growing attention for 'the Web' and 'the Internet'. Throughout this road, researchers and practitioners have designed and implemented different types of strategies, tools, services, and devices to improve learning for a wide range of students. Many studies have been carried out by our community to describe promising technologies, which underpin and benefit multiple educational contexts around the world. However, never before have we seen the increased mainstream adoption of educational technologies observed since the outbreak of the COVID-19 pandemic. The current context gives rise to several questions such as: What is the purpose of education in the current context of societal transformation? How do learning technologies support this new purpose? How do we ensure that technology is a means to make education more inclusive? In case of another similar situation, will institutions, teachers and students be more prepared for this rapid shift to full digital situation (electronic administration, teaching, etc.)? In that sense, this EC-TEL conference provides us with an opportunity to search for answers to some of these questions, and to explore different topics concerning the future of education.

For EC-TEL 2022, 109 research paper contributions were received. All papers were reviewed by at least three members of the TEL community in a double-blind review process, followed by discussions and a meta-review provided by a senior TEL member. As a result, 30 research papers (27.5%) were accepted and presented at the conference. In addition, 21 posters and 10 demos were presented during the conference to fuel the discussions among the researchers. Research, poster, and demo papers can be found in this volume. In addition, the conference offered seven workshops over two days and a doctoral consortium.

We would like to thank all people involved for making this conference possible particularly authors who submitted their contributions to the conference. Thanks also to the members of the Program Committee who provided reviews on papers, discussed them and supported decision making on paper acceptance. We would like to thank the workshop chairs, Sergey Sosnovsky and Patricia Santos; the dissemination chair, Yizhou Fan; the doctoral consortium chairs, Mikhail Fominykh, Ioana Jivet, Jan Schneider, Daniele Di Mitri, and Zacharoula Papamitsiou; and the steering committee representative, Ralf Klamma. We would also like to thank the local organizers, Mar Pérez-Sanagustín and Julien Broisin, for their hard and excellent work for EC-TEL 2022.

July 2022

Isabel Hilliger
Pedro J. Muñoz-Merino
Tinne De Laet
Alejandro Ortega-Arranz
Tracie Farrell

Organization

General Chair

Tinne De Laet	KU Leuven, Belgium

Program Committee Chairs

Isabel Hilliger	Pontificia Universidad Católica de Chile, Chile
Pedro J. Muñoz-Merino	Universidad Carlos III de Madrid, Spain

Poster/Demo Chairs

Alejandro Ortega-Arranz	Universidad de Valladolid, Spain
Tracie Farrell	The Open University, UK

Workshop Chairs

Sergey Sosnovsky	Utrecht University, The Netherlands
Patricia Santos	Universitat Pompeu Fabra, Spain

Dissemination Chair

Yizhou Fan	The University of Edinburgh, UK

Doctoral Symposium Chairs

Mikhail Fominykh	Norwegian University of Science and Technology, Norway
Ioana Jivet	DIPF, Germany
Jan Schneider	DIPF, Germany
Daniele Di Mitri	DIPF, Germany
Zacharoula Papamitsiou	SINTEF, Norway

Local Organization Chairs

Mar Pérez Sanagustín	Institute Recherche Technology de Toulouse, France
Julien Broisin	Institute Recherche Technology de Toulouse, France

Steering Committee Representative

Ralf Klamma	RWTH Aachen University, Germany

Program Committee

Mohsin Abbas	The Open University, The Netherlands
Marie-Helene Abel	Université de Technologie de Compiègne, France
Andrea Adamoli	Università della Svizzera italiana, Italy
Nora'Ayu Ahmad Uzir	Universiti Teknologi MARA, Malaysia
Carlos Alario-Hoyos	Universidad Carlos III de Madrid, Spain
Hamed Alavi	University of Amsterdam, The Netherlands
Patricia Albacete	University of Pittsburgh, USA
Laia Albó	Universitat Pompeu Fabra, Spain
Vincent Aleven	Carnegie Mellon University, USA
Liaqat Ali	Simon Fraser University, Canada
Cristina Alonso-Fernández	Universidad Complutense de Madrid, Spain
Ainhoa Álvarez	University of the Basque Country, UPV/EHU, Spain
Héctor Amado-Salvatierra	Universidad Galileo, Guatemala
Ishari Amarasinghe	Universitat Pompeu Fabra, Spain
Roberto Araya	Universidad de Chile, Chile
Maria Aristeidou	The Open University, UK
Juan I. Asensio-Pérez	Universidad de Valladolid, Spain
Nikolaos Avouris	University of Patras, Greece
Antonio Balderas	University of Cádiz, Spain
Nicolas Ballier	Université de Paris Cité, France
Jordan Barria-Pineda	University of Pittsburgh, USA
Sabine Barthold	TU Dresden, Germany
Jason Bernard	McMaster University, Canada
Anis Bey	Annaba University, Algeria
Lars Birch	Aalborg University, Denmark
Geoffray Bonnin	Université de Lorraine, France
Miguel L. Bote-Lorenzo	Universidad de Valladolid, Spain
François Bouchet	Sorbonne Université - LIP6, France
Yolaine Bourda	CentraleSupélec, France
Anne Boyer	University of Lorraine, France
Bert Bredeweg	University of Amsterdam, The Netherlands
Andreas Breiter	Universität Bremen, Germany
Gert Breitfuss	evolaris next level GmbH, Austria
Julien Broisin	Université Toulouse 3 Paul Sabatier, France
Armelle Brun	Université de Lorraine, France
Ilona Buchem	Beuth University, Germany

Daniela Caballero	McMaster University, Canada
Manuel Caeiro Rodríguez	University of Vigo, Spain
Agustín Caminero	Universidad Nacional de Educación a Distancia, Spain
Lorenzo Cantoni	Università della Svizzera italiana, Italy
Manuel Castro	Universidad Nacional de Educacion a Distancia, Spain
Teresa Cerratto-Pargman	Stockholm University, Sweden
Mohamed Chatti	University of Duisburg-Essen, Germany
Pankaj Chejara	Tallinn University, Estonia
Henrique Chevreux	Universidad Austral de Chile, Chile
Sunhea Choi	University of Southampton, UK
Irene-Angelica Chounta	University of Duisburg-Essen, Germany
Ruth Cobos	Universidad Autónoma de Madrid, Spain
Miguel Ángel Conde	University of León, Spain
John Cook	Frankfurt University, Germany
Audrey Cooke	Curtin University, Australia
Catalina Cortázar	Pontificia Universidad Catolica de Chile, Chile
Mayela Coto	Universidad Nacional, Costa Rica
Mutlu Cukurova	University College London, UK
Mihai Dascalu	University Politehnica of Bucharest, Romania
Sophia Daskalaki	University of Patras, Greece
Tinne De Laet	Katholieke Universiteit Leuven, Belgium
Felipe de Morais	Unisinos, Brazil
Inge de Waard	EIT InnoEnergy, Belgium
Carlos Delgado Kloos	Universidad Carlos III de Madrid, Spain
Stavros Demetriadis	Aristotle University of Thessaloniki, Greece
Carrie Demmans Epp	University of Alberta, Canada
Michael Derntl	University of Tübingen, Germany
Philippe Dessus	LaRAc, Université Grenoble Alpes, France
Daniele Di Mitri	Leibniz Institute for Research and Information in Education, Germany
Darina Dicheva	Winston-Salem State University, USA
Yannis Dimitriadis	University of Valladolid, Spain
Vania Dimitrova	University of Leeds, UK
Monica Divitini	Norwegian University of Science and Technology, Norway
Chaitali Diwan	International Institute of Information Technology Bangalore, India
Juan Manuel Dodero	Universidad de Cádiz, Spain
Hendrik Drachsler	Leibniz Institute for Research and Information in Education, Germany

Benedict du Boulay	University of Sussex, UK
Anastasios Economides	University of Macedonia, Greece
Erkan Er	Middle East Technical University, Turkiye
Maka Eradze	University of Foggia, Italy
Alejandro Fernández	Universidad Nacional de La Plata, Argentine
Baltasar Fernández-Manjon	Universidad Complutense de Madrid, Spain
Rafael Ferreira	Cesar School, Brazil
Angela Fessl	Graz University of Technology, Austria
Anna Filighera	Technical University of Darmstadt, Germany
Olga Firssova	Open University of the Netherlands, The Netherlands
Mikhail Fominykh	Norwegian University of Science and Technology, Norway
Rolf Fricke	Condat AG, Germany
Thomas Gaillat	Université de Rennes 2, France
Félix J. García Clemente	Universidad de Murcia, Spain
Francisco J. García Peñalvo	University of Salamanca, Spain
Jesús Miguel García-Gorrostieta	Universidad de la Sierra, Mexico
Javier García-Zubia	Universidad de Deusto, Spain
Dragan Gašević	Monash University, Australia
Sheridan Gentili	University of South Australia, Australia
Sébastien George	Le Mans Université, France
Michail Giannakos	Norwegian University of Science and Technology, Norway
Carlo Giovannella	University of Tor Vergata, Italy
Eduardo Gómez-Sánchez	Universidad de Valladolid, Spain
Samuel González-López	Technological University of Nogales, Sonora, México
Julián Iñaki Goñi	Pontificia Universidad Católica de Chile, Chile
Bernhard Göschlberger	Research Studios Austria, Austria
Sabine Graf	Athabasca University, Canada
Monique Grandbastien	Universite de Lorraine, France
Wolfgang Greller	Vienna University of Education, Austria
David Griffiths	UNIR-iTED, Spain
Julio Guerra	University of Pittsburgh, USA
Nathalie Guin	LIRIS - Université de Lyon, France
Franziska Günther	TU Dresden, Germany
Nicolás Felipe Gutiérrez Páez	Universitat Pompeu Fabra, Spain
Christian Gütl	Graz University of Technology, Austria
Gabriel Gutu-Robu	University Politehnica of Bucharest, Romania
Joerg Haake	FernUniversitaet in Hagen, Germany
Bastiaan Heeren	Open University, The Netherlands

Valeria Henríquez	Universidad Austral de Chile, Chile
Eelco Herder	Utrecht University, The Netherlands
Ángel Hernández-García	Universidad Politécnica de Madrid, Spain
Davinia Hernández-Leo	Universitat Pompeu Fabra, Spain
Ana Isabel Hibert	The University of Edinburgh, UK
Isabel Hilliger Carrasco	Pontificia Universidad Católica de Chile, Chile
Tore Hoel	Oslo Metropolitan University, Norway
Teresa Holocher-Ertl	Centre for Social Innovation, Austria
Peter Holtz	Leibniz Insitut für Wissensmedien Tübingen, Germany
Adrian Holzer	University of Neuchâtel, Switzerland
Sharon Hsiao	Santa Clara University, USA
Pasquale Iero	The Open University, UK
Francisco Iniesto	The Open University, UK
Andri Ioannou	Cyprus University of Technology, Cyprus
Halszka Jarodzka	Open University of the Netherlands, The Netherlands
Johan Jeuring	Utrecht University, The Netherlands
Ioana Jivet	Goethe University Frankfurt & DIPF, Germany
Srecko Joksimovic	University of South Australia, Australia
Pedro Jose Muñoz Merino	Universidad Carlos III de Madrid, Spain
Jelena Jovanovic	University of Belgrade, Serbia
Rogers Kaliisa	University of Oslo, Norway
Marco Kalz	Heidelberg University of Education, Germany
Anastasios Karakostas	Aristotle University of Thessaloniki, Greece
Reet Kasepalu	Tallinn University, Estonia
Mohammad Khalil	University of Bergen, Norway
Zaheer Khan	University of the West of England Bristol, UK
Michael Kickmeier-Rust	Graz University of Technology, Austria
Ralf Klamma	RWTH Aachen University, Germany
Styliani Kleanthous	Open University of Cyprus and CYENS Centre of Excellence, Cyprus
Roland Klemke	Open University of the Netherlands, The Netherlands
Tomaž Klobučar	Jozef Stefan Institute, Slovenia
Anders Kluge	University of Oslo, Norway
Külli Kori	Tallinn University, Estonia
Panagiotis Kosmas	University of Nicosia, Cyprus
Vitomir Kovanovic	The University of South Australia, Australia
Dominik Kowald	Know-Center, Graz University of Technology, Austria
Milos Kravcik	DFKI GmbH, Germany

Karel Kreijns	Open Universiteit/Fontys University of Applied Sciences, The Netherlands
Birgit Krogstie	Norwegian University of Science and Technology, Norway
Agnes Kukulska-Hulme	The Open University, UK
Mart Laanpere	Tallinn University, Estonia
Elise Lavoué	Université Jean Moulin Lyon 3, LIRIS, France
Marie Lefevre	LIRIS - Université Lyon 1, France
Dominique Lenne	Heudiasyc, Université de Technologie de Compiègne, France
Marina Lepp	University of Tartu, Estonia
Tobias Ley	Tallinn University, Estonia
Amna Liaqat	University of Toronto, Canada
Paul Libbrecht	IUBH Fernstudium, Germany
Andreas Lingnau	Ruhr West University of Applied Science, Germany
Martin Llamas-Nistal	University of Vigo, Spain
Aurelio López-López	INAOE, Mexico
Domitile Lourdeaux	CNRS, France
Margarida Lucas	University of Aveiro, Portugal
Vanda Luengo	Sorbonne Université, France
Piret Luik	University of Tartu, Estonia
Kris Luyten	Hasselt University, Belgium
George Magoulas	Birkbeck College, University of London, UK
Katherine Maillet	Institut Polytechnique de Paris, Télécom SudParis, France
Nils Malzahn	Rhine-Ruhr Institute for Applied System Innovation e.V., Germany
Estefanía Martin	Universidad Rey Juan Carlos, Spain
Alejandra Martínez-Monés	Universidad de Valladolid, Spain
Iratxe Menchaca	University of Deusto, Spain
Agathe Merceron	Berliner Hochschule für Technik, Germany
Vasileios Mezaris	Centre for Research and Technology Hellas, Greece
Christine Michel	Techne, France
Konstantinos Michos	University of Zurich, Switzerland
Alexander Mikroyannidis	The Open University, UK
Constanza Miranda	Johns Hopkins University, USA
Tanja Mitrovic	University of Canterbury, New Zealand
Riichiro Mizoguchi	Japan Advanced Institute of Science and Technology, Japan
Miguel Morales	Universidad Galileo, Guatemala
Anders Morch	University of Oslo, Norway

Pedro Manuel Moreno-Marcos	Universidad Carlos III de Madrid, Spain
Jorge Muñoz-Gama	Pontificia Universidad Católica de Chile, Chile
Juan A. Muñoz-Cristóbal	Universidad de Valladolid, Spain
Rob Nadolski	Open University of the Netherlands, The Netherlands
Stavros Nikou	University of Strathclyde, UK
Nicolae Nistor	Ludwig Maximilian University of Munich, Germany
Alexander Nussbaumer	Graz University of Technology, Austria
Xavier Ochoa	New York University, USA
Alejandro Ortega-Arranz	Universidad de Valladolid, Spain
Viktoria Pammer-Schindler	Graz University of Technology, Austria
Sofia Papavlasopoulou	Norwegian University of Science and Technology, Norway
Abelardo Pardo	University of South Australia, Australia
Ronald Pérez-Álvarez	Universidad de Costa Rica, Costa Rica
Mar Pérez-Sanagustín	Université Paul Sabatier Toulouse III, France
Yvan Peter	Université de Lille, France
Niels Pinkwart	Humboldt-Universität zu Berlin, Germany
Gerti Pishtari	University for Continuing Education Krems, Austria
Hans Põldoja	Tallinn University, Estonia
Elvira Popescu	University of Craiova, Romania
Eyal Rabin	The Open University of Israel, Israel
Juliana Elisa Raffaghelli	University of Padua, Italy
Eric Ras	Luxembourg Institute of Science and Technology, Luxembourg
Marc Rittberger	Leibniz Institute for Research and Information in Education, Germany
Tiago Roberto Kautzmann	Universidade do Vale do Rio dos Sinos, Brazil
Gregorio Robles	Universidad Rey Juan Carlos, Spain
Covadonga Rodrigo	Universidad Nacional de Educación a Distancia, Spain
M. Fernanda Rodríguez Palma	Universidad Finis Terrae, Chile
M. Cristina Rodríguez-Sánchez	Universidad Rey Juan Carlos, Spain
José A. Ruipérez Valiente	University of Murcia, Spain
Nikol Rummel	Ruhr-Universität Bochum, Germany
Merike Saar	Tallinn University, Estonia
Demetrios Sampson	Curtin University, Australia
Teresa Sancho-Vinuesa	Universitat Oberta de Catalunya, Spain
Olga C. Santos	Universidad Nacional de educación a Distancia, Spain
Patricia Santos	Universitat Pompeu Fabra, Spain

Mohammed Saqr	University of Eastern Finland, Finland
Petra Sauer	Beuth University of Applied Sciences, Germany
Maren Scheffel	Ruhr University Bochum, Germany
Daniel Schiffner	Leibniz Institute for Research and Information in Education, Germany
Andreas Schmidt	Karlsruhe University of Applied Sciences, Germany
Marcel Schmitz	Zuyd Hogeschool, The Netherlands
Jan Schneider	Leibniz Institute for Research and Information in Education, Germany
Ulrik Schroeder	RWTH Aachen University, Germany
Yann Secq	Université de Lille, France
Karim Sehaba	LIRIS CNRS, France
Audrey Serna	LIRIS, INSA Lyon, France
Sergio Serrano-Iglesias	Universidad de Valladolid, Spain
Shashi Kant Shankar	Tallinn University, Estonia
Kshitij Sharma	Norwegian University of Science and Technology, Norway
Bernd Simon	Knowledge Markets Consulting, Austria
Andrzej M. J. Skulimowski	AGH University of Science and Technology, Poland
Maxim Skyrabin	Skryabin.PRO, Russia
Alan Smeaton	Dublin City University, Ireland
Sergey Sosnovsky	Utrecht University, The Netherlands
Marcus Specht	Delft University of Technology, The Netherlands
Srinath Srinivasa	International Institute of Information Technology Bangalore, India
Tim Steuer	Technical University of Darmstadt, Germany
Alexander Streicher	Fraunhofer IOSB, Germany
Bernardo Tabuenca	Universidad Politécnica de Madrid, Spain
Stefano Tardini	Università della Svizzera italiana, Italy
Ali Tarhini	Sultan Qaboos Univeristy, Oman
Marco Temperini	Sapienza University of Rome, Italy
Stefan Thalmann	University of Graz, Austria
Paraskevi Topali	Universidad de Valladolid, Spain
Richard Tortorella	University of North Texas, USA
Stefan Trausan-Matu	University Politehnica of Bucharest, Romania
Andrea Vázquez-Ingelmo	University of Salamanca, Spain
Guillermo Vega-Gorgojo	Universidad de Valladolid, Spain
J. Ángel Velázquez-Iturbide	Universidad Rey Juan Carlos, Spain
Rémi Venant	Le Mans Université, France
Olga Viberg	KTH Royal Institute of Technology, Norway

Markel Vigo	The University of Manchester, UK
Ignacio Villagran	Pontificia Universidad Católica de Chile, Chile
Massimo Vitiello	Graz University of Technology, Austria
Joshua Weidlich	Leibniz Institute for Research and Information in Education, Germany
Denise Whitelock	The Open University, UK
Fridolin Wild	Open University, The Netherlands
Jacqueline Wong	TU Delft, The Netherlands

Contents

Who are My Peers? Learner-Controlled Social Comparison in a Programming Course

Kamil Akhuseyinoglu[1](✉), Aleksandra Klasnja Milicevic[2], and Peter Brusilovsky[1]

[1] University of Pittsburgh, Pittsburgh, PA, USA
{kaa108,peterb}@pitt.edu
[2] University of Novi Sad, Novi Sad, Serbia
akm@dmi.uns.ac.rs

Abstract. Studies of technology-enhanced learning (TEL) environments indicated that learner behavior could be affected (positively or negatively) by presenting information about their peer groups, such as peer in-system performance or course grades. Researchers explained these findings by the social comparison theory, competition, or by categorizing them as an impact of gamification features. Although the choice of individual peers is explored considerably in recent TEL research, the effect of learner control on peer-group selection received little attention. This paper attempts to extend prior work on learner-controlled social comparison by studying a novel fine-grained peer group selection interface in a TEL environment for learning Python programming. To achieve this goal, we analyzed system usage logs and questionnaire responses collected from multiple rounds of classroom studies. By observing student actions in selecting and refining their peer comparison cohort, we understand better whom the student perceives as their peers and how this perception changes during the course. We also explored the connection between their peer group choices and their engagement with learning content. Finally, we attempted to associate student choices in peer selection with several dimensions of individual differences.

Keywords: Learner control · Social comparison · Open learner model · Computer science education · Self-regulated learning · Online learning

1 Introduction

Over the last ten years, social comparison approaches have become an essential component of modern online learning tools. Researchers explored social comparison in various forms, such as leaderboards [21], comparative progress visualization [2], learning analytics dashboards [25], and socially-enhanced open learner modeling interfaces [5]. These social comparison approaches demonstrated their

I. Hilliger et al. (Eds.): EC-TEL 2022, LNCS 13450, pp. 1–15, 2022.
https://doi.org/10.1007/978-3-031-16290-9_1

ability to increase learners' participation and contributions [26], help learners navigate more efficiently [16], and improve completion rates in MOOCs [8]. However, the studies on social comparison also demonstrated that it could provide no effect [8] or even negative effect for some groups of learners [19,23]. For example, high-performing learners were not affected by social comparison based on class average [8], while learners exposed to perfect peer performance exhibited declined success and increased drop rate [23]. These findings suggested that mismatches in selecting peer comparison groups could neutralize or negate the positive impact of social comparison. On the other hand, social psychology research states that comparison to similar peers strengthens the positive effect of social comparison [6].

To address the need for a proper peer group selection in social comparison, recent research explored the value of learner control over social comparison features, i.e., allowing learners to choose their peer comparison group [1]. While existing research reported positive results, the explored learner control options were quite limited: Instead of comparing themselves to the whole class, learners could choose the upper or lower part of the class as their peer groups. This paper explores the value of a more advanced interface for fine-grained learner control over social comparison in a Technology-Enhanced Learning (TEL) environment for learning Python programming. This interface allows a learner to choose precisely a segment of the class as the peer comparison group. As an added value, the freedom of choice provided by this interface offers an opportunity to examine how learners identify a segment of a class as their comparison peers. Then, we investigated how these comparison preferences relate to engagement and which factors cause variance in peer-group selections, such as achievement goals and social comparison orientation.

2 Social Comparison in Python Grids

We explored learner-controlled social comparison in a *practice system* designed for Python programming called Python Grids (PG) [1]. For this study, the PG interface was augmented with fine-grained learner-controlled social comparison features. This section reviews the components of the PG: content access interface with learner-controlled social comparison features and the set of available interactive learning tools.

2.1 The Content Access Interface

In the PG, an Open Social Learner Modeling (OSLM) interface [20] (Fig. 1[B-D]) provides access to a set of Python learning content. The interface helps students decide what they need to work on and how much they need to practice freely. In this context, the ability to track personal and peer progress becomes critical to encourage students to practice more and guide them to the most relevant practice content. This ability is the core component of this interface.

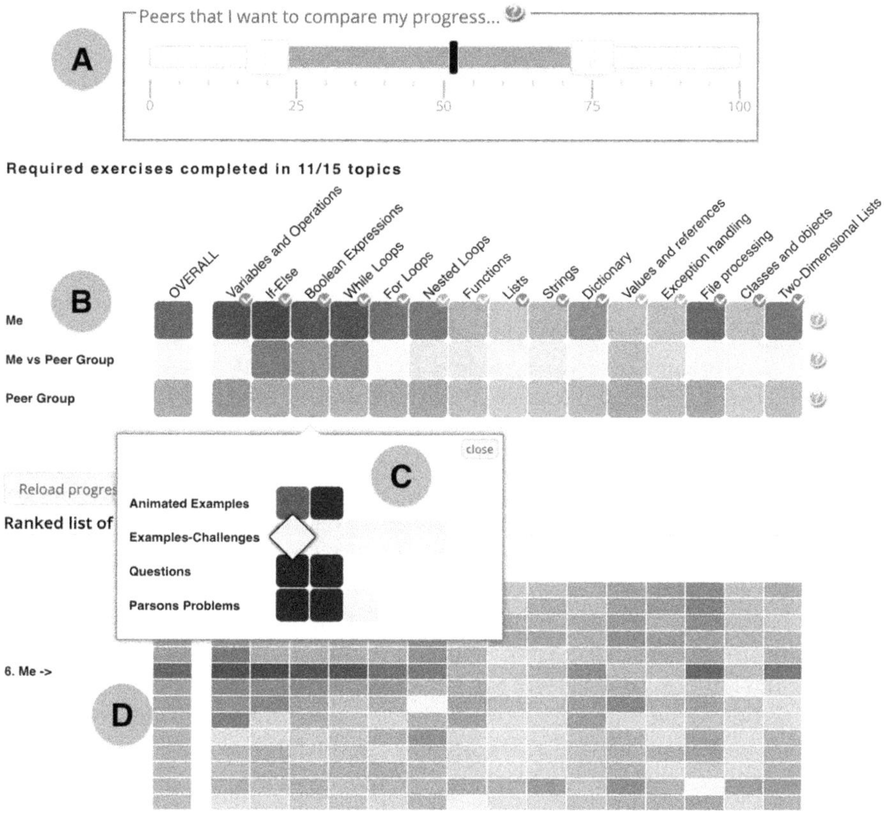

Fig. 1. The PG interface with fine-grained controllable social comparison features (A), OSLM grid (B), a set of learning activities (C), and anonymized ranked list (D).

The columns of the OSLM grid (Fig. 1B) organize the learning content into 15 topics. The rows in the grid visualize the topic-by-topic progress of the student and the comparison peer group while making it easy to compare them to one another. The first row of the grid summarizes the topic-level progress of a learner using a green color of different density. The third row displays an aggregated average progress level of students in the selected comparison peer group (Fig. 1A) using a blue color. The middle *comparison* row presents the progress difference between the learner and the currently selected peer group. The green-colored topics in the middle row represent the topics where the learner is ahead of the comparison group. In contrast, the blue-colored topics show the topics where the comparison group is ahead of the student. In all cases, the darker color indicates a higher level of progress (or progress difference) for that topic. By clicking on a specific topic column, a student accesses the learning content available for this topic. Similar to the topic-level progress visualization, the PG also visualizes content-level progress using the green color density (Fig. 1C). The progress of a topic or content is computed as the ratio of completed activities associated with the topic or content.

2.2 Learner-Control over Social Comparison

In our recent study [1], we explored some options for learner control, but these options were limited, i.e., a learner could compare herself to the upper or lower half of the class in addition to viewing the average progress of the whole class and anonymized ranked list of learners in the class (Fig. 1D). For the current study, we augmented the interface with fine-grained control of the peer comparison group through the comparison slider widget (Fig. 1A). The 0–100 progress scale represents all students in a class ranked by their current total progress in the PG from a student with the lowest progress (marked as 0) to the student with the highest progress (marked as 100). Within this range, each student could set the target comparison group using two sliders. The handles on the comparison slider define the minimum and maximum progress range of the comparison group within the class, i.e., the group that average progress is visualized by the bottom row of the PG interface (Fig. 1B) and which is shown in the anonymized ranked list in detail (Fig. 1D).

In the beginning, the peer group is placed in the middle of the class with the sliders set to the 25–75 range. At any time, the student can change the peer group by moving the handles or dragging the *cyan* colored segment between the handles (i.e., comparison group bar). After each change, the progress visualization in the PG interface and the ranked list are updated accordingly to show only students in the selected peer group. To help students in choosing the peer group, their own relative progress within the class is shown as a red cursor. Note that student progress is automatically displayed by the system and the position of the red cursor could move within the slider widget as the student standing in the class changes. In contrast, the selection of the peer group, i.e., the position of sliders, is fully controlled by students. Altogether, this interface offers students full freedom in deciding who their comparison peers are, i.e., how wide the group is, how far from the bottom of the class it starts, how close to the top of the class it ends, and how it is positioned in relation to student's own progress ranking.

2.3 Learning Activities

Once students decide to practice on a specific topic in the PG, they can "open" a topic and examine the available learning activities by clicking on the topic column. In each topic, the PG provided access to two types of *examples* and two types of *problems* for learning Python programming. Figure 1C shows the practice contents available for the topic of *Boolean Expressions*. Content items are shown as squares organized by the four content types. Example content types include *Animated examples* and *Examples-Challenges*. Animated examples [24] provide interactive visualization of the code execution. Examples-Challenges [15] consist of a single worked example that allows students to examine a solution to a coding problem and one or more "challenge" activities that ask students to

Table 1. Summary of practice with the learning content (N = 122).

	Mean (%)	SD	Med
Number of sessions	8.66 (-)	6.26	7
Unique content accesses	99.5 (41%)	65.5	89.5
Unique questions and Parsons attempted	41.1 (51%)	24.0	41.5
Unique challenges, animated examples worked examples attempted/viewed	58.4 (36%)	47.7	53

find the missing code lines from a set of options. *Questions* and *Parson's problems* are the problem types. Questions [17] are parameterized exercises that test student comprehension of program execution by asking to predict the output of a given program. Finally, Parson's problems [22] are code construction exercises in which students must arrange code lines in the correct order. In this study, students accessed 243 unique content: 81 problems (47 questions and 34 Parsons problems) and 162 examples (39 animated examples, 52 worked examples, and 71 challenges).

3 Research Methodology

3.1 Study Context

We conducted the study with 174 undergraduate students during multiple offerings of an introductory programming course at a large Australian university. The course was delivered online during the study due to the Covid-19 pandemic. The course does not assume any previous programming experience and covers programming fundamentals, including input and output, decision structures, loops, functions, data structures, file I/O, exceptions, and object-oriented programming concepts. One coordinator and two other instructors taught the course using the same syllabus, course materials, and grading policy. The passing grade is 50%, which students must collect through assignments (30%), a project (40%), and class participation (30%). By solving one Question and one Parson's problem for each of the 15 topics in the PG, i.e., 30 problems (37% of the problems in the system), students could receive up to 10% practice credit as a part of the class participation. The practice with the example content types was not counted for the credit. The blue checkmarks on each topic column in Fig. 1B highlight the topics where the student fulfilled the credit requirement.

3.2 Data Collection

We collected data from four course offerings where we kept the PG the same. There were no significant differences between course offerings in learners' practice behavior in the PPG, including overall engagement and usage of the social comparison control features (e.g., the number of problem-solving attempts and peer group changes). Thus, we combined data from these offerings into a single dataset that includes system usage logs, performance measures, and individual learner differences collected through several standard instruments.

System Usage Logs: The system logs include detailed time-stamped records of practice with all learning activities including attempts to Parson's problems, questions, and challenges, viewing animated and worked examples (see Table 1). The logs also contain social comparison actions such as peer group changes and ranking list views (see Table 2). The system continuously recorded the current state of social comparison preferences, such as the orientation of the comparison group bar and the learner's current rank in the class (i.e., red cursor position).

Performance Measures: In the first week of the class, we administered a pretest and several instruments focused on individual differences. The pretest had ten problems related to various Python programming concepts. Due to minimal participation in the post-test, we only considered course grades as the final performance measure.

Instruments: The social comparison orientation (only the ability factor) was measured by the Iowa-Netherlands Comparison Orientation Measure (INCOM) [14], and the achievement goal orientation framework [12] was applied to measure achievement orientations. Researchers demonstrated that both questionnaires are inter-connected in interpreting students' social comparison choices [4]. In this study, we administered these questionnaires mainly to explore their possible link to the comparison preferences observed in the PG.

In analysis, we used the logs from students who attempted at least one learning activity in the practice system. We only used students who gave their consent for the research study and received a final course grade (i.e., did not withdraw from the course). In total, we analyzed the logs of 122 students.

For questionnaire-based analysis, we filtered out students who selected the same option in all items and responded very quickly (in less than 4 min – 1st quartile is used as the threshold). After the initial filtering process, we analyzed the internal consistency of each scale and included the items with a factor loading of at least 0.5 on the appropriate subscale. For the achievement goal orientation, we found three valid constructs: (1) mastery approach (Cronbach's $\alpha = .61$), (2) mastery avoidance ($\alpha = .77$), and (3) performance orientation ($\alpha = .78$) (both performance avoidance and approach items loaded on the same factor). Further, we validated the social comparison orientation (ability factor) items ($\alpha = .62$). As a final step, we calculated a scale score by calculating the mean scores of the selected items related to a subscale and used these scores in our analysis. Not all students participated in the pretest and questionnaire. As a result, we only used students with the complete data for specific analyses[1].

[1] We had complete data for 53 students (43%), including system logs, course grades, pretest, achievement orientation, and social comparison orientation scores.

3.3 Data Analysis Methods

In regression analysis, we checked regression assumptions, including multicollinearity, by calculating the *Variance Inflation Factors (VIF)* and ensuring none of the features had $\sqrt{VIF} > 2$. Then, we performed a backward step-wise feature selection process. We reported regression model results with the features selected by this process. For linear mixed-effects models, we added learner identifier as a random effect which also resolves the non-independence issue of our session-based data. We shared the results of mixed-effects models after confirming that the model fitted better than a random-effect only model using the likelihood ratio test. For count data predictions (e.g., number of learning activities), we used Poisson regression.

3.4 Labeling the Social Comparison Preferences

Researchers have explored the direction of social comparison, i.e., upward and downward comparison (comparing with someone better or worse), to understand the potential effects of social comparison [3,7,10]. Following the prior work, we labeled learners' comparison group changes with a comparison direction to examine their comparison intentions in our analyses.

First, we performed the labeling by checking the absolute position of the selected comparison group on the 0–100 scale (the cyan segment between sliders in Fig. 1A). For the *absolute labeling*, we used the index position of 50 as the fixed reference point, and we labeled the comparison group obtained after each change of sliders by four comparison types: (1) Downward, (2) Upward, (3) Balanced, or (4) Average. Downward/Upward type means that the selected comparison group mainly (or entirely) contains students from the lower-half/higher-half of the class (students below/above the reference point value of 50). The balanced comparison corresponds to the case where the comparison group covers the lower and higher half of the class equally (e.g., the sliders set to the 30–70 range). Lastly, the average type covers the case where the student selected the whole class as the comparison group (i.e., the sliders set to the 0–100 range).

Second, we used the relative position of the comparison group to students' current rank in the class (shown as a red cursor in Fig. 1A) to represent the comparison direction more reasonably. We summarized learners' comparison group selection with a single scalar value for *relative labeling*. This value corresponds to the distance of the learner's current position (i.e., the red cursor) to the midpoint of the selected comparison group (i.e., the cyan segment), and we called this value mid-distance. If this value is below 0, the student's position was lower than the most (or all) of the students in the selected comparison group, i.e., performing a relatively upward social comparison. If it is above 0, the student's position was higher than the most (or all) of the comparison group, indicating a relatively downward social comparison. By using the mid-distance value, we classified each group change as (1) Downward, (2) Upward, (3), or (3) Balanced. This case has no average type since we considered the learner's current position.

Table 2. Summary of social comparison actions and preferences (N = 113).

	M(SD)	Med	Absolute		Relative	
			Upward	Downward	Upward	Downward
Peer group changes	5.7(6.4)	3.0	40%	35%	47%	52%
Ranked list views	4.3(6.6)	2.0	-	-	-	-

4 Results

The focus of our analyses is twofold. First, we want to examine learners' interactions with the social comparison control interface and understand the social comparison preferences they expressed through this interface. Second, we want to examine the association between these preferences and engagement with the practice system. To assure that engagement with the practice system is valuable for learning, we start our analyses by examining the connection between engagement and course performance.

4.1 Engagement with the Python Grids and Course Performance

As shown in Table 1, students extensively used all content types. Notably, they solved significantly more *problems* (Parsons and questions) than the criteria for obtaining the full practice credit (i.e., solving 30 problems) ($t(121) = 5.11, p < .001$), and 71% of them (N = 87) exceeded this threshold. In addition, students practiced with 36% ($M = 58.4$) of the *example* content types, although they were not counted for credit. This data indicated that the students considered the Python Grids (PG) valuable for their learning rather than just a source of credit points.

To assess the relationship between the practice system usage and course performance, we regressed course grades on pretest scores, achievement goal subscale scores, and overall practice amount (i.e., percentage of uniquely accessed learning content). We found a statistically significant regression model ($F(5, 52 = 7.2)$, $adj.R^2 = .35$, $p < .001$) with pretest scores ($B = 5.3, p = .003$), system usage ($B = 15.9, p = .015$), mastery approach ($B = 5.6, p = .004$), and mastery avoidance ($B = 7.5, p < .001$) scores were positively associated with the grades. However, performance orientation was associated with lower course grades ($B = -5.0, p = .011$). Given these results, we observed that working with the practice system was positively associated with higher course grades while keeping prior knowledge and various individual differences constant.

4.2 Social Comparison Preferences

Students used social comparison controls noticeably on average, although the usage differed between students (see Table 2). Most students (83%) used the opportunity to change their comparison peer group at least once ($M = 5.7$).

Similarly, 71% of the students viewed the anonymous ranked list at least once ($M = 4.3$). Also, there was a significant correlation between the number of ranking views and comparison group changes (r = .27, p = .002). Thus, we counted both actions as *social comparison events* in the rest of the analyses.

Following the comparison preference labeling process explained in Sect. 3.4, we could summarize learners' preferences in peer comparison group selection in detail (see Table 2). Out of 639 comparison group changes, 41% of changes were labeled upward, 35% downward, 12% average, and 12% balanced based on the *absolute labeling.* From the *relative labeling* prospect, students preferred downward comparison the most (52%), then upward comparison (47%). Only 1% of the changes were balanced. Thus, according to the absolute labeling, students preferred upward comparison the most. However, the dominance of upward comparison was not present in the relative labeling. This difference might originate from the fact that for high-performing students (e.g., a student at the 5th percentile), there is limited opportunity to perform an upward comparison due to the ceiling effect.

4.3 Social Comparison Events and Engagement

Throughout the semester, learners worked with the practice system in multiple sessions of varying duration and with different intensities. We hypothesized that if social comparison events (i.e., group change and ranking view) influence engagement, we should observe this effect on the total number of learning actions performed in a session (*num-act*), i.e., problem-solving attempts and example views. Thus, we classified all sessions (N = 1057) into two types: those with at least one social comparison event occurred (27%) and those without (73%). Then, we compared the number of learning actions performed in these session types per student. We filtered out students who did not have both types of sessions for this analysis (N = 93). We discovered that students practiced significantly more in sessions when they also performed a social comparison event ($M = 72, Med = 43$) compared to sessions without a comparison event ($M = 40, Med = 27$)($V = 3028, p < .001$). This observation holds for both the example and problem activity types. Moreover, students had a significantly higher chance to increase their in-system progress-based ranking as a result of their practice (19% progress difference) in sessions when they interacted with the social comparison controls ($t(92) = 5.54, p < .001$).

4.4 The Effect of Social Comparison Direction on Engagement

The results reported above revealed a positive association between the usage of social comparison controls and practice. However, this connection might depend on social comparison direction, namely upward or downward. This section assesses the effect of direction on learner engagement.

First, we analyzed the direction effect based on the *absolute* labeling. To perform such an evaluation, we considered learning sessions containing at least one comparison group change (N = 146). This filtering was necessary to concentrate on sessions with explicit group change. We utilized the labeling process described in Sect. 3.4 and calculated the ratio of *upward* social comparison changes (*upward-ratio*) within a session. Then, we predicted the number of learning actions (*num-act*) performed in a session by fitting a linear mixed-effects model with the *upward-ratio* and session duration as fixed effects. We found significant positive effects of the *upward-ratio* ($B = .21, z = 8.5, p < .001$) and the session duration ($B = .95, z = 47.2, p < .001$) on *num-act*. We also found an opposite effect for the *downward* social comparison. These findings highlight the importance of comparison direction, namely *upward* social comparison, on engagement.

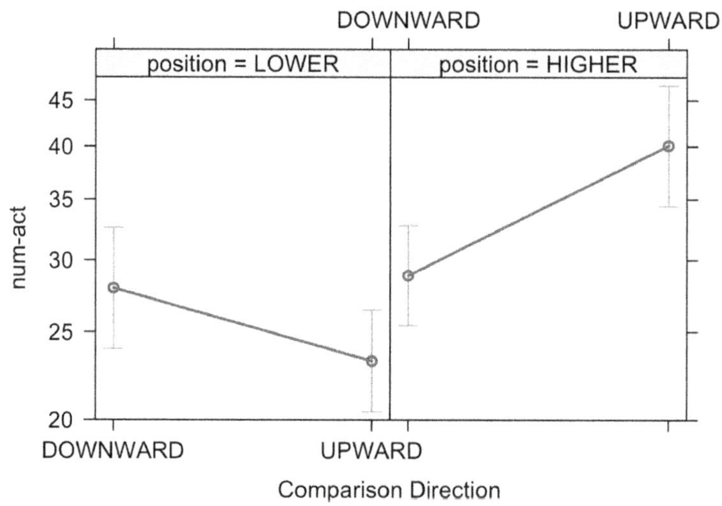

Fig. 2. Predicted number of unique learning activities (*num-act*) for the interaction term (direction*position). Purple bars denote 95% confidence interval. (Color figure online)

Second, we leveraged the relative labeling to examine the comparison direction. We used the *mid-distance* value (as described in Sect. 3.4) and calculated the mean of *mid-distance* for each learner session to represent the comparison direction. Using this mean value, we categorized a session either as an *upward* or *downward* comparison session, e.g., a session was labeled as upward when the mean *mid-distance* was below zero. Additionally, we categorized each session as a *lower* or *higher* standing session by computing the mean of learner position index (on the 0–100 scale). For example, a higher standing session implies the learner is positioned in the higher half of the class (above 50) on average during that session. In this case, we considered sessions containing a comparison group change or the ones that come after the first comparison group change, not necessarily including another comparison change (N = 765 sessions). This filtering was critical in observing the learner's explicit attitude in peer-group selection throughout multiple sessions, given that students could observe their positions without changing their comparison groups. We fitted a linear mixed model with the comparison *direction*, learner *position*, and session duration as fixed effects to predict *num-act* in a session. A significant interaction effect of position and direction was found ($B = .51, z = 7.77, p < .001$), along with a significant effect of session duration on *num-act*. As presented in the interaction effect plot (Fig. 2), the results revealed that students performed more learning actions in lower standing sessions if they were engaged in downward comparison (num-act = 28) compared to upward comparison (num-act = 23). In contrast, if they were in the higher progress state, engaging with upward comparison (num-act = 40) was more effective than downward comparison (num-act = 29). To summarize, this detailed analysis revealed that engagement with the learning activities was associated with the direction of the social comparison and the progress standing of the student.

4.5 How to Explain Learners' Social Comparison Preferences?

We explored the social comparison preferences of learners in Sect. 4.2 to understand the frequency and type of comparison group changes, such as upward or downward comparison. However, in that section, we did not discuss the factors that might affect learners' choice in selecting their peer comparison group.

We started by checking which factors affect the size of the selected comparison group (i.e., having a more expansive comparison group bar in Fig. 1A). A fitted linear mixed model revealed that the higher the learner's current position within the class, the wider the comparison bar is ($B = 3.26, t = 2.604, p = .010$). In addition, being closer to the end of the course was positively associated with choosing a larger comparison group ($B = 2.54, t = 1.992, p = .048$).

How did students increase the size of the comparison group? To modify the size and placement of a peer group, students could adjust either the left or right slider, and their use might be associated with different factors. To understand these factors, we fitted two separate mixed-effects models to predict the position of the left and right slider after controlling for the position of the opposite slider. Regression results indicated that the current standing of the learner in class was statistically significantly and positively associated only with the position of the right slider ($B = 2.91, t = 2.993, p = .003$). On the other hand, closeness to the end of the course was marginally and negatively correlated with only the left slider position ($B = -1.93, t = -1.824, p = .069$). As a result, we concluded that when students advanced in their standing within the class, they increased their comparison group size by adding stronger students (i.e., by moving the upper slider to the right). In addition, while approaching the end of the class, students added weaker students to their peer group by decreasing the position of the lower slider (i.e., moving it to the left).

We extended our analysis by connecting the comparison preferences with the collected self-reported instruments. Thus, we tried to predict the scalar value of *mid-distance* by using the collected instruments (see Sect. 3.2 for details). We fitted a linear mixed model on the session-based data (290 comparison group changes). The results indicated that there was a significant effect of *social comparison orientation score* ($B = -17.76, t = -4.774, p =< .001$) and *performance orientation score* ($B = 9.66, t = 2.757, p = .008$) on *mid-distance*. In other words, socially-oriented students preferred upward social comparison (given the sign of the regression coefficient) while performance oriented students favored downward social comparison. Following the previous analysis, we fitted another linear regression model to predict the size of the comparison group but could not find any significant model.

5 Discussion: Results in the Context of Related Work

In this paper, we report the results of several rounds of classroom studies to explore the effects of learner-controlled social comparison on learner engagement and performance in an online programming practice system. We observed that students used the system extensively throughout the semester and showed that their engagement with the system was positively correlated with the course grades. We also found a link between achievement goals and course performance, where mastery-oriented students finished the course with better grades [11].

The unique design of the user-controlled social comparison interface also enabled us to explore the diverse learner preferences towards social comparison. Social comparison theory states that people want continuous improvement and assess their capabilities and opinions by comparing themselves to similar people [13]. Moreover, the performance-based reward system in education leads students to compare themselves socially [9]. Our analyses show that students paid considerable attention to social comparison features. We also observed a gradual change in their social preferences, which is consistent with the findings of Huguet et al. [18], who argued that social comparison is a dynamic process that changes over time. Our data also demonstrated that students tend to choose the upward social comparison (in absolute labeling) most frequently in a TEL environment, the tendency observed earlier in other contexts [10].

A deeper analysis of social comparison choices yielded more discoveries, which correlate with findings reported in the literature. First, we observed that students practiced significantly more and increased their in-system progress levels in sessions where they also self-assess their current state by interacting with the learner-controlled social comparison features. Researchers presented similar positive effects of social comparison [8,26]. We also highlighted that the direction of the comparison and the progress level of a learner impact the benefit of social comparison. We found that engaging with upward social comparison (in absolute labeling) was positively associated with enhanced practice intensity. Researchers argued that learners tend to perform upward comparison as a means of self-improvement when they also recognize that they can improve their standing [7,18]. Moreover, the progress state of a learner interacted with the comparison direction (in relative labeling) such that performing a comparison that is "matched" to their current state (i.e., performing upward comparison while being in the higher state) was more beneficial on engagement. This interaction could mean that the upward comparison might be beneficial only when students do not feel uneasy about being inferior [3]. We believe that the novel learner-controlled comparison features with OSLM features helped learners choose appropriate peer groups based on their standing, leading to increased engagement.

We concluded our analysis by exploring the factors affecting the comparison preferences. For example, we observed that students added high-performing students into their peer groups based on their standing within the class. Finally, we connected peer group preferences back to learners' differences and discovered that students with higher social comparison orientation favored upward social comparison, while performance-oriented students preferred downward comparison. This finding conforms to earlier observations where researchers found that the performance-avoidance group conducts downward comparison more [4].

6 Prospects and Limitations

Our work demonstrated that fine-grained learner controls on social comparison could increase the effect of social comparison by helping learners find the most appropriate peers. Moreover, we showed that these control features provide valuable insight into students' intentions in the peer-group selection and emerge as a practical technology for future studies. We want to explore learner control more broadly while addressing several limitations of this study in future work. We hope to augment our findings with qualitative analysis to understand how students think and feel while adjusting their comparison groups. Moreover, the online delivery of the programming course could impact students' comparison behavior. Even though we diligently verified our statistical findings, we conducted some of the analysis only with limited data. Also, the authors are conscious of the difference between causality and correlations, and more rigorous study designs are needed to investigate causal effects. Finally, although the system usage was encouraged slightly through course credits, our study might be susceptible to the self-selection bias since the majority of the system use was voluntary. We hope to address these limitations in our future work.

Acknowledgements. This material is partially supported by the National Science Foundation under Grant No. 1822752.

References

1. Akhuseyinoglu, K., Barria-Pineda, J., Sosnovsky, S., Lamprecht, A.-L., Guerra, J., Brusilovsky, P.: Exploring student-controlled social comparison. In: Alario-Hoyos, C., Rodríguez-Triana, M.J., Scheffel, M., Arnedillo-Sánchez, I., Dennerlein, S.M. (eds.) EC-TEL 2020. LNCS, vol. 12315, pp. 244–258. Springer, Cham (2020). https://doi.org/10.1007/978-3-030-57717-9_18
2. Auvinen, T., Hakulinen, L., Malmi, L.: Increasing students awareness of their behavior in online learning environments with visualizations and achievement badges. IEEE Trans. Learn. Technol. **8**(3), 261273 (2018)

3. Blanton, H., Gibbons, F.X., Buunk, B.P., Kuyper, H.: When better-than-others compare upward: choice of comparison and comparative evaluation as independent predictors of academic performance. J. Pers. Soc. Psychol. **76**(3), 420–430 (1999)
4. Bounoua, L., Cury, F., Regner, I., Huguet, P., Barron, K.E., Elliot, A.J.: Motivated use of information about others: linking the 2×2 achievement goal model to social comparison propensities and processes. Br. J. Soc. Psychol. **51**(4), 626–641 (2012)
5. Brusilovsky, P., Somyürek, S., Guerra, J., Hosseini, R., Zadorozhny, V., Durlach, P.J.: Open social student modeling for personalized learning. IEEE Trans. Emerg. Top. Comput. **4**(3), 450–461 (2016)
6. Cialdini, R.B., Wosinska, W., Barrett, D.W., Butner, J., Gornik-Durose, M.: Compliance with a request in two cultures: the differential influence of social proof and commitment/consistency on collectivists and individualists. Pers. Soc. Psychol. Bull. **25**(10), 1242–1253 (1999)
7. Collins, R.L.: For better or worse: the impact of upward social comparison on self-evaluations. Psychol. Bull. **119**(1), 51–69 (1996)
8. Davis, D., Jivet, I., Kizilcec, R.F., Chen, G., Hauff, C., Houben, G.J.: Follow the successful crowd: raising MOOC completion rates through social comparison at scale. In: 7th International Learning Analytics & Knowledge Conference, pp. 454–463 (2017)
9. Dijkstra, P., Kuyper, H., van der Werf, G., Buunk, A.P., van der Zee, Y.G.: Social comparison in the classroom: a review. Rev. Educ. Res. **78**(4), 828–879 (2008)
10. Dumas, F., Huguet, P., Monteil, J.M., Rastoul, C., Nezlek, J.B.: Social comparison in the classroom: is there a tendency to compare upward in elementary school? Curr. Res. Soc. Psychol. **10**(12), 166–186 (2005)
11. Elliot, A.J., Mcgregor, H., Gable, S.L.: Achievement goals, study strategies, and exam performance: a mediational analysis. J. Educ. Psychol. **91**, 549–563 (1999)
12. Elliot, A.J., Murayama, K.: On the measurement of achievement goals: critique, illustration, and application. J. Educ. Psychol. **100**(3), 613 (2008)
13. Festinger, L.: A theory of social comparison processes. Hum. Relat. **7**(2), 117–140 (1954)
14. Gibbons, F.X., Buunk, B.P.: Individual differences in social comparison: development of a scale of social comparison orientation. J. Pers. Soc. Psychol. **76**(1), 129 (1999)
15. Hosseini, R., et al.: Improving engagement in program construction examples for learning python programming. Int. J. Artif. Intell. Educ. **30**(2), 299–336 (2020)
16. Hsiao, I.H., Brusilovsky, P.: Guiding and motivating students through open social student modeling: lessons learned. Teachers College Record **119**(3) (2017)
17. Hsiao, I.H., Brusilovsky, P., Sosnovsky, S.: Web-based parameterized questions for object-oriented programming. In: World Conference on E-Learning, E-Learn 2008, pp. 3728–3735 (2008)
18. Huguet, P., Dumas, F., Monteil, J.M., Genestoux, N.: Social comparison choices in the classroom: further evidence for students' upward comparison tendency and its beneficial impact on performance. Eur. J. Soc. Psychol. **31**(5), 557–578 (2001)
19. Kitsantas, A., Zimmerman, B.J., Cleary, T.: The role of observation and emulation in the development of athletic self-regulation. J. Educ. Psychol. **92**(4), 811–817 (2000)
20. Loboda, T.D., Guerra, J., Hosseini, R., Brusilovsky, P.: Mastery grids: an open source social educational progress visualization. In: Rensing, C., de Freitas, S., Ley, T., Muñoz-Merino, P.J. (eds.) EC-TEL 2014. LNCS, vol. 8719, pp. 235–248. Springer, Cham (2014). https://doi.org/10.1007/978-3-319-11200-8_18

21. Morales-Trujillo, M.E., García-Mireles, G.A.: Gamification and SQL: an empirical study on student performance in a database course. ACM Trans. Comput. Educ. **21**(1) (2021)
22. Parsons, D., Haden, P.: Parsons programming puzzles: a fun and effective learning tool for first programming courses. In: Proceedings of the 8th Australasian Conference on Computing Education, vol. 52, pp. 157–163 (2006)
23. Rogers, T., Feller, A.: Discouraged by peer excellence: exposure to exemplary peer performance causes quitting. Psychol. Sci. **27**(3), 365–374 (2016)
24. Sirkiä, T.: Jsvee & Kelmu: creating and tailoring program animations for computing education. J. Softw.: Evolut. Process **30**(2) (2018)
25. Teasley, S.D.: Student facing dashboards: one size fits all? Technol. Knowl. Learn. **22**(3), 377–384 (2017)
26. Vassileva, J.: Toward social learning environments. IEEE Trans. Learn. Technol. **1**(4), 199–214 (2008)

A Dashboard to Support Teachers During Students' Self-paced AI-Supported Problem-Solving Practice

Vincent Aleven[1(✉)], Jori Blankestijn[2], LuEttaMae Lawrence[3], Tomohiro Nagashima[1], and Niels Taatgen[2]

[1] Human-Computer Interaction Institute, Carnegie Mellon University, Pittsburgh, USA
{aleven,tnagashi}@cs.cmu.edu

[2] Computer Science and Artificial Intelligence, Bernoulli Institute for Mathematics, University of Groningen, Groningen, The Netherlands
n.a.taatgen@rug.nl

[3] Instructional Technologies and Learning Sciences Department, Utah State University, Logan, USA

Abstract. Past research has yielded ample knowledge regarding the design of analytics-based tools for teachers and has found beneficial effects of several tools on teaching and learning. Yet there is relatively little knowledge regarding the design of tools that support teachers when a class of students uses AI-based tutoring software for self-paced learning. To address this challenge, we conducted design-based research with 20 middle school teachers to create a novel real-time dashboard, Tutti, that helps a teacher monitor a class and decide which individual students to help, based on analytics from students' tutoring software. Tutti is fully implemented and has been honed through prototyping and log replay sessions. A partial implementation was piloted in remote classrooms. Key design features are a two-screen design with (1) a class overview screen showing the status of each student as well as notifications of recent events, and (2) a deep dive screen to explore an individual student's work in detail, with both dynamic replay and an interactive annotated solution view. The project yields new insight into effective designs for a real-time analytics-based tool that may guide the design of other tools for K-12 teachers to support students in self-paced learning activities.

Keywords: Teacher dashboards · Problem-solving practice · AI-based tutoring software

1 Introduction

Much research in technology-enhanced learning has focused on creating and evaluating tools that support teachers or instructors in aspects of awareness and classroom orchestration. This work has resulted in novel tools and insight into how best to design these kinds of tools [1, 2, 4, 9, 13, 14, 16, 25]. A small number of classroom studies have

I. Hilliger et al. (Eds.): EC-TEL 2022, LNCS 13450, pp. 16–30, 2022.
https://doi.org/10.1007/978-3-031-16290-9_2

documented beneficial effects of such tools on teaching and learning [13, 16]. The current work focuses on scenarios in which students do individual, self-paced work with an intelligent tutoring system (ITS). This mode of personalized learning is increasingly common in K-12 [19, 23] and often leads to improved learning outcomes compared to instruction without this kind of software [7]. This type of software supports deliberate practice [15] in solving complex problems with "step-based tutoring" [22] and individualized mastery learning [8]. We target "real time" scenarios in which a class of students works with tutoring software, each student working individually at their own pace, and a teacher is available to help the students. The teacher monitors the class and interacts with students (often individually) to provide extra help or encouragement.

Creating teacher support tools for this kind of scenario presents several novel design challenges, compared to past work on teacher analytics tools. First, many existing real-time teacher support tools have been designed with the assumption that a class of students progresses through instructional activities in a relatively synchronized manner. By contrast, ITSs often support personalized mastery learning [8], which means that students proceed in a self-paced manner, work on different problem-solving activities at the same time, and finish milestones at different times [21]. Second, few teacher tools are designed to be used in conjunction with ITSs. These systems are typically capable of producing rich analytics [6], yet much is still unknown regarding how best to leverage these analytics to support teachers in real-time scenarios.

Recent work has started to look at these challenges by creating teacher tools for scenarios in which students ITSs (e.g., [11, 18, 25]) or other classroom scenarios [1, 16]. Some reporting tools designed for use in conjunction with an ITS support detailed monitoring of student progress [3, 5]. Other tools are helpful to teachers during classroom discussions of homework assigned through the system [14] or during lesson planning [25]. Yet other tools were designed to be independent of any learning software [2]. A few of these projects yielded implemented tools for real-time scenarios, including Lumilo, mixed-reality smart glasses that support teachers in real-time scenarios with ITSs [11]. A classroom experiment with Lumilo provides evidence that a real-time analytics tool can measurably change how teachers allocate their time and attention among students, yielding better learning outcomes for students [13]. While Lumilo provides answers to our design challenges, it requires hardware (mixed-reality devices) that is not often available (yet) in schools. Thus, how best to design tools that support teachers in helping students who are engaged in personalized, technology-enhanced, self-paced learning, is still largely an open design problem.

In the current work, we address the question: How might we design a dashboard that displays analytics from (K-12) students' work with an ITS to support teachers in aiding students in real time, during their work with the ITS? Building on the prior work with Lumilo, we conducted a process of human-centered research and design, grounding our designs in data about teachers' goals and needs, uncovered through a range of design activities. We created a new dashboard, named Tutti, within the infrastructure for development of ITSs named CTAT + Tutorshop [3].

The paper is structured as follows: After describing the instructional contexts for which Tutti is designed, we give a brief overview of the design as it is currently implemented (it is fully functioning). In the following sections, we describe the process that led to this design, present some of the insights that resulted from that process and that helped shape the design of Tutti, look at key design features and describe how they are grounded in data from our many interactions with teachers.

2 Context

The current work targets contexts in which students engage in self-paced, personalized learning with AI-based tutoring software, by now a common occurrence in K-12 in the US and elsewhere [16, 23]. It covers scenarios in which students are either present in class or work remotely, either synchronously or asynchronously. Using the tutoring software, they work through assigned problem sets, each targeting a set of knowledge components, also called "skills." The software uses a form of AI plan recognition to assess student work at the level of problem steps and provides guidance in the form of hints and feedback. It also supports individualized mastery learning: Students move on to the next problem set only when they master the skills targeted in the current, as assessed by the system [6]. The design of the tutoring software is grounded in cognitive theory, theory of deliberate practice, and notions of scaffolding/tutoring [15].

When a class of students uses tutoring software, students typically work through assigned problem sets at their own pace. Thus, at any given point in time, different students work on different learning objectives or problem-solving tasks, even when they are working synchronously in the classroom. A teacher monitors the class and helps students in situations that the software is not designed well to handle. Other teacher goals may be to keep students on task, to keep them motivated, as well as to encourage and praise them. In remote learning, much of the communication and progress monitoring is mediated through technology. In in-person scenarios, teachers tend to move around the classroom and can talk to students to better understand their struggles or celebrate their successes. Yet it is not always easy for a teacher to assess who needs help the most, as students may hide their struggle, or, conversely, may ask for help when they do not need it urgently [24]. Further, teachers must be very efficient in their one-on-one interactions with students, as many students may need attention.

The current work builds on a proven technology infrastructure for research and development of ITS called CTAT + Tutorshop [3]. The infrastructure provides tools for building tutoring systems and for deploying and using them in classrooms. It has been used to create many ITSs [3]. It also has many affordances to support the development of analytics tools. Although our examples in the current paper tend to focus on a tutoring system for equation solving, in principle Tutti can work with any tutoring system developed within the CTAT + Tutorshop infrastructure.

3 Overview of Tutti's Design

We briefly overview the design of Tutti in its current implementation. In a later section, we discuss key design features in more detail.

Similar to prior teacher dashboards designed for use with classes that use learning software [11, 16, 25], Tutti has a two-screen design. An *overview screen* (Fig. 1) shows information about each student in a class and is designed to draw the teacher's attention to students who may need help (e.g., students who appear to be struggling or misusing the software) or deserve praise. At the teacher's request, a *deep dive screen* (Figs. 2, 3) shows more information about any given student. This information might help a teacher assess more fully whether communication with any given student is needed (e.g., what skills, problem types, or errors a student is struggling with).

Fig. 1. Overview screen with progress table (left) and stream of notifications (right). The names are not real student names.

The *overview screen* shows a table with information about each student's progress and status (Fig. 1, left). Each of the small squares in the table represents a problem set, filled up (with black) in proportion to how far the student progressed through this problem set. A set of "indicators" capture each student's recent learning experience (shown in the "Status" column in Fig. 1). The indicators were developed and honed with frequent input from teachers in past research on the Lumilo system [11]. The indicators are: Struggle, system misuse (aka "gaming the system"), being off-task, and making good progress (so as to alert the teacher to opportunities for complimenting students). For example, to determine whether a student is struggling, their correctness rate over recent attempts is gauged, using a sliding window over student attempts. As well, the overview screen displays notifications of recent events regarding students' learning with the software (Fig. 1, right). Notifications are generated when the status of an indicator changes or when a given status has persisted for a certain threshold amount of time. For example, an idle indicator ("Zzz") appears when a student has not been working in the tutoring software for 2 min.

The *deep dive screen* (Fig. 2) provides information about a single student's progress through the assigned problem sets (top right), their mastery of the skills targeted in these problem sets (top left), and the problems they have solved (bottom left). The teacher can also look at a student's areas of struggle, defined as skills on which the student has made little progress despite ample practice, a sign that the tutoring software might not be helping the student effectively and that extra help from the teacher could be beneficial. The display of areas of struggle was highly requested by teachers. For even more detail, a teacher can look at a student's current problem solution (as a "remote peek over the shoulder," a feature also found in Lumilo [9]) or at any of a student's past problem solutions in full detail. Tutti offers two ways of doing so, both of which teachers found useful (as described below): Annotated Snapshots (Fig. 2, right panel) and Replay (Fig. 3). Both show a student's stepwise attempts at solving a problem, displayed in the tutor interface. Snapshots provide quick insight into which problem steps were challenging, as indicated by the number of errors and hints, shown with icons in Fig. 2. Replay steps through a student's attempts including errors and hints.

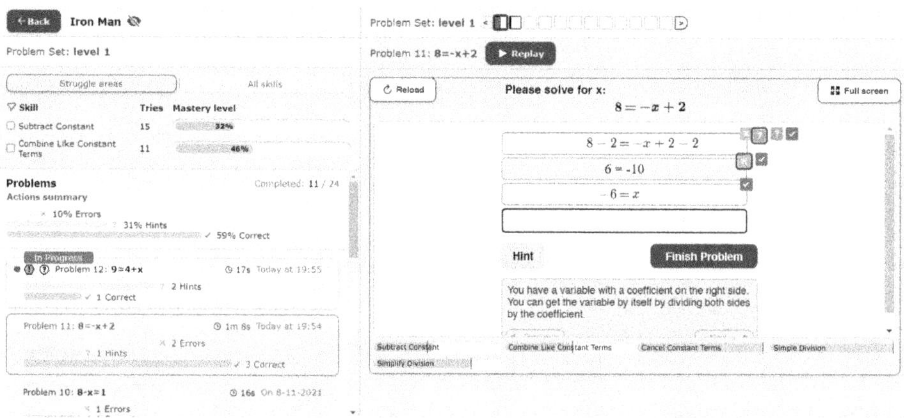

Fig. 2. Deep dive screen with information about an individual student, including areas of struggle, list of solved problems, and an annotated snapshot of a past problem solution (right)

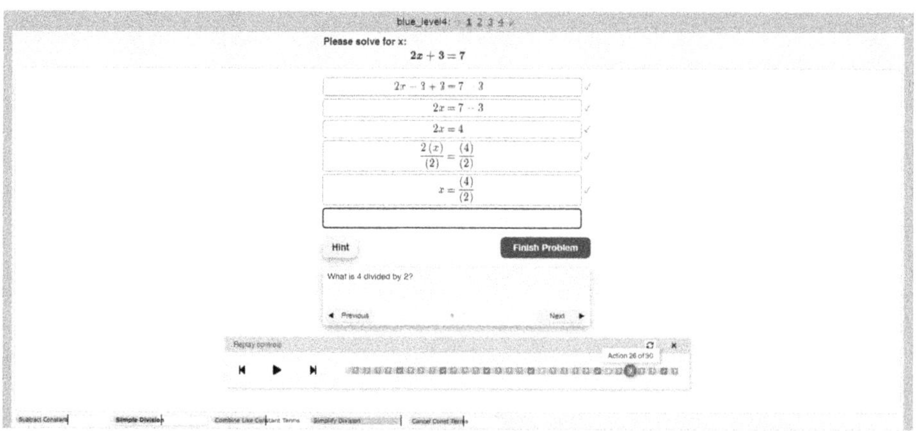

Fig. 3. Screen for replay of a student's solution to one of the tutor problems

4 Research Activities

To create Tutti we carried out a process of user-centered research and design, working with a total of 20 teachers across a range of research activities. In the current section, we describe the activities. In subsequent sections, we present the results.

1. **Discovering teachers' needs.** We conducted needs finding and concept validation exercises with six middle school math teachers from six school districts across the United States during the Fall of 2020. Three teachers were teaching fully remotely and three were teaching in a hybrid model (i.e., in-person instruction two days a week, remote instruction three days a week). We conducted six sessions, each lasting one hour per teacher. These sessions included semi-structured interviews and storyboard-based speed dating exercises [26]. Afterwards, we used affinity diagramming to reveal important themes in the teacher comments [10].
2. **Refining the understanding of teachers' needs.** We conducted speed dating sessions to solicit teachers' feedback, preferences, and motivations [26], prompted by a set of 10 storyboards. The storyboards depicted scenarios with possible dashboard designs that varied along three key dimensions: (1) Whether the instruction is in-person, remote, or a combination, (2) how examples of student work are presented in the analytics tool: as a Snapshot, as Replay, or a Live Feed of a student's screen as they are working in the tutoring software, and (3) options for teacher-student communication (audio, chat, or drawing on a shared representation of the student's problem interface combined with chat balloons). We also asked teachers what additional features and improvements they would like to see, compared to the storyboards. We clustered the resulting quotes to discover themes using affinity diagramming [10].
3. **Scoping and implementing Tutti.** Given that our needs-finding activities revealed an almost desperate need on the part of teachers to be better informed of what their students are doing during instructional sessions, we started implementing the dashboard early on during the project. We pursued the most popular ideas, including notifications of events in the learning software that might need the teacher's attention, and different ways of displaying instances of student work (Snapshots and Replay). Over time, schools gradually started shifting back to in-person instruction, which led us to prioritize features of the dashboard that were most useful for in-person instruction.
4. **Piloting an early implementation of Tutti in remote classrooms.** As the implementation effort was underway, several opportunities arose (during 2020–2021) to conduct a pilot study with an early version of the dashboard, as part of an unrelated research project. Although only the overview screen had been implemented, we figured the Tutti could still be helpful. We asked the teachers who participated in the study if they were interested in using it even though it was not yet in a perfect state. All of them agreed. We used the dashboard with three teachers in three schools in the US. One school was operating in a hybrid mode (with some students participating in-person and others joining remotely) whereas the other two schools operated fully remotely. In all sessions (30 in total), students were assigned individual work with algebra tutoring software. The teachers helped the students while the students were using the software. Experimenters attended each session remotely to provide

help where needed. Before the study, teachers worked through instructional materials about Tutti. During the study, teachers and experimenters had access to and monitored the dashboard.

5. **Testing hi-fi prototypes.** We conducted a series of prototyping sessions with early implementations of the dashboard to hone its design and usability. During these sessions, we interviewed teachers as they interacted with the tool. Four math teachers (grades 6 through 12) and one math director participated, with an average teaching experience of 19 years. One teacher was in Taiwan, the rest were in the US. All participants were asked to think aloud while performing 20 tasks using the dashboard's interactive capabilities. (The dashboard however was not updated in real-time during this study.) They were asked to report any potential problems they noticed, if they were to use it in class. We made many changes to the dashboard because of the findings.
6. **Conducting replay studies.** As a final way of honing the design of Tutti we conducted replay studies, that is, prototyping sessions during which teachers experienced some of the dynamic behaviors of the tool, though outside the real classroom environment. To create the dynamic behaviors, we replayed log data from a class of students (which captures their interactions with the tutoring software) through the dashboard in real time. The tool would update as it would if it were used during the real class session (cf. The Replay Enactments method [11]). In addition to testing usability, the study focused on how teachers would use the dashboard information to support their real-time decisions regarding whom to help. We also asked interview questions about desirable features in the tool. Three math teachers participated, all of whom had participated previously, with on average 19 years of teaching experience, teaching grades 7–12; one teacher taught special education classes. The data that was replayed came from a 6th grade class of 11 students, collected during the pilot study. As a result of the findings from this study, we made many changes to the dashboard.

5 Results from Teacher Interviews

We present insights from the early need finding activities (Research Activity #1).

Learning Process: "I Wish I Could see What They're Doing". All participating teachers described frustration when it came to identifying what students needed or how they were doing. Several of them noted the value in being able to see students' processes and actions as they normally would in their classroom. Several teachers working with MATHia (a commercially available tutoring system for mathematics) described how they used reports generated by the software and the software's live dashboard to understand if the students were working in the tutoring software, completed their assignments, and were on track to master content. They expressed a need for more detailed live information about what students were doing, as existing tools did not allow for remote monitoring. They described requesting or sharing screenshots with students over email or asking students to share their screens during individual meetings via teleconferencing software as a form of remote monitoring. However, not all students would respond or engage in one-on-ones with teachers.

Real-Time: "I Want to Know as Soon as Possible". Teachers wanted to get information about students as quickly as possible, so that they could correct problems immediately and provide timely praise. With remote instruction, teachers felt they could not identify and correct problems immediately as was possible in their normal classrooms. As a result, they could be missing moments of struggle until an assessment; some teachers strongly preferred reaching out and reteaching content to students before they experienced further frustration. Teachers also described missing the ability to quickly provide praise and support. One teacher remarked, "*Encouragement is a huge part of learning, saying, hey, you're moving in the right direction!*"

6 Insights from Storyboard Study

We present insights gained from the study with storyboards, Research Activity #2 listed above, which, as mentioned, focused on three aspects: Instructional context, displaying instances of student work, and technology options for teacher-student communication.

Viewing Specific Instances of a Student's Work is Valuable. Consistent with our earlier findings and those from the Lumilo project [11], the participating teachers unanimously valued the ability to follow students' processes in specific problem instances, both current and past. They viewed the different display options (Snapshots, Replay, Live Feed) as overlapping but complementary. The live problem view was deemed useful primarily for remote scenarios, as it may enable quick feedback and avoids the need for screen sharing by the student. Teachers felt that Replay (more so than Snapshots) enables them to investigate a student's challenges.

Time is of the Essence. Teachers (without prompting) evaluated whether the tool concepts depicted in the storyboards would help them operate efficiently. They found Snapshots attractive because they give quick insight, whereas they questioned whether they would have the time to use Replays or Live Feeds. Chat was viewed as the most efficient communication method, provided it would be well integrated with the dashboard and the tutoring software. The combination of Live Feed with drawing and chat was viewed as an efficient combination for use in remote scenarios. In live scenarios, teachers said they instead preferred to walk up to a student and talk.

Private Communications with Students are Highly Preferable. Consistent with past work on Lumilo [11], teachers valued tool and communication options that would safeguard students' privacy, in the sense that a student's struggles would not be known or visible to the entire class. For example, they did not want to show student names when displaying a Replay or when displaying the full dashboard to the class.

Teacher Attention Might Help Increase Participation in Class. Some teachers stated that students might be more motivated if they felt the teacher was keeping an eye on them - which the dashboard might help them do. They thought it might help to send "wake-up calls" (using chat or audio) to idling students or students misusing the system.

Teacher-Student One-on-One Communications via Chat Might be Useful Especially for Remote Students. Teachers thought audio communication with remote learners would be natural; they unanimously felt "normal interactions" would be possible in this manner (e.g., to redo a problem together with a student). One teacher mentioned that the use of chat in in-person scenarios might support multitask helping (help one student, write another; send a quick message and not interrupt students). They suggested having pre-defined, easily-customizable chat messages.

7 Observations from Remote Classroom Piloting

During the remote classroom pilots (Research Activity #4), teachers' activity with the dashboard's overview screen focused on checking which students were actively working on the tutor. (The Deep Dive screen had not been implemented yet.) During fully-remote sessions, many students had their webcam off, so teachers had no other easy way of ascertaining this information. The need to know who is working during educational technology use in fully-remote sessions has also been reported elsewhere [17]. The study revealed a need for a communication channel built into the dashboard when used for a remote or hybrid instructional mode, so teachers would not need a separate video conferencing tool (e.g., Zoom) to talk to a student.

We also observed that teachers did not make use of the notifications displayed on the dashboard's overview screen. We did not observe any instances, for example, where a teacher reached out to a particular student when a notification showed that the student was struggling. In this remote teaching context, teachers appeared to be occupied more with encouraging students to use the software and reaching out to students who did not make much progress (which could be gleaned from the progress table better than from the notifications) than reacting to indications of struggle. Indeed, during the study sessions, the teachers and experimenters exchanged many private messages regarding who is working on the software and who is not. This is not to say that notifications are not useful. Rather, their utility may depend on context, such as remote/in-person, and other factors (e.g., specific instructional goals teachers may have).

8 Key Design Features with Rationale

Following the storyboards, we narrowed our scope to focus on a smaller set of features that we expected to be useful for teachers. As (so far) teachers valued both Snapshot and Replay for in-class teaching, we decided to keep both, to further explore their complementary strengths through higher-fidelity prototyping. We put the Live Feed on hold, as the teachers said they would not use it often in person. Moreover, a live view had already been explored in past research on Lumilo [11]. We also dropped the communication options. Although some teachers saw use for them in live classrooms, we prioritized the display of analytics. Within this scope, the main design features are: (1) Two-screen design with easy navigation from class overview to student-level deep dive, (2) dual representations of students' status and recent behaviors (progress table and notifications) and (3) two ways of viewing instances of student work (Snapshots and

Replay). These features kept evolving during the subsequent activities (hi-fi prototyping and replay study). In the current section, we provide more detail about these features as they were at the end of the process. We also describe how they are grounded in data gathered during our interactions with teachers.

8.1 Two-Screen Dashboard Design

As mentioned, Tutti combines an *overview screen* (see Fig. 1) that provides information about each student in a class with a *deep dive screen* (Figs. 2, 3) that provides more detailed information about any given student's learning experiences. The information on the overview screen may help teachers get an initial sense of which students might need their attention (Fig. 1). To this end, the overview screen (a) summarizes progress through the problem sets with a simple visualization, (b) summarizes each student's learning state with indicators adopted from Lumilo, and (c) presents notifications of recent events regarding students' learning.

The information on the deep dive screen helps a teacher gain further insight into whether communication with the given student could be beneficial and what it might focus on (e.g., what skills, problem types, or errors a student may be struggling with). The deep dive screen may be a teacher's sole source of information about a student's work in remote scenarios. The deep dive screen provides information about the given student's progress through the assigned problem sets (Fig. 2, top right), with more detail available at the teacher's request including information about a student's skill mastery, areas of struggle (i.e., skills with substantial practice but low mastery; see Fig. 2., top left), and past problems (Fig. 2, bottom left). The problem list helps teachers gain insight into what problems were difficult for the given student, with information such as counts of errors, hints, and correct steps as well as the same indicators of progress and struggle that are used on the overview screen. Teachers can filter the problem list by skill, to select problem instances to inspect using either a Snapshot (Fig. 2, right) or a Replay of the solution (Fig. 3), as described in more detail below.

Teachers can access a student's deep dive screen in multiple ways, a design feature that make it easier to follow leads gathered from information on the overview screen. When the teacher clicks on a notification on the overview screen, the deep dive screen is initialized with information relevant to that notification, namely, the problem set and the problem the student was working on when the notification occurred. Similarly, when the teacher clicks on a student listed in the overview screen, the deep dive screen shows information related to that student's current problem set and problem.

The two-screen design (with a class overview screen and student-specific deep dive screen) is found in other teacher tools as well, including two dashboards used (like Tutti) in conjunction with AI-based tutoring software, Luna [25] and Lumilo [11]. These dashboards share the same raw data—tutor interaction data—and use analytics derived from that data. There are, however, some interesting differences regarding the information displayed on these dashboards, which could be attributed to the different use scenarios for which the dashboards were designed. For example, the overview screen of Luna, which is designed to support lesson planning, provides class aggregates, which are helpful when deciding what topic or examples to discuss in class. By contrast, Tutti only presents student-specific information on its overview screen, which is helpful when deciding which individual student to help. Further, where both Tutti and Lumilo present, on their student-specific deep dive screen, areas of struggle and examples of student work, Lumilo selects the examples for the teacher, whereas in Tutti the teacher has full control over which past problem instances to inspect.

8.2 State-Based and Event-Based Overview of Students' Learning

Although, on Tutti's overview screen (see Fig. 1), there is overlap between the information shown in the progress table and that captured in notifications, teachers preferred to have both representations. They use them for different purposes, and different teachers tend to rely to a greater or lesser extent on the notifications. In remote scenarios, the progress table shows which students are working with the tutoring software at any given moment, information they could not ascertain easily in other ways. The progress table also shows the current indicator values for each student.

The notifications draw teachers' attention to recent events. They are generated when there is a change of status in an indicator variable for a given student (e.g., a student enters the "idle" state or satisfies the definition for struggle). They also change (and are then displayed again at the top of the list) when a status has existed for a certain threshold amount of time. The notifications show how long the status has persisted (e.g., how long the student has been idle), the student, the problem set, and the specific problem the student is working on. Teachers can sort the notifications by student name or recency and can filter the notifications by student, type, or skill. Filtering and sorting can help teachers identify students who need help, as indicated by recent notifications, or simply go student-by-student to check on each student. Filtering by notification *type* makes it easy to view (say) all the struggle notifications and check whether they occur on similar math problems, or to identify all idle students and perhaps address all of them at once. Filtering the notifications by skill helps to ascertain whether there are class-level problems related to any specific skill. (Perhaps a brief mini lecture to the whole class is in order.) Some teachers mentioned that the notifications could help them get students back to work quickly (e.g., when there is no strong evidence of struggle, only an idle indicator or system misuse indicator). One teacher indicated they wanted the notifications to be always visible (i.e., on both the deep dive and overview screens).

8.3 Snapshots and Replay to View Examples of Student Work

Many teachers indicated that viewing specific examples of a student's work is a key way for them to discover what that student finds difficult. Initially, we thought of Snapshots and Replays of student work as *alternative* designs for meeting this need; we expected that teachers would gravitate towards one or the other. We found, however, that *both* were attractive options to teachers, with Replay being slightly preferred. Although an annotated Snapshot would appear to be faster (and time is of the essence, as discussed above), an argument in favor of Replay, in the words of one teacher, is that it is more like what you would see if you interacted with a student.

Snapshots take up more screen real estate, compared to Replay, as the problem steps are annotated with "action icons" that represent each hint, error, and correct action (see Fig. 2, right). The main challenges in designing the Snapshot screen were placing these annotations so they do not cover up the problem steps and showing the order in which the student's actions happened. We tried multiple concepts (e.g., numbering actions and representing multiple similar actions with a single icon). However, showing a row of single-action icons row seemed the most straightforward and easy to interpret. This solution, however, communicates the order of student actions only for tutor interfaces in which the order of problem steps is fixed (e.g., the equation-solving tutor shown in Figs. 2 and 3), and not for tutor interfaces in which the order of steps can vary. At the suggestion of teachers, tapping or hovering on an action icon is used as an intuitive way to show specific errors or hints. We used the same color coding for hints, errors, and correct entries in all parts of the deep dive screen. Snapshots (unlike Replay, for technical reasons) can be applied to the student's current problem, although without automatic live updating. A "Full screen" option for Snapshots helps allocate more screen space, which is useful for large tutor interfaces. The full-screen mode hides the student name, which is useful when the teacher wants to project a problem solution for the whole class to see and discuss. We also added a hide name button (top left, Fig. 2). Teachers strongly wanted to maintain student anonymity when sharing student work.

Key design decisions in creating the Replay functionality were, first, to model the controls after those often used in media players (e.g., video/music); second, to make the bar draggable and minimizable so it does not obstruct the teacher's view; and third, to use a fixed duration for each replayed action (2s; teachers preferred this speed). Teachers commented that they would use Replay for reviewing problem solutions with students, individually or with the whole class. One teacher commented that they would use Snapshots with the more advanced students, as doing so would be efficient, whereas for less advanced students, Replay would be more concrete and recognizable. During the replay study (Research Activity #6) Replay was a popular feature, although teachers also looked at Snapshots often and expressed a liking for them. Teachers suggested several new use cases for Replay. One teacher thought Replay might help them get to know new students more quickly. Another thought it might work as a homework tool for students who are behind. Finally, one teacher suggested Replay together with recording a proof of help might be used in parent-teacher conferences.

9 Discussion and Conclusion

Analytics-based support tools for teachers who run personalized classrooms with AI-based software pose unique design challenges, yet there is relatively little general knowledge regarding the design of such tools. To address this challenge, we created Tutti through user-centered design and prototyping. Teachers found three main design features to be helpful: A design with both a class overview screen and a student-level deep dive screen, multiple views of data about a class of students (a progress table and notifications), and two ways of looking at specific instances of problems solved by a given student, either in the form of a Snapshot (with annotations that show hints and errors) and a Replay of all student step attempts and hints.

The work adopts several design elements from Lumilo, a mixed-reality tool that helps teachers help their students during self-paced, personalized learning [11], but is also different. Tutti uses commonly available hardware (e.g., tablet computers). It adds interactive exploration of students' learning experiences; it features multiple views of student information, ways of quickly finding past problem instances where a student struggled, and teacher control over which past problem instances to inspect. The work confirms the value of the shared design elements and suggests there is value in the new elements (e.g., Snapshots and Replay).

The work's key contributions include new knowledge regarding the design of analytics tools for real-time helping of students during self-paced learning with AI-based tutors, grounded in data about teachers' needs. The work also contributes new insights into teachers' needs during self-paced technology-enhanced learning and how these needs vary by context, such as whether instruction is in-person or remote. Further, the work provides new insight into how the importance of design features of real time analytics-based teacher tools varies by context. Regarding the generality of the work, Tutti is designed for use with any tutor built within CTAT + Tutorshop [3]. We tried out Tutti with several tutors built within this infrastructure and found it can be useful with them, although further generality testing is in order. More broadly, Tutti might be used with any tutoring system that supports stepwise problem-solving practice and tracks student learning of detailed skills. Perhaps some design features could be useful with other forms of technology-enhanced problem-solving practice as well.

Although the design of Tutti is grounded in extensive data of teachers' needs and an early version was pilot-tested in remote teaching scenarios, more classroom piloting with the complete tool is needed. A second limitation is that the design of Tutti is not grounded in data about *students'* needs and preferences. It may help to study these needs for example through Holstein et al.'s multi-stakeholder iterative speed dating method [12]. Finally, it will be interesting to test, in a classroom study how students' learning experiences and outcomes are affected when the teacher uses the dashboard (cf. [13]).

Knowledge regarding the design of support tools for teachers, such as that generated in the current project, may have both practical and theoretical value: Practically, it may serve as a foundation for future projects. Theoretically, it enhances our understanding of how to harness the power of analytics for use by teachers in specific use scenarios.

Acknowledgments. The research was supported by US Dept. of Education (IES) grant R305A180301 and NSF (IIS) grant 1822861 We gratefully acknowledge their contributions. Opinions expressed in the paper are those of the authors, not the sponsor.

References

1. Ahn, J., Campos, F., Hays, M., Digiacomo, D.: Designing in context: reaching beyond usability in learning analytics dashboard design. J. Learn. Anal. **6**, 70–85 (2019)
2. Ahuja, K., Kim, D., Xhakaj, F., Varga, V., Xie, A., et al.: EduSense: practical classroom sensing at scale. Proc. ACM Interact Mob. Wearable Ubiq. Technol. **3**, 1–26 (2019)
3. Aleven, V., McLaren, B., Sewall, J., van Velsen, M., Popescu, O., et al.: Example-tracing tutors: intelligent tutor development for non-programmers. Int. J. Artif. Educ. **26**, 224–269 (2016). https://doi.org/10.1007/s40593-015-0088-2
4. An, P., Holstein K., d'Anjou B., Eggen B., Bakker S.: The TA framework: designing real-time teaching augmentation for K-12 classrooms. In: Proceeding 2020 CHI Conference, pp. 1–17. New York, ACM (2020)

5. Arroyo, I., Woolf, B., Burleson, W., Muldner, K., Rai, D., et al.: A multimedia adaptive tutoring system for mathematics that addresses cognition, metacognition and affect. Int. J. Artif. Educ. **24**, 387–426 (2014). https://doi.org/10.1007/s40593-014-0023-y
6. Baker, R.S., Yacef, K.: The state of educational data mining in 2009: a review and future visions. J. Educ. Data Mining **1**, 3–17 (2009)
7. du Boulay, B.: Recent meta-reviews and meta–analyses of AIED systems. Int. J. Artif. Educ. **26**, 536–537 (2016). https://doi.org/10.1007/s40593-015-0060-1
8. Corbett, A.T., Anderson, J.R.: Knowledge tracing: modeling the acquisition of procedural knowledge. User Model User-adapt. Interact. **4**, 253–278 (1995). https://doi.org/10.1007/BF01099821
9. Gupta, A., et al.: Affective teacher tools: affective class report card and dashboard. In: Roll, I., McNamara, D., Sosnovsky, S., Luckin, R., Dimitrova, V. (eds.) AIED 2021. LNCS (LNAI), vol. 12748, pp. 178–189. Springer, Cham (2021). https://doi.org/10.1007/978-3-030-78292-4_15
10. Hanington, B., Martin, B.: Universal methods of design expanded and revised. Rockport Publishers (2019)
11. Holstein, K., McLaren, B.M., Aleven, V.: Co-designing a real-time classroom orchestration tool to support teacher–AI complementarity. J. Learn. Anal. **6**, 27–52 (2019)
12. Holstein, K., McLaren, B.M., Aleven, V.: Designing for complementarity: teacher and student needs for orchestration support in AI-enhanced classrooms. In: Isotani, S., Millán, E., Ogan, A., Hastings, P., McLaren, B., Luckin, R. (eds.) AIED 2019. LNCS (LNAI), vol. 11625, pp. 157–171. Springer, Cham (2019). https://doi.org/10.1007/978-3-030-23204-7_14
13. Holstein, K., McLaren, B.M., Aleven, V.: Student learning benefits of a mixed-reality teacher awareness tool in AI-enhanced classrooms. In: Rosé, C.P., et al. (eds.) AIED 2018. LNCS (LNAI), vol. 10947, pp. 154–168. Springer, Cham (2018). https://doi.org/10.1007/978-3-319-93843-1_12
14. Kelly, K., Heffernan, N., Heffernan, C., Goldman, S., Pellegrino, J., Goldstein, D.S.: Estimating the effect of web-based homework. In: Chad Lane, H., Yacef, K., Mostow, J., Pavlik, P. (eds.) AIED 2013. LNCS (LNAI), vol. 7926, pp. 824–827. Springer, Heidelberg (2013). https://doi.org/10.1007/978-3-642-39112-5_122
15. Koedinger, K.R., Aleven, V.: Multimedia learning with cognitive tutors. In: Mayer, R., Fiorella, L. (eds.) Cambridge Handbook of Multimedia Learning, 3rd edn., pp. 439–451. Cambridge University Press, Cambridge, UK (2022)
16. Knoop-van Campen C.A.N., Wise A., Molenaar I.: The equalizing effect of teacher dashboards on feedback in K-12 classrooms. Interact. Learn. Env. 1–17 (2021)
17. Nagashima, T., Yadav, G., Aleven, V.: A framework to guide educational technology studies in the evolving classroom research environment. In: De Laet, T., Klemke, R., Alario-Hoyos, C., Hilliger, I., Ortega-Arranz, A. (eds.) EC-TEL 2021. LNCS, vol. 12884, pp. 207–220. Springer, Cham (2021). https://doi.org/10.1007/978-3-030-86436-1_16
18. Olsen, J.K., Rummel, N., Aleven, V.: Designing for the co-orchestration of social transitions between individual, small-group and whole-class learning in the classroom. Int. J. Artif. Educ. **31**, 24–56 (2021). https://doi.org/10.1007/s40593-020-00228-w
19. Pane, J.F., Griffin, B.A., McCaffrey, D.F., Karam, R.: Effectiveness of cognitive tutor algebra I at scale. Educ. Eval. Policy Anal. **36**, 127–144 (2014)
20. Ritter, S., Anderson, J.R., Koedinger, K.R., Corbett, A.: Cognitive tutor: applied research in mathematics education. Psychon. Bull. Rev. **14**, 249–255 (2007). https://doi.org/10.3758/BF03194060
21. Ritter S., Yudelson M., Fancsali S.E., Berman S.R.: How mastery learning works at scale. In: Proceeding 2016 ACM Conference on Learning @ Scale, pp. 71–9, New York ACM (2016)
22. VanLehn, K.: The relative effectiveness of human tutoring, intelligent tutoring systems, and other tutoring systems. Educ. Psychol. **46**, 197–221 (2011)

23. Wang, S., Christensen, C., Cui, W., Tong, R., Yarnall, L., et al.: When adaptive learning is effective learning: comparison of an adaptive learning system to teacher-led instruction. Interact. Learn. Env. 1-11 (2020). https://doi.org/10.1080/10494820.2020.1808794
24. Wood, H., Wood, D.: Help seeking, learning and contingent tutoring. Comput. Educ. **33**, 153–169 (1999)
25. Xhakaj, F., Aleven, V., McLaren, B.M.: Effects of a teacher dashboard for an intelligent tutoring system on teacher knowledge, lesson planning, lessons and student learning. In: Lavoué, É., Drachsler, H., Verbert, K., Broisin, J., Pérez-Sanagustín, M. (eds.) EC-TEL 2017. LNCS, vol. 10474, pp. 315–329. Springer, Cham (2017). https://doi.org/10.1007/978-3-319-66610-5_23
26. Zimmerman, J., Forlizzi, J.: Speed dating: providing a menu of possible futures. She Ji J. Des. Econ. Innov. **3**, 30–50 (2017)

Pyrates: A Serious Game Designed to Support the Transition from Block-Based to Text-Based Programming

Matthieu Branthôme(✉)

Université de Bretagne Occidentale, CREAD - EA 3875, 29238 Brest, France
matthieu.branthome@univ-brest.fr

Abstract. This paper presents a design-based research which focuses on the design and the evaluation of the *Pyrates* online application. This serious game aims to introduce Python programming language supporting the transition from block-based languages. The layout of *Pyrates*' learning environment is inspired from beneficial features of block-based programming editors. In order to evaluate this design, the application has been tested in eight classrooms with French 10-th grade students ($n = 240$). Self-generated activity traces have been collected ($n = 69,701$) and supplemented by a qualitative online survey. The data analysis shows that some of the design choices conduct to the expected effects. The creation of a "programming memo" (synthesized documentation) allows the discovery of algorithmic notions while offering a reference support for the Python syntax. The ease of copy-paste from this memo limits keyboarding. The integration of a syntax analyzer designed for beginners gives students a high level of autonomy in handling errors. However, other choices have rather deleterious impacts. For instance, the creation of a control panel for program executions proves to be dedicated to a trial-and-error programming approach or to "notional bypassing" strategies.

Keywords: Block-based programming · Text-based programming · Python · Scratch · Serious game · Design-based research · Learning analytics

1 Introduction

Over the years, block programming has become one of the preferential modalities for introducing computer coding to younger children [6]. Research has demonstrated the benefits of this approach over the traditional introduction using text-based languages [3,18,25]. At the same time, text-based programming remains overwhelmingly used in high school and college contexts for more advanced computer science instruction. This is even more true in industry, where languages like Python and Java are ubiquitous [19]. Learners who started programming

I. Hilliger et al. (Eds.): EC-TEL 2022, LNCS 13450, pp. 31–44, 2022.
https://doi.org/10.1007/978-3-031-16290-9_3

with blocks may therefore have to switch to text-based programming. How could they be helped in this transition? This is one of the open questions occupying the research field that focuses on introductory programming [14,16,24,26].

A way to assist them is to design intermediate digital environments offering features that support the transition from one coding modality to the other. These bridging environments are intended to be used transitionally before moving to text-based development tools. *Pyrates* online application [20,21] was developed with this objective. It's a serious game [1] which aims at introducing the Python textual language to high school students.

According to Brousseau [8], one of the drivers of learning is feedback from the "learning environment". He defined this learning environment (called *milieu* in French) as the antagonistic system of the learner, the objects (physical, cultural, social, or human) they interacts with. The *Pyrates*' learning environment was designed taking inspiration from block-based programming editors hoping to take advantage of their features.

This contribution focuses on the evaluation of this design. Hence, the addressed research questions are:

- **RQ1:** During classroom testing, do students adopt the designed features? If so, how do they use them?
- **RQ2:** How do students rate these features regarding clarity and utility?

In this paper, the state-of-the-art related to block-to-text transition is first presented (Sect. 2). Next, the design of *Pyrates*' learning environment is outlined (Sect. 3). Then, the methodology adopted to evaluate this conception is described (Sect. 4) and the ensuing results are exposed and discussed (Sect. 5). Finally, the conclusion is followed by some perspectives and extensions (Sect. 6).

2 State-of-the-Art

This literature review is divided into two parts. First, existing applications designed to support the transition from blocks to text are presented. Secondly, the results of scientific works analyzing the intrinsic differences between these two kinds of environments are outlined.

2.1 Existing Applications

Several avenues based on digital applications have been explored to support the block-to-text transition. Following Lin & Weintrop classification [16], three types of environments are distinguished: one-way transition, dual-modality, and hybrid.

One-way transition environments have two views. One view allows the editing of programs using blocks, these programs being automatically converted into a target textual language in the other view. This target language cannot be directly modified, it can only be consulted and possibly executed by users. This is for example the case of the *EduBlocks* application [10] which automatically

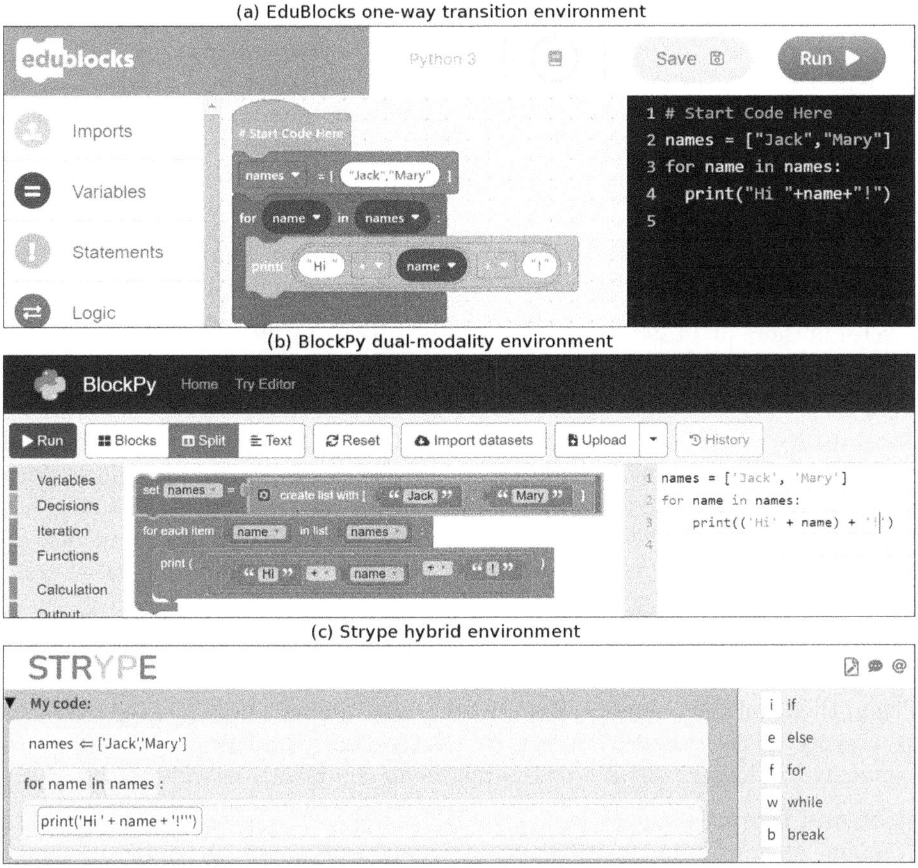

Fig. 1. Examples of the three types of environments

translates assembled block-based programs in Python scripts (see Fig. 1-a). The *Patch* environment [23] presents a similar operation based on Scratch blocks.

Dual-modality environments are structured in the same manner as one-way ones. In addition, programs can be created or modified directly in the textual view. This automatically results in updating the program in the block view. Existing implementations include *PencilCode* [5], which is aimed at learning Javascript and more recently Python [2]. *BlockPy* [4] provides another environment dedicated to Python programming (see Fig. 1-b).

Finally, **hybrid environments** are combining blocks and text in a single view. High-level structures (loops, conditionals, etc.) can be inserted by drag-and-drop or from keyboard shortcuts. Expression-level code is introduced by traditional text editing supported by auto-completion. *Stride* provides teachers with an operational implementation for the Java language [14]. The freshly released *Strype* [15] offers a "frame-based" environment dedicated to Python edition (see Fig. 1-c).

With respect to this classification, there are actually two types of environments: those based on translation (one-way transition and dual-modality) and those based on the fusion of modalities. Each of them has different objectives. On the one hand, to support the transition on the syntactic and concepts transposition aspects. On the other hand, to temporarily hide the drawbacks of textual languages while still benefiting from the advantages of blocks.

2.2 Advantages of Block-Based Environments: Synthesis of the Research literature

Several authors [6,14,24] have analyzed the inherent differences between block-based and text-based programming environments. Their most salient results are summarized below.

Availability of a Command Catalog (ACC). Block programming environments present the user with a browsable "palette" listing all existing blocks organized thematically or conceptually. This allows novice users to discover new concepts or to recall previously acquired ones. In text-based environments, the existence and syntax of code structures must be well-known to programmers.

Reduced number of Significant Elements (RSE). Textual programming languages are made up of many units of information (keywords, typographical signs, etc.). This dense notation is an obstacle for novices because it can overwhelm their working memory. Experienced programmers have learned over time to interpret code in larger chunks. Blocks help to reduce the cognitive load of beginners by showing them how to apprehend commands in wider parts.

Drag and Drop Composition (DDC). Composing programs by dragging and dropping blocks limits the difficulty of typing and searching for typographical signs on the keyboard. The purely mechanical act of typing the program text can be a cognitive and motor obstacle for young learners. The need of keyboarding adds cognitive distractions when correcting the inevitable typing errors.

Absence of Syntactic Errors (ASE). Block-based systems avoid most of the syntax errors thanks to a global and constrained manipulation of the structures. In text-based systems, these errors are numerous and the error messages are generally unclear in their formulation. Interpreting these messages is a far from trivial skill which takes a long time for novices to master.

Execution Control and Visibility (ECV). Block-based environments ease control and improve visibility of program execution. They allow to highlight the block being executed in order to make visible the correspondence between code and action. They may provide a step-by-step mode (set speed, stop and resume execution) or make apparent the current state of variables. These features, not necessarily found in text-based environments, offer to beginners a better understanding of programs execution.

The above comparisons are based on basic code editors. However, some educational text-based environments, like *PyScripter* [22], offer facilitating features such as syntax highlighting, automatic completion, or syntax checking during typing which can help to reduce semantic errors and to limit keyboard input.

3 Design of the Learning Environment

This section reports on *Pyrates*' learning environment design. The presentation is based on Fig. 2 which shows the graphical interface and the different areas of the application.

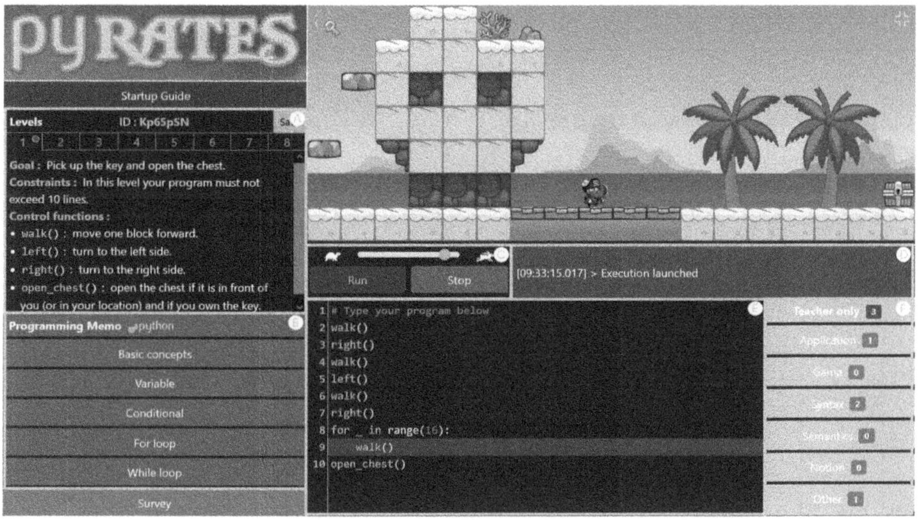

Fig. 2. Different areas of *Pyrates*' graphical interface.

This online application consists of a platform game allowing to control a character using a Python program. This avatar must accomplish various playful objectives. The different levels of this game were designed by implementing the constructivist paradigm which is based on Piaget's psychological hypothesis about adaptive learning [17]. In this way, the algorithmic notions at stake in each level are not explicit but are made necessary by the game problem to be solved. Brousseau [9] qualified these kind of learning situations as "adidactical situations". For the sake of brevity, the game levels' design will not be studied in this paper.

The conception of *Pyrates*' learning environment is presented below. It was designed grounding on the research findings described in Sect. 2.2. Therefore, the features of block programming environments (**ACC** to **ECV**) have been incorporated hoping to take advantage of their benefits.

First, a fixed sidebar was created on the left side of the screen containing, among other elements, a **programming memo** (see Fig. 2-b). This area is inspired by the command catalog present in block-based environments (**ACC**). The memo contents are classified by concepts (basic concepts, variable, conditional, for loop, and while loop) and are accessible by clicking on the different blue buttons. The exposed concepts have been chosen in coherence with the

French mathematics and computer science curriculum. In an effort to guide the students in the exploration of this memo, mouse hovering on a button changes its title by giving an idea of the usefulness of the notion. For example, "variable" becomes "Store information in memory".

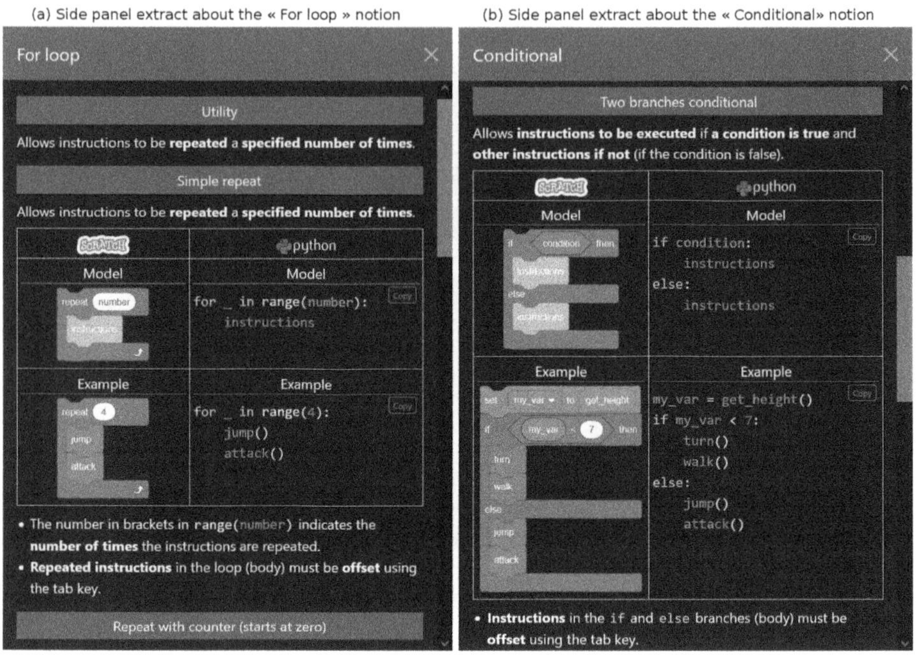

Fig. 3. Two extracts of the programming memo side panel

Clicking on a button causes a side panel appearance detailing the concept in sub-notions (see Fig. 3). Each sub-notion is explained and then illustrated by a **translated generic model and example**. These two programs are expressed both in Python and Scratch languages. Indeed, in France, programming is mainly introduced at lower secondary school using the Scratch block-based language. In this transitional context, Scratch translations of these text-programs are provided. The presence of the Python generic model and its Scratch equivalent is intended to help the learners reducing the number of significant text elements. The goal is to foster the apprehension of Python programs in chunks and not element by element (**RSE**). For example, in the simple repetition case (see Fig. 3-a), students should focus on the number in brackets and consider the rest of the code as a single aggregate.

To limit keyboarding, each piece of Python code is accompanied by a **copy button**. The goal is to encourage the practice of copy-paste to the text editor (see Fig. 2-e). This usage is a kind of substitute to the drag-and-drop characteristic of block-based environments (**DDC**).

Despite these design efforts, it seems presumptuous to consider the disappearance of syntactic errors (**ASE**). Since interpreting error messages is a hindrance for novice programmers, the learning environment has been enhanced with a research-based **syntax analyzer** especially designed for beginners [13]. This module parses the Python code before interpreter execution. It formulates error messages in users' language (only French and English are currently set up) and in a practical register which novices can understand. Moreover, these messages has been marginally amended according to the programming memo terminology. Thus, when a syntax error occurs, an enhanced message is displayed in the console area of the interface (see Fig. 2-d) and the involved code line is red highlighted in the code editing area. An error-free program does not mean that the code is interpretable. Semantic errors (e.g. related to typing) may still appear during interpretation.

Finally, a **control panel** was created (see Fig. 2-c) to improve the supervision of execution (**ECV**). Users can thus launch and stop program execution and adjust its speed using a slider which changes the speed of characters movements by acting on a multiplying factor. This factor is set to 1 (tortoise) at the launch of the game and can go up to 3 (hare). The visualization of the execution (**ECV**) is ensured by the highlighting of the executed line in the code editor area. In this way, the correspondence between code and current action is apparent.

4 Methodology

This section describes the methodology used to evaluate the design choices exposed in the previous section. This methodology relies on field experiments in classrooms. The *Pyrates* software was tested in eight high school classes in France (10th-grade: 14–15 years old). The 240 involved students were Python beginners.

The students used the application during two or three sessions of 55 min each, one or two weeks apart, depending on the class. During the first session, the application and its functioning were quickly introduced before letting the students use it independently during the remaining time. The teacher was asked to intervene only on students' request, or when they had been stuck for a long time. When the teacher interacted with a student, they had to report the content of the given help (application, game, syntax, semantics, notion, other) by clicking on buttons in a reserved frame of the application (see Fig. 2-f).

During these sessions, the application traces the interactions of the students with the learning environment: consultation and copy-paste of contents, syntactic and semantic errors, helps brought by the teacher, launched programs, manipulation of the control panel, etc. These activity traces are automatically generated according to the students' behavior and then exported in a standardized *xAPI* format [12]. This data are completed by an online survey filled in by the students at the end of the experiment. The purpose of this survey is to collect their qualitative point of view on the application.

Consequently, this study data set consists of 69,701 activity traces and 224 survey responses (some students were unable to answer for technical reasons). It was analyzed in an automated way by means of Python programs. Data manipulation and processing relied on *Pandas* library, graphs are generated by *Matplotlib* and *Seaborn* libraries. In an open science approach, the data and the code that led to this paper's figures are shared in an online notebook [7].

5 Results and Discussion

The choices described in Sect. 3 have been evaluated by analyzing the students activity traces. In this study, the following traces were taken into account: consultations of the memo, copy-paste from the memo to the code editor, errors detected by the syntax analyzer and by the interpreter, syntactic and semantic aids given by the teachers during their interventions, manipulations of the speed cursor, and chosen speed during the programs' execution.

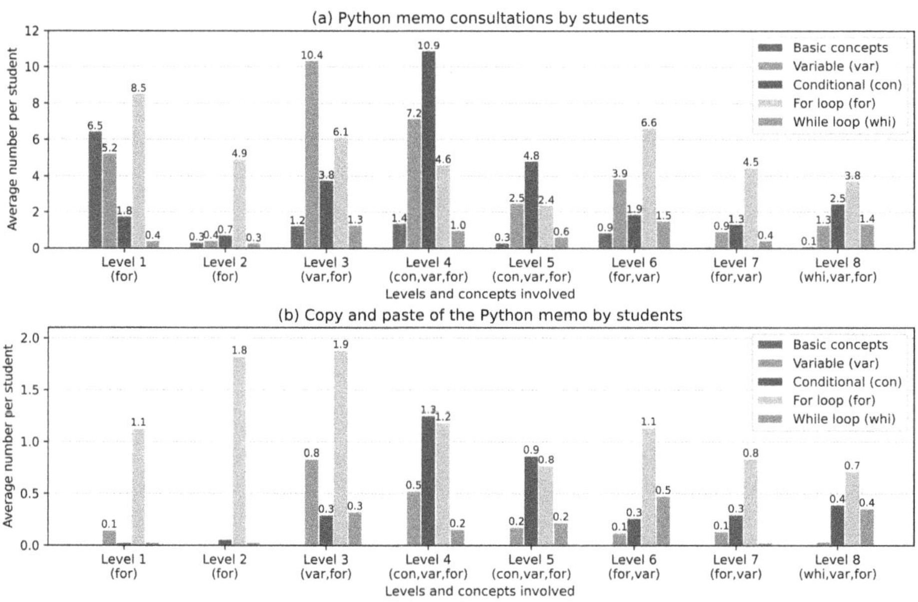

Fig. 4. Consultations and copy-pastes of the Python memo by level

Let us look at programming memo usage. First, Fig. 4-a shows that this memo is frequently consulted by students. It can be noticed that, like the catalog of block-based environments, it supports the discovery of notions. Indeed, each time a new notion is involved in a level (lev 1, lev 3, lev 4, and lev 8), a great variety can be found in the consulted notions. This appears to be the manifestation of a research process. When the concepts have already been used (lev 2, lev 5, and lev 6), the consultation seems to be more focused on the concepts at stake. The hypothesize can be stated that, in this case, the students need to remember concepts' implementing syntax. This reminds the recall function of the block catalog.

Figure 4-b allows to assert that the students almost systematically use the copy-paste function when implementing a notion. Each time a notion is involved in a level, there is, on average, at least one use of copy-paste associated with it. Except for the notion of variable which has a much simpler implementation syntax than the other notions. This practice is similar to the drag-and-drop of blocks, and is able to limit keyboard input and help establish code structures.

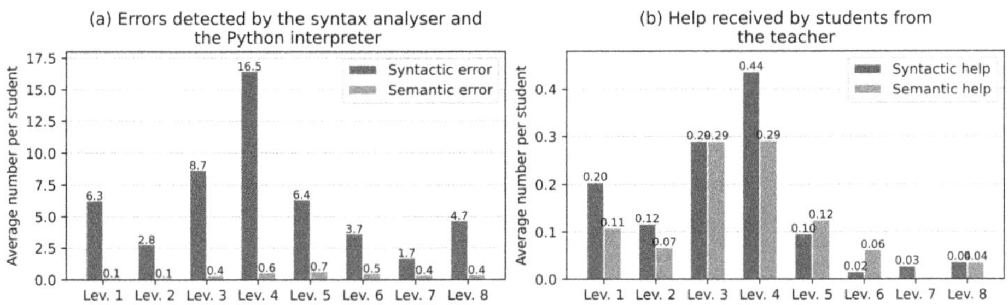

Fig. 5. Errors detected by the application and teacher helps received by students.

Considering errors analysis, the examination of Fig. 5-a shows that syntactic errors (issued from the syntax analyzer) are numerous and in a much higher proportion than semantics ones (issued from the interpreter). Looking at the aids provided by the teachers (see Fig. 5-b), it is remarkable to note that the interventions related to the syntax are very rare. Actually, there is one intervention for every thirty to forty syntactic errors in the first four levels. The students are therefore presumably able to adjust their syntax-erroneous code thanks to feedback from the environment, without asking the teacher.

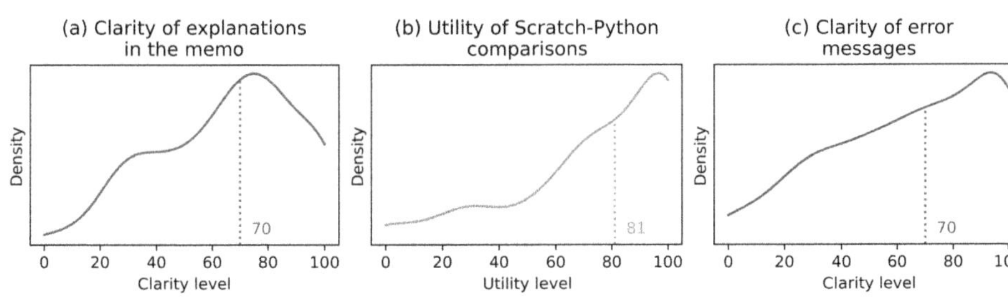

Fig. 6. Results extract from the student survey (score distribution and median).

The traces generated by the application give quantitative insight concerning the use of the memo and the occurrences of the error messages. To go further, these analyses can be qualitatively completed by the survey results. The students had to evaluate several aspects of the application by placing cursors between two extremes ("Not clear" - "Very clear", "Not useful" - "Very useful"), which had the effect of generating a score between 0 and 100. The survey included questions related to the Python memo and the error messages. Figure 6 presents the scores distribution (density) and median for the these questions.

In addition to being extensively consulted by students, the memo's explanations are considered as clear by the majority of them (see Fig. 6-a). Despite this, a group of students can be distinguished around the score of 30 for whom these contents are more confusing. The comparisons with Scratch are judged as useful or even very useful by the great majority of the students (see Fig. 6-b). Finally, the error messages, which we have shown to foster to students' autonomy, are also deemed to be clear by the largest number of respondents.

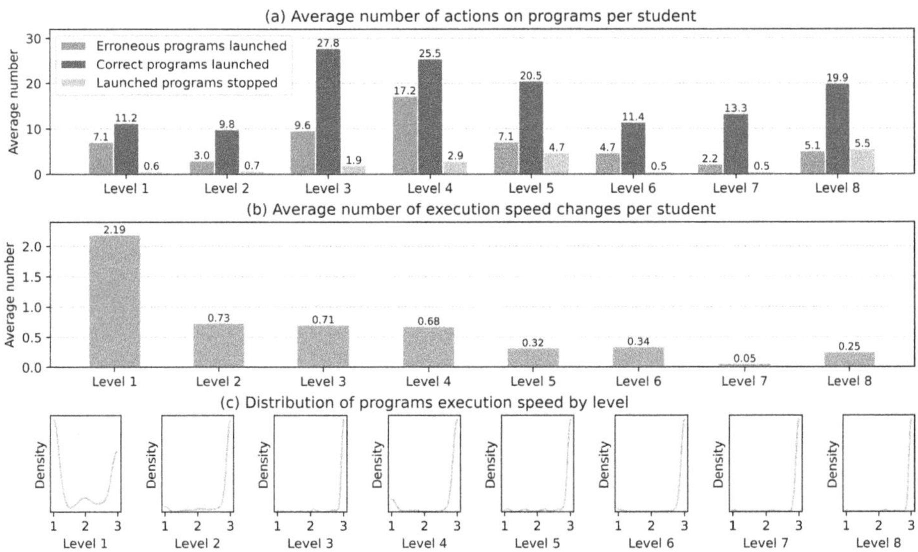

Fig. 7. Data concerning the execution control by level.

Let us now evaluate the use of the program control features. According to Fig. 7-a, there is a very large number of programs run on average per student. Many of them are erroneous, suggesting that students are adopting a trial-and-error programming approach. Numerous correct programs are also launched, which shows that students progress through the game levels in incremental intermediary steps. Program stops are scarce. It is possible to distinguish two types of behaviors depending on the way the levels routes are generated. For a first set of levels with fixed non-random routes (Lev.1, Lev.2, Lev.6, and Lev.7), students use on average between fifteen and twenty launches and almost no stops. In levels containing random-based routes which change with each run (Lev.3, Lev.4,

Lev.5, and Lev.8), students tend to use more launches and to stop some of them. For these random-levels some students adopt a transient operating mode consisting of a series of launch-stop actions until they obtain a random route configuration suitable for their program. This strategy, which can be coined as "notional bypassing", makes it possible to succeed at these levels without implementing the algorithmic notions at stake. These notions are the coding structures based on tests (conditional and while loop). This procedure has very little chance of success because of the large number of different level random routes. These students who remain at any costs in the playful domain are unwilling or unable to enter into notional learning by exploring the learning environment seeking a notion that might allow them to complete the level.

Finally, let us pay attention to the speed change cursor. It is on average rarely used and decreasingly over time (see Fig. 7-b). Figure 7-c shows the distribution (density) of launched programs' execution speeds for each level. From level 2 onwards, the programs are almost all launched at the maximum speed (multiplying factor of 3). The trial-and-error and incremental programming approach earlier described is consistent with this high execution speed. Indeed, three students remarked in the open-ended field of the survey that "the character does not move fast enough". Nevertheless, a marginal practice can be noted in more advanced levels (level 4 and level 5). It consists of returning to slower execution speeds. Observations during the experiments indicate that some students need to follow more easily the executed lines in a step-by-step action mode.

6 Conclusion and Perspectives

To conclude this contribution, its main results can be recalled. The *Pyrates*' learning environment has been designed by incorporating block-based environments features that are thought to be beneficial to students. This design was evaluated by analyzing students' activity and answers to an online survey. Some design choices have the following positive consequences:

- the programming memo is very frequently consulted by the students, it is the support of the discovery and the recall of the concepts;
- the included comparisons with Scratch are considered useful by a large majority of students, they should help the apprehension of Python structures in larger chunks;
- copy and paste from the programming memo is widely practiced, this has the effect of limiting keyboarding;
- the feedback provided by the syntax analyzer via "clear" error messages makes it possible to correct the programs with very little teacher involvement.

The control panel should allow the students to better understand the execution of the programs. We note, very marginally, a reduction in the speed of the character in order to follow the executions in a step-by-step fashion. However, in general, it does not produce the expected results:

- the program launch button is frequently used and the speed control slider is very early set to the maximum in order to adopt a trial-and-error programming approach which do not foster reflection;
- the button allowing to stop the executions is little used, and when it is, it is mostly to try to succeed in some random-based levels using "notional bypassing".

Beyond these results, in comparaison with the applications presented in Sect. 2, it can be stated that *Pyrates* allows to ease the block-to-text transition at the level of syntax and notions transposition (translated generic model and example). The design environment also partially erase the inconveniences of the text modality while profiting from the benefits of the blocks (programming memo, copy button, control panel and syntax analyser). This application therefore offers an intermediate step, a kind of island, allowing a gradual progression from the block bank to the text bank. However, there is still a step to go towards a more classical practice of programming in Python using a text editor and a command line interpreter.

These results must be considered in light of the limitations of the methodology. Since the students were in a naturalistic context, it was difficult to maintain totally similar experimental conditions between different groups, particularly concerning the teacher's activity and the temporal distance between sessions. Moreover, reasoning only on averages allows to identify trends, but masks the disparities of levels and practices between the students observed in classrooms. Lastly, we did not have the opportunity to measure students' actual learning while playing the *Pyrates* game.

Finally, let us mention some perspectives that can extend this work. Edwards [11] argues that beginners in computer science are more successful at learning if they move from a trial-and-error approach to a "reflection-in-action" practice. Therefore, it would be advantageous to modify the execution control possibilities in our application in such a way as to force students to do less action and more reflection. One way could be to limit the number of executions with scores penalties. Furthermore, it would be interesting to exploit activity traces using data mining algorithms in order to highlight different coding strategies used by students. Clustering algorithms could also be used to identify different student profiles.

Acknowledgements. This research was funded by *Region Bretagne*, *Université de Bretagne Occidentale* and *IE-CARE* ANR project. We thank students and teachers who participated in the game evaluation sessions.

References

1. Alvarez, J.: Du jeu vidéo au serious game: approches culturelle, pragmatique et formelle. Ph.D. thesis, Université de Toulouse (2007). https://hal.archives-ouvertes.fr/tel-01240683

2. Andrews, E., Bau, D., Blanchard, J.: From droplet to lilypad: present and future of dual-modality environments. In: 2021 IEEE Symposium on Visual Languages and Human-Centric Computing (VL/HCC), pp. 1–2 (2021). https://doi.org/10.1109/vl/hcc51201.2021.9576355
3. Armoni, M., Meerbaum-Salant, O., Ben-Ari, M.: From scratch to "real" programming. ACM Trans. Comput. Educ. **14**(4), 1–15 (2015). https://doi.org/10.1145/2677087
4. Bart, A., Tibau, J., Tilevich, E., Shaffer, C.A., Kafura, D.: BlockPy: an open access data-science environment for introductory programmers. Computer **50**(05), 18–26 (2017). https://doi.org/10.1109/mc.2017.132
5. Bau, D., Bau, D.A., Dawson, M., Pickens, C.S.: Pencil code: block code for a text world. In: Proceedings of the 14th International Conference on Interaction Design and Children, IDC 2015, pp. 445–448. Association for Computing Machinery, New York (2015). https://doi.org/10.1145/2771839.2771875
6. Bau, D., Gray, J., Kelleher, C., Sheldon, J., Turbak, F.: Learnable programming: blocks and beyond. Commun. ACM **60**(6), 72–80 (2017). https://doi.org/10.1145/3015455
7. Branthôme, M.: Paper's data visualisation notebook (2022). https://nbviewer.org/url/storage.py-rates.org/EC-TEL/data_visualisation.ipynb
8. Brousseau, G.: Le contrat didactique: le milieu. Recherches en didactique des mathématiques **9**(3), 309–336 (1990)
9. Brousseau, G.: Théorie des situations didactiques. La Pensée sauvage, Grenoble (1998)
10. Edublocks. https://app.edublocks.org/. Accessed 14 Apr 2022
11. Edwards, S.H.: Using software testing to move students from trial-and-error to reflection-in-action. In: Proceedings of the 35th SIGCSE Technical Symposium on Computer Science Education, SIGCSE 2004, pp. 26–30. Association for Computing Machinery, New York (2004). https://doi.org/10.1145/971300.971312
12. Kevan, J.M., Ryan, P.R.: Experience API: flexible, decentralized and activity-centric data collection. Technol. Knowl. Learn. **21**(1), 143–149 (2015). https://doi.org/10.1007/s10758-015-9260-x
13. Kohn, T.: Teaching python programming to novices: addressing misconceptions and creating a development environment. Ph.D. thesis, ETH Zurich, Zürich (2017). https://doi.org/10.3929/ethz-a-010871088
14. Kölling, M., Brown, N.C.C., Altadmri, A.: Frame-based editing: easing the transition from blocks to text-based programming. In: Proceedings of the Workshop in Primary and Secondary Computing Education, WiPSCE 2015, pp. 29–38. Association for Computing Machinery, New York (2015). https://doi.org/10.1145/2818314.2818331
15. Kyfonidis, C., Weill-Tessier, P., Brown, N.: Strype: frame-based editing tool for programming the micro: bit through python. In: The 16th Workshop in Primary and Secondary Computing Education, pp. 1–2. Association for Computing Machinery, New York (2021). https://doi.org/10.1145/3481312.3481324
16. Lin, Y., Weintrop, D.: The landscape of block-based programming: characteristics of block-based environments and how they support the transition to text-based programming. J. Comput. Lang. **67**, 1–18 (2021). https://doi.org/10.1016/j.cola.2021.101075
17. Piaget, J.: Léquilibration des structures cognitives. Presse Universitaire de France, Paris (1975)

18. Price, T.W., Barnes, T.: Comparing textual and block interfaces in a novice programming environment. In: Proceedings of the Eleventh Annual International Conference on International Computing Education Research, ICER 2015, pp. 91–99. Association for Computing Machinery, New York (2015). https://doi.org/10.1145/2787622.2787712
19. PYPL - popularity of programming language. https://pypl.github.io/PYPL.html. Accessed 14 Apr 2022
20. Pyrates. https://py-rates.org. Accessed 14 Apr 2022
21. Pyrates pedagogical guide. https://py-rates.org/guide/EN/. Accessed 14 Apr 2022
22. Pyscripter github. https://github.com/pyscripter/pyscripter. Accessed 14 Apr 2022
23. Robinson, W.: From scratch to patch: easing the blocks-text transition. In: Proceedings of the 11th Workshop in Primary and Secondary Computing Education, WiPSCE 2016, pp. 96–99. Association for Computing Machinery, New York (2016). https://doi.org/10.1145/2978249.2978265
24. Weintrop, D.: Block-based programming in computer science education. Commun. ACM **62**(8), 22–25 (2019). https://doi.org/10.1145/3341221
25. Weintrop, D., Wilensky, U.: Comparing block-based and text-based programming in high school computer science classrooms. ACM Trans. Comput. Educ. **18**(1), 1–25 (2017). https://doi.org/10.1145/3089799
26. Weintrop, D., Wilensky, U.: Transitioning from introductory block-based and text-based environments to professional programming languages in high school computer science classrooms. Comput. Educ. **142**, 1–17 (2019). https://doi.org/10.1016/j.compedu.2019.103646

Privacy-Preserving and Scalable Affect Detection in Online Synchronous Learning

Felix Böttger[1(✉)], Ufuk Cetinkaya[2], Daniele Di Mitri[2], Sebastian Gombert[2], Krist Shingjergji[1], Deniz Iren[1], and Roland Klemke[1]

[1] Open University of The Netherlands, Heerlen, The Netherlands
mail@felixboettger.de, {krist.shingjergji,deniz.iren,roland.klemke}@ou.nl
[2] DIPF - Leibniz Institute for Research and Information in Education, Frankfurt, Germany
{cetinkaya,dimitri,gombert}@dipf.de

Abstract. The recent pandemic has forced most educational institutions to shift to distance learning. Teachers can perceive various non-verbal cues in face-to-face classrooms and thus notice when students are distracted, confused, or tired. However, the students' non-verbal cues are not observable in online classrooms. The lack of these cues poses a challenge for the teachers and hinders them in giving adequate, timely feedback in online educational settings. This can lead to learners not receiving proper guidance and may cause them to be demotivated. This paper proposes a pragmatic approach to detecting student affect in online synchronized learning classrooms. Our approach consists of a method and a privacy-preserving prototype that only collects data that is absolutely necessary to compute action units and is highly scalable by design to run on multiple devices without specialized hardware. We evaluated our prototype using a benchmark for the system performance. Our results confirm the feasibility and the applicability of the proposed approach.

Keywords: Affect detection · Action units · Emotion recognition · Privacy

1 Introduction

COVID-19 pandemic forced more than 1.6 billion learners out of school [31], becoming the most challenging disruption ever endured by the global education systems. In many countries, educational institutions were forced to move their regular activities online, relying on remote teaching to continue their education [16]. While the modality of education provision changed from physical to online presence the teaching methods in use remained essentially the same. For example, teachers often favored online synchronous classrooms (i.e., video conferencing tools) over asynchronous activities, discussion forums, or group work.

Physical distancing and learning in isolation posed severe challenges for learners worldwide by hindering their study success [24]. In this context, making education systems more resilient and less vulnerable to future disruptions became

I. Hilliger et al. (Eds.): EC-TEL 2022, LNCS 13450, pp. 45–58, 2022.
https://doi.org/10.1007/978-3-031-16290-9_4

a compelling need. In particular, we have to reconsider how digital technologies can support and better facilitate online and hybrid teaching. Digital education technologies such as *video conferencing tools* and *learning management systems* have made education more accessible and flexible. However, the modes of interaction respective systems implement remain unnatural for teachers and learners as it requires them to sit behind a computer screen for long hours. Furthermore, also communication in an online classroom has limitations. Teachers can perceive the students' affective states in a face-to-face classroom and notice when they are distracted, confused, or tired. This ability is somewhat hindered in online classrooms due to several limitations of the communication tools. For instance, video conferencing tools only show a limited number of participants on screen. Their images are displayed in small portions of the screen, leaving no space for showing body language. Thus, teachers using video conferencing tools cannot observe the non-verbal cues exhibited by the students. In addition, human communication is multimodal by nature [18], and students and teachers need to use a wide array of modes that go beyond the audio-visual support of the webcams and microphones to interact with each other. Such peripheral devices fall short in capturing and conveying non-verbal aspects of human communication such as body posture, facial expressions, prosody and intonation, and physical proximity. This poses a tremendous challenge for both teachers and learners and hinders the teachers' ability to give the classroom timely feedback. Thus, it potentially leads to learners lacking guidance and motivation.

In the last decade, the technological leaps in artificial intelligence have paved the way for novel human-computer interaction methods. State-of-the-art affective computing technologies can automatically recognize non-verbal cues such as gestures and body posture [15], facial expressions [20], and speech intonation [3]. Such technologies can alleviate the challenges of online education by analyzing and aggregating many signals from the microphones and webcams of learners, narrowing the communication modality gap between video conferencing and face-to-face communication. Teachers who are equipped with such information can alter their teaching strategy when needed, such as taking a break or changing the course of the learning activities. Moreover, they can adapt their teaching styles and course structures based on data.

Despite apparent benefits, affective computing systems are not without any risks. Debatably, the most critical threat is the invasion of learners' privacy [6]. Therefore, it is imperative to design such systems in a way that ensures the protection of the same [9]. The designs must adhere to privacy and data protection regulations and must employ privacy-by-design principles [23]. These principles include practices such as purposeful data collection (e.g., collecting and sharing only the data relevant to the teacher), clearly informing the subjects of the method, asking for consent, and using anonymization and aggregation to avoid tracing the data back to individuals.

To address these challenges, we seek to answer the following research question.

How can we enable teachers to sense the affective states of the classroom in online synchronized learning environments in a privacy-preserving way?

This paper addresses these challenges by proposing a pragmatic approach to detecting student affect in online synchronized learning classrooms in a privacy-preserving and highly scalable manner. We present *Sense the Classroom - Live (STC-Live)*, a research prototype that addresses these challenges and can run on many different end-user platforms, thus not requiring costly specialized equipment. Moreover, we evaluate the prototype's performance.

The remaining of this paper is structured as follows. First, Sect. 2 presents the background information on emotions, emotion recognition, and privacy-preserving design in the context of learning. Then, in Sect. 3, we describe the details of STC-Live and the evaluation procedure. Next, Sect. 4 presents the results of the system evaluation. Finally, in Sect. 5, we discuss the results, reflect on them, and conclude our paper.

2 Background

2.1 Emotions and Emotion Recognition in Learning

Emotions are complex reaction patterns involving experiential, behavioral, and physiological elements by which humans attempt to cope with a matter or event [1]. Ekman defined a set of 'basic emotions' [11] as anger, disgust, sadness, happiness, fear, surprise, and neutrality. The primary emotions are universal in how they are expressed and perceived. More complex emotions are nuances or combinations of the basic emotions. A similar term, affective state, refers to longer-lasting emotions and moods. Several studies exist that define affective states in the context of educational sciences [27]. Some of the affective states relevant to educational sciences are engagement, concentration, boredom, anxiety, confusion, frustration, and happiness [8]. Students' emotional states affect their learning experience by influencing their motivation to learn, engagement, and self-regulation [25]. Many studies report pieces of evidence of a relationship between emotional states and learning experience. For example, it is shown that enjoyment and pride positively predicted academic achievement, while the opposite holds for emotions like anger, anxiety, shame, boredom, and hopelessness [28]. The affective states can be perceived by observing nonverbal cues, e.g., gestures, body posture, micro-expressions, and activities such as not actively listening or looking away. Therefore, in recent years, affective computing in education has received widespread attention from researchers [32].

There are many methods and tools to measure emotions in online learning environments [17] that can be categorized into three different areas: psychological, physiological, and behavioral [13]. The psychological measurement methods are based on the self-reporting of emotions, e.g., questionnaires such as the Academic Emotions Questionnaire (AEQ) by Pekrun et al. [26], and self-report systems such as *emot-control* [14]. The physiological measurement methods use sensors to collect signals from the skin, heart, etc. This method requires specific instruments and sensors, making it challenging to use in an online setting [17]. Lastly, the behavioral measurement tools use behavioral expressions to measure emotions in, for example, natural language [10] and facial expressions. Examples in the literature include a system that detects boredom and lack of interest using eye and head movement [19] and a method that uses eyeball movement and head gestures observed from the real-time feed of the students' web cameras to estimate the corresponding concentration levels [30].

2.2 Facial Expressions and Action Units

Facial expression is one of the most effective channels humans use to communicate their emotions [20]. Many studies have documented that basic human emotions are expressed and recognized universally across cultures [21]. Emotions are expressed in the face by combining multiple muscle movements and contractions, i.e., action units (AU). Researchers have developed systematic approaches to categorize and decode action units [12], and such practices have formed a solid basis for automated facial emotion recognition [20].

Table 1. The 20 AUs as classified by the AU detection step of STC-Live

AU1	AU2	AU4	AU5	AU6
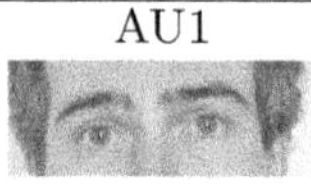	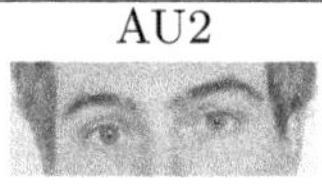	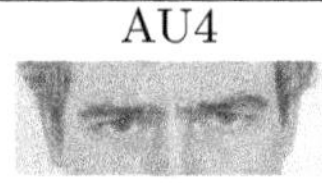	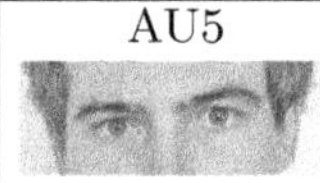	
Inner Brow Raiser	Outer Brow Raiser	Brow Lowerer	Upper Lid Raiser	Cheek Raiser
AU7	AU9	AU10	AU11	AU12
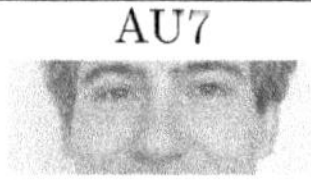	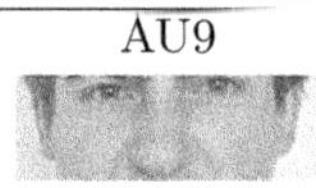	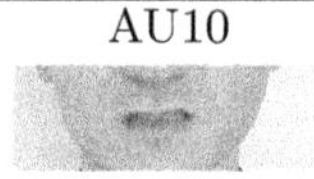	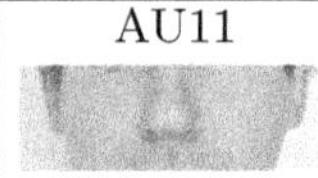	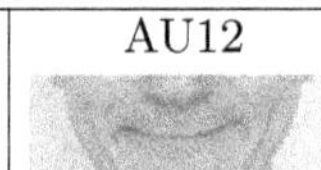
Lid Tightener	Nose Wrinkler	Upper Lip Raiser	Nasolabial Deepener	Lip Corner Puller
AU14	AU15	AU17	AU20	AU23
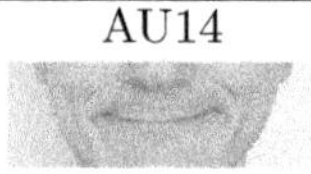	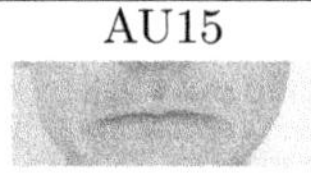	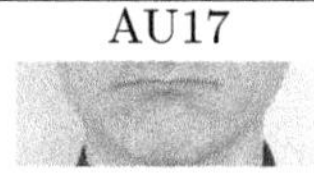	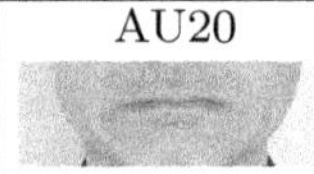	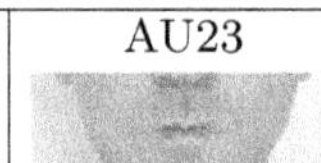
Dimpler	Lip Corner Depressor	Chin Raiser	Lip Stretcher	Lip Tightener
AU24	AU25	AU26	AU28	AU43
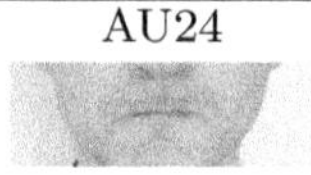	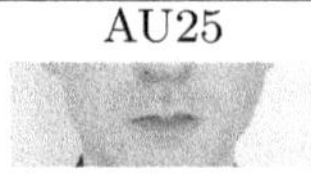	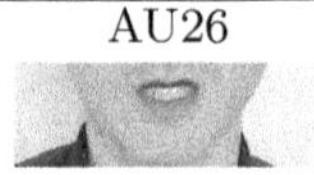	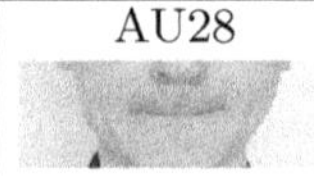	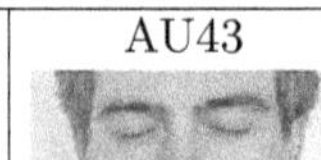
Lip Pressor	Lips Part	Jaw Drop	Lip Suck	Eyes Closed

2.3 Privacy in Learner Emotion Detection

Scheffel et al. [29] identified data privacy as the most critical factor for users' trust in systems processing learner data. According to Drachsler & Greller [9], "there are hesitations regarding, among other things, [...] violation of personal privacy rights; [...] intransparency of the learning analytics systems; [...] the impossibility to fully anonymize data; safeguard access to data; and, the reuse of data for non-intended purposes." For this reason, they conclude, among other aspects, that learner data needs to be "anonymize[ed] as far as possible".

Research on achieving privacy for the specific use case of emotion detection is sparse. Past publications mainly focused on achieving privacy at the machine learning stage by minimizing the possibility of extracting sensitive information from neural networks while maximizing their ability to recognize human emotions [22]. The vector representations produced by these networks are aimed to be sent over the network for downstream classification.

It is debatable what exact types of vector representations are appropriate for preserving privacy in online learner emotion detection, as many representations allow at least for linking attacks. Nonetheless, acquiring vector representations which contain only the data which is absolutely necessary for detecting affect on the client-side and then transferring these to a server for downstream classification reduces sensitivity of the stored data by a large degree. This contributes to preserving the privacy of the classified individuals.

3 Method

In this study, we designed and developed a software prototype that detects the students' affective states in online synchronized learning environments. This section details the proposed system architecture, the collection, storage, and processing of the data, including the action unit detection method based on machine learning. Finally, we report the evaluation of the proposed system.

3.1 System Architecture

STC-Live is a web-based affective learning analytics platform. It uses machine learning models embedded inside the web browser to extract data from the user's webcam without transmitting or storing any video data. Only the outcomes of the machine learning process (i.e., numerical representations of the facial expressions) are transferred to the server, stored inside a database, and displayed to the teacher in an aggregated manner. Additionally, the platform offers a dashboard that visualizes the collected data in real-time. As an open-source project, it can be used as a starting point for similar study designs and adapted for specific requirements.

3.2 System Overview

The system comprises three main components: a) the student-side component that runs on student computers for data collection, b) the server back-end

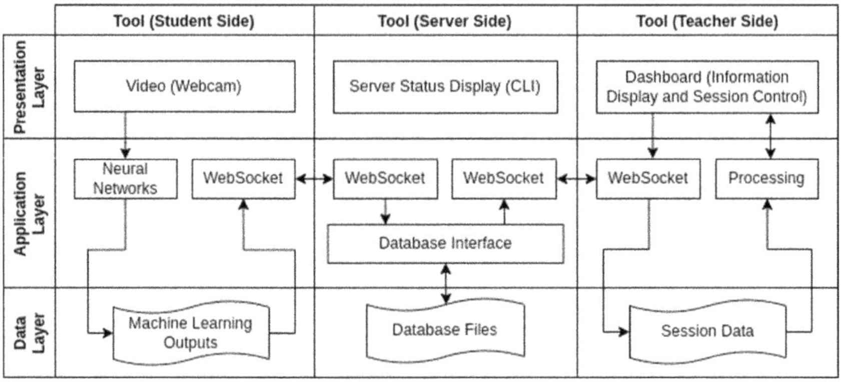

Fig. 1. The system architecture of STC-Live.

component that receives, stores, and forwards the data to the teacher, and c) the teacher-side component that allows session handling and access to the session data (see Fig. 1). The teacher- and student-side components are accessible through a website hosted on the server back-end. This approach ensures multi-platform compatibility without the need to develop and maintain separate code bases for different platforms. From the user's perspective, web-based programs are also more trusted than their native counterparts, as browsers limit the capabilities of web-based programs (e.g., restricted file access, asking users to allow camera/microphone access).

3.3 Student-Side Component: Data Collection

The student-side component is a JavaScript program that runs inside the web browser. It periodically takes an image from the webcam's video feed, which is then used as input for the machine learning pipeline. The machine learning pipeline transforms the images into numerical values representing the facial action units. Consecutively, the numerical values are converted into JSON (Javascript Object Notation) format that contains the following information for each time interval; the prominent emotion detected, timestamp, a list of the spatial coordinates of the 68 facial landmarks, and a list of 5408 Histogram of Oriented Gradient (HOG) values. This JSON object is sent to the server-side tool (back-end) via a WebSocket connection. The images themselves are neither stored nor transferred, therefore avoiding any risk of a privacy breach. The frequency of data collection is configured on the server-side, taking into account the time required to generate a JSON data point. Our recommendation to ensure reliable data collection is for the worst-performing student computer to be used as a baseline for this interval. We evaluate the performance of the data collection tool on different sets of hardware (Sect. 3.6).

Machine Learning Pipeline: The student-side component incorporates a machine learning pipeline (see Fig. 2) that consists of three different neural networks provided by FaceAPI, a commonly used computer vision library for face detection and emotion recognition. Specifically, the pipeline comprises the steps of i) face detection, ii) landmark identification and facial emotion recognition, and iii) AU classification. The first two steps use the following models provided by the FaceAPI; *ssdMobilenetv1*, *faceLandmark68Net*, and *faceExpressionNet*, and the third step uses the *Py-Feat AU classification* model [4].

The face detection step uses *ssdMobilenetv1*, which was trained on the WIDERFACE - dataset [33], and is used to detect the faces on the given image. The model calculates the location of every face and returns a bounding box for each face and a confidence probability associated with the bounding box.

The landmark identification and facial emotion recognition step use *faceLandmark68Net* and *faceExpressionNet* simultaneously. The *faceLandmark68Net* is a lightweight landmark detection network that identifies the location of prominent facial features, i.e., landmarks. It has been trained on approximately 35.000 face images, and it recognizes 68 unique facial landmarks on a given image of a face. In contrast, the *faceExpressionNet* constitutes a Convolutional Neural Network (CNN) that takes an image as an input and returns the predicted emotion.

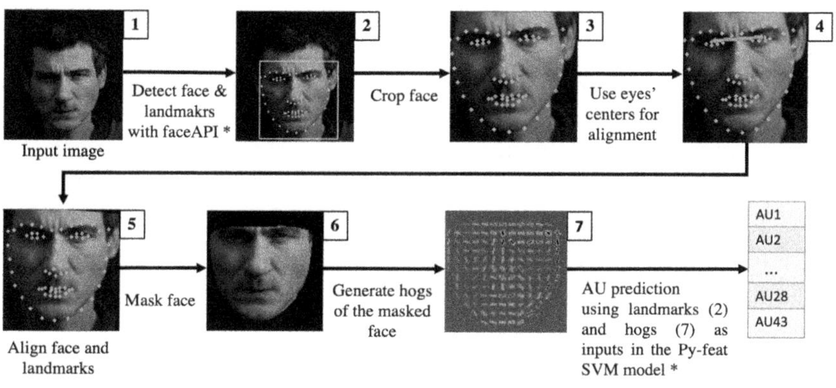

Fig. 2. The pipeline of AU detection. The steps with an asterisk (*) are non-deterministic methods of machine learning algorithms with different performance accuracy measures.

The AU classification step uses the pre-trained Support Vector Machine (SVM) model provided by the Py-Feat [4]. The model receives two vectors as input: the facial landmarks, a (68×2) vector of the landmark locations, and the HOGs, a vector of (5408×1) features that describe an image as a distribution of orientations [7]. The model's output is a list of the AUs classified as present among the 20 possible AUs (Table 1). Pre-processing the image is required for alignment with the input format used for training the classifier [2]. The pre-processing, in summary, consists of the following steps: cropping, resizing, alignment, and masking. In the initial stages, the detected face is cropped from the initial image and resized[1]. Respectively, the detected landmarks are projected in the new image. In the following steps, the cropped face is aligned using the positions of the two eyes and rotating the image so that the line that connects them is horizontal. Similarly, as in the previous step, the detected landmarks are rotated respectively. Lastly, the face is masked using the positions of the landmarks. The vector of the HOG values of the pre-processed image is calculated using eight orientations, 8×8 pixels per cell and 2×2 pixels per block. STC-Live saves the vectors of the HOG values and the landmarks of the pre-processed image, but not the camera image itself, reducing the amount of possibly sensitive data. The data can be used as inputs to the SVM classifier to detect the AUs.

3.4 Server Back-End Component: Data Storage and Transfer

The server-side tool is a Node.js program that functions as a back-end for the distributed system. It receives periodic updates from the student-side component and stores the contained data in a MongoDB database. The current status of all participants of an individual session is bundled and periodically sent to the teacher-side component for visualization. The back-end can run multiple sessions simultaneously, making it possible to have a shared instance. When a new session is created using the web interface, the back-end creates a 12-digit session key, which the students use to enter a session. Access to the session data is only granted to the creator of the session, i.e., the host. The server can be configured to either automatically delete all session data shortly after a session has ended or keep the data in the database for the after-the-fact review. The resource-intensive computation through neural networks is done solely on the students' machines, so the system is highly scalable. It can handle several hundreds of participants in multiple sessions, even on weaker server hardware.

3.5 Teacher-Side Component: Session Management

The teacher-side tool is a JavaScript program that runs inside the teacher's web browser. It connects to the backend via a WebSocket connection used to control the session and receive periodic updates from the back-end. Users can create sessions through a web interface. The session host is granted access to a web-based dashboard that contains real-time information about the current participants' states, such as the detected affective states, as well as the control elements to invite new participants, download all corresponding data, or close the session. Sessions without active participants are automatically closed after a configurable delay.

3.6 System Evaluation

To evaluate the actual performance of our prototype, we created a benchmark scenario that uses the same machine-learning pipeline to extract data from the

[1] The size used is 112×112.

webcam video feed but does not transmit the extracted data to the server. We decided this to ensure that the performance measurement is accurate and not influenced by the stability or speed of the connection to the server. As the machine learning process is by far the most resource-demanding task for the prototype, the results should indicate the overall system performance. The benchmark scenario consisted of 1000 executions of the pipeline, with a new image being passed to the pipeline every second. We measured the time it takes to process the facial data, emotion, and landmark recognition and generate the HOG features, but not the AU detection from these data points as the latter is performed on the server-side. We recorded a video clip of a face moving around to create challenging - but not impossible - situations for face detection. We then tested the actual performance of the system using this pre-recorded video clip[2] on different computers with varying hardware, operating systems, and browsers. We tested the platform on all hardware configurations that were available to us. We have shown that it's feasible to run our platform on lower-end hardware with a status interval of one second, the status interval can be shorter on higher-end hardware.

4 Results

While a correlation between the response time and the systems clock rate and memory size can be shown, performance depends on additional factors such as L1, L2, L3 cache, thermal design and processor architecture. We therefore also report the performance testing results on real hardware configurations. Figure 3 shows a violin plot of the benchmark results, i.e., the distribution of the time required for each pipeline iteration on each computer. The specifications of the computers are listed below the device names. Each graph displays a different number of clusters indicating the concentration of the measurements within that range. The density of the charts indicates a low variance in execution time, suggesting consistent performance. The ThinkPad Yoga 370 and HP Envy x360 15 show occasional spikes of about 900 ms per run. The weakest performer among the tested devices was the ThinkPad T420 running Ubuntu 21.10, with an average run time of 853 ms and occasional spikes to over 1 s.

For most computers, the average data processing time was below the 400 ms mark, except for the ThinkPad T420, with an average time duration of 866 ms. The time needed to initiate the data processing was left out for calculating the average time. While the initialization may take some time, this can be easily compensated for by starting the prototype before the actual teaching session.

Furthermore, we derived regression plots of the average time duration for each device. The average time illustrates the dependent variable, whereas the RAM and clock rate are the independent variables. As Fig. 4 shows, the amount of RAM and the time needed for one pipeline iteration are negatively correlated. With an increase in RAM, we observe a decrease in time duration, which improves the device's overall performance. The regression between the CPU clock

[2] We used a virtual webcam for this purpose.

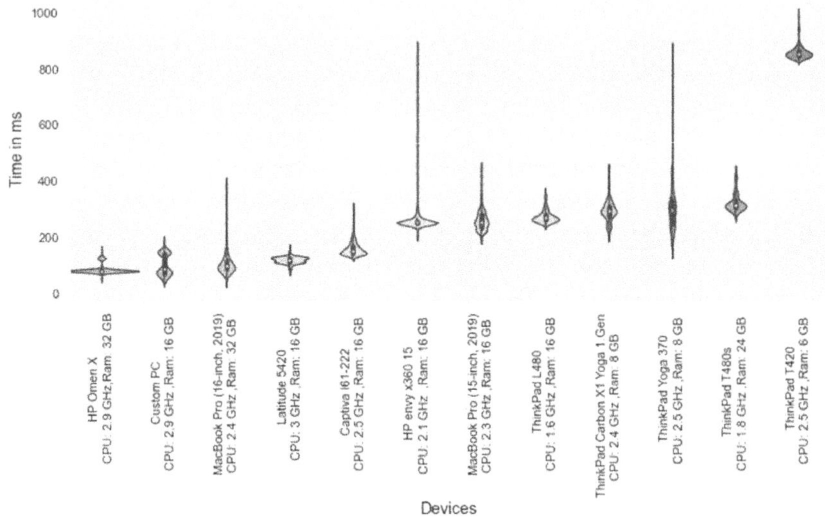

Fig. 3. Violin plot for device performance

and the same execution time also shows a slight negative correlation, as shown in Fig. 4. Unsurprisingly, the results show that better hardware leads to increased performance and, therefore, a decrease in the time needed to run the pipeline on a picture. The most important observation is that, with the scarce exception of a small number of iterations on ThinkPad T420, all iterations finished under a second, which successfully demonstrates the real-time operation capability of the prototype.

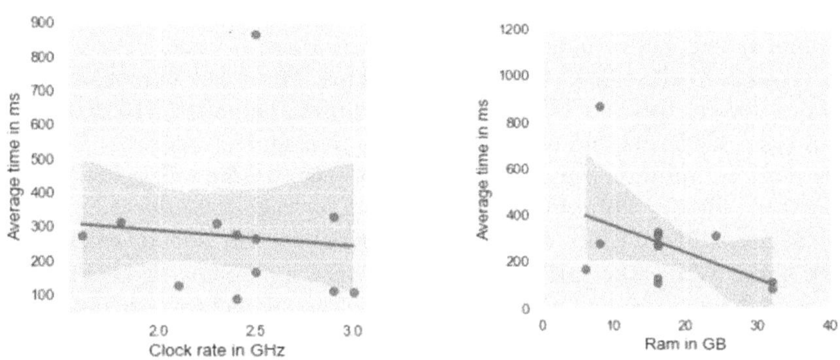

Fig. 4. Average response time vs. hardware specifications

5 Discussion and Conclusion

The forced shift to hybrid learning in most educational institutions during the recent pandemic has affected the majority of learners and teachers throughout the globe. In this study, we aimed to explore the ways to alleviate the challenges posed by non-verbal communication limitations of synchronized online learning. Specifically, we designed STC-Live to automatically detect the learners' affective states and communicate this information to the teachers so that they can sense the overall affective status in the classroom and adapt their teaching style to improve the students' learning experience potentially. Furthermore, we implemented a machine learning pipeline that processes the webcam feed of the students to detect and extract facial expressions without the need to transfer the images to a remote server, thus, preserving the privacy of the student by design. The performance evaluation of the student component of the prototype indicates that it can run on most modern computers without causing resource bottlenecks. Moreover, the distributed architecture of STC-Live makes it highly scalable.

With the continuous advances in machine learning and affective computing, we envision many more automated methods being developed and used in practice soon. However, to reap the benefits of these technologies while avoiding the potential risks, researchers must study the underlying concepts from theoretical and practical perspectives.

An essential concern regarding the use of affective machine learning technologies is the user's privacy. From a student's perspective, there are several concerns. Emotions are highly personal. Therefore, recording and disclosing of emotions can lead towards student profiling and eventually constitute a privacy threat. Educational providers that consider using the proposed technology must inform students and teachers regarding any attempt to analyze emotions automatically, and they must seek students' informed consent to carry out the analysis. From a teacher's perspective, such a data-intensive approach for measuring of the classroom's affective might backfire, as it could be used as an indicator to monitor teachers' performance and undermine their independence. Therefore, we caution against the use of aggregate affective measurements as performance goals and highlight the importance of using such information only for decision support to improve students' learning experience.

This study has implications for both research and practice. We described a method and the implementation details of a prototype that can detect students' affective states in an online classroom. Our method and the open-source prototype can enable educational scientists to study the effect of affective states in synchronized online education. The machine learning pipeline that we propose comprises a novel way of affective state recognition, which practitioners can tailor to fit specific purposes. In practice, such a prototype can be used by teachers in online courses that may alleviate the hardships posed by the lack of non-verbal communication between the teachers and the students, potentially improving the learning experience.

Despite the aforementioned contributions, this study is not without limitations. The first limitation relates to the accuracy of the system. STC-Live incorporates a series of underlying machine learning models which can limit its performance. Additionally, the privacy-preserving design of STC-Live makes it challenging to measure the system's accuracy as a whole. One possible way to overcome this challenge is to conduct a separate experiment in which the participants' video data can be recorded and manually annotated by the researchers. Only then can practitioners compare the system's output against the ground truth annotations created by the researchers. Additionally, the role of affective states in learning must be explored by additional research. For instance, which affective states are relevant, and how can we define them in terms of observable non-verbal cues? The answer to these questions will help us improve the system and communicate the information with the teachers in an optimal way.

Another limitation relates to the privacy of the system. The contribution lies in the possibility to detect action units of students without ever collecting any imagery of them. While not collecting any images of participants certainly improves the privacy aspect of the system, the collected data (HOG values and landmarks) can still be considered sensitive data. Furthermore, linking attacks [5] could allow to identify participants using the stored data. To further improve the privacy of the system, we plan create a model for action unit detection that can be run in the browser, thus eliminating the need to send HOG values and landmarks to the server.

In the future, we will continue our research in affective state detection in learning. Specifically, we will examine how the affective states manifest as non-verbal cues in online education settings. We will study how teachers and students perceive the system, focusing on their preferences and concerns. Finally, a relevant milestone for the proposed system is to evaluate its effect in multiple courses.

References

1. APA dictionary of psychology, emotions. https://dictionary.apa.org/emotions. Accessed 19 Apr 2022
2. Baltruaitis, T., Mahmoud, M.M., Robinson, P.: Cross-dataset learning and person-specific normalisation for automatic action unit detection. In: 2015 11th IEEE International Conference and Workshops on Automatic Face and Gesture Recognition (FG), vol. 06, pp. 1–6 (2015)
3. Bromuri, S., Henkel, A.P., Iren, D., Urovi, V.: Using AI to predict service agent stress from emotion patterns in service interactions. J. Serv. Manag. (2020)
4. Cheong, J.H., Xie, T., Byrne, S., Chang, L.J.: Py-feat: python facial expression analysis toolbox. arXiv abs/2104.03509 (2021)
5. Chiu, W.C., Fritz, M.: See the difference: direct pre-image reconstruction and pose estimation by differentiating hog (2015). https://doi.org/10.48550/ARXIV.1505.00663. https://arxiv.org/abs/1505.00663
6. Correia, A.P., Liu, C., Xu, F.: Evaluating videoconferencing systems for the quality of the educational experience. Distance Educ. **41**(4), 429–452 (2020)

7. Dalal, N., Triggs, B.: Histograms of oriented gradients for human detection. In: 2005 IEEE Computer Society Conference on Computer Vision and Pattern Recognition (CVPR 2005), vol. 1, pp. 886–893 (2005)
8. D'Mello, S.: A selective meta-analysis on the relative incidence of discrete affective states during learning with technology. J. Educ. Psychol. **105**(4), 1082 (2013)
9. Drachsler, H., Greller, W.: Privacy and analytics: it's a delicate issue a checklist for trusted learning analytics. In: Proceedings of the Sixth International Conference on Learning Analytics & Knowledge, LAK 2016, pp. 89–98. Association for Computing Machinery, New York (2016)
10. D'Mello, S., Graesser, A.: Affect detection from human-computer dialogue with an intelligent tutoring system. In: Gratch, J., Young, M., Aylett, R., Ballin, D., Olivier, P. (eds.) IVA 2006. LNCS (LNAI), vol. 4133, pp. 54–67. Springer, Heidelberg (2006). https://doi.org/10.1007/11821830_5
11. Ekman, P.: An argument for basic emotions. Cogn. Emot. **6**(3–4), 169–200 (1992)
12. Ekman, P., Friesen, W.V.: Facial Action Coding System, vol. 1. Consulting Psychologists Press (1978)
13. Feidakis, M., Daradoumis, T., Caballé, S.: Emotion measurement in intelligent tutoring systems: what, when and how to measure. In: 2011 Third International Conference on Intelligent Networking and Collaborative Systems, pp. 807–812. IEEE (2011)
14. Feidakis, M., Daradoumis, T., Caballé, S., Conesa, J.: Measuring the impact of emotion awareness on e-learning situations. In: 2013 Seventh International Conference on Complex, Intelligent, and Software Intensive Systems, pp. 391–396. IEEE (2013)
15. Ghaleb, E., Mertens, A., Asteriadis, S., Weiss, G.: Skeleton-based explainable bodily expressed emotion recognition through graph convolutional networks. In: 2021 16th IEEE International Conference on Automatic Face and Gesture Recognition (FG 2021), pp. 1–8. IEEE (2021)
16. Hodges, C.B., Moore, S., Lockee, B.B., Trust, T., Bond, M.A.: The Difference Between Emergency Remote Teaching and Online Learning (2020). https://er.educause.edu/articles/2020/3/the-difference-between-emergency-remote-teaching-and-online-learning
17. Imani, M., Montazer, G.A.: A survey of emotion recognition methods with emphasis on e-learning environments. J. Netw. Comput. Appl. **147**, 102423 (2019)
18. Kress, G.: Multimodality: A Social Semiotic Approach to Contemporary Communication. Routledge (2009)
19. Krithika, L.B., Lakshmi Priya, G.G.: Student emotion recognition system (SERS) for e-learning improvement based on learner concentration metric. Procedia Comput. Sci. **85**, 767–776 (2016)
20. Li, S., Deng, W.: Deep facial expression recognition: a survey. IEEE Trans. Affect. Comput. (2020)
21. Matsumoto, D., Hwang, H.S.C.: Culture, Emotion, and Expression. Cross-Cultural Psychology: Contemporary Themes and Perspectives, pp. 501–515 (2019)
22. Narula, V., Feng, K., Chaspari, T.: Preserving privacy in image-based emotion recognition through user anonymization, pp. 452–460. Association for Computing Machinery, New York (2020)
23. Newlands, G., Lutz, C., Tamò-Larrieux, A., Villaronga, E.F., Harasgama, R., Scheitlin, G.: Innovation under pressure: implications for data privacy during the Covid-19 pandemic. Big Data Soc. **7**(2), 2053951720976680 (2020)
24. Onyema, E.M., et al.: Impact of coronavirus pandemic on education. J. Educ. Pract. **11**(13), 108–121 (2020)

25. Pekrun, R.: Emotions and learning. Educ. Pract. Series **24**(1), 1–31 (2014)
26. Pekrun, R., Goetz, T., Frenzel, A.C., Barchfeld, P., Perry, R.P.: Measuring emotions in students' learning and performance: the achievement emotions questionnaire (AEQ). Contemp. Educ. Psychol. **36**(1), 36–48 (2011)
27. Pekrun, R., Goetz, T., Titz, W., Perry, R.P.: Academic emotions in students' self-regulated learning and achievement: a program of qualitative and quantitative research. Educ. Psychol. **37**(2), 91–105 (2002)
28. Pekrun, R., Lichtenfeld, S., Marsh, H.W., Murayama, K., Goetz, T.: Achievement emotions and academic performance: longitudinal models of reciprocal effects. Child Dev. **88**(5), 1653–1670 (2017)
29. Scheffel, M., Drachsler, H., Stoyanov, S., Specht, M.: Quality indicators for learning analytics. J. Educ. Technol. Soc. **17**(4), 117–132 (2014)
30. Sharma, P., Joshi, S., Gautam, S., Maharjan, S., Filipe, V., Reis, M.J.: Student engagement detection using emotion analysis, eye tracking and head movement with machine learning. arXiv preprint arXiv:1909.12913 (2019)
31. UNESCO: UN Secretary-General warns of education catastrophe, pointing to UNESCO estimate of 24 million learners at risk of dropping out (2020). https://en.unesco.org/news/secretary-general-warns-education-catastrophe-pointing-unesco-estimate-24-million-learners-0
32. Yadegaridehkordi, E., Noor, N.F.B.M., Ayub, M.N.B., Affal, H.B., Hussin, N.B.: Affective computing in education: a systematic review and future research. Comput. Educ. **142**, 103649 (2019)
33. Yang, S., Luo, P., Loy, C.C., Tang, X.: Wider face: a face detection benchmark. In: IEEE Conference on Computer Vision and Pattern Recognition (CVPR) (2016)

Video-Assisted Self-Regulated Learning (SRL) Training: COVID-19 Edition

Guy Cohen[1], Afrah Assi[1], Anat Cohen[1](✉), Alla Bronshtein[1], Danny Glick[2], Hagit Gabbay[1], and Orit Ezra[1]

[1] Tel Aviv University, Tel Aviv, Israel
{guycohen2,afrahassi}@mail.tau.ac.il, {anatco, allab}@tauex.tau.ac.il
[2] University of California, Irvine, Irvine, USA
glickd@uci.edu

Abstract. The COVID-19 crisis emphasizes the importance of Self-Regulated Learning (SRL), one of today's most valuable skills, with which learners set their learning goals, monitor and control their cognition, motivation, and behavior, and reflect upon them. In the current experimental study, an intervention program based on short online interactive videos was developed to promote SRL skills. This paper presents the impact of the intervention on students' use of SRL skills and grades. It also explores four key pedagogical processes (teacher-student relationships, collaboration, autonomy, and feedback) as mediators for SRL strategies use and grades. The experimental and control groups were randomly assigned (N = 290 students, 18 classes, grades 7–12). Each teacher taught the same subject in two classes for a month, an amount of time that allows intervention to take effect. One of the classes participated in the video-based intervention program (experimental group), whereas the other performed all activities but did not have access to the videos (control group). Data was collected through an SRL and pedagogies usage questionnaire, SRL video prompts, and knowledge tests and was analyzed using the quantitative method. In addition to the theoretical contribution, a practical tool has been developed for educators who wish to employ online SRL training.

Keywords: SRL - Self-Regulated Learning · Video-assisted learning · ERT - Emergency remote teaching · SRL intervention program · COVID-19

1 Introduction

COVID-19 crisis has caused a shift to Emergency Remote Teaching (ERT), catching many teachers unprepared for the transition and families not ready to monitor and facilitate daily home-based learning [34]. Despite the rapid adoption of online learning methods, teachers are expected to adopt practices that ensure successful online learning [56]. Scholars have discussed for a long time the factors that contribute to and inhibit effective online teaching. These factors relate to students, teachers, the learning content, and the learning environment [4, 5, 7]. Effective online teaching relies on several factors, including flexibility in place, time, and pace of learning; collaboration between students and

I. Hilliger et al. (Eds.): EC-TEL 2022, LNCS 13450, pp. 59–73, 2022.
https://doi.org/10.1007/978-3-031-16290-9_5

interpersonal communication; and feedback. Some factors that hinder online learning include inadequate experience in online teaching, insufficient support for and feedback to students; lack of motivation among teachers and students; and especially, insufficient self-regulated learning (SRL) capabilities [13, 57]. SRL involves an active process in which learners set learning goals, monitor and control their cognition, motivation, and behavior, and reflect upon them [46, 64]. Zimmerman's [63] cyclical model of SRL distinguishes three phases: Forethought, Performance, and Self-Reflection. Research has shown that SRL skills can be taught and preserved over time [24] and that balancing them as part of the learning process helps improve learners' achievement and development [46, 59, 64]. A study conducted during the outbreak of the epidemic among schools found that students with SRL skills are less likely to procrastinate and perceive learning experiences more positively [35]. Studies emphasize the importance of developing SRL skills in young adolescents who are in social, emotional, and academic growth and experience further challenges [3]. SRL skills acquired by young adolescents play a significant role in their lifelong learning abilities [51] and academic achievement [62]. These factors all encourage the development of these skills at an early age [20]. For these reasons, SRL skills have become increasingly crucial in the pandemic-ERT [42].

1.1 Video Assisted Self-Regulated Learning (SRL) Training

All students can acquire SRL skills as they are not innate, and teachers can assist students in becoming independent learners. Researchers have found that learners can develop SRL strategies through instruction and training programs regardless of the context in which they are employed [23, 44, 46]. Learning can be more effective when students are exposed to a technological learning environment that encourages them to pursue strategies to become independent learners [61]. Accordingly, researchers have recommended that SRL training be conducted with the help of online learning media, particularly video [24, 37]. Although video usage has increased in recent years, few studies have examined the use of video in SRL training [37, 48]. A preliminary study that implemented a video-based SRL training program in online courses at a large online university in Panama showed that students' perseverance and achievement were influenced by the SRL strategies [30]. In this context, few studies have examined the integration of video-based technologies into SRL training programs among young adolescents while emphasizing the role of technology [24].

1.2 The Role of Pedagogical Processes in SRL Training

Teachers are crucial to developing learning processes and SRL skills in particular [50]. Teachers play a critical role in cultivating and developing SRL skills, in routine settings and in emergencies, such as COVID-19 [12, 13]. By providing an environment that facilitates shared learning and promotes SRL skills among students, teachers can also be instrumental in promoting SRL skills among students with medium-high SRL skills [55]. Pedagogical processes associated with SRL strategies in online settings included teacher-student relationships, collaboration, autonomy, and feedback. Relationships between students and teachers do more than support daily learning pursuits; they also promote students' motivation to become independent learners [58]. Additionally, studies have shown that teaching methods that support students' autonomy can increase their motivation for autonomy, academic engagement, academic achievement, the overall feeling, and SRL skills [16]. Teacher feedback also gives students a significant opportunity to reflect on what they have learned and still need to learn. It also helps close the gap between current understanding and desired learning goals, which are crucial for SRL [15]. Students who receive frequent feedback through conversation, comments, verbal praise, and rewards are more likely to develop their SRL [65]. Furthermore, collaboration directly impacts a learner's internal motivation, hence their ability to learn independently, and is considered an important external factor in online learning environments [18, 26]. While teachers are crucial to developing these skills in children, the subject is so vague for them that most do not attach much importance to learning these skills [60]. Thus, few teachers teach SRL strategies to their students [31].

2 The Present Study

The current study aims to add knowledge on the role of video-based technology and pedagogical processes in developing SRL skills among adolescents during ERT. To this end, an online intervention program utilizing short videos was developed for second-level education during COVID-19. The videos are intended to promote SRL skills. Based on the literature concerning video-assisted SRL training and the role of pedagogical processes in SRL training, a research model has been formulated (see Fig. 1), which consists of three questions:

RQ1. To what extent do (a) SRL training videos influence (c) students' SRL skills and (d) academic achievement?
RQ2. To what extent do (b) pedagogical processes influence (c) students' SRL skills and (d) academic achievement in an ERT during the COVID-19 crisis?
RQ3. Is there an indirect effect of the (a) SRL training videos on (c) students' SRL skills and (d) academic achievement through the (b) pedagogical processes?

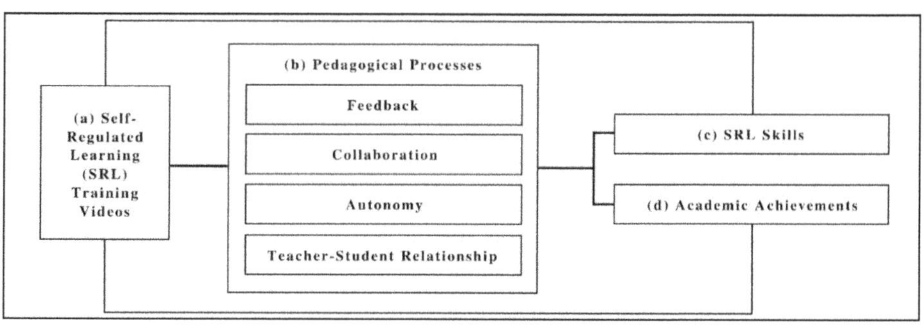

Fig. 1. The proposed research model.

3 Method

3.1 Participants

Nine Israeli teachers participated in the study, six of whom taught in Arabic-speaking schools and three in Hebrew-speaking schools. Two hundred ninety students aged 12–18 participated in the experiment, split into an experimental group (149 students) and a control group (141 students). 66.9% (194) are Arabic-speaking students and 33.1% (96) are Hebrew-speaking students (see Table 1).

Table 1. Study population (N = 290).

	Arabic-speaking students	Hebrew-speaking students	Total
Experimental group	102	47	149
Control group	92	49	141
Total	194	96	290

3.2 Development of the Intervention Program

An online intervention program was created based on previous literature reviews and empirical studies [e.g., 30, 38]. It was designed to be simple so that it could be implemented rapidly in an emergency.

SRL Training Videos. It has been shown that in order to promote SRL, intervention programs must be integrative and incorporate different aspects of learning. Interventions that utilized multiple SRL strategies (cognitive, metacognitive, and motivational) showed the highest effectiveness [9, 21, 46, 52, 53]. To learn about various strategies and their implementation, learners should receive feedback on their learning strategies [9, 47]. Five videos were created to teach SRL skills included in previous intervention programs, which were found to be effective: (1) Planning & Goal Setting, (2) Time Management, (3) Checking for Comprehension, (4) Help-Seeking, and (5) Refection [11, 22, 29, 33, 38, 49]. The teachers also created an introductory video introducing the intervention program to their classes. This video was created by each teacher using the same prewritten script. Adding this extra video allows students to focus on one knowledge subject and link the video content to their natural learning environment.

Scaffolding Support. Scaffolding support during computer-based training enables learners to advance their abilities [49]. For example, using guiding questions (prompts), learners are often asked to perform an activity while thinking about their actions [22, 49]. Hence, all video scripts contained questions encouraging students to self-thinking about the content. Moreover, students were asked several questions at the end of each video that encouraged them to reflect on their learned skills. The videos and questions were distributed via different distribution channels, such as Google Classroom and WhatsApp, according to the teacher's preference.

Pedagogical Processes. The program focuses on four pedagogical processes.

Teacher-Student Relationship. Teachers were asked to discuss their communication expectations with students, including tools and time schedules. In addition, teachers were instructed to encourage students to communicate without fear and in any circumstance during the intervention period. Of course, teachers were asked to be responsive to individuals and groups.

Collaboration. The teachers were advised to promote group learning, create group assignments, facilitate learning resource sharing, and encourage communication between students on academic matters for consultation or assistance. Also, teachers were asked to discuss and find solutions to questions raised by students.

Autonomy. Teachers were asked to offer students permission assignments - a wide range of work topics and submission dates based on various materials available to them (videos, presentations, books, websites). It was also recommended that students choose how they will learn (individually or in groups), the materials they will use, and additional learning topics.

Feedback. Giving as many types of feedback as possible is stressed, including individual, group, class, written, verbal, numerical, as well as discussing performance in general.

3.3 Measures and Instruments

SRL Skills and Pedagogical Processes Questionnaire (SRL-PP). One part of the SRL-PP questionnaire addresses SRL strategies, while the other relates to the use of pedagogies: teacher-student relationships, collaboration, autonomy, and feedback.

SRL Skills. This section of the questionnaire measures how SRL strategies are applied in the three phases of the SRL process as defined by Zimmerman (1998): forethought, performance, and reflection. The questionnaire was constructed based on several questionnaires frequently used in studies related to SRL: OSLQ [6], OSRQ [17], SOLQ [38], MAI & JMAI [54], and MSLQ [25, 45]. First, 29 questions with a Likert scale ranging from 5 to 1 (strongly agree and strongly disagree) were included. Then, all questionnaire was translated into Hebrew and Arabic and tested by a sample of 8 students of the appropriate age group.

Pedagogical Processes. This section is based on a previous questionnaire that examined how students used pedagogical processes [36]. The section consists of 28 items divided into four groups based on the pedagogies included in the study, with a Likert scale score between 5 and 1 (strongly agree and strongly disagree).

Knowledge Tests. In order to measure academic achievement, knowledge tests were composed by the teachers using psychometric rules. The pre-intervention test was based on the content delivered in the month preceding the intervention, and the post-intervention test was based on the content taught during the intervention. Teachers were asked to test knowledge and understanding only, according to Bloom's taxonomy [8].

3.4 Procedure

In the current study, an intensive intervention was conducted for one month, determined in the literature as an adequate period for achieving the study's objectives [23]. Eighteen classes in the 7th-12th grades participated in the study. For each teacher, two classes are taught on the same subject. The classes were randomly divided into experimental and control groups to evaluate the effectiveness of the intervention. The experimental group participated in the video-based intervention program, while the control group performed all the activities without having access to the videos. Students in the experimental group were asked to avoid sharing the video with their schoolmates in the control group.

Teachers participated in online introduction sessions during which the research was introduced, its goal was discussed, and the intervention course was explained. In addition, the teachers received training on writing questions for the tests based on accepted psychometric principles. Each teacher was instructed to make an introduction video that addressed the students in a personal manner in order to stimulate their interest in watching the intervention videos. Three stages of data collection were conducted: prior, during, and immediately after the intervention. Data were collected anonymously, based on a unique code assigned to each student by the teacher. Each teacher provided a separate list of codes for the experimental and control groups.

3.5 Data Analysis

The data was quantitatively analyzed. Exploratory factor analyses (EFA) and confirmatory factor analyses (CFA) were applied to identify the appropriate models and their suitability. Then, in order to answer RQ1, parametric and nonparametric tests were performed to compare the experimental and control groups. In order to answer RQ2, multiple linear regressions were applied to test the relations between pedagogical processes and SRL skills and academic achievements, considering the variance of each other. Finally, to answer RQ3, a path analysis was performed to examine the mediational effect through pedagogical processes.

4 Findings

4.1 The Retrieved Components of SRL and Pedagogy Processes

Two EFA processes were conducted: one to explore the structure of the SRL model out of the SRL questionnaire and the other to construct the PP model based on the PP-usage-related items in the questionnaire. In both processes, the Principal Axis Factoring method with an Oblimin rotation was applied, assuming factors are not orthogonal to each other in both models.

SRL Skills. Twenty-nine items were entered into an EFA, yielding seven indicators of SRL skills: (1) Metacognition (Forethought, Performance & Self-Reflection phases); (2) Excellence orientation (Forethought & Performance phases); (3) Environment management (Performance phase); (4) Student teachers' help-seeking; (5) Online help-seeking; (6) Seeking social assistance (Except teacher); and (7) Peer-to-peer exchange challenging. These factors explained 56.70% of the total variance.

Theoretically, it could be assumed that there is a common factor regarding the help-seeking skill. However, since the help-seeking-related items were not grouped into a unifying factor, a repeated measurement was performed to determine whether the learners responded differently to these items. Indeed, learners' responses to the relevant four items were significantly different (F3 = 30.433, $p < 0.001$).

Pedagogical Processes. Twenty-eight items were entered into an EFA, yielding six indicators of pedagogical processes: (1) Feedback; (2) Collaboration; (3) Autonomy; (4) Student-to-teacher change suggestions; (5) Sharing concerns with the teacher; and (6) Teacher-Student interaction frequency. These factors explained 66.36% of the total variance. Statements relating to the teacher-student relationship and student-to-teacher change suggestions statements have been grouped into unifying factors. Because the factor failed to be statistically significant, they have been kept as stand-alone factors (The Alpha-Cronbach value is relatively low, $\alpha = 0.462$).

Confirmatory factor analyses (CFA) were conducted on items related to SRL skills and on items related to pedagogical processes (post-intervention questionnaire). The CFA supported a model with the seven factors mentioned above linked to SRL skills and with six factors mentioned above linked to pedagogical processes (Fig. 2).

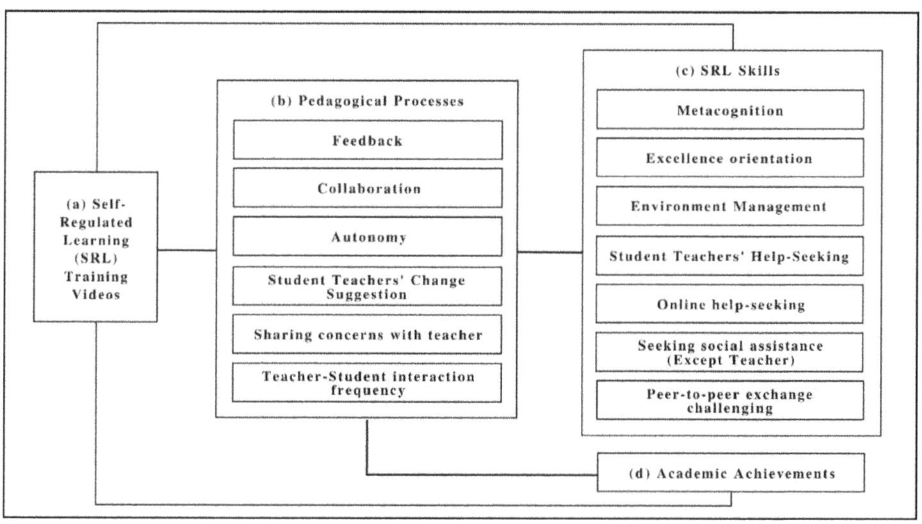

Fig. 2. The revised research model.

4.2 SRL Training Videos Effect (RQ1)

SRL Skills. A comparison was made between the experimental and control groups regarding the differences in the SRL factor values between pre-and post-intervention. As some of the SRL factors are ordinal variables, pre-and post-questionnaire results were compared using the nonparametric Mann-Whitney test for independent samples. Among all the factors representing SRL skills, no significant differences were found between the experimental group and the control group. Thus, it was found that SRL training videos did not influence students' SRL skills.

Academic Achievements. The intervention's effect on academic achievement was examined by comparing the experimental and control groups regarding the changes in knowledge test scores before and after the intervention. As a covariate, grades of the same subject from the semester before the intervention were used to eliminate the effect of students' previous knowledge levels in the same subject. On a repeated measurement test, in which the knowledge tests were compared before and after the intervention, controlling the effect of the previous semester's score, no difference between the experimental and control groups was found. Hence, it was found that SRL training videos did not influence students' academic achievements.

4.3 Pedagogical Processes Effect (RQ2)

The first step in examining the impact of pedagogical processes on SRL skills and academic achievement was evaluating the differences between pre-and post-intervention reports regarding the relevant factors and knowledge test results. Then, using regressions with the Enter method, the prediction of the six differential variables related to pedagogical processes was examined on each of the seven variables related to SRL and the differential variable of knowledge test scores, eliminating the effects of the intervention and previous semester score.

SRL Skills. The seven SRL skills (dependent variables) are presented in Table 2, as well as the pedagogical processes affecting them. The analysis shows that at least one pedagogical process predicts one of six of the SRL skills (Metacognition, Excellence orientation, Environment management, Student teachers' help-seeking, Online help-seeking, and Peer-to-peer exchange challenging).

Academic Achievements. Data analysis revealed that none of the six pedagogical processes predicted knowledge test scores.

4.4 Mediated Relations (RQ3)

Lastly, a path analysis was applied to compute the indirect effects of pedagogical processes. The intervention program variable (experimental and control groups) and the previous semester grade were predictor variables. The mediating variables were the six differences between pre-and post-intervention of the pedagogical process variables. The outcome variables were the seven differences in SRL skills between pre-and post-intervention and the difference between the pre-and post-intervention standardized assessment scores. The results revealed that the indirect effect of SRL video training on SRL skills and academic achievement through pedagogical processes was not statistically significant.

Table 2. A regression analysis of SRL skills and pedagogical processes.

SRL factor	R2	Predictors	β	P Value
Metacognition (Forethought, Performance & Self-Reflection phases)	.49***	Feedback	.32	***
		Autonomy	.17	***
		Teacher-Student interaction frequency	– .08	**
Excellence orientation (Forethought & Performance phases)	.31***	Feedback	.32	***
		Sharing concerns with teacher	.10	*
Environment management (Performance phase)	.44***	Feedback	.45	***
		Collaboration	.30	***
Student teachers' help-seeking	.21**	Feedback	.57	**
Online help-seeking	.19**	Sharing concerns with teacher	.25	**
Seeking social assistance (Except teacher)	.13	Feedback	.31	*
Peer-to-peer exchange challenging	.14*	Feedback	.33	*
		Collaboration	.25	*

* < .05, ** < .01, *** < .001

5 Discussion

5.1 Measurement Model

Based on the questionnaire analysis, it was possible to develop a model that fits well into the measurement of SRL skills. Besides identifying several literature-related factors, such as metacognition & environment management [6, 38], a new factor was identified which combined statements related to excellence orientation, a concept that the literature also discusses in the context of learning and training [19]. In addition, no unifying factor was identified concerning help-seeking, unlike Jansen [38] and Barnard [6]. It may be possible that even though there is a strategic basis for help-seeking in various methods [39], the choice of source of help may have been determined by significant differences between students; thus, the results were not combined. The significant differences between the responses to the four statements relating to help-seeking support this hypothesis. There may be room for refinement of circumstances where assistance is needed [1, 2].

Another model that emerged from the data analysis provides a good fit for pedagogical processes. Factor analysis grouped statements according to three pedagogies that were encouraged during the intervention: feedback, collaboration, and autonomy. These factors follow the literature [16, 26, 58, 65]. In addition, the statements relating to the teacher-student relationship and change suggestions have been gathered into another unifying factor. Even though it is reasonable to assume that willingness to suggest changes is related to the quality of the teacher-student relationship, we chose to examine these variables separately for statistical reasons.

5.2 SRL Training Videos

Several studies have shown that SRL training programs can positively impact SRL skills and performance [23]. Furthermore, over the last few years, researchers and educators have viewed video as a rich and powerful training medium [14, 41]. In the current study, however, the video-based intervention program did not directly affect SRL skills and academic achievements. There are several possible reasons for this. First, the study was carried out at the height of the COVID-19 crisis with frequent transitions from distance learning to hybrid learning or cancellations of sessions. Teachers and students had difficulty adjusting to these changes [5, 27, 56]. Learning and teaching patterns were affected by these changes [40], and it is likely that these changes also affected research engagement. Teachers play an essential role in implementing SRL strategies, and encouraging them in this direction is vital [43]. Apparently, due to its complexity, teachers found it challenging to participate in this period. Other reasons are the lack of time for designing intervention material due to the crisis and variation in the teaching platforms used by teachers. Uniformity in the educational platforms is important for the implementation of the intervention and for monitoring the students' and teachers' progress. Further, the videos might have been more engaging had they been designed within the context of the subject content [32] or had included further interactivity [10] in addition to prompts.

5.3 Pedagogical Processes

This study confirms the strong link between pedagogical processes and SRL skills as described in the literature. Specifically, feedback significantly enhances the use of SRL strategies [15, 65]. Furthermore, both positive and negative effects of pedagogical processes have been found on SRL skills, suggesting that the portion of activation and use of these processes should be considered. A frequent teacher-student relationship, for instance, as a substitute for a help-seeking strategy from other sources, may not be conducive to developing these skills [1, 2]. Future research should investigate this relationship and even identify the optimal integration.

While some pedagogies seem to be associated with some SRL strategies, no pedagogical processes were found to mediate the intervention program. In the study context, it may be that teachers could not operate pedagogies effectively. Consequently, there was no evidence of "pedagogical consumption", and the intervention did not influence such consumption. Also, an improvement in the measurement tool (the questionnaire's statements) might be required.

6 Limitations and Future Directions

The study was conducted from February to June 2021, during a challenging time for the world and the education system in particular. Although this complexity may contribute to the small effect of the intervention on students, other reasons could include the fact that the activity is not mandatory and has a low priority for both students and teachers. Furthermore, the preparation period for the research was quite short. Future studies should recruit more teachers and develop training programs that are further integrated with the subject knowledge and embedded within uniform education platforms.

Like most studies in the SRL field, this study relies heavily on questionnaires [23]. Nevertheless, additional tools may be included to help gather new, more in-depth data about SRL [64]. Other sources of information about student behavior might include situational judgment tests (SJTs), diaries, learning analytics, and focus groups.

7 Conclusion

As a whole, the intervention program implemented in the short-term study did not result in significant changes in student behavior or greater use of SRL strategies. The pandemic-ERT period and other constraints (especially the length of the design process) may have contributed to this outcome. Nevertheless, the study provided valuable insights into research and training tools, especially in ERT. Moreover, the importance of teacher feedback for developing SRL skills was also emphasized, so when planning a future intervention program that supports teacher knowledge alongside students, assessment for learning aspects should be taken into consideration [28].

The study observed low teacher involvement in research operations. Future research should focus on strengthening the relationship with teachers, creating a supportive environment for leading change, reflecting the benefit to teachers, and strengthening their knowledge of SRL.

As for data collection and management, it is worthwhile to collect real-time data from learning management systems. When it comes to having different educational platforms in different schools, it is worth considering a uniform system that is easy to use and will allow real-time information.

One remaining question for future research is whether the intervention should be directly related to the subject knowledge or be more general like the one used in this study. In addition, future research may address how to conduct SRL training in emergencies with the transition between different modes of learning (physical classroom, hybrid, distance learning).

Acknowledgement. This research was supported by the Chief Scientist of the Israeli Ministry of Education.

References

1. Aleven, V., Koedinger, K.R.: Investigations into help seeking and learning with a cognitive tutor. In: Papers of the AIED-2001 Workshop on Help Provision and Help Seeking in Interactive Learning Environments, pp. 47–58 (2001)
2. Aleven, V., McLaren, B., Roll, I., Koedinger, K.: Toward tutoring help seeking. In: Lester, J.C., Vicari, R.M., Paraguaçu, F. (eds.) ITS 2004. LNCS, vol. 3220, pp. 227–239. Springer, Heidelberg (2004). https://doi.org/10.1007/978-3-540-30139-4_22

3. Alderman, M.K., MacDonald, S.: A self-regulatory approach to classroom management: empowering students and teachers. Kappa Delta Pi Rec. **51**(2), 52–56 (2015)
4. Asoodar, M., Vaezi, S., Izanloo, B.: Framework to improve e-learner satisfaction and further strengthen e-learning implementation. Comput. Hum. Behav. **63**, 704–716 (2016)
5. Baber, H.: Determinants of students' perceived learning outcome and satisfaction in online learning during the pandemic of COVID-19. J. Educ. E-Learn. Res. **7**(3), 285–292 (2020)
6. Barnard, L., Lan, W.Y., To, Y.M., Paton, V.O., Lai, S.L.: Measuring self-regulation in online and blended learning environments. Internet High. Educ. **12**(1), 1–6 (2009)
7. Baruth, O., Gabbay, H., Cohen, A., Bronshtein, A., Ezra, O.: Students' perceptions regarding distance learning during the coronavirus outbreak and differences in attitudes between first-year and more advanced students. J. Comput. Assist. Learn. **37**(6), 1666–1681 (2021). https://doi.org/10.1111/jcal.12612
8. Bloom, B.S., Engelhart, M.D., Furst, E.J., Hill, W.H., Krathwohl, D.R.: Taxonomy of Educational Objectives: The Classification of Educational Goals. Handbook I: Cognitive Domain. David McKay Company, New York (1956)
9. Boekaerts, M., Corno, L.: Self-regulation in the classroom: a perspective on assessment and intervention. Appl. Psychol. Int. Rev. **54**(2), 199–231 (2005)
10. Brame, C.J.: Effective educational videos: principles and guidelines for maximizing student learning from video content. CBE Life Sci. Educ. **15**(4), es6 (2016)
11. Broadbent, J., Poon, W.L.: Self-regulated learning strategies & academic achievement in online higher education learning environments: a systematic review. Internet High. Educ. **27**, 1–13 (2015)
12. Cai, R., Wang, Q., Xu, J., Zhou, L.: Effectiveness of students' self-regulated learning during the COVID-19 pandemic. Sci. Insigt. **34**(1), 175–182 (2020)
13. Carter Jr, R.A., Rice, M., Yang, S., Jackson, H.A.: Self-regulated learning in online learning environments: strategies for remote learning. Inf. Learn. Sci. 321–329 (2020)
14. Chen, C.M., Sun, Y.C.: Assessing the effects of different multimedia materials on emotions and learning performance for visual and verbal learning style learners. Comput. Educ. **59**, 1273–1285 (2012)
15. Chen, X., Breslow, L., De Boer, J.: Analyzing productive learning behaviors for students using immediate corrective feedback in a blended learning environment. Comput. Educ. **117**, 59–74 (2018)
16. Cheon, S.H., Reeve, J., Lee, Y., Lee, J.W.: Why autonomy-supportive interventions work: explaining the professional development of teachers' motivating style. Teach. Teach. Educ. **69**, 43–51 (2018)
17. Cho, M.-H., Cho, Y.: Self-regulation in three types of online interaction: a scale development. Distance Educ. **38**(1), 70–83 (2017)
18. Cho, M.H., Jonassen, D.: Development of the human interaction dimension of the self-regulated learning questionnaire in asynchronous online learning environments. Educ. Psychol. **29**(1), 117–138 (2009)
19. Colby, A., Sullivan, W.M.: Strengthening the foundations of students' excellence, integrity, and social contribution. Lib. Educ. **95**(1), 22–29 (2009)
20. de Bruijn-Smolders, M., Timmers, C.F., Gawke, J.C., Schoonman, W., Born, M.P.: Effective self-regulatory processes in higher education: research findings and future directions. A systematic review. Stud. High. Educ. **41**(1), 139–158 (2016)
21. Desoete, A., Roeyers, H., De Clercq, A.: Can offline metacognition enhance mathematical problem solving? J. Educ. Psychol. **95**(1), 188–200 (2003)
22. Devolder, A., van Braak, J., Tondeur, J.: Supporting self-regulated learning in computer-based learning environments: systematic review of effects of scaffolding in the domain of science education. J. Comput. Assist. Learn. **28**(6), 557–573 (2012)

23. Dignath, C., Büttner, G.: Components of fostering self-regulated learning among students. A meta-analysis on intervention studies at primary and secondary school level. Metacogn. Learn. **3**(3), 231–264 (2008)
24. Dresel, M., Haugwitz, M.: A computer-based approach to fostering motivation and self-regulated learning. J. Exp. Educ. **77**(1), 3–20 (2008)
25. Duncan, T.G., McKeachie, W.J.: The making of the motivated strategies for learning questionnaire. Educ. Psychol. **40**(2), 117–128 (2005)
26. Ejubović, A., Puška, A.: Impact of self-regulated learning on academic performance and satisfaction of students in the online environment. Knowl. Manag. E-Learn. **11**(3), 345–363 (2019)
27. Ezra, O., Cohen, A., Bronshtein, A., Gabbay, H., Baruth, O.: Equity factors during the COVID-19 pandemic: difficulties in emergency remote teaching (ERT) through online learning. Educ. Inf. Technol. **26**(6), 7657–7681 (2021). https://doi.org/10.1007/s10639-021-10632-x
28. Fabregat-Sanjuan, A., Pàmies-Vilà, R., Ferrando Piera, F., De la Flor López, S.: Laboratory 3.0: manufacturing technologies laboratory virtualization with a student-centred methodology. J. Technol. Sci. Educ. **7**(2), 184–202 (2017)
29. Garcia, R., Falkner, K., Vivian, R.: Systematic literature review: self-regulated learning strategies using e-learning tools for computer science. Comput. Educ. **123**, 150–163 (2018)
30. Glick, D., Cohen, A., Gabbay, H.: Do student written responses to reflection questions predict persistence and performance in online courses? A text analysis approach. In: Glick, D., Cohen, A., Chang, C. (eds.) Early Warning Systems and Targeted Interventions for Student Success in Online Courses, pp. 1–21. IGI Global (2020)
31. Hamman, D., Berthelot, J., Saia, J., Crowley, E.: Teachers' coaching of learning and its relation to students' strategic learning. J. Educ. Psychol. **92**(2), 342–348 (2000)
32. Hattie, J.A., Biggs, J., Purdie, N.: Effects of learning skills interventions on student learning: a meta-analysis. Rev. Educ. Res. **66**(2), 99–136 (1996)
33. Hattie, J.A.C., Donoghue, G.M.: Learning strategies: a synthesis and conceptual model. NPJ Sci. Learn. **1**, 1–13 (2016)
34. Hodges, C., Moore, S., Lockee, B., Trust, T., Bond, A.: The Difference Between Emergency Remote Teaching and Online Learning (2020). https://er.educause.edu/articles/2020/3/the-difference-between-emergency-remote-teaching-and-
35. Hong, J.C., Lee, Y.F., Ye, J.H.: Procrastination predicts online self-regulated learning and online learning ineffectiveness during the coronavirus lockdown. Personality Individ. Differ. **174**(110673), 1–8 (2021)
36. Horowitz, O.: The contribution of teaching method for the advancement of SRL skills among high school students. MA thesis, Tel Aviv University (2020)
37. Jansen, R.S., van Leeuwen, A., Janssen, J., Conijn, R., Kester, L.: Supporting learners' self-regulated learning in massive open online courses. Comput. Educ. **146**, 103771 (2019)
38. Jansen, R.S., van Leeuwen, A., Janssen, J., Kester, L., Kalz, M.: Validation of the self-regulated online learning questionnaire. J. Comput. High. Educ. **29**(1), 6–27 (2016). https://doi.org/10.1007/s12528-016-9125-x
39. Järvelä, S.: How does help seeking help?–New prospects in a variety of contexts. Learn. Instr. **21**(2), 297–299 (2011)
40. Kufi, E.F., Negassa, T., Melaku, R., Mergo, R.: Impact of corona pandemic on educational undertakings and possible breakthrough mechanisms. BizEcons Q. **11**(1), 3–14 (2020)
41. Ozan, O., Ozarslan, Y.: Video lecture watching behaviors of learners in online courses. Educ. Media Int. **53**(1), 27–41 (2016)
42. Pelikan, E.R., Lüftenegger, M., Holzer, J., Korlat, S., Spiel, C., Schober, B.: Learning during COVID-19: the role of self-regulated learning, motivation, and procrastination for perceived competence. Zeitschrift für Erziehungswissenschaft **24**(2), 393–418 (2021)

43. Perry, N.E., Hutchinson, L., Thauberger, C.: Talking about teaching self-regulated learning: scaffolding student teachers' development and use of practices that promote self-regulated learning. Int. J. Educ. Res. **47**(2), 97–108 (2008)
44. Persico, D., Steffens, K.: Self-regulated learning in technology enhanced learning environments. In: Duval, E., Sharples, M., Sutherland, R. (eds.) technology enhanced learning, pp. 115–126. Springer, Cham (2017). https://doi.org/10.1007/978-3-319-02600-8_11
45. Pintrich, P.R.: A Manual for the Use of the Motivated Strategies for Learning Questionnaire (MSLQ) (1991)
46. Pintrich, P.R.: The role of motivation in promoting and sustaining self-regulated learning. Int. J. Educ. Res. **31**(6), 459–470 (1999)
47. Puustinen, M., Pulkkinen, L.: Models of self-regulated learning: a review. Scand. J. Educ. Res. **45**(3), 269–286 (2001)
48. Raaijmakers, S.F., Baars, M., Schaap, L., Paas, F., van Merriënboer, J., van Gog, T.: Training self-regulated learning skills with video modeling examples: do task-selection skills transfer? Instr. Sci. **46**(2), 273–290 (2017). https://doi.org/10.1007/s11251-017-9434-0
49. Rowe, F.A., Rafferty, J.A.: Instructional design interventions for supporting self-regulated learning: enhancing academic outcomes in postsecondary e-learning environments. MERLOT J. Online Learn. Teach. **9**(4), 590–601 (2013)
50. Rice, M., Oritz, K., Curry, T., Petropoulos, R.: A case study of a foster parent working to support a child with multiple disabilities in a full-time virtual school. J. Online Learn. Res. **5**(2), 145–168 (2019)
51. Schloemer, P., Brenan, K.: From students to learners: developing self-regulated learning. J. Educ. Bus. **82**(2), 81–87 (2006)
52. Schunk, D.H., Swartz, C.W.: Goals and progress feedback: effects on self-efficacy and writing achievement. Contemp. Educ. Psychol. **18**(3), 337–354 (1993)
53. Souvignier, E., Mokhlesgerami, J.: Using self-regulation as a framework for implementing strategy instruction to foster reading comprehension. Learn. Instr. **16**(1), 57–71 (2006)
54. Sperling, R.A., Howard, B.C., Miller, L.A., Murphy, C.: Measures of children's knowledge and regulation of cognition. Contemp. Educ. Psychol. **27**(1), 51–79 (2002)
55. Sulisworo, D., Fatimah, N., Sunaryati, S.S.: A quick study on SRL profiles of online learning participants during the anticipation of the spread of COVID-19. Int. J. Eval. Res. Educ. **9**(3), 723–730 (2020)
56. Taranto, D., Buchanan, M.T.: Sustaining lifelong learning: a self-regulated learning (SRL) approach. Discourse Commun. Sustain. Educ. **11**(1), 5–15 (2020)
57. Viberg, O., Khalil, M., Baars, M.: Self-regulated learning and learning analytics in online learning environments: a review of empirical research. In: Proceedings of the Tenth International Conference on Learning Analytics & Knowledge, pp. 524–533 (2020)
58. Vrieling, E.: Effects of increased self-regulated learning opportunities on student teachers' motivation and use of metacognitive skills. Aust. J. Teach. Educ. **37**, 102–117 (2012)
59. Vrieling, E., Stijnen, S., Bastiaens, T.: Successful learning: balancing self-regulation with instructional planning. Teach. High. Educ. **23**(6), 685–700 (2018)
60. Waeytens, K., Lens, W., Vandenberghe, R.: 'Learning to learn': teachers' conceptions of their supporting role. Learn. Instr. **12**, 305–322 (2002)
61. Wang, T.H.: Developing Web-based assessment strategies for facilitating junior high school students to perform self-regulated learning in an e-Learning environment. Comput. Educ. **57**(2), 1801–1812 (2011)
62. Winters, F.I., Greene, J.A., Costich, C.M.: Self-regulation of learning within computer-based learning environments: a critical analysis. Educ. Psychol. Rev. **20**(4), 429–444 (2008)
63. Zimmerman, B.J.: Developing self-fulfilling cycles of academic regulation: an analysis of exemplary instructional models. In: Schunk, D.H., Zimmerman, B.J. (eds.) Self-regulated Learning: From Teaching to Self-reflective Practice, pp. 1–19. Guilford, New York (1998)

64. Zimmerman, B.: Investigating self-regulation and motivation: historical background, methodological developments, and future prospects. Am. Educ. Res. J. **45**(1), 166–183 (2008)
65. Zimmerman, B., Barry, J.: From cognitive modeling to self-regulation: a social cognitive career path. Educ. Psychol. **48**(3), 135–147 (2013)

An Empirical Study of the Effects of Virtual Currency on Learners in Out of Class Practicing

Darina Dicheva[1(✉)], Lillian Cassel[2], Robert Styer[2], Christo Dichev[1], Breonte Guy[1], and Keith Irwin[1]

[1] Winston-Salem State University, Winston-Salem, NC 27110, USA
{dichevad,dichevc,guybs,irwinke}@wssu.edu
[2] Villanova University, Villanova, PA 19085, USA
cassel@acm.org, robert.styer@villanova.edu
https://www.wssu.edu/profiles/dichevad/

Abstract. As a gamification element, virtual currency (VC) stands for rewards that can be exchanged for virtual or real goods. While some forms of reward-based gamification have been studied extensively, the exploration of the impact of VC on learners is relatively scarce. In particular, there is a lack of studies investigating its effects in different learning contexts. Since VC can evoke perception of benefits with positive impact on course outcomes, it may be experienced as an extrinsic incentive. On the other hand, VC can promote internalized motivation when awarded for accomplishment of certain challenges. To bridge this gap we are conducting a longitudinal study on the impact of VC on student motivation and engagement in different contexts and with different types of learners. The goal of this paper is to empirically investigate whether and how VC can improve the engagement in out-of-class practicing of a certain population of learners in a gamified Discrete Structures course. The study demonstrated a strong positive impact of VC on learners' engagement however VC exhibited no significant impact on students' academic performance and intrinsic motivation.

Keywords: Engagement · Motivation · Gamification · Virtual currency · Case study

1 Introduction

Gamification, the use of game design elements in non-game contexts [5], has become a promising strategy for enhancing learners motivation, engagement, and performance. The driving insight of educational gamification lies in the promise to transfer the motivational potential of games to non-game learning environments. While games use a variety of elements, the range of game elements used

Supported by NSF DUE - 1821189.

I. Hilliger et al. (Eds.): EC-TEL 2022, LNCS 13450, pp. 74–87, 2022.
https://doi.org/10.1007/978-3-031-16290-9_6

for gamifying learning is rather limited and is typically confined to reward structures based on points, forming the so-called reward-based gamification [17,22]. The usual types of rewards commonly include points, badges, and leaderboards and rarely some less common rewards such as virtual currency. Previous studies have shown that reward strategies can encourage learners to keep track of their learning and performance since rewards can serve as indicators of progression and goal accomplishment [25]. In discordance to its popularity, empirical research on reward-based gamification paints a conflicting picture [6,27]: some find positive results [4], others find no or even negative effects, like a decrease in student performance [20]. The emergence of such conflicting results is attributed to poor gamification design [21] by some researchers, or to novelty effects by others [11]. In this context, extending the range of game elements used for studying reward-based gamification can shed new light on the understanding of its mechanisms and potentials for learning. Many games incorporate game design elements that can be redeemed for unlocking or buying objects (e.g., new characters, tools, weapons, stages). Utilizing rewards in such a way can enhance players' motivation and engagement due to the possibility of achieving useful objects and tools, and using them to progress and perform better in the game [25]. While this idea has been transferred to gamification in educational contexts, typically in the form of virtual currency [8], the exploration of its motivational and psychological impact on learners is relatively scarce. This inadequate interest is intriguing as Chang and Wei [1] identified badges and virtual currency as two of the most engaging game elements used in MOOC environments. In their meta-study, Huang et al. [12] provide evidence that not all game elements have the same effect on student learning outcomes. This indicates that it is important to further our understanding about which game design elements work under what circumstances. In order to foster the design of applications that effectively motivate and appeal to individual learners, we need to improve our understanding of the relationship between game elements, such as virtual currency, and the motivation that can emerge in learning activities gamified with them.

As a gamification element, virtual currency (VC) typically stands for all kinds of rewards which can be exchanged with virtual or real goods [12]. It can be viewed also as a reward that has some exchange value within the system. Since virtual currency evokes perception of benefits with positive impact on course outcomes, it may be experienced by learners as an extrinsic incentive. On the other hand, based on Ryan and Deci [28] we can assume that VC can enhance intrinsic motivation when it is awarded for the accomplishment of specific challenges. Unraveling these motivational possibilities suggests studying the psychological effects of VC in different contexts. Furthermore, as of now there is a lack of empirical studies investigating the effects of virtual currency on different learner populations. Recognizing the above gaps, we are conducting a longitudinal study on the impact of the game element virtual currency on student motivation and engagement in different contexts and with different types of learners. The learning activity in focus is student practicing. Practicing is known to be an effective strategy for self-training, yet some students lack motivation to engage or persist in practicing activities [7]. By gamifying this type of learning activities we aim at increasing learners' engagement and, by extension, their academic performance. Thus the goal of the study presented here was to empirically investigate whether and how gamifying learning activities with virtual currency can engender motivation for out-of-class practicing in a "Discrete Structures" course. To improve our understanding of the motivational drivers that influence learners' engagement in the activity, in addition to the motivational scale based on the Self-Determination theory [2], in this study we also used the Expectancy-Value-Cost (EVC) [16] scale as an instrument for estimating the motivational quality (intrinsic vs. extrinsic). In particular, we were interested in finding out why learners value gamified practicing - because it is fun/interesting or because it is useful for completing the course. Specifically, we addressed the following research questions:

RQ1: Does virtual currency encourage more active engagement in out-of-class practicing?
RQ2: Does virtual currency improve students' academic performance?
RQ3: Do gamified activities using virtual currency improve intrinsic motivation?

In the next section we review the related work. The design of the study and the data collection process are described in Sect. 3, and the results of the experiment are reported in Sect. 4. In Sect. 5, we discuss the results and conclude the paper.

2 Related Work

Reward-based gamification is a design method to condition a behavior by affording rewards (e.g., points, badges). While some authors have shown positive outcomes of using reward strategies in improving learners' motivation [19], engagement [23], learning outcomes [19], and enjoyment [21], other studies have found that gamification decreases class participation, exam performance [10,20], motivation [12] and leads to lower knowledge acquisition [20]. Although virtual currency falls in the reward category, it offers more complex motivational mechanism driven by the possibility to earn certain values that enable obtaining of some other desirable objects. In this aspect, the present study aims at bringing extra light to our understanding of the potentials of rewards-based gamification.

Yet, a limited number of papers have studied the effects of VC in different learning contexts and categories of learners. In one of the first experiments with VC, O'Donovan et al. [23] describe their implementation of a gamified game development course with points that could be redeemed for course benefits along with badges, progress bars, and a leaderboard. Although the study concludes that the in-game currency was very well received, its isolated effect was not statistically confirmed. Another early attempt of using VC studied the effects of adding VC along with some social motivators to a peer help system to incentivize learners to help their peers [29]. Essentially, when gamification is driven by several game elements, the isolation of the effect of each one is problematic.

Gamifying a Computer Science course with virtual currency (BitPoints) used together with levels and stars was proposed by Lopes [18]. BitPoints were earned for overcoming obstacles associated with challenges (in practical exercises). The earned BitPoints could be used for purchasing tools/hints for solving other tasks. Explicit evaluation of the VC impact on student learning has not been performed. An alternative kind of VC, in a form of coins, used for gamifying a Software Testing course [20] has been studied recently, but with inconclusive results. Outside of computing subjects, in Duolingo (https://www.duolingo.com/) a type of VC (Lingots) is awarded upon successful completion of some lessons or tasks. This VC can be used to buy prizes (i.e. extra lessons, bonus skills, outfits for the Duolingo mascot). Similarly, in Super Chinese (https://www.superchinese.com/) learners earn coins when they complete a session with no mistakes and make streaks of correct answers. The coins can be used to unlock a full version of the system for a certain time. Regarding math disciplines, virtual currency in a form of eCoins, was used in a Statistics course [4] but in combination with levels, progress feedback, time pressure, and pathways. The earned eCoins could be used to remove parts of a question or an entire question from a test set. Virtual currency, as a feature for enhancing engagement, has also been studied in a MOOC environment, where redeemable points were reported as the second most engaging gamification mechanism [28]. A similar version of VC, called in-course redeemable rewards, was reported in [26]. It was issued to students for completing predefined tasks and could be exchanged for various privileges (e.g., unlock exclusive learning contents, extra attempts and/or more time to perform quizzes, extended due date of assignments). Nonetheless, the subsequent studies [24] did not demonstrate a significant increase in student engagement.

A more systematic exploration of the effect of VC on learners' behavioral and psychological outcomes began with the work of Dicheva et al. [9]. In a Data Structures course gamified with badges, leaderboard, and VC students could earn and spend VC based on rules specified by the instructor. The earning rules were based on the amount, the level of difficulty, and the correctness of the solutions of completed problem-solving exercises. Students could spend their VC on purchases of deadline extensions, re-submission of homework, etc. The idea behind this form of gamification economy was to stimulate students to practice more in order to attain the intended learning outcomes by incentivizing them with purchasable course-related 'benefits'. The reported results of the study confirmed that the targeted motivational effect was achieved but again without isolating the motivational impact of VC from the other elements used to gamify the course. This early work was followed by two consecutive studies with a focus on examining the effect of VC on learners enrolled in a Discrete Math course and in a Computer Networking course. Unlike the previous studies, they studied empirically the individual effect of VC (which was the single gamification element used) in two different contexts (subject and student population) as an initial step towards gaining more generalizable results. These two studies showed that using VC to gamify practicing increased students' engagement, leading to improved academic performance. The present study narrows the focus by preserving the subject (Discrete Structures) but shifting it to a different population of students (with potentially different leaning objectives and attitudes). As the motivational drivers of these two populations may be different, we were interested to examine how they interact with the motivational affordances provided by VC and whether this interaction yields different psychological and behavioral outcomes. Furthermore, we were interested to explore empirically if VC is perceived as an intrinsic or extrinsic motivator by the type of learners participating in this experiment.

3 Case Study

3.1 Course Description

The experiment reported here was conducted in a Discrete Structures course offered at Villanova University. This is a required course for majors and minors in Computer science and computer engineering. It also can fulfill a mathematics requirement which attracts some non-technical students. Students from freshmen through seniors take this class. Because the course is open to all students with no prerequisites, no programming is included. The course is a one-semester treatment of discrete structures covering sets, trees, graphs, logic and proof, mathematical induction, relations, functions, sequences, summations, and elementary combinatorics. In this offering of the course, the textbook was *Discrete Mathematics: An Open Introduction* by Oscar Levin, 3rd edition. (http://discrete.openmathbooks.org/dmoi3.html)

The course structure was fairly traditional, with three midterm exams and a final exam, weekly quizzes, a homework set on each section, and a class participation component. All instructors used the same exams, quizzes, and homework sets. All instructors used the same set of PowerPoint slides, modified from slides used in a previous semester by a different instructor.

3.2 The OneUp Course Gamification Platform

In this study we used the OneUp course gamification platform [9] to gamify the Discrete Structure course. OneUp supports a large set of gamification elements, including experience points (XP), leaderboards, progress bar, avatars, badges, virtual currency, content unlocking, goal setting, challenge duels and callouts, and learning dashboard. It is configurable and the instructor sets which game elements they want to use in their course. Since this study utilized only the game element virtual currency (VC), below is a description of the support for it provided by OneUp.

The use of virtual currency in the gamified environment is governed by rules of two types: VC earning rules and VC spending rules. The earning rules specify in what circumstances the system shall award virtual currency to the students. Each rule specifies a learning activity and a condition related to the student performance in it, as well as how much VC should be awarded to the student if the condition is satisfied. The activities can be either automatically graded by the system practicing quizzes (warm-up challenges) and graded course quizzes (serious challenges), or not automatically graded, for which the instructor has to enter students' scores, such as assignments, labs, projects, attendance, etc. OneUp has an event-based game engine which checks if the defined rules are satisfied for a given student and if so, adds to their account the corresponding VC. Students can check their VC transactions at any moment.

The spending rules specify what the students can buy with the accumulated virtual currency. The spending rules involve typical course-related benefits, such as extending a homework deadline, re-submitting of an assignment, excusing skipping of a class, awarding extra-credit points to a lab or homework, etc. These are offered in the Course Shop, where the students can buy them as in a traditional online shop. The system sends a notification to the instructor for each purchase and also to the student, when the instructor changes the status of the transaction from 'requested' to 'in progress' to 'completed'. It should be noted that both the earning and spending rules are created by the instructor; there are no hard-built rules in the system. The instructor decides what they are comfortable with to offer and creates both kinds of rules in the system interface during the system configuration.

3.3 The Experimental Setting

The experiment occurred in the Spring 2021 semester. Sections were taught by three instructors with a total final enrollment of 82 students. The three instructors carefully coordinated the classes. All used exactly the same slides, the same quizzes, homework, and examinations. One instructor taught in the afternoon in person with a final enrollment of 38 students. One instructor taught the course in the evening in person with a final enrollment of 33 students. The third instructor taught in the day online with a final enrollment of 11 students.

The experimental group consisted of the day sections, for a total of 49 students. The evening students served as the control group. The evening students were the same demographic: full-time undergraduates.

All students in all sections were introduced to the OneUp gamification platform and had access to the practice problems (warm-up challenges) there. The content of the OneUp challenges followed the text's examples and homework questions. The quizzes and exams were written in and administered through Blackboard (using Random Blocks so each student had similar but distinct questions). We closely matched the formats of the quiz, exam, and OneUp warm-up challenge questions. All the students could see that doing warm-up challenges in OneUp provided good preparation for quizzes and exams.

The students in the experimental group had access to virtual currency rewards for doing the warm-ups; the control group did not. Amazingly, we managed to get nearly all the way through the course (week 12 of 14) before the control group students discovered that the other students were earning virtual currency. For evaluation purposes, the final grades used in this study are those obtained before any adjustments due to the virtual currency purchases.

The OneUp platform offers many flexible options for earning and spending virtual currency. The instructors jointly chose the OneUp earning and spending rules and values listed in Table 1.

Table 1. Earning and spending rules.

Earning rule	VC earned
At least 60% on first warm-up on topic	50
At least 5 warm-ups on topic	50
At least 85% on 5 warm-ups on topic	100
At least 90% on a homework	20
Perfect homework score	10
Notable class contribution	20
Spending rule	**VC cost**
Add 10% to quiz	200
Add 2.5% to final	400
Add 1% to midterm	160
Add 10% to a homework	200
Drop lowest quiz	800
Retake quiz	200
One day late homework submission	80
Resubmit a homework	200
Add 2% to participation score	160

3.4 Study Design and Research Methods

We used three complementary methods to answer the research questions. We extracted data from the OneUp logs about student interaction and engagement with the gamified environment to answer the first research question (RQ1). These included students' visits to the gamification-related webpages, how many practice quizzes (warm-up challenges) students have completed, etc. To answer the second research question (RQ2) about the impact of gamifying the course on students' academic performance, we compared the final course grades of the control group and the experimental group. To answer the third research question (RQ3), we conducted a motivational survey with the experimental group. The survey was a modified version of the Basic Psychological Needs Satisfaction Scale - Work Domain [2]. This 21-item scale was chosen because Self-Determination Theory is linked to basic psychological needs, i.e., Autonomy, Competence, and Relatedness [2,13,15]. We hypothesized that these basic psychological needs apply to course work as well, and slightly modified the scale items to reflect this, e.g., "I feel like I can make a lot of inputs regarding how my classwork gets done" vs. "I feel like I can make a lot of inputs regarding how my job gets done".

4 Results

4.1 Student Engagement with the Gamification Platform

This section presents an overview of how the students interacted with the OneUp platform during the study.

The Use of Virtual Currency. To answer the question of how the students from the experimental group used virtual currency in the gamified course, we extracted data from the OneUp transaction log. The data show that the students have earned a total of 64,760 course bucks during the semester, recorded in 774 earning transactions. Each VC earning transaction is a result of satisfying a particular VC earning rule defined by the instructor. The distribution of the transactions by students is given in Fig. 1. It can be seen that 16% of the students have 1 or no earning transactions at all. Those are the students who did not practice in OneUp; some were awarded points by the instructor for participating in class activities. From the students who used OneUp, the majority had between 11 and 20 (30%) or between 21 and 30 (30%) earning transactions, and 11% had more than 30 transactions. Figure 2 shows the actual amount of VC (course bucks) earned by students. As a context, the amount of course bucks specified in the earning rules related to taking warm-up challenges was either 50 or 100. As can be seen, the largest percentage of the students (41%) have earned between 1,001 and 2,000 bucks and 9% more than 3,000. This does show considerable engagement. As to how the students have earned their VC, 51% of the transactions were related to completing 5 warm-up challenges in one topic with results at least 70% correct. This is followed by 37% of the transactions for completing at least 5 challenges in one topic with results at least 85% correct. The latter shows the persistence of the students to keep re-taking some warm-up challenges until they get them correct.

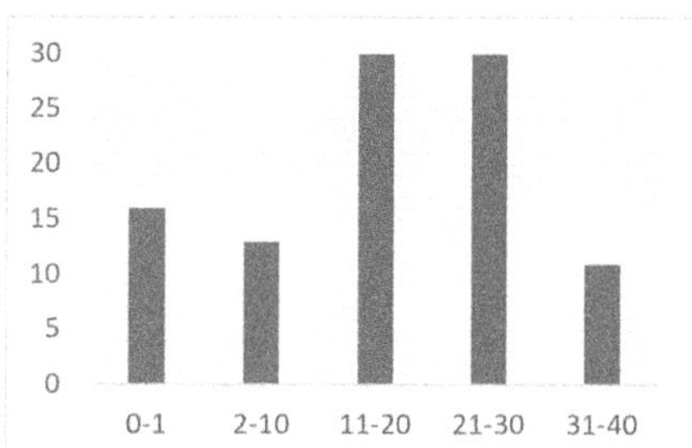

Fig. 1. VC Earn. trans. by students.

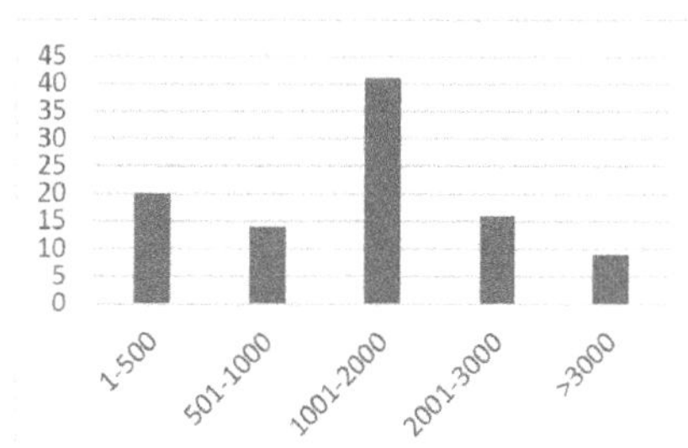

Fig. 2. Earned VC by students.

Regarding the spending of the earned virtual currency, students made 243 purchases in the Course Shop spending 59,620 course bucks. The distribution of the spending transactions by students is shown in Fig. 3. And the distribution of the actual spent bucks in Fig. 4. Note that the highest price in the shop was 800 bucks, the lowest 200, and the average price around 300 bucks.

Most of the students (48%) made up to 5 spending transactions. The 16% that haven't bought anything have never logged in OneUp and have been awarded VC by the instructor for class activities not related to practicing in the platform. Interestingly, most of them have final course grades between 85 and 89 and might have benefited of using the awarded VC, but they never logged in OneUp even for

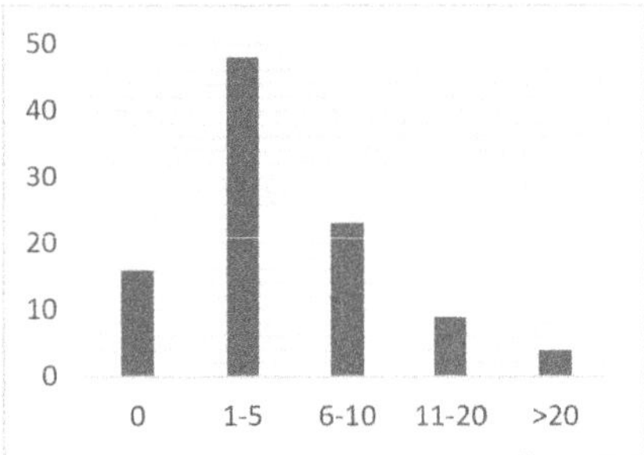

Fig. 3. Spend. trans. by students.

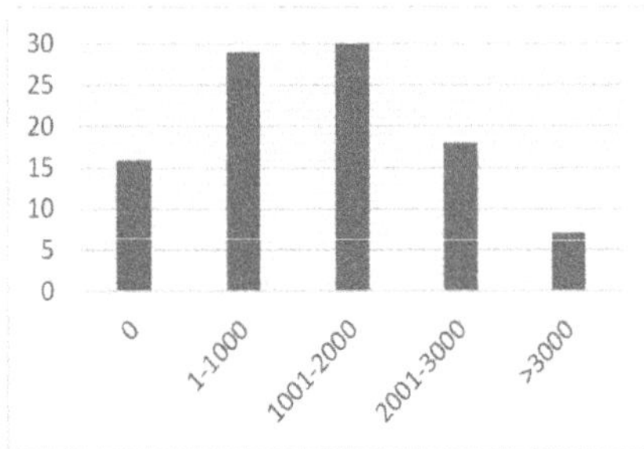

Fig. 4. Spent VC by students.

that reason. A possible explanation is that these students were confident in their knowledge and did not feel they needed additional practicing, so having never been to OneUp, they have not even seen that they have VC to spend. Figure 5 depicts the distribution of the students' spending transactions by category. It shows that students' favorite was buying an extra point on an exam (41%), followed by buying 5 points on the final exam (22%) and adding 10% to a homework grade (11%). It is noticeable that there were not many requests for retaking a quiz and re-submitting or extending the deadline for a homework.

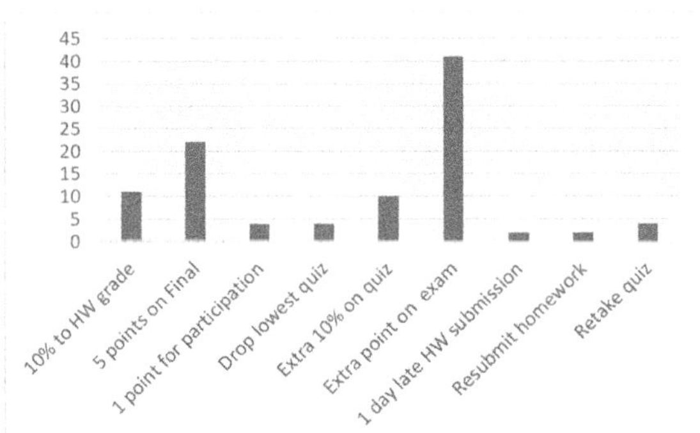

Fig. 5. Spent transactions by category.

We added to the OneUp interface a pop-up question displayed at the time of each spending transaction asking the student for the reason for that particular purchase. 7% of the students did not answer and 13% selected "Prefer not to say". Of those who answered, 50% said that they did it because they worried about their performance in this course, 46% because they had much earned VC and wanted to spend some, and only 4% because they were busy and could benefit from some extra time. Overall, the students made good use of the offered virtual currency in the course. 16% of the students spent all their VC and finished the course with a balance of 0. The majority of the students who were using

OneUp (55%) spent most of their earned VC and had a remaining balance less than 100 course bucks. A likely reason for not spending all earned VC is that the students did not have enough course bucks to purchase a desired item, or that they collected bucks with the intention of making purchases at the end of the course, but then realized that they did not need any of the offered course benefits.

Taking Warm-Up Challenges. To assess whether the use of virtual currency improved the engagement of students in out-of-class practicing, we compared the number of taken warm-up challenges in OneUp by the students in both the control and the experimental groups. The students from the control group took 985 unique warm-up challenges with a total of 1,384 attempts, while the experimental group took 3,674 unique warm-up challenges with a total of 6,485 attempts. The increase of the student engagement with OneUp is striking: the number of warm-up challenges taken from the experimental group is close to 4 times (373%) and the number of challenge attempts is close to 5 times (470%) bigger than those of the control group. Figure 6 shows the percent of students who have taken between 1–50, 51–100, 101–150 and more than 150 unique challenges in both groups. It also shows that 44% of the control group and 30% of the experimental group did not try any challenges. For the experimental group, this is consistent with our previous observation that for each gamified environment, which use is not required, there is a group of students who never participate no matter what kind of gamification is used. Figure 6 shows that the largest percentage of the students in the control group (44%) have taken between 1 and 50 unique challenges, while 23% in the experimental group have taken between 51–100 unique warm-ups and 23% have taken between 101–150 unique warm-ups, with 9% taking more than 150 challenges.

Similarly, Fig. 7 shows that the students in the experimental group have taken many more warm-up challenges. While the largest percentage (35%) of students in the control group who practiced in OneUp fall in the interval of 1–50 challenges taken, the largest percentage from the experimental group (26%) are in the interval 151–250. In addition, 9% have taken more than 250 warm-ups. The average number of warm-up challenge attempts for the control group was 65.90, while for the experimental group it was 162.12.

As can be seen, these results provide a strongly positive answer to our first research question "Does virtual currency encourage more active engagement in out-of-class practicing?" (RQ1).

4.2 Student Academic Performance

With regard to RQ2, we hypothesized that the virtual currency would motivate students to spend more time studying and thus improve their performance [14]. The format of the quizzes closely followed the OneUp warm-up challenges, so we expected a close correlation of challenge attempts to performance on the quizzes. In the following analysis, we compare the day in-person experimental

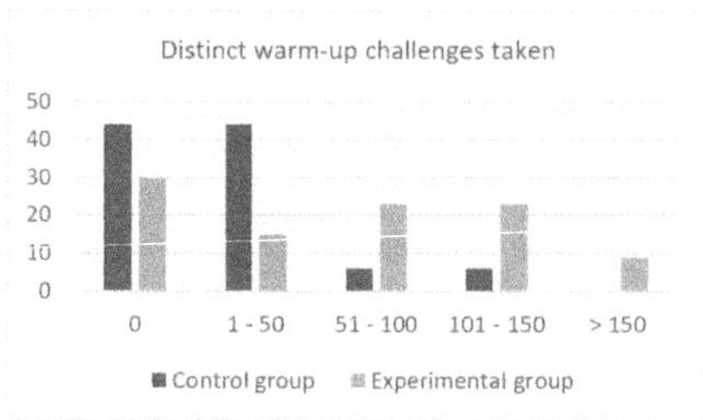

Fig. 6. Distinct warm-ups taken.

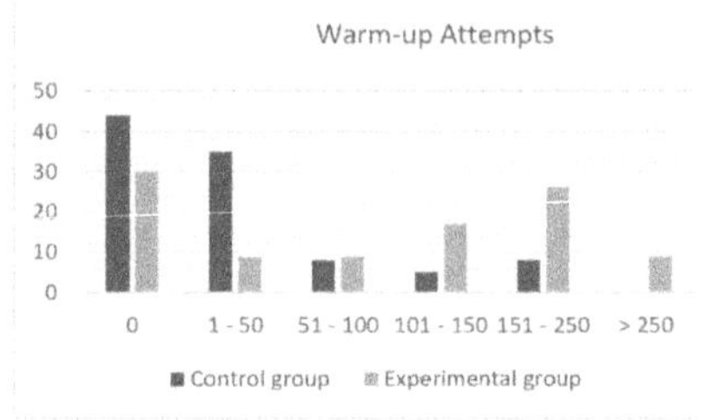

Fig. 7. Warm-up challenge attempts.

group (n = 37) with the evening in-person control group (n = 29). (By removing the online section's data from this analysis, we avoid possible bias due to the format of the class; also the online class was much smaller so including its data does not significantly affect the analysis. Here we also remove students without final grade data who withdrew before the end of the course.)

The analysis does not support the hypothesis. For the experimental group the average grade is 87.73, compared to 85.85 for the control group, essentially no difference (t-test p-value of 48%.) When looking just at the quizzes, the experimental group averaged 84.32 versus 79.40 for the control group, again not significant (t-test p-value of 13%). These results suggest that offering the class virtual currency did not significantly improve student performance (RQ2).

We next analyze the relationship between the number of OneUp warm-up challenges taken by a student (referred to as OneUp score) to their final course grade and also to their quiz grade total. For the experimental group's relation of OneUp score and final grade, $R^2 = 0.045$, while $R^2 = 0.011$ for the experimental group's relation of OneUp score and quiz total. Interestingly, the control group had higher correlations and R^2 values. For the control group's OneUp score and final grade, $R^2 = 0.214$ while $R^2 = 0.129$ for the control group's OneUp score and quiz total. Perhaps future research could explore the conjecture that virtual currency causes students to focus on earning more than on learning, while students who do not earn currency attempt fewer OneUp challenges but focus more intently on learning if they do choose to work on them.

4.3 Motivational Survey

We performed a paired-samples t-test and a stepwise regression to address RQ3 (i.e., Do gamified activities using virtual currency improve intrinsic motivation?). To determine the impact of virtual currency on intrinsic motivation, two measures of intrinsic motivation were employed. The first set of analyses centered on exploring pre- to post-test differences in autonomy, competence, and relatedness as measured by the Basic Psychological Needs scale (e.g., [2,13,15]). The second set of analyses were designed to elucidate a relationship between academic performance as measured by participants' final course grades and participants' task-specific activity perceptions as measured by the Intrinsic Motivation Inventory (IMI; [3]). Factors of the IMI were drawn for the current study because they directly reflect intrinsic motivation (i.e., Interest/Enjoyment), because they are related to behavioral representations of intrinsic motivation (i.e., Perceived Choice), or because they are implicated in internalization of intrinsic motivation (i.e., Value/Usefulness). To perform the analysis, thirty-three matched pairs (i.e., students who took both the pre– and post-test surveys) were extracted from the full dataset. These students were all between the ages of 18 and 25-years-old, with half being drawn from the freshman class, 36.4% from the sophomore class, 11.4% from the junior class, and 2.35% from the senior class. Well over half of the participants (61.4%) were male, whereas 36.4% of participants were female and 2.3% of participants identified as having a non-binary gender. The racial composition of participants was majority White (75%), whereas 15.9% were Mexican/Hispanic/Latin, 4.5% African American, and 4.5% Asian. Further, 34.1% of participants were computer science majors, whereas 15.9% were mathematics majors and the remaining 50% of participants came from various majors. The data were cleaned and negatively worded items recorded in accordance with the previous literature.

The t-test results indicated a significant difference from pre- to post-test on the Relatedness factor of the Basic Need Satisfaction at Work scale. In other words, participants who took both the pre-test and post-test felt more positively about how they related to other students in class after our intervention than before, $t(32) = -2.29$, $p = 0.02$. The stepwise regression analysis was conducted to determine which IMI factors predicted participants' final course grades. Thus, the independent variables (e.g., predictor variables) for this regression model were Interest/Enjoyment, Perceived Choice, and Value/Usefulness and the dependent variable (e.g., outcome variable) was participant's final course grades. For the current study, neither Interest/Enjoyment ($B = -0.07$, $SE = 0.11$, $p = .53$), Perceived Choice ($B = -0.00$, $SE = 0.10$, $p = .94$), nor Value/Usefulness ($B = -0.05$, $SE = 0.15$, $p = 0.72$) emerged as a significant predictor of participants' final course grades, so all three factors were excluded from the final model. For our participants, the final model of the stepwise regression was non-significant indicating that none of the three factors significantly predicted participants' grades.

5 Conclusion

Reward-based gamification is seen as an aid to learner motivation, given that motivation is one of the leading factors of academic success [27]. Although the effect of reward-based gamification in educational context has been addressed in many papers, the number of works that empirically examine the effects of using virtual currency is still limited. Specifically, there is a lack of studies that explore the potential motivational and behavioral effects of VC on learners. On the one hand, VC might function as an extrinsic reward, leading learners to engage in the learning activities in order to earn the desired amount of VC. On the other hand, learners might be motivated to collect VC as a sign of achievements. Yet, it can be perceived as an indicator of their level of learning. Accordingly, one of the goals of this study was to add to the understanding of the effect of VC on learners' behavior and motivation.

While the study results demonstrated a strong positive impact of VC on learners engagement in out-of-class practicing there was no statistically significant difference in the final course grades between the experimental and control group. Thus, inconclusive results were obtained regarding the impact of VC on learners' academic performance. Similarly, no significant relationship was found between learners' intrinsic motivation and their academic performance in the present study. An interesting observed relationship between the individual student OneUp scores to their academic performance suggests further study of a potential influence of VC on the activity outcomes pursued by learners, specifically, shifting their focus on earning virtual bucks rather than learning. While the use of VC as a gamification element is not new, its motivational effect on learners is not sufficiently understood. The present paper aims to expand the current understanding of the motivational mechanisms afforded by the game element virtual currency.

References

1. Chang, J.W., Wei, H.Y.: Exploring engaging gamification mechanics in massive online open courses. Educ. Technol. Soc. **19** (2016)
2. Deci, E., Ryan, R., Gagné, M., Leone, D., Usunov, J., Kornazheva, B.: Need satisfaction, motivation, and well-being in the work organizations of a former eastern bloc country: a cross-cultural study of self-determination. Pers. Soc. Psychol. Bull. **27**, 930–942 (2021)
3. Deci, E.L., Eghrari, H., Patrick, B.C., Leone, D.: Facilitating internalization: the self-determination theory perspective. J. Pers. **62**, 119–142 (1994)
4. Denny, P., McDonald, F., Empson, R., Kelly, P., Petersen, A.: Empirical support for a causal relationship between gamification and learning outcomes. In: Proceedings of the 2018 CHI Conference on Human Factors in Computing Systems (2018)
5. Deterding, S., Dixon, D., Khaled, R., Nacke, L.: From game design elements to gamefulness: defining "gamification". In: Proceedings of 15th MindTrek 2011 Conference: Envisioning Future Media Environments (2011)
6. Dichev, C., Dicheva, D.: Gamifying education: what is known, what is believed and what remains uncertain: a critical review. Int. J. Educ. Technol. High. Educ. **14**(1), 1–36 (2017). https://doi.org/10.1186/s41239-017-0042-5
7. Dichev, C., Dicheva, D., Irwin, K.: Gamifying learning for learners. Int. J. Educ. Technol. High. Educ. **17**(1), 1–14 (2020). https://doi.org/10.1186/s41239-020-00231-0
8. Dicheva, D., Hsin, W.J., Dichev, C., Guy, B., Cassel, L., Irwin, K.: Exploring the effect of virtual currency on learners engagement. ICALT **2021**, 83–87 (2021)
9. Dicheva, D., Irwin, K., Dichev, C.: OneUp: engaging students in a gamified data structures course. In: Proceedings of 50th ACM SIGCSE Conference. ACM (2019)
10. Domínguez, A., de Navarrete, J.S., De-Marcos, L., Fernández-Sanz, L., Pagés, C., Martínez-Herráiz, J.J.: Gamifying learning experiences: practical implications and outcomes. Comput. Educ. **63**, 380–392 (2013)
11. Hanus, M., Fox, J.: Assessing the effects of gamification in the classroom: a longitudinal study on intrinsic motivation, social comparison, satisfaction, effort, and academic performance. Comput. Educ. **80**, 152–161 (2015)

12. Huang, R., et al.: The impact of gamification in educational settings on student learning outcomes: a meta-analysis. Educ. Tech. Res. Dev. **68**(4), 1875–1901 (2020). https://doi.org/10.1007/s11423-020-09807-z
13. Ilardi, B., Leone, D., Kasser, T., Ryan, R.: Employee and supervisor ratings of motivation: main effects and discrepancies associated with job satisfaction and adjustment in a factory setting. J. Appl. Soc. Psychol. **23** (1993)
14. Louw, J., Muller, J., Tredoux, C.: Time-on-task, technology and mathematics achievement. Eval. Program Plan. **31**, 41–50 (2008)
15. Kasser, T., Davey, J., Ryan, R.: Motivation and employee-supervisor discrepancies in a psychiatric vocational rehabilitation setting. Rehabil. Psychol. **37**, 175–188 (1992)
16. Kosovich, J.J., Hulleman, C.S., Barron, K.E., Getty, S.: A practical measure of student motivation: establishing validity evidence for the expectancy-value-cost scale in middle school. J. Early Adolesc. **35**(5–6), 790–816 (2015)
17. Kyewski, E., Krämer, N.C.: To gamify or not to gamify? An experimental field study of the influence of badges on motivation, activity, and performance in an online learning course. Comput. Educ. **118**, 25–37 (2018)
18. Lopes, R.P.: An award system for gamification in higher education. In: 7th International Conference of Education, Research and Innovation, Valencia, pp. 5563–5573 (2014)
19. Luo, Z.: Gamification for educational purposes: what are the factors contributing to varied effectiveness? Educ. Inf. Technol. **27**, 891–915 (2021)
20. de Marcos, L., Domínguez, A., de Navarrete, J.S., Pagés, C.: An empirical study comparing gamification and social networking on e-learning. Comput. Educ. **75**, 82–91 (2014)
21. Nacke, L.E., Deterding, S.: The maturing of gamification research. Comput. Hum. Behav. 450–454 (2017)
22. Nicholson, S.: A recipe for meaningful gamification. In: Gamification in Education and Business (2015)
23. O'Donovan, S., Gain, J., Marais, P.: A case study in the gamification of a university-level games development course. In: Proceedings of the South African Institute for Computer Scientists and Information Technologists Conference, pp. 242–251 (2013)
24. Ortega-Arranz, A.: Supporting practitioners in the gamification of MOOCs through reward-based strategies. Ph.D. thesis, Universidad de Valladolid (2021)
25. Ortega-Arranz, A., Bote-Lorenzo, M.L., Asensio-Pérez, J.I., MartínezMonés, A., Gómez-Sánchez, E., Dimitriadis, Y.: To reward and beyond: analyzing the effect of reward-based strategies in a MOOC. Comput. Educ. **142** (2019)
26. Ortega-Arranz, A., Kalz, M., Martínez-Monés, A.: Creating engaging experiences in MOOC through in-course redeemable rewards. In: Proceedings of the 2018 Global Engineering Education Conference, pp. 1875–1882. IEEE (2018)
27. van Roy, R., Deterding, S., Zaman, B.: Collecting Pokémon or receiving rewards? How people functionalise badges in gamified online learning environments in the wild. Int. J. Hum. Comput. Stud. **127**, 62–80 (2019)
28. Ryan, R.M., Deci, E.L.: Intrinsic and extrinsic motivations: classic definitions and new directions. Contemp. Educ. Psychol. **25**, 54–67 (2000)
29. Vassileva, J., McCalla, G.I., Greer, J.E.: From small seeds grow fruitful trees: how the PHelpS peer help system stimulated a diverse and innovative research agenda over 15 years. Int. J. Artif. Intell. Educ. **26** (2016)

Effects of Course, Gender, and Remediation on both Success Rate and Realism of Undergraduates on Pre-requisites Testing

Julien Douady(✉), Christian Hoffmann(✉), and Nadine Mandran(✉)

Université Grenoble Alpes, CNRS, Grenoble INP, LIG, 38000 Grenoble, France
{julien.douady,christian.hoffmann,
nadine.mandran}@univ-grenoble-alpes.fr

Abstract. When entering higher education, students must become more autonomous in their learning, particularly know how to take stock of their ways of learning: identify what they know, and also what they do not know, then adapt their learning strategies. They must therefore develop metacognitive skills. This article analyzes the responses of 3830 newly arrived undergraduate students through a pre-requisites test including confidence levels. Focus is given on both their success rate, *i.e.,* their achievement at the test, and their realism, *i.e.,* if they were predictive in their confidence judgement. To compute a relevant realism index, previous work by Prosperi [1] is extended to our context. First, an expected course effect is observed: one of the seven proposed courses reveals a lower realism index, and at the same time, its success rate is lower too. Moreover, a gender impact is highlighted: females reach a higher realism index than males and this gap fluctuates over the 4 last years. This gender effect is probably different from the course effect because success rates of males and females remain equivalent, thus success rate and realism seem to be dissociated in this case. Finally, students who perform poorly on the pre-requisites test and choose to take a second session after a remediation period improve their results: both gaps of success rate and realism are closed. That could prove the relevance of the remediation, and/or the effect of metacognition feed-back provided just at the end of the pre-requisites test.

Keywords: Metacognition · Realism index · Gender effect · Undergraduate students · Confidence levels

1 Introduction

Students who enter higher education are expected to become more autonomous in their learning methods. They must be able to care about what they know and what they do not know, and about how to adapt their learning strategies. That means they have to develop their metacognitive skills.

Metacognition as a concept is hard to define, and several authors have attempted to do so. Noël and Leclercq [2] consider it as the set of three processes: judgment, analysis

I. Hilliger et al. (Eds.): EC-TEL 2022, LNCS 13450, pp. 88–101, 2022.
https://doi.org/10.1007/978-3-031-16290-9_7

and regulation of a given performance. Schraw and Moshman [3] distinguish metacognitive knowledge, defined as "*what individuals know about their own cognition and about cognition in general*", and metacognitive regulation, related to "*metacognitive activities that help control one's thinking or learning*". This point of view is further supported by Biasutti and Frate [4], who specify that a metacognitive regulation "*includes the following activities: planning (predicting the products and results, defining the methods and arranging the strategies), monitoring before and during learning (controlling, testing, revising and changing learning strategies and approaches), and evaluating the activities (making judgments about results and ways of performing the tasks)*". Thus, to help students develop their metacognitive skills, instructors need to provide them with relevant and concrete indicators, and knowledge evaluations on Learning Management Systems (LMS) are undoubtedly a valuable opportunity to gather information and calculate such indicators. As emphasized by Schraw and Moshman [3]: "*a number of studies indicates that metacognition knowledge and regulatory skills such as planning are related to evaluation*".

One way to develop the ability to judge one's own performance is to introduce formative assessments using degrees of certainty. Gardner-Medwin and Gahan [5] even speak of "*substantial merits*" for confidence-based assessment. The degree of certainty is the student's estimation of his or her perceived chance of answering a question correctly. Collecting degrees of certainty on a formative test assessing knowledge allows to establish, in addition to the success rate (*i.e.* passing the test, *e.g.,* with 75 out of 100 correct answers), another level of feedback for learners called *realism* (*e.g.,* you were very sure of almost all of your answers, yet almost half are incorrect). These both feedbacks on knowledge and on metacognition seem likely to improve success and develop autonomy in learning. According to Butler *et al.* [6], feedback after a test with degrees of certainty not only improves the results (both on concepts related to initially correct and incorrect answers) but also improves the correspondence between results and confidence, thus the realism: "*it seems more likely that the improvement in metacognitive accuracy is the result of eliminating any discrepancy between perceived and actual correctness of responses*".

Nevertheless, several pitfalls make the use of degrees of certainty tricky. In particular, there are several ways to implement them, some of which are perilous, and there is no consensus on the common LMS used to host standardized assessments. In this article, we propose to look at a crucial situation: students entering higher education, who need to check the prerequisites necessary to succeed in the first year at university via a test on LMS. We explain how to construct a relevant realism index to complement the information provided by the success rate on the test, based on a robust statistical approach that extends Prosperi's [1] previous work to true-false questions. The two research questions we address are (i) do we observe any effects of course or gender on the success rate or realism index, and (ii) does the feedback and remediation given to low-performing students allow them to improve the success rate and/or realism in a second test?

The paper is structured as follows. After reviewing related work in Sect. 2, we present the research context and our data set in Sect. 3. Next, we present the data analysis involving two indicators, success rate and realism index: in Sect. 4, we explain how we calculate these two indicators and in Sect. 5, we present the results. Finally, we discuss the results and conclude on the contribution of this work, its limitations and perspectives.

2 State of the Art

In order to use degrees of certainty to develop students' metacognitive skills, we must address how to collect them, how to calculate an index of realism, and how to formulate metacognitive feedback for students. We review related work on these topics and on gender effects on realism.

Collecting Degrees of Certainty. Although the collection of degrees of certainty seems very relevant to support learning activities, the method used remains subject to discussion, as does the feedback offered to the learner. For the collection of degrees of certainty, some authors use a numerical scale in arbitrary units or in percentages [7] while others prefer a literal scale [8–10]. Some use both: numbers and verbatim [6, 11]. The number of levels on the scale varies: sometimes 3, often 4, and sometimes more. Leclercq [12, 13] has done a detailed analysis of the different strategies. He argues for a percentage use and recommends 6 levels, not necessarily equidistant. In all cases, the value of the research lies in the combination of the success rate and the degree of certainty expressed by the student through a realism index. It is therefore convenient to have a numerical value for the degree of certainty. Some authors then associate an arbitrary number with a degree of certainty initially expressed in literal form [10], which is highly questionable. Sometimes the degree of certainty is even reduced to its simplest binary expression "sure" or "unsure" [9]. Others authors propose a numerical scale to the students, but confuse the numerical value with the ordinal value in the ensuing treatment [6]. Finally, some publications, particularly in the vein of Leclercq's work, use degrees of certainty expressed as percentages, with a numerical value that is meaningful to students [1, 5, 14].

Realism Index. To combine degree of certainty and success rate, several approaches have been examined. Some assume continuity between the variable degree of certainty: for example, in 1973, Brown and Shuford [15] propose the affine function, $y = ax + b$, where y is relative to the degree of certainty, and x to the success rate. A realistic student is one who reaches $a = 1$ and $b = 0$. Other concepts are proposed by Leclerq [16] who calculates indicators named "confidence", "recklessness" and "nuance", by Andriamiseza *et al.* [11] who use "correlation", or by Butler *et al.* [6] calculating "resolution" and "mean-gamma-correlation". But none of these approaches is satisfactory in terms of statistical significance of the degree of certainty. In 2015, Prosperi [1] proposes a novel approach by keeping the discrete character of both the success rate (due to the finite number of questions) and the degree of certainty (by the number of levels). His approach concerns multiple-choice questions (MCQ) and proposes a statistical index that assumes an expanded definition of how a student is considered as "realistic". To keep it simple, Prosperi considers for each degree of certainty, two distinct confidence intervals:

- The first one is due to the finite number of answers given with a particular degree of certainty: *e.g.*, if 25 answers are associated with the 70% degree of certainty, the success rate of these answers can only be associated to a confidence interval of ±2% (if 19/25 answers are correct, success rate is 76%, and if 20/25 answers are correct it reaches to 80%). More precisely, Prosperi assumes that, for a given student, the success rate for the degree of certainty i is called TE_i and is included in an interval $[a_i, b_i]$. He suggests that the extension of this interval can be calculated by the Wilson's method [17] and he chose a 90%-threshold.
- The second one is due to the chosen scale for coding the degrees of certainty: *e.g.*, if the student can express its certainty degrees in between 50%, 60%, 70%, 80%, 90%, and 100%, each level will be associated with a confidence interval of ±5%. For example, the degree of certainty 70% will be associated to the interval [65%, 75%].

Thus, Prosperi considers that a student is realistic for the degree of certainty i if an overlap exists between those two confidence intervals. On the opposite, only if the two intervals are separate, a significant realism-error for this degree of certainty err_i can be calculated (see Fig. 1, adapted from Prosperi, 2015 [1]), and it is always considered a positive value, regardless of whether TE_i is higher or lower than the degree of certainty.

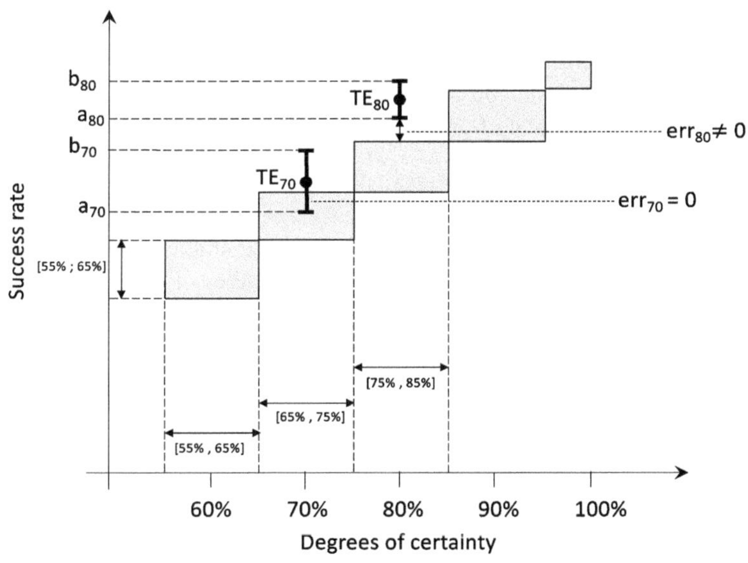

Fig. 1. Example of calculating realism-error err_i for two degrees of certainty: 70% and 80%.

Prosperi considers the different realism-errors for each degree of certainty, with a ponderation given by the frequency of this degree relative to the others. Finally, the calculation of Prosperi's realism index, called *RSN*, is computed by adjusting one normalization parameter β:

$$RSN = \frac{\beta - \sum_i \left(err_i * \frac{NU_i}{NR} \right)}{\beta}$$

where i enumerate the different degrees of certainty, NU_i is the number of utilizations of the given degree of certainty i, and *NR* is the total number of questions. *RSN* gives a number between 0 and 1 (ideally realistic student).

Metacognitive Feedback. As far as feedback is concerned, we identify essentially two types of practices, which often result in different implementations on the common platforms used to host standardized assessments (*e.g.,* Moodle or equivalent). The most common practice is the one introduced by Gardner-Medwin [5, 18] which aims at weighting the final score obtained according to the level of realism. In general, the student gets a bonus if his or her realism is adequate, and a malus if it is not. In some cases, the weighting calculation ensures that the behavior promoted by the scoring system is the most honest behavior possible [18]. An alternative practice, quite opposite, is to propose feedback to students that minimizes the importance of the global score in order to emphasize the realism, especially when it is caught in fault (for example an error with high certainty). This last approach has not been yet implemented on Moodle or any equivalent platform, to the best of our knowledge.

Gender Impact. Finally, it should be noted that the studies diverge as to a possible effect of gender on realism: if some studies report a difference between males and females [9], others on the contrary show no effect. Of these, some studies are in the case where students have been previously trained in the use of degrees of certainty, and it appears that while the gap is erased by training, it did exist before [5]. There are also studies that show that a gender gap exists on success rate, but that it appears to be reduced by using degrees of certainty [7, 19]. We found no recent studies on the impact of gender or re-mediation on undergraduates' realism.

3 Research Context and Data Collection

Our research is supported by a data set collected in an ecological situation (*i.e.* in-field evaluation). When they enter the university, in order to validate their registration in one of the 7 courses (see Table 1) offered as part of the Bachelor of Science and Technology at a French university (Université Grenoble Alpes), all the concerned students - about 1000 each year - have to go through a "welcome day", where they finalize their administrative registration and take both an English and a science pre-requisites test. This is where our data are collected. The pre-requisites test is therefore compulsory and is taken in a computer room on an individual workstation, under the supervision of tutors (advanced students who help solve problems of connection or understanding of the instructions, in particular), and in a limited time. The test is implemented on the local LMS.

The science pre-requisites test was built by a team of teachers from the Science and Technology Bachelor's department who list pre-requisites identified as necessary for success in the first year. Major scientific themes addressed are Biology, Chemistry, Mathematics, Physics, and another one inspired by the MOHICAN project [16], around the understanding of scientific vocabulary and the basic rules of reasoning. Within these 5 topics, the teacher team created several versions of true-false questions of equivalent difficulty for each of the selected pre-requisite, thus constituting a database of questions. Then, for each of the 7 courses offered, a set of relevant prerequisites was selected corresponding to 80 true-false questions that are randomly drawn from the question database during testing.

Table 1. List of courses, total number of students in our sample, and distribution of students (male/female ratio per course)

Code	Course main topics	Nb of students over 2018–2021	% male students	% female students
CB	Chemistry and biology	474	43%	57%
IMA	Applied maths and computer sciences	949	76%	24%
PC	Physics and chemistry	140	39%	61%
PCMM	Physics, chemistry, maths and mechanics	671	68%	32%
SPI	Engineering sciences	327	76%	24%
ST	Geology	124	58%	42%
SV	Biology	1145	33%	67%
TOTAL		**3830**	**56%**	**44%**

Implemented in 2013 [20], this pre-requisites test was redesigned in 2017 with the mandatory capture, for each true-false question, of the associated degree of certainty. The scale chosen for the collection of degrees of certainty is a hybrid scale, mixing words and percentages (see Fig. 2). It is inspired by Leclercq's work [13] but adapted to the case of true-false questions. In particular, if the degree of certainty expressed is of the order of 50%, this means choosing at random.

If the global success rate is less than 75%, the student is invited to sign up for tutoring sessions in the relevant subjects and then is supposed to retake a test a few weeks later. In this case, the second test, optional, is taken on the same platform. It is the same test, *i.e.* the same pre-requisites tested by true-false questions randomly chosen in the common base, as for session 1.

The data include the first test (mandatory and concerning all students) for the years 2018, 2019, 2020, and 2021. The second tests were extracted for the years 2019 and

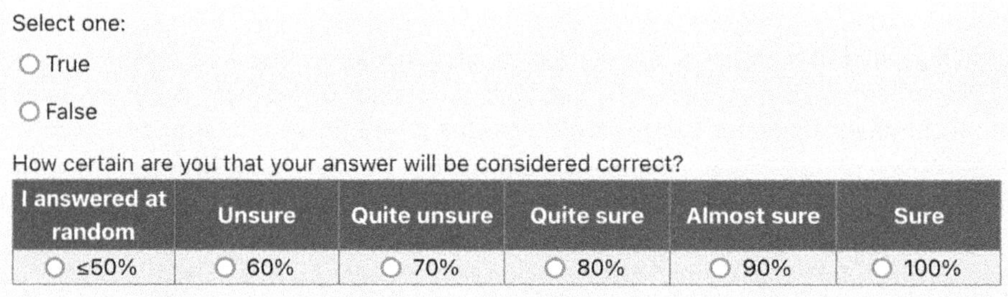

Fig. 2. Students must choose "True" or "False" and associate a degree of certainty.

2021 (in 2018, an error made the data unusable, and in 2020, the COVID19-related situation did not allow communication around the second test). When exporting the results subsequently analyzed, the individual results are fully anonymized. The results used as input are therefore made up of: an anonymity number, the course, the gender, whether it is the first or second test, and for each of the 80 true-false questions, the result (correct or incorrect) and the degree of certainty expressed.

4 Computing both the Success Rate and the Realism Index

In this section, we explain how we computed both indicators: *Success Rate* and *Realism Index*. In our case, assuming that for true-false tests the choice of the lowest degree of certainty is associated with "*I answered at random*", there is no relevant information in the associated answers, either they will be correct or incorrect. We then calculate a relevant score with only the answers associated with higher degrees of certainty (60% up to 100%): it's called *Success Rate* hereafter. The use of this 50% degree of certainty is quite rare: for our sample, only 6.1% of the answers are concerned.

Adapting the work of Prosperi [1], we calculate at first the achievement for each student and for each of the following degrees of certainty: 60%, 70%, 80%, 90%, and 100%. We obtain then the TE_i and the associated intervals $[a_i, b_i]$ as described in Sect. 2. Then we associate an interval for each degree of certainty, *e.g.*, 60% is associated with the [55%, 65%] interval, and so on up to 100% that is associated with the reduced [95%, 100%] interval. Subsequently, we calculate the different realism-errors err_i, with $i =$ 60%, 70%, 80%, 90%, and 100%, for each student.

To choose the β parameter, we must explore the limits of the term $\sum_i \left(err_i * \frac{NU_i}{NR} \right)$.

For an ideally realistic student, it is zero. On the other side of the spectrum, one of the worst cases is obtained for a student who chooses the level of certainty 60% for all answers and for which all answers will be correct; then the err_{60} value reaches 0.35 (TE_{60} is 1.0 and the upper limit of the certainty interval is 0.65) and the other ones are zero, leading to $\sum_i \left(err_i * \frac{NU_i}{NR} \right) = 0.35$. The other worst case consists of a student who answers without any knowledge (the success rate is then around 50%) with the highest level of certainty (100%). Then, following our definition, err_{100} (the only one that is not zero) reaches 0.45, because the random success rate is supposed to be about 0.50 for a true-false test and the lower bound on the certainty interval is 0.95. Then, the value of the term $\sum_i \left(err_i * \frac{NU_i}{NR} \right)$ is assumed to be around 0.45. Therefore, we chose $\beta = 0.45$ in our case.

Then Prosperi's realism index *RSN* is computed. Here, we choose to extend the work of Prosperi, as both the *Success Rate* and the *RSN* indicators are calculated variables whose distribution laws are not known. Moreover, a study of these indicators shows that they do not follow a normal distribution. In these conditions, the classical tests of comparison of means such as the Student test cannot be used. That's why we use the Kruskall and Wallis test [21], a non-parametric rank test, which does not require the normality of the distribution of the variables. We calculate the effect size to assess the strength of the observed effect (using η^2 from h-statistic, see [22] for details) and we use the Dunn test with Bonferroni correction to assess differences between groups. In the same way, to enlarge the dispersion and because of the non-parametric signature of the realism index, we decide to rank the *RSN* over the whole sample, being careful that in case of egality, the lower ranking value is given to all the equal students. We must check that the maximum rank corresponds to an ideally realistic student ($RSN = 1$), and then we renormalize it with respect to the highest rank so that the realism index always remains between 0 and 1 (ideally realistic student).

Note that in our sample, any subpopulation considered above has a significant number of students who achieve $RSN = 1$, so that the global median of ranking is greater than 0.5. We finally obtain a new ranked realism index, hereafter called the *Ranked Realism Index*, which is computed for each given student, just like the *Success Rate.*

5 Results

This section relates the results obtained about the questions introduced before: (i) do we observe any effects of course or gender on the success rate or realism index, and (ii) does the feedback and remediation given to low-performing students allow them to improve the success rate and/or realism in a second test?

First, we observe that our sample shows very stable results over the 4 years of our study, in both the *Success Rate* and the *Ranked Realism Index*, as shown in Fig. 3. The

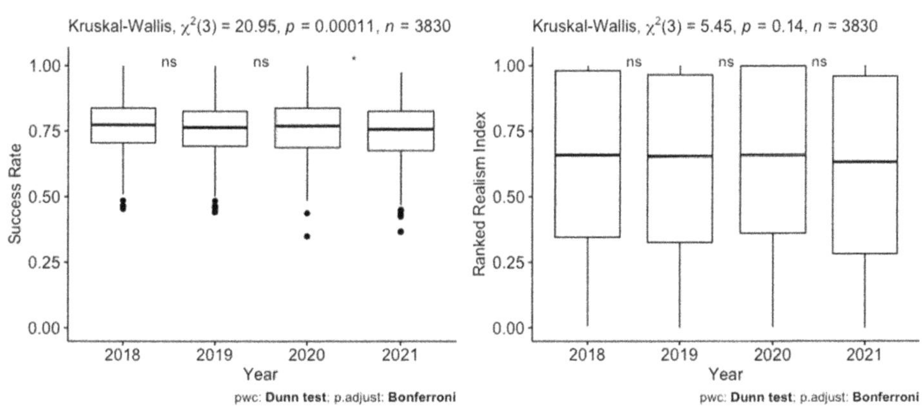

Fig. 3. *Success Rate* and *Ranked Realism Index* for the whole sample per year.

global median is 0.76 for the *Success Rate* and is 0.65 for the *Ranked Realism Index*. If we consider only year-to-year variation, the results show no significant variation over time, except for a slight decrease between 2020 and 2021 in the *Success Rate* (Dunn test with p-value = 0.0048).

Then, we observe substantial differences between the courses, in both the *Success Rate* and the *Ranked Realism Index* (Kruskal-Wallis with p-value <0.0001 for both indicators). As we can see in Fig. 4, the SPI course has the worst results, and the differences with another course such as, for example, the PCMM course, are highly significant (Dunn test with p-value <0.0001 for both indicators). Note that the effect size is small, but close to the small-moderate limit ($\eta^2 = 0.0528$ and 0.0524 respectively, effect size is considered small if $\eta^2 < 0.06$).

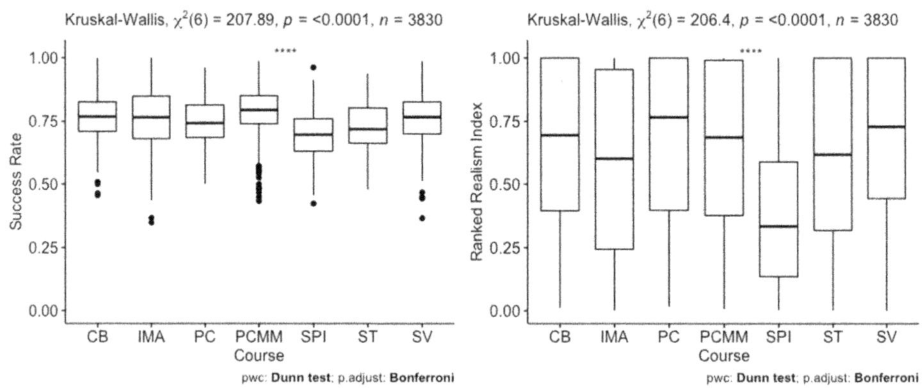

Fig. 4. *Success Rate* and *Ranked Realism Index* for the whole sample per course.

Looking at the overall sample, there is no significant difference in the *Success Rate* between male and female students as we can observe in Fig. 5 – top, left. On the other hand, Fig. 5 – top, right, there is a significant difference in the *Ranked Realism Index* Note that the effect size remains very small in this last case ($\eta^2 = 0.0094$).

Moreover, if we look at the difference in the *Ranked Realism Index* per year, we can see an evolution: on Fig. 5 – bottom, we observe that the gender difference is not significant in 2018 (Kruskal-Wallis with p-value = 0.294). However, it is highly significant in 2019 and 2020 (Kruskal-Wallis with $p < 0.0001$), and in 2021 it is weakly significant (Kruskal-Wallis with p-value = 0.015). The maximum gender gap is achieved in 2020 with a small effect size ($\eta^2 = 0.03$). Note that the differences in the *Success Rate* between genders over the same period are not significant.

Finally, let's consider the students who poorly performed at the test and choose to take a second test session after a remediation period: it is a subpopulation of our whole sample, called *Double-test-sample* (N = 193). The students who only take the first test (because their results were satisfying or because they did not find relevant to take the second test) constitute the *Single-test-sample* (N = 3637). We observe on Fig. 6 (left) that the double-test students obviously have a lower *Success Rate* at the first test (Dunn test with $p < 0.0001$ with a small effect size: $\eta^2 = 0.0399$). We can see that after

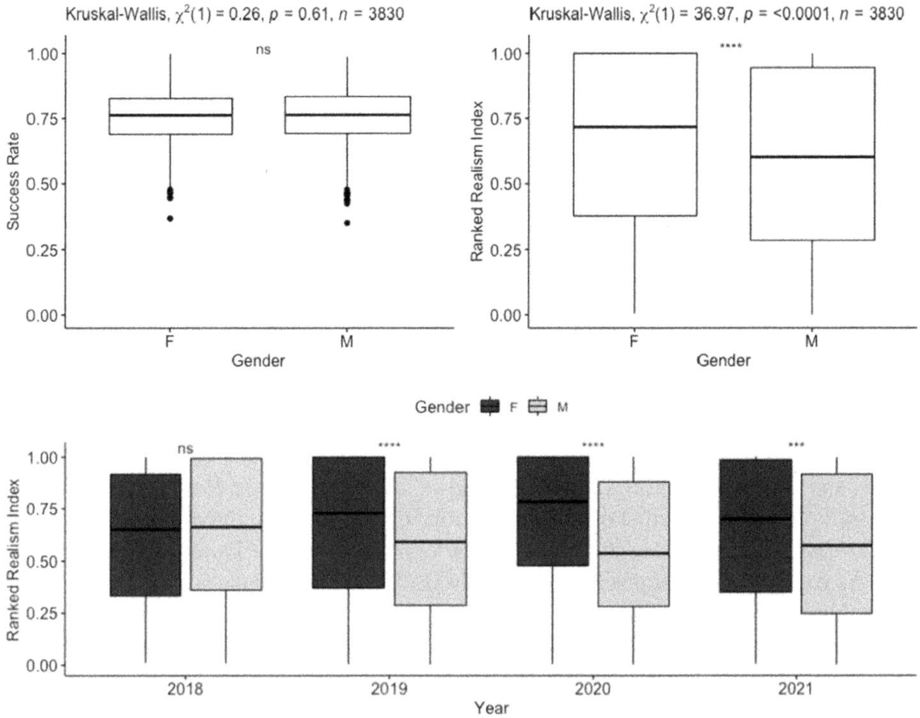

Fig. 5. (Top) *Success Rate* and *Ranked Realism Index* for the whole sample per gender. (Bottom) Evolution of the *Ranked Realism Index* of male and female students over 4 years.

a remediation period, the double-test students totally close the gap at the second test (Dunn test with $p = 0.68$): the "poorly-performing" population obtains the same results than the single-test students.

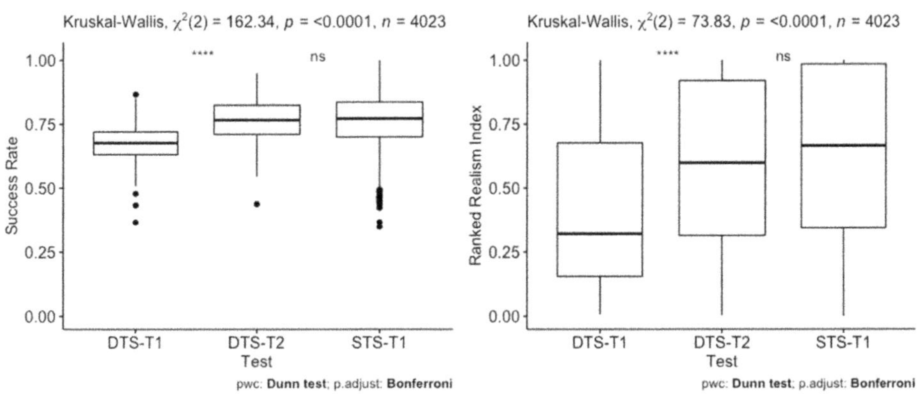

Fig. 6. *Success Rate* and *Ranked Realism Index* for the *Double-test-sample* (DTS, N = 193, T1 = first test and T2 = second test) and for the *Single-test-sample* (STS, N = 3637, T1 = first test).

Moreover, we observe the same behavior with the *Ranked Realism Index*: the difference is significant between the two populations in the first test (Dunn test with $p < 0.0001$ with a small effect size: $\eta^2 = 0.0179$) and the gap is closed in second test (Dunn test with $p = 0.16$), as shown in Fig. 6 (right).

6 Discussion

As shown by the relative stability over the years (see Fig. 3), we can reasonably assume that the reproducibility of the results is good from year to year, and that the variations observed as a function of gender or background are not linked to a less successful or less realistic cohort of students. Concerning the course effect, highlighted in Fig. 4, we expected the SPI course to stand out. Indeed, it is traditionally a course that recruits students with lower high school results, and a higher proportion of technological baccalaureates than general baccalaureates. The SPI sample is therefore significantly different, and this is not surprisingly reflected in both the *Succes Rate* and the *Ranked Realism Index*. The principal question, considering the correlation between *Succes Rate* and *Ranked Realism Index* is if it could be explained by the Dunning-Kruger effect [23]. As explained by Gignac and Zajenkowski [24] "*the Dunning-Kruger hypothesis states that the degree to which people can estimate their ability accurately depends, in part, upon possessing the ability in question*". Consequently, students with lower *Succes Rates* would tend to self-assess their results less well than students who have relatively higher *Success Rates*. Alternatively, it has been proposed that this kind of observations could be explained by a combination of the better-than-average-effect and regression towards the mean [25].

The gender effect observed is sufficiently significant and recurrent to affirm that it is not an artefact. Over the last three years, there is a strong difference between female and male students in terms of realism, but there is no difference in the *Succes Rate*. Thus, the Dunning-Kruger effect cannot be invoked to account for this gap, and the explanation must be sought elsewhere. Since the gap is not observable in 2018, it would be appropriate to look for changes in the high school curriculum for the generation entering university in 2019. To date, we have no credible explanation for the appearance of this gap in 2019 and in subsequent years. At most, we can hypothesize that if the gap is larger in 2020, it may be an effect of the total confinement that French high school students experienced in spring 2020, thus just before they entered university. It is then possible that female and male students did not use the same distance learning strategies, and that this is felt on a metacognitive indicator such as realism, without however affecting the test score.

Finally, concerning the "remediation-effect", it can be explained by several hypotheses. The first would be an effect of the metacognitive feedback offered to the students at the end of the pre-requisite test: the awareness of the discrepancy between the test score and the self-assessment would allow the student concerned to adjust his or her judgment. The second would be an effect related to the tutoring offered, and/or the work done, during the remediation period between the two tests. In this case, the fact of reworking some pre-requisites, and in particular those that were lacking, would allow both the test score and the reliability of the student's judgment of his performance to be improved. The second hypothesis could therefore be in favor of a Dunning-Kruger effect. The first hypothesis could be tested by a study comparing two groups of students, one receiving metacognitive feedback and the other not.

7 Conclusion and Perspectives

By analyzing the answers to a pre-requisite test with degrees of certainty of several thousands of students, enrolled in different courses of the Bachelor of Science and Technology of a French university, we observe an expected course effect by comparing the test results and the realism indices. In a next step of analysis, the relevance of the Dunning-Kruger hypothesis as a possible explanation should be verified, for example by performing the statistical tests proposed by Gignac and Zajenkowski [24]. We also observe a significant gender effect over the last 3 years. If it is difficult to explain why this effect is absent in 2018, it also remains to be explained why it is present in the following years. In any case, it is clear that this effect differs from the previous one since test result and realism seem to be decorrelated. Finally, we observe a probable remediation effect. Here again, the Dunning-Kruger hypothesis should be tested, and the impact of the proposed metacognitive feedback should be studied further.

Regarding the limitations of our approach, following the evolution of the realism index of a single student is often difficult, as the confidence intervals in Prosperi's model become prohibitive, unless one can analyze a large number of responses. Furthermore, we have considered a single test here (with the exception of the "double-test-sample"). In order to better identify what generates realism improvement over time, we need to track a cohort of students on multiple tests that include degrees of certainty. In addition, in an attempt to better understand what enables a given student to regulate his or her learning, the collection of metacognitive comments, written by the student after reviewing his or her results (success and realism), could greatly enrich the analysis.

Acknowledgements. This work is funded by CNRS and LIG. Authors want to thank Hubert Borderiou, who develops specific routines on the local LMS platform, and Astor Bizard and Nadia Brauner-Vettier, who develop specific plug-in for Caseine (a Moodle-like LMS).

References

1. Prosperi, O.: Le réalisme avec degrés de certitude. Mes. Éval. En Éduc. **38**, 121–140 (2015). https://doi.org/10.7202/1036553ar
2. Noël, B., Leclercq, D.: Comment développer des capacités cognitives et métacognitives ? In: Recherches et actions en faveur de la réussite en première année universitaire. Vingt ans de collaboration dans la Commission « Réussite » du Conseil interuniversitaire de la Communauté française de Belgique. CIUF, Bruxelles (2011)
3. Schraw, G., Moshman, D.: Metacognitive theories. Educ. Psychol. Rev. **7**, 351–371 (1995). https://doi.org/10.1007/BF02212307
4. Biasutti, M., Frate, S.: Group metacognition in online collaborative learning: validity and reliability of the group metacognition scale (GMS). Educ. Technol. Res. Dev. **66**(6), 1321–1338 (2018). https://doi.org/10.1007/s11423-018-9583-0

5. Gardner-Medwin, A.R., Gahan, M.: Formative and summative confidence-based assessment. In: 7th International Computer-Aided Assessment Conference, pp. 147–155. Loughborough University, UK (2003)
6. Butler, A.C., Karpicke, J.D., Roediger, H.L.: Correcting a metacognitive error: feedback increases retention of low-confidence correct responses. J. Exp. Psychol. Learn. Mem. Cogn. **34**, 918–928 (2008). https://doi.org/10.1037/0278-7393.34.4.918
7. Gilles, J.-L.: Entraînement à l'autoévaluation: une comparaison filles/garçons à l'université. In: Actes du colloque de l'AIPU. Enseignement supérieur: stratégies d'enseignement appropriées, Hull, pp. 159–166. Université du Québec (1995)
8. Curtis, D.A., Lind, S.L., Boscardin, C.K., Dellinges, M.: Does student confidence on multiple-choice question assessments provide useful information? Med. Educ. **47**, 578–584 (2013). https://doi.org/10.1111/medu.12147
9. Hassmen, P., Hunt, D.P.: Human self-assessment in multiple-choice testing. J. Educ. Meas. **31**, 149–160 (1994). https://doi.org/10.1111/j.1745-3984.1994.tb00440.x
10. Al-Shanfari, L., Demmans Epp, C., Baber, C., Nazir, M.: Visualising alignment to support students' judgment of confidence in open learner models. User Model. User-Adapt. Interact. **30**(1), 159–194 (2020). https://doi.org/10.1007/s11257-019-09253-4
11. Andriamiseza, R., Silvestre, F., Parmentier, J.-F., Broisin, J.: Recommendations for orchestration of formative assessment sequences: a data-driven approach. In: De Laet, T., Klemke, R., Alario-Hoyos, C., Hilliger, I., Ortega-Arranz, A. (eds.) Technology-Enhanced Learning for a Free, Safe, and Sustainable World, vol. 12884, pp. 245–259. Springer, Cham (2021). https://doi.org/10.1007/978-3-030-86436-1_19
12. Leclercq, D.: J'en suis aussi sûr que vous, mais pas avec le même pourcentage de chances, que ce soit hors contexte ou en contexte Deux études sur la variabilité inter-individus des significations métriques données aux degrés de certitude verbaux. Evaluer J. Int. Rech. En Educ. Form. **2**, 89–125 (2016)
13. Leclercq, D.: Une mata-analyse des degrés de certitude exprimés en mots. Evaluer J. Int. Rech. En Educ. Form. 2, 69–105 (2017)
14. Gilles, J.-L.: Qualité spectrale des tests standardisés universitaires - Mise au point d'indices édumétriques d'analyse de la qualité spectrale des évaluations des acquis des étudiants universitaires et application aux épreuves MOHICAN check up '99 [Ph. D., Liège] (2002). https://hdl.handle.net/2268/2217
15. Brown, T.A., Shuford, E.H.: Quantifying uncertainty into numerical probabilities for the reporting of intelligence (1973). https://apps.dtic.mil/sti/pdfs/AD0777063.pdf
16. Leclercq, D.: Diagnostic cognitif et métacognitif au seuil de l'université: le projet Mohican mené par les 9 universités de la communauté française Wallonie Bruxelles. ULg, Liège (2003)
17. Newcombe, R.G.: Interval estimation for the difference between independent proportions: comparison of eleven methods. Stat. Med. **17**, 873–890 (1998). https://doi.org/10.1002/(SICI)1097-0258(19980430)17:8%3c873::AID-SIM779%3e3.0.CO;2-I
18. Khan, K.S., Davies, D.A., Gupta, J.K.: Formative self-assessment using multiple true-false questions on the internet: feedback according to confidence about correct knowledge. Med. Teach. **23**, 158–163 (2001). https://doi.org/10.1080/01421590031075
19. Koivula, N., Hassmén, P., Hunt, D.P.: Performance on the Swedish scholastic aptitude test: effects of self-assessment and gender. Sex Roles **44**, 629–645 (2001). https://doi.org/10.1023/A:1012203412708
20. Hoffmann, C., Douady, J., Buty, C.: Test initial de prérequis : quelles corrélations avec la réussite en première année universitaire? In: Actualité de la Recherche en Éducation et Formation (AREF), Montpellier, France (2013)
21. Howell, D.C.: Statistical Methods for Psychology. Cengage Learning (2012)

22. Tomczak, M., Tomczak, E.: The need to report effect size estimates revisited: an overview of some recommended measures of effect size. TRENDS Sport Sci. **1**, 19–25 (2014)
23. Kruger, J., Dunning, D.: Unskilled and unaware of it: how difficulties in recognizing one's own incompetence lead to inflated self-assessments. J. Pers. Soc. Psychol. **77**, 1121–1134 (1999)
24. Gignac, G.E., Zajenkowski, M.: The Dunning-Kruger effect is (mostly) a statistical artefact: valid approaches to testing the hypothesis with individual differences data. Intelligence **80**, 101449 (2020). https://doi.org/10.1016/j.intell.2020.101449
25. Krueger, J., Mueller, R.A.: Unskilled, unaware, or both? The better-than-average heuristic and statistical regression predict errors in estimates of own performance. J. Pers. Soc. Psychol. **82**, 180–188 (2002). https://doi.org/10.1037/0022-3514.82.2.180

Enhancing Instructors' Capability to Assess Open-Response Using Natural Language Processing and Learning Analytics

Rafael Ferreira Mello[1,2](✉), Rodrigues Neto[1], Giuseppe Fiorentino[1], Gabriel Alves[1], Verenna Arêdes[1], João Victor Galdino Ferreira Silva[1], Taciana Pontual Falcão[1], and Dragan Gašević[2]

[1] Universidade Federal Rural de Pernambuco, Rua Dom Manuel de Medeiros, s/n, Recife, PE 52171-900, Brazil
{rafael.mello,gabriel.alves,taciana.pontual}@ufrpe.br
[2] Monash University, 20 Exhibition Walk, Clayton, VIC 3800, Australia
dragan.gasevic@monash.edu

Abstract. Assessments are crucial to measuring student progress and providing constructive feedback. However, the instructors have a huge workload, which leads to the application of more superficial assessments that, sometimes, does not include the necessary questions and activities to evaluate the students adequately. For instance, it is well-known that open-ended questions and textual productions can stimulate students to develop critical thinking and knowledge construction skills, but this type of question requires much effort and time in the evaluation process. Previous works have focused on automatically scoring open-ended responses based on the similarity of the students' answers with a reference solution provided by the instructor. This approach has its benefits and several drawbacks, such as the failure to provide quality feedback for students and the possible inclusion of negative bias in the activities assessment. To address these challenges, this paper presents a new approach that combines learning analytics and natural language processing methods to support the instructor in assessing open-ended questions. The main novelty of this paper is the replacement of the similarity analysis with a tag recommendation algorithm to automatically assign correct statements and errors already known to the responses, along with an explanation for each tag.

Keywords: Open-response evaluations · Learning analytics · Natural language processing · Recommendation system

1 Introduction

Assessments aim to evaluate students' learning progress. They can be formative, conceived to enable students to address conceptual or behavioral shortcomings;

I. Hilliger et al. (Eds.): EC-TEL 2022, LNCS 13450, pp. 102–115, 2022.
https://doi.org/10.1007/978-3-031-16290-9_8

and summative, with the primary goal of providing a score for the assignment [12]. Unfortunately, assessments are often reduced to the summative function, without the proper feedback [1]. Convincing instructors of the importance of the assessment does not seem to be a problem. However, the demands to provide quality and timely feedback on the assignments performed seem unfeasible due to the work overload in academia.

In this context, many algorithms and educational tools to support the evaluation of different types of answers emerged: online judges to support the analysis of programming activities developed by students [7], dashboards to provide information about responses to multiple-choice questions [3], and automatic grading systems for mathematical problems [14]. Despite the importance of these tools, they are very focused on a limited task/content, or demand considerable engagement from the instructors in the configuration of the environment. For instance, previous works have proposed possible solutions for automatic answer grading [4,16]. However, these solutions require the creation of (i) a possible correct answer for each question, or (ii) content about the topic approached.

In addition to the instructor's engagement in providing information beforehand, there are multiple limitations of the previous automatic answer grading systems: (i) the concerns about the fairness and possible bias of these solutions [13]; (ii) the lack of generalizability of the solutions [16]; and (iii) the insufficient connection with quality feedback (in general these systems only provide a score) [7].

Therefore, this study presents a tool to enhance the instructor's ability to assess open-ended responses without previous interaction with the system. The proposal applies an unsupervised natural language processing approach to generate real-time tag recommendations, which can correspond to errors or correct statements made by students in their answers. The best algorithm evaluated reached an accuracy of 89.39% (in terms of F1-Score) for the tag recommendation. Finally, we provide details on how this approach can be used to increase the reliability and support the provision of quality and timely feedback.

2 Background

2.1 Assessment and Open-Ended Questions

Wiliam [39, p.1] defined assessment as "processes of evaluating the effectiveness of sequences of instructional activities when the sequence was completed." It can be divided into summative assessment, often used as an assessment of learning, which aims to measure if the student has reached the expected standard; and formative assessment or assessment for learning [5], that focuses on providing timely and continuum feedback for students. Many studies have stated that formative assessment is an effective method to improve student achievement [19,39].

Among the many possible instruments to perform formative assessment, open-ended questions allow instructors to understand students' progress, critical thinking, and creativity [35]. However, answers to this type of questions can be complex to evaluate, which can lead to an overload in the assessment activity and demotivation of instructors in providing feedback [7]. This issue motivated the research in automatic algorithms to assess and grade open-ended questions.

2.2 Automatic Open-Response Grading

The Automated Answer Grading (AAG) has been widely studied over the years [4,10,24,33]. There is a wide variety of approaches applied to this goal focusing on different text mining methods such as statistical techniques, natural language processing (NLP), information extraction, clustering, deep learning and mixed-approaches [4,24]. In general, AAG algorithms focus on computing the similarity of the reference answer (provided by the instructor) and a student's answer targeting the provision of a score for the question or a categorical outcome (i.e., 'correct', 'partially correct', 'incorrect') [32].

The initial approaches focused on adopting traditional NLP pipelines with word matching to reach the final grade. For instance, Cutrone and Chang [10] and Siddiqi et al. [33] applied preprocessing steps like spell check, removal of punctuation, removal of stopwords and stemming process to generate a shorter version of the reference and the student's answers before computing the similarity. After this initial step, Cutrone and Chang [10] proposed an approach to compare each word of the answers using wordnet [15], while Siddiqi et al. [33] also considered the sentence structure in the process. Noorbehbahani and Kardan [26] proposed a different approach using the BLUE [28] and ROUGE [21] statistical measures to compute the similarity. BLUE and ROUGE are algorithms to calculate the performance of machine translation and text summarization systems, respectively. They divide the text into n-grams and compare their correlation in different text segments (i.e., reference and student's answers). The main advantage of this method is the decrease in time to predict the similarity. The authors provide experimentation showing that the BLUE method reached better results.

Recently, several deep learning approaches have been proposed for this task [4]. In this case, the methods rely on the application of Long Short-Term Memory (LSTM) and transformers networks to perform the grading of students' answers. The results presented in [4] cannot be directly compared, as they were evaluated on different datasets, but they show the potential of using pre-trained BERT models for this task [6,38].

Although the literature proposes several AAG algorithms, there are several limitations in previous studies: (i) the best-performing algorithms work only for short answers (up to three sentences); (ii) there is still an open concern about the fairness of AAG algorithms [13]; and (iii) the methods focus only on providing a final score for each question without delivering qualitative feedback to assist students to recognize their errors.

In this context, we suggest that using a Learning Analytics approach in combination with NLP could address these concerns.

2.3 Learning Analytics as a Method to Enhance Learning

Learning analytics is defined as "the measurement, collection, analysis and reporting of data about learners and their contexts, for purposes of understanding and optimizing learning and the environments in which it occurs" [22]. As learning becomes ever more digital, an outstanding amount of data have been generated about students' and instructors' interactions with learning environments. Such data can provide insights into how to enhance learning settings for different scenarios.

A learning analytics cycle proposed by Clow [9] explains precisely how educational tools can be used in a technology-mediated learning environment using learning analytics: (1) learners producing (2) data, which are processed into (3) metrics, thereby informing (4) interventions or actions. This cycle has been used in several contexts to provide information to support feedback tools [29], analysis of written activities [2], and support game analytics [34]. In this study, we followed this learning analytics cycle to create the proposed tag recommendation system.

3 Technology Enhanced Assessment of Open-Responses

In this paper, we propose an approach that employs learning analytics and NLP to support instructors in the process of assessing open-ended responses. More specifically, we propose a tag recommendation system to automatically identify errors or correct statements made by students based on the instructors' own previous corrections. The system does not require any other previous data or content to support the recommendation and it learns new tags while the instructors are evaluating the students' assignments.

Figure 1 describes the implementation of each step proposed by Clow [9] for the proposed tag recommendation system: (1) the student interacts with the LMS to answer open-ended questions proposed by the instructor in an activity, which (2) are further assessed by the instructor in the platform, thereby (3) the system generates tag recommendations for the following student answer, (4) that can be accepted or not by the instructor.

The following sections present a brief overview of steps 1–3 proposed in the tool, and then Sect. 4 presents details about the tag recommendation system (step 4), which is the main contribution of this paper.

3.1 Overview of the Tutoria Platform

Tutoria[1] provides support for the correction of written assignments, which can be imported from Google Classroom. After importing the responses, the instructor can choose to navigate per question or student (Fig. 2). This means the instructor can either correct the complete assignment of each student or all students' answers to a specific question.

[1] https://tutor-ia.com/.

Fig. 1. Clow (2012) [9] flow for the proposed tag recommendation system.

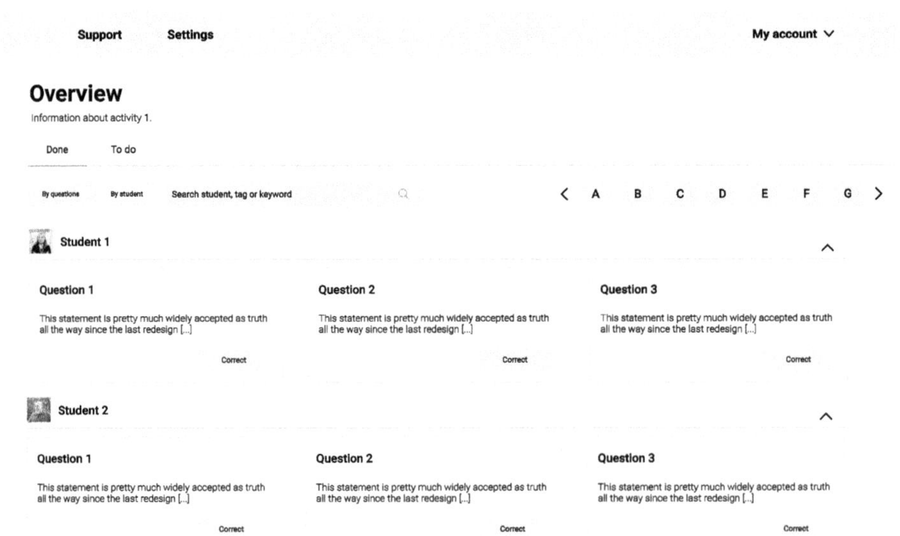

Fig. 2. Home screen with students' activities

Figure 3 presents the correction of an open-ended question of Student 1. This screen shows the question and the student response (1), and the tags assigned by the instructor, which can be created on-the-fly or reused. Tags can also be created without association with a specific text excerpt (2), but as a general comment about the answer (e.g., creativity and originality). Tags must be named and classified in errors or correct statements (3). The inclusion of correct statements tags aims to encourage instructors to include positive comments in their feedback, as usually feedback mostly indicates errors (against good educational practice [17] [25]). Finally, it is possible to indicate the final score that the student reached on this specific question (4).

To ensure quality feedback, each tag must have an explanation associated and written by the instructor. When a tag is reused, the explanation needs not be re-inserted, making the process of correction more efficient, as it is common that many students make similar errors. After finishing the correction of an assignment, the instructor can create a template for the feedback to be received by all students. This template will be filled according to the tags in each student's answer, providing a personalized experience for the students.

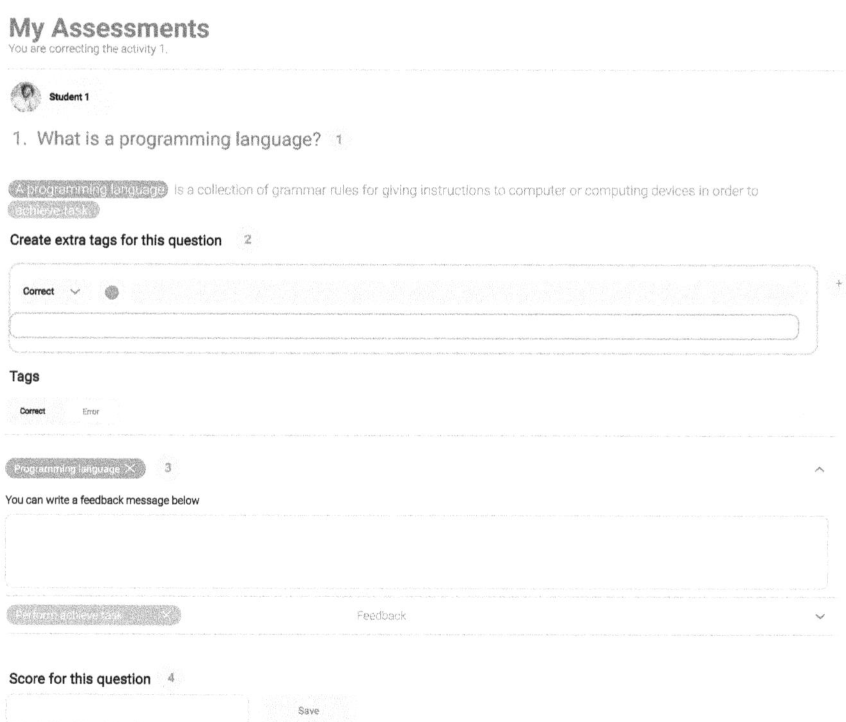

Fig. 3. Assessment of an open-ended question.

3.2 Algorithm for Tag Recommendation

The Tutoria platform incorporates the proposed recommendation system to suggest tags, using NLP techniques (semantic similarity and textual classification) to identify similar excerpts which have previously been tagged. Tag suggestions are automatically shown in the interface for the instructor to accept or reject.

It is important to mention that the tag recommendation approach represents a novelty in relation to the previous algorithms to support open-ended responses evaluation. Instead of performing a textual similarity analysis between a reference and the student's answer, this approach matches small pieces of the text with a previous correction. The following section presents details about the NLP steps to execute the recommendations.

4 Method

4.1 Data and Course Design

The educational data used in this paper corresponds to an assignment extracted from a fully-online undergraduate course about Basic Informatics, which explores topics related to hardware, software, networks, operational system, among others.

This course included a series of instructional videos about different topics that were used in combination with online assignments containing multiple-choice and open-ended questions. Every two weeks, new videos and assignments were provided for the students. These assignments accounted for 50% of the final mark. In the offering of the course analyzed, a total of 47 students answered the first assignment, containing five open-ended questions.

The instructor of this course, with a background in computer science, agreed to use the Tutoria platform to assess the open-ended responses without the tag recommendation system in order to generate the tags for each response manually and produce the gold standard in this study. Thus, in this study we evaluated the recommendation system based on the tags included by one instructor. Table 1 presents the details of the number of tags divided by each question. It shows the (1) number of students' responses; (2) number of unique tags that the instructor included; (3) total number of tags, including the repetition of the same tag for different responses; and (4) maximum number of unique tags that can be suggested if the system recommends all unique tags for all student responses. In this experiment we evaluated answers with 100–200 words.

4.2 Text Processing and Feature Extraction

As the first step of our analysis, we used NLP techniques to process the text and extract features. The similarity measures adopted in this study need to be applied just to the words. Therefore, we removed punctuation, multiple spaces, and Unicode characters. In addition, we also applied methods that rely on Term Frequency–Inverse Document Frequency (TF-IDF) scores and Bidirectional Encoder Representations from Transformers (BERT), which are described below.

Table 1. Distribution of tags per question.

Question	Responses	Unique tags	Total number of tags	Potential recommendation
Q1	33	4	35	132
Q2	33	4	42	132
Q3	47	10	98	470
Q4	47	3	63	141
Q5	47	4	37	188
Total	207	25	275	1063

TF-IDF Features. TF-IDF is one of the most used approaches in text mining models to extract features from texts [23]. This algorithm converts textual documents (e.g. students' responses) to a vector consisting of the term counts [23], in this case the TF-IDF values. The current study adopted the traditional TF-IDF technique [23].

BERT. We also adopted BERT in order to include a state-of-the-art deep learning approach in the comparison. BERT is a word embedding approach that considers the context of each word, which has been shown to increase the performance in several NLP applications [11]. Previous studies have shown the potential of using BERT in Automated Short Answer Grading systems [4]. It is important to mention that we have not done any data preparation in our dataset before using BERT, as suggested by the previous studies [4,11].

4.3 Similarity Measures and Evaluation

The similarity measures evaluated in this paper are composed of statistical methods to perform string matching, word matching and the deep learning approach using BERT. The outcome of each similarity measure is a number from 0 to 1, where 1 means the highest similarity. Based on the previous studies, we decided to use a similarity threshold equal to 0.7 to define the text that should receive a tag recommendation [4,10,24,33].

The first group evaluated is based on string matching similarity measures that seek to find substrings with overlaps at the character level. The most known method is the Levenshtein distance, which counts the number of modifications that should be done to change one string into the other [40]. The following list outlines the measures that were evaluated in this group.

Levenshtein: We used the classical implementation of the Levenshtein distance.
Partial ratio: This algorithm performs the similarity matching of the shortest string with all substrings of the same length.
Token Sort Ratio: This measure performs a tokenization process to clean the string before the final matching using the Levenshtein distance.

Partial Token Sort Ratio: It uses the Token Sort Ratio tokenization with the Partial ratio substrings matching.
Token Set Ratio: This method uses the Token Sort Ratio, but it also adds a stopword removal process before the final matching with Levenshtein distance.
Partial Token Set Ratio: It is similar to the Token Set Ratio, but it uses the Partial ratio similarity instead of the Levenshtein distance.
Fuzzy Search: It uses Levenshtein distance to search for a group of similar substrings instead of evaluating the entire text.
Edit Distance: This measure uses the Jaro-Winkler distance [37] to compute the final similarity.
Rapidfuzz: This is a faster version of the Edit Distance similarity.

The second group is based on word matching by applying a different n-gram composition. It uses the TF-IDF scores to vectorize the analyzed texts, computing the similarities using:

1-gram: It compares the similarity of each word in both texts.
2-gram: It compares the similarity of each pair of words in both texts.
3-gram: It compares the similarity of each segment of three words in both texts.
4-gram: It compares the similarity of each segment of four words in both texts.
n-gram: It uses all the previous similarities (1, 2, 3 and 4-gram) to compute the final score.

Finally, we also evaluated the performance of the BERT model in this study. Unlike the word matching methods, BERT encapsulates one vector per word, not per sentence. It means that the similarity, in this case, compares two matrices. The main idea is to have semantic information about the words being compared. However, it increases the time to have the final result.

To evaluate the performance of the proposed similarity measures, we adopted the traditional machine learning measures Precision (P), Recall (R), and F1-score, largely used in this context [23]. In short, precision measured the number of tags recommended that the instructor accepted as a correct tag; and recall assessed the number of relevant tags for a specific response that the system failed to recommend. The F1-score is the harmonic mean between precision and recall. Moreover, we also evaluated the performance in terms of time to recommend the tag, as it is a critical issue for the practical use of the proposed approach.

5 Results

The results presented in this section show the performance of each similarity measure for the recommendation of 25 tags for 207 students' responses (see Sect. 4.1 for more details). In the worst-case scenario, the system would recommend 1063 tags, the total number of tags for each question multiplied by the number of responses. Table 2 presents the results of each similarity algorithm that was evaluated using precision, recall, F1-Score and the time to run the recommendation for all responses in seconds.

In general, all algorithms reached good results in terms of precision. In the worst case, the Levenshtein similarity reached 0.80. It means that the algorithms managed to recommend tags for instructors correctly. In contrast, multiple algorithms obtained recall lower than 0.50. In other words, they overall suggested a small number of tags, which means that the system has not recommended tags for most of the questions and the instructor had to do it manually, maintaining a similar workload of not using the proposed approach.

Three similarity measures achieved F1-Score higher than 0.80: Partial Token Set Ratio, TF-IDF 1-gram, and BERT. These algorithms reached a balance between precision and recall, and were the most adequate algorithms for this task. However, BERT was the slowest one taking 93.28 s to perform the tag predictions, while Partial Token Set Ratio made the same recommendations in 0.08 s.

Table 2. Results of each similarity algorithm in the tag recommendation task.

#	Similarity algorithm	Precision	Recall	F1-score	Mean time	Median time
1	Levenshtein	0.80	0.01	0.01	00.02	00.03
2	Partial Ratio	0.98	0.32	0.48	00.06	00.29
3	Token Sort Ratio	0.94	0.02	0.03	00.05	00.07
4	Token Set Ratio	0.97	0.43	0.59	00.05	00.06
5	Partial Token Set Ratio	0.91	0.88	0.89	00.08	00.20
6	Partial Token Sort Ratio	0.96	0.25	0.39	00.07	00.25
7	Fuzzy Search	0.90	0.42	0.57	01.22	26.95
8	Edit Distance	0.93	0.62	0.74	01.03	01.04
9	Rapidfuzz	0.93	0.60	0.72	00.86	00.87
10	TFIDF 1-gram	0.90	0.74	0.81	05.10	05.10
11	TFIDF 2-gram	0.98	0.06	0.10	04.84	04.83
12	TFIDF 3-gram	0.98	0.02	0.03	04.78	04.75
13	TFIDF 4-gram	0.96	0.01	0.02	04.71	04.62
14	TFIDF n-gram	0.94	0.19	0.31	05.27	05.39
15	BERT	0.89	0.79	0.83	93.28	107.86

6 Discussions

6.1 Interpretation of the Results

The proposed method of evaluating open-ended responses using tag recommendation is an entirely new approach in the field of AAG, as the previous works focused on the comparison of students' entire answers with reference answers provided by the instructor [4,10,24,33]. Although there is previous literature on tag recommendation systems [36], to the best of our knowledge, no similar analysis has been done in focusing on the AAG. It is important to mention that due to the original nature of this study, it was not possible to compare our approach with previous work directly.

The results obtained for the tag recommendation algorithms evaluated in this study indicated that the measures intended to analyze the similarity at a single word level (Partial Token Set Ratio, TFIDF 1-gram, and BERT) reached better results. Although we cannot generalize this result (due to the limited dataset used in the evaluation), this behavior was expected as the recommendation system works at the level of a single question, which generally is restricted to a specific topic. Previous literature on NLP methods demonstrates that word-based methods achieve good results for the analysis of texts from a specific domain [8].

Another relevant factor revealed in the experimentation is that all algorithms managed to recommend tags correctly, as the precision results were overall high. This recommendation tends to reduce the number of tags removed by the instructor during the process of evaluating a specific question. Previous literature shows that presenting information that is not relevant to the stakeholders (i.e., instructors) could demotivate the use of a specific tool or visualization [18].

Finally, the deep learning algorithm used (BERT) was the slowest one. We expected this outcome as deep learning algorithms generally require more processing time [4,27]. However, this approach can be beneficial in the analysis of questions with a broader possibility of answering or even an extension of the proposed tag recommendation system to evaluate essays or longer texts [20].

6.2 Implications

The findings of the study showed that the use of the proposed tag recommendation approach is promising for the analysis of open-ended responses in practical settings. Not only could the proposed approach support the assessment of open-ended questions, but it also has implications related to reliability, generalizability and the improvement in the connection between the assessment and timely feedback [7,13,16].

Moreover, using an artificial intelligence method (i.e., the tag recommendation system) allows instructors to reuse previously defined correct statements and errors, potentially reducing the workload to assess open-ended activities, which increases the reliability and consistency in grading students' activities [31] and potentially reduces bias in the assessment [13].

Furthermore, the proposed approach increases the generalizability of the previous methods used for assessing open-ended questions as it does not require the initial reference answer provided by the instructors [16,32]. Therefore, it could be easily adopted in different learning settings without a previous adaptation or effort from the instructors, which is a critical condition to facilitate the adoption of learning analytics tools [30]. However, it is important to note that this approach has a cold start problem. In other words, the instructor needs to assess several students' activities to receive effective tag recommendations.

The approach can effectively be used together with existing approaches for the automatic provision of feedback as the tags provide tangible indicators about students' performance on each specific question. It could be used, for instance, to feed the OnTask tool [29] that has been largely used to generate feedback about multiple-choice questions.

7 Limitations and Directions for Future Research

The limitations of the present study include: (1) The size and the nature of the dataset used. The dataset adopted to evaluate this study comprised a relatively small number of responses (207) produced by students enrolled in a single course (basic informatics). Although this can interfere with the generalizability of the proposed approach, the novelty of the paper is still relevant (no previous work has made tag recommendation for this problem) and several previous works in the field of educational text mining evaluated their studies with fewer data [16]. In future work, we intend to assess the same similarity algorithm using data collected from other courses and possibly written in different languages. (2) In this study, we have evaluated different similarity measures with different natures, including string and word similarity and deep learning. Yet, other possible solutions for this task could be explored, for instance, LSTM networks, clustering, and topic modelling. Moreover, the use of white-box or explainable artificial intelligence algorithms is also a target in the future. (3) This study has not evaluated the application of the proposed approach in practice to assess instructors' potential benefits and satisfaction with the tag recommendation algorithm. However, such an algorithm is already integrated with the Tutoria platform, and we have already scheduled initial experiments in real-world settings. Finally, evaluating the system with larger texts, i.e., essays, is also important.

Acknowledgment. This research was partially supported by the RNP, FACEPE (APQ-0749-1.03/21), and fellowship 310888/2021-2 of the National Council for Scientific and Technological Development - CNPq.

References

1. Andriamiseza, R., Silvestre, F., Parmentier, J.-F., Broisin, J.: Recommendations for orchestration of formative assessment sequences: a data-driven approach. In: De Laet, T., Klemke, R., Alario-Hoyos, C., Hilliger, I., Ortega-Arranz, A. (eds.) EC-TEL 2021. LNCS, vol. 12884, pp. 245–259. Springer, Cham (2021). https://doi.org/10.1007/978-3-030-86436-1_19
2. Barthakur, A., et al.: Understanding depth of reflective writing in workplace learning assessments using machine learning classification. IEEE Trans. Learn. Technol. (2022)
3. Bodily, R., et al.: Open learner models and learning analytics dashboards: a systematic review. In: Proceedings of the 8th International Conference on Learning Analytics and Knowledge, pp. 41–50 (2018)
4. Bonthu, S., Rama Sree, S., Krishna Prasad, M.H.M.: Automated short answer grading using deep learning: a survey. In: Holzinger, A., Kieseberg, P., Tjoa, A.M., Weippl, E. (eds.) CD-MAKE 2021. LNCS, vol. 12844, pp. 61–78. Springer, Cham (2021). https://doi.org/10.1007/978-3-030-84060-0_5
5. Brown, S.: Assessment for learning. Learn. Teach. High. Educ. **1**, 81–89 (2005)
6. Camus, L., Filighera, A.: Investigating transformers for automatic short answer grading. In: Bittencourt, I.I., Cukurova, M., Muldner, K., Luckin, R., Millán, E. (eds.) AIED 2020. LNCS (LNAI), vol. 12164, pp. 43–48. Springer, Cham (2020). https://doi.org/10.1007/978-3-030-52240-7_8

7. Cavalcanti, A.P., et al.: Automatic feedback in online learning environments: a systematic literature review. Comput. Educ.: Artif. Intell. **2**, 100027 (2021)
8. Chowdhary, K.: Natural language processing. Fundam. Artif. Intell. 603–649 (2020)
9. Clow, D.: The learning analytics cycle: closing the loop effectively. In: Proceedings of the 2nd International Conference on Learning Analytics and Knowledge, pp. 134–138 (2012)
10. Cutrone, L.A., Chang, M.: Automarking: automatic assessment of open questions. In: 2010 10th IEEE International Conference on Advanced Learning Technologies, pp. 143–147. IEEE (2010)
11. Devlin, J., Chang, M.W., Lee, K., Toutanova, K.: BERT: pre-training of deep bidirectional transformers for language understanding. In: Proceedings of NAACL-HLT, pp. 4171–4186 (2019). https://doi.org/10.18653/v1/N19-1423
12. Dixson, D.D., Worrell, F.C.: Formative and summative assessment in the classroom. Theory Pract. **55**(2), 153–159 (2016)
13. Erickson, J.A., Botelho, A.: Is it fair? Automated open response grading. In: International Conference on Educational Data Mining (2021)
14. Erickson, J.A., Botelho, A.F., McAteer, S., Varatharaj, A., Heffernan, N.T.: The automated grading of student open responses in mathematics. In: Proceedings of the Tenth International Conference on Learning Analytics & Knowledge, pp. 615–624 (2020)
15. Fellbaum, C.: WordNet. In: Poli, R., Healy, M., Kameas, A. (eds.) Theory and Applications of Ontology: Computer Applications, pp. 231–243. Springer, Cham (2010). https://doi.org/10.1007/978-90-481-8847-5_10
16. Ferreira-Mello, R., André, M., Pinheiro, A., Costa, E., Romero, C.: Text mining in education. Wiley Interdisc. Rev.: Data Min. Knowl. Discov. **9**(6), e1332 (2019)
17. Freeman, R., Lewis, R.: Planning and Implementing Assessment. Routledge (2016)
18. Gibson, D., Ifenthaler, D.: Adoption of learning analytics. In: Ifenthaler, D., Gibson, D. (eds.) Adoption of Data Analytics in Higher Education Learning and Teaching. AALT, pp. 3–20. Springer, Cham (2020). https://doi.org/10.1007/978-3-030-47392-1_1
19. Hattie, J.: Visible Learning for Teachers: Maximizing Impact on Learning. Routledge (2012)
20. Hussein, M.A., Hassan, H., Nassef, M.: Automated language essay scoring systems: a literature review. PeerJ Comput. Sci. **5**, e208 (2019)
21. Lin, C.Y.: Rouge: a package for automatic evaluation of summaries. In: Text Summarization Branches Out, pp. 74–81 (2004)
22. Long, P.D., Siemens, G., Conole, G., Gašević, D. (eds.): Proceedings of the 1st International Conference on Learning Analytics and Knowledge (LAK 2011). ACM, New York (2011)
23. Manning, C., Schutze, H.: Foundations of Statistical Natural Language Processing. MIT Press (1999)
24. Marın, D.R.P.: Automatic evaluation of users' short essays by using statistical and shallow natural language processing techniques. Advanced Studies Diploma Work, University of Madrid (2004)
25. Nicol, D.J., Macfarlane-Dick, D.: Formative assessment and self-regulated learning: a model and seven principles of good feedback practice. Stud. High. Educ. **31**(2), 199–218 (2006)
26. Noorbehbahani, F., Kardan, A.A.: The automatic assessment of free text answers using a modified bleu algorithm. Comput. Educ. **56**(2), 337–345 (2011)

27. Otter, D.W., Medina, J.R., Kalita, J.K.: A survey of the usages of deep learning for natural language processing. IEEE Trans. Neural Netw. Learn. Syst. **32**(2), 604–624 (2020)
28. Papineni, K., Roukos, S., Ward, T., Zhu, W.J.: Bleu: a method for automatic evaluation of machine translation. In: Proceedings of the 40th Annual Meeting of the Association for Computational Linguistics, pp. 311–318 (2002)
29. Pardo, A., Jovanovic, J., Dawson, S., Gašević, D., Mirriahi, N.: Using learning analytics to scale the provision of personalised feedback. Br. J. Edu. Technol. **50**(1), 128–138 (2019)
30. Pontual Falcão, T., et al.: A penny for your thoughts: students and instructors' expectations about learning analytics in Brazil. In: LAK22: 12th International Learning Analytics and Knowledge Conference, pp. 186–196 (2022)
31. Ragupathi, K., Lee, A.: Beyond fairness and consistency in grading: the role of rubrics in higher education. In: Sanger, C.S., Gleason, N.W. (eds.) Diversity and Inclusion in Global Higher Education, pp. 73–95. Springer, Singapore (2020). https://doi.org/10.1007/978-981-15-1628-3_3
32. Sahu, A., Bhowmick, P.K.: Feature engineering and ensemble-based approach for improving automatic short-answer grading performance. IEEE Trans. Learn. Technol. **13**(1), 77–90 (2019)
33. Siddiqi, R., Harrison, C.J., Siddiqi, R.: Improving teaching and learning through automated short-answer marking. IEEE Trans. Learn. Technol. **3**(3), 237–249 (2010)
34. da Silva, G.C., Rodrigues, R.L., Amorim, A.N., Mello, R.F., Neto, J.R.O.: Game learning analytics can unpack Escribo play effects in preschool early reading and writing. Comput. Educ. Open **3**, 100066 (2022)
35. Stanger-Hall, K.F.: Multiple-choice exams: an obstacle for higher-level thinking in introductory science classes. CBE-Life Sci. Educ. **11**(3), 294–306 (2012)
36. Vairavasundaram, S., Varadharajan, V., Vairavasundaram, I., Ravi, L.: Data mining-based tag recommendation system: an overview. Wiley Interdisc. Rev.: Data Min. Knowl. Discov. **5**(3), 87–112 (2015)
37. Wang, Y., Qin, J., Wang, W.: Efficient approximate entity matching using Jaro-Winkler distance. In: Bouguettaya, A., et al. (eds.) WISE 2017. LNCS, vol. 10569, pp. 231–239. Springer, Cham (2017). https://doi.org/10.1007/978-3-319-68783-4_16
38. Wang, Z., Lan, A.S., Waters, A.E., Grimaldi, P., Baraniuk, R.G.: A meta-learning augmented bidirectional transformer model for automatic short answer grading. In: EDM (2019)
39. Wiliam, D.: What is assessment for learning? Stud. Educ. Eval. **37**(1), 3–14 (2011)
40. Yujian, L., Bo, L.: A normalized Levenshtein distance metric. IEEE Trans. Pattern Anal. Mach. Intell. **29**(6), 1091–1095 (2007)

Exploring the Connections Between the Use of an Automated Feedback System and Learning Behavior in a MOOC for Programming

Hagit Gabbay(✉) and Anat Cohen

School of Education, Tel Aviv University, Ramat Aviv, P.O.B 39040, 69978 Tel Aviv, Israel
hagitgabbay@mail.tau.ac.il, anatco@tauex.tau.ac.il

Abstract. Automated Testing and Feedback (ATF) systems are widely applied in programming courses, providing learners with immediate feedback and facilitating hands-on practice. When it comes to Massive Open Online Courses (MOOCs), where students often struggle and instructors' assistance is scarce, ATF appears to be particularly essential. However, the impact of ATF on learning in MOOCs for programming is understudied. This study explores the connections between ATF usage and learning behavior, addressing relevant measures of learning in MOOCs. We extracted data of learners' engagement with the course material, code-submissions and self-reported questionnaire in a Python programming MOOC with an ATF system embedded, to compile an overall and unique picture of learning behavior. Learners' response to feedback was determined by sequence analysis of code submission, identifying improved or feedback-ignored re-submissions. Clusters of learners with common learning behaviors were identified, and their response to feedback was compared. We believe that our findings, as well as the holistic approach we propose to investigate ATF impact, will contribute to research in this field and to effective integration of ATF systems to maximize learning experience in MOOCs for programming.

Keywords: Automated feedback · MOOCs for programming · Clustering · Learning analytics

1 Introduction and Related Work

1.1 Automated Testing and Feedback (ATF) Systems

Writing and executing code is the basis for learning a programming language and developing programming skills [36]. An accurate, detailed and timely feedback on the correctness and quality of the code may promote learning and increase practice effectiveness [33]. Large scale courses, however, make assessing the great volume of submissions and giving individual feedback nearly impossible [17]. Therefore, Automated Testing and Feedback systems (ATF) are often offered as a learning tool, providing immediate feedback and allowing unlimited resubmissions [22]. Recent reviews of literature reveal that ATF tools and systems are widely available, developed using different technologies and

I. Hilliger et al. (Eds.): EC-TEL 2022, LNCS 13450, pp. 116–130, 2022.
https://doi.org/10.1007/978-3-031-16290-9_9

methodologies [9, 22, 30]. Feedback may refer to syntax errors, the correctness of results or efficiency of the code [15, 36]. It may consist of only result correctness, or it might include a detailed explanation of the error or hints for solving it [22, 35]. In response to feedback, the learner is required to take two steps: decide whether to resubmit or waive, and to engage in an active practice of identifying and correcting the errors [29].

Behavioral characteristics of learners using the ATF system have been studied mainly through analyzing the programs submitted to the system and the feedback received. Learners' progress through code assignments, for example, was analyzed in [28] using cluster analyses based on variables harvested from ATF logs. Machine learning algorithms were applied on code solutions submitted for course assignments to identify attrition points and predict dropouts [37]. These and similar studies, however, did not analyse learning behavior in light of all course resources, including content consumption and solving non-code exercises.

Regarding affective measures, studies have suggested that the automated feedback enhances satisfaction and sense of learning [3, 4]. Learners perceive the automated feedback as enhancing learning and increasing motivation and engagement [30]. However, results concerning the system's impact on performance in the course, represented by scores of final exam or concluding assignment, were inconclusive (e.g. [6, 16]).

1.2 Massive Open Online Courses (MOOCs) and Learning Behavior Measures

Recent years have seen an increase in MOOCs in a variety of subjects. Learners in MOOC are usually diverse in their motivation for learning, as well as in their demographics and previous background [1]. Despite high enrollment rates, a high percentage of learners do not complete their learning due to variety of reasons including the lack of prior knowledge, struggling with course materials, and the need to self-regulate learning [38]. MOOCs, on the other hand, are not necessarily for credit and completing the course is not the ultimate goal [13]. Different measures should therefore be applied to evaluate learning outcomes and success in MOOCs [12, 23]. A common indicator of learning outcomes in MOOCs is learner's engagement, measured by [20, 23] as the degree of interaction with course materials, e.g. watching videos and attempt to solve exercises. Persistence is another common measure, defined by learner's determination to complete assignments and the achieved progress in study units [20]. Grades achieved on exercises and assignments determine the performance in the course [18].

Applying cluster analysis, researchers identified learning behavioral patterns and categorized learner by common patterns. In a key study [23] identified four major groups of MOOC learners: completers (learners who completed most assignments), auditors (completed few exercises but engaged in watching videos), disengaging (stopped participating after solving few exercises), and sampling (watched only few videos along the course). Similar studies proposed from three up to seven clusters, categorizing learners based on various sets of learning characteristics (e.g. [2, 21]). The most common variables used were the number of videos watched, in-video questions answered, exercises and assignments submitted, and social engagement such as activity discussion forums. In current research, we considered the suggested measures of learning behavior in MOOCs and applied cluster analysis in order to investigate the connections between ATF usage and learning patterns.

1.3 ATF Effectiveness in MOOCs for Programming

MOOCs for programming have the potential to teach programming to a broad and diverse audience [26]. The high demand for computer professionals have led to an abundance of courses, with large numbers of enrolees [24]. Independent programming learning, however, is challenging. In addition to learning the programming principles and syntax of the language, code assignments pose a significant difficulty, especially in MOOCs where assistance from faculty or peers is scarce. Hence, automated feedback is of particular importance, with the potential of supporting learners, prevent frustration and even dropout [24]. Moreover, the flexibility of practicing and receiving feedback at any time is appropriate to the nature of the MOOC's learning [31]. The majority of studies on ATF focus on frontal courses, or online courses offered as part of a curriculum. It is likely that students in these courses interact extensively with the faculty, which enhances their learning [34], and might "overshadow" the impact of ATF on learning outcome [17]. In MOOCs, the impact of ATF system may be more significant. Yet, the effect of ATF on learning in MOOCs is under studied.

Currently, most research on automated feedback in MOOCs focuses on increasing error detection and feedback accuracy, with few reported on future intention to investigate the impact of the suggested ATF on learning [24, 27]. In other studies, factors to consider when developing ATF systems for MOOCs have been discussed, but no empirical results were presented [36]. According to a several studies, ATF is perceived by learners as improving performance and increasing engagement [7, 25]. The researchers [14] suggested that learners who formally registered to an ATF system were more engaged when solving code assignments than those who used the system partially, but not formally. No differences in performance or completion rates were observed. To summarize, there seems to be some evidence to indicate that automated feedback has the potential to support learners and enhance learning success in MOOCs for programming. Yet, there is still a lack of empirical research and a comprehensive picture of how the system is affecting learning behavior and outcomes.

1.4 Research Questions

In order to harness the potential of ATF in MOOCs, it is necessary to gain a better understanding of how the system influences learning behavior. Using a quantitative approach and an empirical design, the current study examines the relationship between ATF use and learning patterns in a MOOC, referring to relevant measures of learning in MOOCs. We suggest a comprehensive picture of learners' behavior, combining data of ATF usage, learners' interactions with course materials and their perception of the effect of ATF on learning. To that end, we pose the following research questions:

RQ1: Are the characteristics of learning behavior related to the interaction with course materials similar to those of ATF usage?
RQ2: What are the connections, if any, between the patterns of learning behavior and learners' responses to the automated feedback on code assignments?
RQ3: What is learners' perception with regard to the impact of ATF on learning?

2 Setting

2.1 The Course and ATF System

Our research field is a MOOC to learn the Python programming language, offered on Edx-based platform for MOOCs. The course was designed for beginners and no prior background in programming or Python is required. It consists of nine learning units, from the basics of programming in Python to the use of functions, data structures and working with files. The content is delivered through videos, in which short ungraded comprehension questions are embedded. Each unit includes closed exercises (e.g. multiple choice or text fill-in exercises, referred to as CE hereafter), answering of which is followed by an indication of correct/incorrect answer and a numeric grade. In addition, in order to provide learners with hands-on experience, code-writing assignments of different difficulty levels are offered. Programs ranging from a few lines of code to several dozen lines are required as solutions. To get the most out of the practice, learners are encouraged to submit their code solutions to the ATF system integrated into the course.

The system we implemented is INGInious, an open-source software, supporting several programming languages and suitable for online courses (for more details on INGInious, see [11, 19]). Upon submission, the INGInious runs the code against a predetermined set of test scenarios and provides an instant feedback message, consisting of a grade and a textual component. Adapted to each assignment and error-type, the text may include varying levels of feedback (e.g. correct/incorrect, expected correct answer or more elaborated feedback), as classified by [35]. The system is incorporated into the course as an external tool, and registration is necessary for access. It is configured to allow unlimited re-submission of solutions.

Each cycle of the course is open for learning for six months. All course resources are available upon enrollment, enabling a self-paced mode of learning. It is offered free of charge, although a certificate can be earned for a small fee. Learners interested must, in addition to paying the fee, complete 70% of the closed exercises and submit a concluding project, with a weighted grade of 70 (out of 100). The course staff review the project and provides written feedback.

2.2 Population

The data for the present study were collected during the course cycle of June-December 21'. The research population consists of all learners who registered to the ATF system and submitted code-assignments at least once (N = 899). Among them, 655 (72.86%) filled out a demographic questionnaire. In terms of gender distribution, 73.28% of respondents identified as male, 26.57% as female and 0.15% as non-identified. The reported age ranged between less than 11 to over 75, with 15.57% under the age of 18, the majority (66.26%) in the range of 18–34 and 18.17% above. Based on self-reported prior knowledge, 32.67% of respondents had programming skills but did not know Python, 15.57% had prior Python knowledge, and 52.21% had no prior knowledge related to the course content.

3 Method

3.1 Operational Measures of Learning Behavior

In the context of the current study, learning behavior consists of engagement, persistence and performance (Table 1):

- **Engagement** is measured using variables related to watching videos, completing closed exercises and submitting code-assignments.
- **Persistence** is determined by the number of "touched" units, i.e. the number of units a learner interacted with video or a closed exercise or submitted a code-assignment.
- **Performance** is defined by the mean grade of closed exercises and the mean grade of code-assignments. The highest grade achieved in all attempts for each exercise or assignment was considered.

3.2 Data Resources and Pre-processing

It is one of the main goals of this study to present a comprehensive picture of learners' behavior in the course. Therefore, we have gathered and analyzed data from multiple sources, as follows:

1. **Learning Activity Log**, including all events of learner's interactions with course material. We pulled out three types of event: playing video, answering of comprehension questions, and attempts to answer closed exercises. Video replays for the same learner within the same video have been reduced to one event.
2. **ATF System Log**, containing records of code submissions. Each record includes the submitter ID, the submitted code, testing results and the generated feedback.
3. **Learners' Responses to Self-reported Questionnaires.** Two questionnaires were administrated: one for demographic details including age, gender, and prior knowledge of programming and Python. The second one, titled as "learning experience", collected learners' perspectives of the impact of ATF on learning. Using a 5-point Likert scale, learners were asked questions about system's contribution to engagement and learning effectiveness (e.g. "The system contributed to the motivation to complete more tasks in the course").

The research was conducted under the rules of ethics, while protecting privacy and maintaining the security of information, and in accordance with the approval of the university ethics committee.

3.3 Definition of "Response to Feedback"

In order to obtain a learner's response to feedback on a particular submission, we compared two consecutive submissions of the same code-assignment [32]. Three response types were defined: *any improvement* (AI), meaning an error detected in a particular submission has been fixed in the next one; *no improvement* (NI), when the same errors appeared in two consecutive submissions, and *getting worse* (GW), where the score of

Table 1. Learning behavior calculated measures

Learning behavior	Learning component	Variable	Description
Engagement	Course materials	Watched video	Percent of watched videos (out of the 29 videos in the course)
		Watched units	Number of units in which at least one video was watched (0–9)
		Active-watched ratio	Ratio between the number of videos in which the learner solved comprehension questions and the total number of videos watched (0–1)
		Solved closed exercises (CE)	Percent of CE a learner attempted, out of the 39 CE in the course (0–100)
		Solved units	Number of units in which at least one closed exercise was attempted (0–9)
		Mean attempts in CE	Mean attempts per closed exercise
	ATF usage	Submitted assignments	Percent of code assignments for which the learner has submitted a solution, out of the 53 code assignments in the course (0–100)
		Submitted units	Number of units in which at least one assignment was submitted (1–9)
		Mean attempts in assignments	Mean of attempts per code assignment
Persistence	Course resources and ATF	Units touched	Number of units in which the leaner watched a video or attempted an exercise or submitted an assignment (1–9)

(*continued*)

Table 1. (*continued*)

Learning behavior	Learning component	Variable	Description
		Max unit touched	The most advanced "touched" unit (1–9)
Performance	Course resources	CE grade	The mean grade in CE (0–100)
	ATF usage	Submission score	The mean score in submitted assignments (0–100)

the following submission was lower. An empty value was assigned as the response to feedback for the last submission of each assignment or in case only one attempt was made for an assignment by the learner. The degree of improvement in response to feedback for each learner was determined as follows:

$$\text{Positive Response to Feedback (PRF)} = \sum (\text{AI responses})/(\text{AI} + \text{NI} + \text{GW}) \quad (1)$$

The PRF ranges from 0 to 1, and its complement to 1 reflects non-improved responses.

4 Data Analysis and Findings

4.1 Learning Behavior - A Comprehensive Picture (RQ1)

For the purpose of analyzing the connections between learning behavior in the various learning components, the forementioned variables (Table 1) were extracted for each learner and descriptive data were generated, summarized in Table 2. Examining the correlation of the variables representing interactions with course materials and those representing ATF usage revealed the following results: the mean percentage of solved CE and submitted code-assignments, as well as the mean number of solved units and submitted units, were found to be strongly correlated ($r(897) = .76$ and $r(897) = .82$, respectively, $p < .001$). Similarly, a strong positive correlation was found between the percent of watched video and submitted assignments ($r(897) = .63, p < .001$), although lower than the correlation between watched video and solved CE ($r(897) = .81, p <$ $.001$).

However, the mean grade on CE and the mean score on submissions were found to be weakly correlated ($r(897) = .22$, $p < .001$), while no correlation was found between the number of attempts in these two types of tasks. We further discuss this in Subsect. 5.

Even though the variables associated with solving CE and those associated with submitting code assignments correlated, the mean values of "paired" variables from these two sets differed significantly, as visualized in Fig. 1. A Shapiro-Wilk test of normality distribution was statistically significant, indicating a univariate normality deviation of learning behavior variables. Thus, the nonparametric Wilcoxon signed-rank test was used for the comparison. When compared to the percentage of code assignments learners

Table 2. Descriptive data of learning behavior variables (N = 899)

Learning component	Variable	Mean	SD	Mdn
Course materials	Watched video (percent)	41.40	30.70	34.00
	Watched units	4.17	2.88	3
	Active-watched ratio	0.38	0.23	0.4
	Solved CE (percent)	36.60	32.50	26.00
	Solved units	4.01	3.02	3
	Mean attempts in CE	2.23	1.45	2
ATF usage	Submitted assignments (percent)	26.50	32.20	8.00
	Submitted units	3.51	2.94	2
	Mean attempts in assignments	4.22	3.45	3.12
Course materials and ATF usage	Units touched	4.62	2.93	4
	Max unit touched	4.80	2.99	4
Course materials	CE grade	81.80	34.20	100
ATF usage	Submission score	67.99	35.43	82.76

submitted and the mean score they received for those assignments, more CE were completed, with higher grades achieved. The mean number of attempts per CE, however, was lower than the mean number of attempts per code assignment. Wilcoxon test indicated that these differences were statistically significant ($p < .001$).

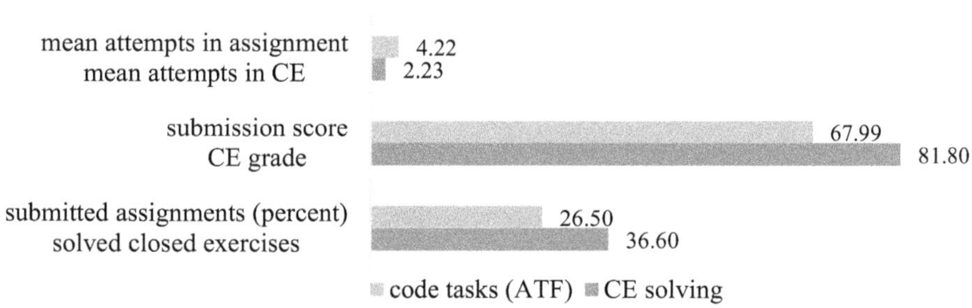

Fig. 1. Learning behavior regarding solving CE and submitting code assignments

Cluster Analysis: Prior to clustering, PCA was applied to identify a subspace that carries the meaningful information with minimal redundancy (e.g. high-correlated variables) in the high-dimensional data in hand [5]. Five "differentiating" variables were identified, representing over 62.6% explained variance: watched video, submitted assignments, mean attempts in assignments, CE grade and submission score. K-mean cluster analysis was then performed with pre-defined number of five clusters, based on the elbow method plot and silhouette score [39]. The features of the clusters and mean values of differentiating variables are presented in Table 3.

Table 3. Identified clusters: mean values of five differentiating variables and max unit touched

	Name	Size	Watched video	Submitted assigns	Mean attempts per assign	CE grade	Submission score	Max unit touched
1	Mid-course learners	299	0.33	0.16	3.13	95.20	88.11	4.09
2	Completers, high performers	213	0.78	0.78	3.73	97.30	92.25	8.385
3	Content oriented mid-learners	189	0.36	0.06	3.20	94.00	21.34	4.063
4	Touched and left	123	0.15	0.05	4.01	20.00	50.95	2.472
5	Trail-error ATF users	75	0.28	0.11	12.87	87.00	64.44	3.173

The mean value of max unit touched was also calculated for each cluster, to add the persistence to the learning patterns observed. The clusters were named as follows: (1) "mid-course learners": those who reached about the middle of the course, interacting to some extent with all course resources, and achieving fairly high grades. This is the largest group of learners. (2) "Completers, high performers": learners with highest performance and completing rates, while medium submission rate per code assignment. This pattern was the second in number of learners. (3) "Content oriented mid-learners": the third group in size, characterized by reaching to similar stage as the mid-course learners, while watching video content but rarely using the ATF system (may have solved code assignments without submitting to the system). (4) "Touched and left": those who log in but showed almost no engagement with course materials and actually dropped out shortly after they started. (5) "Trail-error solvers": those who submitted few code-assignments with many attempts, showing low persistence and performance. This was the least frequent behavior pattern.

4.2 The Response to Feedback (RQ2)

In examining the learners' response to feedback, an interesting finding emerged, indicating that only in 36% of resubmissions, learners corrected the indicated error and resubmitted (mean PRF = 0.36, SD = 0.24, N = 796). Note that for learners who attempt only one solution per assignment (11.8% of learners), the PRF variable is empty as there was no consequent submission and thus no response to feedback. PRF was found to positively correlate with mean score on code assignments ($r(791) = .46$, $p < .001$), and negatively with mean attempts per assignment ($r(791) = -.25$, $p < .001$), suggesting that positive response to feedback shorten the way to correct solution.

Next, we compared PRF among the various clusters to examine how learners with different learning patterns responded to feedback. Levene's test indicated that the equality of variance assumption was not met, thus we use the non-parametric Kruskal Wallis test one-way ANOVA-by-Rank for the comparison [8].

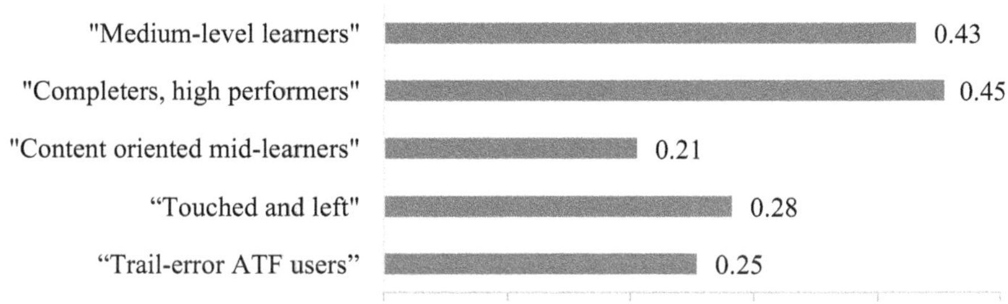

Fig. 2. Mean values of PRF of the five learning behavior clusters (N = 791)

Findings suggest a connection between higher PRF and higher engagement and performance, where learners in the "Completers, high performers" cluster tend to correct and resubmit most often in compared to all other groups. The "mid-course learners" were next in line to fix errors and resubmit, whereas learners in clusters 3, 4, 5 were less likely to respond positively (Fig. 2). Kruskal Wallis test indicated statistically significant difference among the clusters regarding mean PRF ($H(4) = 196.64$, $p < .001$).

The differences were examined applying pairwise multiple comparisons using the nonparametric Dunn's test, which is suitable for unequal sample sizes such as cluster sizes in our case [40]. Significant difference was found between clusters 1 and 2 ($p_{bonf} = .003$), as well as between each of these two and each of the other three 3, 4, 5 ($p_{bonf} < .001$). No significant differences were found, however, among clusters 3, 4 and 5.

4.3 Learners' Perception of ATF Effects (RQ3)

We analyzed learners' responses to the "learning experience" questionnaire as supporting evidence, therefore applying descriptive statistics only. As indicated by 102 responses we received, learners tend to perceive that using the ATF system improves engagement, performance, and motivation for deeper learning. Treating "I strongly agree" and "I agree" (4 and 5 in Likert scale) as a consent, the majority of respondents agreed with the statements that the option to correct and resubmit prompted them to make an effort for a higher score (91.15%) and using the ATF system motivated them to be more engaged in solving CE and assignments (84.32%). Using the system enhanced coding skills, according to 84.31% of respondents, and 76.47% believed it enabled them to develop more correct solutions. According to 86.27% of those who responded, code testing and immediate feedback make learning more effective, and 84.31% found that the immediate feedback helped them progress more rapidly. Nevertheless, it is noteworthy that while the results indicate a positive impact of the system, about 53% of learners who answered the questionnaire completed eight or more learning units of the course, i.e. were characterized by high persistence and engagement.

5 Discussion

Regarding the first research question, positive correlations between variables associated with interactions with course materials and those related to ATF suggest that learners are generally consistent in their learning behavior. Those who consume content and solve closed exercises also choose to practice and submit code assignments. Yet, despite the similarity in trends, learners attempted and succeeded in solving more closed exercises relative to the number of code assignments submitted to the ATF and solved correctly. Referring to Bloom's taxonomy, [25] suggest that closed exercises assess only the degree of understanding of the main concepts while code assignments address higher and more complex levels of cognitive skills, thus being more challenging. The difference in learners' behavior regarding these two types of tasks may be explained, therefore, by their ability or determination to deal with the cognitive effort required for code assignments. Moreover, identifying and correcting errors in the code, as needed in code writing, is a difficult practice especially for beginners [10] and may result in increased number of resubmissions in comparison to solving close exercises.

Five clusters of learners with common learning behavior patterns emerged from the cluster. The identification of two groups of "extreme behaviors" - the "excelled" learners and those who dropout early, along with a third group of "mid-learners", is similar to results of previous studies applying clustering of MOOC learners (not specifically MOOCs for programming, e.g. [2]). Two additional groups were identified, based on their ATF usage patterns: those who reached half the course but rarely submitted code assignments ("content oriented mid-learners") and those exhibiting trial-and-error behavior in their ATF usage ("trial and error ATF users"). Combining these two data sources, i.e. course and ATF logs, enable us to characterize learners' behavior in more comprehensive way. To the best of our knowledge, this is the first study to use both course and ATF behavioral data for clustering.

Examine the effect of automated feedback on learning outcomes, as stated in RQ2, was one of the major goals of our study. Results offer evidence that a positive response to feedback (PRF) enhances the probability of reaching a correct answer, and even shortens the way until success. Less positive finding, however, is that in 64% of resubmissions the error pointed out by the ATF was not corrected, and the learner received the same feedback message again. An earlier study analyzing submissions for code assignments found a high percentage of non-improved submissions as well [28]. The loop of resubmitting and getting the same error-message can cause frustration and even dropout [37]. Adding the option to change the wording of feedback in a situation of identical repeated submissions may result in a "rescue" and a faster move towards a correct solution. In addition, identifying code assignments in which this phenomenon is particularly prevalent is recommended, to avoid potential attrition points in the course.

The connection between learning behavior and the response to feedback was demonstrated by comparing the value of PRF among the clusters we characterized. Findings indicated that learners in groups with lower level of engagement and persistence, and relatively low performance (clusters 3, 4, 5), responded positively less frequently, were unable to correct errors, or did not submit again. In contrast, however, the percentage of positive responses was highest among the "Completers, high performers" (cluster 2). Feedback has been found to be associated with higher performance in previous studies, concerning frontal programming courses [16, 32]. Regarding the measures relevant to learning outcomes in MOOCs, our findings suggest that the positive response to feedback is significantly associated with success in the investigated MOOC.

As for RQ3, learners' perceptions regarding the impact of ATF on learning support the previous findings. In accordance with early studies both in the context of frontal and online programming courses (e.g. [30]) learners reported higher motivation for engagement in course assignments and considered the ATF as enhancing programming skills and learning effectiveness.

6 Conclusions and Future Work

In this study, we present a comprehensive picture of learning behavior in a MOOC for programming with an embedded ATF system. We believe that combining all the data into a single holistic picture is a significant contribution to advancing research in the field. Moreover, the indicated connections between ATF use and learning behavior may support the assumption that the automated feedback facilitates engagement, persistence, and performance. Nevertheless, we must be cautious in this context, and further research is needed to confirm the causal connection. It is primarily due to a limitation arises from the nature of the learning environment of the course, which includes an external interpreter enabling learners to actively solve code assignments, without receiving feedback, or having any indications in the analyzed data. Future research be undertaken with a setup allowing the comparison of these data as well, might bring additional insight into the effect of automated feedback. To maximize ATF effectiveness, however, exploring the causes of the high percentage of feedback-ignored resubmissions is suggested, as well as the impacts of feedback characteristics on learning behavior.

Acknowledgement. Our thanks to the Azrieli foundation for the award of a generous Azrieli Fellowship, which allowed this research. We thank the anonymous reviewers for their constructive comments.

References

1. Alario-Hoyos, C., Estévez-Ayres, I., Pérez-Sanagustín, M., Kloos, C.D., Fernández-Panadero, C.: Understanding learners' motivation and learning strategies in MOOCs. Int. Rev. Res. Open Distrib. Learn. **18**(3), 119–137 (2017). https://doi.org/10.19173/IRRODL.V18I3.2996
2. Anderson, A., Huttenlocher, D., Kleinberg, J., Leskovec, J.: Engaging with massive online courses. In: WWW 2014 - Proceedings of the 23rd International Conference on World Wide Web, pp. 687–697 (2014). https://doi.org/10.1145/2566486.2568042
3. Benotti, L., Aloi, F., Bulgarelli, F., Gomez, M.J.: The effect of a web-based coding tool with automatic feedback on students' performance and perceptions. In: SIGCSE 2018 - Proceedings of the 49th ACM Technical Symposium on Computer Science Education, pp. 2–7 (2018). https://doi.org/10.1145/3159450.3159579
4. Cai, Y.-Z., Tsai, M.-H.: Improving programming education quality with automatic grading system. In: Rønningsbakk, L., Wu, T.-T., Sandnes, F.E., Huang, Y.-M. (eds.) ICITL 2019. LNCS, vol. 11937, pp. 207–215. Springer, Cham (2019). https://doi.org/10.1007/978-3-030-35343-8_22

5. Carreira-Perpinán, M.: A review of dimension reduction techniques. Department of Computer Science. University of Sheffield. Technical report CS-96-09, pp. 1–69 (1997)
6. Cavalcanti, A.P., Barbosa, A., Carvalho, R., et al.: Automatic feedback in online learning environments: a systematic literature review. Comput. Educ.: Artif. Intell. **2**, 100027 (2021). https://doi.org/10.1016/J.CAEAI.2021.100027
7. Chan, M.M., De La Roca, M., Alario-Hoyos, C., Plata, R.B., Medina, J.A., Rizzardini, R.H.: MOOCMaker-2017 perceived usefulness and motivation students towards the use of a cloud-based tool to support the learning process in a Java MOOC. In: International Conference MOOC-MAKER, pp. 73–82 (2017)
8. Chan, Y., Walmsley, R.P.: Learning and understanding the Kruskal-Wallis one-way analysis-of- variance-by-ranks test for differences among three or more independent groups. Phys. Ther. **77**(12), 1755–1762 (1997). https://doi.org/10.1093/ptj/77.12.1755
9. Combéfis, S.: Automated code assessment for education: review, classification and perspectives on techniques and tools. Software **1**, 3–30 (2022). https://doi.org/10.3390/software1010002
10. Denny, P., Luxton-Reilly, A., Carpenter, D.: Enhancing syntax error messages appears ineffectual. In: The 2014 Conference on Innovation & Technology in Computer Science Education, pp. 273–278 (2014). https://doi.org/10.1145/2591708.2591748
11. Derval, G., Gego, A., Reinbold, P., Benjamin, F., Van Roy, P.: Automatic grading of programming exercises in a MOOC using the INGInious platform. In: European Stakeholder Summit on experiences and best practices in and around MOOCs (EMOOCS 2015), pp. 86–91 (2015)
12. Evans, B.J., Baker, R.B., Dee, T.S.: Persistence patterns in massive open online courses (MOOCs) **87**, 2, 206–242 (2016). http://dx.doi.org/10.1080/00221546.2016.11777400, https://doi.org/10.1080/00221546.2016.11777400
13. Feklistova, L., Luik, P., Lepp, M.: Clusters of programming exercises difficulties resolvers in a MOOC. In: Proceedings of the European Conference on e-Learning, ECEL, vol. 2020-Octob, pp. 563–569 (2020). https://doi.org/10.34190/EEL.20.125
14. Gallego-Romero, J.M., Alario-Hoyos, C., Estévez-Ayres, I., Delgado Kloos, C.: Analyzing learners' engagement and behavior in MOOCs on programming with the Codeboard IDE. Educ. Tech. Res. Dev. **68**(5), 2505–2528 (2020). https://doi.org/10.1007/s11423-020-09773-6
15. Gordillo, A.: Effect of an instructor-centered tool for automatic assessment of programming assignments on students' perceptions and performance. Sustainability **11**(20), 5568 (2019). https://doi.org/10.3390/su11205568
16. Gusukuma, L., Bart, A.C., Kafura, D., Ernst, J.: Misconception-driven feedback: results from an experimental study. In: ICER 2018 - Proceedings of the 2018 ACM Conference on International Computing Education Research, pp. 160–168 Association for Computing Machinery, Inc., New York (2018). https://doi.org/10.1145/3230977.3231002
17. Hao, Q., Wilson, J.P., Ottaway, C., Iriumi, N., Arakawa, K., Smith, D.H.: Investigating the essential of meaningful automated formative feedback for programming assignments. In: Proceedings of IEEE Symposium on Visual Languages and Human-Centric Computing, VL/HCC, pp. 151–155. IEEE Computer Society (2019). https://doi.org/10.1109/VLHCC.2019.8818922
18. Hew, K.F.: Promoting engagement in online courses: what strategies can we learn from three highly rated MOOCS. Br. J. Edu. Technol. **47**(2), 320–341 (2016). https://doi.org/10.1111/bjet.12235
19. INGInious [software] (2014). https://github.com/UCL-INGI/INGInious
20. Jung, Y., Lee, J.: Learning engagement and persistence in massive open online courses (MOOCS). Comput. Educ. **122**, 9–22 (2018). https://doi.org/10.1016/j.compedu.2018.02.013
21. Kahan, T., Soffer, T., Nachmias, R.: Types of participant behavior in a massive open online course. IRRODL **18**(6), 1–18 (2017). https://doi.org/10.19173/irrodl.v18i6.3087

22. Keuning, H., Jeuring, J., Heeren, B.: A systematic literature review of automated feedback generation for programming exercises. ACM Trans. Comput. Educ. **19**(1), 1–43 (2018). https://doi.org/10.1145/3231711
23. Kizilcec, R.F., Piech, C., Schneider, E.: Deconstructing disengagement: analyzing learner subpopulations in massive open online courses. In: ACM International Conference Proceeding Series, pp. 170–179 (2013). https://doi.org/10.1145/2460296.2460330
24. Krugel, J., Hubwieser, P., Goedicke, M., et al.: Automated measurement of competencies and generation of feedback in object-oriented programming courses. In: 2020 IEEE Global Engineering Education Conference (EDUCON), pp. 329–336. IEEE (2020)
25. Krusche, S., Seitz, A.: Increasing the interactivity in software engineering MOOCs-a case study. In: Proceedings of the 52nd Hawaii International Conference on System Sciences, pp. 7592–7601 (2019)
26. Luik, P., et al.: Participants and completers in programming MOOCs. Educ. Inf. Technol. **24**(6), 3689–3706 (2019). https://doi.org/10.1007/s10639-019-09954-8
27. Marin, V.J., Pereira, T., Sridharan, S., Rivero, C.R.: Automated personalized feedback in introductory Java programming MOOCs. In: Proceedings - International Conference on Data Engineering, pp. 1259–1270 (2017). https://doi.org/10.1109/ICDE.2017.169
28. McBroom, J., Yacef, K., Koprinska, I., Curran, J.R.: A data-driven method for helping teachers improve feedback in computer programming automated tutors. In: Penstein Rosé, C., et al. (eds.) AIED 2018. LNCS (LNAI), vol. 10947, pp. 324–337. Springer, Cham (2018). https://doi.org/10.1007/978-3-319-93843-1_24
29. Narciss, S.: Feedback strategies for interactive learning tasks. In: Spector, J.M., Merrill, M.D., Van Merriënboer, J., Driscoll, M.P. (eds.) Handbook of Research on Educational Communications and Technology, pp. 125–144. Lawrence Erlbaum Associates, Mahaw, New York (2008)
30. Pettit, R., Prather, J.: Automated assessment tools: too many cooks, not enough collaboration. J. Comput. Sci. Coll. **32**(4), 113–121 (2017)
31. Pieterse, V.: Automated assessment of programming assignments. In: 3rd Computer Science Education Research Conference on Computer Science Education Research, vol. 3, pp. 45–56 (2013). http://dx.doi.org/10.1145/1559755.1559763
32. Qian, Y., Lehman, J.: Using targeted feedback to address common student misconceptions in introductory programming: a data-driven approach. SAGE Open **9**, 4 (2019). https://doi.org/10.1177/2158244019885136
33. Rafique, W., Dou, W., Hussain, K., Ahmed, K.: Factors influencing programming expertise in a web-based e-learning paradigm. Online Learn. J. **24**(1), 162–181 (2020). https://doi.org/10.24059/olj.v24i1.1956
34. Restrepo-Calle, F., Ramírez Echeverry, J.J., González, F.A.: Continuous assessment in a computer programming course supported by a software tool. Comput. Appl. Eng. Educ. **27**(1), 80–89 (2019). https://doi.org/10.1002/cae.22058
35. Shute, V.J.: Focus on formative feedback. Rev. Educ. Res. **78**(1), 153–189 (2008). https://doi.org/10.3102/0034654307313795
36. Staubitz, T., Klement, H., Renz, J., Teusner, R., Meinel, C.: Towards practical programming exercises and automated assessment in massive open online courses. In: Proceedings of 2015 IEEE International Conference on Teaching, Assessment and Learning for Engineering, TALE 2015, pp. 23–30 IEEE (2015). https://doi.org/10.1109/TALE.2015.7386010
37. Vinker, E., Rubinstein, A.: Mining code submissions to elucidate disengagement in a computer science MOOC. In: LAK22: 12th International Learning Analytics and Knowledge Conference (LAK22), pp. 142–151 (2022). https://doi.org/10.1145/3506860.3506877
38. Wong, J., Baars, M., Davis, D., Van Der Zee, T., Houben, G.J., Paas, F.: Supporting self-regulated learning in online learning environments and MOOCs: a systematic review. Int. J.

Hum.-Comput. Interact. **35**(4–5), 356–373 (2019). https://doi.org/10.1080/10447318.2018.1543084

39. Yuan, C., Yang, H.: Research on K-value selection method of K-means clustering algorithm. J **2**(2), 226–235 (2019). https://doi.org/10.3390/J2020016
40. Zar, J.H.: Biostatistical Analysis. Prentice Hall, New York (1999)

Integrating Podcasts into MOOCs: Comparing Effects of Audio- and Video-Based Education for Secondary Content

Daniel Koehler(✉), Sebastian Serth, Hendrik Steinbeck, and Christoph Meinel

Hasso-Plattner-Institute, University Potsdam, Potsdam, Germany
{daniel.koehler,sebastian.serth,hendrik.steinbeck}@hpi.de

Abstract. Multimedia learning methods can enrich any online learning scenario. However, traditional Massive Open Online Courses (MOOCs) often put the learner into classroom-like situations without considerably varying presentation formats. By conducting a study and analysis of multimedia elements such as interviews and podcasts, we lay a foundation for future research in the field of multimedia learning. This research studies video-based and audio-based education methods for secondary learning content. We explore both the conscious and subconscious effects of the different formats. In our quantitative assessment of more than 900 learners, we did not observe any significant differences in quiz performance between learners of the two groups. Although our recurring learners are used to video-based learning methods, the audio-based teaching methods were accepted and rated "easy to follow" by more than 80% of our learners. However, we observe that the learners enjoy *traditional podcasts* with a single presenter the least. Our work adds to the field of multimedia online teaching and shows that enriching courses with audio-based education methods proves beneficial for asynchronous learning offers.

Keywords: Podcasts · MOOCs · Multimedia learning · Online learning

1 Introduction

Teachers in traditional secondary and tertiary education classrooms have learned to apply varying teaching methods to keep the learners' attention [19]. Such variation has already seen tremendous success. Nevertheless, few online-learning courses use variable teaching methods or a variety in presentation formats to increase learner engagement. Notably, the COVID-19 pandemic of recent years triggered an incredible growth of online education [1]. While traditional education such as from schools or universities has moved online, many additional offers for personal and adult education in the form of Massive Open Online Courses (MOOCs) have been created [2,13]. Unfortunately, recent studies show

I. Hilliger et al. (Eds.): EC-TEL 2022, LNCS 13450, pp. 131–144, 2022.
https://doi.org/10.1007/978-3-031-16290-9_10

that the current state of MOOCs concerning learner interaction and educational best practices is not en-par with face-to-face learning, yielding less learner success [9,14].

Traditional online courses primarily consist of video material interlaced with additional exercises such as multiple-choice quizzes to engage the learners and ensure that the course content is appropriately understood. Trends show that the use of interactive learning content (e.g., drag-and-drop exercises or H5P[1] elements) has already increased largely [5]. Nevertheless, new knowledge in online education is still primarily provided in video-based learning or as additional literature proposed in the course.

In addition to visual learning, people consume much information and knowledge by simply listening. This behavior has been observed over the last centuries, for example, by the ongoing popularity of (informational) radio [17]. However, recently, podcasts as a sole medium of entertainment and information sharing have seen a massive surge of consumers. Podcasts have increasingly become a part of everyday life as seen in rising listener counts, such as the increase of 30% in podcast listeners over the past three years[2]. Similarly, podcasts have started being used more and more as a medium for traditional education, which had to move online [3,11,20,21].

To identify possibilities to improve online education, we conducted a study to evaluate if educators can integrate podcasts into online education as a video-equivalent teaching medium. Therefore, we formulate the following research questions:

RQ1. How does the form of content presentation (e.g., podcasts, interviews, videos) affect learners' perception? (c.f. Sect. 4.1)
RQ2. How do audio-based teaching methods compare to video-based education in regard to learning success? (c.f. Sect. 4.2)
RQ3. Which differences regarding learner acceptance and learning success can a teacher observe when comparing audio-only and video-based education? (c.f. Sect. 4.3).

2 Background and Related Work

Traditionally, video-based online education in the context of MOOCs features audio-visual learning items—*videos*. These are usually open to any student to watch and learn the content.

Very similar regarding the availability and openness are *podcasts*. They convey knowledge in an audio-only format. Podcasts can be seen as the continued development of radio, proliferating and available on almost any topic of interest on various streaming platforms such as Spotify or Apple Podcasts [18]. Educational podcasts often rely on additional material such as the so-called show-notes, often referencing texts or articles available for download to the listeners [6].

[1] H5P is a JavaScript Framework for interactive exercises, Website: https://h5p.org/.

[2] Statistics from https://www.buzzsprout.com/blog/podcast-statistics (Retrieved Feb. 5th, 2022).

2.1 Comparing Audio-Based and Video-Based Education Methods

To the best of our knowledge, despite the rising popularity of podcasts and the positive aspects they provide, the impact of the delivery medium of educational material on learner success is not yet investigated thoroughly. Some fellow researchers explicitly exclude the comparison from their work [8].

Comparisons between audio- and video-based education have been performed with a small group of students (N = 94) by Shqaidef et al. in the field of dental education [16]. Their research identified that no significant difference exists between the two learning groups for basic knowledge, such as easy recall tasks. However, for analytical questions, the scores of students experiencing video-based education were significantly higher. Limitations of their work are the relatively small group of assessed students. Further, in-depth study material, namely the printed presentation slides, was provided to the students. The way of knowledge presentation is therefore not considered audio-only anymore.

Fellow researchers Daniel and Woody have studied 48 students of a psychology course using podcasts for delivering *new content* [7]. However, they explicitly state that "the use of audio podcasts remains untested for delivering *secondary content* that reinforces, extends, and contextualizes the primary concepts of a course or concept". Further, they raise awareness for the challenge of carefully selecting fitting content for audio-only education, as educators can not convey every learning item or topic without visual support similarly effectively.

Our study fills in the gaps of previous research by comparing the learning success of different forms of content presentation using videos and podcasts.

3 Study Material and Study Design

The following sections describe the content presentation forms to be studied, the study design, and the execution of the same.

3.1 Learning Material for the Study

In previous work, we discussed our process of selecting appropriate content to teach in an audio-only podcast [10]. We decided on using podcasts for *secondary content* in new learning items, which we added to our course, within so-called *Deep Dive* sections. In those sections, we reiterate key learning content, highlighting interconnections or differences between various terminologies, technologies, and functionalities previously explained. To gain a holistic view of the impact of the presentation medium, we created three *Deep Dive* sections for our study. These multiple *Deep Dive* sections allow room for subjectivity regarding the perceived difficulty or learning result between the different learning topics.

For example, one of our *Deep Dive* elements in our online course on cybersecurity reiterates on digital signatures. In previous learning elements, the technical background of digital signatures has been presented, which leaves the *Deep Dive* to target practical implementations and the security goals achieved with digital signatures.

3.2 Content Presentation Forms

In previous work, we assessed which presentation methods might be suitable for evaluation in more detail [10]. We decided to offer the learning content from the *Deep Dive* sections using three different teaching methods as shown in Table 1.

Table 1. Overview of the different presentation forms and the thereby manipulated variables.

Presentation Method	Number of Presenters	Video Available
Interview Video	2	Yes
Interview Podcast	2	No
Traditional Podcast	1	No

Interview Video. Learners in our MOOC platform are used to video-based education formats. As the control group for visual education, we present content from two speakers in an interview format without any additional visualizations.

Interview Podcast. One of the elements under close survey for this work is our *interview podcast*. To ensure that we teach the same content as in the corresponding interview video, we took the audio from the video and presented it as an audio-only podcast.

Traditional Podcast. Finally, we evaluate the impact that the number of presenters in a podcast has by comparing a single presenter to multiple presenters. After recording the interviews, we recorded this audio to ensure we presented similar content in the one-person podcast. Hence, we picked the significant questions from the interview podcast and elaborated on the same ideas and challenges while only having one presenter.

With our approach of recording the different elements, we are confident that the knowledge and content we present in all three podcast variants are the same. To assess the learners' learning success, we provided identical quizzes and tests, regardless of the content variant they had.

3.3 Study Design

We performed the study in the context of one of our Massive Open Online Courses. Our study plan is preregistered with *osf.io*[3] and thus available to fellow researchers[4].

[3] Open Science Framework, Website: https://osf.io.

[4] *Survey Preregistration: Consuming Security: Evaluating Podcasts to Promote Online Learning Integrated with Everyday Life*: https://osf.io/grqek (DOI: 10.17605/OSF.IO/GRQEK.

As presented in Table 1, the two main variables that we modify within this study are the *Number of Presenters* as well as the *Availability of Video Content.*

In our online course and study, we presented learners with a total of three *Deep Dive* sections in which we compared the different presentation methods. In each section, users are first shown the *learning item*, i.e., the interview video or one of the two audio-only podcasts. Afterwards, learners answer a *content quiz* and finally, they are asked to complete one *survey* for feedback in each *Deep Dive* section. Users are assigned to one of the three different forms of content presentation when they visit the first *Deep Dive* section. This assignment is performed in a round-robin principle and stays consistent for the other *Deep Dive* sections. Thus, we present a single user content in only one of the presentation forms throughout our course.

As we collect feedback from learners with one survey for each of the three *Deep Dive* sections, we have fine-granular data, which further allows us to reflect on changes in the users' answers. These might occur because a specific topic might have been more or less suitable for the podcast format as the others or because the learners' perception could change over time, i.e., with repeated presentation of a specific learning medium.

Survey Design. The perception of learners was measured using a quantitative survey questionnaire. Due to the high count of participants in a MOOC, we are confident that a survey is the only reasonable proxy for quantitative measurement of learners' perceptions. We asked the learners to answer it after consuming the respective learning material. The survey was optional, and we did not offer rewards or incentives.

We divided the surveys into multiple question groups. First, we asked the users to provide feedback on the content of the learning item. This feedback is collected using various 5-point Likert scale [12] questions. While the learning content remained identical during all the different learning variants, this question block allows us to capture subconscious differences among the users and their understanding of the content.

The next block of 5-point Likert scale questions targeted the *type* of learning content. Recurring users in our online courses are used to traditional education videos, showing the teacher and presentation slides. This section explicitly required the users to assess whether they liked and enjoyed the new type of learning (i.e., our interview video or podcasts).

The third block of 5-point Likert scale questions references the connection between the presenter and the learner. We attempted to identify whether the learner felt that a particular form of teaching might be particularly engaging or boring.

Finally, we calculated the Net Promoter Score (NPS) [15] of our *Deep Dive* sections. The NPS assesses the likelihood of users recommending an experience to friends and divides them into *promoters*, *passives* and *detractors* based on their responses. The final score (ranging from -100 to $+100$) allows us to compare the different formats against each other easily.

3.4 Learning Success

Besides the questionnaires we asked the users to fill out, we collected implicit feedback on the learning items by providing the learners with an ungraded quiz in the learning platform. This provides us with quantitative data to measure the learning success of the different presentation forms. Therefore, we prepared our course so that learners of any content variant first consume their *Deep Dive* learning content. Next, we present them with the survey for their particular variant. Finally, they can take an ungraded quiz to evaluate their learning success from the previous learning item. Those quizzes followed the same design as usual ungraded quizzes offered after each video unit, ensuring that learners are already familiar with the format. Assessing the success of a teaching form by comparing learners' success for the different groups in the quiz helps us derive implicit insights on the content presentation.

4 Results and Analysis

Table 2. Overview over the enrolled number of learners in the course and the corresponding rate of completion of the different surveys, quizzes and learning items. *Quiz Completions* showing unique users, some of which took the quiz without previously accessing any of the learning items.

		Interview Video	Interview Podcast	Traditional Podcast
Course Enrollments			3,969	
Active Learners			2,815	
Deep Dive 1	Interacting Users	312	280	302
	Survey Results	142	111	104
	Quiz Completions		1,121	
Deep Dive 2	Interacting Users	231	225	213
	Survey Results	104	79	76
	Quiz Completions		909	
Deep Dive 3	Interacting Users	192	176	173
	Survey Results	65	59	56
	Quiz Completions		874	
Course Completion			1,186 (42% of Active Learners)	

We performed the study in this work performed alongside a cybersecurity MOOC in English language. 3,969 Participants have initially registered with our online course, out of which 1,186 participants (42% of active learners, i.e., those visiting at least one item) have completed the course. As described in Subsect. 3.3, we randomly assigned the learners into three groups to be able to compare the different learning and content presentation types. For each learner, we offered a total of three *Deep Dive* elements in which we presented the learning content in the assessed form. We presented the learners with the same presentation form across all three *Deep Dive* sections. Each of the *Deep Dive* elements was accompanied by one survey per group of learners. Additionally, each *Deep Dive* element was accompanied by an identical quiz for learners of all three groups. Table 2 shows the exact number of participants and completions per learning element in the course.

We derived the NPS over all of the nine different learning items out of the three presentation categories. The calculated scores rank the *Interview Video* the best (NPS: 7) followed by the *Interview Podcast* (NPS: −4) and finally the *Traditional Podcast* with an NPS of −7. In the following sections, we analyze in more detail which aspects of the teaching content were particularly liked or disliked by the learners.

4.1 Acceptance of New Presentation Formats

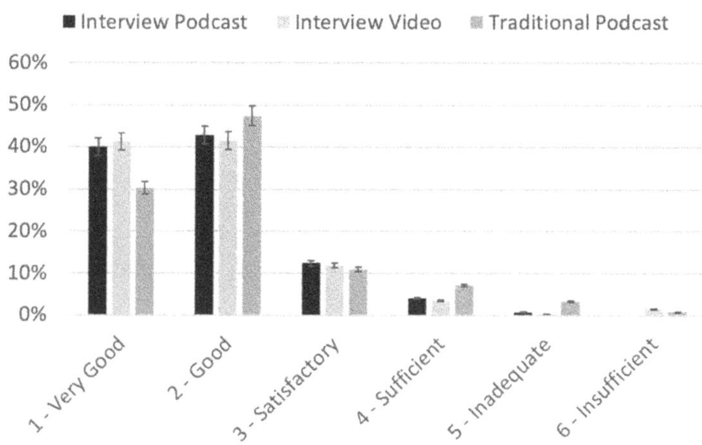

Fig. 1. Distribution of the school grades that the learners assigned to the learning content. Whiskers show standard deviation. N = 804

Independent of the actual learning success, in the field of lifelong learning and adult education, keeping learners' attention and motivation is of particular importance [4]. We, therefore, tested the overall acceptance of our *Deep Dive* elements and the three different presentation formats by asking the learners to rate the items using school grades ranging from *1 - Very Good* to *6 - Insufficient*. Figure 1 shows that the lowest-rated content out of the three was the *Traditional Podcast* with an average grade of 2.18. The next-best rated type of learning was the *Interview Video*, which was on average graded with a 2.03. With another 15% increased grade, *Interview Podcast* was the best-graded type of learning item at an average grade of 1.73.

To judge the acceptance of the new education formats, we further assessed access statistics of the different learning items. Throughout all learning items, we observe that 91% of active course participants at that point also access our optional Deep Dives. This falls in line with statistics from other courses in which 92% of learners accessed optional items.

4.2 Analysis of Learning Success

The main target for any education form is to convey knowledge. We retrieved implicit feedback on the quality and success of educating learners by assessing their performance during the course and, e.g., weekly graded exams.

Figure 2 shows a box-plot of the course performance that the learners of the three different presentation forms achieved. The course performance is almost identical for all three variants (Median: 0.86), with non-significant differences in-between the three groups (measured with a one-way ANOVA, $p = 0.68$). We thus conclude that all three presentation formats fulfilled the task of providing and reinforcing knowledge to our learners. This verifies results from related work identifying that for teaching basic knowledge, audio-based and video-based education serve equally good [16]. The × indicated in the chart marks the mean course performance (Interview Video: 0.83; Interview-Podcast: 0.82; Traditional Podcast: 0.82).

Having identified that all three presentation methods yielded similar good results regarding the learners' course performance, we also analyzed the learners' conscious feedback on whether they understood the presented content. The Likert scale presented in Fig. 3 containing the results of our first *Deep Dive* section shows two major results:

(1) The content in all three education forms was understandable to at least 89% of our learners.

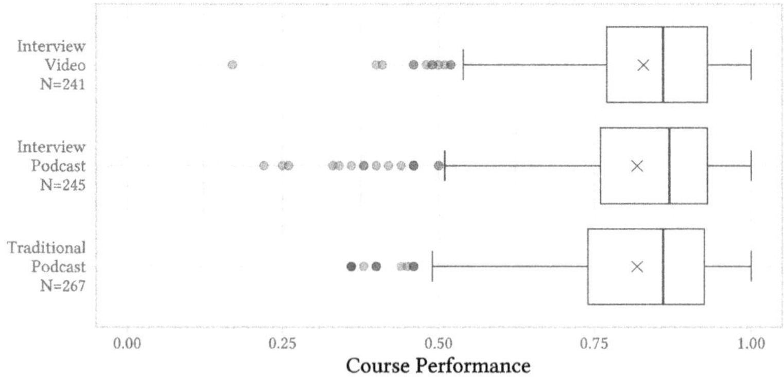

Fig. 2. Course performance of learners partitioned by the different Deep Dive presentation formats. Black lines mark median values, × the mean. N = 753

(2) The surveys show a differentiation of eight percentage points between learners agreeing with the question of whether the content was understandable between the variants *Video* (89%) and *Interview Podcast* (97%). This finding is particularly surprising, as the (audio-) content in the interview podcast was identical to the spoken content in the video. This could indicate that being forced to concentrate on audio-only content might lead to learners understanding that content better.

However, the results from the other two *Deep Dive* sections do not confirm that hypothesis. Both other surveys show the comprehensibility of the *Traditional Podcast* slightly worse than that of the Interviews, with the *Interview Videos* rated best (*Traditional Podcasts*: 89%, 89%; *Interview Podcasts*: 93%, 94%; *Interview Videos*: 96%, 97%). It appears to be generalizable that content prepared by two speakers in the form of an interview or dialogue is better understandable.

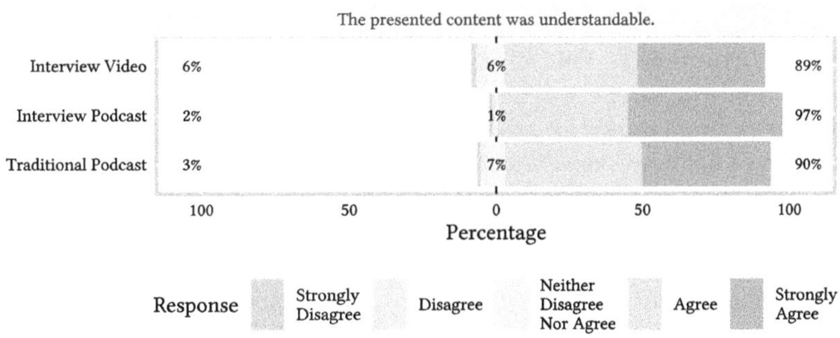

Fig. 3. Likert scale answers whether the content was understandable, as taken from the surveys of *Deep Dive* 1, N(Total) = 357

4.3 Comparison of the Presentation Forms

Having identified that the content appealed to the learners and adequately served its function in educating our participants properly, we analyzed and considered other variables closer.

In our survey, we collected feedback on the two modified variables (*Video Availability, Number of Presenters*) for all learning types. Table 3 provides an overview of the results for the different presentation forms. For each of the variables and the respective presentation method, we highlight how the variable is used in the offered teaching content and which option of the variable is preferred by the learners as taken from the surveys.

Table 3. Overview of learners' preferences for modified variables. Highlighted are the stronger preferred variants. Color-coded in Mint-Green are cases where user preference is identical to the way the variable is presented. Highlighted in Beige are the cases where learners preferred a different variant than the one they experienced.

	Variable	Interview Video	Interview Podcast	Traditional Podcast
Speaker	**Count**	2	2	1
	Preferred Single	5%	15%	33%
	Preferred Multiple	86%	66%	24%
	Indecisive	9%	19%	43%
Media	**Video Available**	Yes	No	No
	Preferred Video	53%	45%	44%
	Preferred Audio	30%	20%	23%
	Indecisive	17%	35%	33%

Number of Speakers. One of the variables we experimented with was the number of speakers in the learning element. Therefore, some of our questions asked the users to imagine the other presentation forms they did not experience. One example of such are learners of the *Interview Podcast* being presented with the statement "I think multiple speakers are confusing for audio content". In the surveys, 66% of learners disagreed with that statement, implying that they preferred multiple speakers. Table 3 highlights such feedback.

For the *Number of Speakers*, the data shows stronger tendencies towards two speakers as seen in the 66% or even 86%. However, this does not appear to be of universal truth, as the listeners of the *Traditional Podcast* responded with a (slight) tendency toward a *Single Speaker*. One might argue that learners tend to prefer the variant which they experienced. However, the listeners of the *Traditional Podcast* with only one speaker were most indecisive. We conclude that the learners who listened to only one presenter in a podcast were least happy with their way of presentation.

Video Availability. For *Video Availability*, the hypothesis from before—that learners tend to prefer the variant of the variable that they have been presented with—does not appear to hold. Of the learners who watched a video, 53% selected that they preferred it. However, even for learners who did not watch a video, the majority (45% and 44%) would have preferred to see a video in addition to the podcast. The same applies to the indecisive learners: The learners presented with a podcast showed twice the amount of indecisiveness.

We observe similar results when analyzing whether the learners are interested to see more content in the presented form (Fig. 4). User's interest for more *Interview Podcasts* has decreased from 50% to 40% throughout the three *Deep Dive* sections. However, at the same time, interest in more content in the form of *Interview Videos* has increased from 50% to 69%. Therefore, we conclude that while one standalone podcast is retrieved positively, recurring learning content is most positively perceived in video form. Since videos are the primary way of presenting content in our MOOCs, this result aligns with the expected outcome.

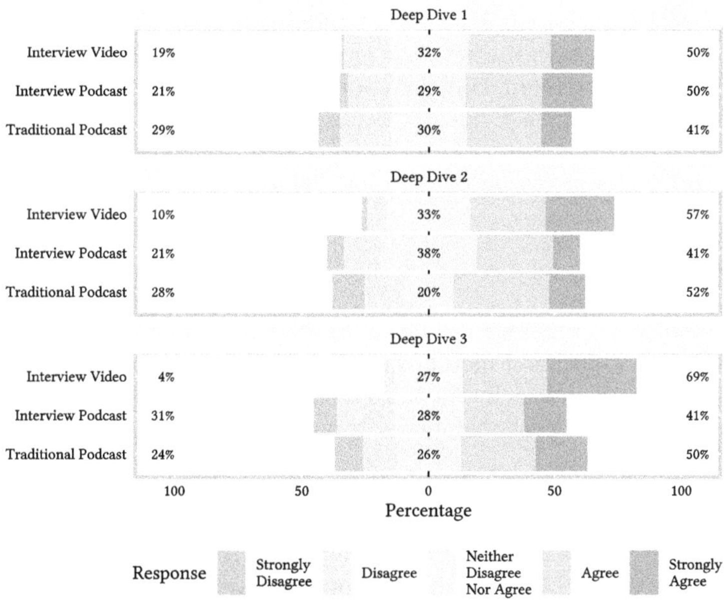

Fig. 4. Answers to the statement "I'd like to see more content in this form" grouped by the different *Deep Dive* elements.

5 Limitations

The study at hand was created in the very narrow context of cybersecurity with a relatively limited sample of learners (on average survey completions per Deep Dive N = 265). Further, we presented podcast elements for the first time in this MOOC, which could lead to a "novelty" effect for our learners. On the other hand, our learners are used to video-based education and might have biased the results against podcasts.

6 Future Work

Our study opens the research space for comparing audio-only to video-based education, particularly for secondary content. However, some questions are still missing generalizable answers. Therefore, we aim to investigate the following ideas and questions in future research:

1. The regular video units and podcasts we presented in the course were of similar length, with 10 to 15 min on average. Platforms such as Apple Podcasts or Spotify feature popular podcasts with lengths of up to 90 min. As such, the optimal length of a podcast remains to be evaluated.
2. In future online courses for broader audiences, we will reiterate similar experiments and the questions at hand. This should help normalize, e.g. the "novelty" factor that podcasts had in the study at hand.
3. In our videos and podcasts, both the interviewer and the interviewee are members of our teaching team. However, educators could use the interview format to integrate experts on a specific topic. We aim to investigate the impact of different interview partners and their level of expertise on the learner's interest in the interview-based learning elements.

7 Conclusion

The presented work tackles one deficit of current online courses: the lack of diverse content presentation methods and not relying on visual information. To enable more diverse and inclusive learning formats, we investigated the effects of using audio-only podcasts compared to video-based online education for secondary learning content.

Previously, the question of whether audio-based education might be of a substantial benefit or a suitable alternative to video-based online education was often omitted or barely touched by other research [7,8,16]. Similarly, we hardly see podcasts integrated into established online learning platforms, such as the platform operated by us, openHPI[5], or other (international) platforms such as Coursera or Edx.

Our study compared three different presentation methods: (1) *Interview Video*, (2) *Interview Podcast*, (3) *Traditional Podcast*. Learners were randomly assigned to the different education groups. Throughout the course, we presented them with three *Deep Dive* learning items in their respective education format, followed by a survey and a content quiz to evaluate active feedback and subconscious learning results. We were able to derive the following results regarding our research questions:

RQ1. How does the form of presentation affect learners' perception?

We identified that the learners perceived the educational character of the presented content throughout all three methods positively (80%, 82% and 83%). When asked to assign school grades from 1 (*Very Good*) to 6 (*Insufficient*) to the different course items, the *Interview Podcast* scored best, with an average grade of 1.73 (*Interview Video*: 2.03; *Traditional Podcast*: 2.18).

RQ2. How does audio- and video-based teaching contribute to learning success?

[5] https://open.hpi.de.

Our study did not show significant differences in learning success between the analyzed groups. Instead, all learners performed similarly well with averages of about 86% performance in the course. Regarding the conscious feedback, our surveys show that, generally, the content of the *Interviews* was rated slightly (6%) better understandable throughout all learning items.

RQ3. Which differences can be observed when comparing audio-only and video-based education techniques?

Our analysis shows a tendency towards multiple speakers compared to a single speaker. Further, comparing the availability of video, learners preferred video-based education. However, this might be because our recurring learners are used to video-based education.

Comparing results between the different *Deep Dive* sections raised the assumption that the *Interview Podcast* is primarily appreciated if only used rarely, e.g., once or twice per course. This is supported by the fact that over the three *Deep Dive* sections, the appreciation for the *Interview Podcasts* dropped (by 23%). In contrast, the appreciation of *Interview Videos* has increased by 38%.

7.1 Takeaways for Researchers and Teachers

The essential question of this work on video- or audio-based education still shows indecisiveness amongst learners. We account this uncertainty to personal preferences, a relatively small amount of survey answers, or the inconclusiveness of learners used to video-based education. However, we see that no presentation form is superior for learning success. Video-based and audio-only education methods can account for specific needs during an online course. As a seldom integration of podcasts for multimedia learning showed great resonance by the learners, we advise any content creator, educator, or teacher to identify the content they can add as an interview-styled podcast to their courses.

References

1. Adedoyin, O.B., Soykan, E.: Covid-19 pandemic and online learning: the challenges and opportunities. Interact. Learn. Environ. 1–13 (2020)
2. Arima, S., Yasui, M., Okawa, K.: Re-design classroom into MOOC-like content with remote face-to-face sessions during the COVID-19 pandemic: a case study in graduate school, p. 299–302. Association for Computing Machinery, New York (2021). https://doi.org/10.1145/3430895.3460163
3. Berk, J., Trivedi, S.P., Watto, M., Williams, P., Centor, R.: Medical education podcasts: where we are and questions unanswered. J. Gen. Intern. Med. **35**(7), 2176–2178 (2020)
4. Brammer, S.E., Punyanunt-Carter, N.M.: Getting the attention of online learners. Commun. Educ. **71**(2), 155–157 (2022)

5. Ch, S.K., Popuri, S.: Impact of online education: a study on online learning platforms and EDX. In: 2013 IEEE International Conference in MOOC, Innovation and Technology in Education (MITE), pp. 366–370. IEEE (2013)
6. Cho, D., Cosimini, M., Espinoza, J.: Podcasting in medical education: a review of the literature. Korean J. Med. Educ. **29**(4), 229 (2017)
7. Daniel, D.B., Woody, W.D.: They hear, but do not listen: retention for podcasted material in a classroom context. Teach. Psychol. **37**(3), 199–203 (2010). https://doi.org/10.1080/00986283.2010.488542
8. Drew, C.: Edutaining audio: an exploration of education podcast design possibilities. Educ. Med. Int. **54**(1), 48–62 (2017). https://doi.org/10.1080/09523987.2017.1324360
9. Julia, K., Marco, K., et al.: Educational scalability in MOOCs: analysing instructional designs to find best practices. Comput. Educ. **161**, 104054 (2021)
10. Koehler, D., Serth, S., Meinel, C.: Consuming security: evaluating podcasts to promote online learning integrated with everyday life. In: 2021 World Engineering Education Forum/Global Engineering Deans Council (WEEF/GEDC), pp. 476–481. IEEE (2021)
11. König, L.: Podcasts in higher education: teacher enthusiasm increases students' excitement, interest, enjoyment, and learning motivation. Educ. Stud. **47**(5), 627–630 (2021)
12. Likert, R.: A technique for the measurement of attitudes. Arch. Psychol. **22**, 5–55 (1932)
13. Mejía, K., Escoto, B., Barahona, J., Flores, O.: Designing a MOOC to prepare faculty members to teach on virtual learning environments in the time of Covid-19. In: 2020 IEEE Learning With MOOCS (LWMOOCS), pp. 96–99 (2020). https://doi.org/10.1109/LWMOOCS50143.2020.9234381
14. Oh, E.G., Chang, Y., Park, S.W.: Design review of MOOCs: application of e-learning design principles. J. Comput. High. Educ. **32**(3), 455–475 (2020). https://doi.org/10.1007/s12528-019-09243-w
15. Reichheld, F.F.: The one number you need to grow. Harv. Bus. Rev. 12 (2003). https://hbr.org/2003/12/the-one-number-you-need-to-grow
16. Shqaidef, A.J., Abu-Baker, D., Al-Bitar, Z.B., Badran, S., Hamdan, A.M.: Academic performance of dental students: a randomised trial comparing live, audio recorded and video recorded lectures. Eur. J. Dent. Educ. **25**(2), 377–384 (2021)
17. Spiker, J.: The development of radio. R. Luthra, Encyclopedia of life support systems, pp. 105–136 (2009)
18. Spinelli, M., Dann, L.: Podcasting: The Audio Media Revolution. Bloomsbury Publishing USA (2019)
19. Spitzer, D.R.: Motivation: the neglected factor in instructional design. Educ. Technol. **36**(3), 45–49 (1996). http://www.jstor.org/stable/44428339
20. Strickland, B.K., Brooke, J.M., Zischke, M.T., Lashley, M.A.: Podcasting as a tool to take conservation education online. Ecol. Evol. **11**(8), 3597–3606 (2021)
21. Tarchichi, T.R., Szymusiak, J.: Continuing medical education in the time of social distancing: the case for expanding podcast usage for continuing education. J. Contin. Educ. Heal. Prof. **41**(1), 70–74 (2021)

The Digitalization of Teaching Practices in K-12 Education: Insights from Teachers' Perspective

Panagiotis Kosmas[1,2,4](✉), Demos Michael[1,3], Efi Nisiforou[1,4], and Charalambos Vrasidas[1,4]

[1] Center for the Advancement of Research and Development in Educational Technology (CARDET), Nicosia, Cyprus
{kosmas.p,nisiforou.e,vrasidas.c}@unic.ac.cy, demos.michael@cardet.org
[2] Cyprus University of Technology, Limassol, Cyprus
[3] Department of Education, University of Cyprus, Nicosia, Cyprus
[4] School of Education, University of Nicosia, Nicosia, Cyprus

Abstract. The reopening of schools and the returning to normal after the emergency experience of online teaching brought to the line new realities in educational practice for both teachers and students. It is now crucial to reflect on the consequences of this experience and rethink the prospects of using digital tools and online learning. The previous remote learning experience could be conceived as an opportunity for the educational community to take advantage of the benefits online teaching offers and adopt those practices that could further develop the teaching experience. This paper examines the reality in K-12 schools after the pandemic investigating the incorporation of seven digital teaching strategies into teachers' daily routines. The study adopts a mixed methodology approach analysing quantitative data from an online survey of 392 in-service teachers and qualitative data from two focus groups. The results show that an essential percentage of teachers continue to use some practices of the distance learning model to enhance learning and communication in the classroom. The use of these strategies was directly and indirectly affected by teachers' attitudes towards the distance learning model and their perceptions of the challenges faced during the pandemic. Implications for policy and practice are drawn.

Keywords: Digital teaching strategies · Distance learning model · Post COVID-19 era · Online teaching · K-12 education · Teachers

1 Introduction

There is much discussion about how COVID-19 is changing many areas of our lives and education landscape. After more than two years of the pandemic, the investigation on what are the long-term and permanent effects on teaching and learning has been set off. Terms such as online education, distance learning, or education information technology are no longer extraneous to school communities. Several authors noted that education

I. Hilliger et al. (Eds.): EC-TEL 2022, LNCS 13450, pp. 145–158, 2022.
https://doi.org/10.1007/978-3-031-16290-9_11

would never be the same after COVID-19 [1–3]. However, the extent to which education is now digitally transformed remains a question.

The disease outbreak in Cyprus started in March 2020, when the government imposed the first national lockdown for around three months. As in most countries worldwide, local primary and secondary education schools shifted to a new reality from one day to another. The distance learning model vastly replaced the conventional physical attendance in schools, gradually forming the new regular education. Teachers strived to employ digital methods and practices by integrating technology and available digital tools to maintain the educational process. Although this transition was imposed by the circumstances of that period, it is still unclear whether teachers continue to employ such practices in the post-COVID-19 era as long-term effects of the pandemic.

This study aims to investigate whether K-12 education in Cyprus changed after the pandemic regarding the teaching practices and methods adopted by the teachers. As a further investigation, we explore the influence of two factors related to the attitudes and perceptions of teachers on the adoption of digital teaching strategies in the classrooms after the lockdowns. This study serves as an evidence-based effort offering some critical considerations regarding the effects of the distance learning model applied during the pandemic and contributing to the discussion on rethinking education in the post-COVID-19 era.

Despite the initial research conducted, no academic work focuses exclusively on the impact of COVID-19 on the digitalization of teaching practices in K-12 education in Cyprus. This research highlights critical insights from the teachers' perspective regarding using online practices in the classroom. Based on teachers, those practices could further enhance the learning experience of both students and teachers, providing opportunities for collaboration, communication, and digital skills development. The examination focuses on seven practices as strategies to improve learning. Quantitative and qualitative data were collected through a parallel mixed-method design to address the research questions of this study:

1. Which digital teaching strategies are used in K-12 education in Cyprus after the pandemic of COVID-19, and to what extent? Which aspects comprise these digital teaching strategies?
2. Which factors affect the use of these digital teaching strategies after the pandemic, related to teachers' attitudes towards the distance learning model for K12 education and perceptions about the challenges faced during the pandemic? (see Fig. 1).

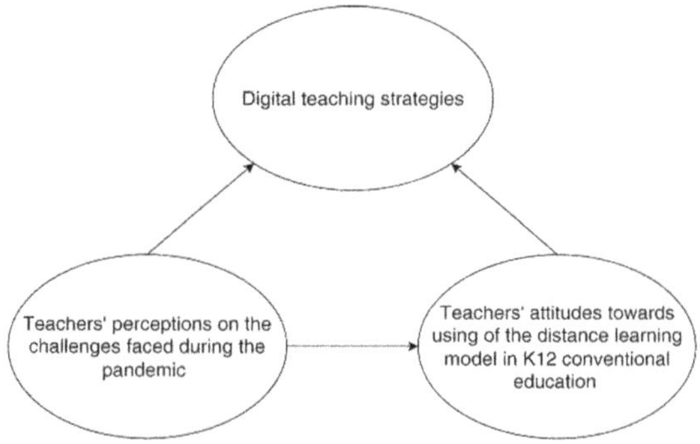

Fig. 1. The hypothesized model on the direct and indirect effects on the use of digital teaching strategies (research question 2)

2 Rethinking K-12 Education After COVID-19

Indisputably, the COVID-19 has caused an immeasurable global impact on more than 191 educational systems worldwide [4]. The national lockdowns had interrupted conventional schooling in response to the virus contagion. They forced institutions to switch to a 100% online modality, making remote learning the de facto method of education provision for varying periods [5, 6]. The immersive effects have demanded urgent attention and solutions to address the difficulties and limitations associated with the rapid adoption of digital technologies and the transformation of educational infrastructures.

Studies conducted around the world reached some common conclusions regarding the impact of COVID-19 on education regarding digital teaching practices and strategies; teachers are compelled to make concerted efforts to develop creative approaches to online teaching that they might not have prepared for in the past. This was attempted by exploiting existing infrastructures or designing new pedagogical delivery concepts. However, new methodologies required specific preparation time and familiarisation with devices and platforms. Teachers would also collaborate with colleagues and teaching staff to exchange ideas and support each other [7–10].

The crisis stimulated innovative approaches and teaching methodologies incorporating digital tools during teachers' daily practice [11]. Digital-driven education innovations can now be spotted everywhere, generating a "trend" in schools and classrooms [12]. For example, teachers would monitor and assess students' performance through quizzes and rubric-based assessment tools, although they face great difficulties monitoring and verifying students' learning [6, 12].

The mass response by governments to support the education systems for implementing online learning solutions worldwide would possibly lead to new foundations for transforming schools based on the demands of high digitalized societies [4]. The use of digital tools and platforms were explored as valuable opportunities that came to stay in education even when face-to-face teaching resumes [12]. This mass swift has shown that the potential to transform the future of learning is possible, provided that systems are appropriately supported, and technology is leveraged to complement a skilled teaching staff [10].

2.1 Challenges and Boundaries for Change

When designed and implemented deliberately, online learning might offer equal benefits as conventional face-to-face schooling. However, emergency remote teaching due to COVID-19 was far from that [13]. Still, effective and meaningful online learning can be pursued if teachers have adequate time to plan and realize the full scope of using digital tools and platforms [14]. Affordability and acquisition of appropriate digital devices, availability of good quality internet, suitability of working conditions at schools and houses, and catering for the unique needs of students are only some of the factors that should be strategically addressed in basic education's online learning. Moreover, teachers' and students' lack of digital education recourses and low digital literacy were among the main boundaries reported for a smooth transition [9, 15]. However, neither the time nor the resources were adequate for such preparation. At the same time, social isolation and emotional and psychological distress over adjusting to the new reality imposed further challenges to distance learning [12, 16, 17]. Considering these factors, the COVID-19 has undoubtedly highlighted the inadequacies and inequalities in the education systems.

Results from European studies varied in the outcomes of applying online learning during the pandemic. For example, Kruszewska and her colleagues [7] found that despite the vast experience teachers could gain from engaging in remote education, they did encounter numerable issues that hindered their efforts to teach online. These includes the absence of information technology equipment in students' homes, lack of communication and motivation among students, and decreased learning efficiency. Similarly, a research in Finland [18] showed that while some teachers indicated remarkable resilience and capacity to respond to the challenge of digitalizing their practices, others have struggled, as it required the integration of digital tools efficiently and in a way that benefits students' performance. Lavonen and Salmela-Aro [19] identified that teachers suffered from stress, weakening the learning conditions.

The switch to more digitalized solutions to learning has motivated institutions to become more accepting of the use of modern technologies [20]. Empirical evidence suggests that teachers' intention to use online learning is highly correlated with their readiness to incorporate such methods into their practices, prior experience and ICT skills [21]. At the same time, students' attitudes toward using computers, their self-efficacy to browse the internet for educational purposes, and teachers' positive attitudes toward e-learning were significant factors contributing to their motivation for learning [17]. Online learning has also imposed more freedom and flexibility on physically challenged students, who can participate in learning through virtual environments, thus limiting movement requirements [12]. As a result, suitable pedagogies for online education depend on teachers' expertise and exposure to ICT tools for communication, collaboration, and content creation. Therefore, the extent to which schools and society adapt efficiently to online teaching is highly debatable when speaking in the long term.

2.2 The Case of Cyprus

Cyprus has not been an exception for transitioning to online education. In-school operation of all public and private schools in the country was suspended in March 2020, when the first national lockdown was imposed, recalling all institutions to act for synchronous and asynchronous distance learning [22].

During the pandemic, most teachers used Microsoft Teams (as suggested by the Ministry of Education) as their preferred platform to communicate with students and deliver teaching, in addition to the use of email, Facebook (Messenger) and ZOOM [23]. Nevertheless, as in many other countries worldwide, many teachers in Cyprus working in public schools struggled to shift their daily teaching practices into online modes, as they did not have adequate prior experience using online tools. Therefore, they had to receive specific training and overcome various technical and pedagogical challenges to establish an efficient online learning process. In contrast, private schools proved to be much more prepared to cope with such requirements, with students having fewer issues accessing ICT and internet connections [24, 25].

3 Methods

3.1 Sampling Process and Participants

A parallel mixed-method design was used to obtain data for this study [26, 27]. Data collection took place in June-July during the summer after the school year 2020–2021. The subjects of this study are teachers of K-12 education in Cyprus.

An online questionnaire was administered electronically through an official announcement[1] of the Cyprus Pedagogical Institute to all country's primary and secondary schools. Data were collected as a part of a larger survey on teachers' best practices, challenges and recommendations about the distance learning model applied during COVID-19 in Cyprus. The questionnaire was developed by the CARDET research team, who have long experience in educational technology topics and approved by the Cyprus Pedagogical Institute. A total of 411 teachers filled in the online questionnaire administered in the Greek language. Pre-primary education teachers (n = 19) were excluded from this study as they consist of a very small and not relevant cluster for this study. Consequently, the sample consists of 392 teachers (24.7% male, 75.0% female, 0.3% other). Most of the participants work in public schools (n = 349, 89.0%), while the rest in private schools (n = 43, 11.0%). Around half of them are teachers in primary education schools (i.e., grades 1–6; n = 207, 52.8%) and the other half work in secondary education schools (i.e., grades 6–12; n = 185, 47.2%). From the latter group, 73 teachers are employed in lower secondary schools (i.e. grades 7–9), 90 in upper secondary schools (i.e., grades 10–12), and 22 in technical schools. The participants held either a master's degree (n = 246, 62.8%), a bachelor's degree (n = 116, 29.6%), or a doctoral degree (n = 30, 7.7%). The sample is reliable at 95% (Confident interval [CI] = .05) of the total population of teachers in Cyprus, which is 10,863 for the year 2019–2020, according to the latest data from the National Statistical Service [28].

Two focus groups were conducted in parallel with the questionnaire distribution, based on a semi-structured guide, which provided the qualitative data of this study. Eight primary school teachers formed the first group, and six teachers comprised the group of secondary education. The conversations were recorded, transcribed, and content analysed [29].

[1] The official announcement of the Cyprus Pedagogical Institute can be accessed here.

3.2 Measures

Digital Teaching Strategies. The use of seven digital teaching strategies by teachers after the pandemic, along with the conventional teaching in the classroom, was answered on a scale from 1 (Every day) to 5 (Never). The items emerged during a preliminary analysis of how COVID-19 changed teaching in Cyprus. During this process, the research team consulted the Cyprus Pedagogical Institute, which was continuously communicating with the schools during the 3-month lockdown (i.e. May-June 2020). Examples of digital teaching strategies provided are "Use of the digital classroom in combination with the conventional classroom", "Create online activities for student collaboration", or "Provide personalised supportive teaching to students through technology (e.g. MS Teams, chat)". Further analysis of the properties of this scale is presented in the section on results, as the investigation of this measure falls under the first research question.

Teachers' Attitudes and Perceptions. Two items were used to observe the attitudes of teachers towards the distance learning model for K-12 education: "If properly designed, the distance learning model can bring just as good results as the conventional teaching" and "I want to continue to use the distance learning model in combination with conventional teaching (blended learning)". The items were answered on a Likert scale ranging from 1 (Totally disagree) to 5 (Totally agree). With the later item, we refer to combining online learning with face-to-face class time as supplementary, which is used to build upon the content discussed in the classroom. Other studies provided evidence that this learning modality can benefit students as they can independently review the course and interact with the online material at their own pace, which may result in better performance, higher motivation and lower anxiety [30]. The reliability of the factor representing teachers' attitudes towards applying the distance learning model in K-12 conventional education was measured using the Spearman's Rho coefficient and estimated at .408 ($p > .01$), which indicates a significant correlation [31].

Last, teachers' perceptions of the challenges faced during the pandemic were captured through a scale addressing four main issues: the additional time required to prepare a distance learning lesson, the lack of educational material in digital formats, the lack of interaction with students, and the physical, mental and emotional exhaustion of students and themselves. A higher score on the scale indicates that the challenge was more important for the teacher (1 = Not important, 3 = Very important). Cronbach's alpha for this latent scale was satisfactory ($\alpha = .66$). Confirmatory factor analysis (CFA) was conducted for both measures added in the same model to examine their relationship and test if these measures are consistent with the researchers' understanding of the nature of the construct. Model's properties were assessed using the maximum likelihood method: chi-square test, Comparative Fit Index ($CFI > 0.95$), Root Mean Square Error of Approximation ($RMSEA < 0.05$), Standardized Root Mean Square Residual ($SRMR \leq 0.05$), and 90% Confidence Interval of $RMSEA < 0.08$. Results indicated a good model fit, χ^2 $(7) = 15.08$, $p < .05$; $CFI = 0.98$; $RMSEA = 0.05$, 90% CI [0.01; 0.09], $SRMR = 0.03$, after a minor correction on the distribution of standardized residuals. Factor loadings were .55 and .75 for teachers' attitudes and ranged from .39 to .77 for teachers' perceptions of challenges ($p < .05$). The correlation between the two factors was estimated at $-.381$ ($p < .05$). Based on these results, the structural model, including both latent variables, was evaluated as acceptable for use in the following analyses.

3.3 Data Analysis

As per the parallel mixed-method design, qualitative and quantitative data were collected in the same phase of the research, analysed separately, and discussed together [27]. First, the two focus groups were scrutinised using content analysis to identify patterns and new themes. Second, apart from the factor analysis to assess the psychometric properties of each scale, we used Structural Equation Modelling (SEM) [32] to estimate the direct and indirect effects of attitudes and perception on the use of digital teaching strategies (see research question 2). Analyses were conducted using SPSS v.20.0.0 and EQS 6.4 software [33]. Last, the qualitative data were used to confirm or complement the quantitative results and triangulate our findings.

4 Results

4.1 Quantitative Results

The analysis of the seven given digital teaching strategies in K-12 education in Cyprus showed that teachers barely tended to do so in their daily practice. The mean of all items was well above the average (from 3.18 to 4.18), indicating that they employ these strategies weekly or monthly. The most usual strategy identified deals with their professional practice (i.e., use of technology to communicate with colleagues) rather than directly involving technology in the classroom (M = 3.18, SD = 1.36). The assignment of tasks via MS Teams or other tools and the combination of digital and conventional classrooms were two strategies applied at least monthly. Less frequently, teachers created online activities for student collaboration (see Table 1).

Correlation and comparable analysis (Pearson correlation and t-test for independent samples) followed to identify whether any digital teaching strategy is related to teachers' characteristics (i.e., gender, age, educational attainment level, years of experience, education level employed). The results revealed no significant relationships or differences (male vs female), apart from the case educational level used (primary vs secondary). The t-test showed statistically significant differences in the means of seven items between the two groups. Teachers in secondary education schools frequently used the seven digital teaching strategies more than their colleagues in primary schools.

Since the scale was developed and administered for the first time, we ran an exploratory factor analysis (EFA) and then a confirmatory factor analysis (CFA) based on the results. The principal component analysis (PCA) with Varimax orthogonal rotation was used for the EFA. The KMO test was good, .829, and the analysis extracted two factors. The first factor represented the digital teaching strategies to enhance learning (5 items) and explained 36.48% of the total variance. Factor loadings ranged from .57 to .82. The second factor comprised the digital teaching strategies for communication (2 items) and explained 23.70% of the remaining variance (total variance explained 60.19%). Factor loadings were .88 and .65. Factors' reliabilities were .78 (Cronbach's alpha) and .35 (Spearman's rho), respectively (see Table 2).

The two subscales were entered into one CFA model to evaluate their psychometric properties. Results indicated a good model fit, χ^2 (12) = 36.38, p < .001; CFI = 0.96; RMSEA = 0.07, 90% CI [0.05; 0.09], SRMR = 0.04, after a minor correction on the

Table 1. Frequency of use of seven digital teaching strategies

	Mean	SD
Use technology to communicate with colleagues (e.g., video conference)	3.18	1.36
Assign tasks via MS Teams (or other digital tools)	3.41	1.51
Use of the digital classroom in combination with the conventional	3.43	1.48
Use technology to communicate with parents/guardians (e.g. emails, etc.)	3.56	1.39
Create a space for asynchronous communication in the afternoon	3.70	1.42
Provide individualised supportive teaching to students through technology	3.78	1.29
Create online activities for student collaboration	4.18	1.21

Note. Items were listed on a scale where 1 = Every day, 2 = 2–3 times a week, 3 = Once a week, 4 = Sometimes a month, and 5 = Never. N = 392

Table 2. Factor loadings of items on the two factors extracted by varimax rotation

#		Factors*		h^2
		I	II	
q01	Use of the digital classroom in combination with the conventional classroom	**.82**	−.17	.69
q02	Create a space for asynchronous communication	**.73**	.16	.64
q03	Assign tasks via MS Teams (or other digital tools)	**.69**	.38	.55
q04	Create online activities for student collaboration	**.63**	.26	.48
q05	Provide individualised supportive teaching	**.57**	.43	.54
q06	Use technology to communicate with parents/guardians (e.g. emails, MS Teams)	−.03	**.88**	.78
q07	Use technology to communicate with colleagues	.37	**.65**	.57
	Eigenvalues	3.09	1.13	
	Percentage of variance	36.48	23.70	
	Cumulative percentage of variance	36.48	60.19	

Note.
***Factor I:** Digital teaching strategies to enhance learning
Factor II: Digital teaching strategies for communication

distribution of standardized residuals. Factor loadings ranged from .52 to .78 for digital teaching strategies to enhance learning and were .47 and .80 for digital teaching strategies for communication ($p < .05$). The correlation between the two subscales was estimated at .692 ($p < .05$). These evaluation indices confirmed the measurement fit of all items and the structural fit between the latent variables as emerged from the EFA; therefore, the two-factor model was allowed for use to form the hypothesised model.

The structural analyses were conducted in four phases regarding the second research question. First, the factor of teachers' attitudes was regressed on the two subscales of digital teaching strategies. The exact process followed with the teachers' perceptions as the independent variable. Then, a model was constructed to observe if teachers' perceptions affect teachers' attitudes. Last, the factors were incorporated into one structure to form the hypothesised model. However, after the analysis preceded the digital teaching strategies (research question 1), the hypothesised model emerged (see Fig. 2).

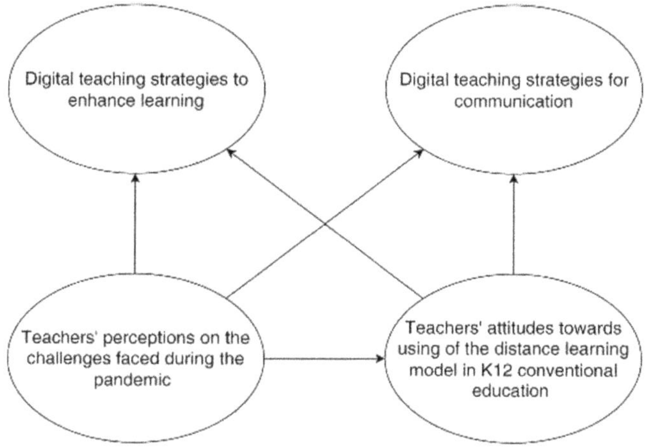

Fig. 2. The emerged hypothesised model on the direct & indirect effects of the use of digital teaching strategies

The regression analysis of teachers' perceptions of digital teaching strategies to enhance learning showed no statistically significant effect. Similarly, the effect on digital teaching strategies for communication was very low (i.e., −.07). The model did not show a good fit either. Thus, these effects were excluded from the final model. The regression of teachers' attitudes on the same subscales showed low to moderate negative effects on digital teaching strategies (−.385 on digital teaching strategies to enhance learning and −.256 on digital teaching strategies for communication). The analysis of the two independent factors revealed that teachers' perceptions of the challenges faced during the pandemic have a negative effect (−.381) on their attitudes towards using the distance learning model after the pandemic. Based on these results, we structured the final model (Fig. 3). Model fit was good, χ^2 (52) = 131.97, $p < .001$; CFI = 0.93; RMSEA = 0.06, 90% CI [0.05; 0.08], SRMR = 0.06. Teachers' attitudes were found to negatively affect teachers' perceptions (−.350, $p < .05$), meaning that those who considered the challenges during the pandemic less important expressed more positive attitudes towards adopting the distance learning model along with the conventional classroom. Therefore, teachers' perceptions of challenges only indirectly affected digital teaching strategies through teachers' attitudes towards the distance learning model. The direct effect of teachers' attitudes on digital teaching strategies to enhance learning and communication was estimated at −.402 and −.251 correspondingly (at $p < .05$). These effects indicate that positive attitudes toward the distance learning model foresee more frequent use of the digital teaching strategies.

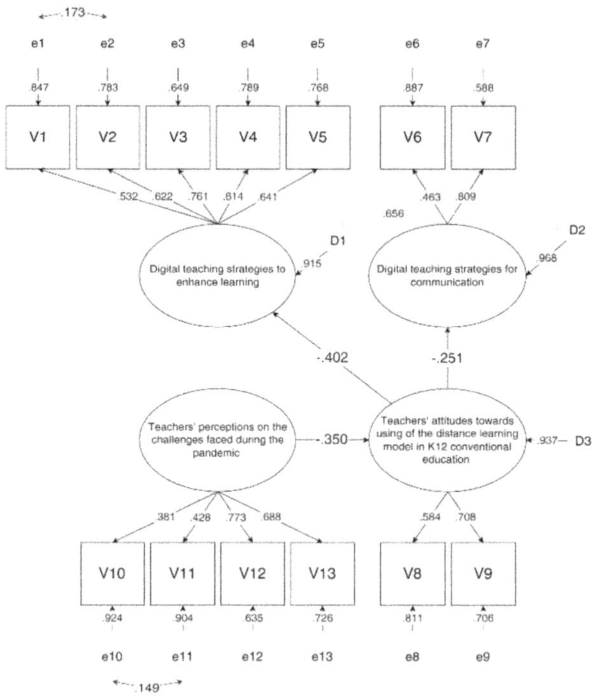

Fig. 3. The final model and estimated direct and indirect effects on the use of digital teaching strategies. Note. All effects are statistically significant at $p < .05$.

4.2 Qualitative Results

The data from the focus groups led to the triangulation of the above findings, as emerged from the qualitative analysis. During the focus groups, teachers were asked to provide their opinion if the distance learning model was used or could be exploited after the pandemic as a step toward a blended K-12 education. Responses were informative beyond the quantitative results, revealing further insights on why teachers continued using digital teaching strategies after the pandemic or not.

In secondary education, the attitudes towards the blended learning model were more optimistic than those in primary education: "*We uploaded many lessons online, so they are now there. If structured better, we can use them in the future and next year*". A teacher said, "*I would demand it to dedicate one day of the week for distance learning*". On the other hand, the hybrid model was, in many cases, imposed by the circumstances because some students in the classrooms needed to stay home to stop the chain of contamination. Primary education teachers found coping with the hybrid model challenging. A teacher explains, "*I had to react very fast in everything. In the beginning, I allowed children to interact [with those at home] to make the lesson more engaging and interactive. However, I soon had to interrupt them and choose the student to talk to. Good organisation and time management were required.*"

Several digital tools were used in classrooms as a 'heritage' from the pandemic era. A primary education teacher said, "*We used some tools such as Kahoot and Padlet because we have already learned them. [...] Also, something I saw that worked well was chatting communities and online spaces for communication and for students to upload their assignments*". In secondary education, teachers also mentioned several digital tools; "*I used MS Teams for communication as a group chat and OneNote. I told them [students] now you know how to use your online notebook, assignments will be done and corrected there.*" Similar practices were adopted by secondary teachers, such as "*worksheets and exercises for homework were uploaded in MS Teams*".

As observed in the quantitative results, teachers used digital means for communication with colleagues; "*As a school principal, I did not teach to classrooms, but I used MS Teams for teleconferences with my school staff*". In secondary education, teachers mentioned that "*we met several times with colleagues during afternoons and days off to discuss several things*". Others added that online meetings are a handful in cases where teachers live in different towns with other schools and attend the seminars.

In summary, teachers' experience with the distance learning model opened new approaches to teaching. They appeared confident to discuss the possibilities of integrating new tools and practices in their daily practice, if not new teaching models. However, several limitations exist that do not allow a complete transition even if desired and accepted by the education stakeholders, including themselves, as evidenced by the quantitative analyses. How they experienced those limitations appears to be decisive in their attitudes and integration of digital tools into their daily practice.

5 Discussion

Our study falls under the global discourse to explore whether the urgent need for continuing schooling and the adoption of online methods and tools to achieve remote education due to the COVID-19 pandemic turned over a new leaf for K-12 education, as questioned by more researchers [34]. Nevertheless, looking at the bigger picture, with technology integration in education, schools are no longer seen as classrooms in the traditional sense where knowledge is merely imparted upon students [15]. According to the literature, there is no one-size-fits-all pedagogy for online learning; it is dependent upon factors such as the subject under study, such as the adequate provision of training or technical infrastructure to enable the incorporation of digital tools [12]. The question that arises, therefore, is the extent to which this new reality could redefine education and reimagine it beyond the inflexible and outdated models that most systems continue to apply today.

In this article, we examine the use of seven digital teaching strategies after the pandemic in K-12 education in Cyprus. Factors related to teachers' attitudes toward the distance learning model and teachers' perceptions of the challenges faced during the pandemic were selected to examine their effect on the use of digital teaching strategies. Our results reveal that K-12 education teachers in Cyprus now use digital teaching practices for communication, task assignment and digital classroom management.

Secondary teachers adopted digital teaching practices to a greater extent than primary teachers to provide educational opportunities to all students. As argued during the interviews, secondary education teachers found it easier to adopt digital strategies because their students appear familiar and competent with technology. On the contrary, primary education teachers should contact parents or guardians instead of reaching out to their students, as essential guidance and support from an adult are required during distance learning. However, the presence of an adult was not always feasible in many cases. This fact generates important implications for integrating certain digital practices based on students' education level.

The structural equation analyses revealed that teachers' positive attitudes towards the distance learning model foresee a more frequent use of the referred digital teaching strategies. This effect was more substantial on the digital teaching strategies to enhance learning than strategies for communication. Teachers' perceptions of challenges during the pandemic had a moderate negative impact on these attitudes. This highlights that perceived limitations and deficiencies of the distance learning experience during lockdowns influenced whether teachers are willing to adopt a digitally-friendly approach. This is important for policymakers and school leaders to consider. Should conventional teaching continue to be supported using online methods, it is necessary to invest in teachers' professional development and real-time guidance to overcome the pandemic upset. Considering the benefits of technology-enhanced learning, the digital transformation of education should be a core concern among governments, seeking ways to empower teachers and schools to act as leaders in the digitalisation of classrooms [18].

The global crisis has shown us the lucrative side of online teaching and learning and the benefits of sermonizing teachers and students at any time, in any part of the world, destroying any barriers that conventional methods could not [20]. Online teaching could be equally creative, innovative, and interactive as traditional modes to attract students' attention and facilitate knowledge. There are undoubtedly gaps in remote learning, yet, it has a great potential to continue as part of the teaching proccss if appropriately designed. Taking all into consideration, important questions arise regarding the role of distance education in reshaping digitalization after the pandemic. The policymakers' role is crucial in addressing those for a holistic integration of digital strategies into the teaching reality.

Acknowledgements. The research team would like to thank the Cyprus Pedagogical Institute (Ministry of Education, Culture, Sport and Youth) for the ongoing support during the implementation of this research and for participating teachers for sincerely expressing their views.

References

1. Kalantzis, M., Cope, B.: After the COVID-19 crisis: why higher education may (and perhaps should) never be the same. ACCESS: Contemp. Issues Educ. **40**(1), 51–55 (2020)
2. Riley, N.S.: K-12 Education Will Never Be the Same After Covid-19. Bloomberg Opinion, N.PAG. (2021). Accessed 14 Apr 2022
3. Yarrison, B.G.: "To seek a newer world": honors in virtual reality. Honors Pract. **17**, 185–194 (2021)

4. United Nations: Policy Brief: Education during COVID-19 and beyond (2020). https://www.un.org/development/desa/dspd/wp-content/uploads/sites/22/2020/08/sg_policy_brief_covid-19_and_education_august_2020.pdf. Accessed 14 Apr 2022
5. Yu, L.: Analysis and enlightenment of user agreements based on the three smart teaching tools of rain classroom. Manag. Sci. Eng. **14**(1) (2020)
6. Almonacid-Fierro, A., Vargas-Vitoria, R., de Carvalho, R.S., Fierro, M.A.: Impact on teaching in times of COVID-19 pandemic: a qualitative study. Int. J. Eval. Res. Educ. (IJERE) **10**(2), 432 (2021)
7. Kruszewska, A., Nazaruk, S., Szewczyk, K.: Polish teachers of early education in the face of distance learning during the COVID-19 pandemic – the difficulties experienced and suggestions for the future. Education 3–13 **50**(3), 304–315 (2020)
8. Meinck, S., Fraillon, J., Strietholt, R.: The impact of the COVID-19 pandemic on education international evidence from the responses to educational disruption survey (2022)
9. Schleicher, A.: The Impact of Covid-19 on Education Insights from Education at a Glance (2020)
10. The World Bank, UNESCO and UNICEF: The State of the Global Education Crisis: A Path to Recovery. The World Bank, Washington D.C. (2021)
11. Dwivedi, Y.K., et al.: Impact of COVID-19 pandemic on information management research and practice: transforming education, work and life. Int. J. Inf. Manag. **55**, 102211 (2020)
12. Pokhrel, S., Chhetri, R.: A literature review on impact of COVID-19 pandemic on teaching and learning. High. Educ. Future **8**(1), 133–141 (2021)
13. Hodges, C., Moore, S., Lockee, B., Trust, T., Bond, A.: The Difference Between Emergency Remote Teaching and Online Learning (2020)
14. Di Pietro, G., Biagi, G., Costa, P., Karpiński, Z., Mazza, J.: The likely impact of COVID-19 on education: reflections based on the existing literature and recent international datasets. Publications Office of the European Union, Luxembourg (2020)
15. Cheng, X., Pellegrini, M., Zhou, L., Cheung, A.C.K.: Not only survival but stronger: the impact of alarming invader of SARS-CoV-2 on global education. Sci. Insights Educ. Front. **7**(2), 835–860 (2020)
16. Dias, A., Scavarda, A., Silveira, H., Scavarda, L.F., Kondamareddy, K.K.: The online education system: COVID-19 demands, trends, implications, challenges, lessons, insights, opportunities, outlooks, and directions in the work from home. Sustainability **13**(21), 12197 (2021)
17. Wang, X.Y., Li, G., Malik, S., Anwar, A.: Impact of COVID-19 on achieving the goal of sustainable development: E-learning and educational productivity. Econ. Res.-Ekonomska Istraživanja 1–17 (2021)
18. Iivari, N., Sharma, S., Ventä-Olkkonen, L.: Digital transformation of everyday life – how COVID-19 pandemic transformed the basic education of the young generation and why information management research should care? Int. J. Inf. Manag. **55**, 102183 (2020)
19. Lavonen, J., Salmela-Aro, K.: Experiences of moving quickly to distance teaching and learning at all levels of education in Finland. In: Reimers, F.M. (ed.) Primary and Secondary Education During Covid-19, pp. 105–123. Springer, Cham (2022). https://doi.org/10.1007/978-3-030-81500-4_4
20. Dhawan, S.: Online learning: a panacea in the time of COVID-19 crisis. J. Educ. Technol. Syst. **49**(1), 5–22 (2020)
21. Ngabiyanto, Nurkhin, A., Widiyanto, Saputro, I.H., Kholid, A.M.: Teacher's intention to use online learning; an extended technology acceptance model (TAM) investigation. In: Journal of Physics: Conference Series, vol. 1783, no. 1, p. 012123 (2021)
22. CEDEFOP: Cyprus: Responses to the Covid-19 outbreak. CEDEFOP (2020). Accessed 10 Apr 2022

23. Vrasidas, C., Kosmas, P., Nisiforou, E., Michael, D.: The Implementation of Distance Education in Cyprus Schools. CARDET Press (2020)
24. Nisiforou, E.A., Kosmas, P., Vrasidas, C.: Emergency remote teaching during COVID-19 pandemic: lessons learned from Cyprus. EMI **58**(2), 215–221 (2021)
25. Sofianidis, A., Meletiou-Mavrotheris, M., Konstantinou, P., Stylianidou, N., Katzis, K.: Let Students Talk about Emergency Remote Teaching Experience: Secondary Students' Perceptions on Their Experience During the COVID-19 Pandemic (2021)
26. Cohen, L., Manion, L., Morrison, K.: Planning educational research. In: Research Methods in Education. Routledge Editors, New York (2011)
27. Creswell, J.W., Plano Clark, V.L.: Designing and Conducting Mixed Methods Research, 2nd edn. SAGE Publications (2011)
28. Statistical Service of Cyprus (2021). https://library.cystat.gov.cy/Documents/Publication/ABSTRACT-2019-EN-270521.pdf
29. Chi, M.T.: Quantifying qualitative analyses of verbal data: a practical guide. J. Learn. Sci. **6**(3), 271–315 (1997)
30. Poon, J.: Blended learning: an institutional approach for enhancing students' learning experiences. J. Online Learn. Teach. **9**(2), 271–289 (2013)
31. Eisinga, R., Grotenhuis, M.T., Pelzer, B.: The reliability of a two-item scale: Pearson, Cronbach, or Spearman-Brown? Int. J. Public Health **58**(4), 637–642 (2012)
32. Kline, R.B.: Principles and Practice of Structural Equation Modeling, 4th edn. Guilford Press (2015)
33. Bentler, P.M.: EQS 6, Structural Equations Program Manual. Multivariate Software Inc., Encino (2006)
34. Zhao, Y., Watterston, J.: The changes we need: education post COVID-19. J. Educ. Change **22**(1), 3–12 (2021). https://doi.org/10.1007/s10833-021-09417-3

Representation-Driven Mixed Initiative in Computer Supported Collaborative Learning in Secondary Education

Marco Kragten[1](✉), Monique Pijls[1], Emile Jaspar[1], Malou Sprinkhuizen[1], and Bert Bredeweg[1,2]

[1] Faculty of Education, Amsterdam University of Applied Sciences, Amsterdam, The Netherlands
m.kragten@hva.nl

[2] Faculty of Science, Informatics Institute, University of Amsterdam, Amsterdam, The Netherlands

Abstract. We investigate a computer supported approach in which pairs co-construct a qualitative representation of the dynamics of the industrial revolution in a shared workspace. A key feature of this approach concerns the use of a meta-vocabulary for representing cause-and-effect relationships that facilitates the use of a predefined norm-representation to automatically steer the collaborative learning process. In particular, it provides focus on the set of ingredients that the learners should use. Additionally, the workspace offers each learner pair information about progress and content-related support. An evaluation study was executed in a real classroom. A workbook provided information for constructing the representation and gave advise on how to approach this task together. However, most pairs took an alternative approach and divided their actions in the shared workspace in an unbalanced way. Three types of task division occurred that showed differences in the number of errors and the number of requests for support. From this result, we formulate future directions for the development of a pedagogical approach that stimulates collaborative learning with qualitative representations and the support offered by the software.

Keywords: Knowledge representation · Computer supported collaborative learning · Secondary education · Systems thinking

1 Introduction

Creating a representation (e.g., diagram, graph, concept map) of a knowledge domain requires students to actively construct and translate concepts from one mode to another, which promotes deep learning [1–3]. Collaboration enforces this process of translation, since it supports students in making their ideas explicit, while the shared visual representation focuses the discussion in the group [4]. In the present study, we investigate how pairs co-construct a qualitative representation in a shared workspace.

I. Hilliger et al. (Eds.): EC-TEL 2022, LNCS 13450, pp. 159–172, 2022.
https://doi.org/10.1007/978-3-031-16290-9_12

Collaborative learning (CL) is a pedagogical approach in which two or more students share a common goal [5]. Effective collaboration does not happen spontaneously by placing students in a group and offering them a task. Collaboration is difficult and students need support throughout the learning process. A computer can support collaboration between students, i.e., computer supported collaborative learning (CSCL), which has a positive effect on learning [4, 6]. Students should be guided to balance their participation so that they are equally involved in active, constructive and interactive learning activities [7, 8], for instance by scripting the division of work [9], creating group awareness by displaying the contribution of group members [10], or training [11]. Teachers find it difficult to provide adequate support to students in a CL situation [12]. CSCL could alleviate this by providing automatic content-related and collaboration-related support to students [4, 6], and by providing teachers with real-time insight into the learning process on which they are able to take action [10].

Visual representation tools have a positive effect on CL [4] and each representation has its own affordances and constraints [1, 3]. Qualitative representations are logic-based descriptions of systems and their behaviour. The vocabulary of qualitative representations consists of ingredients such as entities, quantities and causal relationships with which a system can be described in a formal, non-numerical way [13]. Students can, alone or together, create their own representation of a system or reconstruct a predefined target representation. Note that, the function and vocabulary of qualitative representations differs from concept maps [14]. Concept maps use nodes and links and have no further typing in terms of the knowledge representation language. In a concept map there are usually various correct ways to represent a knowledge domain. This makes it a challenge, for computers, teacher, or students, to monitor the process and assess the progress and quality of the concept map [15].

Qualitative representations provide specific opportunities to support the collaborative learning process. When students reconstruct a predefined target representation, automatic content-related support can be given, i.e., an algorithm can compare student's representation with this norm representation and give hints to improve the former [16]. The vocabulary of qualitative representations makes it possible to conduct a fine-grained analysis per ingredient. This allows errors to be corrected and misconceptions to be avoided. Uncorrected errors and misconceptions are known pitfalls when students create their own representation [17]. Furthermore, creating (or reconstructing) a representation and CL are both complex tasks and the induced cognitive load might hamper learning. Automatic support can reduce this cognitive load because support is available immediately [18].

Another affordance of qualitative representations is that the action log provides real-time information about the individual and group learning processes, e.g., student's activities compared to other group members or other groups [10]. The challenge is to decide which information is critical and how to present these to students and teachers. When critical moments are detected automatically, they can be used to generate cues [19]. This reduces the burden on behalf of the teacher and gives the teacher the opportunity to provide further (more advanced) support where necessary.

In the present study, learner pairs in a history class are given the task to co-construct a qualitative representation that explains the dynamics of the industrial revolution. Content-related support based on a predefined (yet for the learners hidden) norm-representation is offered. Our main question with this study is: How do pairs co-construct a qualitative representation together in a shared workspace? Do they divide the work? How do they interact with the automated content-related support that detects errors? Do they co-construct 'shared' relationships in the representation? These insights help us to further develop a pedagogical approach for CL when creating qualitative representations and to add and optimize content-related and collaboration-related support.

2 Method

2.1 Participants

The lesson was conducted in a mixed pre-college and pre-university class (K-10) of a school in the northwest of the Netherlands. The school participates in a four-year project in which researchers, teacher educators and teachers jointly develop and implement lesson series in which students learn by constructing qualitative representation [13, 20].

All students ($n = 40$) constructed qualitative representations in previous lessons, so they were already familiar with the vocabulary. In these previous lessons, students made representations individually.

2.2 Development of the Qualitative Representation and Workbook

The lesson was jointly designed by the school's history teachers, teacher educators and researchers. Several sessions were spent to come to a consensus about the predefined norm-representation of the industrial revolution (Fig. 1). Note that, other choices were possible here because the causal mechanisms of the industrial revolution are part of ongoing scientific discourse [21] and the learning goals as prescribed by the Dutch national curriculum are partly implicit about the causal mechanisms that need to be learned.

A workbook was developed to guide students in constructing the representation. The scheduled duration of the lesson was 100 min and was conducted at the students' school during regular class time.

2.3 Qualitative Representation

The DynaLearn software (https://dynalearn.eu/) supports creating qualitative representations at multiple levels of complexity [13, 20]. At each level new ingredients are available to describe system behaviour. In the present study, students created a qualitative representation at level 2. Qualitative representations distinguish *entities* (physical objects or abstract concepts) and *quantities* (changeable features of an entity) within a system. Entities can be structurally related to each other by adding a *configuration*. Quantities can have causal relationships with other quantities and a direction of change (δ). At level 2, causal relationships are either positive (+) or negative (–). A positive relationship indicates that a change in the source causes a change in the target in the same direction. A negative relationship indicates that a change in the source causes a change in the target in the opposite direction. Once a qualitative representation is constructed, it can be used to simulate the system. Opposing influences lead to ambiguity: multiple system behaviours may occur. For this, *initial values* need to be assigned to some quantities (i.e., the direction of change at the start).

Figure 1 shows the complete qualitative representation of the industrial revolution. There are four entities (*Country*, *Industry*, *Agriculture*, and *Population*), three configurations (e.g., *Country has Industry*), 17 quantities, 26 causal relationships (only positive causal relationships were used) and 24 ingredients that need to be named (i.e., entities, configurations and quantities). Students were provided a template in which the four entities and for each of them a quantity (*Political stability, Mechanisation, Productivity*, and *Growth*) was already prepared in advance.

The consensus with the teachers was to select *Political stability* as the initial cause that sets the industrial revolution in motion. The representation thus reads as follows: if *Political stability* increases *Investments* increase (there is increasing confidence among investors with regard to the business climate), an increase of *Investments* causes an increase of *Knowledge*, etc.

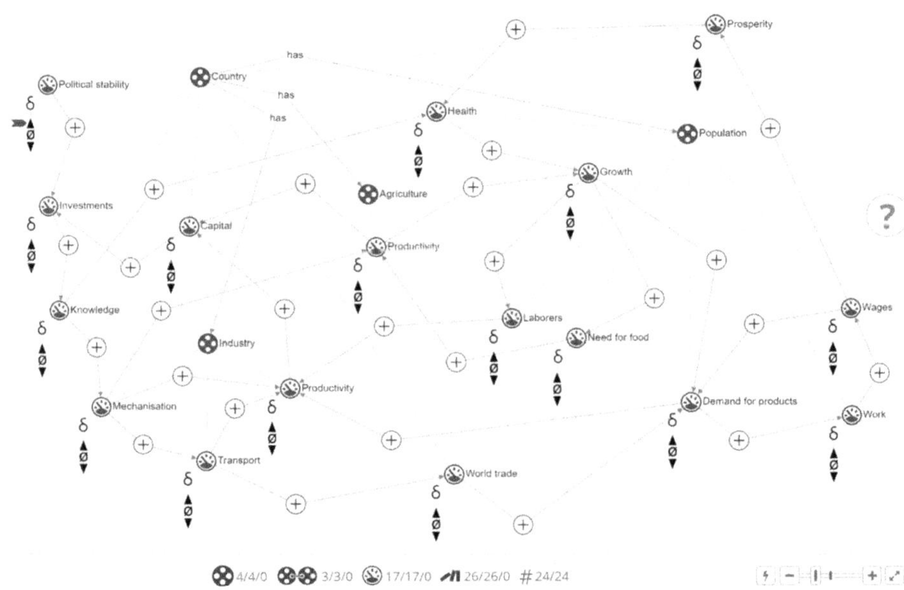

Fig. 1. Qualitative representation of industrial revolution.

The status bar at the bottom of the canvas informs students about their progress per type of ingredient. The status bar in Fig. 1 shows, among others, that (*i*) four entities need to be constructed, (*ii*) four are already constructed, and (*iii*) zero of these are wrong (all four are correct). The numbers in the status bar become green when all ingredients of a certain type are constructed. When an error has been made (i.e., a difference with the norm representation has been detected), the question mark on the right side of the canvas turns red. Students can click the question mark to receive a hint about where the error is located and the type of error (e.g., "Causal relationship between wrong quantities.").

2.4 Workbook

At the beginning of the lesson, students are asked to form pairs and sit next to each other. Both students work on their own computer.

The workbook contains four tables (one for each entity) and text as two forms of information for the students for constructing the representation. Both students had this information and were instructed to read through it once before continuing. Each table contains descriptions of the associated quantities. For example, the table of the entity *Population* contains the description "Compensation, usually in the form of money, paid to employees for services rendered". Students had to link these descriptions to the available quantities in the representation (i.e., *Wages*). If students found a match, they could add the quantity to the entity in the representation. Students could use the text about the industrial revolution to derive the appropriate cause-effect relationships. For example, the text contained the line "The yields of agriculture increased spectacularly, partly as a result of the application of scientific knowledge, which, for example, made it possible to make better agricultural implements". Based on this information, students were expected to infer that they should construct the causal relationships between *Knowledge*, *Mechanisation*, and *Productivity* (of entity *Agriculture*).

The workbook also contains instructions on how the students could divide the work. One student could be responsible for part 1 of the representation (i.e., quantities and causal relations of *Country* and *Industry*) and the other student for part 2 (i.e., *Agriculture* and *Population*). The students were advised to first add the quantities to the correct entity by using the tables. Next, they could add the causal relations in their own part by reading the text. Finally, they could jointly add the causal relationships between quantities of the shared part, i.e., causal relationships from part 1 to part 2 and vice versa (e.g., increase in *Laborers* of entity *Population* causes an increase of *Productivity* of entity *Industry*).

The above described approach was chosen because it is expected to induce active, constructive and interactive learning activities [7]. Note that pairs could ignore the recommended approach. During the lesson, there was no further steering on following the approach.

2.5 Data Analysis

The action log of the software is used for analysis of the construction process of the representation. Firstly, we focus on how pairs approach the joint construction of quantities and causal relationships in part 1, part 2 and the shared part. Students can create, modify or delete quantities and causal relations in the representation. The number of actions performed by each student of the pairs on quantities and causal relations in the parts of the representation are described. Secondly, a cluster analysis (k-means) was performed to distinguish clusters of pairs that demonstrate similar types of task division with regard to actions on causal relations in the parts. For this, we determined the ratio of the number of actions on the parts for each pair (Eq. 1).

$$ratio\ of\ actions\ in\ part = 1 - \frac{|actions\ in\ part_{student\ 1} - actions\ in\ part_{student\ 2}|}{actions\ in\ part_{student\ 1} + actions\ in\ part_{student\ 2}} \quad (1)$$

A score of zero means no joint actions on that part and a score of one means that both students performed exactly the same number of actions. Analysis of *within groups sum of squares differences* per cluster size was used to determine the optimum cluster size. Thirdly, we analysed per cluster the sequence of actions on quantities and causal relationships in time. Fourth, we analyzed per cluster how representation progress, errors, and content-related support were related. Finally, we analyzed by a non-parametric Kruskal-Wallis test if there were differences per cluster with regard to (1) how much time was spent on the representation, (2) completion of the representation, and (3) the number of actions performed.

3 Results

3.1 Actions on Quantities

Figure 2 presents the number of actions performed by each student of the 20 pairs (A-T) on quantities (Q) and causal relations (C) in part 1, part 2 and the shared part of the representation.

On average, students performed 13.80 ($SD = 9.31$) actions on quantities in part 1 and 14.65 ($SD = 8.16$) action in part 2. None of the pairs divided the work on quantities in such a way that each had an own part. In six pairs (B, C, F, K, P, R) all actions related to quantities were performed by one of the students. In 12 pairs (A, D, E, G, J, L, M, N, P, Q, S, T) actions on quantities in part 1 were performed by both students and actions in part 2 by one of the students. In one pair (I) actions on quantities in part 2 were performed by both students and actions in part 1 by one of the students. In two pairs (H, O) both students performed actions on quantities in part 1 and 2.

There are differences between pairs in the ratio in which both performed action on quantities in parts 1 and/or 2. For example, student 1 of pair G performed 39 actions in part 1 whereas student 2 only performed 4 actions. Actions of Pair Q on part 1 are more balanced, student 1 has 9 actions and student 2 has 8 actions.

3.2 Actions on Causal Relations

On average, students performed 75.85 ($SD = 53.85$) actions on causal relations in part 1 and 63.05 ($SD = 40.52$) actions in part 2. In five pairs (D, F, K, R, T) all actions on causal relations in part 1 and part 2 of the diagram were performed by one of the students. In 11 pairs both students performed actions on causal relations in part 1 and part 2 of the diagram (A, C, E, G, H, I, L, M, N, Q, S). In four pairs (B, J, O, P) actions on causal relations in part 1 were performed by both students and actions in part 2 by one of the students. There are no pairs where all actions in part 1 were performed by one student and actions in part 2 by both students.

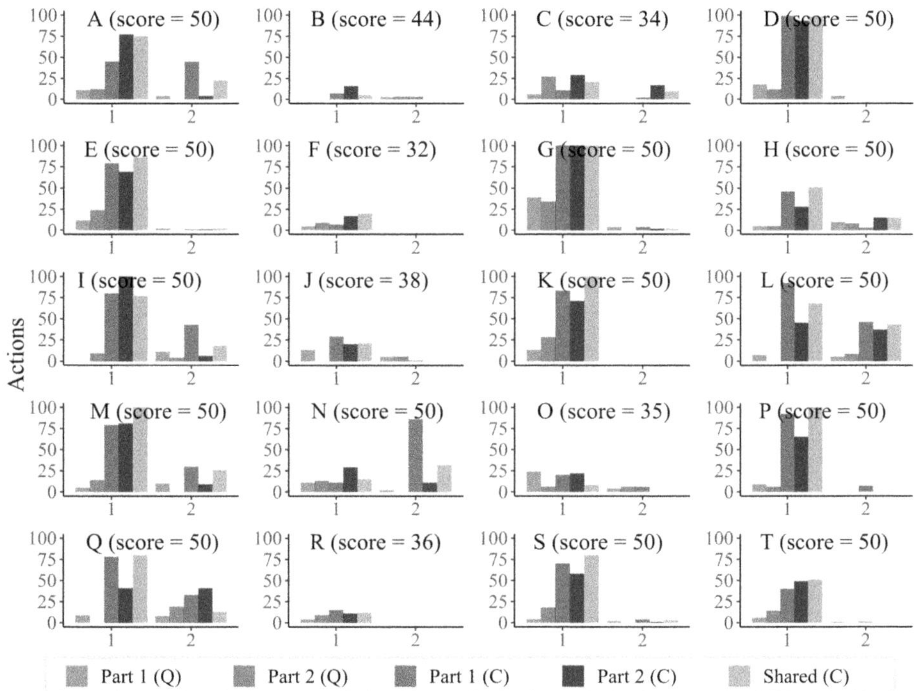

Fig. 2. Actions performed by each student (1–2) of pairs (A-T) on quantities (Q) and causal relations (C) in part 1, part 2 and the shared part of the representation. There is a limit on the y-axis of 100 to make comparison easier.

On average, students performed 76.0 ($SD = 54.27$) actions on causal relations in the shared part. In 11 pairs (A, C, E, G, H, I, L, M, N, Q, S) both students performed actions in the shared part. Note that, for the latter pairs both students also performed actions in both parts of the diagram. In 9 pairs (B, D, F, J, L, O, P, R, T) the actions on the shared part of the diagram were performed by one of the students. With regard to the latter, in all cases this is the student with the highest total number of actions on quantities and causal relations in part 1 and 2.

There are differences between the pairs in the ratio in which both students performed actions on quantities in part 1, part 2 and the shared part. There are also differences *within* pairs in the ratio in which both performed actions on quantities in parts 1, part 2 and the shared part. For example, student 1 and 2 of pair A both performed 45 actions in part 1, student 1 performed 77 actions in part 2 and student 2 performed 4 actions, and student 1 performed 75 actions in the shared part and student 2 performed 23 actions.

3.3 Cluster Analysis

Most of the actions (77%) during the lesson were devoted to making the causal relationships in part 1, part 2 and the shared part. The ratio of actions by both students on causal relationships was calculated for each part and was used as input for cluster analysis. Analysis of *within groups sum of squares differences* per cluster size led to the conclusion that the optimum cluster size is three. Figure 3 shows the results of the cluster analysis.

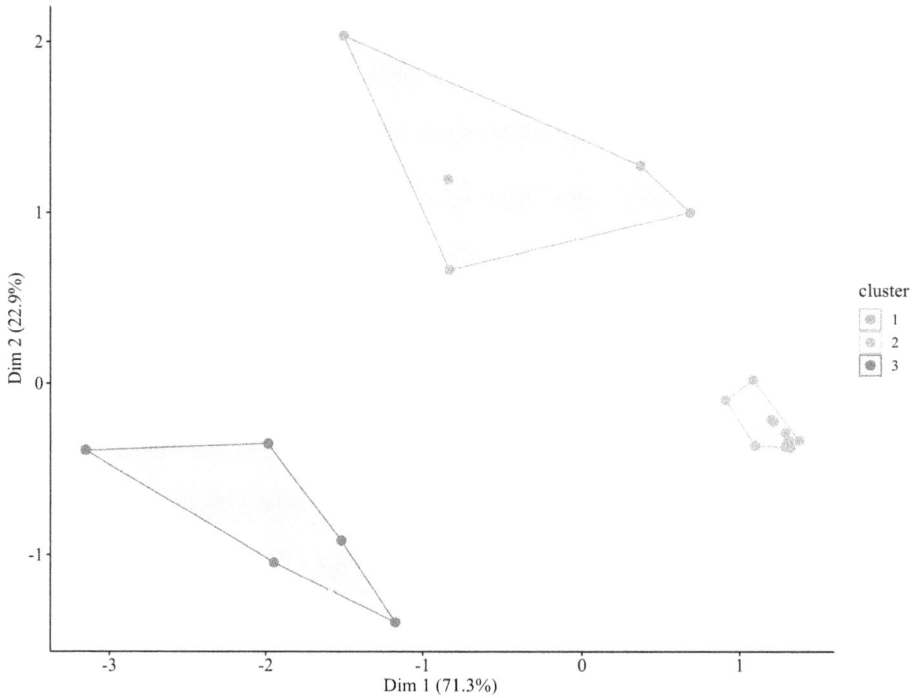

Fig. 3. Cluster plot with a three cluster solution.

Cluster 1 contains 5 pairs (A, B, I, M, O). The cluster mean for the ratio of actions is 66.22% for part 1, 7.75% for part 2 and 24.61% for the shared part. So students in this cluster mainly performed joint actions on part 1 and somewhat on the shared part. Actions in Part 2 were mostly performed by one of the students. Cluster 2 contains 10 pairs (D, E, F, G, J, K P, R, S, T). The cluster mean for the ratio of actions is 4.26% for part 1, 0.86% for part 2 and 1.35% for the shared part. In this cluster, the actions in the representation were almost completely performed by one of the students. Cluster 3 contains 5 pairs (C, H, L, N, Q). The cluster mean for the ratio of actions is 38.36% for part 1, 77.78% for part 2 and 55.85% for the shared part. For the pairs in cluster 3, both students performed a considerable amount of actions on causal relations in all parts of the representation.

3.4 Sequence of Actions in Time

Figure 4 presents the sequence of actions students performed on quantities (Q) and causal relations (C) in part 1, part 2 and the shared part. Students of pairs (A, B, I, M, O) in cluster 1, mainly collaborated on causal relations of part 1 and somewhat on the shared part. Pairs A, I and M completed the representation (score = 50). The general trend for the sequence of actions of the latter pairs is that at the beginning of the lesson both students performed actions in their own part and for some time they both worked on the representation at the same time. At the end of the lesson, one of the students performed all actions and completed the representation. Pairs B and O performed fewer actions and did not complete the representation. Their actions were more spread out over the lesson, but it seems that they mainly performed actions simultaneously at the beginning of the lesson. The sequence of actions for all pairs in cluster 1 mainly followed the order as recommended in the workbook. On a fine-grained scale the actions on causal relations of different parts were often intertwined. For instance, student 1 of pair I seemed to focus on actions on causal relations in the shared part at approximately 65 min but some actions on the shared part were made early in the lesson and actions on causal relations in part 1 and 2 were also still performed.

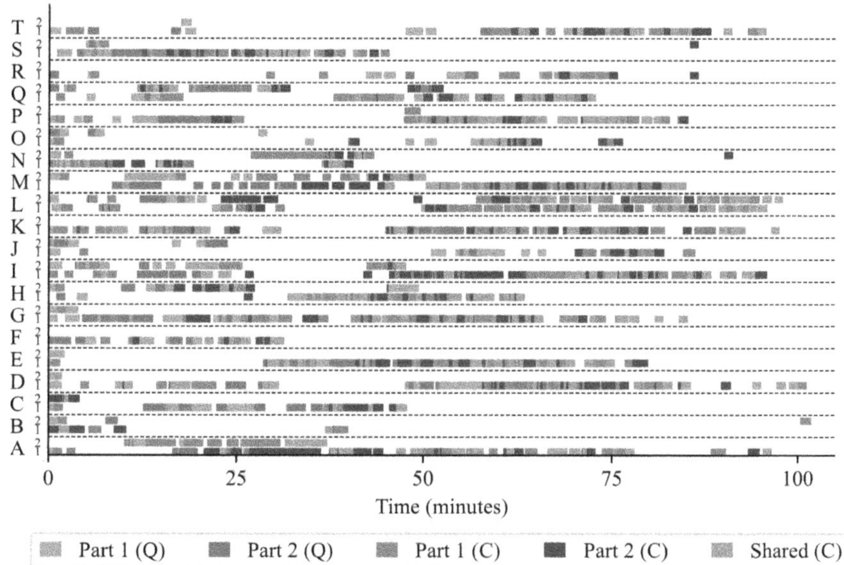

Fig. 4. Sequence of actions of each student (1–2) of pairs (A–H) on quantities (Q) and causal relations (C) in part 1, part 2 and the shared part.

In cluster 2 (D, E, F, G, J, K P, R, S, T) one of the students of the pair performed almost all actions on causal relations in the representation. Seven pairs (D, E, G, K P, S, T) completed the representation. The students that performed the actions of pairs E, G, P, S and T mainly followed the sequence as recommended in the workbook. The sequence of actions on quantities and causal relations of the student of pair D and K were more mixed. For instance, student 1 of pair D already started creating causal relations in the joint part before most actions of quantities in part 1 and 2 were performed. Pair F, J, and R did not finish the representation. These students also mainly followed the sequence of actions as recommended in the workbook.

In cluster 3 (C, H, L, N, Q) both students performed a considerable number of actions on causal relations in all parts of the representation. The pairs H, N, Q, and L completed the representation. The latter pairs differ in the extent to which actions were performed on the representation at the same time. For example, students 1 and 2 of pair H did not often perform actions at the same time. Student 2 mainly performed actions at the beginning of the lesson, and student 1 mainly performed actions at the end of the lesson. In contrast, students of pair L performed many actions at the same time. At the end of the lesson, both students of pair L also performed actions to complete the shared part of the representation. Pair C did not complete the representation. At the beginning of the lesson, student 2 of pair C focused on creating causal relationships in part 2. Later in the lesson, student 1 added the quantities and the causal relations to the representation.

3.5 Errors and Content-Related Support

Figure 5 shows the number of errors and requests for content-related support per cluster as pairs made progress in the representation. Representation progress is the current score at a particular point in the construction process. Note that the construction process varies per pair and that any representation with a current score of 30 points may look different. However, the analysis of the sequence of actions in time (Sect. 3.4) shows that most pairs constructed the representation as suggested in the workbook to some extent.

In cluster 1, few errors were made in the beginning of the construction process. There were two periods in the construction process where the number of errors were increasing. The first period was at a representation progress of approximately 20 to 28 and the second period was when the representation was nearly finished. The peak in the first period coincides with the moment in the construction process where most quantities were added and the first causal relationships were constructed. The number of possible causal relationships that can be constructed was large at that moment and it is possible that the students had initial difficulties with interpreting the text and translating it into the representation. In the second period, when the representation was almost finished, the last causal relationships need to be constructed. These causal relationships were probably difficult to find, either because they were less explicitly mentioned in the text, but also because the number of ingredients in the representation was large at that moment and students might have had difficulties keeping an overview. The number of request for support during the construction process was related to the number of errors.

In cluster 2 the number of errors was slightly increasing in the beginning of the construction process and when the representation was nearly finished. The number of requests for support were relatively high in the beginning of the construction process. This period coincides with the moment when quantities were added to the entities. The number of requests for support were low when the representation was nearing completion. One of the students was performing actions in this cluster and this probably made it immediately clear that the notification (the question mark turns red) was the result of their own action and they could probably fix the error without asking for more extensive support by clicking the question mark.

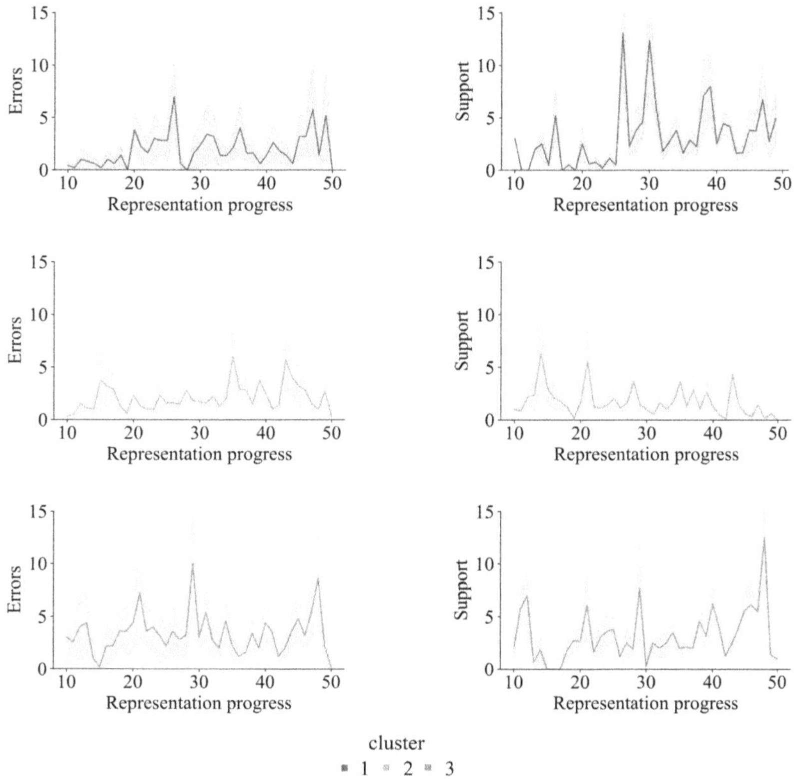

Fig. 5. Number of errors, requests for content-related support and representation progress per cluster.

Cluster 3 showed much variation in the number of errors throughout the construction progress. As in cluster 1, there was an increase in the number of errors around a representation progress of approximately 20–30 and when the representation is nearing completion. During the construction process, the number of requests for content-related support was in sync with the number of errors. The number of requests for support were relatively high when te representation was nearly finished. In this cluster, students were jointly working on the shared part of the representation in this period. The support function detects and reports all errors to both students (the question mark turns red). This might have been confusing when both students worked simultaneously. The increase in the number of requests for support may be explained by the fact that it was not clear to students whether their action or that of their partner was wrong.

3.6 Differences Per Cluster

Kruskal-Wallis test showed that there was no statistically significant difference in time spent on the representation between the cluster ($\chi^2(2) = 2.36$, $p = 0.31$) with a mean time spent of 96.0 (*SD* = 6.47) for cluster 1, 83.8 (*SD* = 17.9) for cluster 2 and 95.7 (*SD* = 11.1) for cluster 3. Also no significant differences ($\chi^2(2) = .19$, $p = 0.91$) were found between completion of the representation for cluster 1 (*M* = 45.8, *SD* = 6.57), cluster 2 (*M* = 45.6, *SD* = 7.23) and cluster 3 (*M* = 46.8, *SD* = 7.16). Furthermore, there was no statistically significant difference in the total number of actions performed on the representation between the clusters ($\chi^2(2) = .09$, $p = 0.95$), with a mean number of actions of 210 (*SD* = 155) for cluster 1, 228 (*SD* = 176) for cluster 2 and 217 (*SD* = 101) for cluster 3.

4 Discussion and Conclusion

The present study examines how pairs co-construct a qualitative representation about the industrial revolution in a shared workspace. Students were advised on how to approach this task together. We expected that the approach would ensure active involvement, a sense of responsibility for completing the model and discussion about the parts, as well as the whole, in both students [7]. However, pairs could ignore the advised approach. Students were supported by the built-in content-related support function and they could monitor their progress by checking the status bar.

It is notable that none of the pairs divided the work into the two parts as recommended in the workbook. Three types of task division occurred: (*i*) for most pairs one student performed all actions on quantities and causal relationships in the representation. This does not mean that the other student was inactive, they could also contribute, for example, by thinking along and reflecting on the actions that the other student made in the representation. The debriefing of the lesson with the teachers and researchers involved provided anecdotal evidence to support the latter. (*ii*) Some pairs worked together on the entire representation, and (*iii*) some pairs worked together on part 1 and somewhat on the shared part.

Most pairs followed the sequence of constructing the quantities and causal relationships as recommended in the workbook. Students of pairs that divided the work to some degree did not necessarily perform their actions simultaneously. In many occasions we found that either one student or the other was performing actions at a certain moment. We also found differences between the three types of task division and the number of errors and the number of requests for support during the construction progress. Pairs that more or less worked together made more errors when the first causal relationships were constructed than pairs where one student performed most of the actions. For all types, there was an increase in the number of errors when the representation was almost ready. For pairs who worked together on the shared part, the number of requests for support increased during this period. Type of task division was not related to time spent on the representation, completion of the representation, and number of actions performed.

In conclusion, it is not self-evident that students jointly create a knowledge representation in which the work is distributed in a balanced way, even if the task, the software and the recommended approach are aimed at this. Students are likely not used to working this way and may not have sufficient collaboration skills to adapt to the recommended approach. They may misinterpret 'collaboration' by constructing together all quantities and relations and step over the phase of individual construction to enforce co-construction [7]. Following the results, we can formulate future directions for the development of a pedagogical approach that stimulates CL with qualitative representations and the support that is offered by the software.

Key to the approach should be that all students are active and that interaction is induced. For this, it might be useful to train students explicitly in collaboration on the representation [11] and to emphasize why it is important to alternate individual construction and discussions on shared construction.

The software could be extended with a dashboard that offers real-time collaboration-related support to students and teachers [22]. The action log and the norm representation are two features of qualitative representations that facilitate the development of such functionality. The dashboard could, for instance, provide insight into the extent to which the members of the group are making progress, making errors or using content-related support. A teacher dashboard, possibly with an automated advice function [23], could support teachers to offer guidance to groups that are unable to reach a satisfactory outcome together. Collaboration-related support could also be enhanced with a script that gives guidance about how to interact [19]. The results of the present study suggest that such critical moments can be distinguished, e.g., an uneven distribution of the number of actions in a certain amount of time, too much working on the same ingredients, many errors and use of content-related support in a short period.

The content-related support function could provide more customized help for each student of the pair. At this moment, both students get the same notifications (the question mark turns red and the status bar shows there is an incorrect ingredient) if an error is made by either student. If both students perform actions simultaneously in the representation, it may not be clear for whom the notification is intended.

To conclude, qualitative representations have specific affordances and constraints and provide opportunities for CL that need to be explored. The present study discusses how students work together in such a learning environment and provides indications for further development of this approach and (automated) support.

References

1. Disessa, A.A.: Metarepresentation: native competence and targets for instruction. Cogn. Instr. **22**(3), 293–331 (2004)
2. Nesbit, J.C., Adesope, O.O.: Learning with concept and knowledge maps: a meta-analysis. Rev. Educ. Res. **76**, 413–448 (2006)
3. Prain, V., Tytler, R.: Learning through constructing representations in science: a framework of representational construction affordances. Int. J. Sci. Educ. **34**(17), 2751–2773 (2012)
4. Chen, J., Wang, M., Kirschner, P.A., Tsai, C.C.: The role of collaboration, computer use, learning environments, and supporting strategies in CSCL: a meta-analysis. Rev. Educ. Res. **88**(6), 799–843 (2018)
5. Dillenbourg, P.: What do you mean by collaborative learning. In: Dillenbourg, P. (ed.) Collaborative-Learning: Cognitive and Computational Approaches, pp. 1–19. Elsevier, Oxford (1999)

6. Wang, M., Cheng, B., Chen, J., Mercer, N., Kirschner, P.A.: The use of webbased collaborative concept mapping to support group learning and interaction in an online environment. Internet High. Educ. **34**, 28–40 (2017)
7. Chi, M.T.H.: Active-constructive-interactive: a conceptual framework for differentiating learning activities. Top. Cogn. Sci. **1**(1), 73–105 (2009)
8. Komis, V., Avouris, N., Fidas, C.: Computer-supported collaborative concept mapping: study of synchronous peer interaction. Educ. Inf. Technol. **7**(2), 169–188 (2002)
9. Fischer, F., Kollar, I., Stegmann, K., Wecker, C.: Toward a script theory of guidance in computer-supported collaborative learning. Educ. Psychol. **48**(1), 56–66 (2013)
10. Han, J., Kim, K.H., Rhee, W., Cho, Y.H.: Learning analytics dashboards for adaptive support in face-to-face collaborative argumentation. Comput. Educ. **163**, 104041 (2021)
11. Eshuis, E.H., ter Vrugte, J., Anjewierden, A., Bollen, L., Sikken, J., de Jong, T.: Improving the quality of vocational students' collaboration and knowledge acquisition through instruction and joint reflection. Int. J. Comput.-Support. Collab. Learn. **14**(1), 53–76 (2019). https://doi.org/10.1007/s11412-019-09296-0
12. Van Leeuwen, A., Janssen, J.: A systematic review of teacher guidance during collaborative learning in primary and secondary education. Educ. Res. Rev. **27**, 71–89 (2019)
13. Forbus, K.D.: Qualitative Representations: How People Reason and Learn About the Continuous World. MIT Press, Cambridge (2019)
14. Novak, J.D., Cañas, A.J.: The origins of the concept mapping tool and the continuing evolution of the tool. Inf. Vis. **5**(3), 175–184 (2006)
15. McClure, J.R., Sonak, B., Suen, H.K.: Concept map assessment of classroom learning: reliability, validity, and logistical practicality. J. Res. Sci. Teach. **36**(4), 475–492 (1999)
16. Spitz, L., Kragten, M., Bredeweg, B.: Exploring the working and effectiveness of norm-model feedback in conceptual modelling – a preliminary report. In: Roll, I., McNamara, D., Sosnovsky, S., Luckin, R., Dimitrova, V. (eds.) AIED 2021. LNCS (LNAI), vol. 12749, pp. 325–330. Springer, Cham (2021). https://doi.org/10.1007/978-3-030-78270-2_58
17. Ainsworth, S.: DeFT: a conceptual framework for considering learning with multiple representations. Learn. Instr. **16**, 183–198 (2006)
18. Martínez, A., Dimitriadis, Y., de la Fuente, P.: Interaction analysis for formative evaluation in CSCL. In: Llamas-Nistal, M., Fernández-Iglesias, M.J., Anido-Rifon, L.E. (eds.) Computers and Education, pp. 227–238. Springer, Dordrecht (2003). https://doi.org/10.1007/978-94-017-1122-7_19
19. Vogel, F., Wecker, C., Kollar, I., Fischer, F.: Socio-cognitive scaffolding with computer-supported collaboration scripts: a meta-analysis. Educ. Psychol. Rev. **29**, 477–511 (2017)
20. Bredeweg, B., et al.: DynaLearn–an intelligent learning environment for learning conceptual knowledge. AI Mag. **34**(4), 46–65 (2013)
21. Ó Gráda, C.: Did science cause the industrial revolution? J. Econ. Lit. **54**(1), 224–239 (2016)
22. Matuk, C., Tissenbaum, M., Schneider, B.: Real-time orchestrational technologies in computer-supported collaborative learning: an introduction to the special issue. Int. J. Comput.-Support. Collab. Learn. **14**(3), 251–260 (2019)
23. van Leeuwen, A., Rummel, N., van Gog, T.: What information should CSCL teacher dashboards provide to help teachers interpret CSCL situations? Int. J. Comput.-Support. Collab. Learn. **14**(3), 261–289 (2019). https://doi.org/10.1007/s11412-019-09299-x

When and How to Update Online Analytical Models for Predicting Students Performance?

Chahrazed Labba(✉) and Anne Boyer

University of Lorraine, CNRS, LORIA, Nancy, France
{chahrazed.labba,anne.boyer}@loria.fr

Abstract. One of the main concerns in online learning environments is the identification of students with learning difficulties. Conventionally, analytical models trained offline on pre-prepared datasets are used to predict student performance. However, as learning data become progressively available over time, this learning method is no longer sufficient in real-world applications. Nowadays, incremental learning strategies are increasingly applied to update online analytical models by re-training them on newly received data. Various online incremental learning approaches have been proposed to overcome different issues such as catastrophic forgetting and concept drift. However, no approach addresses the question of when to update the model and how to determine whether the new data provide important information that the model should learn. In this paper, we propose a method for determining when an online classifier that predicts student performance and receives a real-time data stream, should be updated. In addition, we use a typical approach that maintains balanced old and new data examples to re-train the model when necessary. As a proof of concept, we applied our method on real data of k-12 learners enrolled in an online physics-chemistry module.

Keywords: Incremental learning · Distance learning · K-12 learners · Machine learning · Classification

1 Introduction

Learning from anywhere, at any time and at one's own pace has become a reality through the use of e-learning platforms. One of the main concerns in such a context is the high failure rate among the learners. Multiple research works focused on elaborating analytical models to predict students performance. Conventionally, most of these models operate in batch mode by reading and processing the entire training set, with the strong assumption that the data is static and always available in advance. Indeed, the learning data become progressively available over time. It is impossible to collect all relevant training examples at once, and the models must therefore be updated to incorporate the unlearned knowledge

I. Hilliger et al. (Eds.): EC-TEL 2022, LNCS 13450, pp. 173–186, 2022.
https://doi.org/10.1007/978-3-031-16290-9_13

encoded in the new data received over time. Thus, the traditional methods of training and evaluating models are no more sufficient in real-world applications.

To address this challenge, incremental learning is increasingly used to ensure continuous adaptation of online analytical models based on newly received data. The use of online incremental learning has revealed many challenges, including concept drift and catastrophic forgetting. Both of these problems have been widely addressed and many approaches have been proposed [1,8,12] to overcome their impact on the model efficiency. However, none of the incremental learning approaches addresses the question of when to update the model, which in turn raises the question of how to determine whether the newly received data provides relevant information that the model should learn. Addressing the frequency of updating an online model is of high importance. In the distance education, each student has his own pace to learn, which results in variations in the students engagement, regularity and reactivity. There are periods during the school year when most students are active, while the rest of the time only a few of them use the e-learning platform continuously. This variation in the learning behavior has an impact on the quantity and the quality of the generated data over time. According to the existing definitions [4,5,13], incremental learning is a dynamic strategy that consists in processing the stream data as soon as it becomes available due to limited memory resources. This method can lead to frequent and unnecessary updates of the models.

In this paper, we propose an incremental learning process for determining when an online classifier that predicts student performance and receives a real-time data stream, should be updated. Our process invokes the retraining process: i) when new classes are detected in the newly received data; ii) when the forgetting value in each detected class is below a certain threshold and iii) when a class label is seen but never predicted. The forgetting value within a class is the difference between the two accuracy values over two successive time intervals. To overcome the problems related to concept drift and catastrophic forgetting, our process uses a typical approach that consists in maintaining a balanced training set of old and new data to train the model when necessary. An algorithm is proposed to update the exemplar set continuously as long as the data is generated to re-train the model when necessary. As a proof of concept, we used a real-world scenario of k-12 learners adopting 100% online education. Our process is applied with an Artificial Neural Network (ANN) to predict students at risk of failure.

The rest of the paper is organized as follows: Sect. 2 presents the related work. Section 3 introduces the proposed incremental learning process. In Sect. 4 and Sect. 5, we present respectively the case study description and the experimental results. The Sect. 6 presents the conclusions and the future works.

2 Related Work

Online incremental learning is an Artificial intelligence (AI) technique that refers to the circumstance of a permanent online adaptation of the analytical model according to the constantly received data flow over time [4,5,13]. This technique has been used to fulfill adequately various learning analytics objectives among which predicting students performance [1,6,7], image classification [10,14] and text classification [11]. Most of the existing works focus either on solving the problem of catastrophic forgetting and concept drift, or on comparing incremental online algorithms. When it comes to predicting student performance incrementally, most of the research is oriented towards the comparison of incremental algorithms. In [7], the authors compared four classifiers that can run incrementally. The aim is to recommend the suitable algorithm to use in assessing students performance within an incremental learning context. In [1], the authors compared three approaches of incremental learning to determine the suitable way to handle students stream data. The used approaches include instance-based, batch-based and ensembling of instance-based incremental learning. In [6], the authors proposed an incremental learning technique that combines an incremental version of Naive Bayes, the 1-NN and the WINNOW algorithms. The aim is to predict the student's performance within a distance education environment by using incremental ensemble based on a voting methodology.

The use of incremental learning is more developed, especially for image classification. In [5], the authors proposed an incremental learning framework to overcome the problem of catastrophic forgetting when learning new classes and the problem of data distribution over time referred as concept drift. The framework was tested to classify images using the CIFAR-100 and ImageNet-1000 datasets. In [12] the authors presented a novel framework that can incrementally learn to identify various chest abnormalities by using few training data. the framework is based on an incremental learning loss function that infers Bayesian theory to recognize structural and semantic inter-dependencies between incrementally learned knowledge representations. In [8], the authors compared eight popular incremental methods representing different algorithm classes using stationary and non-stationary datasets. A set of metrics including the accuracy, the robustness and the error classification rate are used to assess the algorithms.

Existing incremental learning methods address a variety of issues, such as catastrophic forgetting, but none address the issue of when to update a model. In this paper, we propose a new incremental learning method that considers the optimal time to update a model by reducing the number of unnecessary updates while maintaining good performance stability.

3 Proposed Approach for Incremental Learning

This section starts with a formal introduction to the problem of when and how to update an online analytical model using stream data (Sect. 3.1). Then it presents an overview of the proposed incremental learning process (Sect. 3.2).

3.1 Problem Formalization

Online incremental learning [8] is a subset of incremental learning, which is further constrained by runtime and the ability to provide lifelong learning with limited data when compared to offline learning. In general, these constraints are related to real-world applications in which new data is generated sequentially over time, thereby contradicting the strong assumption of total data availability.

Assume $\mathcal{M}_1$, $\mathcal{M}_2$, .., $\mathcal{M}_k$ a sequence of models that is computed on stream data (D_1, Y_1), (D_2, Y_2),.., (D_k, Y_k) as shown in the Fig. 1.

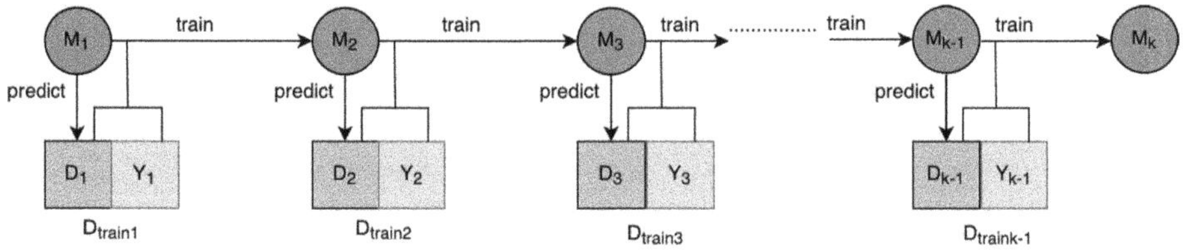

Fig. 1. An incremental online scenario

Each D_i represents a block of new data ($x_i | i \in \{1, m\}$), which it has at least one element and no more than m elements. Usually, the size of the block is limited due to memory constraints [5]. Each Y_i represents the set of true labels. $D_{traini} = (D_i, Y_i)$ represents the data used to update the model $\mathcal{M}_i$ to create the model $\mathcal{M}_{i+1}$ that will be used to predict D_{i+1}.

As shown in Fig. 1, the principle of incremental learning is that each time new data is available, the model update is invoked. This, however, may necessitate frequent updates of the online model, which is both time and resource intensive. Defining *when to invoke the re-train* is of high importance. If the model $\mathcal{M}_i$ can accurately predict D_i, there is no need to update it; it can still be used to process the data D_{i+1}. In other words, if the model maintains a certain level of performance stability, it means that the new data does not contain any new knowledge that the model is unable to handle.

Further, one of the difficult challenges in incremental learning is catastrophic forgetting. Suppose the model $\mathcal{M}_i$ is trained on j classes and we invoke its train on $D_{traini} = (D_i, Y_i)$ that contains p new classes. In theory, the model can predict all classes well (j+p), but in practice, the model's stability on the old j classes decreases significantly due to a lack of representation of these classes when training on new ones.

In this work, we propose a new online incremental learning process that aims to reduce the frequency of updating a model while maintaining a certain performance stability over time. To address the problems related to catastrophic forgetting, our method uses a typical approach [3,5,9] that consists in maintaining a balanced training set of old and new data to train the model when necessary.

3.2 Learning from a Train Exemplar

To address the common issues of incremental learning (e.g. catastrophic forgetting), we adopt a common approach [3,5,9] that has been widely applied: we

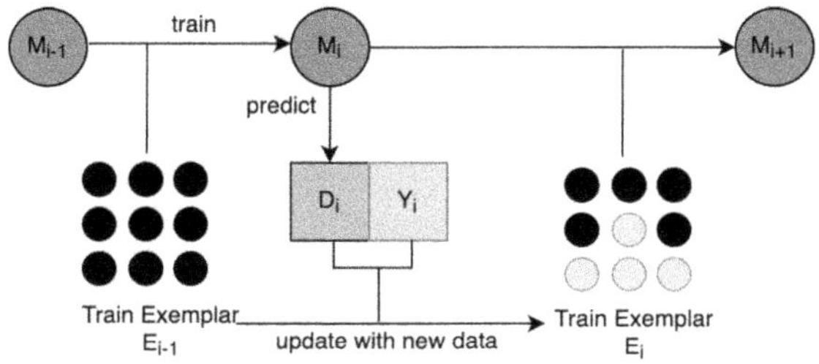

Fig. 2. Exemplar set

use a small exemplar of both old and new data. In our work, the exemplar set is updated each time new data are received. The new data may contain both new data classes and new observations of old classes. As shown in Fig. 2, we no longer use only newly received data to train the model; instead, we use an exemplar set created previously and updated it with new samples from the received stream data. Exemplar samples are selected at random, but with each update, we seek to preserve an equal representation of all learned data classes. Algorithm 1 depicts the entire process of updating the exemplar set.

The Algorithm 1 takes as input the exemplar to update $\mathcal{E}$, the received data (D, Y), the number of samples m to store in $\mathcal{E}$ and the ratio of the classes R. This ratio defines the representation of the classes within the exemplar (e.g. if we have 3 class labels, R is equal to 1/3). The Algorithm provides as output an updated version of the exemplar $\mathcal{E}$.

It all starts with cleaning up the old exemplar $\mathcal{E}$ (Line 1–Line 8). The algorithm checks the number of samples in $\mathcal{E}$ for each old class (Line 3). If this number is strictly greater than the new representation ratio, the algorithm removes the extra samples at random in order to meet the class representation condition (Line 4). Otherwise, there is no need to delete the old observations (Line 6).

The next step is to update the exemplar with the new data. We distinguish between two types of updates: i) the exemplar is updated with the new detected class labels (if any) (Line 9–Line 16), and ii) the exemplar is updated with the new observations for the old class labels (Line 17–Line 25). For the first kind of update, the algorithm first determines whether the number of samples in the new data exceeds the allowed representation ratio (Line 10–Line 11). If this is the case, the algorithm selects samples at random to store in $\mathcal{E}$. The number of selected samples must meet the representation condition. Else, all samples are kept in $\mathcal{E}$ (Line 14). For the second type of update the algorithm checks, for each class, whether the number of samples for old observations meets the representation ratio condition (Line 18–Line 19). If this is the case, all of the old data that have new observations are updated (Line 20). Otherwise, the algorithm updates the old data with new observations (Line 22). Then, it selects samples at random from the new observations of old classes to store in $\mathcal{E}$ while satisfying the representation condition (Line 23).

Algorithm 1. Build the exemplar set

Require: $\mathcal{E}, (D, Y), m, R$
Ensure: $\mathcal{E}$
$(D_{old}, Y_{old}) \leftarrow get\_old\_class(\mathcal{E})$
for $(c \in Y_{old})$ **do**
  if $(|D_{old_c}| > (m * R))$ **then**
    $\mathcal{E} \leftarrow remove\_extra\_observations(\mathcal{E}, (D_{old_c}, c))$
  else
    No need to remove
  end if
end for
$(D_{new}, Y_{new}) \leftarrow get\_new\_data((D, Y))$
for $(c \in Y_{new})$ **do**
  if $(|D_{new_c}| > (m * R))$ **then**
    $\mathcal{E} \leftarrow put(\mathcal{E}, select\_random((D_{new}, Y_{new}), R, m))$
  else
    $\mathcal{E} \leftarrow put(\mathcal{E}, (D_{new_i}, c))$
  end if
end for
$(D_{new_{obs}}, Y_{old_{obs}}) \leftarrow get\_new\_observations\_for\_old\_class((D, Y))$
for $(c \in Y_{old_{obs}})$ **do**
  if $(|D_{new_{obs_c}}| == (m * R))$ **then**
    $\mathcal{E} \leftarrow update(\mathcal{E}, D_{old_c}, D_{new_{obs_c}})$
  else
    $\mathcal{E} \leftarrow update(\mathcal{E}, D_{old_c}, D_{new_{obs_c}})$
    $\mathcal{E} \leftarrow put(\mathcal{E}, select\_random(D_{new_{obs_c}}, Y_{old_{obs}}))$
  end if
end for

In the next section, we present how the use of the exemplar fits into the overall incremental learning process.

3.3 Incremental Learning Process to Update an Online Model

Our incremental learning process (Algorithm 2) takes as input: i) the stream data $D = (D_1, .., D_n)$ as it arrives over time; ii) the true label $Y = (Y_1, .., Y_n)$ associated to the stream data[1]; iii) the ML model $(\mathcal{M})$, iv) the allowed forgetting value $(\mathcal{F})$ and v) m the number of samples to store in the exemplar trainset.

The Algorithm 2 starts by iterating over the prediction times (Line 1). If the prediction time corresponds to the beginning of the time interval (Line 2), we train the model on the received data during that time (Line 3). This first moment corresponds to the beginning of the school year, when all students are given a class label. Indeed, to overcome the cold start problem, students can be considered all successful, all at risk of failure, or their historical information can be used to assign them to a specific class among the predefined ones.

[1] e.g. Y_1 represents the set of true labels for the stream data D_1.

Algorithm 2. Incremental Learning Process

Require: $\mathcal{D} = ((D_1, Y_1), .., (D_n, Y_n)), \mathcal{M}, \mathcal{F}, m$
1: **for** i in $(1..n)$ **do**
2:   **if** $(i == 1)$ **then**
3:     $\mathcal{M} \leftarrow$ **fit**$(\mathcal{M}, (D_i, Y_i))$
4:     $\mathcal{C} \leftarrow$ **get-seen-class**(Y_i)
5:     $\mathcal{E}_i \leftarrow$ **build-trainset**$((D_i, Y_i), m, 1/|\mathcal{C}|)$
6:     $A_{last} \leftarrow \emptyset$
7:   **else**
8:     $c \leftarrow |\mathcal{C}|$
9:     **List_preds** $\leftarrow$ **predict** $(\mathcal{M}, D_i)$
10:     $A_i \leftarrow$ **Score-Accuracy**$(List\_preds, Y_i)$
11:     $\mathcal{C}_i \leftarrow$ **get_current_detected_class**(Y_i)
12:     $\mathcal{C} \leftarrow$ **unique_class** $(\mathcal{C} \cup \mathcal{C}_i)$
13:     $\mathcal{E}_i \leftarrow$ **update Exemplar set**$(\mathcal{E}_{i-1}, (D_i, Y_i), m, 1/|\mathcal{C}|)$
14:     **if** $(|\mathcal{C}| > c)$ **then**
15:       $\mathcal{M} \leftarrow$ **fit**$(\mathcal{M}, \mathcal{E}_i)$
16:     **else**
17:       $OK \leftarrow$ **true** , $j \leftarrow 0$
18:       **while** (**OK and** $j < |\mathcal{C}|$) **do**
19:         **if** $(A_{ij} == 0)$ **then**
20:           $\mathcal{M} \leftarrow$ **fit**$(\mathcal{M}, \mathcal{E}_i)$
21:           $OK \leftarrow$ **false**
22:         **else if** $(A_{last_j} > A_{ij})$ **then**
23:           $a_j \leftarrow$ **compute_forget** (A_{last_j}, A_{ij})
24:           **if** $(a_j > \mathcal{F})$ **then**
25:             $\mathcal{M} \leftarrow$ **fit**$(\mathcal{M}, \mathcal{E}_i)$
26:             $OK \leftarrow$ **false**
27:           **end if**
28:         **end if**
29:         $j \leftarrow j + 1$
30:         $A_{last} \leftarrow A_i$
31:       **end while**
32:     **end if**
33:   **end if**
34: **end for**

Then (line 4), we recuperate the learned classes during the first training time. Later, we build the first trainset (Line 5). The *build-trainset* function takes as parameters the received data (D_1), the true labels (Y_1), the number of samples to store (m) and the ratio of each learned class ($1/|\mathcal{C}|$). The samples are selected randomly, but the learned classes are equally represented in order to address the issue of under-represented classes. The algorithm uses the list A_{last} to save the accuracy values of the model for the most recent prediction time (Line 6). For the following intervals, the algorithm starts by saving the number of the classes already seen (Line 8). Then, the last calculated model is used to predict the classification of the received stream data (D_i) (Line 9). Then it calculates the current accuracy scores for the seen class labels (Line 10). C_i that corresponds to the list of class labels detected in Y_i is identified (Line 11) and the set of seen classes $\mathcal{C}$ is updated (Line 12). Later, the exemplar train-set is updated using the Algorithm 1 (Line 13). The train-set is updated each time new data is received, regardless of whether or not a model is updated. The aim is to maintain an up-to-date train-set that will serve to train the model when necessary. There are three cases to start model training: If new classes are detected in the labeled new received data (Line 14), the model's train is invoked using the recently updated exemplar set ($\mathcal{E}_i$). If no new classes are found, the model's accuracy per class is checked: if the current accuracy score equals zero than the training is invoked (Line 19–Lline 21). Else, the accuracy is compared to that computed during the last prediction time to see if it has improved or decreased(Line 22). If the second case, the algorithm verifies if the forgetting value within the learned classes does not exceed a given threshold ($\mathcal{F}$) (Line 23–Line 24). If it is so, the model's train is invoked (Line 25). It is sufficient to detect a drop in accuracy in one class to start the training phase.

4 Case Study

The Cned[2] offers a diverse range of courses entirely online to k-12 students located all over the world (173 countries). These students come from a variety of demographic backgrounds and are unable to attend regular schools for a variety of reasons. The Cned offers the courses through a Learning Management System (LMS) and provides with it a set of applications such as an education management system that allows administrative tracking of the students. Our case study in this work consists of K-12 students enrolled in the physics-chemistry course during the 2017 2018 school year. There are 46 weeks in the school year and 671 enrolled students.

To predict students performances on weekly-basis, the problem is formalized as a n-classification problem. The classification consists of three classes: high risk (≤8), medium risk (<8 and ≤12) and success (>12). On each week w_i, a student is defined by a tuple $X = (f_1, .., f_m, y)$ where $f_1, .., f_m$ are the features and y is the class label. The student class may vary from one week to another based on his/her performance. The selected features are extracted from the two data sources including the LMS (moodle) and the education management system (GAEL).

We distinguish the following indicators [2] calculated based on the used features:

- Demographic data: it represents information such as the gender, the age, has or not a scholarship, and repeating or not the year. These data are provided by the education management system.
- Performance: this indicator denotes the submitted exams and the grades.

[2] Centre national d'enseignement à distance: https://www.cned.fr.

- Engagement: it described the learner activity on the LMS. The only way to track learners engagement is through their interaction with the LMS content.
- Regularity: it denotes the progress made by the learner in terms of achieved LMS activities and the number of submitted exams through GAEL.
- Reactivity: It is denoted by the time taken to submit an exam as well as the time between successive connections to the LMS.

The aim is to predict students at risk of failure as early as possible while taking into account the progressive availability of data over time. To address the issue of a cold start, all students are classified as having a high risk of failing during the first week. This classification will evolve over time based on the students performance.

5 Experiments

As a proof of concept, the incremental learning process was tested with the ANN model. Prior to the assessment, a set of experiments were performed to determine the suitable parameters for our model, including defining the optimizer (SGD) and the learning rate (0.01). Several configurations were used to evaluate the effect of process parameters on the number of model updates as well as its accuracy. Furthermore, to demonstrate our process's efficiency in reducing the number of model updates while maintaining good performance stability, we compared it to an incremental process that has full access to all previous data and is trained each week. The second process is ideal for an incremental model because all data is available and training is performed on a weekly basis.

5.1 Impact of the Forgetting Value and Exemplar Set Size

Our incremental learning process is based on two key parameters including the exemplar set size and the forgetting value (see Sect. 3). The first specifies the number of the samples to be used when re-training the model. While the second shows the rate of forgetting we can tolerate per class label.

Various configurations were used to test the proposed incremental learning process (see Table 1). Each configuration differs in the size of the exemplar set and the forgetting value. Overall, three exemplar sizes (80, 100 and 150) were used, each with ten forgetting values (from 1% till 10%).

Table 1. Configurations

Exemplar set size	Forgetting value
80	1%, 2%, 3%,4%, 5%, 6%, 7%, 8%, 9%, 10%
100	
150	

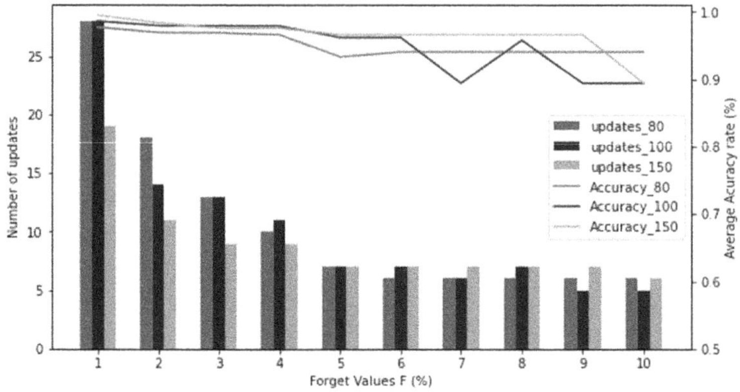

Fig. 3. Number of updates and average accuracy per exemplar size and forgetting value

The Fig. 3 depicts the variation in the number of model updates as well as the average of accuracy as a function of exemplar size and forgetting value. The weekly accuracy values are used to calculate the average accuracy (over a period of 46 weeks).

Regardless the exemplar size, we notice, in overall, that the number of updates decreases while the forgetting value increases. This is to be expected, as increasing forgetting values give the model a lot more space to forget what it has learned. While a minor forgetting value may result in frequent updates. As shown in Fig. 3, for allowed values of 1%, we find the highest number of updates (28, 28, and 19 updates respectively for exemplar sizes 80, 100 and 150). While for a value of 10%, we notice the smallest number of updates (6, 5 and 6 updates respectively for exemplar sizes 80, 100 and 150).

The average accuracy associated with the lowest forgetting values and thus frequent updates is, indeed, the highest. However, for fewer updates, the average accuracy remains high ($\geq$90%), even though it gradually decreases as the forgetting value increases.

Despite the decrease in the number of updates as the forgetting value increases, the model has maintained good stability, which can be attributed to the use of an updated exemplar set. As explained in Sect. 3, the exemplar set is used to store observations for old and new classes over time. Furthermore, when creating this exemplar, we consider an equal representation of all classes to allow the model to learn the knowledge gained over time more effectively. Equal class representation is considered, since the received data over time already present imbalances with respect to the "medium risk failure" class. Consequently, with a non-equal representation this class is not well detected, especially when the samples are selected randomly when building the exemplar set. The number of samples in the exemplar influences both the number of updates and the average accuracy. Increasing this number does not always ensure the smallest number of updates and the highest average accuracy. For example, using an exemplar

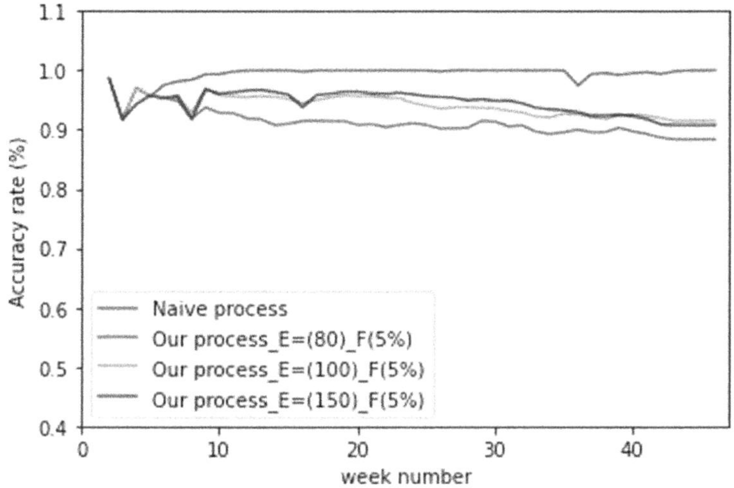

Fig. 4. Accuracy over weeks

set of size 100, for half of the time resulted in an equal or higher number of updates than using an exemplar set of size 80. Furthermore, it demonstrated a high variation in average accuracy when compared to the rest, even though this variation was not significant. While, in overall, the use of the exemplar set with a size 150 samples resulted in less number of updates and better average accuracy. Furthermore, for each exemplar set size, we observe that the number of updates is stable or only slightly varies on an interval of forgetting values for each exemplar set size. For example, for the exemplar set with a size 80, on the interval [6%, 10%], the average accuracy is stable, and the number of updates is equal to six. This can be explained by the fact that most of the detected forgetting values were less than 6%, requiring no model update. Thus, in this case, the number of updates is mostly identified when a new class is detected or when the accuracy of a given class equals zero.

In summary, the forgetting value and the size of the exemplar set are relevant parameters for reducing the number of updates and increasing the stability of the model performance in the context of incremental learning. The goal of this article is not to identify and fix these parameters, but rather to demonstrate how they can be incorporated into a full incremental learning process to reduce unnecessary updates while maintaining good stability.

5.2 Assess Our Proposal to an Incremental Process with Full Data Access

In this experiment, we compared the efficiency of our proposal to an incremental learning process that has full access to old data and trains the model weekly. The second procedure does not take into account the use of the forgetting value and the exemplar set for training. The model update is invoked 46 times (over the

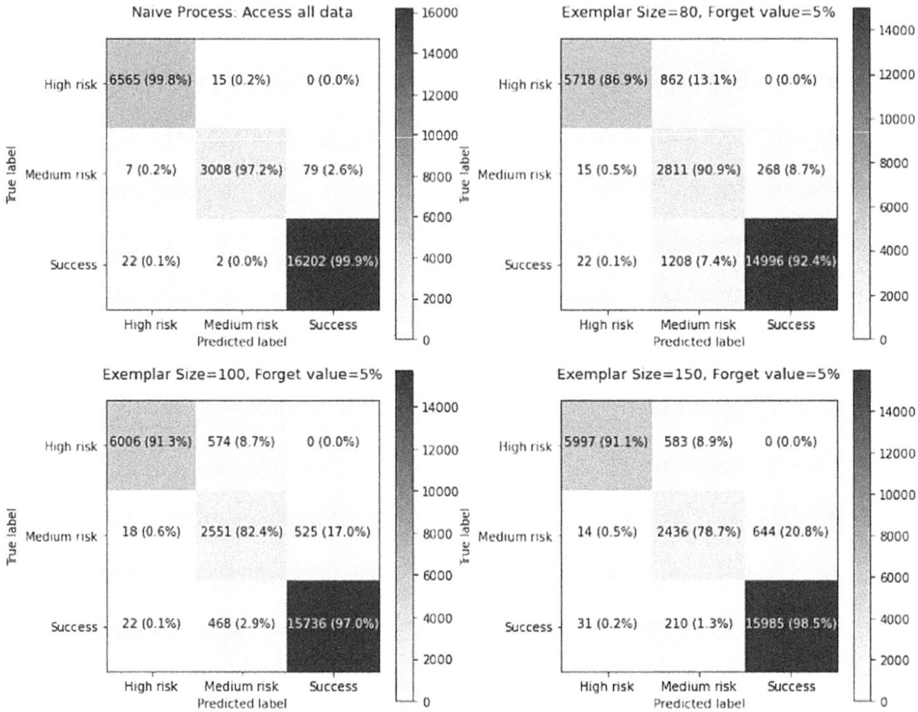

Fig. 5. Confusion matrix

46 weeks). For the rest of the paper, this second process is denoted as the naive process. For this experiment, we consider the results of the model trained with a forgetting value of 5% for each of the exemplar set sizes (80, 100, 150). The Fig. 4 presents the evolution of the accuracy of the four ANN models over the weeks. The model with the highest accuracy values over time is the one that was trained weekly using a process that has full access to all of the data. However, the rest of the models, which were only trained 7 times over the 46 weeks using our incremental learning process, were able to maintain high accuracy values of 90% or higher.

The overall accuracy does not reflect the actual performance of a classifier. Thus, in the Fig. 5, we present the confusion matrix of the four models over all weeks. The model trained using the naive incremental process is represented by the first confusion matrix. It has the highest accuracy values across all classes, and we used it as a reference to evaluate the efficacy of our incremental learning process when training the rest of the models with different exemplar set sizes.

Indeed, with our incremental process, we find that increasing the sample size does not always improve the model's accuracy across all classes. When detecting the medium risk class, training the model with 80 samples outperforms training it with larger numbers of samples (100, 150). Indeed, this could be a result of the sample selection strategy used when creating the exemplar set. When it comes to class representation, the data distribution is not homogeneous during the first few weeks. As a result, the total number of samples determined by the fixed rate cannot always be guaranteed (e.g. 30% of the number of samples should be in the medium-risk category or only 10% are available). However, with a smaller number of samples we can reach the full proportions of the different classes more quickly than by using a larger number of samples. The rapidity is addressed in terms of the number of the week at which we begin to have a complete representation of all classes of students in the selected samples with respect to the predefined rate for each class. We believe it is important to determine the appropriate threshold that should be used as the size of the exemplar set. Since the goal of our experiments is to detect students in difficulty (high and medium risk), we can say that for a fixed forgetting value (5%), the appropriate size of the example set is 80. Indeed, high-risk students have the lowest accuracy value when compared to the rest (100, 150), but students who are not well detected are classified as medium risk. As a result, they will be notified in both cases. Furthermore, with 80 as the exemplar size, the proportion of students who are actually at medium risk and were classified as successful is low (only 8.7%), compared to the rest (100: 17%, 150: 20.8%).

6 Conclusion

In this paper, we addressed the question of when to update online analytical models and how to determine whether the new data provide important information that the model should learn. We proposed an incremental learning process that determines when an online classifier that predicts student performance and receives a real-time data stream, should be updated. Our method invokes the retraining process: i) when new classes are detected in the newly received data; ii) when the forgetting value in each detected class is below a certain threshold and iii) when a class label is seen but never predicted. In addition, we use a typical approach that maintains balanced old and new data examples to re-train the model when necessary. As a proof of concept, we applied our method on real data of k-12 learners enrolled in an online physics-chemistry module. The experimental results show that the forgetting value and the size of the exemplar set are relevant parameters for reducing the number of updates and maintaining the stability of the model performance in the context of incremental learning. Further, we found that increasing the exemplar set size does not always improve the classifier's accuracy across all the classes. Both parameters can be set based on the requirements and the desired outcome.

The current work presents some limitations that we tried to mitigate when possible: i) currently, the proposed incremental process has been evaluated using only the ANN, as the method, rather than the model, makes the most significant contribution and ii) we defined fixed rates for the samples representing each of the class labels when creating the exemplar set for training. This representation, however, cannot always be insured because the number of samples available may be less than what is required.

In the future, we plan to compare the use of our incremental learning process with other classifiers, such as the random forest. Furthermore, we are interested in improving the process of building the exemplar set, particularly as it's currently based on a random selection of samples.

References

1. Ade, R., Deshmukh, P.: Instance-based vs batch-based incremental learning approach for students classification. Int. J. Comput. Appl. **106**(3) (2014)
2. Ben Soussia, A., Roussanaly, A., Boyer, A.: An in-depth methodology to predict at-risk learners. In: De Laet, T., Klemke, R., Alario-Hoyos, C., Hilliger, I., Ortega-Arranz, A. (eds.) EC-TEL 2021. LNCS, vol. 12884, pp. 193–206. Springer, Cham (2021). https://doi.org/10.1007/978-3-030-86436-1_15
3. Castro, F.M., Marín-Jiménez, M.J., Guil, N., Schmid, C., Alahari, K.: End-to-end incremental learning. In: Proceedings of the European Conference on Computer Vision (ECCV), pp. 233–248 (2018)
4. Gepperth, A., Hammer, B.: Incremental learning algorithms and applications. In: European Symposium on Artificial Neural Networks (ESANN) (2016)
5. He, J., Mao, R., Shao, Z., Zhu, F.: Incremental learning in online scenario. In: Proceedings of the IEEE/CVF Conference on Computer Vision and Pattern Recognition, pp. 13926–13935 (2020)
6. Kotsiantis, S., Patriarcheas, K., Xenos, M.: A combinational incremental ensemble of classifiers as a technique for predicting students' performance in distance education. Knowl.-Based Syst. **23**(6), 529–535 (2010)
7. Kulkarni, P., Ade, R.: Prediction of student's performance based on incremental learning. Int. J. Comput. Appl. **99**(14), 10–16 (2014)
8. Losing, V., Hammer, B., Wersing, H.: Incremental on-line learning: a review and comparison of state of the art algorithms. Neurocomputing **275**, 1261–1274 (2018)
9. Masana, M., Liu, X., Twardowski, B., Menta, M., Bagdanov, A.D., van de Weijer, J.: Class-incremental learning: survey and performance evaluation on image classification. arXiv preprint arXiv:2010.15277 (2020)
10. Ristin, M., Guillaumin, M., Gall, J., Van Gool, L.: Incremental learning of random forests for large-scale image classification. IEEE Trans. Pattern Anal. Mach. Intell. **38**(3), 490–503 (2016). https://doi.org/10.1109/TPAMI.2015.2459678
11. Shan, G., Xu, S., Yang, L., Jia, S., Xiang, Y.: Learn#: a novel incremental learning method for text classification. Expert Syst. Appl. **147**, 113198 (2020)
12. Sirshar, M., Hassan, T., Akram, M.U., Khan, S.A.: An incremental learning approach to automatically recognize pulmonary diseases from the multi-vendor chest radiographs. Comput. Biol. Med. **134**, 104435 (2021)
13. Yang, Q., Gu, Y., Wu, D.: Survey of incremental learning. In: 2019 Chinese Control and Decision Conference (CCDC), pp. 399–404. IEEE (2019)
14. Zhao, H., Wang, H., Fu, Y., Wu, F., Li, X.: Memory efficient class-incremental learning for image classification. IEEE Trans. Neural Netw. Learn. Syst. (2021)

Computational Thinking: Focus on Pattern Identification

Marielle Léonard[1,2](✉), Yvan Peter[1], Yann Secq[1], and Cédric Fluckiger[2]

[1] University of Lille, CNRS, Centrale Lille, UMR 9189 CRIStAL, Lille, France
{marielle.leonard,yvan.peter,yann.secq}@univ-lille.fr
[2] University of Lille, ULR 4354 - CIREL - Centre Interuniversitaire de Recherche en Éducation de Lille, 59000 Lille, France
cedric.fluckiger@univ-lille.fr

Abstract. This article focuses on pattern identification in the context of pupils aged 9 to 15 who are learning programming at school. In this context, programming puzzles that involve moving a robot on a 2D grid using a block-based programming language is common. We consider the ability to identify and formally characterize recurring structures within data or processes, to be a fundamental skill of computational thinking. In this article, we study the case where the *motif* (i.e. repeating unit) can be identified visually from the grid (obstacles, target...) for tasks involving the use of a loop. We ask what makes *motif* identification, and thus problem solving, difficult in this context. We provide a quantitative analysis based on the success rates of a hundred tasks from an online programming contest (200,000 participants). We have identified relevant features of the *visual motif*, which led us to specify five categories according to the degree of correspondence between the *visual motif* (2D grid) and the *algorithmic motif* (corresponding loop based program).

Keywords: Computational thinking · Pattern · Pattern identification · Loop · Computer science education · Quantitative analysis · Large-scale study

1 Introduction

Computer Science (CS) education has recently been reintroduced into school curricula in many countries. In France, CS content has been included in compulsory school curricula since 2016. For students aged 9 to 12, programming is part of the mathematics curriculum[1]. The prescribed task is to control a robot or a character on a screen using a block-based programming language. For students aged 12 to 15, they are expected to be able to "Write, develop and execute a simple program."[2]. But what does "a simple program" mean?

[1] Cycle 3 curriculum in effect in 2020, mathematics, space and geometry section.
[2] Cycle 4 curriculum in effect in 2020, mathematics, theme E - algorithmic and programming.

I. Hilliger et al. (Eds.): EC-TEL 2022, LNCS 13450, pp. 187–200, 2022.
https://doi.org/10.1007/978-3-031-16290-9_14

For this age group, using loops is one of the objectives of the school curriculum, along with sequences of instructions, conditional instructions and variables. At first, it could be considered that a program including a single loop, without nesting, conditional statements or explicit variables, is a simple program for students to write.

In previous studies [11], we set up pedagogical scenarios to explore how primary school students deal with programming tasks whose solution focuses on the use of a loop. The results from these case studies led us to consider the identification of patterns, redundancies, as essential to deal with this type of task. Especially, a recurring difficulty has been identified: the transition from one to several instructions inside the loop.

In this article, we want to improve our analysis of pattern identification when solving loop-focused programming tasks. Our two research questions are:

1. **RQ1** What does pattern recognition consist in, in the context of visual programming puzzles resolution?
2. **RQ2** What are the parameters that make pattern recognition difficult when getting started with solving loop-focused tasks?

To answer these questions, we mobilized elements of the theory of conceptual fields by G. Vergnaud [16] to conduct an *a priori* analysis. This allows us to distinguish several elements involved in pattern recognition and to identify parameters that can explain the difficulty of the problems. Then, we carried out a large-scale statistical analysis based on the success rates of 101 loop-focused programming tasks from the 2018 to 2021 editions of the Algorea french programming contest, which is organized by the France-ioi association. This statistical analysis validates the relevance of the identified parameters.

In the next section, we introduce the context of this research: the concept of *motif* and our analysis framework based on *classes of situations*. We then present the analysis of the programming tasks as well as the experimental setting before presenting the statistical analysis of the results for these tasks. We conclude by suggesting perspectives to go further in our understanding of the process of learning the basics of programming.

2 Theoretical Framework

2.1 From Pattern to Motif

In computer science, the word *pattern* is used in works about *design patterns* in the field of software engineering [4]. It is also associated with a specific skill in the scope of computational thinking, for which we can find various expressions: "looking for patterns" [21], "pattern recognition" [6], "identifying and making use of patterns" [3].

Some works more specifically mention the notion of loop, the focus of this paper. Gouws et al. [5] have defined a framework for describing computational thinking skills based on a literature review. This framework contains a category called "Patterns and Algorithms", in which the notion of loop is taken as an example. Rich et al. [12] define learning trajectories, including goals and examples of associated activities, one of which deals with iterative structures. The authors mention the importance of the perception of redundancy because it is intimately linked to the initiation to the notion of loop. Unfortunately, they do not provide any analysis of pattern identification activities.

On the other hand, in mathematics education, some works address this question of pattern identification. For Collins & Laski [2], a pattern is a sequence with a replicable regularity, which can vary along one or more dimensions. Liljedahl [7] proposes to distinguish two categories of patterns: *repeating patterns* and *number/growing patterns* (Fig. 1). The first corresponds to a cyclic structure generated by the repetition of a discernible unit. This definition is used in several works [9,18,20]. The second corresponds to a pattern parameterized by one or more pieces of information.

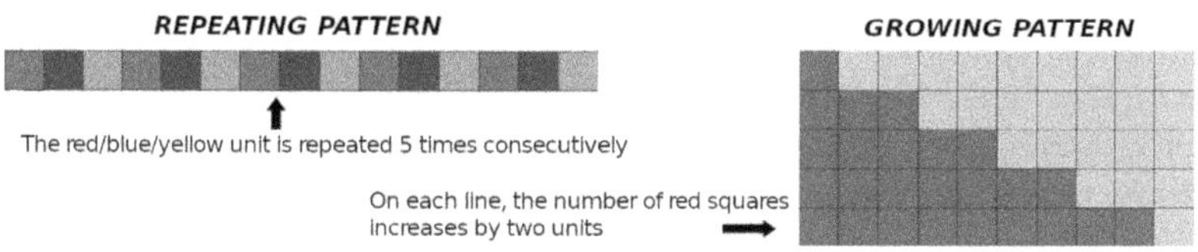

Fig. 1. Two categories of pattern in early mathematical education

For the previous authors, a pattern denotes the whole sequence, while our focus is on the repeating unit. In our work, we choose to use the word *motif* for the unit of repetition. With this meaning, the term *motif* is usually used in the artistic or literary field: "an idea that is used many times in a piece of writing or music"[3], "a design which is used as a decoration or as part of an artistic pattern"[4]. Drawing inspiration from the previous definitions, we define a *motif* in our context as **an entity that can be identified within a set, because it is repeated identically or with predictable variations.**

Liljedahl [7] lists different tasks related to the concept of pattern: copying a pattern, continuing a pattern, finding missing elements in a pattern, transferring a pattern from one representation to another, identifying the unit of repetition, i.e., identifying the *motif*. Based on experiments conducted with young children aged 3 to 6, Warren et al. [18] designed a pedagogical sequence and establish a progression in the difficulty of these tasks [19,20]. In this progression, the identification of the *motif* is the most difficult task and it is the one that reveals the understanding of the structure of the pattern [19]. Indeed, the term-to-term matching strategy, which consists in processing the elements of the pattern one by one without considering it as a whole, is systematically defeated during the activity of *motif* identification [2].

[3] Cambridge Dictionary.

[4] Collins Dictionary.

In our context, we are interested in the activity of *motif* identification in the field of computer science education. More specifically, we study *motif* identification when pupils deal with loop-focused programming tasks. We consider that the distinction proposed by Liljedahl [7] is a beginning of characterization of the forms of complexity of pattern abstraction, in particular the transition from directly observable (visual) patterns to unobservable patterns (changes of state of the environment, even similarity processes in the context of design patterns). We propose to specify what *motif* identification is in our context (**RQ1**) and to study in more detail, the characteristics of the *motifs* to be identified and their relation with the difficulty of the task (**RQ2**).

2.2 Classes of Situations

We aim to characterize and categorize the motifs to be identified when solving loop-focused programming tasks. For this purpose, we rely on the concept of class of situation developed by Vergnaud within the theory of conceptual fields [16]. Vergnaud takes a constructivist and cognitivist approach to learning. He aims to understand conceptualization, especially in the case of complex cognitive tasks, of which computer programming is a part. The unit of analysis is the subject/situation couple, where situation is used in the sense of a task. Vergnaud's hypothesis is that any finalized action is based on a *conceptualization-in-act*, that is to say that the actions of the subject reflect a cognitive activity that remains most often implicit, including for the subject itself. In computer science education, the conceptual field theory was used by Rogalski [13,14] to study *computer literacy* in high school and more recently by Spach [15] to analyze educational robotics situations. In our context, we place ourselves in this theoretical framework to study situations where the goal of the subject is to design a computer program that solves a loop-focused task.

Vergnaud invites us to analyze the situations the subject is confronted with, by grouping them into classes. This categorization can be considered from the point of view of the expert, by an analysis of the characteristics of the situations, and from the point of view of the subject, by studying the way in which he deals with the situations. The expert relies on the identification of situation variables aimed at differentiating close situations. The change in value of a situation variable may affect the structure of the subject's processing of the situation. This makes it possible to define two distinct classes of situations.

Vergnaud also insists on the progressiveness of the conceptualization, which should be considered over a long period of time. In a study on additive structures in the mathematic field, Vergnaud & Durand [17] asked 28 pupils in each level from grades 1 to 5, to solve additive tasks whose answer is strictly the same numerically, but for which the formulation of the task induces a different reasoning. They thus identified classes of situations which correspond to levels of difficulty in the resolution of these additive tasks. Their results show an effect of the age on students' ability to solve these tasks.

In this article, we propose to refine the definition of the concept of *motif* in relation to RQ1 and to characterize difficulties related to the motif identification activity when dealing with loop-focused type situations in a programming context (RQ2). We rely on the works carried out around the concept of pattern and we mobilize the concept of class of situation to categorize loop-focused tasks. We are also inspired by the study by Vergnaud & Durand [17] which we have transposed into our context. The following section details the methodology and the experimental framework that we used to carry out this study.

3 Methodology and Experimental Setting

Our work is based on the analysis of the characteristics and results from a selection of 101 different loop-focused tasks that come from the 2018 to 2021 editions of the Algorea french programming contest. They consist in programming puzzles [10] involving a virtual robot on a grid, using the Scratch language. Their common point is that the sequence of actions to be performed by the virtual robot includes redundancy, which must be identified to solve the problem. The reference solution therefore involves a loop or several loops in sequence, but no nested loops. For the study of these programming situations, we considered the two points of view indicated by Vergnaud. First, we carried out an analysis of the programming tasks from the point of view of the expert, also called *a priori* analysis, which led us to identify the parameters that have a potential impact on the difficulty. Then we analyzed the activity of the subjects confronted with these situations during their participation in the Algorea competition, through the success rates noted for these problems.

3.1 *A Priori* Analysis: *Visual Motif* and *Algorithmic Motif*

When dealing with a loop-focused problem involving programming a virtual robot on a grid, one has to consider two kinds of *motifs*. The first one is a **visual motif**, which is observable on the grid. It consists of adjacent cells, which may contain visually salient elements (marked cell, or containing an object). This can be related to the concept of data which is one of the core concepts of computer science [1].

The second kind of *motif* is the **algorithmic motif**, which is related to the concepts of algorithm and machine, two other core concepts of computer science [1]. The *algorithmic motif* consists of actions to be executed one after the other by the machine, actions which are induced both by the pattern identified in the data and by the specificities of the machine. A series of actions in a fixed chronological order constitutes this *algorithmic motif* and in our context it is induced by the *visual motif* but it is also dependant on the possible actions (i.e., robot language, orientation system). The *algorithmic motif* is only observable during the actual execution of the actions. For instance, in the relative orientation system, the rotational actions of the robot are not matched with any element of the grid. In a program designed in the Scratch language, the *algorithmic motif* corresponds to the sequence of blocks inside the repeat block.

Solving a loop-focused programming problem in our context therefore requires identifying the *visual motif* on the grid, matching this *visual motif* with the actions to be performed by the virtual robot on this same grid, and expressing this *algorithmic motif* with the Scratch programming language.

For each of these *motifs*, *visual* then *algorithmic*, we identify several parameters or characteristics, which correspond to variables of situation in the sense of Vergnaud [16]. For the *visual motif*, we consider the number of cells it occupies on the grid, the presence of visually salient elements within the *visual motif* and the presence of decorative elements on the grid. For the *algorithmic motif*, we retain the number of actions constituting the *motif* and the presence of actions that are not part of the pattern (corresponding to instructions outside of the loop). As a variable of situation, we also study the degree of correspondence between the *visual motif* and the *algorithmic motif*. These are the parameters that will drive our analysis of the difficulty of the programming problems.

3.2 Experimental Setting

The virtual robot programming situations that we study come from the Algorea online contest, whose programming environment is shown in Fig. 2.

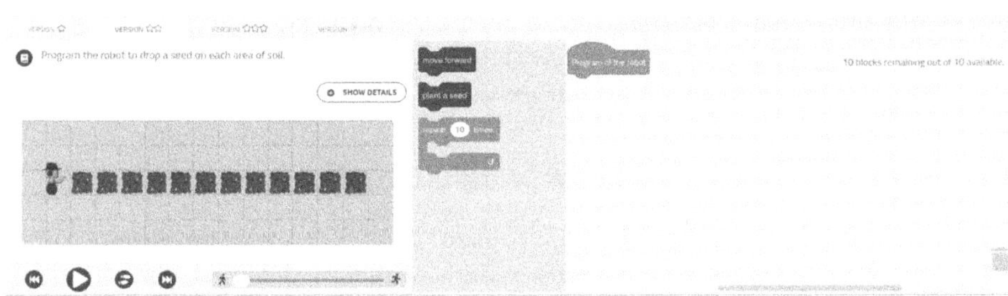

Fig. 2. Algorea contest programming environment (Situation 1, where the *visual motif* covers a single cell)

This environment is suitable for our study on *motif* identification. On the one hand, for loop-focused tasks, the repeat block is the only available control structure block. The subject quickly infers that he is in the situation where he needs to use this repeat block. On the other hand, the total number of blocks that can constitute a program is limited, which forces pupils to make use of this repeat block. However, the number of trials is not limited, which allows a trial and error strategy.

In total, the Algorea competition involves more than 200,000 participants each year, from grade 4 to grade 12 (9 to 18 years old). In the context of this study, we are only interested in the individual results of pupils from grades 4 to 9 (9 to 15 years old), who selected the Scratch language. This represents between 6,000 and 75,000 participants depending on the round of the contest. Studied participants are distributed over the 6 class levels, with an over-representation of middle school students. Thus, we do not control the size of the sample studied, which varies depending on the round but remains substantial. In addition, the competition takes place in school or at home, so in real life conditions. However, we consider that the large sample size compensates for the variations of the participation context.

4 Analysis and Results

For each situation, we collect the success rate by class level, i.e. the quotient of the number of participants who succeeded in the task over the number of participants who opened the task. As a preliminary to the study on the identification of *motifs*, we proceeded to some analysis of a more general nature. On the one hand, we checked the robustness of our data concerning success rates. When considering all class levels together, a chi-square test of independence allows us to verify that all differences in success rates between two situations are statistically significant with a p-value less than 0.01. For a particular class level, a success rate difference of 5% units between two situations is significant for the middle school levels (p-value < 0.02). Only a few situations for the elementary level, whose numbers are smaller, lead to differences in success rates of 5% units that are less statistically robust.

On the other hand, Fig. 3 confirms that, as expected, the success rate decreases when the number of instructions in the reference solution increases. However, we notice a significant dispersion of values on the vertical axis, sometimes by more than 50% units, which tells us that other situational variables influence the success rate. The identification and study of these variables are the subject of the following sections. To this end, for each characteristic identified in the Sect. 3.1, we calculate the median of the success rates and the interquartile range, as indicators of the distribution of the data. At first, we focus on the *visual motif* which allows a first categorization of the tasks. We then complete and refine the analysis by also considering the *algorithmic pattern*.

4.1 Visual Motif

In this section, it is the visual aspect of the pattern that matters, regardless of the actions that the virtual robot has to perform.

Concerning the number of cells over which the *visual motif* extends, we can very clearly distinguish two classes of situations (Fig. 4). For a first class of situation, the *visual motif* consists of a single cell of the grid (example Fig. 2). The success rate of these tasks is high as early as elementary school. The interquartile range is low, which means that this characteristic is significant in explaining the success rate. On the other hand, the interquartile range is much higher if the *visual motif* extends over several cells (examples Fig. 6). In this case, other variables contribute significantly to the value of the success rate.

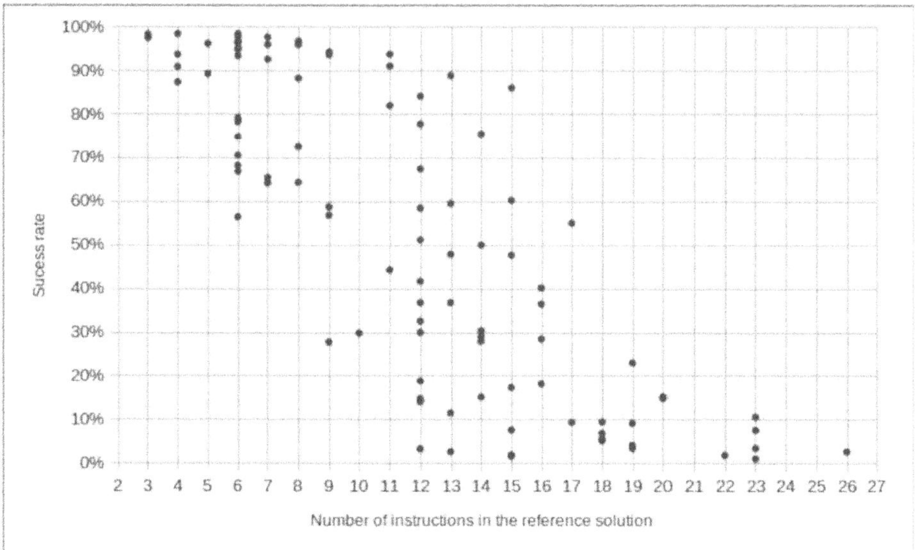

Fig. 3. Success rate scatter plot depending on the number of instructions in the reference solution (linear correlation rate −0.81; p-value < 0.05 on the Bravais-Pearson test)

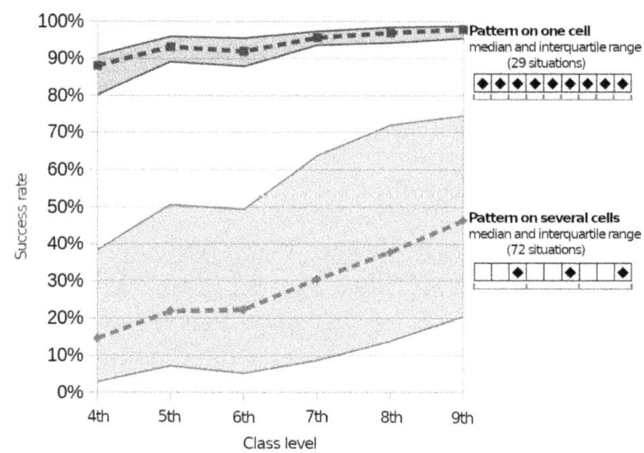

Fig. 4. Two classes of situations: situations where the *motif* is limited to a single cell, and situations for which the *motif* extends over several cells

For 70 situations for which the *visual motif* extends over several cells, we study the adjacent cells which are not part of the same *motif.*

When adjacent identical cells with a visually salient element do not belong to the same *motif* (examples Fig. 6: situations 3 and 4), the success rate is low (Fig. 5: red curve), and this is more pronounced with younger students. However,

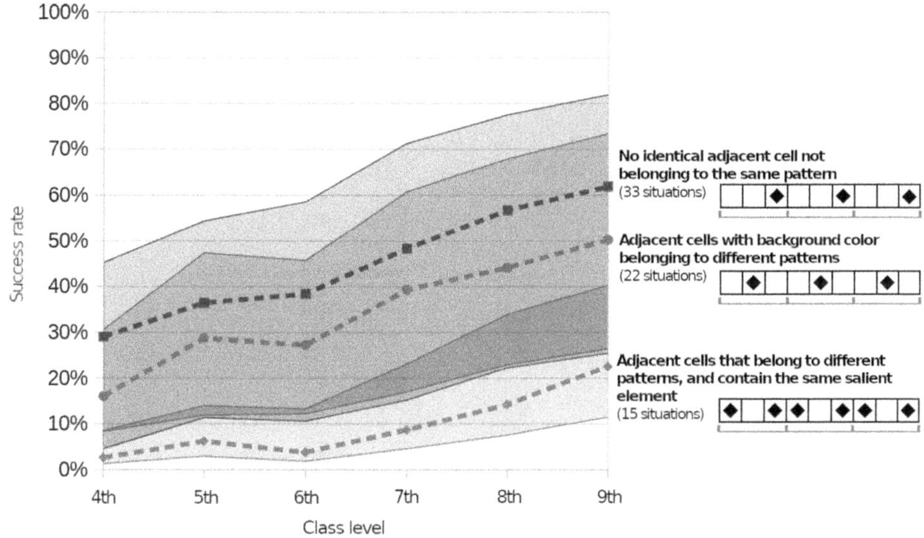

Fig. 5. Study of adjacent cells not belonging to the same *visual motif*

when two adjacent empty cells belong to different *motifs*, the success rate is close to that of situations without identical adjacent cells belonging to different *motifs*. This result leads us to think that the salient elements are taken as privileged reference points during the identification of the *visual motif*. Identical salient elements on adjacent cells are perceived as part of the same visual entity. When they do not belong to the same *motif*, this makes the *motif* less visible and therefore more difficult to identify.

We show in the same way, the effect of the presence of decorative elements on the grid, that is, visual elements that are not on the expected path of the robot, but make the cells look different from regular empty cells, or may be forbidden cells for the robot. For lack of space, we only give for each modality, the value of the median (Q2) and the interquartile range (IQR) for all the class levels taken together, with the unit being the percentage point of the success rate. Depending on how they are arranged, the decorative elements are more of a help or a source of difficulty. When they completely constrain the path of the robot (Q2: 60.0, IQR: 31.3), they constitute an aid compared to situations without decorative elements (Q2: 51.1, IQR: 58.0). If not, they seem to act as distractors and are a source of difficulty (Q2: 27.7, IQR: 49.0). This difficulty becomes massive when these decorative elements make some *motifs* visually different (Q2: 3.2, IQR: 3.3). Thus the study of the characteristics of the *visual motifs* shows that the nature of the elements present on the grid has an effect on the complexity of the situation. The easier the *motif* is to visually isolate, the more likely the situation is resolved by pupils. Conversely, factors that disrupt the visibility of the *motif* negatively impact the success rate of the situation.

4.2 Matches Between *Visual Motif* and *Algorithmic Motif*

Once the *visual motif* on the grid has been identified, it is necessary to deduce the matching *algorithmic motif.* We distinguish 5 classes of situations concerning the correspondence between *visual motif* and *algorithmic motif.* For the first three classes, all the *visual motifs* are the same, which is no longer true for the last two classes.

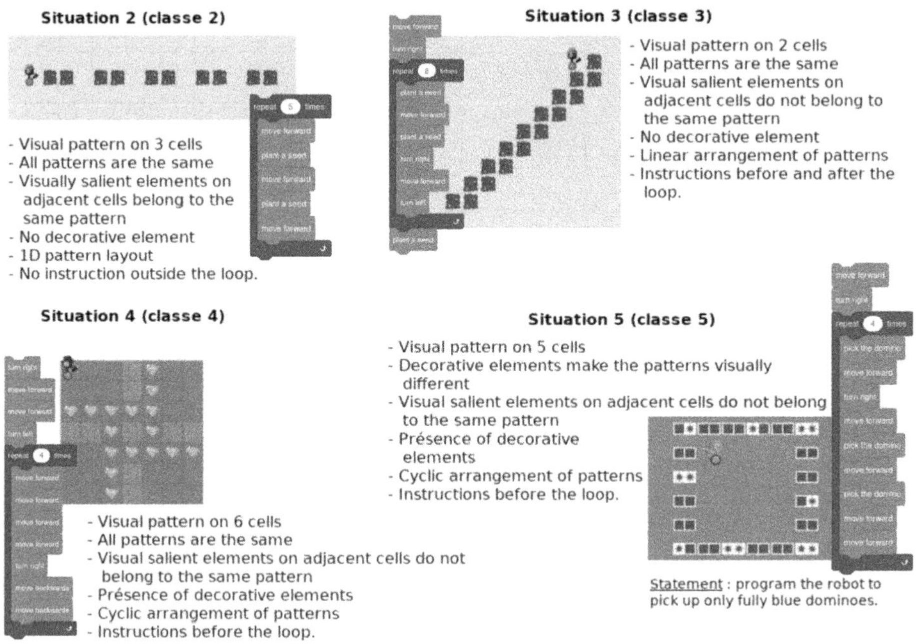

Fig. 6. Prototypical example of a situation for each class defined for the correspondence between *visual motif* and *algorithmic motif*

A first class of situation, very distinct, and which we have already identified in the previous section, concerns situations where the *motif* is limited to a single cell (example in Fig. 2). The other classes are represented in Fig. 6. We put in a second class, situations where the *motif* extends over multiple cells, and for which we have a strict correspondence between *visual motif* and *algorithmic motif.* Each movement action of the robot is identifiable by the boundary between two cells, while the other actions are identifiable by a visually salient element. These are the situations where the movement of the robot is only possible in one direction, and the situations for which the orientation of the robot is absolute (north, south, east, west). A third class corresponds to situations where several states of the robot on the same cell are visually identical, making the correspondence between visual pattern and algorithmic only partial. These are the situations where the robot has a relative orientation, and for which the pivoting actions of the robot are not observable before the execution of the program. To solve these situations, it is necessary to mentally simulate the pivoting actions of the robot, by representing them on the appropriate cells and by keeping the orientation of the robot in memory. The fourth class concerns situations in relative orientation for which the arrangement of *motifs* is cyclical. The *visual motifs* are identical but each rotated by a quarter turn compared to the previous one. Finally, for the fifth class, the correspondence between *visual motif* and *algorithmic motif* is hindered, and it is necessary to disregard certain visual elements. That is, either visual salient elements or decorative elements are equivalent but visually different, or several *visual motifs* are partially superimposed, disturbing the visibility of each of them.

The 5 classes of situations defined above correspond to a gradation in the difficulty of matching *visual motif* and *algorithmic motif* (Fig. 7). The situations of class 1, for which the correspondence between the two *motifs* is attached to the cell, are solved well by most pupils from elementary school. However, situations of class 5, which require much more abstraction skills, are still difficult for most middle school students. The interquartile zones of classes 1 and 5 do not overlap with those of the other classes of situations. We deduce that the degree of correspondence between *visual motif* and *algorithmic motif* strongly determines the difficulty of these situations. On the other hand, classes 2, 3 and 4 have partially overlapping interquartile areas, which means that other variables also impact the difficulty of these situations in a significant way. These are also classes of situations where we observe the strongest progression during the 6 class levels studied.

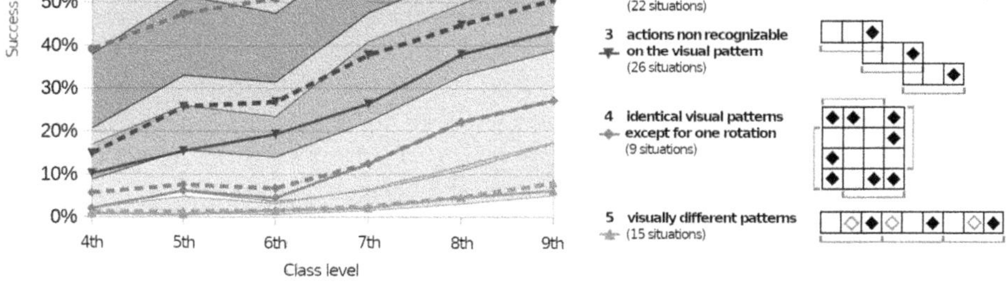

Fig. 7. Study of the correspondence between *visual motif* and *algorithmic motif*

Concerning the *algorithmic motif* expressed in Scratch language, we further show that the success rate is correlated with the number of instructions in the loop (linear correlation rate of −0.79) and that the situation is significantly less successfully resolved when it is necessary to place instructions outside the loop, especially before the loop. We think that this last difficulty is linked to the identification of the position of the robot to be considered for the beginning of the pattern, i.e. the robot has to move to reach the beginning of the pattern. This position need to be mentally anticipated.

5 Conclusion and Perspectives

We show in this study that a loop-focused programming puzzle, even if the solution includes only one loop, is not necessarily a simple task. When solving this type of problem, pattern identification skill is essential, especially the identification of the repeat unit. We have specified the definition of a *motif* in this context. More precisely for programming puzzles that involve moving a virtual robot on a 2D grid, the identification of a *visual motif* and of the corresponding *algorithmic motif* are required (**RQ1**). Using a quantitative analysis of one hundred loop-focused tasks, we have characterized factors that make it difficult to identify the *visual motif* and we have established a gradation in the difficulties encountered, in particular for the matching of visual and algorithmic *motifs* (**RQ2**). Among the difficulties identified, we find the one, already identified in a previous study [8], related to the association of the programming situation with orientation in space.

Our contribution to knowledge concerns the understanding of what pattern identification covers in the situation of programming a virtual robot on a grid. This contribution makes it possible to better understand the obstacles encountered when starting learning computer science. The practical implication addresses teachers, by helping them to understand the difficulties of their students and to design relevant courses.

Further work is underway to continue this study. On the one hand, can we consider that a student has mastered the notion of loop when he has solved programming problems by trial and error, which is possible in this context? On the other hand, we know that motif identification is not the only issue in the treatment of loop-focused situations. Once the *motif* has been identified, the *motifs* have to be counted, which can lead to other difficulties that remain to be analyzed. To refine our understanding, we need more precise data. This is why we have set up a collection of activity traces at several scales. Apart from the success rates collected at the national level analyzed in this article, we have traces of activities at the class level and video recordings of contest participation at the individual level. Class-wide activity traces should allow us to distinguish between expert solving procedures and trial-and-error successes. As for the analysis of the video recordings, we seek to identify indicators that reflect the reasoning, the conceptualization-in-action [16] of the participant (expert procedure, errors). The objective will then be to match these indicators with the traces of activity in order to scale up, i.e. to make the link between the three collection scales.

Acknowledgements. This work is supported by the Digital Transition for Teaching Interreg project (https://teachtransition.eu). We would also like to thank the France-IOI association for providing the success rates for the Algorea contest.

References

1. Berry, G.: L' Hyperpuissance de l'informatique: algorithmes, données, machines, réseaux. Odile Jacob (2017)
2. Collins, M.A., Laski, E.V.: Preschoolers' strategies for solving visual pattern tasks. Early Child. Res. Q. **32**, 204–214 (2015)
3. Csizmadia, A., et al.: Computational thinking-a guide for teachers (2015)
4. Gamma, E., Helm, R., Johnson, R., Johnson, R.E., Vlissides, J.: Design Patterns: Elements of Reusable Object-oriented Software. Pearson Deutschland GmbH (1995)
5. Gouws, L.A., Bradshaw, K., Wentworth, P.: Computational thinking in educational activities: an evaluation of the educational game light-bot. In: Proceedings of the 18th ACM conference on Innovation and technology in computer science education, ITiCSE 2013, pp. 10–15. Association for Computing Machinery, Canterbury (2013). https://doi.org/10.1145/2462476.2466518
6. Hsu, T.C., Chang, S.C., Hung, Y.T.: How to learn and how to teach computational thinking: suggestions based on a review of the literature. Comput. Educ. **126**, 296–310 (2018). https://doi.org/10.1016/j.compedu.2018.07.004
7. Liljedahl, P.: Repeating pattern or number pattern: the distinction is blurred. Focus Learn. Probl. Math. **26**(3), 24–42 (2004)
8. Léonard, M., Peter, Y., Secq, Y.: Reconnaissance et synthèse de motifs redondants avec des élèves de 6–7 ans MOTIFS.MOTIFS.MOTIFS. < = > 3 x MOTIFS. 3 x MOTIFS (2020). https://hal.univ-lille.fr/hal-02971775
9. Papic, M.: Promoting repeating patterns with young children - more than just alternating colours! Aust. Primary Math. Classroom **12**(3), 8–13 (2007)
10. Pelánek, R., Effenberger, T.: Design and analysis of microworlds and puzzles for block-based programming. Comput. Sci. Educ. 1–39 (2020)
11. Peter, Y., Secq, Y., Léonard, M.: Reconnaissance de motifs redondants et répétitions: introduction à la Pensée Informatique. STICEF (Sci. Technol. l'Inf. Commun. Pour l'Éduc. Format.) **27**(2) (2020)
12. Rich, K.M., Strickland, C., Binkowski, T.A., Moran, C., Franklin, D.: K-8 learning trajectories derived from research literature: sequence, repetition, conditionals. In: Proceedings of the 2017 ACM Conference on International Computing Education Research, ICER 2017, pp. 182–190. Association for Computing Machinery, Tacoma (2017). https://doi.org/10.1145/3105726.3106166
13. Rogalski, J.: Acquisition de savoirs et de savoir-faire en informatique. Cahiers Didactique Math. (43) (1987)
14. Rogalski, J., Vergnaud, G.: Didactique de l'informatique et acquisitions cognitives en programmation. Psychol. Française **32**(4) (1987)
15. Spach, M.: Activités robotiques à l'école primaire et apprentissage de concepts informatiques: quelle place du scénario pédagogique? Les limites du co-apprentissage. Ph.D. Thesis, Université Sorbonne Paris Cité (2017)
16. Vergnaud, G.: La théorie des champs conceptuels. In: Recherches en didactique des mathématiques, vol. 10/2.3. La Pensée Sauvage (1991)
17. Vergnaud, G., Durand, C.: Structures additives et complexité psychogénétique. Rev. Française Pédag. 28–43 (1976)

18. Warren, E., Cooper, T.: Using repeating patterns to explore functional thinking. Aust. Prim. Math. Classr. **11**(1), 9 (2006)
19. Warren, E., Miller, J.: Exploring four year old indigenous students' ability to pattern. Int. Res. Early Child. Educ. **1**(2), 42–56 (2010)
20. Warren, E., Miller, J., Cooper, T.: Repeating patterns: Strategies to assist young students to generalise the mathematical structure. Australas. J. Early Child. **37**(3), 111–120 (2012). https://doi.org/10.1177/183693911203700315
21. Wing, J.M.: Computational thinking. Commun. ACM **49**(3), 33–35 (2006). https://doi.org/10.1145/1118178.1118215

Towards Modelling the Technology Integration in Elementary School. A Diachronic Study of Teachers' Digital Practices During and After Covid-19 Lockdown

Christine Michel(✉) and Laëtitia Pierrot(✉)

University of Poitiers, TECHNE (UR-20297), 86000 Poitiers, France
{christine.michel,laetitia.pierrot}@univ-poitiers.fr

Abstract. Different studies have highlighted changes in pedagogical practices in elementary school and several of them question the potential impact of lockdown. The objective of our research is: to analyse the TEL practices of French elementary school teachers in 2020 and 2021, to determine and qualify the levels of technological integration, and to identify the factors explaining the (non-) integration of technology. We conducted a survey and analysed the responses of 572 teachers on their practices and work contexts in 2020 and 2021. By combining a cluster analysis technique on the reported practices and a covariance analysis between the obtained classification and other variables, we identified 3 groups of practices (stabilized, emerging, underdeveloped) and 5 classes of teachers (traditional, interpretative, reproductive, explorer, innovator) according to the way they use technology in vs. outside of the classroom and for traditional vs. constructive learning methods. The impact factors are personal (like the perception of the added value of TEL), contextual (like the equipment offered at the school) and related to the experience of remote work in 2020 (like the feeling of isolation). In the light of our results, we propose recommendations: to foster greater digital integration that goes hand in hand with teachers' professional development and to conduct future diachronic analysis of practices.

Keywords: Teaching practices · Technology integration · Digital uses · Adoption model

1 Introduction

The teacher plays a decisive role in the learner's success, through his or her choice of teaching method and ability to manage the class [1]. Teaching methods include verifying the learners' understanding regularly or explicating the course's structure for instance. The quality of classroom management is reflected by continuous supervision of the class or by providing an emulation system to reinforce certain student behaviours. More generally, these teaching practices describe activities implemented to target specific knowledge for learners. The introduction of technology into the classroom transforms these teaching practices. In France, like in other countries, introducing technology into

I. Hilliger et al. (Eds.): EC-TEL 2022, LNCS 13450, pp. 201–214, 2022.
https://doi.org/10.1007/978-3-031-16290-9_15

the class is part of an institutional prescription: since 2013, "elements of digital culture" appear among teachers' expected skills. Teachers must mobilize them to vary didactic content and evaluation format and modalities while contributing to learners' digital skills development.

In this context, studies on the integration of technology in schools focus on teaching practices with technology. We conducted a literature review and observed diverse ways of analysing these practices. First, teaching practices can refer to tasks or activities mediated by digital tools (1.1) or to the use of digital resources (1.2). Furthermore, the recent context related to Covid-19 has contributed to a renewal of the issues related to the integration of technology in schools (1.3). In terms of methods, two main approaches exist (1.4): a descriptive approach, generally associated with qualitative research methods, which complements a rather quantified and modelling approach. Our previous contribution consisted in proposing a digital integration model while considering teachers' professional activity in primary and secondary schools while home-working during the first lockdown of 2020. In this paper, we aim to start from this model to determine how teaching and digital practices evolved, after the 2020 lockdown. Following the presentation of our literature review and our model in this section, we present the study we conducted in 2021 and the main results we obtained in the next ones.

1.1 TEL Activities in Pedagogical Practices

We apprehend the role and place of technology in teaching or learning activities using a theoretical framework built on the activity theory [2] completed by the contributions of the instrumental approach [3] on the one hand, and the process described by the didactic triangle [4] on the other hand. Thus, the introduction of a technical object, such as a digital resource, a website, an application, or a service in a pedagogical situation mainly fulfils three educational functions: training on basic digital skills, accessing and searching for information or supporting a learning activity. For this article, we focus on the third function.

574 Belgian elementary school teachers had their practices studied and classified through a cluster analysis [5]. For this purpose, the authors differentiated the declared teaching practices according to "traditional" or "constructivist" teaching methods and obtained four profiles: teachers who declare both traditional and constructivist practices, with high intensity (cluster 1) or low intensity (cluster 4), those who have rather traditional (cluster 3) or rather constructivist (cluster 2) practices. By crossing these profiles with the reported digital uses, they observed that teachers with constructivist practices have greater use of technology. Chuang *et al.* [6] conducted a study on technology integration among 320 Taiwanese primary and secondary school teachers. In this study, integration depends primarily on internal factors, specifically teachers' perceptions of the effects of technology on student learning. In addition, participants chose to integrate technology or not according to how these technologies aligned or not with their practices.

Spiteri *et al.* [7] also examined the factors explaining technology integration in primary teachers' practices, through a literature review that includes 27 studies from 2010 to 2016. From this work, they elaborated a conceptual map with four main dimensions. The first identified dimension relates to the *school culture*, which favours the development of digital practices when the school allows and supports collaborative work, provides training time for teachers, and integrates projects with technology on a local scale. The second dimension is *teachers' technology knowledge*: which technology, when to use them and why, based on the knowledge of themselves, their students, and the technology. In addition, the technology integration into their practices depends on their teaching experience: longer teaching experience contributes to developing more technical knowledge and therefore using it more optimally. The third dimension focuses on *teachers' attitudes toward digital use.* This dimension focuses on beliefs and perceptions of being effective when using technology. The literature review conducted by the authors shows that these factors do not only depend on the availability of equipment, but also on the importance they attach to it to have beneficial effects on their students (in terms of motivation or academic success for example). The fourth and final dimension concerns *teachers' skills.* To develop the use of technology, the studies cited in the literature review point to their ability to pick constructivist or student-centred pedagogical approaches, particularly through project-based activities, thus echoing the results cited above [5, 6].

In the French context, Dioni [8] notes that there is an "active" minority of teachers who develop their practices to reduce possible inequalities between students. Moreover, there is a distinction in teachers' practices between "digital" practices, relating to the perceived expectations that the school institution has for them, and "personal" practices, which they carry out outside the institution and of which they are not always aware [9]. This tension between institutional (and normative) practices and other personal practices also appears while using digital resources.

1.2 Use of Digital Resources

Digital resources can include static or interactive content. They describe resources that teachers use or transmit in or outside the classroom [10]. Resources include institutional material resources (or curriculum materials), which comply with the curriculum imposed by the educational institution, and those personally produced by teachers (teacher materials) [11]. As with the factors influencing the integration of technology into practice, strong links exist between teachers' beliefs and conceptions (what they think of their role, their mission), their disciplinary knowledge (and their freedom to follow the curriculum or not) and the use they make of institutional resources: these decisions are part of their professional development, and refer to their "sense of professionalism", their ability to adapt and improvise [12].

Teachers mobilize resources inherited from their initial training or more experienced colleagues [13] and "raw" resources extracted and collected from sites or manuals or proposed by groups to build up their corpus of resources.

In Chinese rural schools [14], the authors have observed widespread use of "traditional" resources (digital or multimedia training aids) and a minority of "innovative" resources (video, specialized software for example). Their analysis, based on a two-level model, leads them to conclude that the use of digital resources can be explained mainly on an individual level (the teacher): 80% of the total variance is attributed to intra-individual differences (mainly age, attitude towards the use of resources, teachers' prior knowledge and teaching experience). In this way, contextual (school) factors are less important. The authors, therefore, recommend considering individual teacher characteristics (or more directly taking teachers into account in digital plans) to facilitate the integration of digital resources into teaching practices.

1.3 The Covid-19 Context

School closures imposed by the Covid-19 health context led to numerous studies examining the experience of distance learning motivated by educational continuity. In Scotland, the practices of some 60 primary school teachers were followed from March to June 2020 through in-depth interviews [15]. The participants of the study expressed the feeling of a certain pressure to offer a wide range of digital services, which placed them in a constant search for new tools.

In Spain, the activities of 1403 primary and secondary school teachers during lockdown were collected through a questionnaire [16], distinguishing them according to whether they were part of traditional or constructivist pedagogical approaches and whether they targeted the acquisition of procedural, verbal or behavioural knowledge or their evaluation. Their analysis shows a predominance of traditional type activities, mainly conducted by teachers with little teaching experience; these activities mainly target the acquisition of verbal and behavioural knowledge. Based on these results, they established 4 teacher profiles: the group of "passive" teachers whose activity with technology is the least intense, and mainly according to a traditional approach, the group of "active" teachers, whose activity is more important than that of the passive teachers, still according to a mainly traditional and minority constructivist approach, the "traditional" teachers whose activity is equivalent to the previous group but with a more marked predominance towards traditional activities and the group of "interpretative" teachers whose activity is the most important and mobilizes both traditional and constructivist approaches. Primary school teachers were over-represented in the first group.

In the British context, two studies have examined the resources mobilized during the lockdown of 2020 and 2021. The first one highlights the engagement of students which was higher when schools relied on specific resources for learning, at the school level, notably through VLEs [17]. On the other hand, when comparing the 2020 and 2021 lockdowns, more active strategies implemented (including the use of video conferencing tools) could be observed during the second lockdown [18].

1.4 Approaches to Accounting for Practices

The works cited in the previous section are divided according to whether they rely on a modelling or a descriptive approach. In the first case, as summarized by Taherdoost [19], the studies were based on models relating to the integration of technology [5, 6, 14, 16–18] and mobilised surveys by questionnaire with a representative aim. In the second case, the authors use more qualitative approaches while intending to conduct more in-depth analyses of the motivations or purposes of the practices, which are less generalizable [8–10, 12, 15].

In a previous study [20], we proposed a model of technology integration that considers elementary and middle school teachers' practices related to the use of a virtual learning environment (VLE) and other digital tools based on data from a questionnaire including closed and open-ended questions and in-depth interviews on the tasks performed during the first lockdown of 2020. This integration model derives from a multidimensional classification [21] to differentiate teachers' behaviours according to the main purposes they were pursuing (activity design, resource delivery, facilitation, verification, communication, and self-study).

Among the 279 primary school teachers surveyed in 2020, the main reported practices with digital tools were motivated by the objectives of resource transmission (integration level 1), to which were added objectives of design (level 2), communication (level 3), self-training and verification (level 4) and finally facilitation (level 5). Most (142/279) of the teachers interviewed are located in class 4 and class 5, with a "pragmatic" [22] use distributed between the services offered by the institution (the VLE) or not and motivated by the imperative need to remain in contact with the students during the schools' closing [23].

1.5 Research Questions

The analysis of the literature shows that different studies have highlighted changes in teaching practices in elementary school to support a learning activity with the use of digital resources and technologies. Several studies question the potential impact of the lockdown. The objective of our research is to determine how teaching and digital practices evolved in France, after the 2020 lockdown. Our first research question is to determine the levels of technology integration, based on the activities implemented by teachers at school and out-of-school (RQ1). More specifically, what is the contribution of resources found on the internet, transmitted by colleagues or the institution in the integration of TEL? Our goal is also to describe the diversity and intensity of practices in 2021. Our second research question is to explain these levels of digital tools integration (RQ2) based on the individual and contextual factors identified in the previous section. More specifically, the objective is to determine whether the educational experience during the lockdown played a role in the integration of technology in the mainstream context. More broadly, we seek to measure the quality and representativeness of our approach to analyse the dynamics of technology integration in schools (RQ3).

2 Study on Technology Integration

Context of the Study and Research Questions Addressed. The study is part of the French ministerial program "Territoires Numériques Éducatifs" (Digital Education Territory) launched in September 2020 in the two pilot departments of Aisne and Val d'Oise to contribute to the improvement of educational efficiency with technology in times of pandemic as well as in ordinary times[1]. In this context, the objective of the study is to make a diagnosis of the evolution of teachers' digital practices. We proposed a questionnaire[2], organized into 4 parts (Personal characteristics, Work context, Practices in

[1] https://www.education.gouv.fr/les-territoires-numeriques-educatifs-306176.

[2] Questionnaire: https://techne.labo.univ-poitiers.fr/wp-content/uploads/sites/63/2019/07/questionnaire.png.

2021/2020/2019, Experience during the Home Confinement) and 108 questions, from January to February 2021 to all teachers in the two departments via their professional email address.

Participants. We collected 1224 complete questionnaire responses, these include 572 primary school teachers, representing 10% of each department's total share of teachers. In the Aisne department, 133 responses (out of 1336 elementary school teachers in 2019–20) were mainly from females (114), with an average age of 40 years and 15 years of service. In the Val-d'Oise department, the 439 responses (out of 4181 elementary school teachers in 2019–20) were also mostly from females (374), with an average age of 40 and 13 years of teaching seniority.

Method. We used discretization and standardization with the scale data. We identified teachers' technology use strategies over the two time periods by averaging responses on how they performed different academic tasks. We modelled the levels of technology integration (RQ1) using a 5-level K-means classification techniqueto group teachers according to their declared practices while using technology in and outside of the classroom (TIM21) and during the lockdown (TIM20) by considering questions related to practices over these two periods. We only calculated the TIM20 classification on the 525 responses from teachers who taught remotely during the period. We chose a five-level classification to be consistent with the TIM scale of technology integration [21]. Indeed, this TIM scale considers 5 levels: entry, adoption, adaptation, infusion, and transformation [21]. A matrix describes, for each level, the possible uses of technologies according to the type of learning (active, collaborative, etc.) proposed by the teacher. The TIM matrix does not consider the teacher's administrative and preparation activities. We will consider them as communication, information and design activities [20]. We performed the calculation of K-means on the normalized values. We ordered the obtained classes based on empirical studies on traditional and innovative behaviours identified in the literature.

In addition, we performed an analysis of the covariance (0.05 level of significance) between the TIM21 classification and other variables to identify if there were any explanatory factors (RQ2). The variables considered were: 8 personal variables, the 29 context variables, the practices in 2019 and 2020 (32 variables), and 29 experience variables during the first confinement. We identified a total of 18 variables considered significant and calculated mean values by integration levels for them. We used Excel and XLStat to perform all statistical analyses (bivariate or multivariate analyses).

3 Results

3.1 The Current Level of Technology Integration (RQ1)

Tables 1 and 2 show the ratio of teachers who performed different practices during the 2020 lockdown and in normal work mode, according to the TIM20 and TIM21 integration levels and all levels combined. Thus, a value of 1 means that all teachers at that level used that practice. Traditional (resp. Constructivist) activities are shown in

Table 1. Percentage of activities during the lockdown according to the technology integration levels TIM20 and TIM21.

Practices during lockdown	TIM 20-1	TIM 20-2	TIM 20-3	TIM 20-4	TIM 20-5	TIM 21-1	TIM 21-2	TIM 21-3	TIM 21-4	TIM 21-5	Mean 20	Mean 21
Sending homework	1,00	0,93	0,97	0,97	0,93	0,93	0,93	0,97	0,97	1,00	**0,96**	**0,96**
Online coaching	0,00	0,70	1,00	0,97	0,99	0,66	0,84	0,86	0,91	0,83	**0,73**	**0,82**
Telephone coaching	1,00	0,00	1,00	0,71	0,86	0,57	0,74	0,77	0,75	0,81	**0,71**	**0,73**
Prescription for online resources	0,48	0,58	0,76	0,94	0,69	0,56	0,70	0,66	0,77	0,78	**0,69**	**0,70**
Prescription for CNED system	0,12	0,04	0,00	1,00	0,49	0,11	0,20	0,24	0,25	0,39	**0,33**	**0,24**
Sending self-made resources	0,17	0,20	0,36	0,26	0,49	0,23	0,30	0,33	0,50	0,39	**0,30**	**0,35**
Virtual classes (in sub-groups)	0,22	0,19	0,00	0,00	1,00	0,22	0,33	0,39	0,37	0,42	**0,28**	**0,34**
Virtual classes (whole class)	0,10	0,15	0,06	0,29	0,33	0,11	0,19	0,16	0,15	0,36	**0,19**	**0,20**

Table 2. Percentage of activities in regular context according to the integration level TIM 21.

Use in the Classroom, Activity	TIM 21-1	TIM 21-2	TIM 21-3	TIM 21-4	TIM 21-5	Mean	Use outside the Classroom, Activity	TIM 21-1	TIM 21-2	TIM 21-3	TIM 21-4	TIM 21-5	Mean
Percentage Of Teachers	24%	25%	25%	19%	7%		***Percentage Of Teachers***	24%	25%	25%	19%	7%	
							Programming, scripting	0,74	0,94	0,98	0,93	0,97	**0,92**
Collective visualization of	1,00	1,00	1,00	1,00	1,00	**1,00**	Preparation of educational material	0,72	0,97	0,94	0,95	0,97	**0,91**
Consultation of resources	1,00	1,00	1,00	1,00	1,00	**1,00**	Communication with parents	0,69	0,88	0,85	0,93	0,90	**0,85**
Search for information	0,83	0,90	0,77	0,95	0,95	**0,88**	Communication with colleagues	0,64	0,85	0,92	0,92	0,90	**0,85**
Use of exercisers	0,35	0,67	0,22	0,87	0,68	**0,56**	Administrative tasks	0,64	0,86	0,87	0,92	0,92	**0,84**
Individual production	0,24	0,54	0,27	0,66	0,68	**0,48**	Evaluation	0,54	0,69	0,94	0,82	0,92	**0,78**
Collective production	0,24	0,58	0,24	0,62	0,66	**0,47**	Resource - Personal	0,51	0,64	0,84	0,86	0,82	**0,73**
Communication	0,18	0,42	0,13	0,56	0,58	**0,37**	Communication with institution	0,45	0,74	0,83	0,79	0,77	**0,71**
Students sharing online resources	0,19	0,38	0,13	0,50	0,45	**0,33**	Resource-Peers	0,52	0,66	0,72	0,78	0,77	**0,69**
Evaluation	0,05	0,04	0,07	0,61	0,37	**0,23**	Resource-Internet	0,45	0,71	0,60	0,83	0,74	**0,67**
Programming activities	0,01	0,01	0,00	0,02	0,97	**0,20**	Follow-up	0,20	0,45	0,63	0,65	0,82	**0,55**
Educational games	0,02	0,15	0,02	0,15	0,29	**0,13**	Resource-Institutional	0,20	0,29	0,26	0,34	0,41	**0,30**
							Correction	0,06	0,04	0,33	0,32	0,49	**0,25**

purple (resp. Blue). The communication (resp. Information and design) activities are presented in orange (resp. Black).

According to the TIM20 classification, the practices reported during the lockdown with technology are of the "traditional" type with the transmission of resources and the use of online resources for all levels. These practices are the more accessible ways to integrate technology tools. The level of integration is distinguished according to the mode of follow-up (by phone for class 1 and by email for class 2), the type of resources used for the design (online resource for class 3, institutional for class 4 and self-produced for class 5). These differences are less visible in 2021 with a more homogeneous behaviour at all levels which means that these practices are becoming more widespread. The strongest progression in 2021 is online coaching, which can be considered as an adaptation of practices over the period. Constructive activities such as virtual classroom facilitation or the design of personal resources are progressing but remain low. These practices are being adopted. The use of institutional resources will decrease in 2021 to the benefit of resources created by teachers.

The integration of technology tools is quite segmented in 2020 (see Table 1) with specific choices for each class (identifiable by 0's and 1's on some lines) whereas it is more inclusive and cumulative in 2021: the technologies integrated by class 2 are those of class1 plus others, etc. In the regular context (see Table 2), the most developed activities are "traditional" learning activities in the classroom: whole class or individual resource presentation and information retrieval. Technology tools are then used more and more according to the TIM level for activities outside the classroom: designing scenarios or digital resources, communicating with parents or other teachers and administrative tasks (class 2), evaluating students, and improving personal resources (class 3), self-training through internet research or collaboration between colleagues (class 4), monitoring and correcting students' work (class 5). Teachers in classes 4 and 5 also use technology for classroom activities for constructivist activities: exercise, individual and collective production of documents, communication between students (class 4), and programming and educational games (class 5). Uses outside of the classroom follow a regular progression. On the other hand, uses in the classroom, such as collaborative and constructivist TEL uses, are stopped for classes 1 and 3. Further studies must be done to understand why these practices can't be regularly adopted. Uses of exercisers and programming software seem to be good leverage for new teaching practice transformations.

3.2 Explanatory Factors

Of all the variables tested, only 18 variables were significant to explain the composition of the TIM integration classes21: 5 items were related to the added value of technology, 4 items to the context (the school identification, the fact that the school equipped the teacher with a computer and the classes with peripheral devices, and that the teacher himself had devices) and 9 items to the experience during the lockdown (previous experience, integration level TIM20, reorganization of the work at school and professional isolation). These variables are marked in bold in Table 1 and Tables 3, 4 and 5.

Personal Variables. Table 3 shows the mean values for the perceived usefulness of technology, overall ("benefits of technologies") and for different educational purposes.

Table 3. Average score attributed to technology value according to the TIM21 level.

Perceived value of technologies	TIM21-1	TIM21-2	TIM21-3	TIM21-4	TIM21-5	Mean
Benefits of technologies	0,81	0,85	0,86	0,89	0,95	**0,87**
Improve the quality and diversity of documents	0,67	0,83	0,77	0,84	0,89	**0,80**
Promote openness to the world	0,65	0,69	0,68	0,78	0,76	**0,71**
Train students to the use of technologies	0,50	0,64	0,63	0,78	0,84	**0,68**
Educate students about issues affecting technologies	0,42	0,57	0,54	0,59	0,79	**0,58**
Train students to information retrieval	0,39	0,57	0,51	0,63	0,74	**0,57**
Allow individualized and personalized work for students	0,43	0,45	0,44	0,61	0,79	**0,55**
Facilitate group activities and collaboration between students	0,25	0,31	0,43	0,44	0,76	**0,44**
Facilitate students' personal work at home	0,23	0,28	0,32	0,40	0,68	**0,38**
Stimulate students' creativity	0,14	0,21	0,26	0,38	0,53	**0,30**
Allow the inclusion of disabled students	0,16	0,23	0,23	0,36	0,47	**0,29**
Improve the evaluation of learning	0,06	0,11	0,21	0,24	0,71	**0,27**

All teachers feel that technology is useful (0.87/1) especially for improving the quality of documents (0.8) and openness to the world (0.71). Overall, in the higher TIM21 levels, the feeling of usefulness is greater, which corroborates the link between the feeling of usefulness and the uses. More specifically, 5 criteria play a role in integration. Some are shared by all classes, such as training students in technology, while others are mainly identified by class TIM21–5, such as facilitating group or homework, improving evaluation or stimulating creativity. With averages of 0.68, 0.44 and 0.38, it seems quite easy to convince teachers on the first 3 criteria (train students, facilitate work at home or in a group) by giving them examples of uses. The last two (creativity and evaluation) seem to be further away from the teachers' values and practices.

Contextual Variables. The level of equipment is relatively similar for all teachers. However, they feel that they are better equipped to work at home than at school. The fact that the school provides the equipment is a factor in technology integration, mainly concerning peripherals devices: a printer and hard drives at home and an interactive whiteboard (IWB) at school. In only 23 schools out of the 94, the technology integration exceeds the level TIM21–4 in a significant way. Further study is needed to understand the reasons for this by analysing the school culture [8] (Table 4).

Table 4. Average score attributed to equipment according to TIM21 integration level.

Context	TIM21-1	TIM21-2	TIM21-3	TIM21-4	TIM21-5	Mean
Home equipment provided by the school	0.31	0.43	0.33	0.42	0.51	0.38
Satisfaction home equipment	0.59	0.63	0.62	0.65	0.58	0.62
Home : Digital interface	0.35	0.41	0.41	0.39	0.49	0.40
Home : Tangible interface	0.02	0.02	0.02	0.02	0.11	0.02
Home : Peripheral devices	0.27	0.34	0.37	0.37	0.44	0.34
Satisfaction school equipment	0.49	0.57	0.49	0.55	0.57	0.53
School : Digital interface	0.30	0.42	0.33	0.42	0.51	0.38
School : Tangible interface	0.05	0.09	0.08	0.22	0.18	0.11
School : Peripheral devices	0.20	0.35	0.33	0.41	0.48	0.33
School network satisfaction	0.41	0.54	0.46	0.54	0.38	0.48
Use of personal equipment at school	0.53	0.54	0.66	0.61	0.62	0.59
School Id	0.24	0.25	0.25	0.19	0.07	0.20

Experience Variable. Several practice variables had a significant impact on technology integration: uses before COVID (in bold in Table 5) and activities during lockdown (in bold in Table 1). Using technology before COVID favours integration with 0.76 and 0.88 in TIM21–4 and 5. As described earlier, having carried out in 2020, the traditional type of training activities (sending homework, prescribing resources found on the Internet) consolidated carrying out traditional activities in 2021 but did not allow the introduction of constructivist teaching activities in the classroom. On the other hand, the fact that teachers were designing their own resources in 2020 had an impact on out-of-class use: they found it easier to search for information on the Internet or to communicate with other teachers. Similarly, having accompanied students on the phone or by email in 2020 helped the teachers in 2021 to follow students online.

Unlike the studies cited by Spiteri *et al.* [7], skills did not impact technology integration. Teachers report being poorly trained (0.25) but having a proficient level of technical or teaching skills (resp. 0.65 and 0.69) and not having suffered from a lack of skills in 2020 (0.32 and 0.03) while having built useful skills during this time (0.86).

The professional isolation linked to the lockdown and the changes induced in the way of working at school have also significantly influenced the integration of technology, especially for classes 3 and 4 (Table 5a). Overall, teachers believe that the way they work at school has changed (Table 5b). Teachers communicate more with parents (0.81 and 0.73). To a lesser extent, they share their resources and practices more (resp. 0.63 and 0.67) and exchange with each other (0.56, 0.44, 0.40) or help each other (0.40).

Some behaviours are specific to class 5 teachers: they engage in more collaborative practices with joint preparation activities (0.67), which significantly impacts technology integration, and they participate in virtual teacher communities (0.63).

Table 5. (a) Average score attributed to experience according to TIM21 integration level and (b) focus on "change at school" variable

Experience	TIM21-1	TIM21-2	TIM21-3	TIM21-4	TIM21-5	Mean	Perceived changes in work at school	TIM21-1	TIM21-2	TIM21-3	TIM21-4	TIM21-5	Mean
Satisfaction with initial training	0.23	0.21	0.24	0.19	0.37	**0.25**	More frequent exchanges with parents	0.71	0.82	0.84	0.88	0.88	**0.81**
19 : Use before COVID	0.52	0.66	0.46	0.76	0.88	**0.66**	Advice to parents on supporting schoolwork	0.71	0.72	0.73	0.75	0.92	**0.73**
20 : Lack of technical skills	0.36	0.33	0.33	0.38	0.22	**0.32**	Sharing resources	0.67	0.40	0.81	0.67	0.88	**0.63**
20 : Lack of pedagogical skills	0.03	0.02	0.03	0.03	0.06	**0.03**	Sharing practices	0.67	0.27	0.71	0.63	0.63	**0.57**
20 : Lack of digital resources	0.19	0.23	0.27	0.19	0.19	**0.21**	More frequent exchanges with the school	0.44	0.53	0.74	0.50	0.80	**0.56**
21 : New COVID skills	0.54	0.58	0.60	0.74	0.64	**0.62**	Mutualization of resources	0.67	0.20	0.58	0.50	0.93	**0.49**
21: Usefulness of new comp	0.83	0.78	0.89	0.90	0.90	**0.86**	More frequent exchanges with administrative information	0.33	0.44	0.48	0.52	0.52	**0.44**
20 : Professional isolation	0.30	0.31	0.48	0.41	0.31	**0.36**	Distribution of printed materials	0.33	0.39	0.48	0.47	0.44	**0.42**
21: Change in work at school	0.08	0.11	0.33	0.34	0.42	**0.76**	More frequent exchanges individually	0.44	0.33	0.51	0.29	0.67	**0.40**
21 : Change in work outside of school	0.05	0.11	0.25	0.27	0.24	**0.26**	More mutual aid	0.33	0.27	0.56	0.35	0.53	**0.38**
21 : Change in parent relationship	0.67	0.72	0.84	0.85	0.69	**0.18**	**More collaborative preparation**	0.11	0.13	0.44	0.50	0.67	**0.30**
21: Technical Skills	0.53	0.63	0.66	0.69	0.72	**0.65**	Participating in virtual communities	0.00	0.40	0.39	0.37	0.63	**0.29**
21: Teaching Skills	0.64	0.65	0.69	0.72	0.77	**0.69**	Distribution of computer materials	0.02	0.06	0.09	0.07	0.08	**0.06**

4 Discussion

Emerging Student-Centred Approaches Over the Period. To answer the first research question (RQ1), our study shows that overall, teachers have greater use of technology in ordinary times. Considering practices' nature and evolution, three groups appear: stabilized practices, emerging ones, and underdeveloped ones. Stabilized practices, mainly related to "traditional" pedagogical approaches: communicating and preparing/planning/designing activities outside the class and, disseminating resources in the classroom. This result is consistent with similar studies cited above [5, 6, 12]. Stabilized practices are, most of the time, combined with diversified emerging practices enhanced by the lockdown: tasks in relation to resource work, evaluation/follow-up and communication with the school. In 2021, teachers used few institutional resources and more resources shared by peers, found on the Internet or made by themselves. We need to examine whether containment has helped in setting up a new framework that limits institutional/normative "pressure" [8, 9]. Finally, underdeveloped practices include the use of educational games, communication and collaboration activities and we must analyse if this observation falls under the pragmatism approach identified in Spanish primary school teachers [16].

Different dynamics of technology integration can be observed. In classes 1 and 3, the teachers prefer to integrate technology first in activities that do not directly involve the students (preparation of lessons, communication with parents, administrative tasks) and then in activities that take place in the classroom. Class 1 is a group with a "traditional" profile [16] characterized by low activity while group 3 attaches a lot of importance to the preparation of material and is similar to a "reproductive" profile [16]. Classes 2, 4 and 5 are “interpretative” [16]: teachers use traditional and constructive practices (i.e. student-centred approaches) according to the situation. Class 4 performs more self-training to diversify the modes of implementation, they can be described as “interpretative explorers” while class 2 renews themselves less and are rather “interpretative followers”. Class 5 uses technologies for more complex practices such as programming and are “innovators”. Unlike the innovation curve, which is bell-shaped, the curve of technology integration in schools (see Fig. 1) follows a horizontal asymptote. The traditional group remains large. To make this group evolve, it is necessary to train them mainly in the practices of groups 2 and 3.

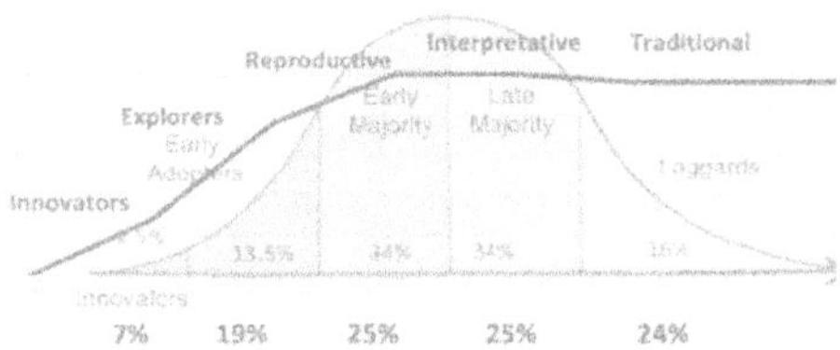

Fig. 1. The curve of technology integration in schools [22]

We identify two leverage effects that should be considered. First, it is essential to offer a limited and rationalized range of technology to teachers, who in any case will concentrate on those they consider most suitable for them and their students [6, 7, 14, 15]. For this reason, we recommend involving teachers as much as possible in the choice of technology and providing design training for pedagogical activities. Second, the stabilization and emergence of “personal” rather than institutional practices mark a milestone in the professional identity of teachers [12]. It appears that lockdown has opened up the possibility for more transfers of practices developed outside the classroom. To maintain this openness, institutions should recognize and value the activities of teachers who deviate from the normative framework by encouraging peer sharing during in-service training.

Factors Explaining Technology Integration (RQ2). Our results are in line with the work on the perceived usefulness of technology that precedes its actual use [6, 8]. Referring to the traditional/constructivist classification of Tondeur *et al.* [5], teachers are aware that technology is useful in general but not to support constructive learning or train students in digital skills. Our study shows that skill variables do not impact technology integration, which contrasts with previous work [7]. Teachers reported having been poorly trained, but still having good technical and pedagogical skills. They declared that they had learned during the COVID, that they had not experienced a lack of skills, yet they only partially integrated them into their practices, mainly for traditional activities. An incorrect self-evaluation of their skills can explain this paradox: having insufficient training, they consider that the personal efforts made to integrate technology are adapted. It is therefore essential to provide teachers with examples of constructive practices with technology to help them identify their limits in terms of technical and pedagogical skills and to encourage the implementation of these practices. In addition, it would be interesting to accompany them in a professional certification such as the PIX[3], as it is required for students.

We believe that the dissemination of information is not a highly effective way to raise teachers' awareness of the added value of technology or the implementation of practices. Teachers are much more sensitive to direct communication with expert teachers, present in schools or in online communities. Thus, workshops or awareness-raising would be much more effective in supporting digital-related changes, in particular, integrating more constructive practices in the classroom. The context in which technology is deployed also influences the integration of technology, mainly the availability of equipment: to promote this integration, it seems necessary to systematically provide teachers with personal computers so that they can use them at home. In this way, the development of practices in and out of the classroom [10] can be facilitated, as well as the work of monitoring and developing effective resources [11]. Classrooms should also be systematically equipped with broadcasting and interaction devices such as IWBs or visualizers to match the most common activities of primary school teachers.

Analysis of our Approach to Measuring TEL Integration. To answer the third research question (RQ3), our approach, which combines a classification of practices and an analysis of the covariance, allowed us to see how teachers deploy strategies to integrate these technologies into their practices both outside and inside the classroom. In addition to observing an intensification of its usage that increased between 2020 and 2021, we were able to follow the evolution and stabilization of certain practices, while identifying the factors explaining these dynamics. Although initially responding to different objectives (the previous study focused more on the use of the VLE), the study presented here complements our previous results to provide an overview of the main practices conducted among French primary school teachers. In addition, our approach allowed us to cover practices that were not necessarily included in the TIM. While the matrix focuses on practices in the classroom, the analysis of our data highlights behaviours related to uses mainly in the classroom (classes 2, 4 and 5) or outside (1 and 3). This constitutes a step forward in the analysis of teachers' activity in relation to the TEL continuum. The method can nevertheless be questioned on different aspects.

Data Collection and Analysis. Some variables, such as the use of software or the websites used, are not well described in this study, which is more focused on the technical means. The analysis of the "other" open-ended questions in the questionnaire should be carried out to identify the software, in particular the exercises, and the Internet resources that teachers most often choose to use. Moreover, our study highlights a lack of information about certain phenomena. The surprising results regarding teachers' self-assessment of skills suggest that these data are biased or inaccurate. To have a more accurate measure of skill levels, it would be preferable to use PIX-type certification scores, but they are not used in France. It would also be interesting to refine the questions based on the expectations of school directors or government agencies. Similarly, we have identified that some schools have specific characteristics that hinder the integration of TELs, but we do not know whether these are organizational, material or related to the socio-demographic

[3] https://pix.fr/.

characteristics of students and families. To continue the study, we propose to analyse the 92 complementary answers of the school directors.

Diachronic Analysis of Practices. Does a diachronic analysis of different practices observed show an evolution in practices? For each practice, no: some are abandoned while others emerge. It is therefore impossible to compare strictly the same practices. However, the classification method allows teachers to be grouped by class of practices and our study shows that comparing classes makes sense. Diachronic studies can accurately follow the life cycle of established practices by questioning teachers regularly about how they are carried out but can also include or eliminate others because they are innovative or abandoned. A preliminary study in selected schools, in the form of interviews and focus groups, would allow for this and for the inclusion of possibly emerging impact factors that the questionnaire could measure on a larger scale. We have conducted a series of 50 interviews with teachers, principals, parents and children. We will analyse them soon to complete the results of this study, but also to identify those new factors that could be useful to observe in other future studies.

5 Conclusion

We conducted a study to determine the levels of technology integration, based on the activities implemented by teachers at school and out-of-school in 2021, one year after the confinement. Through the analysis of 572 primary school teachers' responses to a questionnaire, we identify 5 classes of teacher profiles: traditional, interpretative, reproductive, explorers, and innovators. We found also that the curve of digital tools integration in school is not following the classical innovation curve. It is characterized by horizontal asymptotes representing a large group of traditional teachers. Emerging student-centred approaches are also more intense than in the classical curve. We identify 3 main factors explaining technology non-integration: a lack of value in using technology to support constructive learning, a lack of equipment especially in a classroom, and a lack of collaboration culture between teachers in school. Our study shows that skill variables do not impact technology integration, which contrasts with previous work. This is explained by a lack of professional certification in digital uses. We propose various perspectives to promote technology integration and refine the approaches to measuring TEL integration.

References

1. Hattie, J.: Visible Learning: A Synthesis of Over 800 Meta-Analyses Relating to Achievement. Routledge, USA (2008)
2. Davydov, V.V.: The content and unsolved problems of activity theory. In: Perspectives on Activity Theory, pp. 39–52. Cambridge University Press, Cambridge (1999)
3. Rabardel, P., Bourmaud, G.: From computer to instrument system: a developmental perspective. Interact. Comput. **15**, 665–691 (2003)
4. Augustsson, G., Boström, L.: Teachers' leadership in the didactic room: a systematic literature review of international research. Acda Didactica Norge. **10**(3) (2016)

5. Tondeur, J., Hermans, R., van Braak, J., Valcke, M.: Exploring the link between teachers' educational belief profiles and different types of computer use in the classroom. Comput. Hum. Behav. **24**, 2541–2553 (2008)
6. Chuang, H.-H., Weng, C.-Y., Huang, F.-C.: A structure equation model among factors of teachers' technology integration practice and their TPCK. Comput. Educ. **86**, 182–191 (2015)
7. Spiteri, M., Rundgren, S.-N.C.: Literature review on the factors affecting primary teachers' use of digital technology. Technol. Knowl. Learn. **25**(1), 115–128 (2018). https://doi.org/10.1007/s10758-018-9376-x
8. Dioni, C.: Métier d'élève, métier d'enseignant à l'ère numérique. 29 (2008)
9. Epstein, M., Bourgeois, N.: A statistical analysis of French teachers' blogs: beyond institutional perspectives Some changes in the teaching profession made visible by the study of their blogs. French J. Media Res. Web 2.0 Places of Perception Transformations Societies (2018)
10. Ratompomalala, H., Bruillard, É.: Quelle gestion des ressources éducatives par les enseignants de sciences ? Questions Vives. Recherches en éducation (2019)
11. Reverdy, C.: Du programme vers la classe: des ressources pour enseigner. Dossier de veille de l'IFÉ (2014)
12. Mars, E.: Professional standards, teacher careers and the enactment of professional judgement: an exploration of the discourses. In: Joint Australian Association for Research in Education and Asia-Pacific Educational Research Association Conference, p. 24, Sidney (2012)
13. Diekema, A., Olsen, M.: The notion of relevance in teacher information behavior. Proc. Am. Soc. Inf. Sci. Technol. **49**(1), 1–9 (2012)
14. Wang, J., Tigelaar, D.E.H., Admiraal, W.: Connecting rural schools to quality education: rural teachers' use of digital educational resources. Comput. Hum. Behav. **101**, 68–76 (2019)
15. Brown, J., McLennan, C., Mercieca, D., Mercieca, D.P., Robertson, D.P., Valentine, E.: Technology as thirdspace: teachers in scottish schools engaging with and being challenged by digital technology in first COVID-19 lockdown. Educ. Sci. **11**, 136 (2021)
16. Pozo, J.-I., Pérez Echeverría, M.-P., Cabellos, B., Sánchez, D.L.: Teaching and learning in times of COVID-19: uses of digital technologies during school lockdowns. Front. Psychol. **12**, 1511 (2021)
17. Lucas, M., Nelson, J., Sims, D.: Schools' responses to Covid-19: pupil engagement in remote learning. National foundation for Educational Research (2020)
18. Montacute, R., Cullinane, C.: Learning in lockdown: research brief. The Sutton Trust (2021)
19. Taherdoost, H.: A review of technology acceptance and adoption models and theories. Procedia Manufact. **22**, 960–967 (2018)
20. Michel, C., Pierrot, L., Solari-Landa, M.: VLE limits and perspectives for digital integration in teaching practices. In: De Laet, T., Klemke, R., Alario-Hoyos, C., Hilliger, I., Ortega-Arranz, A. (eds.) EC-TEL 2021. LNCS, vol. 12884, pp. 96–109. Springer, Cham (2021). https://doi.org/10.1007/978-3-030-86436-1_8
21. Kozdras, D., Welsh, J.: Enter the matrix: a pedagogy for infusing technology. In: Society for Information Technology and Teacher Education International Conference, pp. 536–541. Association for the Advancement of Computing in Education (AACE) (2018)
22. Rogers, E.M.: Diffusion of Innovations. Free Press, USA (2003)
23. Pace, C., Pettit, S., Barker, K.: Best practices in middle level quaranteaching: strategies, tips and resources amidst COVID-19. Becoming **31**(1), 2–13 (2020)

Learning to Give a Complete Argument with a Conversational Agent: An Experimental Study in Two Domains of Argumentation

Behzad Mirzababaei[1(✉)] and Viktoria Pammer-Schindler[1,2]

[1] Know-Center GmbH, Graz, Austria
bmirzababaei@know-center.at
[2] Graz University of Technology, Graz, Austria
viktoria.pammer-schindler@tugraz.at

Abstract. This paper reports a between-subjects experiment (treatment group N = 42, control group N = 53) evaluating the effect of a conversational agent that teaches users to give a complete argument. The agent analyses a given argument for whether it contains a claim, a warrant and evidence, which are understood to be essential elements in a good argument. The agent detects which of these elements is missing, and accordingly scaffolds the argument completion. The experiment includes a treatment task (Task 1) in which participants of the treatment group converse with the agent, and two assessment tasks (Tasks 2 and 3) in which both the treatment and the control group answer an argumentative question. We find that in Task 1, 36 out of 42 conversations with the agent are coherent. This indicates good interaction quality. We further find that in Tasks 2 and 3, the treatment group writes a significantly higher percentage of argumentative sentences (task 2: $t(94) = 1.73$, $p = 0.042$, task 3: $t(94) = 1.7$, $p = 0.045$). This shows that participants of the treatment group used the scaffold, taught by the agent in Task 1, outside the tutoring conversation (namely in the assessment Tasks 2 and 3) and across argumentation domains (Task 3 is in a different domain of argumentation than Tasks 1 and 2). The work complements existing research on adaptive and conversational support for teaching argumentation in essays.

Keywords: Educational conversational agent · Intelligent tutoring · Argumentation · Toulmin's model of argument

1 Introduction

Being able to argue is an essential skill for participation in everyday and professional life [18], and for participation in society [9,20]. "It is in argument that we are likely to find the most significant way in which higher-order thinking and reasoning figure in the lives of most people" [19]. Based on this understanding, research has been carried out on different challenges regarding how to teach

I. Hilliger et al. (Eds.): EC-TEL 2022, LNCS 13450, pp. 215–228, 2022.
https://doi.org/10.1007/978-3-031-16290-9_16

argumentation. One strand of research focuses on including argumentation within teacher education [10,12]. Such works investigate guidelines and teaching strategies for teachers in order to encourage students to justify better their opinions. A related line of investigation is interested in designing learning environments and course instructions, and assessing their impact on the argumentation skills of students [15].

This work takes up a related and newer line of research that focuses on computer-mediated environments for teaching argumentation [2,31]. A fundamental motivation underlying such research is the promise of scalability in the face of large class sizes while still being able to give feedback specifically to each learner. The importance of such personal feedback, adapted to each learner's prior knowledge or task performance is in turn a foundational motivation for research in adaptive learning support [4]. Such feedback is of course also important for learning how to argue, as has been found in research investigating teaching strategies for argumentation skills [7]. This is the research strand that we continue and complement. Our particular approach to this challenge is to study a conversational agent for teaching argumentation directly within conversations. The underlying rationale is that good argumentation is expected and helpful in many private, professional and public conversations.

2 Related Work

Educational conversational agents have been studied across different age groups, such as primary school, apprentices (e.g., [34]), or university students (e.g., [28]).

They can also take on different roles. In educational scenarios, the agents usually act as a tutor (e.g., [3]) or as a peer (e.g., [33]). However, in collaborative learning settings, they act as a moderator. For instance, in [26], a chatbot was developed to increase engagement and collaboration in discussion among students. Educational agents have also been studied across a range of topics, such as mathematics [3], medicine [17], and computer science [24]. All these agents teach factual knowledge. They therefore also encode domain knowledge, albeit in different ways. For instance, in [3], the authors used the language AIML (Artificial Intelligence Markup Language) to encode the mathematical knowledge. In [24], the agent's knowledge which was about SQL queries was represented as a list of constraints written by SQL experts.

Furthermore, a number of adaptive environments exist that make use of technologies for understanding text-based argumentation; not all for educational purposes. In non-educational settings, agents have been studied that act as a discussion partner [22,27] or a persuader [6]. As a discussion partner for argumentation, the goal of the agent is only selecting or generating the most relevant argument in order to have a coherent argumentative dialogue. For instance, in [22], the goal of the agent is to keep the conversation alive by generating an argument or selecting the best argument from a pre-defined list. In [27], an agent is presented that focuses on keeping the conversation meaningful so long as the users want to continue. These agents do not give feedback in an educational sense to user statements within the conversation. As a persuader, the goal of agents is to persuade users regarding controversial topics. In [6], the authors were interested in persuading the user to accept a conversational agent's stance about meat consumption. They tried to maximise the chance of persuasion by selecting the best argument or counterargument from the agent's knowledge base.

In educational settings, the goal is to teach argumentation. In [31], the authors have created an intelligent tutoring system that gives feedback to students on an argumentative peer review. The students were asked to read a discussion between two teachers about a specific topic and then write a review about the discussion. The system is turn-based in the sense that the users write a review and then receive feedback. The students can then improve the review and receive further feedback. The feedback and hints include argumentation theory, highlighting argumentative components, an individual summarising feedback based on the number of automatically identified argumentative components, and last but not least, a readability score which is calculated based on [14]. In [2], the authors have created four different interfaces that help students to make further revisions to their argumentative writings. The difference between interfaces was in the unit span of revision analysis (sentence and sub-sentence) and the level of surface and content revisions. The surface revision contains the changes that are about grammar, fluency and organisational changes. However, the content revisions include meaningful textual changes such as claim, reasoning and rebuttal. The authors' main focus was on having an effective interface to help users to improve their essays. They found that the most effective interface was the interface that showed the details of the surface and content revisions at the sentence level.

At the time of writing, the above two are examples for adaptive computational systems that teach argumentation (e.g., [2,31]) that we know of. Both deal with longer argumentative texts, and the tutoring systems support learners in an iterative process of improving their writing, i.e. during the learning process, the learners write an argumentative text and then receive feedback by which they understand how to improve the text. Further, in the above two studies, the domain of argumentation is the same.

Adjacent to such research, our goal has been to develop an educational conversational agent that teaches a good argumentation structure within a conversation, rather than give feedback on an artefact developed outside the conversation (e.g., feedback on an argumentative essay written prior to the tutorial conversation). Naturally, argumentation, as given within a conversation, will be shorter and needs to be more compact than argumentation developed carefully over one or more pages in writing. Furthermore, we evaluate our intervention, the educational conversational agent, on two different argumentative domains in order to study whether the argument structure that the agent teaches can be transferred to a different domain of argumentation.

3 Conversational Agent

The conversational agent that we have developed acts as a tutor towards the student with the goal to convey knowledge about good argumentation by developing a good argument in a concrete example together with the student. Technically, we have implemented the agent using Bazaar framework [1][1].

The knowledge about what constitutes a good argument is based on Toulmin's model of arguments [29]. Based on this model, a good argument has three core components: a claim, evidence, and a warrant. The claim is an argument or assertion that states our position regarding a specific issue. The evidence is a piece of knowledge that supports the claim. The warrant interprets how the evidence proves the claim. This model has already been widely used in research in educational settings, e.g., to assess students' opinions [15], to evaluate students' essays [16], and in online discussions to support the consolidation of opinions [32].

At the beginning of the conversation, the agent asks a question that demands an argumentative answer. If the user's argument is missing one of the three core components (claim, warrant, evidence), the agent explains which elements it understands the argument to already have and which to be missing, and asks the user to complement the answer by adding the missing elements.

In the experiment described in this work, the agent asks questions of the type "*Is X intelligent or not? Why?*" X was replaced either by an animal (snakes, monkeys and sharks) or with an AI-enabled technology (Google search engine and self-driving cars). An example question asked to study participants therefore was "*Is a self-driving car intelligent or not? Why?*"

To identify which of the three core components are given in a user response, we used classifiers that were created and evaluated specifically for this type of question in our previous work [23]. The resulting classifiers achieve an accuracy of 0.91 for detecting whether a claim exists in a given argument, 0.89 for detecting whether the warrant exists in a given argument, and 0.83 for detecting whether evidence is given in the argument (ibid). While our previous work focused on classifier accuracy, the work presented here focuses on the effect of such a tutorial dialogue on learning Toulmin's argument structure.

Figure 1 shows one of the dialogues within our experiment. The introduction, greeting, and ending parts of the dialogue were removed. Figure 2 shows the complete flowchart of the agent. Note that the agent asks three times for each missing core component and gives repeatedly stronger and more direct hints to help users to fill the structural gap in their answers. If more than one component is missing, the agent prioritises the missing elements along the following sequence: Claim, warrant, and evidence. This means, that if all three components are missing, the agent will step-by-step scaffold the creation of a structurally complete argument.

[1] https://github.com/DANCEcollaborative/.

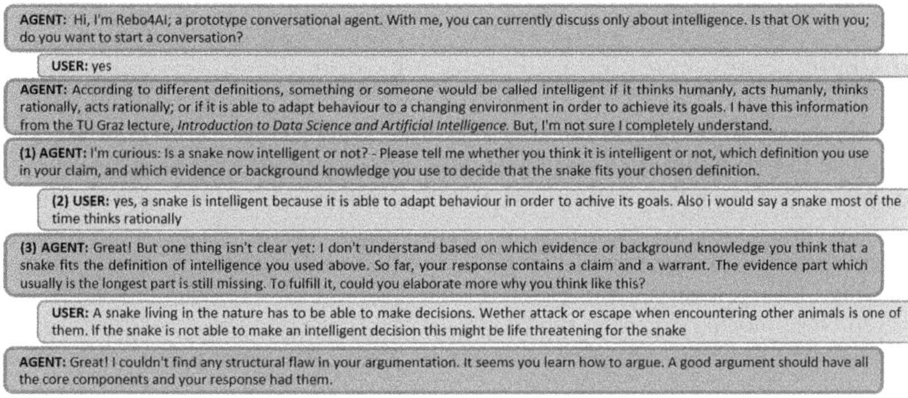

Fig. 1. A coherent conversation is taken from our study. (1): The agent asks its initial question. (2): the user answer is missing an element in the argumentation. (3): the agent identified the missing component and asked for it. Finally, the user completed the argumentation by adding evidence.

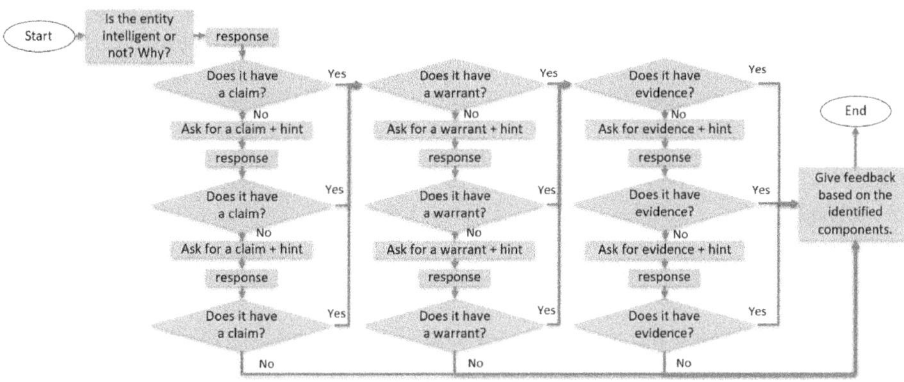

Fig. 2. The different states that the agent reaches based on user responses.

4 Research Questions

In this paper we ask and answer the following research questions, all with respect to the given experiment:

RQ1 - Classifier accuracy: How accurately do the used classifiers detect the existence of a claim, warrant and evidence respectively?

RQ2 - Conversation coherence: How coherent are the tutorial conversations?

RQ3 - Learning: Do users learn to structure arguments using the three core components of Toulmin's model of argument (claim, warrant, evidence) in the same argumentation domain as in the conversation with the agent?

RQ4 - Learning transfer: Can users apply the learned argument structure to a different domain of argumentation than is discussed in the conversation with the agent?

The questions are hierarchical in the sense that with each research question we are aiming to ascertain a specific quality of the agent and the user-agent interaction, and each quality is the foundation for the quality that we are assessing in the next question. For instance, if the classifiers that we used in the investigated agent is not reasonably accurate in the here presented experiment (RQ1), then it is highly unlikely that tutorial conversations are coherent (RQ2). If conversations overall were incoherent, then we would expect that this has a negative impact on whether users actually learn to argue well with the given agent (RQs 3 and 4). On the other hand, the different qualities do not constitute strictly necessary preconditions. For instance, we have designed the agent's dialogue structure in a way, that some classifier inaccuracy is covered by the way the agent phrases its responses.

The contribution of this paper towards literature lies in answering RQs 3 and 4 on whether a tutorial conversation leads to the learning of the taught argumentation structure (Toulmin's model). This complements existing work on computational environments for teaching argumentation in longer texts (e.g., [2,31]). Both the underlying computational methods needed to understand and feedback arguments are different, due to different lengths and styles of argumentation in essays and in conversations.

5 Method

5.1 Procedure

In order to answer the above research questions, we conducted a between-subjects experiment with two groups (treatment and control group). The experiment was a voluntary assignment set in a university lecture, named "Introduction to data science and artificial intelligence", at the Technical University of Graz. Before conducting the experiment, all materials were piloted within our research team.

The experiment contains three tasks. The overall procedure is shown in Fig. 3. At the beginning of the experiment, all participants receive information about the tasks, and necessary learning materials that explain Toulmin's model of argument and that give foundational information from the two different domains of argumentation used in the experiment tasks. These two domains of argumentation are: What is intelligence? Related learning materials describe different definitions of intelligence. We call this domain of argumentation the "intelligence domain"; it is used in Tasks 1 and 2. The second domain of argumentation is ethics, and related learning materials are about utilitarian and deontological ethics. We call this domain of argumentation the "ethics domain"; it is used in Task 3. The information about the tasks as well as learning materials remained accessible to study participants throughout the experiment.

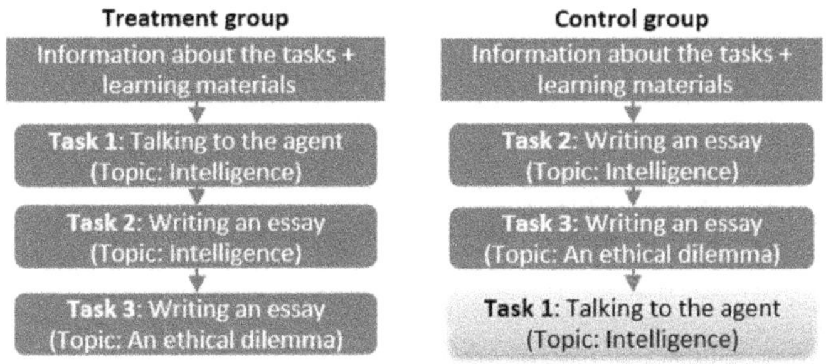

Fig. 3. The between-subjects study design.

The treatment group first exercises using Toulmin's argument structure in the intelligence domain (Task 1) with the agent. Then, the treatment group is given Task 2, which is also in the intelligence domain. Here the users simply answer the argumentative question without receiving feedback. Finally, the treatment group answers an argumentative question in the ethical domain (Task 3).

The control group starts with Tasks 2 and then Task 3. Note that the control group finishes with Task 1, which contains the intervention. This task was included for the control group as the experiment was an optional assignment in a university course, so that all students who decided to participate in the experiment would have the opportunity to talk to the conversational agent, and such that all students would have three argumentative tasks. The control group's performance on Task 1 was not used for the purpose of this study.

The data collected from Task 1 done by the treatment group answers RQs 1 and 2. The comparison of the performance on Task 2 between the treatment and control group answers RQ3 on whether the conversation with our tutorial agent helps learners to learn Toulmin's argument structure in the same domain of argumentation. The comparison of the performance on Task 3 between the treatment and the control group answers RQ4 on whether learners can transfer the learned argument structure to a different domain of argumentation.

5.2 Materials: Argumentation Topics and Tasks

Tasks 1 and 2 are about intelligence. In these tasks, the participants were asked to decide "*Is X intelligent? Why?*". X was substituted either with a type of animal or by a (type of) AI-enabled technology. For animal categories we used: sharks, eagles, monkeys, and snakes. For the AI-enabled technologies, we used: the Google search engine and self-driving cars. The two categories "animal" and "AI-enabled technology" are ontologically different, such that we can expect different lines of argumentation regarding their intelligence. In both categories, one can argue for both intelligence and non-intelligence of the entities, depending on the underlying definition of intelligence.

In Task 3, the participants were confronted with the trolley problem. By this we mean, the participants need to answer this: *There is a trolley coming down the tracks and ahead, there are five people tied to the tracks and are unable to move. The trolley will continue coming and will kill the five people. There is nothing you can do to rescue the five people EXCEPT that there is a lever. If you pull the lever, the train will be directed to another track, which has ONE person tied to it. What do you do? Please, justify your decision.*

The choice of argumentation topics has been made such that the questions are structurally similar: By relying on different definitions, in one case of intelligence, in the other about what constitutes ethical behaviour, one can argue always for both types of answers (intelligent yes/no; pull the lever yes/no).

5.3 Participants

Study participants were recruited in an introductory university lecture, named "Introduction to data science and artificial intelligence", at the Technical University of Graz. The experiment was contextualised in the lecture as an optional bonus task for which points were received based on the most complete argument given in any of the three tasks. Overall 95 students participated in the experiment fully, i.e. such that they completed all three tasks in the treatment group or at least Tasks 2 and 3 in the control group. We randomly and equally split all the students into two groups. However, because of technical problems we had to exclude some participants who could not finish all the tasks. Finally, 42 participants were in the treatment group and 53 in the control group.

5.4 Data Annotation

In all tasks, we annotated the user statements sentence by sentence. By statements we mean: Every user response of the treatment group to an argumentative question of the conversational agent in Task 1 (depending on into which branches of the adaptive dialogue structure the user enters this could be more than once in a single conversation) and responses to the argumentative question given in Tasks 2 and 3. All the sentences have been annotated by four coders (including the first author), such that for each of them, we express which of the three core components of Toulmin's model (claim, warrant, evidence) is contained. Therefore, for each component, a binary value was defined to indicate the existence of the component. Then we called a sentence argumentative if it contains at least one of the core components. Furthermore, for Task 1, we annotated the conversations of the treatment group based on coherence. Similar to the core components, a binary value was defined to show whether a conversation is coherent or not.

Before starting the annotating process, the first author created a codebook in which the details about identifying the core components of Toulmin's model were explained. The annotation process was done in three rounds. In the first round, we randomly selected 25% of data that was independently annotated by all raters based on the codebook. The goal of this round was to reach a shared agreement on codes, and clarify and update the codebook where necessary.

In the second round, we randomly selected another 25% and assigned them to all four annotators. We computed inter-rater reliability and discussed the remaining differences in order to further improve the codebook and shared agreement.

For the 50% of data, annotated in the first two rounds, we had four ratings for each statement. Where we could not reach an agreement, we selected the final annotation based on the majority.

In the third round, we divided the rest of the data among all annotators for coding based on the codebook.

Overall, the data as analysed for the purpose of this paper therefore contains 51 single responses written by the treatment group in Task 1, 904 sentences written by both groups in Task 2, and 600 sentences written by both groups in Task 3. The dataset is published on Zenodo[2]. Doccano [25] was used for annotating the data.

5.5 Inter-rater Agreement

We used Fleiss kappa [13] to measure agreement among the coders. Based on [21], the values below 0 are understood as a poor agreement, between 0 and 0.20 as slight, between 0.21 and 0.4 as fair, between 0.41 and 0.6 as moderate, between 0.61 and 0.80 as substantial, and above 0.80 as almost perfect inter-rater reliability. However, we also note that not all the natural language processing tasks are not the same and we cannot define a specific threshold for all computational linguistic tasks [5].

In Tasks 1 and 2 which were about intelligence, the κ value for argumentative sentences was 0.69. We call a sentence argumentative if it contains at least one of the core components. The κ value for the claim, warrant and evidence were 0.90, 0.80 and 0.77 respectively. In Task 3, which was about an ethical dilemma, we achieved moderate inter-rater reliability for argumentative sentences, $\kappa = 0.58$. There was a substantial agreement for the claim ($\kappa = 0.77$). However, the warrant ($\kappa = 0.36$) and evidence ($\kappa = 0.42$) components turned out to be not easily distinguishable [11,30]. We, therefore, did not use warrant and evidence annotations for comparing the groups on Task 3. Additionally, in Task 1, with respect to the coherence coding, we reached a significant agreement ($\kappa = 0.83$).

5.6 Data Analysis

RQ1 (classifier accuracy) and RQ2 (coherence of tutorial conversations) in principle assess the qualities of the conversational agent. For assessing classifier performance (RQ1) in Task 1, we used the classifiers trained in our previous work [23]. For each core component, a separate classifier was trained. We report the macro-average F1 score for each classifier over the 51 argumentative statements from Task 1 of the treatment group. The macro-average F1 score indicates the average of F1 scores of all classes. For assessing the coherence of tutorial conversations (RQ2), we report the number of coherent conversations in Task 1 of the treatment group expressed as an absolute number and as the ratio of all 42 conversations (Sect. 5.4).

---

[2] https://doi.org/10.5281/zenodo.6627040.

RQs 3 and 4 ask whether participants in the treatment group have learned Toulmin's argument structure. As the conversational agent in Task 1 specifically points out missing components from Toulmin's model, we hypothesised that students would learn to include all elements in the subsequent Tasks 2 and 3. In other words, we expect the treatment group to significantly more often use claims, warrants or evidence in their responses to questions in Tasks 2 and 3.

In order to measure this, we define that a sentence is argumentative if it contains at least one of the core components (a claim, warrant or evidence). We further define the ratio of argumentative sentences in the response to the question in either Task 2 or 3 to be the number of argumentative sentences in the user response divided by the overall number of sentences in a response. Using these definitions, we compare the treatment and the control group with a t-test on the ratio of argumentative sentences in Tasks 2 and 3. Additionally, to get more insights into the results, we do the same analysis for each Toulmin's core component separately. This means that we compare the treatment and the control group with a t-test on the ratio of sentences that contain a claim, warrant or evidence respectively. For RQ 4, which means to compare responses on Task 3, we only do this analysis for the claim component, since we did not reach sufficient inter-rater reliability for the warrant and evidence component (see Sect. 5.5).

6 Results

Regarding *RQ1 (classifier accuracy)*, we evaluate the performance of the classifiers using the macro-average F1 score based on data from Task 1. The macro-average F1 scores of the classifiers for detecting the existence of claims, warrants and evidence are 0.72, 0.91 and 0.77 respectively. These values are typically understood as very good classifier performance. Further, they are comparable to the classifiers' performance on a dataset collected outside the conversational agent environment in earlier own work [23], where the respective values were 0.77, 0.88 and 0.71. Inaccuracy is covered by the way the agent phrases its responses.

Regarding *RQ2 (conversation coherence)*, we find that 85% (36 out of 42) of dialogues are coherent. This is a bit lower but comparable with the proportion of coherent conversations in related work on a reflective conversational agent [34], in which 97% (149 out of 153) of conversations were coherent.

Regarding *RQ3 (learning the argument structure, measured by a task within the same argumentation domain)*, we find that the treatment group ($N = 42$, $M = 0.83$, $SD = 0.18$) compared to the control group ($N = 53$, $M = 0.76$, $SD = 0.21$) has a significantly higher percentage of argumentative sentences in Task 2, $t(94) = 1.73$, $p = 0.042$ (see Table 1). To have more insight into this result, we compared the two groups in a more fine-granular manner per core component (claim, warrant, evidence). The only significant result is related to the claim component. The treatment group ($M = 0.26$, $SD = 0.25$) compared to the control group ($M = 0.16$, $SD = 0.1$) has a significantly higher percentage of sentences with a claim in their responses, $t(94) = 2.45$, $p = 0.007$. Overall, the results show that the treatment group has learned Toulmin's argument structure, but the effect is mainly visible on one of three argument elements, namely the claim.

Table 1. The ratio of argumentative sentences to all sentences based on each core component in Tasks 2 and 3.

Group	# of sentences	% of arg. sentences	% of sent. with a claim	% of sent. with a warrant	% of sent. with evidence
Task 2					
Treatment	358	**0.762**	**0.159**	**0.315**	**0.497**
Control	546	0.697	0.130	0.238	0.468
Task 3					
Treatment	252	**0.662**	**0.297**	–	–
Control	348	0.494	0.221	–	–

Regarding *RQ4 (learning transfer, measured by a task within the same argumentation domain)*, we again compared the responses of both groups based on the proportion of argumentative sentences. The treatment group's responses ($M = 0.68$, $SD = 0.25$) compared to the control group's responses ($M = 0.59$, $SD = 0.27$) has a significantly higher ratio of argumentative sentences, $t(94) = 1.7$, $p = 0.045$. Because of the low inter-rater reliability on Task 3 for the components warrant and evidence, we only did the more fine-granular analysis for the component "claim". Different than for RQ3, however, the treatment group's responses do not contain a higher ratio of sentences with a claim than the control group's responses. Overall, these results show that the participants of the treatment group have transferred Toulmin's argument structure also to a new argumentation domain. Our results cannot be used to make a more fine-granular statement that distinguishes between the effect in terms of single core components.

Further, we see that in both Task 2 and Task 3, the control group wrote more sentences. Proportionally more of them were non-argumentative, however, i.e. not actually needed for the argument. In other words, the control group had more difficulties coming to the point and justifying it. Table 1 summarises the results for both RQ3 and RQ4.

7 Discussion

In summary, participants in the treatment group, who had an adaptive-tutoring conversation with the conversational agent (Task 1), wrote significantly more argumentative sentences, both in the same domain of argumentation (Task 2) in which the teaching took place, and in a different domain of argumentation (Task 3). This is encouraging, as it shows the feasibility of using scalable tools such as a conversational agent to teach the basics of argumentation, as would be useful based on the understanding of the importance of argumentation in many areas of life. Our study further shows that it is possible to conduct a coherent conversation with a conversational tutorial agent. This is an important indicator of user experience and hence teaching quality.

We make two additional observations that highlight that future research is needed: For Task 2, at a fine-granular level, the treatment group and control group differed statistically significantly only in terms of the claim component. We interpreted this in the sense that the claim, in this task, was the easiest argumentative element. However, in Task 3, the difference between the proportion of sentences that contained claims was not significant. This could be due to the nature of the question, which was about an ethical dilemma situation in which at least one person would die and making one final decision is challenging. Further, we have noticed low inter-rater reliability in differentiating between warrant and evidence in Task 3. Overall, this leads us to suspect that the ethical dilemma is - in terms of Toulmin's structure of argument - substantially different from the discussion of which type of thing to consider intelligent and which not. In order to be able to effectively use Toulmin's model as a structure for a good argument in computational environments that teach argumentation - because such environments are in many ways more strictly bound to a pre-defined structure than human teachers - it will be necessary to develop systematic knowledge about what kinds of arguments Toulmin's model of argument is suitable for.

Secondly, our study illustrates that the tutorial conversation had the desired positive effect when compared with no intervention. However, our study cannot make comparative statements towards other interventions, amongst them technically simpler ones like asking study participants to re-work their answers after re-reading educational material about Toulmin's argument structure (comparable to the time spent on Task 1). Further experiments are needed to make statements about the efficiency of the agent in comparison to other interventions.

Finally, there is a range of wider-reaching directions for exciting future research. For instance, structural argument assessment, as is done by the conversational agent studied in this paper, could be complemented by content-wise argument assessment. For this, additional approaches from argument mining such as clustering of arguments could be useful [8]. Such content-based assessment of arguments is the basis for further teaching strategies, such as teaching by giving counter-arguments.

8 Conclusion

We presented a conversational agent that teaches Toulmin's model of argument via an argumentative task. By conducting a between-subjects experiment, we showed that study participants learned what they should - Toulmin's model of argument - and could apply it both in the same (Task 2) and in a new domain of argumentation (Task 3). This demonstrates the fundamental possibility that an AI-enabled tool can teach a structure for argumentation, which learners can then transfer to a setting outside the tutoring conversation as well as to a different argumentation domain. Our work advances teaching argumentation in education as follows: This work indicates that Toulmin's model is a suitable structure to computationally analyse relatively short argumentation, as found in conversations. This work also constitutes one of the still few examples of an educational conversational agent that teaches a skill (argumentation), rather than facts.

Acknowledgements. This work was supported by the "DDAI" COMET Module within the COMET—Competence Centers for Excellent Technologies Program, funded by the Austrian Federal Ministry (BMK and BMDW), the Austrian Research Promotion Agency (FFG), the province of Styria (SFG) and partners from industry and academia. The COMET Program is managed by FFG.

References

1. Adamson, D., Dyke, G., Jang, H., Rosé, C.P.: Towards an agile approach to adapting dynamic collaboration support to student needs. Int. J. Artif. Intell. Educ. **24**(1), 92–124 (2014)
2. Afrin, T., Kashefi, O., Olshefski, C., Litman, D., Hwa, R., Godley, A.: Effective interfaces for student-driven revision sessions for argumentative writing. In: Proceedings of the CHI, pp. 1–13 (2021)
3. Aguiar, E.V.B., Tarouco, L.M.R., Reategui, E.: Supporting problem-solving in Mathematics with a conversational agent capable of representing gifted students' knowledge. In: IEEE 47th HICSS, pp. 130–137. IEEE (2014)
4. Aleven, V., McLaughlin, E. A., Glenn, R. A., Koedinger, K.R.: Instruction based on adaptive learning technologies (2017)
5. Artstein, R., Poesio, M.: Inter-coder agreement for computational linguistics. Comput. Linguist. **34**(4), 555–596 (2008)
6. Chalaguine, L.A., Hunter, A.: A persuasive chatbot using a crowd-sourced argument graph and concerns. Front. AI Appl. **326**, 9–20 (2020)
7. Dawson, V.M., Venville, G.: Teaching strategies for developing students' argumentation skills about socioscientific issues in high school genetics. Res. Sci. Educ. **40**(2), 133–148 (2010). https://doi.org/10.1007/s11165-008-9104-y
8. Daxenberger, J., Schiller, B., Stahlhut, C., Kaiser, E., Gurevych, I.: ArgumenText: argument classification and clustering in a generalized search scenario. Datenbank-Spektr. **20**(2), 115–121 (2020)
9. Duschl, R.A., Osborne, J.: Supporting and promoting argumentation discourse in science education. Stud. Sci. Educ. **38**(1), 39–72 (2002). https://doi.org/10.1080/03057260208560187. Routledge
10. Erduran, S.: Promoting ideas, evidence and argument in initial science teacher training. Sch. Sci. Rev. **87**(321), 45 (2006)
11. Erduran, S.: Methodological foundations in the study of argumentation in science classrooms. In: Erduran, S., Jiménez-Aleixandre, M.P. (eds.) Argumentation in Science Education. Science & Technology Education Library, vol. 35, pp. 47–69. Springer, Dordrecht (2007). https://doi.org/10.1007/978-1-4020-6670-2_3
12. Erduran, S., Ardac, D., Yakmaci-Guzel, B.: Learning to teach argumentation: case studies of pre-service secondary science teachers. Eur. J. Math. Sci. Technol. Educ. **2**(2), 1–14 (2006)
13. Fleiss, J.L.: Measuring nominal scale agreement among many raters. Psychol. Bull. **76**(5), 378 (1971)
14. Flesch, R.: Marks of readable style: a study in adult education, no. 897. Teachers College Contributions to Education (1943)
15. Georgiou, M., Mavrikaki, E., Halkia, K., Papassideri, I.: Investigating the impact of the duration of engagement in socioscientific issues in developing Greek students' argumentation and informal reasoning skills. Am. J. Educ. Res. **8**(1), 16–23 (2020)
16. Habernal, I., Gurevych, I.: Argumentation mining in user-generated web discourse. Comput. Linguist. **43**(1), 125–179 (2017)

17. Jagtap, R., Phulare, K., Kurhade, M., Gawande, K.S.: Healthcare conversational chatbot for medical diagnosis. In: Handbook of Research on Engineering, Business, and Healthcare Applications of Data Science, pp. 401–415. IGI Global (2021)
18. Kelly, T., Weaver, R.: The goal structuring notation-a safety argument notation. In: Proceedings of the Dependable Systems and Networks Workshop on Assurance Cases, p. 6. Citeseer (2004)
19. Kuhn, D.: Thinking as argument. Harv. Educ. Rev. **62**(2), 155–179 (1992)
20. Kuhn, D.: Science as argument: implications for teaching and learning scientific thinking. Sci. Educ. **77**(3), 319–337 (1993)
21. Landis, J.R., Koch, G.G.: The measurement of observer agreement for categorical data. Biometrics **33**(1), 159–174 (1977)
22. Le, D.T., Nguyen, C.T., Nguyen, K.A.: Dave the debater: a retrieval-based and generative argumentative dialogue agent, pp. 121–130 (2018)
23. Mirzababaei, B., Pammer-Schindler, V.: Developing a conversational agent's capability to identify structural wrongness in arguments based on Toulmin's model of arguments. Front. Artif. Intell. **4** (2021). https://doi.org/10.3389/frai.2021.645516. https://www.frontiersin.org/articles/10.3389/frai.2021.645516. ISSN 2624-8212
24. Mitrovic, A.: An intelligent SQL tutor on the web. Int. J. Artif. Intell. Educ. **13**(2–4), 173–197 (2003)
25. Nakayama, H., Kubo, T., Kamura, J., Taniguchi, Y., Liang, X.: Doccano: text annotation tool for human (2018)
26. Neto, A.J.M., Fernandes, M.A.: Chatbot and conversational analysis to promote collaborative learning in distance education. In: 2019 IEEE 19th International Conference on Advanced Learning Technologies, vol. 2161, pp. 324–326. IEEE (2019)
27. Rakshit, G., Bowden, K.K., Reed, L., Misra, A., Walker, M.: Debbie, the debate bot of the future. In: Eskenazi, M., Devillers, L., Mariani, J. (eds.) Advanced Social Interaction with Agents. LNEE, vol. 510, pp. 45–52. Springer, Cham (2019). https://doi.org/10.1007/978-3-319-92108-2_5
28. Suleman, R.M., Mizoguchi, R., Ikeda, M.: A new perspective of negotiation-based dialog to enhance metacognitive skills in the context of open learner models. Int. J. Artif. Intell. Educ. **26**(4), 1069–1115 (2016)
29. Toulmin, S.E.: The Uses of Argument. Cambridge University Press, Cambridge (2003)
30. Van Eemeren, F.H., Grootendorst, R., Kruiger, T.: Handbook of Argumentation Theory: A Critical Survey of Classical Backgrounds and Modern Studies, vol. 7. De Gruyter Mouton (2019)
31. Wambsganss, T., Kueng, T., Soellner, M., Leimeister, J.M.: ArgueTutor: an adaptive dialog-based learning system for argumentation skills. In: Proceedings of the CHI, pp. 1–13 (2021)
32. Wang, W., Arya, D., Novielli, N., Cheng, J., Guo, J.L.: ArguLens: anatomy of community opinions on usability issues using argumentation models. In: Proceedings of the ACM 2020, vol. 20, pp. 1–14 (2020)
33. Winkler, R., Söllner, M., Leimeister, J.M.: Enhancing problem-solving skills with smart personal assistant technology. Comput. Educ. **165**, 104148 (2021)
34. Wolfbauer, I., Pammer-Schindler, V., Rosé, C.: Rebo junior: analysis of dialogue structure quality for a reflection guidance chatbot. In: Proceedings of the EC-TEL 15th, pp. 14–18 (2020)

Video Segmentation and Characterisation to Support Learning

Abrar Mohammed(✉) and Vania Dimitrova(✉)

School of Computing, University of Leeds, Leeds, UK
{a.mohammed1,v.g.dimitrova}@leeds.ac.uk

Abstract. The predominance of using videos for learning has become a phenomenon for generations to come. This leads to a prevalence of videos generating and using open learning platforms. However, learners may not be able to detect the main points in the video and relate them to the domain for their study. This can hinder the effectiveness of using videos for learning. To address these challenges, our research aims to develop automatic ways to segment videos, characterise them and finalise the segmentation work by aggregating adjacent segments within a video with the same focus of domain topic(s) or topic-concept(s). We present a framework for automated video segmenting and characterising to support learning (VISC-L). We assume that the domain we are processing videos from has been computationally presented (via ontology). We are using the Deep learning BERT-BASE-Uncased model with a binary classifier to identify the focus topic of each segment. Then we use a semantic tagging algorithm to identify the focus concept within the topic. The adjacent segments within a video with the same focus topic/concept are aggregated to generate the final characterised video segments. We have evaluated the usefulness of watching the identified segments and characterisations compared with video segmentation provided by Google.

Keywords: Video-based learning · Video transcript · Text analytics · Domain ontology · Video characterisation · Video aggregation

1 Introduction and Related Work

The use of videos for learning has increased rapidly. It offers the flexibility of having visual and auditory channels that make it easier for learners to get the information and to support their learning [11,14]. There is a massive amount of freely available videos that learners have access to. Not only does learning from such videos take up a significant amount of time for watching, but, crucially, it can be hard for the learners to identify key points in the videos and link these points to the study domain [3,21].

Manual Video Segmentation and Characterisation. A widely used approach for video segmentation and characterisation is manual annotation. A common technique when using videos for learning is note-taking which makes a reference of important points mentioned within a segment in a video [10]. This

I. Hilliger et al. (Eds.): EC-TEL 2022, LNCS 13450, pp. 229–242, 2022.
https://doi.org/10.1007/978-3-031-16290-9_17

allows learners to identify relevant video segments and to indicate key points in these segments. However, such video annotation requires manual effort. In [5], segmenting videos has been done by teachers who provide the sections in the videos related to specific courses. In order to improve learner engagement and to aid the digesting of the learning material, teachers in [22] characterise learning videos by highlighting the contents with a phrase or a keyword or by adding questions. While such characterisation is closely linked to the learning goals set by the teachers, it is subjective and does not scale across different domains.

Characterising videos can also be done by learners. For instance, teachers have asked learners to annotate videos and test the effect of it on their learning [16]. Though learner annotation can improve engagement with videos, it is dependent on learner engagement (e.g. high self-efficacy learners engage better) and their prior knowledge (e.g. learners may not be able to see key points).

Automatic Segmentation and Characterisation. Recent works have developed approaches for automating the process of video segmentation. This falls into two categories - using learner interactions and using video content. In [17] learners' comments while watching videos are aggregated to identify "high attention intervals" which refer to key points noted by learners. These intervals are used to facilitate interaction with videos by offering an interactive visualisation interface. While using learner interaction data to segment and characterise videos which can give the learners reactions and perspective, the segmentation depends on the learner engagement and learners may not appropriately capture the key points in the videos. Alternative approaches focusing on the video content are proposed. To detect teaching practices (presenting, guiding, administration) in recorded lessons of trainee teachers, acoustic features from the audio and text feature from the transcripts are used in [21]. Machine learning models, trained by using annotations by expert observers, are dependent on the availability of previously annotated segments which may not always be practical.

Recent video segmentation approaches based on video content utilise state-of-the-art tools in natural language processing and tap into the availability of knowledge models. MOOC video lectures were automatically segmented in [6] by using a neural network over adjacent sentences; the neural network was trained on Wikipedia pages. To characterise the video segments, topics are extracted from slide titles. In [7], topical segmentation of lecture videos is performed by using a domain knowledge graph. A BERT model is used to compute the semantic similarity between different concepts in the video. [4] uses different text sources (transcript, slide text, hand written text on whiteboards) to segment and annotate videos. The segmentation is based on the transition between slides, while the annotation uses Wikidata and DBPedia to find the entity type and to compute semantic similarity between tokens in the video segment's text. All existing approaches have evaluated only the technical performance of their segmentation algorithms; their usefulness to aid learning has not been assessed.

In this paper, we address the following research question:

How to automatically segment and characterise videos to support learning?

We present a generic ontology-underpinned framework, called VISC-L, which uses video transcripts to segment, characterise and link videos to the domain knowledge covered in the segments. Similarly to the last approaches, we use existing knowledge models, in the form of a domain ontology, to identify the domain concepts as well as use the ontology hierarchy and a language model based on BERT to identify focus topics and concepts for each video segment. Our work has a key difference from previous approaches. While none of them assesses the effect on learning, we provide here an evaluation study with users to examine the effect of the segmentation and characterisation in a learning context. We compare with a state-of-the-art video segmentation and characterisation interface that is available for YouTube videos[1].

The main contributions of the work presented here is: (a) a novel framework for segmenting and characterising videos by using video transcripts and linking them to domain concepts; (b) application of the framework in a representative learning domain (presentation skills); (c) evaluating the usefulness of video segmentation and characterisation for learning and drawing wider implications for adoption. The work is part of broader research that explores how to generate video narratives to support learning by linking video segments to help learners to identify and link key points in videos.

The paper is organised as follows. Section 2 outlines the VISC-L framework, and Sect. 3 presents how VISC-L is applied in the Presentation Skill domain. A user evaluation study is presented in Sect. 4, and Sect. 5 is a conclusion.

2 Framework for Video Segmentation and Characterisation for Learning (VISC-L)

The proposed framework for Video Segmentation and Characterisation for Learning (VISC-L) is presented in Fig. 1. It includes three main steps: selecting initial segments, characterising those segments, and aggregating the segments based on common domain topics.

Input. VISC-L is based on two assumptions. Firstly, it is assumed that the **video transcript** relates to the domain which will be learned (e.g. the videos can be lectures/tutorials/conversations linked to a specific topic). Hence, the text in the video transcripts is taken as an input. The second assumption is that there is a **domain ontology** $\Omega = \{C, H\}$ which includes the relevant domain concepts C $\neq \phi$ linked in a concept hierarchy H. Available ontologies - The Linked Open Data Cloud:[2] can be used or the ontology can be developed with domain experts. The later is used in this work. We use $c_i \subset c_j$ to denote that c_i is a subclass of c_j. The top level concepts in the concept hierarchy define the main domain topics $\{T_1, ..., T_m\}$. In order to identify the main topics in the video transcripts, as part of the characterisation step (see below), **training data** with domain topics as labels are needed. This can either be created with expert annotators or collected from past user interactions (the later is followed in the application of VISC-L presented in the next section).

[1] Offered by Google, produced by Google Video AI https://cloud.google.com/video-intelligence/.

[2] The Linked Open Data Cloud https://lod-cloud.net/.

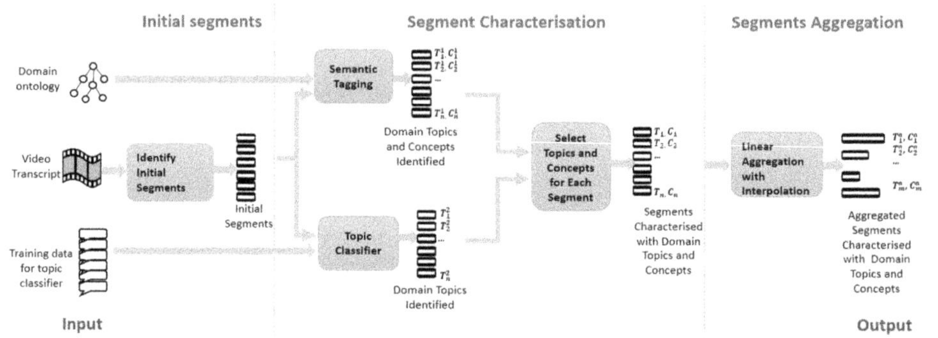

Fig. 1. Video segments characterisation and aggregation framework. Notice that T means a set of focus topics and C means a set of focus concepts within the focus topics, e.g. T_1C_1 means there is a focus concept C_1 in the focus topic T_1.

Output. The output of VISC-L is a set of aggregated video segments with a start and end time in the corresponding video. Each aggregated video segment i is characterised with a set of domain focus topics T_i^a (top concepts in Ω) and a set of concepts C_i^a from the focus topics which are mentioned in the transcript of the video segment (for every c_i from C_i^a, $c_i \subset T_i^a$).

Initial Segments. Our video segmentation approach is inspired by text-tilling in text summarisation [12] - starting with smaller units (e.g. sentences) and aggregating them to get larger coherent units (e.g. paragraphs). Hence, we include an initial segmentation step where the video transcripts are cut into small segments that are used as a starting point for aggregation. Initial segments can be done by using a certain number of text lines (e.g. the approach presented in the next section) or by using pre-defined segments (e.g. high attention intervals from past interactions [18]).

Segment Characterisation. In order to aggregate the initial segments, we need to identify what domain content is presented in each segment. This is done during the segment characterisation step which links each video segment i with a set of focus topics T_i and a set of concepts C_i. To do so, we propose using two algorithms: semantic tagging and topic classification.

The first algorithm is **semantic tagging** which was developed in our previous work [18]. This algorithm links each video segment to focus topics and concepts by mapping the terms from the ontology to the text in the video transcript. It first pre-processes the transcript[3], including: tokenise the transcript, clean it from stop words and punctuation, select nouns and noun phrases and match the ontology terms to the noun phrases. If there is a match, the ontology concept c_i will be identified (tagged to the text), noting also the path to reach a top level concept (i.e. linking to a focus topic T; $c_i \subset T$). As a result, each segment i is linked to a set of focus topics and their corresponding concepts;

[3] We have used Natural Language Tool Kit (NLTK) https://www.nltk.org/.

we denote this as $<T_i^1, C_i^1>$ (where (see footnote 1) indicates that this is an output from the first segment characterisation algorithm). A key challenge for this algorithm is word sense disambiguation. This is not that prominent with carefully selected videos. However, if the videos are selected automatically from open social spaces, there will be a high risk of word sense ambiguity. Hence, we need to disambiguate the topics based on the context, which is done with the second algorithm.

The second algorithm is a **topic classifier** which identifies a domain topic based on the context of that topic. Following the latest development in natural language processing, we use Bidirectional Encoder Representations from Transformers (BERT) [8] as a topic classifier. BERT embeds pre-trained deep bidirectional representations from unlabeled text by jointly conditioning on both left and right context in all layers. Accordingly, it can be fine tuned with just one additional output layer to create state-of-the-art models for different language tasks, topic classification in this case. First, the BERT model is fine-tuned using training data with domain topic labels (which is part of the input for VISC-L). Then, the fine-tuned model is used as a classifier to link each segment i to its domain topics T_i^2 (where (see footnote 2) indicates that this is an output from the second segment characterisation algorithm).

The last step in segment characterisation is to **combine the outputs from both algorithms**. For each segment i, the outcomes from the two algorithms $<T_i^1, C_i^1>$ and T_i^2 are combined by intersecting the focus topics $T_i = T_i^1 \cap T_i^2$ and selecting the concepts C_i from C_i^1 that belong to T_i. Hence, each segment is characterised by $<T_i, C_i>$ (a set of focus topics T_i and their concepts C_i).

Segments Aggregation. Following the text-tilling approach [12], small segments will be aggregated into larger segments. To maintain the flow of information within adjacent segments, we have developed an aggregation algorithm based on thematic progression theory [2]. It states that a good written text should have a relation between theme, (the main clause), and rheme, ("the remainder of the message where the Theme is developed") [2]. Three patterns for coherent text are suggested: *Constant theme* (when the first theme in one sentence is carried on and used at the beginning of the second sentence); *Linear theme* (the important message in a rheme of one sentence is carried on into following clause as a theme in the second sentence), and *Split theme* (a development of a rheme with important information to be used as themes in subsequent clauses in the following sentence). Relating to video segments and using the characterisation, we associate the focus topic with the segment's theme and the focus concepts with the segment's rheme. We propose a **linear aggregation with an interpolation algorithm** (see Algorithm 1). The linear theme pattern was selected as the most appropriate, as it allows keeping a continuous focus topic and at the same time take into account the specific concepts within that topic. Some segments can be without characterisation which can be because the speaker is silent or is digressing from the domain. If we look strictly for adjacent segments, these *gap segments* which break the topic flow will lead to starting a new aggregate. To smoothen the aggregation, we use interpolation. If the segments before and after a *gap segment* have common focus concepts, it is assumed that the common concepts are spread across the three segments. Hence, the *gap segment* will be interpolated in the aggregated segment.

3 Application of VISC-L in a Presentation Skill Domain

3.1 Input and Initial Segments

Domain and Ontology. To apply VISC-L we have selected the Presentation Skill domain which represents a transferable skill that can assist learners in transmitting their message or to convince others with their ideas [9,15]. This domain is supported by a domain ontology designed by [1]. The main topics T in this ontology are Delivery, PresentationAttribute, Structure and Visual Aids. Each topic has its own concepts C and this domain ontology has 302 concepts.

Video Selection and Initial Segmentation. If there is no pre-selected set of videos related to the domain, the ontology can be used to collect videos from available social platforms (like YouTube). Following the concept hierarchy, a search schema can be developed, similarly to [19]. For example, using a combination of $<Domain, T_i, C_i,$ "*tutorial*"$>$ as search terms, videos with tutorials related to the topic T_i in the domain can be collected. We have implemented this search schema using the library youtube-search-python[4]. We have applied a time filter so that each video duration should be >3 min and selected the videos that associate with the YouTube generated transcript. As a result, we have collected 63 videos that have a corpus of 110594 tokens. Then, we applied the Initial segmentation step from VISC-L on the 63 collected video transcripts and generated 2382 segments.

Training Data for the Topic Classifier. To fine tune the BERT-BASE-Uncased model, we used the training data which we obtained from the six studies conducted on the [17] learning platform. The domain of the videos used in [17] is the Presentation skill domain where the students can write comments or rate other students' comments. The total number of participants who watched the videos was 38 and they wrote 2038 comments. These comments had been labelled by other students with the domain topics: Delivery, Structure and VisualAids; notice that the topic PresentationAttribute is missed from the labels- we have solved this issue in the semantic tagging step below.

Segment Characterisation. The characterisation of video segments includes two steps: semantic tagging and a topic classifier. With **Semantic tagging** we have applied the semantic tagging algorithm, as demonstrated in Sect. 2, which has two inputs: the transcript of the 2382 segments generated from the Initial segmentation step in VISC-L, and the ontology [1] of the Presentation skill domain. The transcript of each segment has been tokenized, cleaned and POSTAGed to get the resulted nouns and noun phrases to be semantically tagged to the

[4] https://pypi.org/project/youtube-search-python/.

Algorithm 1: VISC-L algorithm. The input is the list of the segments from the videos with their focus topic FT and concepts FC. We aggregate the segments from the same video

```
   Data: S = {s1, s2, .., sn}; n ≥ 0; s =< FT, FC > where
         FT, FC ≠ φ,CurrentSeg=φ,NextSeg=φ,PreviousAgg=False,AggList=[],Gap=φ, i = 0
   Result: AllAgg = {S1a, S2a, .., Sma}; m <> 0
 1 while i < n do
 2     CurrentSeg=Si;
 3     if PreviousAgg=False then
 4         NextSeg=Si+1; FocusC ← CurrentSeg ∩ NextSeg
 5         if FocusC <> φ then
 6             if Gap ≠ [] then
 7                 AggList ← CurrentSeg, Gap, NextSeg
 8             else
 9             AggList ← CurrentSeg, NextSeg;i ← i + 2; PreviousAgg = True
10         else
11         if Gap = [] then
12             Gap ← NextSeg; i ← i + 1; Go to Step 3 ;
13         else
14             AllAgg ← CurrentSeg;AggList, FocusC ← [];CurrentSeg= Gap; i ← i + 1;
                Go to step 3
15         end
16     else
17         if PreviousAgg=True then
18             FocusC ← CurrentSeg ∩ FocusC;
19             if FocusC <> φ then
20                 if Gap = [] then
21                     AggList ← CurrentSeg; i ← i + 1 ;
22                 else
23                     AllAgg ← CurrentSeg, Gap; Gap ← []; i ← i + 1;
24                 end
25             else
26             AllAgg ← AggList, CurrentSeg; AggList ← []; CurrentSeg= Gap;
27             Gap = [];FocusC = []; i ← i + 1; PreviousAgg=False;
28         else
29         end
30     end
31 end
32 if i = n then
33     CurrentSeg = Si ;FocusC ← CurrentSeg ∩ FocusC;
34     if FocusC <> φ then
35         if Gap = [] then
36             AggList ← CurrentSeg; AllAgg ← AggList; AggList = []
37         else
38             AggList ← CurrentSeg, Gap; Gap ← []; AllAgg ← AggList; AggList = []
39         end
40     else
41         if Gap = [] then
42             AllAgg ← AggList, CurrentSeg; AggList ← []
43         else
44             AllAgg ← AggList, Gap, CurrentSeg; AggList, Gap, FocusC ← [];
                PreviousAgg=False;
45         end
46     end
47 end
```

ontology terms to decide the focus topic/concept $<T_i^1, C_i^1>$. This algorithm also succeeds in noticing the topic, PresentationAttribute, and collect its concept. To overcome the issue of word sense ambiguity mentioned in Sect. 2 by identifying the tokens in the transcript that are contextually related to the domain, we need the topic classifier model.

The second step is the **Topic classifier**. To select the best Deep learning model to be considered as the VISC-L Topic classifier, we have conducted two experiments. First, we compared different pre-trained BERT models (Roberta Base [13], Distill Bert [20] and BERT-BASE-Uncased [8]) as topic classifiers. These models are widely used for topic modelling and semantic analysing tasks. After we fine-tuned the models with our training data, we passed the 2382 video segments generated from the initial segmentation step to the models to be classified with the domain topics. To choose the best model, we compared between their precision, recall and F1-score values. Hence, BERT-BASE-Uncased has been selected as it gives higher (precision, recall and F1-Score) results and is better to be used as a binary classifier as shown in Table 1.

To get the final segment characterisation, we run the step of **Combining the characterisation results** identified from the semantic tagging and the topic classifier. For instance, a segment i has two characterisations, one from the semantic tagging algorithm $<T_i^1, C_i^1>$ and one from the topic classifier model $<T_i^2>$. The final characterisation of the segment i is the result of combining the two characterisations: $<T_i, C_i> = <T_i^1, C_i^1> \cap <T_i^2>$. This means, the focus topic is the one identified in both characterisations. Notice that the topic *PresentationAttribute* can only be recognised by the semantic tagging algorithm as mentioned in Sect. 2.

Table 1. BERT-BASE-Uncased model as multiple and binary classifier result.

Topic	Multiple classifier			Binary classifier		
	Precision	Recall	F1-score	Precision	Recall	F1-score
Delivery	0.89	0.94	0.92	0.91	0.93	0.92
Structure	0.76	0.74	0.75	0.69	0.71	0.70
Visual Aids	0.97	0.85	0.91	1.00	0.87	0.93

Characterisation Outcome. The final characterisation result revealed that 1877 segments have been characterised with a focus topic(s) and concept(s). However, there are 505 segments with no characterisation. The average segment duration is 14 s with (STDV = 6) and the average number of focus topic(s)/concept(s) per segment is (1 and 2) respectively. According to the characterisation results, 62% of all segments focus only on one topic while 30% focus on two topics and 7% of all segments focus on three topics. The number and type of the focus topic(s) within the segments can inform the next step in our framework which is the aggregation of video segments. Additionally, the segments' characterisation can inform their usage for learning (useful for creating video-segment-narratives). For example, to get an in-depth focus of the concepts within a topic, the segments with one focus topic can be used. Whereas, to find the relationship between two topics, the segments with two focus topics can be helpful, e.g. 10% of segments (the higher percentile) focus on the topics Delivery and Structure together. The segments that focus on three topics could be used as introductory segments to the domain by mentioning most of its topics.

The characterisation results showed that more segments have the same focus topic which can be aggregated together to get longer segments with the same focus topic and concept. Before we commenced the aggregation step, we first evaluated the characterisation of the single segments.

Characterisation Evaluation. In order to evaluate the characterisation of the single segments, we have asked an external expert to asses the accuracy of the characterisation of 137 random segments taken from the 2382 segments that we have characterised from all the videos. The expert is a researcher who has some work done on the same domain of this work (Presentation skills). We provided the expert with the topics and concepts in the domain ontology with their hierarchy to be familiar with the nature of the video segments' characterisation. The expert has been asked to do the following: add new topics or concepts if it is thought to be missed from the characterisation, mark the assigned topic or concept to segment as wrong if they thought it was irrelevant or leave the characterisation if it was correct. The overall number of topics/concepts that were assessed was 345. By analysing the evaluation results, we found that the new suggested concepts from the evaluators either added to the ontology if it was relevant to the domain or ignored if it was irrelevant. To measure the agreement between the expert and our characterisation, we ran the Cohen Kappa formula. The agreement value we got from the formula was 0.91 which is 90%, proving a high agreement between our characterisation and the expert.

Linear Aggregation with Interpolation. We ran the third step of VISC-L on the characterised segments to aggregate them based on their focus topic/ concept. The input to the aggregation Algorithm 1 is the video segments with their final characterisation. The algorithm compares the adjacent segments $i, i{+}1$ within a video and checks their focus topic and concept $<T_i, C_i>, <T_{i+1}, C_{i+1}>$. It checks whether they intersect with each other and have some similar concept(s) $FocusC = <T_i, C_i> \cap <T_{i+1}, C_{i+1}>$. If $FocusC \neq \phi$ then these segments will be aggregated and their final characterisation will be $<T_i^a, C_i^a>$, which is the focus topic and concept of the aggregates. The duration of the aggregates starts from the beginning of the first segment and finishes at the end of the last segment in the aggregate. If $FocusC = \phi$, then the second segment $i+1$ will be a gap segment and the algorithm will check the intersect between the first and third segment $FocusC = <T_i, C_i> \cap <T_{i+2}, C_{i+2}>$. If $FocusC \neq \phi$ then the segment $i, i+1, i+2$ will be aggregated - this is the reason we call it aggregation with interpolation. Otherwise, if $FocusC = \phi$, the first segment i will be saved as a single segment and a new aggregation will start from the segment $i{+}1$ which will be considered as the first one. The aggregation result revealed that the number of the segments decreases to become 933 (where the original number was 2382).

This showed that many adjacent segments have the same focus topic and concept. This is proved with the increase in the percentage of the segments (67.7%) that focus on one topic and concept. Subsequently, the size of the new aggregates has been increased with an average duration of 36 s. Furthermore, the predominant topics, after aggregating the segments, are still the topics Delivery with (29.1% of the segments) and Structure with (20.6% of the segments). There is a decrease in the number of segments that focus on two topics (13%). Nevertheless, the topics Delivery and Structure stand out as the more correlated topics among other topics which highlighted that they are necessary to understand each other. On the other hand, the topic Presentation Attribute appears alongside other topics in the aggregates instead of being a unique focus topic. This indicates that this topic is better to be demonstrated by presenting its relationship with other topics.

4 User Study

To evaluate the usefulness of the characterised video segments to support learning, we have conducted a user study focusing on soft-skills (giving presentations).

4.1 Experimental Setup

Participants. 18 people (10 Male, 7 Female and 1 other) took place in the study; 16 PhD students from the University of Leeds and 2 from Industry. 13 participants were 18–29 years old and 5 participants were above 30 years. The training level is varied: 13 have some training, the rest either have a lot of training or received no training before. Their presentation experience is varied: 10 have a Medium level, 5 have either an experienced level or little experience. 12 participants are native English speakers. 10 participants watch YouTube videos every week for learning and every day for other purposes, whereas the rest use YouTube occasionally.

Materials and Procedure. 8 videos have been selected for the study, based on: their popularity, the duration of the video should be between >4 and <6 min so the study will not last for more than one hour. A survey (using Google Forms) was prepared to assess the learning effect, perceived usefulness, cognitive demand and usability, comparing the VISC-L and Google algorithm. The participants went through the following steps in the survey: 1. Read and accept the consent form, 2. Complete a short pre-study section to collect their profiles, 3. Watch several suggested video-segments with characterisation generated using one of the algorithms (VISC-L or Google), 4. Give feedback on the video-segments and the provided characterisation, 5. Provide a short video summary, 6. Give feedback on the usability and usefulness of the recommended video-segments for learning about giving presentations, Repeat [3–6] with segments generated by the other algorithm (Google or VISC-L).

The study was approved by the ethical committee of the Faculty of Engineering and Physical Sciences, University of Leeds.

Data Analysis. Due to the limited number of participants, when comparing the VISC-L and the Google algorithm with regard to learning effect, perceived usefulness, cognitive demand and usability, we use the non-parametric Mann Whitney U-test, there was no statistical significance at $p < 0.05$.

4.2 Results

To assess the **Learning effect** of watching the video segments, we compared the participants' domain terms mentioned in the pre-test with the new domain terms mentioned after watching the video segments generated by either VISC-L or the Google algorithms. During the pre-test, an average of 6 terms (STDV = 5.9) were mentioned by the participants. After watching VISC-L segments, the participants named on average 7 (STDV = 4.6) new terms, while after watching the Google segments, the participants named on average 7 (STDV = 4.8) new terms. With both algorithms (no significant difference), the video segments with characterisation led to identifying new domain terms.

Perceived usefulness comparison between the characterisation of VISC-L and Google considered whether participants managed to identify and link main points in the videos to the topics in the domain and to identify key points and focus on them. The results presented in Fig. 2-**A** showed that in general, the characterised segments were LIKELY to meet their goals. The participants preferred the characterisation generated by Google more because the language used was extracted directly from the transcript and was easy to recognise in the video, while VISC-L was referring to key domain concepts related to the transcript.

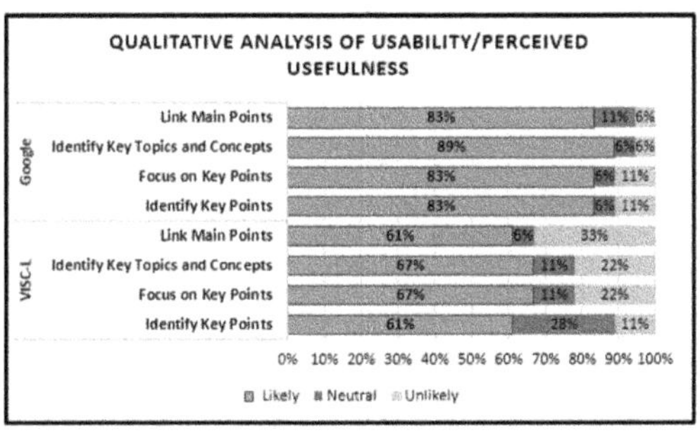

A

		Mental	Effort	Frustration	Performance
VISC-L	AVG	9.39	7.22	9.89	11.89
	STDV	2.93	2.94	5.07	6.04
Google	AVG	7.89	7.39	8.18	10.65
	STDV	3.72	5.01	5.13	6.13

B

Fig. 2. A: Perceived usefulness of the characterised video segments for learning using VISC-L and Google. **B:** Cognitive demand results of the characterised video segments for learning using VISC-L and Google. The values range from 1 (low) to 20 (high).

Furthermore, participants were asked what they found positive or negative when watching characterised video segments generated by VISC-L or Google. For **both VISC-L and Google Positives** the participants found that the segments offered them a strategy for learning and were good to help them focus as these segments were short and with description. For **VISC-L Negatives** the participants noticed that the characterisation was scripted and not in a natural way while for **Google Negatives** they found that some descriptions did not match with the video content, commented that there were too many segments within some videos, and pointed at inaccurate starting times.

Cognitive demand was assessed using the NASA-TLX questionnaire[5], including mental demand, effort, frustration, and performance - the results are showed in Fig. 2-**B**. Participants were asked to provide comments to justify their scores. For **Mental Demand** they reported that the video segments generated with both VISC-L and Google had low Mental demand and required low **Effort**. This is because the segments were short, easy to watch and the characterisation helped the participants to focus on a single topic. Meanwhile, high mental demand and effort was reported because some of the video content added little or no new knowledge or the description was not in-line with the video or did not specify the focus topics. With regard to **Frustration**, for VISC-L, 4 participants reported high frustration because they found some segments' characterisation did not align with the actual content. While with Google, 5 participants gave high frustration because they found some segments' start time was inaccurate or the characterisation was incomplete. Regarding **Performance**, there was similar feedback for both segments generated with VISC-L and Google. Participants gave high performance as they found the segments were very good at explaining the key terms and helped them to think of the domain topics. Whereas, few participants reported low performance as they did not enjoy some of the video content and did not feel they learned new things.

To assess **Usability**, we asked the participants to rank whether the segments were useful and the characterisation was helpful for learning presentation skills. The number of participants given as an average and standard deviation for each ranked factor. For VISC-L segments, an (avg = 0.47, STDV = 0.36) found that the segments were useful but an (avg = 0.30, STDV = 0.26) found that these segments were not useful. In comparison, for Google segments, an (avg = 0.54, STDV = 0.34) found these segments were useful but an (avg = 0.24, STDV = 0.23) found these segments were not useful. Furthermore, we tested whether the characterisation of the segments was helpful or not. For VISC-L characterisations, an (avg = 0.46, STDV = 0.29) found that the characterisation was helpful but an (avg = 0.39, STDV = 0.30) found that these characterisations were unhelpful. For Google characterisations, an (avg = 0.60, STDV = 0.26) found them helpful but an (avg = 0.26, STDV = 0.17) found that the characterisations unhelpful. These results indicate that the participants agreed that the using of characterised video segments for learning was helpful.

5 Conclusion and Future Work

We proposed the generic video segmentation and characterisation framework VISC-L to support learning. It was applied in a presentation skills domain.

[5] https://humansystems.arc.nasa.gov/groups/tlx/.

An evaluation study examined the usefulness and usability of video segmentation and characterisation, comparing VISC-L and Google. The results from the study gave two indications. Firstly, they indicated that using characterised video segments could improve learners' domain knowledge, as the learners were able to identify new domain terms. Secondly, the results showed that there was no statistical significant difference between VISC-L and Google video segmentation and characterisation. With regards to learning effect, for both VISC-L and Google, there was improvement in learning because there were unique new terms mentioned in the summaries after watching the videos. Hence, the study provides support for using segmentation with characterisation to support learning. The perceived usefulness of segmentation and characterisation with Google was slightly better than VISC-L. Participants' feedback indicated that the format used to present the characterisation has influenced the usefulness - the natural language descriptions offered by Google were easier to follow than the list of concepts offered in the VISC-L interface. The usability with both VISC-L and Google shows that their generated characterised segments were helpful.

Having a characterisation in the form of terms linked to a domain ontology will allow us to develop algorithms for connecting video segments to create video narratives (combining several segments) to focus on specific domain concepts. We will combine VISC-L with the Google approach: VISC-L to extract the concepts and Google to create initial segments and to formulate titles. VISC-L is currently being applied in healthcare where we focus on awareness of patients' health-related quality of life needs, using online videos with patient stories.

Acknowledgments. The authors wish to thank the participants in the user study. The authors thank Prof. Tanja Mitrovic and her colleagues at the University of Canterbury New Zealand for sharing the user interaction data, which was used to fine-tune the BERT model. The work on VISC-L is partially funded by the European Union's Horizon 2020 research and innovation programme under grant agreement No 825750 (InADVANCE project).

References

1. Abolkasim, E.N.A.: Semantic approach to model diversity in a social cloud. Ph.D. thesis, University of Leeds (2019)
2. Bloor, M., Bloor, T.: The Practice of Critical Discourse Analysis: An Introduction. Routledge (2013)
3. Bywater, J.P., Floryan, M., Chiu, J.L.: DiSCS: a new sequence segmentation method for open-ended learning environments. In: Roll, I., McNamara, D., Sosnovsky, S., Luckin, R., Dimitrova, V. (eds.) AIED 2021. LNCS (LNAI), vol. 12748, pp. 88–100. Springer, Cham (2021). https://doi.org/10.1007/978-3-030-78292-4_8
4. Cagliero, L., Canale, L., Farinetti, L.: VISA: a supervised approach to indexing video lectures with semantic annotations. In: 2019 IEEE 43rd Annual Computer Software and Applications Conference, vol. 1, pp. 226–235. IEEE (2019)
5. Castro, M.D.B., Tumibay, G.M.: A literature review: efficacy of online learning courses for higher education institution using meta-analysis. Educ. Inf. Technol. **26**(2), 1367–1385 (2019). https://doi.org/10.1007/s10639-019-10027-z

6. Das, A., Das, P.P.: Automatic semantic segmentation and annotation of MOOC lecture videos. In: Jatowt, A., Maeda, A., Syn, S.Y. (eds.) ICADL 2019. LNCS, vol. 11853, pp. 181–188. Springer, Cham (2019). https://doi.org/10.1007/978-3-030-34058-2_17
7. Das, A., Das, P.P.: Semantic segmentation of MOOC lecture videos by analyzing concept change in domain knowledge graph. In: Ishita, E., Pang, N.L.S., Zhou, L. (eds.) ICADL 2020. LNCS, vol. 12504, pp. 55–70. Springer, Cham (2020). https://doi.org/10.1007/978-3-030-64452-9_5
8. Devlin, J., Chang, M.W., Lee, K., Toutanova, K.: BERT: pre-training of deep bidirectional transformers for language understanding. arXiv:1810.04805 (2018)
9. Di Gangi, P.M., Goh, S.H., Lewis, C.C.: Using social media to support presentation skill development in traditional classroom environments. J. Organiz. End User Comput. (JOEUC) **29**(3), 68–91 (2017)
10. Dodson, S., Roll, I., Harandi, N.M., Fels, S., Yoon, D.: Weaving together media, technologies and people: students' information practices in flipped classrooms. Inf. Learn. Sci. (2019)
11. Haridakis, P., Hanson, G.: Social interaction and co-viewing with YouTube: blending mass communication reception and social connection. J. Broadcast. Electron. Media **53**(2), 317–335 (2009)
12. Hearst, M.A.: TextTiling: a quantitative approach to discourse segmentation. Comput. Linguist. **23**(1), 33–64 (1997)
13. Huertas-Garcıia, Á., Huertas-Tato, J., Martín, A., Camacho, D.: CIVIC-UPM at CheckThat! 2021: integration of transformers in misinformation detection and topic classification. (2021)
14. Khan, M.L.: Social media engagement: what motivates user participation and consumption on YouTube? Comput. Hum. Behav. **66**, 236–247 (2017)
15. Maican, C., Cazan, A.M., Lixandroiu, R., Dovleac, L., Maican, M.A.: Exploring the factors influencing the use of communication and collaboration applications. J. Organ. End User Comput. (JOEUC) **33**(4), 94–124 (2021)
16. Mirriahi, N., Jovanović, J., Lim, L.-A., Lodge, J.M.: Two sides of the same coin: video annotations and in-video questions for active learning. Educ. Tech. Res. Dev. **69**(5), 2571–2588 (2021). https://doi.org/10.1007/s11423-021-10041-4
17. Mitrovic, A., Dimitrova, V., Weerasinghe, A., Lau, L.: Reflective experiential learning: using active video watching for soft skills training. In: Proceedings of the 24th International Conference on Computers in Education. Asia-Pacific Society for Computers in Education (2016)
18. Mohammed, A., Dimitrova, V.: Characterising video segments to support learning. In: Proceedings of the 28th International Conference on Computers in Education. Asia-Pacific Society for Computers in Education (in print) (2020)
19. Pritoni, M., et al.: Metadata schemas and ontologies for building energy applications: a critical review and use case analysis. Energies **14**(7), 2024 (2021)
20. Sanh, V., Debut, L., Chaumond, J., Wolf, T.: DistilBERT, a distilled version of BERT: smaller, faster, cheaper and lighter. arXiv preprint arXiv:1910.01108 (2019)
21. Schlotterbeck, D., Uribe, P., Jiménez, A., Araya, R., van der Molen Moris, J., Caballero, D.: TARTA: teacher activity recognizer from transcriptions and audio. In: Roll, I., McNamara, D., Sosnovsky, S., Luckin, R., Dimitrova, V. (eds.) AIED 2021. LNCS (LNAI), vol. 12748, pp. 369–380. Springer, Cham (2021). https://doi.org/10.1007/978-3-030-78292-4_30
22. Tseng, S.-S.: The influence of teacher annotations on student learning engagement and video watching behaviors. Int. J. Educ. Technol. High. Educ. **18**(1), 1–17 (2021). https://doi.org/10.1186/s41239-021-00242-5

Assessing the Quality of Student-Generated Short Answer Questions Using GPT-3

Steven Moore([✉]), Huy A. Nguyen, Norman Bier, Tanvi Domadia, and John Stamper

Carnegie Mellon University, Pittsburgh, PA 15213, USA
StevenJamesMoore@gmail.com

Abstract. Generating short answer questions is a popular form of learnersourcing with benefits for both the students' higher-order thinking and the instructors' collection of assessment items. However, assessing the quality of the student-generated questions can involve significant efforts from instructors and domain experts. In this work, we investigate the feasibility of leveraging students to generate short answer questions with minimal scaffolding and machine learning models to evaluate the student-generated questions. We had 143 students across 7 online college-level chemistry courses participate in an activity where they were prompted to generate a short answer question regarding the content they were presently learning. Using both human and automatic evaluation methods, we investigated the linguistic and pedagogical quality of these student-generated questions. Our results showed that 32% of the student-generated questions were evaluated by experts as high quality, indicating that they could be added and used in the course in their present condition. Additional expert evaluation identified that 23% of the student-generated questions assessed higher cognitive processes according to Bloom's Taxonomy. We also identified the strengths and weaknesses of using a state-of-the-art language model, GPT-3, to automatically evaluate the student-generated questions. Our findings suggest that students are relatively capable of generating short answer questions that can be leveraged in their online courses. Based on the evaluation methods, recommendations for leveraging experts and automatic methods are discussed.

Keywords: Question generation · Question quality · Question evaluation

1 Introduction

Students generating short answer questions has been proven to support their learning of new instructional content [4, 9]. As students generate questions, they deeply engage with the subject matter and utilize critical thinking skills [13]. This process leverages student engagement in ways that provide meaningful data around student interaction integrated with new student-generated learning assets that can support future learners [15]. This is known as a form of learnersourcing, where students complete activities that produce content which can then be leveraged by future learners [20]. Several systems to support students in the generation and sharing of questions have been leveraged by

I. Hilliger et al. (Eds.): EC-TEL 2022, LNCS 13450, pp. 243–257, 2022.
https://doi.org/10.1007/978-3-031-16290-9_18

thousands of students [14, 19]. This usage has led to the student-authoring of nearly a million questions, while also supporting research demonstrating that student question generation can lead to positive learning outcomes [18].

On the other hand, the quality of student-generated questions can widely vary [26]. While existing learnersourcing tools can scaffold this process and guide students towards generating better questions, they often require external systems [14, 19]. Additionally, evaluating the multitude of student-generated questions presents another challenge, with past research relying on experts, other students, or automated methods [24]. Automated methods often rely on the surface-level features of the question, such as the readability of text length, without including the pedagogical value it adds to a course. Recent research has developed and utilized a rubric for human evaluation of automatically generated questions that includes both linguistic and pedagogical criteria [16, 31]. However, these criteria have not seen wide adoption in automated evaluation methods, largely due to the difficulties associated with encoding them in a machine-interpretable way.

In this work, we explored how students could contribute short answer questions with minimal scaffolding and how we could assess their quality using machine learning models that match expert evaluations. We deployed a short answer question generation activity into seven instances of an online college-level chemistry course. From the student responses, we evaluated the quality of the short answer questions, determining if they were of sufficient quality, with respect to their pedagogical value, to be used in the course. The student-generated questions were also assessed for their cognitive level, in terms of Bloom's taxonomy [21]. Following this, we explored automatically evaluating the questions for their quality and cognitive level using a state-of-the-art language model. This study investigates the following research questions: (RQ1) *Can students generate high quality and educationally meaningful short answer questions?* (RQ2) *Can students generate short answer questions that target higher order cognitive processes with minimal prompting and scaffolding*? (RQ3) *Can we automatically assess the quality and cognitive level of a student-generated question with sufficient accuracy?*

Our work makes the following contributions towards learnersourcing and question evaluation. First, we demonstrate that students can create high-quality questions with a simple prompt that can be added to virtually any learning platform. Second, we present an expert evaluation process investigating the quality and cognitive level of student-generated questions. Third, we evaluate the usefulness of using a state-of-the-art language model in classifying educational questions, in an effort to make this process scalable and potentially saving instructor time. Ultimately, our work demonstrates how students can generate high quality questions with minimal scaffolding and how language models might be leveraged to assist in the quality and pedagogical evaluation of short answer questions.

2 Related Work

2.1 Students Generating Short Answer Questions

Previous work has explored leveraging learnersourcing for the creation of short answer questions and found that this process is beneficial to student learning, as it increases their engagement with the material and invokes critical thinking [9]. The quality of the student-generated questions can range depending on the study, influenced by factors such as the education level of the students and the domain of the course [4]. It is desirable to have students generate questions that assess the content in the course that they are making the questions for, but that has not already been assessed by an existing question, as it creates more practice opportunities [27]. Additionally, it is more beneficial for student learning if they generate questions that use higher order cognitive processes according to Bloom's revised Taxonomy. The revised Bloom's Taxonomy consists of six hierarchical categories, where each category corresponds to the cognitive processes that answering the question requires, from remembering a piece of information to combining information in a new way to create a new pattern or structure [21]. Research has shown that short answer questions typically assess at the lower levels of Bloom's Taxonomy, although it is possible for them to assess at all levels [12].

2.2 Evaluating the Quality of Student-Generated Questions

To evaluate student-generated questions, previous work typically leverages student performance data on the questions, using item response theory (IRT) techniques, or uses human experts to evaluate the questions according to a set of criteria [22]. Relying on IRT techniques that require student performance data on the questions can be detrimental to the learning process, because if the questions being used have not been first vetted for their quality, then they may be poorly constructed which can negatively impact students' performance and achievement [10]. In addition to IRT, previous research has leveraged experts or other students to review student-generated questions using a rubric consisting of different criteria such as language coherence, correctness, or the perceived difficulty [4, 23]. The criteria used in these past studies often focus on the surface-level aspects of the question, rather than including the pedagogical value of them, such as how well they might fit back into a given course or assess relevant content that has previously not been assessed. There has been a 9-item rubric used in two previous studies [16, 31] that assess both the linguistic and pedagogical qualities of questions in their expert evaluation. Unlike previous studies that utilize human evaluation, this rubric requires the evaluators to have domain knowledge of the questions and keep in mind how the question might be used in a course teaching the given domain. In the present study, we adopt this rubric to evaluate the student-generated short answer questions, as it is comprehensive, easy to interpret, and includes the pedagogical aspects of a question.

2.3 Automatically Evaluating Student-Generated Questions

A challenge in evaluating questions, whether automatically generated or created by students, is that human evaluation can be subjective, influenced by their prior knowledge and linguistic preferences [3]. To overcome this subjectivity, researchers commonly use automatic methods of evaluating questions [11]. These methods often utilize metrics related to the readability and explainability of the question, such as the popular natural language processing (NLP) ones of BLEU and METEOR [29]. These metrics are not appropriate for the present study, as we take a pedagogical perspective in evaluating the questions and previous research has indicated these metrics do not correlate with human evaluation [23]. Other automatic evaluation work has utilized deep learning methods and language models to evaluate the quality of questions, comparing it to the same evaluation done by a set of human experts [8, 28]. While these studies have achieved a model to expert human matching of 81%, surpassing the previous baseline of 42%, they focus their evaluation on the surface-level features of the questions, such as the length, word choice, or grammar, without considering the pedagogical value it might bring to a course [28].

In addition to automatically evaluating the quality of questions, previous work has looked to automatically classify questions according to which level of Bloom's Taxonomy they fit into [17, 30]. These studies have achieved classification accuracies ranging from 70% to 87%, however they note that the performance is limited by the training data used and that categorization was more accurate for the lower levels of Bloom's Taxonomy [37]. The automatic evaluation methods used in these, and many other prior studies are on questions that typically assess reading comprehension, at the lower cognitive levels of Bloom's Taxonomy, and do not require domain knowledge [2]. This is different from the questions used in the present study, which are at an advanced education level and contain domain knowledge, rather than the more basic recall and comprehension type questions traditionally used.

3 Learning Platform and Data Collection

The present study takes place in a digital courseware platform known as the Open Learning Initiative (OLI). OLI is an open-ended learning environment that offers courses from a variety of domains and consists of interactive activities and diverse multimedia content [5]. OLI consists of instructional content and low-stakes, also known as formative, activities. These activities consist of a variety of question types such as multiple-choice questions, short answer, and dropdown style questions. Students work through different modules in the system, akin to chapters in a textbook, where they are presented with instructional text and videos. Low-stakes activities are embedded throughout these instructional materials, providing the students with feedback and practice opportunities to assess the concepts they are learning.

The data used in this study was collected from a week-long module in seven instances of an introductory chemistry course taught at a community college in the western U.S. The course consists of first- and second-year undergraduates from varying degree backgrounds, with most of the students pursuing a chemistry-related degree. The data comes from the fall semester of 2021, when the introductory chemistry course was offered in the OLI system. In total, the data consists of 143 students and their contribution to the short answer generation activity. The OLI content the students used during the week when our data was collected covers the topics of pH, buffers, and amino acids. There are a total of 38 low-stakes activities embedded throughout the pages of this module. Every activity provides the students with detailed instructional feedback, for both incorrect and correct responses.

We focus on an activity that was added to the course that involves each student generating a short answer question. In the chemistry course, this activity is found on a page contains four paragraphs of instructional text, three worked examples, and eight multiple-choice questions. This activity is presented in the same low-stake format as the other activities found throughout the course, as students do not receive a grade for their participation or the quality of their response in the activity. It prompts students to generate a short answer question, by asking them to "*Create a short answer question that can be correctly answered based on the content covered in this module*". In the activity, students are first prompted to write the question text in the provided text box on the top part of the activity and then write the answer to the question in the bottom text box. The instructions for the self-explanation are intentionally brief and similar prompts have been used in related studies by [1, 36].

4 Data Analysis

4.1 Human Evaluation

The 143 student-generated short answer questions were evaluated by two experts to assess their quality and Bloom's taxonomy level. The two experts had content knowledge in chemistry, multiple years of teaching experience, familiarity with the OLI course, and ample previous experience coding qualitative student data. To first evaluate the quality of the questions, the two experts used a 9-item rubric that has been used in previous studies for assessing the linguistic and pedagogical quality of questions [16, 31]. This rubric contains 9 hierarchical criteria, shown in Table 1. These criteria are asked to the two experts in the order, from top to bottom, that they are presented in the table. Eight of the rubric criteria involve binary (yes/no) responses. The only non-binary item is *information needed*, which consists of three unique options, where each corresponds to the location of the information the students need to know in order to successfully answer the question.

The rubric items are hierarchical by nature, meaning that if certain criteria are answered as "no", then the remaining items will be marked as "not applicable". These criteria are bolded in Table 1. For example, if the experts answer "no" to the *answerable* rubric item, then the three items that follow will be marked as "not applicable". This contributes to avoiding distortion of the rubric criteria distributions for questions that are not ratable across certain items and helps to save the expert evaluators' time. The inter-rater reliability (IRR) values between the two evaluators for each rubric item are also reported in Table 1. It includes the percentage agreement and Cohen's Kappa κ statistic [25] as a measure of IRR for all rubric items. These items are at either a near perfect or substantial level of agreement between the two raters. Two of them, *domain related* and *central*, had perfect agreement, as all of the student-generated questions pertained to chemistry content covered in the current OLI module.

If the expert evaluators answer "yes" to all the binary rubric items and answer any of the three options for *information needed* then we consider that to be a high quality question. In line with previous research, meeting all the rubric criteria suggests that the question is both linguistically and pedagogically sound [16, 31]. Additionally, the last rubric criteria *would you use it* asks the evaluators if they would use the student-generated question if they were teaching the course and using the OLI materials. As the evaluators are familiar with the OLI content and have prior teaching experience, they can judge the pedagogical quality of the student-generated questions. However, we acknowledge that despite the two expert evaluators' backgrounds and high IRR they can still interpret

Table 1. The hierarchical 9-item rubric used to evaluate the questions; the bolded criteria stop the review process if answered as "no". The bracketed numbers indicate agreement percentage between raters and Cohen's κ value for each item.

Rubric item	Definition
Understandable (97.20%, κ = 0.83)	Could you understand what the question is asking?
DomainRelated (100%, κ = 1.0)	Is the question related to the Chemistry domain?
Grammatical (96.15%, κ = 0.82)	Is the question grammatically well formed, i.e. is it free of language errors?
Clear (98.46%, κ = 0.83)	Is it clear what the question asks for?
NotRephrasing (89.52%, κ = 0.66)	Does the question assess course content that has not been assessed by an existing question in the course?
Answerable (99.19%, κ = 0.88)	Are students probably able to answer the question?
InformationNeeded (88.14%, κ = 0.73)	(op) Information presented directly and in one place only in the text (dp) Information presented in different parts of the text (te) A combination of information from the text with external knowledge
Central (100%, κ = 1.00)	Do you think being able to answer the question is important to work on the topics covered by the current module?
WouldYouUseIt (82.35%, κ = 0.62)	If you were a teacher working with the OLI module in your class, would you include this question in the course?

the student-generated questions in different ways as influenced by their prior knowledge and linguistic preferences [3].

In order to assess the cognitive level of the student-generated questions, the two expert evaluators utilized Bloom's revised Taxonomy [21]. This taxonomy, shown in Table 2, has been applied to educational questions in prior research [17, 37]. It consists of six different levels, where each one corresponds to the cognitive processes involved in answering the question. Using these six taxonomy levels, the two expert evaluators classified each student-generated question to a level, depending on what cognitive process is required to answer it. Note, only student-generated questions that had no "non applicable" answers to the nine rubric criteria were evaluated in this way, resulting in a total of 120 of the 143 (84%) questions being assigned one of the six levels as agreed upon by the two expert evaluators. While there are six levels to the taxonomy, the student-generated questions in this study were all assigned to the first four levels, as none of the questions targeted the cognitive processes of *evaluate* or *create*. The omission of these two levels was not by design, however they are less common for short answer questions typically found in courses, which are more likely to assess the first four levels of Bloom's taxonomy [30]. Additionally, while assessing the questions using the 9-item rubric and for Bloom's taxonomy, the two expert evaluators had disagreements, as indicated by the Kappa values in Table 1. The discordant criteria for such questions were discussed between the two raters, resulting in them reaching a consensus on the categorization of the question.

Table 2. Six levels of Bloom's revised Taxonomy [21] in ascending cognitive order from lowest to highest, along with their operational definitions.

Bloom's level	Definition
Remember	Retrieve relevant knowledge from long-term memory
Understand	Construct meaning from instructional messages, including written communication
Apply	Carry out or using a procedure in a given situation
Analyze	Break down the learning material into constituent parts and determine how parts relate to one another and to an overall structure
Evaluate	Make judgments based on criteria and standards
Create	Put elements together to form a coherent whole or to reorganize into a new structure

The IRR between the two expert evaluators for applying Bloom's revised Taxonomy to the student-generated questions was assessed via percentage of agreement (81.67%) and Cohen's Kappa ($\kappa = .74$), suggesting a substantial level of agreement. This agreement level is akin to previous studies that applied Bloom's revised Taxonomy to student-generated questions [35]. In accordance with previous research [21, 34], we define a student-generated question as assessing a low cognitive level if it was evaluated to be at the *remember* or *understand* levels. Conversely the question is said to assess at a high cognitive level if it was evaluated to be at the *apply*, *analyze*, *evaluate*, or *create* levels. Typically, multiple-choice and short answer questions rely on the cognitive processes associated with lower cognitive levels, although both question types can assess higher levels [33]. It is desirable to have questions assessed at a higher level, as it is more beneficial for student learning [21].

4.2 Automatic Evaluation Using GPT-3

Our second evaluation method utilizes GPT-3, a language model with up to 175 billion parameters trained on a large dataset of text scraped from the internet [6]. We selected this language model for our evaluation due to it being state-of-the-art for multiple natural language processing tasks and being the largest publicly available transformer language model. It is a high-performing and popular language model choice for text classification, with recent applications in classifying emails [32] and determining if news articles were real or fake [7]. In this work, we used GPT-3 to perform classification on the student-generated questions in two different ways. We avoided using typical automated question generation evaluation criteria such as BLEU or METEOR, as they have been proven to not correlate with human evaluation and do not have pedagogical implications [29].

First, we used it for binary classification to see if it could classify the student-generated questions as being low or high quality, matching the evaluation of the two experts. To make this classification, we first fine-tuned a GPT-3 Ada model on the LearningQ dataset [8], which is publicly available and contains 5,600 student-generated short answer questions from Khan Academy. Each question in this dataset was evaluated by two expert instructors and assigned a label corresponding to if it was *useful for learning* or *not*. The researchers for the LearningQ dataset defined a question as being *useful for learning* akin to several of the rubric criteria we utilized in this study. They based their evaluation on the following three criteria: (i) concept-relevant, seeking information on the concepts taught in the course; (ii) context-complete, providing enough information to be answerable by other students; and (iii) not-generic, meaning the question asks about a course concept not on another topic or of another style, such as asking for learning advice. Additionally, the questions in the LearningQ dataset came from a variety of domains, which included STEM courses and a single humanity one. No preprocessing was performed on the questions used to fine–tune the model; they were used as-is from the publicly available dataset along with their corresponding binary labels. Fine-tuning the model with default hyperparameters suggested by the documentation[1] took approximately 10 min and incurred a cost of $0.21. Upon completion, we passed in the student-generated questions as the GPT-3 model's input, obtaining the output as a binary label indicating if it rated each question as useful for learning (*high quality*) or not (*low quality*).

Secondly, we used another instance of the GPT-3 Ada model to perform multiclass classification using Bloom's revised Taxonomy levels. We once again use GPT-3 Ada, which was selected due to its low cost and effectiveness at classification tasks that are less nuanced, with comparable performance to the Davinci model. We wanted to determine if GPT-3, fine-tuned on example questions from each level, could perform similarly to the two expert evaluators. To fine-tune the model, we utilized a dataset consisting of 100 questions mapped to each of six Bloom's revised Taxonomy levels, for a total of 600 questions [34]. These 600 questions were assigned to a level of Bloom's revised Taxonomy by a pedagogical expert and this dataset has been used in ample previous studies involving fine-tuning and classification tasks. In the present student, the expert evaluation of the student-generated questions only identified four of the six Bloom's levels that were applicable to the questions. However, we included questions from the two unused Bloom's levels in the fine-tuning process, because if the model was accurate, we could utilize it for future datasets that may contain questions at that cognitive level. For this dataset, we performed no preprocessing on the questions used to fine–tune the model; they were used as-is from the publicly available dataset along with their corresponding Bloom's revised Taxonomy labels. We once again fine-tuned the model with default hyperparameters which took approximately 5 min and incurred a cost of $0.08. Upon completion, the student-generated questions were passed as the GPT-3 model's input, outputting Bloom's labels for each question.

[1] We used the default hyperparameters as suggested in https://beta.openai.com/docs/guides/fine-tuning.

5 Results

We first begin with our human evaluation by experts, using the 9-item rubric, across all 143 student-generated short answer questions. As indicated in the Data Analysis section, the rubric criteria are hierarchical and they can be marked as "not applicable", causing the following rubric items to be ignored. For example, if a question was marked "not applicable" for the first rubric criteria of *understandable*, that would reduce the question pool for the other eight criteria. We report the percentage relative to the remaining questions, followed by the absolute percentage, i.e. (relative %/absolute %).

RQ1: *Can students generate high quality and educationally meaningful short answer questions?* We found that 91% of the student-generated short answer questions were rated *understandable.* All the questions rated as *understandable*, were also rated *domain related* (100%/91% total). Most questions were also free of *grammatical* errors (90%/82% total), which includes typos and punctuation mistakes. As a question's clarity is related to the understandability of the question, there were also many questions (95%/87% total) that were evaluated as being *clear*. If a question assessed course content that has not been assessed by an existing question found somewhere in the module, then it was marked as *not rephrasing* (84%/73% total). This is one of the lowest rubric criteria percentages and also presented a challenge for the evaluators to find agreement on, as they achieved a Cohen's Kappa of $\kappa = .66$.

The evaluation shows that most of the questions are rated as *answerable* by future students in the course (97%/84% total). Similar to the criteria about being domain related, the *central* criteria (100%/84% total) was perfect for the remaining pool of questions. This not only means the question relates to the chemistry, but it specifically targets a concept that is addressed in the current module. According to the evaluators, knowledge required for answering the questions is obtained in *one place* (68%/57% total) or in *different places* (30%/25% total) throughout the module. However, there were two questions that were evaluated as needing both the instructional *text and external knowledge* (2%/1% total).

If the pH of my solution increased significantly after adding an unknown compound, was the mystery compound added a base or acid?	How do you know which unit to start with?
Calculate the pH of a solution containing acetic acid (pKa = 4.75) with an R value of 10^-2.	What causes an molecule to be more acidic than others?

Fig. 1. The two questions on the left are evaluated as being high quality and the two questions on the right are low-quality, due to being vague (top) and grammatically incorrect (bottom).

As described in the Data Analysis section, a question was categorized as high quality if it passed all nine rubric criteria, including being evaluated as *would you use it* (38%/32% total). In total, 46/143 (32%) student-generated short answer questions met this criterion by passing all nine rubric items and were deemed to be of high quality. Figure 1 shows two questions evaluated as high quality and two questions evaluated as low-quality. The question in the upper-right was evaluated as not being *understandable* and the question in the bottom-right was not *grammatical.*

RQ2: Can students generate short answer questions that target higher order cognitive processes with minimal prompting and scaffolding? In order to assess the cognitive-level of the student-generated questions, the evaluators applied Bloom's Taxonomy to them. Due to some of the questions having certain rubric criteria marked as "not applicable" and thus ending the review, 120/143 (84%) student-generated questions were assigned a Bloom's Taxonomy level by the evaluators. The majority categorization was remember (52%), with understand (25%) and apply (20%) being tagged to a similar number of questions, followed by analyze (3%). An example of the student-generated questions corresponding to each of these four Bloom's Taxonomy levels is shown in Table 3.

Table 3. An example of a student-generated question assessed at each of the four levels of Bloom's Taxonomy present in this study.

Student-generated question	Bloom's level
What is the point in a titration curve that indicates the pKa value of a weak acid?	Remember
Imagine an acidic solution with a low pH. If a strong base is added to the solution, what happens to the pH in relation to the pKa?	Understand
If 10 mL of a diprotic weak acid is fully deprotonated with 20 mL of 0.5M NaOH, how many moles of the acid and NaOH are there?	Apply
When stomach acid enters the esophagus, typically with a pH of 1.5 to 3.5, calcium carbonate is often used to combat this. Why would calcium carbonate be a good substance for this problem?	Analyze

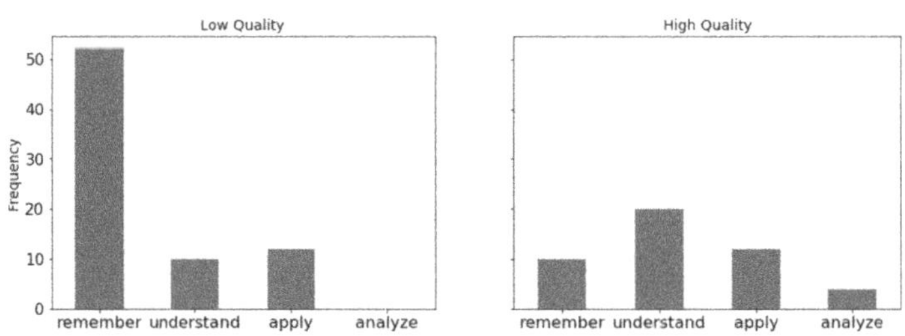

Fig. 2. The distribution of the four Bloom's Taxonomy levels between questions evaluated as low and high quality.

Prior research [21, 30] has indicated that questions at the *apply* level and above are categorized as targeting higher order cognitive processes. As a result, 28/120 (23%) questions tagged with Bloom's Taxonomy were evaluated as assessing at this higher level. Since Bloom's Taxonomy level was not included in the criteria for a high-quality question, we investigated if there was a correlation between the two measures. Fisher's exact test revealed that there was a strong statistically significant association between the quality of the question and the cognitive level ($p = .003$). Figure 2 shows the distribution of Bloom's Taxonomy levels between questions evaluated as being low and high quality.

RQ3: *Can we automatically assess the quality and cognitive level of a student-generated question with sufficient accuracy?* We utilized the first fine-tuned GPT-3 model to classify the quality of the student-generated questions as either low or high quality. The model agreed with the human evaluation for 57/143 questions (40%). In the cases they disagreed, 85/86 mismatches were interpreted as having high quality by GPT-3 but low quality by expert raters. There were only 13/143 questions (9%) the model classified as low quality, suggesting it was overestimating the quality of the questions, as 97/143 (68%) were evaluated by the experts as being low quality. Figure 3 provides a confusion matrix for the quality classifications made by the model.

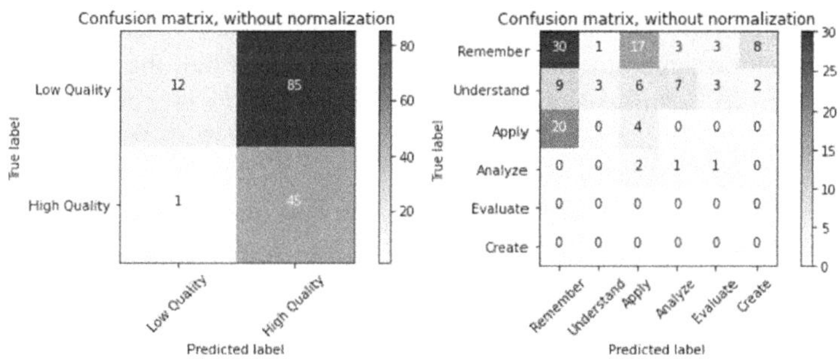

Fig. 3. Confusion matrices for the classification of a question's quality (left) and Bloom's revised Taxonomy (right).

We used the second fine-tuned GPT-3 model to classify the 120 student-generated questions to which the expert evaluators had assigned a Bloom's Taxonomy level. The results of the model compared to the expert evaluation, including the percentage of matches for each Bloom's Taxonomy level between the two, are shown in Table 4. In total, the model matched the expert evaluation for 38/120 (32%) student-generated questions. The GPT-3 model has a similar distribution of *remember* and *apply* questions, although they are often not correctly applied to the questions according to the expert evaluation. Additionally, GPT-3 classified 17 of the questions into the two highest cognitive levels that were not observed in our student-generated questions. Additionally, Fig. 3 also provides a confusion matrix for the classification of Bloom's revised Taxonomy between the expert human evaluators and the model.

Table 4. A breakdown of the six Bloom's revised Taxonomy and the number of questions the experts and GPT-3 tagged to each level.

Bloom's level	Remember	Understand	Apply	Analyze	Evaluate	Create
Expert Evaluation	62	30	24	4	0	0
GPT-3	59	4	29	11	10	7
Matching %	48%	10%	4%	25%	0%	0%

6 Discussion and Conclusion

In this research, we utilized human experts and automatic methods to evaluate the quality and cognitive level of student-generated short answer questions. We found that students were able to contribute high quality questions, as evaluated by a 9-item rubric that contained criteria assessing the linguistic and pedagogical features of the questions. In total, 32% of the student-generated short answer questions were evaluated as being high quality, indicating that the evaluators could use them in the course in their present condition. Students generated these questions through a simplistic prompt consisting of a single sentence instruction and two textboxes embedded into a digital learning platform. Previous research often has an overall lower percentage of high-quality questions and utilizes external systems or scaffolding methods that require the students to spend more time on the question generation activity [1, 4]. We believe that the implementation we used in this study keeps students more engaged in the learning process, by allowing them to create the question in a more natural context as they work through the instructional text and assessments in the platform.

The cognitive processes that the student-generated questions target were evaluated by the two expert evaluators, which identified 23% of the questions as assessing at a high cognitive level and the remaining 77% assessing the lower two cognitive levels. This majority distribution of the short answer questions assessing at the *remembering* and *understanding* cognitive levels is in line with findings from previous work [2, 37]. These questions that assess the first two cognitive levels can still be effective, particularly when students are first learning new concepts, where they might need to first learn essential terminology, methods, and formulas [21].

Automatic evaluation of the student-generated questions for both their quality and cognitive level was suboptimal compared to previous work leveraging different language models [8, 28], however, such prior research often evaluates questions that are mostly at the *remembering* cognitive level and often involve basic reading comprehension with no domain-related knowledge being assessed, which are more appropriate for students at lower education levels [22]. The student-generated questions in this study were at the post-secondary education level, assessed chemistry knowledge, and often included domain terminology. These differences between questions used in prior research in this study likely contributed to the difficulty the two GPT-3 models had, even when they were fine-tuned on relevant data for the classification tasks. The percentage of expert-matching classifications the models achieved for the quality (40%) and cognitive level (32%) could provide an initial estimation of the questions' value.

The main limitation of this study comes from the dataset, as the 143 student-generated short answer questions that were analyzed were all in the domain of chemistry. Including student-generated questions from other domains could lead to more generalizable findings. Question evaluation often entails human annotations as the ideal criterion to compare automatic methods against; however, there is a subjective nature to human ratings. While we tried to reduce subjectivity by using a detailed rubric for the human evaluation and achieving a high IRR for each criterion, there still lies the potential for different evaluation depending on who is doing the evaluation. Finally, the results of the GPT-3 model were suboptimal, often overestimating the quality of the student-generated questions or misclassifying the Bloom's revised Taxonomy level. The results of these classifications were influenced by the datasets used to fine-tune them, which was limited by public datasets that classify the educational quality of the question and the cognitive level.

This work demonstrates that students can generate short answer questions that are both linguistically and pedagogically sound without requiring an external tool or scaffolding. In total, we found that 32% of all the student-generated questions were evaluated as being high quality by the expert evaluators. Across all the questions that were classified according to Bloom's revised Taxonomy, 23% were evaluated as assessing high cognitive levels. Our results highlight how students in the context of an online course can create short answer questions that can readily be implemented into the course, providing new assessment opportunities for essential concepts. While the automatic evaluation may be improved with more robust datasets for fine-tuning, it offers a sufficient first pass classification that may assist experts in their evaluation of the questions. This research helps demonstrate one way to help scale online learning and improve educational resources, by leveraging the students in a course. It opens further opportunities for engaging students in the process of question generation and leveraging both humans and language models to assist in the evaluation process.

This research was supported by the National Science Foundation (Award #2135159).

References

1. Aflalo, E.: Students generating questions as a way of learning. Act. Learn. High. Educ. 1469787418769120 (2018)
2. Amidei, J., Piwek, P., Willis, A.: Evaluation methodologies in automatic question generation 2013–2018. In: Proceedings of the 11th International Conference on Natural Language Generation, pp. 307–317 (2018)
3. Amidei, J., Piwek, P., Willis, A.: Rethinking the agreement in human evaluation tasks. In: Proceedings of the 27th International Conference on Computational Linguistics, pp. 3318–3329 (2018)
4. Bates, S.P., Galloway, R.K., Riise, J., Homer, D.: Assessing the quality of a student-generated question repository. Phys. Rev. Spec. Top.-Phys. Educ. Res. **10**(2), 020105 (2014)
5. Bier, N., Moore, S., Van Velsen, M.: Instrumenting courseware and leveraging data with the open learning initiative. In: Companion Proceedings 9th International Conference on Learning Analytics & Knowledge, pp. 990–1001 (2019)
6. Brown, T., et al.: Language models are few-shot learners. In: Advances in Neural Information Processing Systems, vol. 33, pp. 1877–1901 (2020)
7. Chan, A.: GPT-3 and InstructGPT: technological dystopianism, utopianism, and "Contextual" perspectives in AI ethics and industry. AI Ethics 1–12 (2022)
8. Chen, G., Yang, J., Hauff, C., Houben, G.-J.: LearningQ: a large-scale dataset for educational question generation. In: Twelfth International AAAI Conference on Web and Social Media (2018)
9. Chin, C., Brown, D.E.: Student-generated questions: a meaningful aspect of learning in science. Int. J. Sci. Educ. **24**(5), 521–549 (2002)
10. Clifton, S.L., Schriner, C.L.: Assessing the quality of multiple-choice test items. Nurse Educ. **35**(1), 12–16 (2010)
11. Clinciu, M.-A., Eshghi, A., Hastie, H.: A study of automatic metrics for the evaluation of natural language explanations. In: Proceedings of the 16th Conference of the European Chapter of the Association for Computational Linguistics: Main, pp. 2376–2387 (2021)

12. Das, S., Mandal, S.K.D., Basu, A.: Identification of cognitive learning complexity of assessment questions using multi-class text classification. Contemp. Educ. Technol. **12**(2), ep275 (2020)
13. Denny, P.: Generating practice questions as a preparation strategy for introductory programming exams. In: Proceedings of the 46th ACM Technical Symposium on Computer Science Education, pp. 278–283 (2015)
14. Denny, P., Hamer, J., Luxton-Reilly, A., Purchase, H.: PeerWise: students sharing their multiple choice questions. In: Proceedings of the Fourth international Workshop on Computing Education Research, New York, NY, USA, pp. 51–58 (2008)
15. Denny, P., Tempero, E., Garbett, D., Petersen, A.: Examining a student-generated question activity using random topic assignment. In: Proceedings of the 2017 ACM Conference on Innovation and Technology in Computer Science Education, pp. 146–151 (2017)
16. Horbach, A., Aldabe, I., Bexte, M., de Lacalle, O.L., Maritxalar, M.: Linguistic appropriateness and pedagogic usefulness of reading comprehension questions. In: Proceedings of the 12th Language Resources and Evaluation Conference, pp. 1753–1762 (2020)
17. Huang, J., et al.: Automatic classroom question classification based on bloom's taxonomy. In: 2021 13th International Conference on Education Technology and Computers, pp. 33–39 (2021)
18. Khosravi, H., Demartini, G., Sadiq, S., Gasevic, D.: Charting the design and analytics agenda of learnersourcing systems. In: LAK21: 11th International Learning Analytics and Knowledge Conference, pp. 32–42 (2021)
19. Khosravi, H., Kitto, K., Williams, J.J.: RiPPLE: a crowdsourced adaptive platform for recommendation of learning activities. J. Learn. Anal. **6**(3), 91–105 (2019)
20. Kim, J.: Learnersourcing: improving learning with collective learner activity. Massachusetts Institute of Technology (2015)
21. Krathwohl, D.R.: A revision of Bloom's taxonomy: an overview. Theory Pract. **41**(4), 212–218 (2002)
22. Kurdi, G., Leo, J., Parsia, B., Sattler, U., Al-Emari, S.: A systematic review of automatic question generation for educational purposes. Int. J. Artif. Intell. Educ. **30**(1), 121–204 (2020)
23. van der Lee, C., Gatt, A., van Miltenburg, E., Krahmer, E.: Human evaluation of automatically generated text: Current trends and best practice guidelines. Comput. Speech Lang. **67**(2021), 101151 (2021)
24. Lu, O.H., Huang, A.Y., Tsai, D.C., Yang, S.J.: Expert-authored and machine-generated short-answer questions for assessing students learning performance. Educ. Technol. Soc. **24**(3), 159–173 (2021)
25. McHugh, M.L.: Interrater reliability: the kappa statistic. Biochemia Medica **22**(3), 276–282 (2012)
26. Moore, S., Nguyen, H.A., Stamper, J.: Examining the effects of student participation and performance on the quality of learnersourcing multiple-choice questions. In: Proceedings of the Eighth ACM Conference on Learning@ Scale, pp. 209–220 (2021)
27. Papinczak, T., Peterson, R., Babri, A.S., Ward, K., Kippers, V., Wilkinson, D.: Using student-generated questions for student-centred assessment. Assess. Eval. High. Educ. **37**(4), 439–452 (2012)
28. Ruseti, S., et al.: Predicting question quality using recurrent neural networks. In: Penstein Rosé, C., et al. (eds.) AIED 2018. LNCS (LNAI), vol. 10947, pp. 491–502. Springer, Cham (2018). https://doi.org/10.1007/978-3-319-93843-1_36
29. Scialom, T., Staiano, J.: Ask to learn: a study on curiosity-driven question generation. In: Proceedings of the 28th International Conference on Computational Linguistics, pp. 2224–2235 (2020)

30. Shaikh, S., Daudpotta, S.M., Imran, A.S.: Bloom's learning outcomes' automatic classification using LSTM and pretrained word embeddings. IEEE Access **9**, 117887–117909 (2021)
31. Steuer, T., Bongard, L., Uhlig, J., Zimmer, G.: On the linguistic and pedagogical quality of automatic question generation via neural machine translation. In: De Laet, T., Klemke, R., Alario-Hoyos, C., Hilliger, I., Ortega-Arranz, A. (eds.) EC-TEL 2021. LNCS, vol. 12884, pp. 289–294. Springer, Cham (2021). https://doi.org/10.1007/978-3-030-86436-1_22
32. Thiergart, J., Huber, S., Übellacker, T.: Understanding emails and drafting responses–an approach using GPT-3. arXiv e-prints (2021)
33. Wang, Z., Manning, K., Mallick, D.B., Baraniuk, R.G.: Towards blooms taxonomy classification without labels. In: Roll, I., McNamara, D., Sosnovsky, S., Luckin, R., Dimitrova, V. (eds.) AIED 2021. LNCS (LNAI), vol. 12748, pp. 433–445. Springer, Cham (2021). https://doi.org/10.1007/978-3-030-78292-4_35
34. Yahya, A.A., Toukal, Z., Osman, A.: Bloom's Taxonomy–based classification for item bank questions using support vector machines. In: Ding, W., Jiang, H., Ali, M., Li, M. (eds.) Modern Advances in Intelligent Systems and Tools, pp. 135–140. Springer, Heidelberg (2012). https://doi.org/10.1007/978-3-642-30732-4_17
35. Yu, F.Y., Cheng, W.W.: Effects of academic achievement and group composition on quality of student-generated questions and use patterns of online procedural prompts. In: 28th International Conference on Computers in Education, ICCE 2020, pp. 573–581 (2020)
36. Yu, F.-Y., Liu, Y.-H.: Creating a psychologically safe online space for a student-generated questions learning activity via different identity revelation modes. Br. J. Educ. Technol. **40**(6), 1109–1123 (2009)
37. Zhang, J., Wong, C., Giacaman, N., Luxton-Reilly, A.: Automated classification of computing education questions using Bloom's taxonomy. In: Australasian Computing Education Conference, pp. 58–65 (2021)

Designing Playful Intelligent Tutoring Software to Support Engaging and Effective Algebra Learning

Tomohiro Nagashima[1(✉)], John Britti[2], Xiran Wang[1], Bin Zheng[1], Violet Turri[1], Stephanie Tseng[1], and Vincent Aleven[1]

[1] Carnegie Mellon University, Pittsburgh, PA 15213, USA
{tnagashi,aleven}@cs.cmu.edu, {xiranw,binzheng,vturri,stseng2}@andrew.cmu.edu

[2] Georgia Institute of Technology, Atlanta, GA 30332, USA
jbritti3@gatech.edu

Abstract. In designing learning technology, it is critical that the technology supports both learning and engagement of students. However, achieving both aspects in a single technology design is challenging. We report on the design and evaluation of Gwynnette, intelligent tutoring software for early algebra. Gwynnette was deliberately designed to enhance students' algebra learning and engagement, integrating several playful interaction and gamification features such as drag-and-drop interactions, an alien character, and sound effects. A virtual classroom experiment with 60 students showed that the system significantly enhanced both engagement and conceptual learning in early algebra, compared to the older version of the same software. Log data analyses gave insights into how the design might have affected the outcomes. This study demonstrates that a deliberate design of learning technology can help students learn and engage well in an unpopular subject such as algebra, a challenging dual goal in designing learning technologies.

Keywords: Intelligent tutoring system · Engagement · Algebra

1 Introduction

When designing learning technology, it is critical that the technology is designed to support both learning and engagement of students [1]. An engaging technology with no learning support might entertain students but would not result in meaningful learning. On the other hand, a learning technology with no engaging features would not fully engage students in the learning activity, even if the activity is well designed to support learning. Designing learning technology for enhancing both learning and engagement is critical particularly in disciplines in which many students have a hard time succeeding, such as early algebra. Early algebra is considered as a "gatekeeper" course to advanced learning in Science, Technology, Engineering, and Mathematics (STEM) domains [2]. Many students, especially in the United States, fail to gain important knowledge and skills in algebra, including conceptual understanding and procedural skills [3, 4]. The

I. Hilliger et al. (Eds.): EC-TEL 2022, LNCS 13450, pp. 258–271, 2022.
https://doi.org/10.1007/978-3-031-16290-9_19

difficulty in learning algebra may be partly attributed to the complexity of the symbolic notation system and prior practices in arithmetic problem solving [5] but may also come from a lack of student engagement. Indeed, it is very typical of students to perceive algebra as not being enjoyable [6].

How might one design learning technology that enhances both learning and engagement in algebra? Even though a number of systems have been shown to enhance students' algebra learning, such as Intelligent Tutoring Systems (ITSs) [7–9], the important question of how these effective technologies can also be designed for student engagement has received rather little attention [10]. Of a few attempts that have been made, learning environments with playful interactions and gamification have been developed and tested in the domain of early algebra. For example, *DragonBox* (https://dragonbox.com/products/algebra-12) is an algebra game in which learners drag and drop cards with "dragons" and other associated monsters that represent numbers and variables in equations, with the goal of isolating the variable [7, 11]. DragonBox has also a number of other entertaining elements in the game, including the "dragons" and sounds for various interactions in the system [11]. Another gamified learning environment, *From Here to There!* (FH2T, https://graspablemath.com/fh2t.html), also employs drag-and-drop interactions to help students understand the structure of algebraic expressions and how to change them using formal algebraic strategies [12, 13].

Empirical studies show, however, that these technologies have not yet achieved the goal of supporting both effective learning and engagement. For instance, researchers experimentally compared DragonBox against *Lynnette*, an effective ITS for algebra with no enjoyable elements [7]. Although secondary-school students found DragonBox more engaging than Lynnette (as self-reported by students), students who had used DragonBox performed poorer on a posttest, suggesting a poor learning effect. FH2T has also been evaluated in experimental studies, compared against a non-gamified condition involving problem sets with hints and feedback in *ASSISTments* (https://new.assistments.org) [12]. The findings show that FH2T helps students gain conceptual understanding of algebra compared to ASSISTments. Despite its success, prior studies on FH2T have not directly measured how engaging it is compared to other software [14], making it difficult to understand whether and how it may influence student engagement when learning in FH2T. To sum, although some environments for learning algebra have been shown engaging and others have been shown effective in algebra, no studies have rigorously measured both student learning *and* engagement how it compares with learning and engagement in other learning environments.

In the current study, we deliberately designed an ITS (called *Gwynnette*) based on an existing ITS (i.e., Lynnette) with the goal of enhancing both learning and engagement. Gwynnette embeds several playful features to make student learning effective and engaging. We present findings from a randomized controlled experiment in a virtual classroom environment with 60 secondary-school students, in which we compared Gwynnette against an older version of the same software (i.e., Lynnette) with no playful features. The results showed that Gwynnette enhanced students' engagement and learning; students spent considerably more time using the system and gained more conceptual understanding of algebra than those who used Lynnette. We describe the design principles, findings of the experiment and a detailed analysis of the log data to examine how students interacted with the software and how the interaction and the design of the software might have contributed to student learning and engagement.

2 Gwynnette

2.1 Design Principles

To develop a playful learning environment that can be both engaging and effective in supporting algebra learning, we designed an ITS for early algebra named Gwynnette (Fig. 1). Gwynnette was designed based on Lynnette, an existing ITS for algebra learning which has no common entertaining features [7]. Based on literature review and evaluation of designs in existing software (e.g., design evaluation of DragonBox by [7]), we added the following features in Gwynnette: playful drag-and-drop interactions to enact equation transformations in solving algebra problems, and enjoyable gamification elements including a game theme, sound effects, and a character guide. In this section, we briefly describe these design features. These features were designed following a user-centered design approach; we iteratively prototyped, tested, and improved ideas and artifacts with school teachers and students through virtual interview sessions and pilot use in a secondary-school classroom before the final implementation.

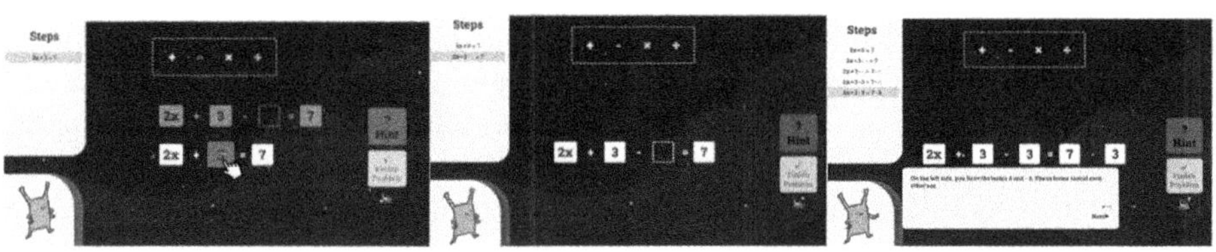

Fig. 1. The main interactions in Gwynnette are drag-and-drop manipulations of equations. Users would drag operators and numbers to manipulate given equations (left). Once an operator (e.g., a "−" symbol) has been dropped onto the appropriate area (e.g., the "3" in the equation), a square box appears (middle). Users can type in a number in the box to fill in the box (right). Users can also request hints anytime (here the hint says, "On the left side, you have the terms 3 and −3. These terms cancel each other out").

Focused Practice of Algebraic Manipulations with Drag-and-Drop Interactions. Using Gwynnette, students can enact equation transformations through its drag-and-drop interactions. As shown in Fig. 2, users can drag operators (e.g., the "+" sign) to an equation to transform the state of the equation. They can also drag a constant term (a number) or a variable term onto another like term to simplify equations. When learners make an error, an "Undo" button appears so that leaners can move back to the previous state. Like other learning environments introduced above [12], such dynamic interactions may be effective by focusing students' practice on equation transformations, rather than also having to take care of arithmetic calculations. This may help students learn "conceptual knowledge that underlies procedures" [4], including the concept of *doing the same thing to both sides* (i.e., when subtracting 3 from the left-hand side of $2x + 3$

= 7, students also need to subtract 3 from the other side of the equation) and the concept of equivalence [9]. Practice on equation transformations may help students focus their attention and cognitive effort to important algebraic thinking rather than arithmetic errors [9].

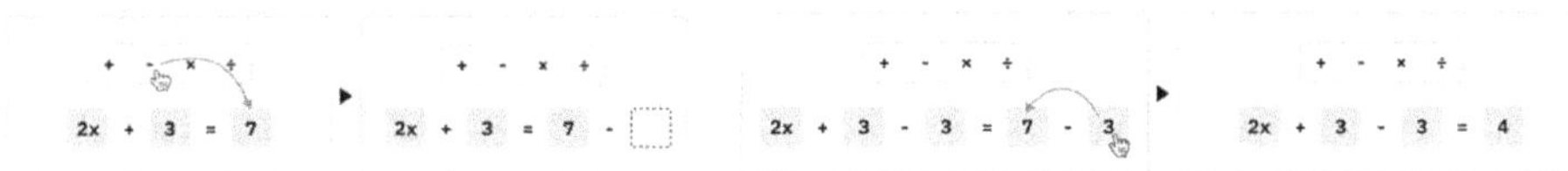

Fig. 2. Drag-and-drop interactions for adding an operator to a given equation (left) and simplifying an equation (the interface takes care of the arithmetic, right). Arrows show the location where the element being dragged will be dropped.

In designing the drag-and-drop interactions for manipulating equations, we made several design decisions aimed at helping learners effectively acquire algebra concepts, based on the findings from [7] and honed through design iterations with teachers and students. For instance, when learners drag a correct operator to one side of an equation, the system requires that the learner's next action is to drag the same operator to the other side to help learners understand the principle of *doing the same thing to both sides of an equation* [9]. This deliberate design was added to help students focus on important conceptual moves while avoiding "over-scaffolding" learners [7]. Also, to further emphasize the principle of doing the same thing to both sides, the system also requires learners to wait to type in a number in the added square box until they first add a square box to each side of the equation (Fig. 3). This deliberate interaction design may help learners focus their cognitive effort and attention to the important concept. Prior work has not considered this design. For example, in FH2T, when a learner drags a number from one side to the other side of an equation, the system automatically presents subtraction of that number on both sides of the equation (and then automatically flips the sign attached to the dragged number as learners progress in the game). It seems possible that doing so may remove a critical difficulty from the task, limiting students' opportunity to learn to handle it through practice, a form of over-scaffolding.

The drag-and-drop interactions might also be perceived as a playful form of solving equations [15]. Solving equations using a drag-and-drop interaction is considerably different from a typical form of instruction and practice that involves writing out equations and their solution steps (as transformed equations). Using such a new way of solving problems might bring a new, engaging, and pleasant experience to students. However, even with the potential effectiveness, playful drag-and-drop interactions could also be unhelpful in enhancing algebra learning. For example, in the drag-and-drop interactions we implemented, users never get an experience of typing in or writing out equations and performing arithmetic operations. Without practicing those skills, users who use the drag-and-drop interactions to solve problems might not be able to apply their learned knowledge to typical algebra problems that ask students to write out equations and their solution steps in a paper or on a computer screen.

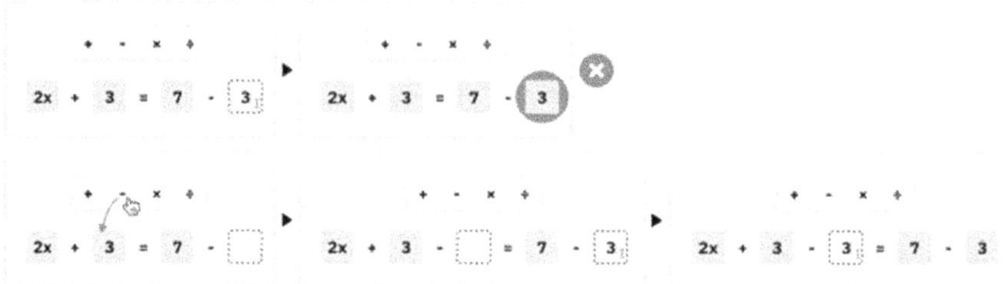

Fig. 3. Gwynnette facilitates the use of an algebra principle of *doing the same thing to both sides* before typing in a number in the added square. The system does not let users, after dragging one operator to one side, type in a number in the added square before dragging the same operator to the other side of the equation (top). Users need to first drag the same operator to both sides (creating two blank squares, bottom). The arrow shows that the negative sign is being dragged onto the "3." The green feedback indicates that the action is correct while the red feedback shows that the system rejects the input as an error. (Color figure online)

Space Travel Theme. Many gamified learning environments employ a fantasy theme (e.g., a monster adventure theme [16]) for their game context. Such a fantasy context helps create an immersive and engaging environment in which other elements (e.g., narratives) can also be integrated [17].

In designing our tutoring software, we adopted a theme of space travel, in which the learner becomes a space traveler exploring planets by solving problems. We conducted multiple design sessions with eight secondary-school students, exploring what feelings they have regarding the use of the space theme. An informal theme analysis found that students, regardless of their age or gender, have a positive view towards the theme.

Alien Guide. Use of avatars and characters is a common strategy employed widely across playful, gamified learning environments. By interacting with such characters, learners may gain a sense of autonomy [17] and therefore engage in their learning. We designed an alien character that guides the learner's space travel by helping them solve algebra problems. This alien gives feedback and hint messages in response to students' problem-solving performance and requests (Fig. 1).

Sound Effects. We also implemented sounds in the system, another popular element in many tools that are designed to enhance student engagement [18]. Specifically, we added voice sounds for the alien and sounds for the drag-and-drop interactions. For example, when a learner finishes a problem, the alien celebrates it with the sound, "ta da!" while it says "hmm" when a learner makes an error. After user study sessions with students and math teachers, to accommodate their preferences and potential simultaneous use in classroom settings, we added the option for learners to turn the sounds on and off at any time (Fig. 1, right).

3 Classroom Experiment

To experimentally examine the effect of Gwynnette on student learning and engagement, we conducted a classroom experiment at two public secondary schools in the U.S. Our research questions asked if Gwynnette, which was deliberately designed to enhance student learning and engagement in algebra, would (RQ1) improve students' conceptual and procedural learning in algebra (i.e., effect on learning) and (RQ2) help students engage with the software (i.e., effect on engagement). We also investigated (RQ3) how the design elements in the software affect students' interactions and learning processes (i.e., effect on learning processes).

3.1 Method

Participants. Twenty 6th, 55 7th, and 19 8th grade students across five classes in two public schools from two different school districts in the U.S. participated (total $n = 94$). Six of the 55 7th graders were also enrolled in the school's "Math Support" class, where students received additional instruction towards the goal of meeting state standards. The study happened in 2020, during which both schools were operating under a remote synchronous instructional mode due to the COVID-19 pandemic (i.e., teachers and students had synchronous classes via a videoconferencing system [19]). Students joined from their home using their own devices or school-provided devices (laptop or tablet).

Materials. To measure student learning of domain knowledge and skills in early algebra, we developed a web-based pretest and posttest based on items in the literature [9]. Each test included seven conceptual knowledge items (CK) and five procedural knowledge items (PK). CK items asked students to provide conceptual reasoning in solving algebra problems through multiple-choice or open-ended questions. PK items asked students to solve equations in an open-ended format (i.e., students typed in their answer and solution steps in a blank box). Two isomorphic versions were created and assigned to students in a counterbalanced way as the pretest and posttest.

Also, we measured students' self-reported engagement and enjoyment with the system using Intrinsic Motivation Inventory (IMI) [20]. IMI is a validated survey instrument developed to measure subjective experiences related to a psychological intervention. We only used the items related to enjoyment and engagement, which consisted of seven 7-point survey items [7]. Additionally, we also measured how long students used the system as a behavioral indicator of engagement [21].

The students in the study used two versions of intelligent algebra learning software, namely, a *playful* version (i.e., Gwynnette) and an *unplayful* version (i.e., Lynnette). These versions share the same algebra content and the core tutoring functionality; they both guide students through step-by-step problem solving and provide on-demand hints and feedback. Lynnette does not have the unique features of Gwynnette that were presented earlier. While Gwynnette allows students to solve equations through drag-and-drop manipulations, Lynnette has students type in problem-solving steps (i.e., transformed equations) into input fields (Fig. 4). Due to this difference, Lynnette software also asks students to perform the arithmetic computations involved in solving equations. In Gwynnette, computations are performed by the system. Additionally, Lynnette also allows students to skip intermediate problem-solving steps, which is not available in Gwynnette as its interaction design emphasizes the step-by-step problem solving that involves conceptual understanding. Other features were kept consistent across the two systems. In the study, we assigned the same sets of problems of 14 levels in both software versions (Table 1). Each problem level (Levels 1–10) has 2–4 problems. Level 11–14 included 8–15 problems with varying difficulty levels taken from Levels 1–10 (for advanced students). Teachers shared that most students have seen or practiced only Levels 1–4, but several advanced students had seen all levels before the study.

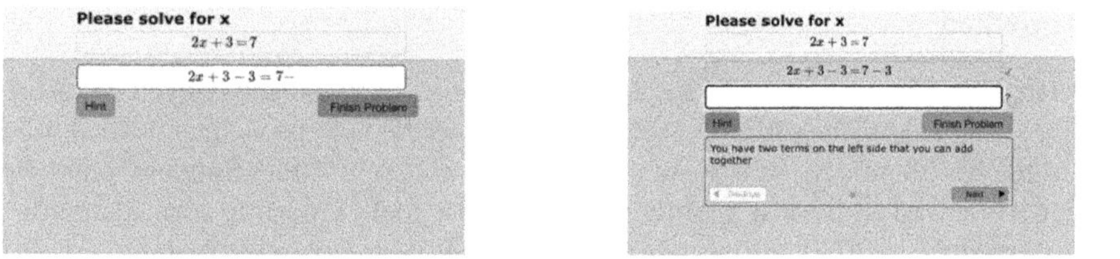

Fig. 4. To solve problems in Lynnette, users type in solution steps. (left) Users can click on the "Hint" button to request hints anytime (right).

Table 1. Problem levels, types of equation problems, and examples implemented in both Gwynnette and Lynnette.

Level	Equation type	Example	Level	Equation type	Example
1	One step	$x + 3 = 5$	8	Variables on both sides	$2x + 6 = 3x$
2	Two step (negative)	$6 - x = 3$	9	Variables and constants on both sides	$4x + 11 = x + 2$
3	One step (division)	$2x = 6$	10	Variables and constants on both sides (negative)	$-2x + 2 = -5x + 8$
4	Two step (division)	$2x + 3 = 7$	11	Mix	
5	Simplify first	$-3x + 5 - 3 = 14$	12	Mix	
6	With parentheses	$2(2x + 1) = 6$	13	Mix	
7	Parentheses, more steps	$1 + 2(2x - 1) = 7$	14	Mix	

Procedure. The study took place during four regular virtual mathematics class periods in each school. Experimenters joined the classes remotely through a video conferencing system. Students were also encouraged to use the assigned software version (see the assignment below) outside of the regular class periods. We allowed for such unmoderated use of the software in order to accommodate students' various needs during their remote learning and teachers' requests [19]. Students in each class were randomly assigned to either Gwynnette condition ($n = 47$) or Lynnette condition ($n = 47$). Students in each condition worked with the respective software version. Six students in the Math Support class were pre-identified and randomly assigned to the groups among them.

Students first worked on the pretest for 20 min. Students then watched a brief video on how to use both systems. In each of the second and third periods, students spent 20–30 min using the assigned software (the total study session time given in both conditions was about 50 min). On the final day, students took the posttest and the IMI survey. Students were given access to both versions after the study (data logging had stopped before we gave access to the tutor versions).

3.2 Results

Of the 94 students, 60 students completed all study activities (32 in the Gwynnette condition, 28 in the Lynnette condition). The high attrition rate was expected given the difficulty of conducting the study remotely. For example, teachers had to support students through a videoconferencing system and were not able to walk around the classroom to support students when necessary, which is typically done in in-person studies [19]. We included the 60 students in the final sample for the analyses. No statistically significant difference was found between the conditions on the dropout rate, X^2 $(1, N = 94) = .74$, $p = .39$.

Results on Learning. All student responses for the open-ended questions were coded for whether student answers were correct or incorrect by two researchers (*Cohen's kappa* = .86) and disagreements were resolved through discussions. Table 2 shows students' mean pretest and posttest scores. To test RQ1 (i.e., effect on learning), we conducted two separate linear regressions, with conceptual knowledge posttest score (CK) and procedural knowledge posttest score (PK) as the dependent variable, respectively. In both models, condition (Gwynnette or Lynnette, coded as 1 or 0) served as a predictor, and pretest score was added as a covariate to control for students' incoming knowledge. Results showed that students in the Gwynnette condition significantly outperformed those in the Lynnette condition on CK ($\beta = .78$, $t(57) = 2.10, p = .04$) but no difference was found on PK ($\beta = .45$, $t(57) = 1.08$, $p = .28$) (Fig. 5, left). Across the conditions, there was a significant pretest-to-posttest gain on CK ($\beta = 2.02$, $t(57) = 5.43, p < .01$) but not on PK ($\beta = .59$, $t(57) = 1.42, p = .16$).

Table 2. Mean pretest and posttest scores (standard deviations) in each condition.

Condition	CK (*max* = 7)		PK (*max* = 5)	
	Pretest	Posttest	Pretest	Posttest
Gwynnette	2.94 (1.44)	3.56 (1.74)	1.25 (1.52)	2.12 (1.84)
Lynnette	2.61 (1.81)	2.71 (1.80)	1.39 (1.83)	1.61 (1.97)

Results on Engagement. For RQ2 (i.e., effect on engagement), we analyzed students' ratings from the IMI survey. We took the mean score from the seven items for each student (*range:* 1–7). The mean score in the Gwynnette condition was 5.20 ($SD = 1.14$), whereas it was 4.80 ($SD = 1.26$) in the Lynnette condition. A Welch two-sample t-test showed that this difference is not statistically significant, $t(55.12) = 1.28, p = .21$.

To further understand student engagement, we also measured students' total time spent working on the system, a behavioral indicator for engagement [21]. In this study, the time spent working on the software was not controlled; students were encouraged to use the software outside the class periods. Therefore, a longer period of system use indicates higher engagement (i.e., the student used the system outside the class periods) On average, students spent 54.03 min ($SD = 34.47$) with Gwynnette while those with Lynnette spent 27.98 min ($SD = 22.69$), about a half the amount of time as the Gwynnette condition (Fig. 5, right). A Welch two-sample t-test revealed that this difference was statistically significant, $t(53.98) = 3.50, p < .01$.

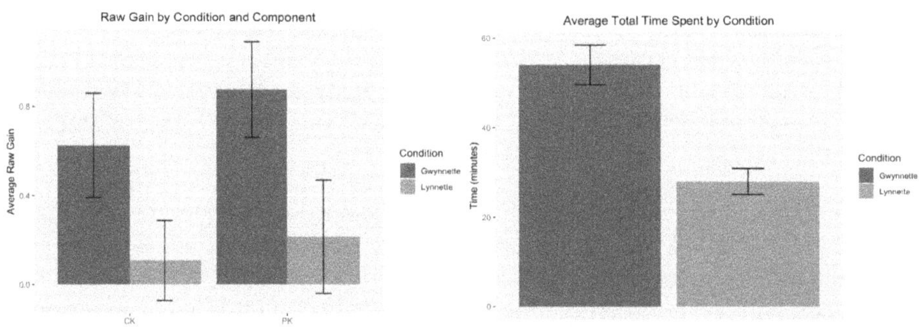

Fig. 5. Students' raw gain scores on the two test components (conceptual and procedural knowledge, left) and total time spent on the system (right). Error bars show standard errors.

System Log Data Analysis. To examine RQ3 (i.e., effect on learning processes), we analyzed the log data gathered from the software. Specifically, we investigated students' learning process measures, including average time spent per problem, average number of hints used per problem, and error rate (i.e., proportion of incorrect attempts for each problem-solving attempt in the system). Table 3 shows descriptive statistics for these measures. We conducted three separate linear regressions, with one of the three process measures as the dependent variable in each model, and condition and prior knowledge as predictors for all the models. These models revealed that students with Gwynnette had a significantly lower error rate ($\beta = -0.17, t(57) = -3.87, p < .01$) but spent more time on each problem ($\beta = 39.15, t(57) = 2.60, p = .01$), compared to those with Lynnette. No significant difference was found on the frequency of hint use. Also, students with Gwynnette solved significantly more problems ($M = 25.8$ problems, $SD = 14.4$) than those with Lynnette ($M = 18.1$ problems, $SD = 10.7$) ($\beta = 7.48, t(57) = 2.32, p = .02$). This difference is likely due to the significantly more time spent by students who learned with Gwynnette. Indeed, the number of problems solved and total time spent were strongly correlated ($r = .81, p < .01$).

Table 3. Learning process measures (standard deviations in parentheses) in each condition.

Condition	Error rate	Time spent on each problem (sec.)	Hint requests per problem
Gwynnette	0.29 (0.20)	136.0 (61.4)	1.83 (2.52)
Lynnette	0.47 (0.22)	98.5 (66.2)	1.89 (2.74)

What Design Features Might Explain the Observed Differences? The results above raise a question, "what made Gwynnette more effective and engaging?" Although it is not possible to tease apart causal effects of each design feature, we investigated two additional questions to get further insights into the potential mechanism involved: 1) *How do students' interaction patterns in each system relate to their learning outcomes?* and 2) *Are there any pain points in the system that students struggle with?*

First, we took a closer look at the dataset in each condition separately 1) to examine behaviors that are related to the distinctive features in each system. For Gwynnette, one of the deliberate design choices was to encourage the learning of *doing the same thing to both sides of an equation*, important conceptual knowledge [9] by not allowing students to type in a number in the blank box before creating another blank box on the other side of the equation (Fig. 3). To examine if this interaction design might have something to do with students' conceptual learning, we calculated the number of instances where students tried to type in a number in the added box before doing the same thing to both sides of an equation (to which the system gave feedback saying, e.g., "You need to drag the plus sign to the other side of the equation before choosing what to add"). We found that, of the 32 students in the Gwynnette condition, all but two at least once tried to type in a number before dragging an operator to both sides of an equation. On average, this action was performed 4.86 times ($SD = 4.46$) per student. The number of times this action was performed was strongly, negatively correlated with students' pretest score on CK items ($r = -.35, p = .048$); however, there was no significant relations between this action and their conceptual knowledge posttests score nor the gain from pretest to posttest on students' conceptual knowledge. In other words, students with high prior knowledge of algebra concepts were more likely to avoid such a behavior than those with lower prior knowledge, but their performance with this interaction in the system does not predict their learning.

For the dataset from the Lynnette condition, we examined if students showed a "guess-and-check" behavior [22] by calculating the number of instances where students, for their first attempt, typed in "$x =$ [a number]" (e.g., "$x = 3$") without showing any intermediate steps (Gwynnette requires step-by-step solutions and preempts guess-and-check strategies). The "guess-and-check" behavior is considered an informal, unideal strategy in solving algebra problems [22]. We investigated this behavior because it could indicate lower conceptual learning and lower engagement with the system (i.e., "gaming the system" behavior [23]). Of the 28 students in the Lynnette condition, 20 students showed the behavior at least once, with the average number of times being 15.8 ($SD =$ 18.5) per student. Correlational analyses showed no relationships between the number of times students used guess-and-check and their conceptual pretest score, conceptual posttest score, and pretest-posttest gain score on conceptual knowledge. However, we found that students who used this strategy tended to spend less time with the system ($r = -.41$, $p = .03$), suggesting that students who used this strategy tended not to engage with the system.

Next, we explored 2) how the interaction patterns changed over time, to examine any pain points in the system that students encountered. Figure 6 (left) shows a visualization of distributions in error rate for each problem set as side-by-side boxplots. One can expect that, within each problem set, learners would normally show some errors but subsequently errors would decline over time as they make progress in the system. As can be observed, students in the Gwynnette condition show smaller variance overall, especially after the first two levels. However, the error rate in the Lynnette condition generally shows a greater variance, indicating that some students in the Lynnette condition solved problems with very few errors while others in the same condition made many incorrect attempts. This may be an indication that, while most of the students who learned with Gwynnette were able to quickly learn how to use the drag-and-drop interactions, a new way to solve equations, after some practice, some students in the Lynnette condition did not become fluent in using the "type-in" interaction to solve equations, even after practice. Furthermore, students in the Lynnette condition had greater difficulty compared to those with Gwynnette especially in levels 5, 8, and 10 (Fig. 6, right). These levels are where the *simplify-before-transform* problems (i.e., students first need to subtract/add constant or variable terms before starting to use operators to transform equations), problems with variable terms on both sides of an equation, and problems with negative numbers in a complex equation format were introduced, respectively (Table 1). These factors (e.g., negative numbers and variable terms in "unusual places") are reported to have a strong influence on students' problem-solving performance [24].

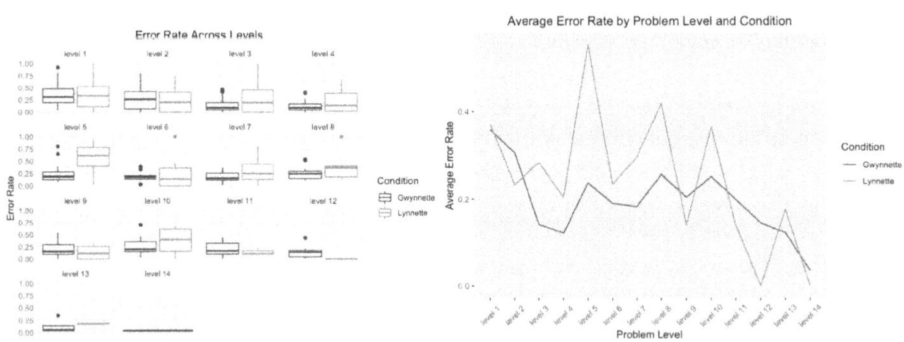

Fig. 6. Distributions of error rates across problem levels (left). Means of error rates across problem levels, plotted as a line chart (right). In both graphs, patterns seen across Levels 12–14 do not inform consistent insights as there were only 9 students in total who reached Level 12 problems (Gwynnette: $n = 7$, Lynnette: $n = 2$).

4 Discussion and Conclusion

We tested whether the deliberate design of playful features in algebra learning software can help enhance student learning and engagement through a controlled classroom experiment. Gwynnette had several playful interaction and gamification features, including drag-and-drop interactions, a space theme, an alien guide, and sounds. Lynnette had no such features; instead of transforming equations through dragging and dropping, students typed in transformed equations. The results of the experiment showed that students who used Gwynnette learned more conceptual knowledge in algebra than those with Lynnette. Students with Gwynnette also showed greater problem-solving efficiency, demonstrated by the overall lower error rate in the system. As well, students engaged significantly more with Gwynnette than with Lynnette, as measured by the total time spent working with the system. There was no statistically significant difference between the conditions in students' ratings on the IMI survey, therefore we cannot fully establish the effect on engagement. However, their ratings correlated positively with the total time spent working on the system ($r = .33$, $p < .01$), and we view the behavioral measure as more compelling evidence than students' self-report. Despite the extended use of the software, however, students with Gwynnette did not outperform those with Lynnette on procedural knowledge. This result suggests less effective procedural learning, possibly due to the new format for solving equations on the interface (i.e., their practice did not transfer to the performance on the posttest).

It is interesting to ask how the design features may have contributed to improved engagement and conceptual learning. Although our study design does not allow us to attribute any outcomes to specific design elements, we can make somewhat speculative inferences based on the design of the systems and findings. For instance, the fact that students with Gwynnette had a lower error rate suggests that the playful drag-and-drop interactions brought about a smooth learning experience. It may also be that the playful features might have led to greater enjoyment, resulting in longer use of the system, hence greater learning gains. As well, the drag-and-drop interactions in Gwynnette perhaps allowed students to focus on the transformations, rather than dealing with arithmetic calculations. This focus may have led to greater conceptual learning. Also, we found that students' explicit action of *doing the same thing to both sides of an equation* had a positive association with students' conceptual knowledge on the pretest, which disappeared on the posttest. This might imply that students' interactions with (and learning from) this deliberate aspect of the drag-and-drop design, rather than whether they performed well or not with the specific action, had a positive influence on conceptual learning. Students with Lynnette, on the other hand, had to perform arithmetic calculations when solving equations, which may have contributed to the greater difficulty that students in the Lynnette condition experienced for new problem types. Also, some students with Lynnette tended to skip problem-solving steps using the "guess-and-check" strategy. Although those who used "guess-and-check" frequently spent less time on each problem ($r = -.63$, $p < .01$), they also did not finish all problem and rather tended to stop using it early ($r = -.41$, $p = .03$), indicating lower engagement.

The current study makes a design contribution that the deliberate design of playful features in a learning technology can help achieve the challenging goal of supporting both learning and engagement in algebra. The features helped students engage with algebra, a notoriously unpopular subject among students [6], with double the time spent. Practically, the study offers an example that designing for a playful learning experience with learning technology can support students' remote learning during difficult times (e.g., a pandemic). Studies report that it is highly challenging for students to engage with school work during remote learning [19, 25]. By allowing for unmoderated system use outside of the class time, we found that students with Gwynnette spent twice as much time (and learned more).

We acknowledge several limitations of the study. First, the study tested very specific design features in the domain of early algebra. We do not know if the findings will generalize across domains. Some of the added features were domain-independent (e.g., alien guide, space theme, and sounds), but at least one of them (drag-and-drop interactions for solving equations) may not be. Second, the study was conducted during the COVID-19 pandemic where students, teachers, and experimenters were all connected virtually. It is possible that the findings would have looked different if the study had been conducted in the in-person classroom where teachers were able to help students as they would have done *normally*. Finally, we cannot attribute the results to specific features in the system. Future studies could experimentally test the question.

Acknowledgements. This research was supported by NSF Award #1760922. We thank Martha W. Alibali, Max Benson, Jenny Yun-Chen Chan, Octav Popescu, Jonathan Sewall, and all the participating teachers and students.

References

1. Nguyen, H., Harpstead, E., Wang, Y., McLaren, B.M.: Student agency and game-based learning: a study comparing low and high agency. In: Penstein Rosé, C., et al. (eds.) AIED 2018. LNCS (LNAI), vol. 10947, pp. 338–351. Springer, Cham (2018). https://doi.org/10.1007/978-3-319-93843-1_25
2. Spielhagen, F.R.: Closing the achievement gap in math: the long-term effects of eighth-grade algebra. J. Adv. Acad. **18**, 34–59 (2006)
3. Rittle-Johnson, B., Siegler, R.S.: The relation between conceptual and procedural knowledge in learning mathematics: a review. Dev. Math. Skills **338**, 75–110 (1998)
4. Crooks, N.M., Alibali, M.W.: Defining and measuring conceptual knowledge in mathematics. Dev. Rev. **34**, 344–377 (2014)
5. McNeil, N.M., Alibali, M.W.: Why won't you change your mind? Knowledge of operational patterns hinders learning and performance on equations. Child Dev. **76**, 883–899 (2005)
6. Norton, S., Irvin, J.: Developing positive attitudes towards algebra. In: Proceedings of the 30th Annual Conference of the Mathematics Education Research Group of Australasia, pp. 561–570 (2007)
7. Long, Y., Aleven, V.: Educational game and intelligent tutoring system: a classroom study and comparative design analysis. ACM Trans. Comput.-Hum. Interact. **24**, 1–27 (2017)
8. Pane, J.F., Griffin, B.A., McCaffrey, D.F., Karam, R.: Effectiveness of cognitive tutor algebra I at scale. Educ. Eval. Policy Anal. **36**, 127–144 (2014)
9. Nagashima, T., Bartel, A., Silla, E., Vest, N., Alibali, M.W., Aleven, V.: Enhancing conceptual knowledge in early algebra through scaffolding diagrammatic self-explanation. In: Gresalfi, M., Horn, I.S. (eds.) Proceedings of the 14th International Conference of the Learning Sciences, pp. 35–43. International Society of the Learning Sciences (2020)

10. Jackson, G.T., McNamara, D.S.: Motivation and performance in a game-based intelligent tutoring system. J. Educ. Psychol. **105**, 1036–1049 (2013)
11. Siew, N.M., Geofrey, J., Lee, B.N.: Students' algebraic thinking and attitudes towards algebra: the effects of game-based learning using Dragonbox 12+ App. Res. J. Math. Technol. **5**, 66–79 (2016)
12. Chan, J.Y.-C., Lee, J.-E., Mason, C.A., Sawrey, K., Ottmar, E.: From Here to There! A dynamic algebraic notation system improves understanding of equivalence in middle-school students. J. Educ. Psychol. **114**, 56–71 (2021)
13. Ottmar, E., Landy, D., Goldstone, R.: Teaching the perceptual structure of algebraic expressions: preliminary findings from the pushing symbols intervention. In: Proceedings of the Annual Meeting of the Cognitive Science Society (2012)
14. Hulse, T., Daigle, M., Manzo, D., Braith, L., Harrison, A., Ottmar, E.: From Here to There! Elementary: a game-based approach to developing number sense and early algebraic understanding. Educ. Technol. Res. Dev. **67**, 423–441 (2019)
15. Schneider, B., Jermann, P., Zufferey, G., Dillenbourg, P.: Benefits of a tangible interface for collaborative learning and interaction. IEEE Trans. Learn. Technol. **4**, 222–232 (2011)
16. Ruan, S., et al.: Supporting children's math learning with feedback-augmented narrative technology. In: Proceedings of the Interaction Design and Children Conference, pp. 567–580. ACM, New York (2020)
17. Xi, N., Hamari, J.: Does gamification satisfy needs? A study on the relationship between gamification features and intrinsic need satisfaction. Int. J. Inf. Manag. **46**, 210–221 (2019)
18. Kim, J.T., Lee, W.-H.: Dynamical model for gamification of learning (DMGL). Multimed. Tools Appl. **74**(19), 8483–8493 (2013). https://doi.org/10.1007/s11042-013-1612-8
19. Nagashima, T., Yadav, G., Aleven, V.: A framework to guide educational technology studies in the evolving classroom research environment. In: De Laet, T., Klemke, R., Alario-Hoyos, C., Hilliger, I., Ortega-Arranz, A. (eds.) EC-TEL 2021. LNCS, vol. 12884, pp. 207–220. Springer, Cham (2021). https://doi.org/10.1007/978-3-030-86436-1_16
20. McAuley, E., Duncan, T., Tammen, V.V.: Psychometric properties of the intrinsic motivation inventory in a competitive sport setting: a confirmatory factor analysis. Res. Q. Exerc. Sport. **60**, 48–58 (1989)
21. Marwan, S., Price, T.W., Chi, M., Barnes, T.: Immediate data-driven positive feedback increases engagement on programming homework for novices. In: CSEDM@EDM (2020)
22. Chu, J., Rittle-Johnson, B., Fyfe, E.R.: Diagrams benefit symbolic problem-solving. Br. J. Educ. Psychol. **87**(2), 273–287 (2017). https://bpspsychub.onlinelibrary.wiley.com/doi/full/10.1111/bjep.12149?casa_token=iTS6Ofbs5n0AAAAA%3AZbCl5bJe2zKN6zI8RmcsOa60AKPV88Gq6q4UkS85-Mo_nncux2dKNjVr2pXUQNqdTwnCDzOLLiO1f9ot
23. Baker, R., Walonoski, J., Heffernan, N., Roll, I., Corbett, A., Koedinger, K.: Why students engage in "gaming the system" behavior in interactive learning environments. J. Interact. Learn. Res. **19**, 185–224 (2008)
24. Long, Y., Holstein, K., Aleven, V.: What exactly do students learn when they practice equation solving?: refining knowledge components with the additive factors model. In: Proceedings of the 8th International Conference on Learning Analytics and Knowledge, pp. 399–408. ACM, Sydney (2018)
25. Stelitano, L., Doan, S., Woo, A., Diliberti, M., Kaufman, J.H., Henry, D.: The digital divide and COVID-19: teachers' perceptions of inequities in students' internet access and participation in remote learning. Data note: Insights from the American Educator Panels. Research Report. RAND Corporation (2020)

Towards Generalized Methods for Automatic Question Generation in Educational Domains

Huy A. Nguyen(✉), Shravya Bhat, Steven Moore, Norman Bier, and John Stamper

Carnegie Mellon University, Pittsburgh, PA 15213, USA
hn1@cs.cmu.edu

Abstract. Students learn more from doing activities and practicing their skills on assessments, yet it can be challenging and time consuming to generate such practice opportunities. In our work, we examine how advances in natural language processing and question generation may help address this issue. In particular, we present a pipeline for generating and evaluating questions from text-based learning materials in an introductory data science course. The pipeline includes applying a text-to-text transformer (T5) question generation model and a concept hierarchy extraction model on the text content, then scoring the generated questions based on their relevance to the extracted key concepts. We further evaluated the question quality with three different approaches: information score, automated rating by a trained model (Google GPT-3) and manual review by human instructors. Our results showed that the generated questions were rated favorably by all three evaluation methods. We conclude with a discussion of the strengths and weaknesses of the generated questions and outline the next steps towards refining the pipeline and promoting natural language processing research in educational domains.

Keywords: Question generation · Concept extraction · Question evaluation

1 Introduction

As online education continues to expand during and after the COVID pandemic, the need for effective and scalable assessment tools emerges as a pressing issue for instructors and educators. On one hand, frequent formative assessments are crucial in reinforcing student learning in an online environment, where the learning experience may be undermined by a multitude of factors, including the lack of motivation [1] and student-teacher interaction [19]. On the other hand, summative assessments that rely on human grader evaluation, such as group projects and essays, are difficult to carry out at scale, making multiple-choice and short-answer questions, which are amenable to automatic grading, a more practical alternative. Consequently, amid many other logistical issues that arise from emergency online education [16], instructors often find themselves having to generate a large question bank to accommodate this new learning format. In turn, this challenge motivates the need for supporting instructor efforts via methods that automatically generate usable assessment questions based on the learning materials, in a way that requires minimal inputs from instructors and domain experts.

I. Hilliger et al. (Eds.): EC-TEL 2022, LNCS 13450, pp. 272–284, 2022.
https://doi.org/10.1007/978-3-031-16290-9_20

Recent advances in natural language processing (NLP), question answering (QA) and question generation (QG) offer a promising path to accomplishing this goal. While QA has been a longtime area of interest for NLP researchers, with wide applications ranging from beating the Jeopardy! challenge [14] to supporting modern intelligent assistants [12], QG has only garnered attention in recent years. Much of the interest in QG stems from the large number of BERT-based models trained on very large corpuses that demonstrate the ability to generate interesting results in open domains [49]. QG in educational domains is an even narrower focus, but holds great potential in transforming the way assessments are generated and conducted [39]. Most theories of learning emphasize repeated practice as an important mechanism for mastering low-level knowledge components, which altogether contribute to the high-level learning objectives [20]. We therefore envision that having the ability to generate questions on-demand would accommodate students' varying levels of learning needs, while allowing instructors to allocate resources to other components of the course.

Our work presents an initial step towards realizing this capability. We applied state-of-the-art Text-To-Text Transfer Transformer (T5) models [45] on conceptual reading materials from a graduate-level data science course to generate potential questions that may be used for assessment. We then evaluated these questions in three different ways. First, we conducted a separate concept hierarchy extraction process on the reading materials to extract the important concept keywords and scored each generated question based on how many such keywords it contains. Second, we applied a fine-tuned GPT-3 model to classify the questions as either pedagogically sound or not. Finally, we had two data science instructors perform this same classification task manually. Our results contribute key insights into the feasibility of applying state-of-the-art NLP models in generating meaningful questions, with a pipeline that generalizes well across learning domains.

2 Background

Recent advances in deep learning have revitalized many areas of artificial intelligence. Within the fields of NLP and QG, significant progress has been made since the introduction of neural transformer-based methods [42], particularly deep bidirectional transformers (BERT [11]), which differ from previous language models in their training approach (masked language modeling and next sentence prediction) as well as their subsequent learned representation of text from both sides (left and right) of the sentences. We summarize recent NLP improvements that are pertinent to QG below.

While BERT could help address the problem of handling long sequences that a traditional recurrent neural network encounters, its initial performance in QG was rather poor, as it did not consider the decoding results of previous steps while producing tokens [7]. Lopez et al. [28] solved this issue with fine-tuning techniques on a single pre-trained language model to design a QG system that generates robust questions at reduced training cost and time. Subsequent research also investigated ways to encode common sense and domain knowledge in the QG process, with Jia et al. [18] utilizing concept-relevant knowledge triples from ConceptNet, a freely available knowledge graph, and Wang et al. [43] building custom knowledge graph models to prevent the generation of irrelevant and uninformative questions. More recently, Liu [24] attempted to increase the relevance of generated questions with an attention-based, sequence-to-sequence model that incorporates target answer information into the question generation process. QG models have also been used to generate training corpora for Question Answering tasks [3].

A subset of QG research involves generating questions specifically for educational purposes, to be used as assessment materials [2]. Towards automatically generating educationally usable questions, previous work has investigated targeting certain cognitive levels of questions, including high-level ones that require synthesis and evaluation or low-level ones that focus on recall [47]. For example, recent work has used the GPT-2 model to generate mathematical word problems at varying levels of difficulty [9]. This approach was found to yield high quality questions, as judged by both automatic and human evaluation, with the capability of altering the perceived difficulty of generated questions. Related work by Liu et al. [27] also investigated automatically generating educational questions in math, with a knowledge graph as the source document for their model. The generated questions were evaluated as coherent, diverse and reflective of real-life scenarios that students may encounter. However, a recent review of question generation for educational purposes found that, while methods for producing educationally valid questions are improving, there is a greater need to properly evaluate them [22].

Question evaluation is traditionally split into two core methods, based on whether the evaluation is performed by trained machine learning models or expert human judges. Automatic assessment of questions often involves the use of evaluation metrics such as BLEU and ROGUE, which quantify how close the generated question text is to an existing human-generated text [31]. However, recent work has reported interpretability issues with these metrics, along with a lack of correlation between them and human evaluation [41]. At the same time, Sha et al. [37] found that using BERT to classify student forum posts based on the question type, post sentiment and confusion level achieved similar results as human evaluators. For human evaluation, a recent meta analysis found that over half of the reviewed research involved criteria related to grammar, fluency, topic relevance, and naturalness [9, 13, 47], most frequently on a numerical scale [4]. Previous work involving human evaluation of questions has also utilized different rubrics, such as being useful or not useful for learning [8] or being shallow or deep [34]. In line with these approaches, our work also employs both automated and expert labeling of the generated questions, so as to arrive at a holistic evaluation of their usability.

Another metric for evaluation involves how much the generated questions align with the "ground truth" data, such as reference questions created by human experts [36]. In educational QG, we expect assessment items to match the target skills of the corresponding unit and module, which raises the need to identify these skills from the learning material. A recent effort in automating this task was carried out by the researchers behind MOOCCubeX [46], an open-access, educational data repository created with the aim of supporting research on adaptive learning in massive open online courses. This framework is capable of performing data processing, weakly supervised fine-grained concept graph mining, and data curation to re-organize data in a concept-centric manner. The published toolkit also assists with the creation of new datasets for adaptive learning and concept mining. In our work, we will examine how well the generated questions match the knowledge concepts identified by MOOCCubeX.

3 Methods

3.1 Dataset

We used the learning materials from a graduate-level introductory data science course at an R1 university in the northeastern United States. The course has been offered every semester since Summer 2020, with class sizes ranging from 30–90 in general. The course content is divided into the conceptual components and the hands-on projects. Students learn from six conceptual Units, further broken down into sixteen Modules, each consisting of several data science Topics such as *Feature Engineering* and *Bias-Variance Trade-off*. Each Module consists of reading assignments, ungraded formative assessments and weekly quizzes serving as graded summative assessments. Students also get to practice with the learned concepts through seven hands-on coding projects, which are evaluated by an automatic grading system. In the scope of this work, we will focus on generating questions from the textual content of the six Units in the course, using the pipeline introduced in the following section.

3.2 Question Generation Pipeline

The overall pipeline for question generation and evaluation consists of six steps. First, we extract the learning materials from an online learning platform which hosts the course. This extracted data is in XML format, which preserves not only the text content but also its hierarchy within the course structure, i.e., which Unit, Module and Topic each paragraph of text belongs to. We scraped the text content from the XML files using the Beautiful Soup library[1]. From this point, the resulting text data was input to two separate processes, Concept Hierarchy Extraction and Question Generation.

Concept Hierarchy Extraction. This process was carried out by the MOOCCubeX pipeline [46], which performs weakly supervised fine-grained concept extraction on a given corpus without relying on expert input. As an example, given a paragraph that explains Regression, some of the extracted concepts include *least-squared error*, *regularization*, and *conditional expectation*; these could be viewed as the key concepts which students are expected to understand after reading the materials. A researcher in the team reviewed the generated concepts and manually removed those which were deemed invalid, including prepositions (e.g., *'around'*), generic verbs (e.g., *'classifying'*) and numbers (e.g., *'45'* – this is part of a numeric example in the text, rather than an important constant to memorize).

Question Generation. For this process, we applied Google's T5 [45], which is a transformer-based encoder-decoder model. Since its pre-training involves a multi-task structure of supervised and unsupervised learning, T5 works well on a variety of natural

---

[1] https://www.crummy.com/software/BeautifulSoup/bs4/doc/.

language tasks by merely changing the structure of the input passed to it. For our use case, we collect all the text within each Topic (which typically consists of 3–6 paragraphs), prepend this text by a header name (which is the name of either the Topic itself, or the corresponding Module, or the corresponding Unit), and input the resulting corpus to T5 (see an example in Fig. 1). In this way, we generate three questions for each Topic in the course. Our rationale for including the header name in the T5 input text is to inform the model of the high-level concept which the generated questions should center around. We had previously tried extracting answers from the text content using a custom rule-based approach with a dependency parse tree, but found that this resulted in the creation of more nonsensical than sensible questions; in comparison, incorporating the headers led to higher quality questions. Before applying the model to our dataset, we also fine-tuned it on SQuAD 1.1 [32], a well known reading comprehension dataset of questions curated by crowd workers on Wikipedia articles and a common benchmark for question-answering models.

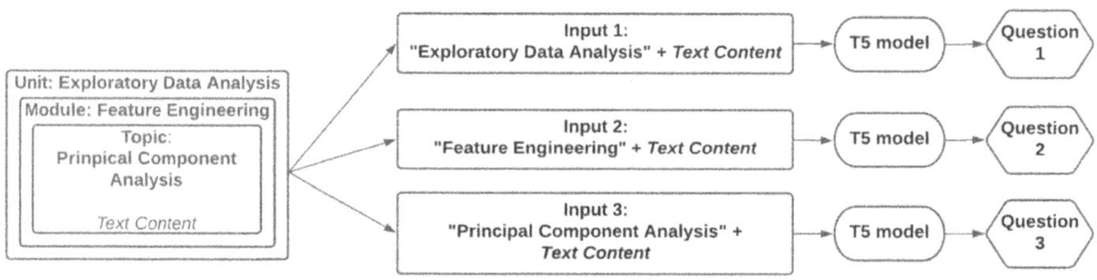

Fig. 1. Example question generation process for the text content in one Topic.

3.3 Evaluation

We evaluated the generated questions with three different methods as follows.

Information Score. This is a set of custom metrics that denote how relevant each question is to the key concepts identified in the Concept Hierarchy Extraction step. We denote this set of key concepts as C. For every generated question q, we further denote $T(q)$ as the set of tokens in it and compute the *information score* as the number of tokens in q that coincide with an extracted concept,

$$IS(q) = \frac{1}{|T(q)|} \sum\nolimits_{t \in T(q)} 1(t \in C). \tag{1}$$

where the division by q's length is to normalize the metric so that longer questions are not inherently favored. With this formulation, higher scores indicate better questions that touch on more of the key learning concepts.

GPT-3 Classification. We used a GPT-3 classification model [6], as it has been a popular choice for text classification tasks such as detecting hate speech [10] and text sentiment

[48]. Our classification task involves rating each question as either *pedagogically sound* or *not*. A pedagogically sound question is one that pertains to the course content and is intended to assess the domain knowledge of the student. An example of a question classified as pedagogically sound in a Physics course is "*Why can't voltage-gated channels be placed on the surface of Myelin?*". A question is classified as not sound if it is vague, unclear, or not about assessing domain knowledge. For example, the question "*What programming language do I need to learn before I start learning algorithms?*" is a valid question, but it is classified as not sound, as it pertains to a course prerequisite rather than assessing domain knowledge.

To make these classifications, we first fine-tuned the GPT-3 model with default parameters on the LearningQ dataset [8]. This dataset is publicly available and contains 5600 student-generated questions from Khan Academy. Each question contains a label to indicate if it is useful for learning or not, as annotated by two expert instructors. No preprocessing was performed on the questions used to fine–tune the model; they were used as-is from the publicly available dataset along with their corresponding binary labels. Fine-tuning the model with default hyperparameters[2] took approximately 10 min and incurred a cost of $0.21. Next, we passed in the T5-generated questions as the GPT-3 model's input, obtaining the output as a set of binary rating labels.

Expert Evaluation. To further validate the quality of the questions, as well as that of the classification model, we had two expert raters with 5 + years of teaching experience in the domain of data science rate each question. Following the same classification process as in previous work [8], the two raters indicated if each question was pedagogically sound or not. We measured the Inter-Rater Reliability (IRR) between the two raters and found they achieved a Cohen's kappa of $\kappa = 0.425$, with similarity in 75.59% of the question ratings, indicating a moderate level of agreement [23]. The remaining discordant questions were discussed between the two raters until they reached a consensus on their classification.

4 Results

Following the pipeline introduced in Sect. 2, we generated a total of 219 questions across the three header levels - Topic, Module and Unit. 16 questions were removed due to being duplicates[3], leading to a final set of 203 unique questions. Table 1 shows a number of example generated questions, along with their information scores and GPT-3 model evaluation. Among the 203 questions, 151 (74.38%) were classified as pedagogically sound by the GPT-3 model. To compare this classification with the human raters' consensus, which rated 115 (56.7%) questions as pedagogically sound, we constructed a confusion matrix as shown in Table 2. We observed that the model agreed with human raters in 135 (66.50%) instances; in cases where they disagreed, most of the mismatches (52 out of 68) were due to the GPT-3 model overestimating the questions' soundness.

[2] We used the hyperparameter set suggested in https://beta.openai.com/docs/guides/fine-tuning.

[3] With our question generation routine (Fig. 1), the text content in each Topic was used as input three times, which could lead to duplicate questions, even if the accompanying header names were different.

Table 1. Example generated questions across different header levels and soundness ratings.

Generated question	Header level	IS	GPT-3 rating	Expert rating
What is the process of using domain knowledge to extract features from raw data?	Module	0.5	Sound	Sound
What are two types of decision trees?	Topic	0.57	Sound	Sound
What is the tradeoff between bias and variance?	Unit	0.375	Sound	Sound
What is used to evaluate clustering when labeled data is not present?	Module	0.33	Sound	Sound
What are two methods that can be used to improve a regression model?	Unit	0.53	Sound	Sound
What is the term for PCA?	Topic	0.16	Sound	Not sound
What is the main topic of the Data Wrangling module?	Topic	0.2	Not sound	Not sound
What is one of the easiest techniques to implement?	Topic	0.22	Not sound	Not sound
What is the title of the Information Design Unit?	Topic	0	Not sound	Not sound
What is the name of the pattern that is used in the module on regression?	Module	0.2	Not sound	Not sound

Table 2. Confusion matrix for comparing GPT-3 and expert evaluations.

	Expert: Not sound	Expert: Sound
GPT-3: Not sound	36	16
GPT-3: Sound	52	99

We followed up with a qualitative review of the questions rated as not sound by human experts to better understand (1) what separated them from the questions rated as sound, and (2) why the GPT-3 model might still rate them as sound. For (1), we identified two important requirements that a question generally needs to meet to be considered sound by human experts. First, it has to thoroughly set up the *context* (e.g., what is the scenario, how many responses are expected) from which an answer could be reasonably derived. An example question that satisfies this category is "*What are* ***two*** *types of visions that a data science team will* ***work with a client*** *to develop?*," where the bolded terms are important contextual factors which make the question sound. Without these terms, the question would become "*what are the types of vision that a data science team will develop?*," which is too ambiguous. We further note that sound questions with thorough contexts tend to be longer, because they necessarily include more information to describe such contexts. At the same time, short questions may still be considered sound by expert raters if they target a sufficiently *specific* concept. For example, "*what is a way to improve a* ***decision tree's performance****?*" is considered sound because the bolded term is very specific. On the other hand, a similar-looking question such as "*what is a way to analyze business data*" is not sound, due to "*analyze business data*" being too broad. It is this second requirement of *specificity* that the GPT-3 model fails to recognize. Many of the questions rated as sound by GPT-3, but not by human raters, are similar to ones such as "*What are two types of data science tasks?,*" which could not be used as a stand-alone assessment question due to a lack of specificity.

Next, we examined whether our IS metric, which calculates the number of important concepts that a question encapsulates, aligns with its pedagogical soundness. Figure 2 (left) shows the distribution of information scores for the questions in each class (pedagogically sound or not), within each type of header level. A one-way ANOVA showed that, among the questions generated with the Topic header names, there was a significant difference in IS between questions rated as pedagogically sound and those rated as not sound by human experts, $F(1, 68) = 8.60, p < .01$. In this case, the pedagogically sound questions ($M = 0.39, SD = 0.14$) had higher IS values than their counterparts ($M = 0.30$, $SD = 0.12$). However, the difference in IS between these two groups was not significant among the questions generated by the Unit header names, $F(1, 66) = 0.07, p = .79$, or the Module header names, $F(1, 63) = 0.41$, $p = .53$. Figure 2 (right) shows the same distribution based on the GPT-3 model's ratings; in this case, however, the IS between sound and non-sound questions were similar across all three header levels.

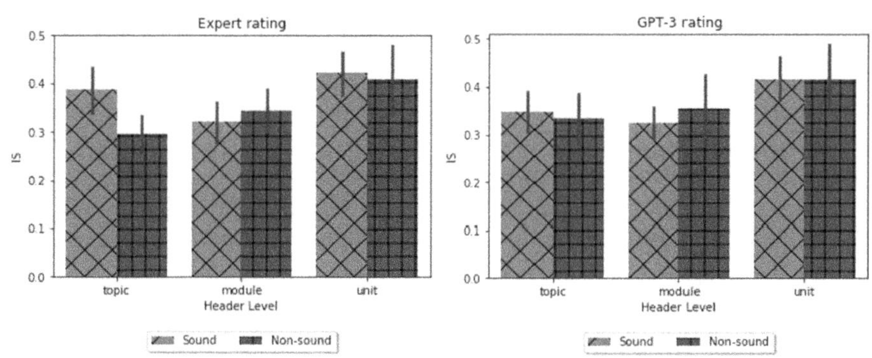

Fig. 2. Distribution of information score at each header level, partitioned by expert ratings (left) and GPT-3 ratings (right).

Finally, we examined which level of header tended to yield the most pedagogically sound questions, based on human ratings. We observed that the number of sound and non-sound questions were respectively 35 and 35 at the Topic level, 37 and 28 at the Module level, and 43 and 25 at the Unit level. Among the sound questions, those generated with the Unit headers were the most common, while those generated with the Topic headers were the least. Conversely, among not-sound questions, those generated with the Topic header were the most common. These distributions suggest that the Topic levels were not suitable for question generation.

5 Discussion

In this work, we propose and evaluate a domain-independent pipeline for generating assessment questions based on instructional materials in an introductory data science course. Our research is motivated by the general lack of practice opportunities in online higher education, as well as the high labor cost in manual question generation, which was reported to be approximately 200 h for one course [35]. Furthermore, the ability to generate questions on-demand can greatly assist adaptive and personalized learning technologies, especially in the context of mastery learning where students are prompted to continue practicing until they reach mastery [33]. To this end, our work makes use of state-of-the-art language models for question generation, concept extraction and question evaluation, in addition to custom scoring metrics and expert labeling as additional validation measures. In general, we found a moderate level of agreement between the three evaluation methods – information score, GPT-3 classification and human judgment – which all rate a high percentage of the generated questions as capturing important concepts or being pedagogically sound. We discuss the features of the generated questions and the possibilities of extending the proposed pipeline as follows.

We saw that the GPT-3 model, fine-tuned on the LearningQ dataset [8], was able to replicate 66.50% of the two expert raters' consensus, which is well above chance. The model appeared to learn that long questions are likely sound, which is a reasonable assumption as these questions might contain more relevant contextual information. However, it also classified a number of short questions as sound, despite the lack of specificity which human evaluators could easily recognize. As the LearningQ dataset did not contain data science questions, it is no surprise that our model was not particularly good at distinguishing between specific data science concepts (e.g., "*decision tree's performance*") and ambiguous ones (e.g., "*business data*"). Additional fine-tuning of the GPT-3 model on a new dataset with questions and expert-generated labels that are closer to our learning domain would therefore be a promising next step.

When treating the expert classification of question soundness as the ground truth labels, we were able to draw a number of comparisons. First, we found that the sound questions generally had higher information score values than those rated as not sound (Fig. 2), suggesting that our rationale for the formulation of these metrics (i.e., that higher scores reflect more concepts captured and therefore higher quality) was justified. Our qualitative review further showed that pedagogically sound questions differ from non-sound questions primarily in their context and specificity. While the current information score metric doesn't capture how specific the terms used in each question are, this task has been explored in previous work [17] and could be incorporated in the next iteration of the question evaluation process in our pipeline. Critically, this evaluation method, which combines concept extraction with information score computation, could be applied in many other learning domains, as it represents a general strategy of identifying high quality and pedagogically sound questions. Second, we found that combining the instructional content with a summary of this content (e.g., the header names) could lead to better question generation with T5. In our case, the header names at the Module and Unit levels were shown to result in more sound questions than those at the Topic level.

At the same time, there are ample opportunities to further promote the adoption of our pipeline across different learning domains. First, more research is needed to investigate question generation when the learning contents are not entirely textual, but may include multimedia components, such as math formulas and images. Recent advances in the area of *document intelligence* [5, 15, 30], combining NLP techniques with computer vision, might be particularly helpful in this direction. Second, there remains the need to diversify the generated questions, so as to meet a wider range of assessment goals. In particular, most of our current questions start with "what" (e.g., those in Table 1), which are primarily geared towards *remembering* information. Incorporating other question types in the generation pipeline could elicit more cognitive processes in Bloom's taxonomy [21] – for example, "how" questions can promote *understanding* and "why" questions are designed for *analyzing* – which in turn contribute to better student learning. This diversifying direction is also an area of active research in the NLP and QG community [40, 44].

In addition, the proposed pipeline is generalizable yet also customizable to individual domains, so as to enable higher quality questions. As previously mentioned, the fine-tuning steps for both T5 and GPT-3 could be carried out on datasets that are closely related to the learning contents and with cross-validated hyperparameter tuning to better fit the dataset. Similarly, the concept extraction process could be enhanced with a combination of machine-generated and human-evaluated skill mappings, which have been shown to yield more accurate knowledge models across several works [25, 26, 38]. Finally, the question evaluation criteria may also benefit from subject matter experts' inputs to closely reflect the distinct nature of the learning domain; for example, chemistry assessments could potentially include both conceptual questions (e.g., "*what is the chemical formula of phenol?*") and scenario-based questions (e.g., "*describe the phenomenon that results from mixing sodium metal and chlorine gas?*").

Finally, we should note the limitations that may influence the interpretation of our results. First, the text input to our T5 model was the content of an entire Topic, consisting of 3–6 paragraphs. Constructing more fine-grained inputs at the paragraph or sentence level could potentially yield more targeted questions, although at the cost of a larger number of questions for human experts to evaluate. This direction could be viable once the evaluation metrics have been refined to more closely replicate expert judgments, allowing them to be applied at scale on large question corpuses. Second, while the human raters' pedagogical soundness ratings provide preliminary evidence of the generated questions' usability, there remains the need to empirically validate their impacts on student learning. To this end, we plan to deploy the pedagogically sound questions identified in this work to formative assignments in the next iteration of the data science course. As shown in prior research [29], the low-stake formats, such as optional quizzes, can still yield crucial insights on student performance while not impacting the overall grades. In this way, they are highly useful for experimenting with new assessment items, especially those not generated by instructors and domain experts, such as in the present study.

6 Conclusion

Our work raises attention to the potential of applying state-of-the-art NLP models in automated question generation. Through applying this process on learning materials from a data science course, we highlight a number of ideas that merit additional investigation in future works. First, we propose an initial method of scoring the quality of automatically generated questions, which provide instructors with the ability to recognize pedagogically sound questions and give the field a baseline to derive comparable methods. Second, we identified the potential of incorporating summary data in the input to QG models, such as Google's T5, to improve the quality of the generated questions. Third, we demonstrated the use of a fine-tuned GPT-3 model in classifying question quality, which in turn serves as a potential feature to add to future models of question quality.

In addition to these contributions, we are also making our full pipeline and results available[4] in hopes of providing a baseline for the community to use and improve on the proposed methods. We believe that achieving generalized, usable methods of automatic question generation will likely require multiple techniques in an ensemble approach to produce content at a sufficiently high quality. Our long term goal is to create generalized QG methods in a widely available open format that use an ensemble of scoring metrics, with the expectation that different metrics will produce better results in different domains. The field of QG for specific educational domains needs a baseline for measuring improvement and we envision this research as a starting point.

References

1. Aguilera-Hermida, A.P.: College students' use and acceptance of emergency online learning due to COVID-19. Int. J. Educ. Res. Open. **1**, 100011 (2020)
2. Ai, R., Krause, S., Kasper, W., Xu, F., Uszkoreit, H.: Semi-automatic generation of multiple-choice tests from mentions of semantic relations. In: Proceedings of the 2nd Workshop on Natural Language Processing Techniques for Educational Applications, pp. 26–33 (2015)
3. Alberti, C., Andor, D., Pitler, E., Devlin, J., Collins, M.: Synthetic QA corpora generation with roundtrip consistency. arXiv preprint arXiv:1906.05416 (2019)
4. Amidei, J., Piwek, P., Willis, A.: Evaluation methodologies in automatic question generation 2013–2018 (2018)
5. Baviskar, D., Ahirrao, S., Potdar, V., Kotecha, K.: Efficient automated processing of the unstructured documents using artificial intelligence: a systematic literature review and future directions. IEEE Access **9**, 72894–72936 (2021)
6. Brown, T., et al.: Language models are few-shot learners. Adv. Neural. Inf. Process. Syst. **33**, 1877–1901 (2020)
7. Chan, Y.-H., Fan, Y.-C.: A recurrent BERT-based model for question generation. In: Proceedings of the 2nd Workshop on Machine Reading for Question Answering, pp. 154–162 (2019)
8. Chen, G., Yang, J., Hauff, C., Houben, G.-J.: LearningQ: a large-scale dataset for educational question generation. In: Twelfth International AAAI Conference on Web and Social Media (2018)

[4] https://github.com/MCDS-Foundations/data-science-question-generation.

9. Cheng, Y., et al.: Guiding the growth: difficulty-controllable question generation through step-by-step rewriting. arxiv preprint arXiv:2105.11698 (2021)
10. Chiu, K.-L., Alexander, R.: Detecting hate speech with gpt-3. arXiv preprint arXiv:2103.12407 (2021)
11. Devlin, J., Chang, M.-W., Lee, K., Toutanova, K.: Bert: Pre-training of deep bidirectional transformers for language understanding. arXiv preprint arXiv:1810.04805 (2018)
12. Dimitrakis, E., Sgontzos, K., Tzitzikas, Y.: A survey on question answering systems over linked data and documents. J. Intell. Inf. Syst. **55**(2), 233–259 (2019). https://doi.org/10.1007/s10844-019-00584-7
13. Du, X., Shao, J., Cardie, C.: Learning to ask: neural question generation for reading comprehension. arXiv preprint arXiv:1705.00106 (2017)
14. Ferrucci, D., et al.: Building watson: an overview of the DeepQA project. AI Mag. **31**(3), 59–79 (2010)
15. Han, B., Burdick, D., Lewis, D., Lu, Y., Motahari, H., Tata, S.: DI-2021: the second document intelligence workshop. In: Proceedings of the 27th ACM SIGKDD Conference on Knowledge Discovery & Data Mining, pp. 4127–4128 (2021)
16. Hodges, C.B., Moore, S., Lockee, B.B., Trust, T., Bond, M.A.: The difference between emergency remote teaching and online learning (2020)
17. Huang, H., Kajiwara, T., Arase, Y.: Definition modelling for appropriate specificity. In: Proceedings of the 2021 Conference on Empirical Methods in Natural Language Processing, pp. 2499–2509 (2021)
18. Jia, X., Wang, H., Yin, D., Wu, Y.: Enhancing question generation with commonsense knowledge. In: China National Conference on Chinese Computational Linguistics, pp. 145–160. Springer (2021) https://doi.org/10.1007/978-3-030-84186-7_10
19. Kalman, R., Macias Esparza, M., Weston, C.: Student views of the online learning process during the COVID-19 pandemic: a comparison of upper-level and entry-level undergraduate perspectives. J. Chem. Educ. **97**(9), 3353–3357 (2020)
20. Koedinger, K.R., Corbett, A.T., Perfetti, C.: The knowledge-learning-instruction framework: bridging the science-practice chasm to enhance robust student learning. Cogn. Sci. **36**(5), 757–798 (2012)
21. Krathwohl, D.R.: A revision of Bloom's taxonomy: an overview. Theor. Pract. **41**(4), 212–218 (2002)
22. Kurdi, G., Leo, J., Parsia, B., Sattler, U., Al-Emari, S.: A systematic review of automatic question generation for educational purposes. Int. J. Artif. Intell. Educ. **30**(1), 121–204 (2020). https://doi.org/10.1007/s40593-019-00186-y
23. Landis, J.R., Koch, G.G.: The measurement of observer agreement for categorical data. Biometrics **33**, 159–174 (1977)
24. Liu, B.: Neural question generation based on Seq2Seq. In: Proceedings of the 2020 5th International Conference on Mathematics and Artificial Intelligence, pp. 119–123 (2020)
25. Liu, R., Koedinger, K.R.: Closing the loop: automated data-driven cognitive model discoveries lead to improved instruction and learning gains. J. Educ. Data Min. **9**(1), 25–41 (2017)
26. Liu, R., McLaughlin, E.A., Koedinger, K.R.: Interpreting model discovery and testing generalization to a new dataset. In: Educational Data Mining 2014. Citeseer (2014)
27. Liu, T., Fang, Q., Ding, W., Li, H., Wu, Z., Liu, Z.: Mathematical word problem generation from commonsense knowledge graph and equations. arXiv preprint arXiv:2010.06196 (2020)
28. Lopez, L.E., Cruz, D.K., Cruz, J.C.B., Cheng, C.: Transformer-based end-to-end question generation. arXiv preprint arXiv:2005.01107, vol. 4 (2020)
29. Moore, S., Nguyen, H.A., Stamper, J.: Examining the effects of student participation and performance on the quality of learnersourcing multiple-choice questions. In: Proceedings of the Eighth ACM Conference on Learning@ Scale, pp. 209–220 (2021)

30. Motahari, H., Duffy, N., Bennett, P., Bedrax-Weiss, T.: A report on the first workshop on document intelligence (DI) at NeurIPS 2019. ACM SIGKDD Explor. Newsl. **22**(2), 8–11 (2021)
31. Novikova, J., Dušek, O., Curry, A.C., Rieser, V.: Why we need new evaluation metrics for NLG. arXiv preprint arXiv:1707.06875 (2017)
32. Rajpurkar, P., Zhang, J., Lopyrev, K., Liang, P.: Squad: 100,000+ questions for machine comprehension of text. arXiv preprint arXiv:1606.05250 (2016)
33. Ritter, S., Yudelson, M., Fancsali, S.E., Berman, S.R.: How mastery learning works at scale. In: Proceedings of the Third (2016) ACM Conference on Learning@ Scale, pp. 71–79 (2016)
34. Ruseti, S., et al.: Predicting question quality using recurrent neural networks. In: Penstein Rosé, C., et al. (eds.) artificial intelligence in education. LNCS (LNAI), vol. 10947, pp. 491–502. Springer, Cham (2018). https://doi.org/10.1007/978-3-319-93843-1_36
35. Rushkin, I., et al.: Adaptive assessment experiment in a HarvardX MOOC. In: EDM (2017)
36. Sai, A.B., Mohankumar, A.K., Khapra, M.M.: A survey of evaluation metrics used for NLG systems. arXiv preprint arXiv:2008.12009 (2020)
37. Sha, L., et al.: Which hammer should i use? A systematic evaluation of approaches for classifying educational forum posts. Int. Educ. Data Min. Soc. (2021)
38. Stamper, J.C., Koedinger, K.R.: Human-machine student model discovery and improvement using DataShop. In: Biswas, G., Bull, S., Kay, J., Mitrovic, A. (eds.) International Conference on Artificial Intelligence in Education, pp. 353–360. Springer (2011). https://doi.org/10.1007/978-3-642-21869-9_46
39. Steuer, T., Bongard, L., Uhlig, J., Zimmer, G.: On the linguistic and pedagogical quality of automatic question generation via neural machine translation. In: European Conference on Technology Enhanced Learning, pp. 289–294. Springer (2021) https://doi.org/10.1007/978-3-030-86436-1_22
40. Sultan, M.A., Chandel, S., Astudillo, R.F., Castelli, V.: On the importance of diversity in question generation for QA. In: Proceedings of the 58th Annual Meeting of the Association for Computational Linguistics, pp. 5651–5656 (2020)
41. Van Der Lee, C., Gatt, A., Van Miltenburg, E., Wubben, S., Krahmer, E.: Best practices for the human evaluation of automatically generated text. In: Proceedings of the 12th International Conference on Natural Language Generation, pp. 355–368 (2019)
42. Vaswani, A., et al.: Attention is all you need. In: Advances in Neural Information Processing Systems, vol. 30 (2017)
43. Wang, S., et al.: PathQG: neural question generation from facts. In: Proceedings of the 2020 Conference on Empirical Methods in Natural Language Processing (EMNLP), pp. 9066–9075 (2020)
44. Wang, Z., Rao, S., Zhang, J., Qin, Z., Tian, G., Wang, J.: Diversify question generation with continuous content selectors and question type modeling. In: Findings of the Association for Computational Linguistics: EMNLP 2020, pp. 2134–2143 (2020)
45. Xue, L., et al.: mT5: a massively multilingual pre-trained text-to-text transformer. arXiv preprint arXiv:2010.11934 (2020)
46. Yu, J., et al.: MOOCCubeX: a large knowledge-centered repository for adaptive learning in MOOCs. In: Proceedings of the 30th ACM International Conference on Information & Knowledge Management, pp. 4643–4652 (2021)
47. Zhang, R., Guo, J., Chen, L., Fan, Y., Cheng, X.: A review on question generation from natural language text. ACM Trans. Inf. Syst. (TOIS) **40**(1), 1–43 (2021)
48. Zhong, R., Lee, K., Zhang, Z., Klein, D.: Adapting language models for zero-shot learning by meta-tuning on dataset and prompt collections. arXiv preprint arXiv:2104.04670 (2021)
49. Zhu, F., Lei, W., Wang, C., Zheng, J., Poria, S., Chua, T.-S.: Retrieving and reading: a comprehensive survey on open-domain question answering. arXiv preprint arXiv:2101.00774 (2021)

Learners' Strategies in Interactive Sorting Tasks

Norbert Noster[1(✉)], Arnon Hershkovitz[2], Michal Tabach[2], and Hans-Stefan Siller[1]

[1] University of Würzburg, 97074 Würzburg, Germany
{norbert.noster,hans-stefan.siller}@mathematik.uni-wuerzburg.de
[2] School of Education, Tel Aviv University, 6997801 Tel Aviv, Israel
{arnonhe,tabachm}@tauex.tau.ac.il

Abstract. Using examples and non-examples is a common technique to demonstrate concepts' characteristics and boundaries. Based on their properties, certain objects are accepted as examples or non-examples intuitively, while others are accepted or neglected non-intuitively. This 2*2 classification is powerful when designing technology-enhanced learning experiences in which feedback could be provided in real-time. That is, feedback could be based not only on the correctness of student response, but also on the specifics of the objects with which they were engaged. Following this framework, we developed an interactive sorting task that aims at strengthening elementary school students' understanding of reflective symmetry. We studied learners' interaction with the objects presented to them, and their success. Our study included 29 elementary school students (ages 9 to 12) from both Israel and Germany. We used screen recording to code participants' shape-movements, and defined quantitative measures of these movements. Our findings support the need for designing feedback that takes into consideration object's properties and students' behavior.

Keywords: Mathematics education · Feedback · Interactive tasks

1 Introduction

Interactive tasks allow learners to construct knowledge in a student-centered, dynamic process that commonly involves hands-on, personal inquiry with concrete problems, and metacognitive support [1]. In mathematics education, such environments—GeoGebra[1], The Geometer's Sketchpad[2], and Desmos[3]—have been used in numerous educational processes and settings, overall with favorable outcomes [2].

Interactive tasks enable the learning process not only to be monitored at its end, but also during it, hence may support learners with formative assessment. One way of doing so is by providing learners with real-time feedback that relates to the learner's performance or understanding [3]. Therefore, it is crucial to identify students' strategies while solving problems in an interactive task, in order to design a feedback system that would respond to them. To meet this goal, we set-up the following research questions:

[1] http://www.geogebra.org.
[2] https://www.dynamicgeometry.com.
[3] https://www.desmos.com.

I. Hilliger et al. (Eds.): EC-TEL 2022, LNCS 13450, pp. 285–298, 2022.
https://doi.org/10.1007/978-3-031-16290-9_21

1) Impact of feedback on success

    a) To what extent is immediate feedback noticed?
    b) Does noticing immediate feedback lead to success?

2) Relations between shape categorization and success

    a) What are the differences in correct classification on first attempt[4] between examples and non-examples for reflective symmetry?
    b) What are the differences in correct classification on first attempt (see Footnote 4) between intuitive and non-intuitive examples of reflective symmetry?

3) Relationships between solving strategies and success

    a) What is the relationship between number of steps[5] in which each shape was chosen to be classified for the first time and overall student success?
    b) What is the relationship between number of steps (see Footnote 5) between similar shapes being classified and overall student success?

2 Background

2.1 Concept Image

The term concept image is used "to describe the total cognitive structure that is associated with the concept, which includes all the mental pictures and associated properties and processes" [4]. This highlights the cognitive structure that resembles the information one individual links to a concept. The information itself does not necessarily have to be correct and may be erroneous. Three elements can be derived from this definition: mental pictures, associated properties, and processes. Within this study we examine reflective symmetry as a topic from the field of Euclidian Geometry.

Visual information in the form of images is what we understand as mental pictures, within the framework of concept images. Learners are often presented with examples of certain concepts [5], which serves as one of the first steps for the development of geometric thought according to Van Hiele's model [6]. Regarding reflective symmetry, there may be different kinds of plane figures, which serve as prototypical examples.

Mental pictures as prototypical (visual) examples can only represent a concept (e.g., reflective symmetry) to a certain extent and can be problematic for applying or recalling aspects of a concept [7]. This may be related to previous findings according to which learners struggle with lines of symmetry being inclined and neither horizontally nor vertically oriented [8]. This indicates a lack of concept images containing prototypes with non-horizontal/-vertical aligned lines of symmetry.

Information about properties is also part of the concept image and can be of use, when mental (prototypical) images fail. This may be definitions on a rather formal level. Within

[4] This is because students can correct themselves using the automatically provided feedback.

[5] Step indicates the order in which a shape was moved.

the topic of reflective symmetry, a link to processes is likely, since students of younger age are often introduced to this concept by folding a plane figure on a piece of paper or using a mirror as line of symmetry. It is just later that more formal aspects of reflective symmetry are being taught and extend ideas of folding/ mirroring by determining distances between points of a plane shape and the line of symmetry. Therefore, it is likely that students' concept images not only consist of formal information but also of less formal information about actions associated with symmetry.

A valid method for investigating a concept image as a cognitive structure are sorting tasks, in which learners are asked to sort items based on pre-defined categories—or to come up with their own categories according to which subsets of items could be arranged. They serve as an effective tool to elicit issues of organization and context for investigating cognitive structures [9]. Compared with other types of tasks—like writing, or even recalling—sorting tasks are easier accessible, hence are more able to tap into a learners' knowledge structure that can be distorted by difficult production tasks [10]. Therefore, this kind of task has been used for learning and assessment in various disciplines [10–12]. Sorting tasks with predefined categories are relatively easy to implement as interactive tasks that support the learner with immediate feedback, as objects could be a-priori tagged with their correct classification.

2.2 Intuitive and Non-intuitive (Non-) Examples

There are multiple ways for determining (non-)reflective symmetry of an object. Having in mind how points are reflected it is possible to follow rules for constructing reflections by using necessary construction tools [13]. In the case of polygons, it is sufficient to reflect corner points of a figure since direct connections between points as lines are unambiguous. To do so, it is necessary to define a line that the points are reflected by (what we refer to as line of symmetry) and compare the resulting halves.

These approaches consider properties of reflective symmetry without necessarily using prototypical examples. Such examples may serve as reference objects for deriving implications of reflective symmetry and properties for other objects (e.g., a rectangle is symmetrical, therefore a square is symmetrical as this is a special case of a rectangle). This raises the question whether learners argue reflectiveness for objects individually or also make use of relationships between shapes.

Considering the different possibilities for arguing reflective symmetry, it is necessary to also take a closer look at different types of examples that shall be examined. Since (prototypical) examples are part of the concept image, the question arises of their nature. We found the taxonomy developed by Tsamir et al. [14] extremely useful for our study. This taxonomy uses a 2*2 categorization of objects regarding a given property, based on them being examples/non-examples and intuitive/non-intuitive. Tsamir et al. found that about 80% of children's and prospective elementary school teachers' first non-example for a triangle was a circle. This had led them to the assumption that there are shapes that are more likely to be stated as (non-)examples for a given geometric property than others. Therefore, it is assumed that intuitive (non-)examples being more easily recalled from the concept image than non-intuitive (non-)examples. Furthermore, there seems to be no need for justification of intuitive (non-)examples as their properties appear self-evident [15]. Notably, intuitive as well as non-intuitive examples and non-examples should be included into teaching of geometric concepts [14]. Therefore, we made use of this categorization in constructing our task within the digital environment (see Sect 4.3).

2.3 Problem-Solving Strategies in Interactive Tasks

The use of online learning environments allows for a continuous monitoring of the learning throughout the learning process. Most relevant to the current study are studies of how students are engaged with online learning environments [16]. Even more specifically, we are interested in the ways by which students interact with open-ended tasks that allow for dynamic exploration in a trial-and-error manner rather than with close-ended tasks that simply require answering questions.

One prominent example of researching problem-solving strategies in open-ended learning environments is the study of science inquiry skills, which enables science researchers and educators to detect higher-order skills like designing controlled experiment [17]. Detecting cognitive and meta-cognitive skills while learning opens a gate for further explorations of relationships between such skills and learning outcomes [18].

In the context of mathematics education, attempts have been taken to analyze learners' interaction with online learning environments in a nuanced way, using log-based measures like page visits, time on task, or repetition [19–21]. These attempts are successful—at least to some degree—to prove relationships between interaction patterns and outcome measures, which may be seen as a validation of this approach. That is, real-time interaction patterns may indeed serve as a good proxy to learning.

3 Methodology

Students at elementary schools are the targeted audience for this interactive task. For this exploratory study, we chose a convenient sample of $N = 29$ elementary school students (9–12 years old) from both Israel and Germany. In Israel $n_1 = 12$ students were recruited through personal and professional networks of the research team. In Germany, a 4th grade classroom was recruited with $n_2 = 17$ participants. In both countries, the sample contained students from different skill levels.

3.1 Research Field

Reflective symmetry in two-dimensional geometry is studied early in the elementary school grades of both countries. By 4th-grade, students in both countries are expected to understand this concept, to identify lines of symmetry, and to correctly classify shapes based on reflective symmetry-related characteristics.

3.2 Research Population

The participants in our study were of age 9–12 years ($M = 10$, $SD = 0.9$), with a gender distribution of 12 female to 17 male participants. We are aware of a statistically significant difference in age between the two country-based groups (Mann-Whitney's

W-value = 38, at $p < 0.01$, and with Rank-Biserial Correlation of 0.63), however none of the research variables proved a difference between these two groups; also, there were no gender differences between the country-based groups, with $\chi^2(1) = 2.26$, at $p = 0.13$. Therefore, we treated the whole population as one group.

3.3 Research Tool and Process

Our main research tool was an applet integrated, designed and developed using GeoGebra. We choose GeoGebra as it allows designing a task with great flexibility at no cost, as well as logging students' actions (for future use). The applet providing the task presents users with seven quadrilaterals, which they are asked to classify (see Fig. 1). The quadrilaterals consist of both intuitive, as well as non-intuitive examples and non-examples (see Table 1). The classification is based on the existence of at least one line of symmetry and is done by dragging the shapes into one of two regions. Immediate feedback is available in the form of an updated cumulative count of correct and incorrect classifications. Users can keep dragging shapes from anywhere to anywhere on the screen. We ran the applet on either tablets or touch-screen laptops.

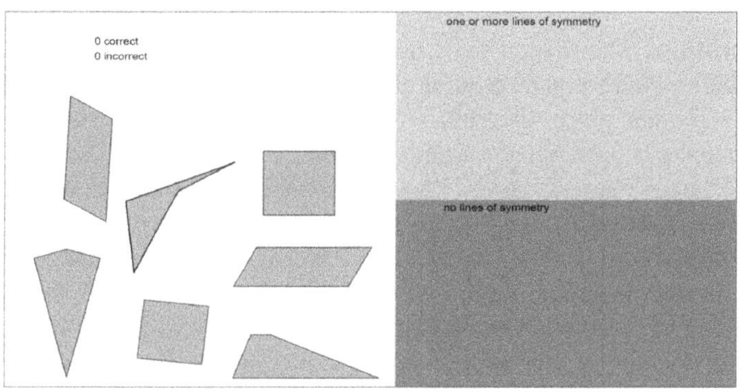

Fig. 1. The GeoGebra applet used in this study.

Table 1. 2x2 shape classification [14].

	Intuitive		Non-Intuitive	
Example	Square	Kite	Tilted Square	
Non-Example	Irregular	Trapezoid	Parallelogram	Rotated Parallelogram

3.4 Data Collection, Preparation, Analysis

Data Collection. The data collection took place in early March 2022. Members of the research team had met with each of the participants individually. In Israel, these meetings took place in the students' homes, after getting approval from their parents; in Germany, these meetings took place in school, after getting approvals from their parents, the responsible teachers as well the school management. First, the researcher made sure – by asking them directly about it – that the participant was familiar with the concept of reflective symmetry and was able to classify shapes based on this property. Then, the researcher presented the participant a similar applet—focusing on a non-symmetry-related classification task—which had the very same graphical interface and made sure that the participant got familiar with the interface, with how to engage with the applet, as well as the feedback mechanism. Finally, the researcher presented the participant the symmetry applet and made sure the instructions are clear. The participant was then let to use the applet by themselves until they stated that they were done. Each such meeting was a few (up to approx. 5) minutes long. While using the applet, we captured the screen, and used these recordings for our analysis. Also, the researcher instructed the participant to think-aloud while using the applet, and to continuously comment on their reasoning; we audio-recorded the participants for future analyses.

Data Preparation. The videos were manually coded with the basic unit of analysis being a shape-movement, that is, dragging and dropping a shape from one place on the screen to another place. Overall, we had 266 shape-movements, with number of shape-movement per participant ranging between 7–21 (M = 9.2, SD = 3.0), with the most common ones being from the "pool" (the area where all the shapes are located when the applet is initiated) to either the symmetry (107, 40% of all shape-movements) or the no-symmetry (109, 41%) areas. There were 37 shape-movements (14%) from either the symmetry or no-symmetry areas to the other area, and 13 shape-movements (5%) from either the symmetry or no-symmetry areas back to the pool. For each shape-movement, we documented the following fields: action ID (across the whole population, to make each movement distinguishable), user ID (so that movements can be linked to the corresponding student), user-action number (count of actions for each user ID), country, object dragged, area from which the object was dragged [pool, symmetry, no symmetry], area in which the object was dropped [pool, symmetry, no symmetry], correct classification [yes, no, N/A (in case of dropping at the pool)]. These fields were used for calculating the variables.

Data Analysis. Due to the relatively small population size, we used non-parametric statistical tests, that is, testing for differences between independent groups using Mann Whitney test, between paired samples using Wilcoxon's Signed-Rank test, and for correlations using Spearman's rho. Analyses were conducted in JASP 0.16.

3.5 Research Variables

Independent Variables. Serve as proxies to students' feedback noticing and strategies.

Feedback Noticing After [Correct/Incorrect] Classification. For each incorrect object classification, we checked whether the student had immediately moved that object to another area [True/False]. Similarly, for each correct object classification, we checked whether the student had not moved that object in the immediate next step [True/False]. These are proxies for feedback noticing.

First Time [Shape] Moved. For each student, each of these seven variables (one per shape) holds the serial number of the action in which that student moved this shape from the pool area for the first time (whether it was correctly or incorrectly classified).

Steps Between [Squares/Parallelograms] First Moves. Our two pairs of similar shapes denote two different cases – the two squares are both examples for reflective symmetry, with one being intuitive and the other being non-intuitive; the two parallelograms are both non-intuitive non-examples. These two variables measure to what extent students recognized the similarity within each of these pairs of shapes, and to what extent they understood that this similarity denotes on keeping the property of symmetry (or non-symmetry). For each student and for each of these pairs, we calculated the number of steps between first attempts to classify the two shapes within the pair.

Dependent Variables. Success was a dependent variable at the student-level.

Normalized Final Correct Classifications ($M = 0.79$, $SD = 0.19$). We calculated the ratio of final correct score to the total number of shape-movements, because not all participants achieved a perfect score of 7 correct classifications before declaring that they had finished. Otherwise, the number of shape-movements as a proxy to knowledge of (reflective) symmetry would be sufficient. This ratio normalized the final score. Note that there were no significant differences in success between the two country-based groups, with Mann-Whitney's W-value = 119.5, at $p = 0.45$.

4 Findings

4.1 Feedback Noticing (RQ1)

Noticing Immediate Feedback (RQ1a). Overall, we had 50 instances relevant to identifying feedback noticing after incorrect classification, that is, cases in which a student incorrectly classified an item and took another action after it; of these, in 18 cases (36%) the feedback was unnoticed, that is, the next action did not consist of moving the incorrectly classified object. Conversely, of the 174 instances relevant to identifying feedback noticing after correct classification, students were noticing feedback, that is, did not move the correctly classified object, in 172 cases (99%).

Success and Feedback Noticing (RQ1b). Averaging at the student level, *Feedback Noticing After Incorrect Classification* takes an average of 0.38 ($SD = 0.38, N = 21$), and it was found to be not significantly correlated with *Normalized Final Correct Classifications*, with $\rho = 0.12$, at $p = 0.61$. *Feedback Noticing After Correct Classification* was not relevant for this test, due to a ceiling effect.

4.2 Empirically Validating the Research Framework (RQ2)

This research question aims at validating our theoretical framework. We did so by testing for correct classification on first attempt, taking into consideration that each shape is either an example or non-example for reflective symmetry, and whether it is an intuitive or non-intuitive (non-)example (see Table 2). Overall, the square (intuitive example) and the irregular quadrilateral (intuitive non-example) were the easiest to classify, with all but one of the participants succeeding on their first attempt (however, in different stages of the process, as is reported below, in Sect. 4.2). The parallelogram and rotated parallelogram (non-intuitive non-examples) were the most difficult to classify, with only 18 and 16 of the participants (respectively) succeeding on their first attempt.

Table 2. Number (%) of participants who correctly classified each of the quadrilaterals on first attempt, and the average step number in which each shape was first chosen for classification.

Shape	Type	# (%) Succeeded	Avg. (SD) step no. first moved
Square	Intuitive example	28 (97%)	1.6 (1.0)
Irregular quadrilateral	Intuitive non-example	28 (97%)	4.9 (4.2)
Tilted square	Non-intuitive example	26 (90%)	3.9 (2.1)
Trapezoid	Intuitive non-example	26 (90%)	6.2 (3.0)
Kite	Intuitive example	20 (69%)	5.9 (3.5)
Parallelogram	Non-intuitive non-example	18 (62%)	4.4 (1.5)
Rotated parallelogram	Non-intuitive non-example	16 (55%)	4.4 (2.0)

Differences in Difficulty Between Examples and Non-Examples (RQ2a). We counted the cases in which each of the examples (square, tilted square, kite) and non-example (irregular, trapezoid, parallelogram, rotated parallelogram) shapes were correctly classified on first attempt. The examples were correctly classified in 85% of the cases (74 of 87), while the non-examples were correctly classified in only 76% of the cases (88 of 116). This difference is, however, not statistically significant, with $\chi^2 = 2.6$, at $p = 0.11$. Findings are summarized in Table 3 (right).

Differences in Difficulty Between Intuitive and Non-Intuitive (RQ2b). We counted the cases in which each of the intuitive (square, kite, irregular, trapezoid) and non-intuitive (tilted square, parallelogram, rotated parallelogram) shapes were correctly classified on first attempt. The intuitive shapes were correctly classified in 88% of the cases (102 of 116), while the non-intuitive shapes were correctly classified in only 69% of the cases (60 of 87). This difference is statistically significant, with $\chi^2 = 11.1$, at $p < 0.05$. Findings are summarized in Table 3 (left).

Table 3. Correctness in first attempt, by (non-)intuitive (left) and (non-)example (right)

	Correct	Incorrect		Correct	Incorrect
Intuitive	102 (50%)	14 (7%)	Example	74 (36%)	13 (6%)
Non-intuitive	60 (30%)	27 (13%)	Non-example	88 (43%)	28 (14%)

4.3 Relationships Between Solving Strategies and Success (RQ3)

First Shape Chosen to be Classified (RQ3a). Notably, the square was by far the most popular shape to be classified on the very first attempt, with 69% of the participants (20 of 29) doing so. Other shapes were each chosen by only 1–3 of the participants to be classified on first attempt. Therefore, the seven variables accounting for the step-number in which each of the shapes were first chosen to be classified is more indicative on students' order-strategy compared to considering the first shape alone. From these variables, we observed that, on average, the tilted square was chosen for classification relatively early in the process, while the trapezoid and the kite were chosen for classification relatively late. Findings are summarized in Table 2.

When testing for correlations between each of these seven variables and *Normalized Final Correct Classifications*, we found that three such variables proved statistically significant relationships. The later the parallelogram was first chosen to be classified – the higher was student success, with $\rho = 0.39$, at $p < 0.05$. The earlier the kite or tilted square were first chosen to be classified – the higher was student success, with $\rho = -0.41$ and $\rho = -0.38$, respectively, both at $p < 0.05$.

Importantly, we observed that the German participants tended to classify the kite earlier in the process, compared with the Israeli participants (M = 4.5, SD = 1.7 and M = 8.0, SD = 4.4, respectively). This could be explained by the fact that the kite – an intuitive example – was located on the left-hand side of the pool area and recalling that German is a left-to-right language while Hebrew is a right-to-left language. However, in-depth studies on cultural differences are still pending.

Other shapes did not prove difference in this manner; this included the other intuitive example, i.e., square, probably due to a ceiling effect, as it was the most frequent shape to be classified on the very first attempt.

Steps Between Attempts to Classify Pairs of Similar Shapes (RQ3b). On average, *Steps Between Squares First Moves* was 2.6 (SD = 1.9), and *Steps Between Parallelograms First Moves* was 1.9 (SD = 1.3). This difference is marginally significant, with Wilcoxon's Signed-Rank W-value = 38.5, at $p = 0.07$. Note that the distances between each of the pairs—as they appeared on the screen—were relatively similar (see Fig. 1), hence this parameter cannot explain the difference in steps.

We found that *Steps Between Squares First Moves* was negatively correlated with *Normalized Final Correct Classification*, with $\rho = -0.40$, at $p < 0.05$, that is, the closer a student attempted to classify both squares, the higher was their success. There was no relationship between *Steps Between Parallelograms First Moves* and *Normalized Final Correct Classification* ($\rho = -0.10$, at $p = 0.36$).

These findings indicate on the importance of recognizing similarity between shapes of different types. Note that the two parallelograms are both non-intuitive examples, while the two squares are either an intuitive example or a non-intuitive example.

5 Discussion

We used visual information, along with immediate feedback, to study cognitive processes required for building a concept image. Using an interactive sorting task that included both intuitive and non-intuitive shapes, that served as either example or non-example, we explored the process of analyzing and justifying (to self) symmetry-related properties. Overall, our findings point out to the importance of non-intuitive (non-)examples in this process (RQ2b). Contrary to previous findings, we found no evidence for differences in the identification of examples or non-examples (RQ2a) [14, 22]. Therefore, non-intuitive shapes should be presented to students more often. Importantly, our findings help in designing effective feedback to sorting tasks.

5.1 Recommended Strategies for Problem-Solving

Indeed, we observed a few strategies of completing the sorting task, which—based on the very nature of the problem, i.e., classifying—are overall governed by the order by which shapes were chosen to be classified. Based on our findings of the relationships between such strategies and success, we can derive a few recommendations for learners engaged in similar tasks. Note that these recommendations are relevant for different phases of the task-solving process.

Start with the Easiest Sub-Task. Many students started by classifying the square, which at the same time was also one of the easiest shapes to classify (and therefore in practice this strategy was not associated with success, due to a ceiling effect). Notably, we found that an indication for success was relatively early attempts to classify the kite, an intuitive example (RQ3a), as well as relatively-late attempts to classify the parallelogram, a non-intuitive non-example, which led us to this recommendation.

Once a Sub-task is Correctly Accomplished, Look for Similar Sub-tasks. Another indication for success was relatively close attempts to classify both squares (RQ3b), which also has to do with the benefit of relatively early attempts to classify the tilted square (RQ3a; as the square was highly frequently chosen in the first step). Hence, this recommendation, which echoes the notion of the importance of using analogies while solving problems [23]. Recently, Palmér and van Bommel's [24] emphasized the importance of explicitly using similar problems as part of young children's learning. Note that this strategy is enabled by the immediate feedback the system gives to learners. This strategy, however, is not always linked to success as is the case with the pair of parallelograms; note that the two parallelograms are both non-intuitive non-examples, which may have made them more difficult to classify in the first place.

When Left with the More Difficult Sub-Tasks, Compare them with what has Already Been Accomplished. Implementing the two previous strategies will leave students with the more difficult subtasks, however with a set of examples and non-examples, both intuitive and non-intuitive. This set of worked examples could help them to identify more complex similarities or dissimilarities [23].

5.2 Contribution to the Development of Automatic Feedback

The identification of beneficial strategies is of great importance for designing an automatic elaborate feedback system that would support learners in real-time, throughout the learning process. Here lies another important advantage of using interactive tasks, as they can automatically and continuously store learner actions in log files, and this data can be used to detect various behaviors, to respond to them, and to help in assessment. This is indeed our next step following the findings of this study.

While there are already designs providing elaborate feedback similar tasks [25], our approach differs in that it provides (non-)examples instead of asking learners to elicit (non-)examples. This allows for presenting learners with non-intuitive (non-)examples, which they are unlikely to produce themselves. Additionally, it is not restricted to inner-mathematical objects, so that learners can be asked to classify extra-mathematical objects as well [26]. Often, the feedback function, even as it could immediately lead students to the correct answer, was not (immediately) used in the cases of incorrect classifications (RQ1a), which highlights the need to make the feedback more prominent for them to serve as a learning opportunity, as feedback in these cases seems to be linked to success (RQ1b). Correctly classified objects serve as reference for identifying similarities regarding the given property.

5.3 Possible Application in Intelligent Tutoring Systems

Intelligent Tutoring Systems not only provide feedback to learners but also assign further tasks according to a learner's performance. The 2*2 framework of intuitive/non-intuitive examples/non-examples and our findings can be of use for assigning tasks. Following our findings, that intuitive (non-)examples are easier to classify than non-intuitive ones, the learners should be presented with intuitive objects first. Once they are classified correctly, tasks including non-intuitive tasks should be provided. In case of incorrect classification of non-intuitive objects, similar intuitive objects (from a previous task) can be presented and have learners compare them, serving as a learning opportunity to analyze their mistake. This way learners can be systematically confronted with examples demonstrating boundaries and unusual cases representing properties of a given concept. Using the notions of (non-)intuitiveness for task assignment can also be helpful to systematically test for boundaries of learners' knowledge.

5.4 Implications for the Design of Digital Tasks

Our findings are of importance for designing digital tasks as well. We point out to the importance of using both examples and non-examples for supporting the enhancement of children's concept image. Also, we emphasize the importance of incorporating both intuitive and non-intuitive (non-)examples, as they help distinguish between levels of proficiency, as well as for supporting beneficial feedback. Importantly, the 2*2 framework of intuitive/non-intuitive examples/non-examples can be implemented in numerous educational contexts and settings, which is one of its strengths.

5.5 Conclusions and Limitations

We demonstrated how student's engagement with an interactive sorting task in mathematics can derive various strategies, and that some of them were beneficial for solving the task successfully. The findings of this study could serve as foundations for the development of an elaborate feedback mechanism, as well as a basis for task assignment loops in intelligent tutoring systems. Of course, this study has limitations; mostly, it is about the sample size being rather small and about having examined only one applet in a specific educational context. Despite these limitations we believe that our findings, based on this unique approach we took, are meaningful.

Acknowledgment. We thank the Bavarian Funding Programme for the Initiation of International Projects (BayIntAn) for supporting this project.

References

1. Hannafin, M., Land, S., Oliver, K.: Open Learning Environments: Foundations, Methods, and Models. In: Reigeluth, C.M. (ed.) Instructional-Design Theories and Models: A new paradigm of instructional theory -, vol. II, pp. 115–140. Routledge, New York, NY (2009)
2. Cevikbas, M., Kaiser, G.: A systematic review on task design in dynamic and interactive mathematics learning environments (DIMLEs). Mathematics. **9**, 399 (2021). https://doi.org/10.3390/MATH9040399
3. Hattie, J., Timperley, H.: The power of feedback. Rev. Educ. Res. **77**, 81–112 (2007). https://doi.org/10.3102/003465430298487
4. Tall, D., Vinner, S.: Concept image and concept definition in mathematics with particular reference to limits and continuity. Edu. Stud. Math. **12**(2), 151–169 (1981). https://doi.org/10.1007/BF00305619
5. McKinney, C.W., Larkins, A.G., Ford, M.J., Davis, I.I.I., J.C.D.: The effectiveness of three methods of teaching social studies concepts to fourth-grade students: an aptitude-treatment interaction study. Am. Edu. Res. J. **20**, 663–670 (1983). https://doi.org/10.2307/1162820
6. Crowley, M.L.: The van Hiele model of the development of geometric thought. In: Montgomery Lindquis, M. (ed.) Learning and Teahching Geometry, K-12, 1987 Yearbook of the National Council of Teachers of Mathematics, pp. 1–16. National Council of Teachers of Mathematics, Reston, VA (1987)

7. Presmeg, N.: Visualization and Learning in Mathematics Education. In: Lerman, S. (ed.) Encyclopedia of Mathematics Education, pp. 636–640. Springer, Berlin, Gremany (2014)
8. Kuchemann, D.: Children's difficulties with single reflections and rotations. Math. Sch. **9**, 12–13 (1980)
9. Miller, G.A.: A psychological method to investigate verbal concepts. J. Math. Psychol. **6**, 169–191 (1969). https://doi.org/10.1016/0022-2496(69)90001-7
10. Tang, H., Clariana, R.: Leveraging a sorting task as a measure of knowledge structure in bilingual settings. Technol. Knowl. Learn. **22**(1), 23–35 (2016). https://doi.org/10.1007/s10758-016-9290-z
11. Smith, J.I., et al.: Development of the biology card sorting task to measure conceptual expertise in biology. CBE Life Sci. Educ. **12**, 628–644 (2013). https://doi.org/10.1187/cbe.13-05-0096
12. Eli, J.A., Mohr-Schroeder, M.J., Lee, C.W.: Exploring mathematical connections of prospective middle-grades teachers through card-sorting tasks. Math. Educ. Res. J. **23**, 297–319 (2011). https://doi.org/10.1007/s13394-011-0017-0
13. Miyakawa, T.: Reflective symmetry in construction and proving. In: Proceedings of the 28th International Conference of Psychology of Mathematics Education, pp. 337–344. Bergen, Norway (2004)
14. Tsamir, P., Tirosh, D., Levenson, E.: Intuitive nonexamples: the case of triangles. Educ. Stud. Math. **69**, 81–95 (2008). https://doi.org/10.1007/s10649-008-9133-5
15. Fischbein, H.: Intuition in Science and Mathematics: An Educational Approach, 1st edn. Kluwer, New York, NY (2002)
16. Dewan, M.A.A., Murshed, M., Lin, F.: Engagement detection in online learning: a review. Smart Learn. Environ. **6**(1), 1–20 (2019). https://doi.org/10.1186/s40561-018-0080-z
17. Gobert, J.D., Sao Pedro, M., Raziuddin, J., Baker, R.S.: From log files to assessment metrics: measuring students' science inquiry skills using educational data mining. J. Learn. Sci. **22**, 521–563 (2013). https://doi.org/10.1080/10508406.2013.837391
18. Zhang, Y., et al.: Can strategic behaviour facilitate confusion resolution? The interplay between confusion and metacognitive strategies in Betty's Brain. J. Learn. Anal. **8**, 28–44 (2021). https://doi.org/10.18608/jla.2021.7161
19. Crossley, S.A., Karumbaiah, S., Ocumpaugh, J., Labrum, M.J., Baker, R.S.: Predicting math identity through language and click-stream patterns in a blended learning mathematics program for elementary students. J. Learn. Anal. **7**, 19–37 (2020). https://doi.org/10.18608/jla.2020.71.3
20. Derr, K., Hübl, R., Ahmed, M.Z.: Monitoring the Use of Learning Strategies in a Web-Based Pre-course in Mathematics. In: Ifenthaler, D., Mah, D.-K., Yau, J.-K. (eds.) Utilizing Learning Analytics to Support Study Success, pp. 119–141. Springer, Cham (2019). https://doi.org/10.1007/978-3-319-64792-0_8
21. Haleva, L., Hershkovitz, A., Tabach, M.: Students' activity in an online learning environment for mathematics: the role of thinking levels. J. Educ. Comput. Res. **59**, 686–712 (2021). https://doi.org/10.1177/0735633120972057
22. Tsamir, P., Tirosh, D., Levenson, E., Barkai, R., Tabach, M.: Early-years teachers' concept images and concept definitions: triangles, circles, and cylinders. ZDM Math. Educ. **47**(3), 497–509 (2014). https://doi.org/10.1007/s11858-014-0641-8
23. Gick, M.L.: Problem-solving strategies. Educ. Psychol. **21**, 99–120 (1986). https://doi.org/10.1080/00461520.1986.9653026
24. Palmér, H., van Bommel, J.: Young students posing problem-solving tasks: what does posing a similar task imply to students? ZDM Math. Educ. **52**(4), 743–752 (2020). https://doi.org/10.1007/s11858-020-01129-x

25. Harel, R., Olsher, S., Yerushalmy, M.: Designing online formative assessment that promotes students' reasoning processes. In: Proceedings of the 14th International Conference on Technology in Mathematics Teaching, pp. 181–188 (2019). https://doi.org/10.17185/duepublico/70762
26. Noster, N., Hershkovitz, A., Siller, Hans.-S., Tabach, M.: Students' strategies for identifying reflective symmetry of extra-mathematical shapes in a digital environment. In: ERME Topic Conference on Mathematics Education in the Digital Age. Nitra, Slovakia (2022)

Adapting Learning Analytics Dashboards by and for University Students

Katia Oliver-Quelennec[1,2,3(✉)], François Bouchet[1], Thibault Carron[1], Kathy Fronton Casalino[3], and Claire Pinçon[2]

[1] Sorbonne Université, CNRS, LIP6, 75005 Paris, France
{francois.bouchet,thibault.carron}@lip6.fr
[2] Univ. Lille, CHU Lille, ULR 2694 - METRICS: Évaluation des technologies de santé et des pratiques médicales, 59000 Lille, France
{katia.quelennec,claire.pincon}@univ-lille.fr
[3] Univ. Lille, GIVRE, DAPI, Lille, France
kathy.casalino@univ-lille.fr

Abstract. Learning Analytics Dashboards (LADs) are becoming a key element in enabling learners to monitor their learning, plan and actually learn. However, LADs are sometimes not completely adapted to students, who are rarely involved in their design. Moreover, even when they are, the implemented LADs are often the same for all students, whereas previous works have shown the value of adapted LADs. Here we investigate which adaptations are requested by students, and attempt to identify which data and visualizations are suitable depending on the student's profile. More specifically, we consider dynamic profiles as students' expectations can vary over the course duration. By using LADs co-design sessions both online and on-site, we collected needs from N = 386 university students from different disciplines and degree level, split in 108 groups (2 to 4 students). After a manual annotation, we identified a total of 54 types of data and indicators, divided into 12 thematics. Our first analysis confirmed some previous results, particularly on the use of peer comparisons that do not fulfill every student's needs. And we noticed other expectations according to the student's learning context or the academic period. Future work will benefit from these results to define a model of adapted LADs.

Keywords: Dashboard · Learning analytics dashboard · Indicator · Co-design

1 Introduction

Technology-Enhanced Learning is nowadays widely developed for both distance and face-to-face learning, which allows us to collect and analyze a large amount of traces of learning activities in order to help learners. By analyzing the data collected, we can understand how users learn with technology, develop new learning tools and offer a unique learning path for each learner. In the field of possibilities provided by learning analytics, Learning Analytics Dashboards (LADs)

I. Hilliger et al. (Eds.): EC-TEL 2022, LNCS 13450, pp. 299–309, 2022.
https://doi.org/10.1007/978-3-031-16290-9_22

are a particularly popular approach to support learning. In recent years, several reviews have shown the growing interest in LADs [4,11,17–19]. But they also revealed the need for further research to design LADs showing a better grounding in learning sciences and learning theories, in particular due to the lack of specific visualizations for the activities of learning and teaching. Sahin and Ifenthaler [17, p. 18] identified the need to involve stakeholders to define "which metrics are important" to them. Recent work by Ahmad et al. [2, p. 66] has also concluded "that it is necessary to keep students and their opinions in the loop". In the case of students' LADs, previous works [16,21] concluded that students needed adapted LADs with personalized displays. To meet this need, co-design tools have been developed to involve students in the design of LADs [5,7,8,14,15]. This approach is all the more important as, even if indicators and visualizations used in LADs can be helpful for the student, e.g. to be aware of their progress [11], it can also have negative consequences, e.g. peer comparison in some contexts [20,21]. The importance of involving students in the design of LADs having been demonstrated, we will focus in the next part on the content of these LADs, in particular on indicators and visualizations that compose them.

1.1 Previous Works

Schwendimann [19, p. 37] defines a Learning Dashboard as "a single display that aggregates different indicators about learner(s), learning process(es) and/or learning context(s) into one or multiple visualizations". Several studies considered existing indicators and their associated visualizations for LAD. Indicators' definitions vary according to the context. Glahn et al. [6, p. 2] provides one that is quite generic: "Indicators are mechanisms to provide simplified information that are valuable to a task. With some background knowledge we can understand the meaning of an indicator without the need of knowing about the details of the underlying process or mechanism". In a review on LA indicators, Morais Canellas [13, p. 107] defines a learning analytics indicator as "a calculated (quantitative or qualitative) measure [computability property] linked to a behaviour or an activity instrumented by the [traceability property] of one or more learners, visible to a user [visibility property] and which can be used to calculate other indicators". LADs are composed of several kinds of indicators and even if some general definitions exist, Ifenthaler [9, p. 168] said "standards for indicators, visualizations, and design guidelines that would make learning analytics pedagogically effective are lacking". In the literature [3,7,8,12], we can find studies describing various indicators used in students' LADs, but to the best of our knowledge, there is no consensus on a single exhaustive list of indicators for students' LADs or even on a single way to categorize them. Ifenthaler and Yau [10] worked on indicators to support success in predicting learning outcomes, and although some of them can be used in LADs, they focused on identifying students at-risk and did not attempt to cover all the expectations of students' LADs. Depending on the studies, LADs' indicators can be classified in different categories. We can use the aforementioned definition from [19] to consider three categories: indicators about learner(s), learning process(es) and/or learning context(s). According to Jivet et al. [12], indicators used in LADs can be of two kinds: learning behaviour indicators, which provide information at the "learning process level", and content progress indicators, which provide information at the "task level". A study from Gartner [1] on LA indicators classified them in four different types of analysis based on the nature of the performed analysis and which are increasing both in terms of value for the stakeholders and in terms of difficulty to compute them: descriptive (what happened?), diagnostic (why did it happen?), predictive (what will happen?) and prescriptive (what should be done?).

Some previous works to produce LADs for students involved them in different phases, from conception to prototyping. Hilliger et al. [8, p. 118] identified that "the design of any dashboard should anticipate that its use could have a different effect depending on the context and the targeted user". With this approach, they defined indicators "relevant at the moment of choosing courses" [p. 127] for a dashboard with a specific objective. This observation highlights the implicit need to consider indicators that are relevant at a given moment in time. For this reason, Gras et al. [7] developed an interactive dashboard which can be customized by first year university students, implying that "one size may not fit all" when it comes to students' LADs.

Overall we see that all these studies seem to define indicators and visualization(s) for students's LADs with specific objectives and an adaptation to a learning context. However there is a lack of works around the generalizability of LADs indicators (1) to different students in the same context or (2) to different learning contexts.

1.2 Objectives

In this paper, we try to investigate the need for LADs' adaptation through a different approach than in previous works. Namely, we seek to understand the needs for student LADs, not for an artificially imposed goal, but for a goal chosen by each student themselves. The underlying assumption is that students may be more at ease to propose their ideal indicators when they do so in a real context (a given course they are registered to) and for a goal that they deem relevant in the first place. Then using data from these numerous co-design sessions organized with university students, we tried to identify which indicators (and to a lesser extent, which visualizations) are spontaneously wished for by students depending on several elements of context such as their discipline, the study duration (short or long), their level (undergraduate or graduate), the moment in the semester (at the beginning of a course, during an ongoing course or towards the end of it, right before the final exam). More precisely, we attempted to answer the following research questions:

- RQ1: Is there a set of indicators for students' LAD that cover their expectations?

- RQ2: Are there shared expectations of students for their LAD? I.e. are there frequently wished for indicators desired by a majority of students who have a same objective for their LAD?
- RQ3: Are there different expectations of students for their LAD, depending on their learning context (study duration, level) and/or moment in the semester according to the LAD's objective?

2 Material

To answer our research questions, we organised LAD co-design sessions using a co-design tool (PADDLE or ePADDLE method [14]), online or in face-to-face sessions, with students in different contexts presented in Table 1. In this paper we use data from a total number of 108 groups of 2 to 4 students (N = 386 students overall). Each group was asked to design a LAD for a specific objective among 6 possible ones (monitoring, planning, communication, evaluation, evolution, remediation) that they were choosing themselves at the beginning of the session. A co-design session lasted an average of 91 min (SD = 25 min). For each LAD, we collected a list of indicators defined by students with a name, a description, one or more visualization(s) and a drawing of the final dashboard (see Fig. 1 for some examples of such dashboards). LADs produced by the students contain an average of 7.04 indicators or data (SD = 2.17).

Table 1. The 7 different contexts of students participating in co-design sessions

Study program	Study years	Period in the semester	Study duration	Co-design conditions	Number of groups	Number of students
Humanities	1	Middle	5	Face-to-face	2	4
Pharmacy	2	Beginning	6	Face-to-face	23	91
Pharmacy	2	End	6	Online	34	121
Pharmacy	5	Middle	6	Face-to-face	1	3
Pharmacy	5	End	6	Face-to-face	1	2
Pharmacy	5	Middle	6	Face-to-face	29	107
IT	1	End	2	Online	18	58
				Total	108	386

3 RQ1: Set of Indicators for Students' LAD

3.1 Method

From the raw data, for each indicator defined by a group of students, we inferred a generic title to be able to compare the content of the different LADs. For each of the 108 LADs, we have listed indicators wished for by students and the associated desired visualization(s) they described or drew.

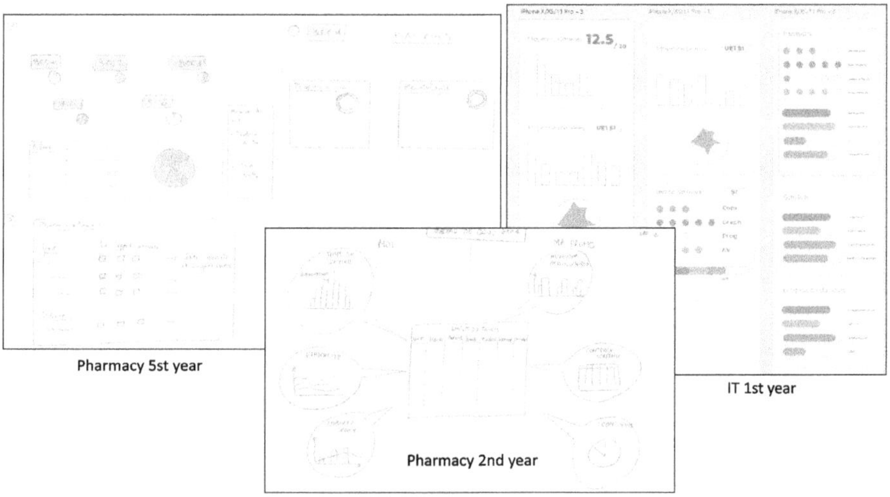

Fig. 1. Examples of LAD drawing produced by students

3.2 Results and Discussion

Overall, we listed 761 data and indicators with their visualization(s). After coding with generic titles, we obtained 54 indicators divided into 12 thematics using 24 different visualizations. Some thematics (monitoring, planning and communication) overlap with the objectives of the LADs. It is worth noting that not all of the 54 indicators wished for by students match the definitions of a LAD indicator from [12] or [13], as students sometimes wish for information that is not directly linked to their learning but which they consider useful in order to plan their learning session (such as weather or personal agenda). Figure 2 shows all 54 indicators and data sorted by the percentage of groups that listed them. We can observe that no single indicator corresponds to all LADs (the most requested indicator, which is the grade, is asked for by 60% of students) and that there is a limited number of data and indicators desired by the majority of students.

We can see that the needs expressed are not limited to indicators, but students also ask for data, whether related to learning or not. We have chosen to keep indicators and data in our analysis because the LADs designed by the students are coherent sets. This is in line with Jivet's findings: "different tools should complement dashboards and be seamlessly integrated in the learning environment and the instructional design" [11, p. 93]. In our study, students may have defined learning environments rather than LADs.

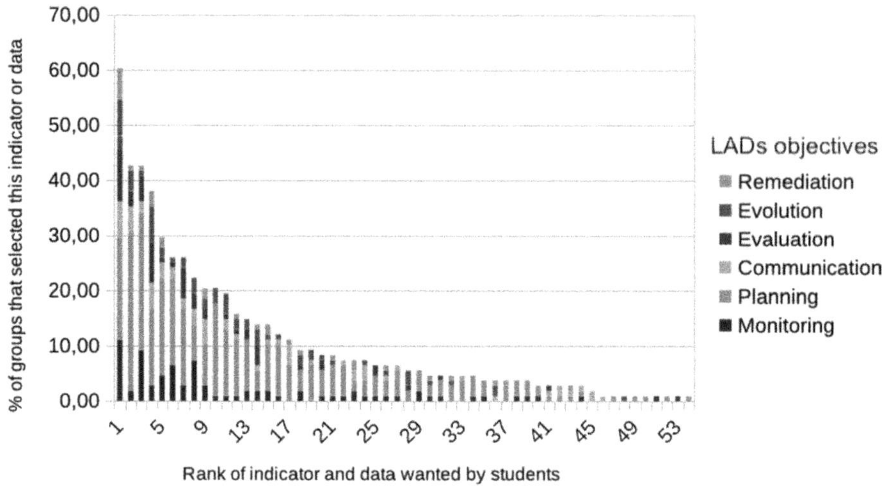

Fig. 2. Indicator and data sorted by the number of groups that selected them

4 RQ2: Prevalence of Most Frequent Learning Indicators by Objectives

4.1 Method

Using the list of 54 indicators identified in RQ1, we looked for the 5 most wanted data and indicators by objective (monitoring, planning, communication, evaluation, evolution, remediation) and analyzed also the associated visualization chosen.

4.2 Results and Discussion

We obtained 17 items presented in Table 2. Almost all data and indicators listed in Table 2 were whished for by groups of different kinds of study except those marked with *. We can observe that some data and indicators are shared by different objective, by different study program but, none is wished by all groups. For the 5 most wanted data and indicators, students expressed different needs in visualization for each data or indicators (between 5 and 17 different visualizations).

By comparing the desired data and indicators according to the LADs' objectives, we have identified some items that are shared by several learning contexts, but none of them is validated for all situations. Even if the grade seems to be wanted by a majority of groups, this data can be represented by different visualizations. This indicator is suitable for only 35% of LAD with a planning objective, perhaps because the planning objective groups together several sub-objectives such as planning one's work for the semester or planning one's revisions. The

Table 2. Compilation of the 5 most wanted data and indicators including ex-aequo for each objective (monitoring[MON], planning[PLA], communication[COM], evaluation[EVA], evolution[EVO], remediation[REM]) presented by % of groups concerned

Thematics	Data and indicators	Rank	LADs' objectives					
			MON N = 15	PLA N = 54	COM N = 10	EVA N = 11	EVO N = 12	REM N = 6
Monitoring	Inventory of time spent and/or time remaining	7	20	28	20	55	17	0
	State of play and/or remaining work	3	67	50	20	45	8	17
Planning	Timetable	2	13	57	50	27	33	17
	To do list	6	47	31	20	9	8	0
Communication	Help	23	13	4	20	0	0	33
	Useful contacts*	17	0	13	40	0	0	17
Course	Course content	9	20	15	50	18	17	33
	Description of the course, resources, and activities	11	7	24	20	9	33	0
	Knowledge requirements*	28	0	4	0	9	25	0
Learning	Comparison with peers	4	20	28	50	73	58	50
	Formative assessment*	14	13	7	10	36	25	17
	Status of knowledge or skills (acquired and/or to be acquired)	8	53	13	30	27	25	0
Method	Difficulties and adaptation*	15	13	17	10	0	8	33
Evaluation	After evaluation	18	7	0	0	0	0	33
	Date	5	33	35	30	9	17	33
	Grade	1	80	37	70	91	83	100
Personal life	Private organisation, leisure and free time	10	7	33	0	0	25	0

*Data or indicator whished for by students from only one kind of study program.

peer comparison indicator, which is often proposed in LADs, varies greatly, ranging from 20% to 72% of groups depending on the objective. This result confirms the need to adapt the LADs to the learning context and target, as identified in previous works. To go further, we should explore, for the same learning context (same student cohort, same study program, same year, same LAD objective), if there are shared expectations of students for their LAD.

5 RQ3: Links Between Indicators and Need Profiles

5.1 Method

To identify a possible link between indicators and need profiles, we looked at the variation of expressed needs and selected the 5 data and indicators which varied the most for:

- the study year: first, second and fifth year,
- the moment when the co-design session took place: at the beginning, the middle or the end of the semester.

To complete this approach, additional analysis were conducted using SAS software (SAS v9.4, SAS Institute Inc., Cary, NC, USA). Categorical variables are presented as absolute numbers and percentages. Chi-square tests or Fisher's exact tests were used as they seem appropriate to compare proportions of a categorical variable. When a statistically significant result is found, Cramer's V was used to estimate the strength of association between the variables. A two-tailed type I error rate of 0.05 was considered for statistical significance.

5.2 Results and Discussion

According to different learning context variables, we have identified various wishes by exploring the variations in the needs expressed by students.

Variation Between Study Year. According to the study year, indicators which varied most are presented in Table 3. We identified statistically significant links for several thematic with some study year:

- 1st year students are less interested by indicators and data of the thematic information ($p = 0.03 < 0.05$, $V = 0.22$) with 0% vs. 23% of 2nd and 5th year students who wanted this kind of indicators (medium association).
- 1st year students are also less interested in planning data than the others ($\chi^2 = 7.35$, $p = 0.02 < 0.05$, $V = 0.26$) with 35% for 1st year vs. 65% and 71% for 2nd and 5th year (medium association).
- 1st year students are mainly more interested about data and indicators about project ($p < .0001$, $V = 0.62$) with 50% of 1st year vs. >2% for the others (strong association).
- finally, data about personal life interested mainly 2nd year students ($p = 0.0057 < 0.05$, $V = 0.31$) with 33% vs. 5% for 1st and 10% for 5th year (medium association).

Table 3. The 5 data and indicators which varied the most according to the study year presented by % of groups concerned

Thematics	Data and indicators	1st year	2nd year	5st year
Learning	Comparison with peers	25	43.86	35.48
Planning	To do list	20	49.12	45.16
Course	Course content	5	28.07	16.13
Evaluation	Coefficients	0	17.54	22.58
Learning	Formative assessment	0	15.79	19.35

1^{st}year students seem to expect less information to implement a learning strategy (coefficient, formative assessment). On the other hand, the are more interested with data and indicators about project management. In our study, 1st year students came from two different academic programs and 2nd and 5th year from another academic program which could bias the results. The majority of first year students are in an IT course with a project-based pedagogical approach, which can explain the high interest for this kind of indicators. All 2nd year students are pharmacy students and they have just passed the 1st year of health studies, which means a very intense 1st year. This could explain the importance of personal life for them, and they hope to find some leisure time. To refine this first result, data from several academic programs would be needed for each sample. And the type of study (duration, thematic, pedagogical approach) should probably also influence students' expectations. The year of study should be coupled with this information to refine this result.

Variation Between Moment in the Semester. The results of the variations in students' expectations over time are presented in the Fig. 3. These results seem globally aligned with what one might naturally expect to observe. At the beginning, students need to plan the semester with basic information (timetable, evaluation's date, expected working time) and consider planning personal life. The information on planning decreases in the middle and at the end of the semester. They are replaced by two kinds of indicators, a learning one with the status of knowledge or skills (acquired and/or to be acquired) and a monitoring one the state of play and/or remaining work, probably to be ready for the exams. We have often seen LADs adapted to the learning context or/and adaptable by the students, but to our knowledge, no adaptation has been provided by the system according to the time. To go further to refine our results, adaptation over time by the system should be explored as an additional adaptation possibility.

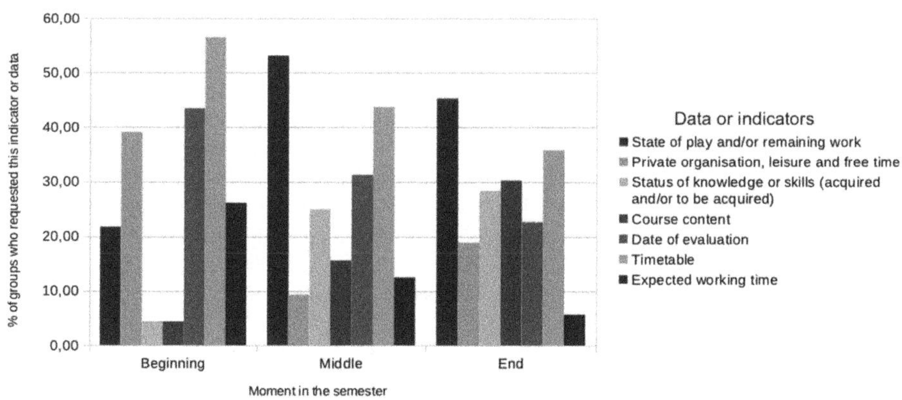

Fig. 3. Variation over time (% of groups who requested these indicators broken down by moment)

6 Conclusion

As previous work has identified, LADs for students need to be adapted to the learning context and by students. We wish to pursue this line of work by investigating whether there were shared data or indicators between LADs with different objectives and whether it was possible to identify adaptation needs according to different variables linked to the learning context. Our results seem to indicate that there are some data and indicators more often desired by students, but in all cases, they remain specific according to the objective of the LAD. It seems that the needs of students change over time, depending on the time in the semester (beginning, middle and end). Students would like useful information to plan at the beginning of the semester and at the end of the semester, they seem to prefer indicators to assess the knowledge and skills acquired and the progress in the remaining work. This result opens new possibilities to adapt LADs according to time. Our next steps will be to try to define from these results an adaptive LAD model for students and to experiment on real LADs with students.

References

1. Gartner Says Advanced Analytics is a Top Business Priority. https://www.gartner.com/en/newsroom/press-releases/2014-10-21-gartner-says-advanced-analytics-is-a-top-business-priority
2. Ahmad, A., et al.: What indicators can i serve you with? An evaluation of a research-driven learning analytics indicator repository, pp. 58–68 (2022)
3. Arriaran Olalde, I.N., Ipiña Larrañaga, N.: Indicators needed to design a student dashboard from lecturers' perspectives: a qualitative study. In: 5th International Conference on Higher Education Advances (HEAd 2019). Universitat Politècnica València (2019)
4. Bodily, R., Verbert, K.: Review of research on student-facing learning analytics dashboards and educational recommender systems. IEEE Trans. Learn. Technol. **10**(4), 405–418 (2017)
5. Dabbebi, I., Gilliot, J.M., Iksal, S.: User centered approach for learning analytics dashboard generation. In: CSEDU 2019, vol. 2, pp. 260–267 (2019)
6. Glahn, C., Specht, M., Koper, R.: Smart indicators to support the learning interaction cycle. Int. J. Cont. Eng. Educ. Lifelong Learn. **18**, 98–117 (2007)
7. Gras, B., Brun, A., Boyer, A.: For and by student dashboards design to address dropout. In: Companion Proceedings 10th International Conference on Learning Analytics & Knowledge (LAK20), Workshop on Addressing Drop-Out Rates in Higher Education (ADORE 2020). Frankfurt, Germany (2020). https://hal.inria.fr/hal-02974682
8. Hilliger, I., et al.: For learners, with learners: identifying indicators for an academic advising dashboard for students. In: Alario-Hoyos, C., Rodríguez-Triana, M.J., Scheffel, M., Arnedillo-Sánchez, I., Dennerlein, S.M. (eds.) EC-TEL 2020. LNCS, vol. 12315, pp. 117–130. Springer, Cham (2020). https://doi.org/10.1007/978-3-030-57717-9_9
9. Ifenthaler, D.: Learning analytics for school and system management. In: OECD Digital Education Outlook 2021 : Pushing the Frontiers with Artificial Intelligence, Blockchain and Robots. OECD Publishing (2021)

10. Ifenthaler, D., Yau, J.Y.K.: Reflections on different learning analytics indicators for supporting study success. Int. J. Learn. Anal. Artif. Intell. Educ. (iJAI) **2**(2), 4–23 (2020)
11. Jivet, I., Scheffel, M., Drachsler, H., Specht, M.: Awareness is not enough: pitfalls of learning analytics dashboards in the educational practice. In: Lavoué, É., Drachsler, H., Verbert, K., Broisin, J., Pérez-Sanagustín, M. (eds.) EC-TEL 2017. LNCS, vol. 10474, pp. 82–96. Springer, Cham (2017). https://doi.org/10.1007/978-3-319-66610-5_7
12. Jivet, I., Wong, J., Scheffel, M., Valle Torre, M., Specht, M., Drachsler, H.: Quantum of choice: how learners' feedback monitoring decisions, goals and self-regulated learning skills are related. In: LAK21: 11th International Learning Analytics and Knowledge Conference, pp. 416–427. ACM (2021)
13. Morais Canellas, C.: Métamodèle d'analytique des apprentissages avec le numérique. Ph.D. thesis, Sorbonne université (2021)
14. Oliver-Quelennec, K., Bouchet, F., Carron, T., Pinçon, C.: Can a learning analytics dashboard participative design approach be transposed to an online-only context? In: 18th International Conference Cognition and Exploratory Learning in Digital Age, p. 9 (2021)
15. Prieto Alvarez, C., Martinez-Maldonado, R., Anderson, T.: Co-designing learning analytics tools with learners, pp. 93–110. Taylor & Francis (10 2018)
16. Roberts, L.D., Howell, J.A., Seaman, K.: Give me a customizable dashboard: personalized learning analytics dashboards in higher education. Technol. Knowl. Learn. **22**(3), 317–333 (2017)
17. Sahin, M., Ifenthaler, D.: Visualizations and dashboards for learning analytics: a systematic literature review. In: Sahin, M., Ifenthaler, D. (eds.) Visualizations and Dashboards for Learning Analytics. Advances in Analytics for Learning and Teaching, pp. 3–22. Springer, Cham (2021). https://doi.org/10.1007/978-3-030-81222-5_1
18. Scheneider, T., Lemos, R.: Use of learning analytics interactive dashboards in serious games: a review of the literature. In. J. Innov. Educ. Res. **8**(3), 150–174 (2020)
19. Schwendimann, B.A., et al.: Perceiving learning at a glance: a systematic literature review of learning dashboard research. IEEE Trans. Learn. Technol. **10**(1), 30–41 (2017)
20. Tan, J.P.L., Koh, E., Jonathan, C.R., Yang, S.: Learner dashboards a double-edged sword? Students' sense-making of a collaborative critical reading and learning analytics environment for fostering 21st century literacies. J. Learn. Anal. **4**(1), 117–140 (2017)
21. Teasley, S.D.: Student facing dashboards: one size fits all? Technol. Knowl. Learn. **22**(3), 377–384 (2017)

The Evaluation of One-to-One Initiatives: Exploratory Results from a Systematic Review

Gerti Pishtari[1](✉), Edna Milena Sarmiento-Márquez[2], Kairit Tammets[2], and Jaan Aru[3]

[1] University for Continuing Education Krems (Danube University Krems), Dr. Karl Dorrek 30, 3500 Krems an der Donau, Austria
gerti.pishtari@donau-uni.ac.at

[2] Tallinn University, Narva mnt 25, 10120 Tallinn, Estonia
msm@tlu.ee, kairit@tlu.ee

[3] University of Tartu, Ülikooli 18, 50090 Tartu, Estonia
jaan.aru@ut.ee

Abstract. While one-to-one initiatives (that equip each student and teacher with digital devices) have been widely implemented, no systematic review has explored how they are being evaluated. The contribution of this paper is twofold. First, we present exploratory insights from a systematic review on the evaluation of one-to-one initiatives. We focus on the relations inside the related research community and explore the relevant research topics that they have considered, through bibiliometric network analyses and topic modeling. Second, this paper contributes to existing guidelines about systematic reviews with an example that applies the mentioned analyses after the manual in-depth review of the papers (usually they are applied in parallel, or afterwards). Results depict a fragmented community, with little explicit collaborations among the research groups, but that shares a common body of literature providing good practices that can inform future one-to-one implementations. This community has considered a common set of topics (including, the implementation of educational technologies, mobile learning and classroom orchestration). Future evaluations of one-to-one initiatives would benefit if grounded in pedagogical theories and informed by learning analytics. Our approach enabled us to understand the dynamics of the related community, identify the core literature, and define guiding questions for future qualitative analyses.

Keywords: One-to-one computing · Evaluation · Bibliometric network analysis · Topic modeling · Systematic literature review

1 Introduction

One-to-one (1:1) initiatives aim to better support teaching and learning practices by providing to each student and/or teacher a digital device (e.g., laptops,

I. Hilliger et al. (Eds.): EC-TEL 2022, LNCS 13450, pp. 310–323, 2022.
https://doi.org/10.1007/978-3-031-16290-9_23

or tablets) [13]. Such initiatives go beyond the mere matching of stakeholders and devices, as apart from supporting the creation of physical and digital infrastructures, they are guided by specific pedagogical objectives and target teachers' professional development. Depending on the socioeconomic context, 1:1 initiatives have different pedagogical goals. For instance, when applied in low-income schools, they have targeted bridging the digital divide, or providing equal opportunities to students [17], while in economically developed contexts goals have included aspects such as collaborative learning, or self-regulated learning [7].

Related research has found that granting each student a device can partially bridge the digital divide, promote collaborative learning, improve communication between teachers and students, and ameliorate student writing skills and engagement, among others [7]. Nevertheless, 1:1 initiatives experience several challenges, as apart from concerns related to students' screen time and behavior [18], they require extensive teacher training, a positive attitude toward change (both from teachers and school managers), as well as offering continuous pedagogical support to teachers [13,18]. Indeed, the sustainability of 1:1 initiatives over time is a notable issue [7]. For these reasons the evaluation of 1:1 initiatives is a central aspect to the related research community [3].

There exist several works describing the implementation and evaluation of specific 1:1 initiatives (e.g., [2,5,19]). Moreover, previous systematic reviews on 1:1 initiatives have mainly focused on the impact of such initiatives [6,7,11], or factors influencing their implementation [1,13,16]. To the best of our knowledge, no systematic review has inquired about how 1:1 initiatives have been evaluated (including all, the contexts of the evaluations, methodologies used, and outcomes), which would create awareness about existing good practices about evaluating 1:1 initiatives, context-dependent guidelines, and potential research gaps.

The current paper presents the first exploratory analyses of a systematic review about the evaluation of 1:1 initiatives. Our first goal is to understand the dynamics inside the research community that has evaluated these initiatives. Namely, we focus on the co-authoring patterns between the researchers, the awareness that researchers have of each-others' work, and on identifying the core literature around the evaluations of 1:1 initiatives. Our second goal is to explore the main research topics considered by the papers under review. To deal with it, we explore both explicit topics (e.g., keywords explicitly mentioned in the papers under review) and latent topics (emerging from the automatic analysis of the textual content of the papers). To achieve these goals we apply a set of automatic analyses based on bibliometric network analyses and topic modeling (further explained in the Methodology section).

These analyses are not uncommon in systematic reviews and can provide useful insights on the maturity and the structure of a research community, can help to identify the relevant literature around a topic, and to discover latent topics found in the textual content of large sets of papers that cannot be easily analysed manually (see, for instance [14]). Nevertheless, the common practice in systematic reviews has been to conduct these analyses after, or in parallel with the in-depth qualitative analyses of the papers, once the researchers have gone manually through all the selected papers. Thus, this paper, apart from providing awareness about research evaluating 1:1 initiatives (based on the two main goals above), also contributes to the body of literature on conducting systematic reviews with an example that uses the mentioned quantitative analyses before starting with the manual filtering process and in-depth analyses of the selected papers (see the Methodology section). In the Discussion section we further discuss the benefits that we identified from following this approach, by emphasising that they served as a starting point that not only provided useful insights about the considered research community, but that also lead to the formulation of a set of guiding questions that will inform future manual analyses.

In the rest of this paper, Sect. 2 presents the related work, while Sect. 3 the methodology. In Sect. 4 we discuss the results and reflect about our approach, while Sect. 5 concludes the paper and presents the future work.

2 Related Work

2.1 Existing 1:1 Computing Initiatives

The first school-wide 1:1 initiative was implemented in 1990 in Australia, after which similar programs have been broadly implemented elsewhere [8]. Nowadays, there exist several similar initiatives, such as Bring Your Own Device, where students are encouraged to use their devices at school, or One Laptop Per Child that targets developing countries [8]. The scope of 1:1 programs is determined by the initiating institutions that usually consist of the central/local government, school administrators [13], but also teachers and parents that might be involved in the decision-making [17].

The impact of 1:1 initiatives is still an open issue. For instance, it is clear that merely providing devices it is not enough (such as by trying to close the digital divide between low and high-income students and expecting that the learning results will improve). More recent initiatives are also targeting specific pedagogical interventions (e.g., that aim to enhance the learning practices of the low-income students) [1]. Targeted learning practices and objectives include self-regulated learning, developing problem-solving skills, or career readiness [13,18]. The evaluation of 1:1 initiatives is a crucial aspect. As these initiatives continue to grow, expand and target a multitude of teaching and learning practices, it is important that they also focus on the quality and rigor of their evaluation [3], as when the assessment of the impact of 1:1 initiatives is not accurate, it might affect the transferability and sustainability of the related good practices [2,17].

2.2 Related Reviews on 1:1 Computing

There exist several reviews on 1:1 computing. Some consider the implementation of 1:1 initiatives, by rather focusing on the factors that influence it (e.g., [11]), or on specific contexts (e.g., [7] focuses on primary and secondary schools). Other reviews report on the impact of 1:1 initiatives, mentioning that demographic factors and the size of the program can impact the outcomes [1], or that such initiatives can have positive effects in several subjects (such as mathematics, or English) [18]. While the evaluation process has not been considered in existing 1:1 reviews, a related review in computing education reported that the evaluation has usually been ad-hoc, as for instance it has not followed standardised practices (e.g., using national assessment tests to measure the impact of implementing educational technologies) [3]. Various 1:1 reviews also call for further large-scale research on the evaluation process of 1:1 initiatives [6,13]. Moreover, no review on 1:1 computing has analysed the relations inside the related research community, which would provide evidence among others, about the collaboration patterns inside the research community, if there exist a common body of literature that can guide future 1:1 implementations, and on the most important research topics considered (which could help identifying research gaps).

3 Methodology

Following the guidelines for systematic reviews from Kitchenham and Charters [10], we defined a search query with keywords representing the main research topic (i.e., 1:1 computing) and our focus (e.g., evaluation). We opted for the following query, due to the number of papers it yielded and their relevance: *("1:1 computing" OR "one to one computing" OR "1:1 computing" OR "1:1 laptop*" OR "one to one laptop*" "1:1 laptop*") AND ("evaluat*" OR "measur*" OR "assess*")*. The asterix (meaning *followed by any list of characters*) was used to include multiple versions of a keyword (e.g., evaluation, evaluations, etc.).

We applied this query on April 30, 2021 on 8 databases relevant for Technology Enhanced Learning, or TEL (represented in Fig. 1). We also considered the first 100 results on Google Scholar to identify potentially relevant grey literature, resulting in a total of 6537 papers. Next, to standardize the process, as different databases apply different filtering criteria, we automatically filtered the papers based on whether the query was found in the title, abstract and keywords of each of them, resulting in 201 papers. The first two authors of this paper separately reviewed the main parts of the resulting papers (namely, title, abstract and keywords) and discarded the ones that were out of scope (e.g., not related to an educational context), not written in English, or not accessible online (even after contacting the authors). Doubtful cases were discussed between all the co-authors, until reaching an agreement. This process resulted in 175 papers, considered for the automatic analyses.

To conduct the automatic analyses, we were guided by the following research questions (RQ): ***RQ1.*** *To what extent is the research community that has evaluated 1:1 computing initiatives interrelated, based on existing collaboration patterns, awareness of each-others work, and the related literature that has been considered?* ***RQ2.*** *What are the main research topics that have been considered by the body of literature evaluating 1:1 computing initiatives?* To respond to RQ1, we focused on three themes (see Fig. 2). To analyse the collaboration patterns

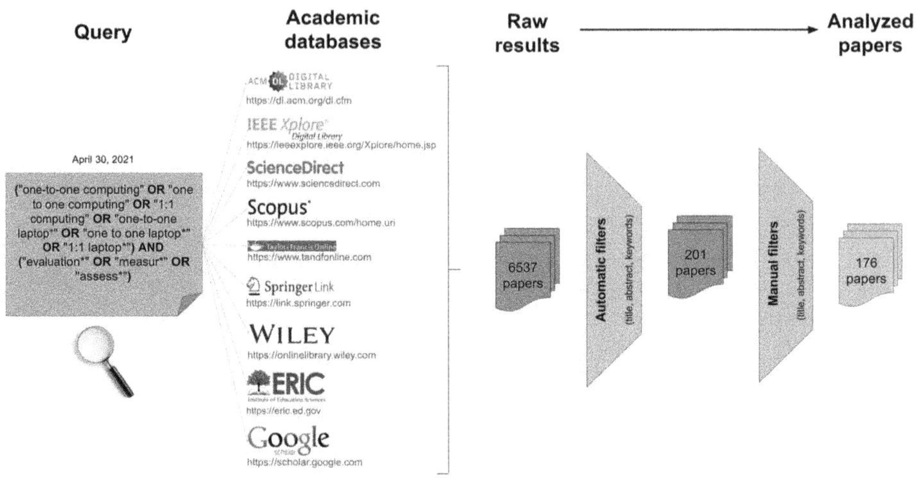

Fig. 1. Stages of the systematic review.

mentioned in RQ1, we considered the *co-authorship* network of the researchers involved in the papers under review (theme 1.1 in Fig. 2), To understand the awareness that researchers had about each-others' work, we analysed the network of *co-citations* between the authors (theme 1.2 in Fig. 2). Regarding the *considered literature*, we focused on the network of specific sources co-cited by at least two of the papers under review (theme 1.3 in Fig. 2).

Fig. 2. Research questions, related themes and data analyses methods.

To respond to RQ2, we considered both explicit (theme 2.1 in Fig. 2) and implicit topics (theme 2.2 in Fig. 2) found in the papers. To identify explicit topics, we analysed the *the co-occurrence of the keywords* by visualising the network of keywords found in at least two of the papers. Similar keywords (e.g., classroom orchestration, orchestration, etc.) were considered as being the same one. To produce the bibliographic network we used Vosviewer[1].

[1] https://www.vosviewer.com/.

Regarding implicit topics, we applied Latent Dirichlet Allocation (LDA), a machine learning technique that is used for topic modeling and that automatically identifies the latent topics found in a group of documents, by statistically allocating words to topics and topics to documents (e.g., by clustering the text found in the documents into specific topics based on the words included in them, and by statistically specifying the probability that a given topic is found in a given document). We applied LDA to the textual versions of the 175 papers, excluding the authors' names, affiliations, and references. We did not limit the number of topics per document (meaning that one document could include several topics). To choose the optimal number of overall topics, we used LDATuning[2], which compares four different metrics and that resulted in 13 topics. The LDA algorithm was implementation using the LDAvis[3] package in RStudio[4].

To make sense of the similarities between the 13 topics, we grouped them based on a Principal Component Analysis (PCA) plotted in a two-dimensional space, where topics closer to each other tend to have similar features (see the Results section). The first two authors of this paper interpreted the resulting topics, by considering the word-maps produced by the algorithm for each topic (i.e., the most relevant words for each topic), the PCA, and the knowledge that they had on the papers that were related to each topic. Figure 2 summarises the RQs, their related themes and data analyses methods used.

4 Results

We identified 175 papers published from 2006 to 2021, from which 148 were journal papers, 12 conference papers, 11 project reports, 3 book chapters, and 1 PhD thesis. The full list of papers can be found online[5]. This section presents the results alongside the RQs and the corresponding themes.

RQ1: Relation Patterns of the Research Community that Has Evaluated 1:1 Initiatives

Theme 1.1. Co-authorship. Figure 3 depicts a fragmented research community, composed of multiple research groups that have evaluated 1:1 initiatives and that have had little explicit collaborations. Few researchers have collaborated on more than one paper (depicted with colors).

Theme 1.2. Citations Among Authors. From 477 researchers that co-authored the papers under review, 57 (12%) co-cited each other. Figure 4 depicts their network, in which we distinguished 10 different clusters when grouping authors based on the co-authoring patterns presented in theme 1.1. (represented by different colors in Fig. 4). Not surprisingly, co-authors of multiple papers tend to cite each other (represented by stronger connections within the clusters).

---

[2] https://github.com/nikita-moor/ldatuning.

[3] https://github.com/cpsievert/LDAvis.

[4] https://www.rstudio.com/.

[5] https://bit.ly/1to1CompFullListPapers.

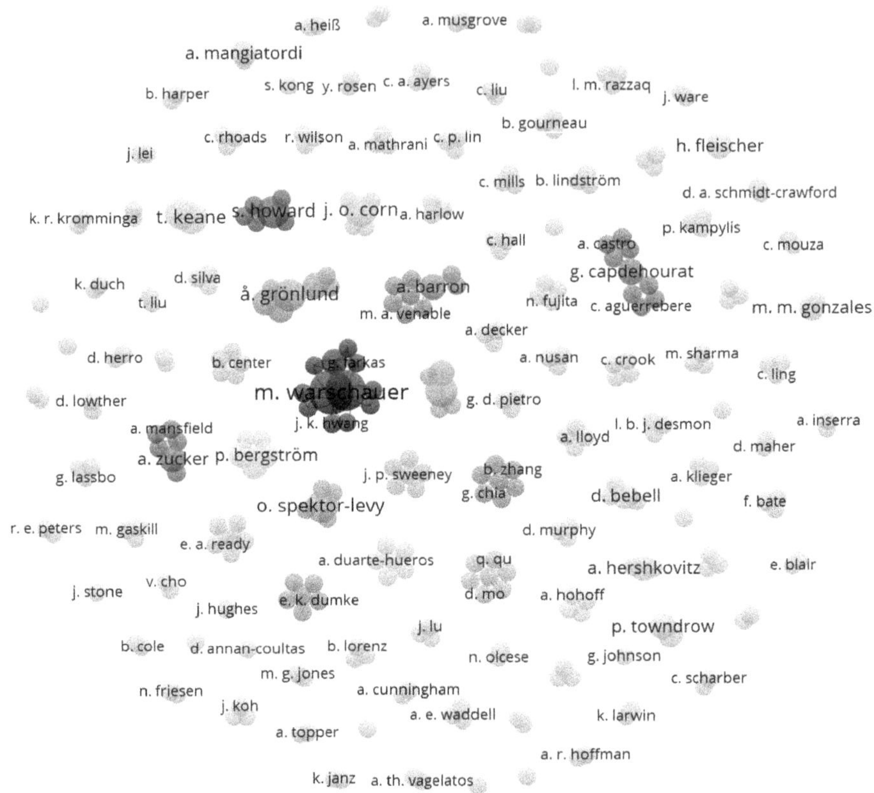

Fig. 3. Network of the co-authorship of the papers under review visualising the names of the first authors. With colors, groups of researchers that have co authored more than one paper. (Color figure online)

Theme 1.3. Considered Literature. Apart from explicit collaboration patterns and/or knowledge of each-others' work (discussed in the previous themes), we also checked whether the community of research that has evaluated 1:1 initiatives was implicitly related, by checking the network of co-citations of the literature that they had considered (i.e., citations found in more than one paper). From 1005 unique sources, 156 were co-cited. To focus on the main literature, in Fig. 5 we show the network of the co-cited sources that had at least 10 citations on semanticscholar.org (resulting in 31 papers, which full list can be found online[6]). We noticed in Fig. 5 that various of the main authors are also found in the previous two themes, which might suggest a group of core authors in 1:1 computing. Furthermore, we noticed four different clusters (depicted with different colors in Fig. 5. Various co-cited papers were literature reviews (rather systematic, or not) in 1:1 computing (with green, in Fig. 5). We have already mentioned some

[6] https://bit.ly/1to1CompLiteratureCoCited.

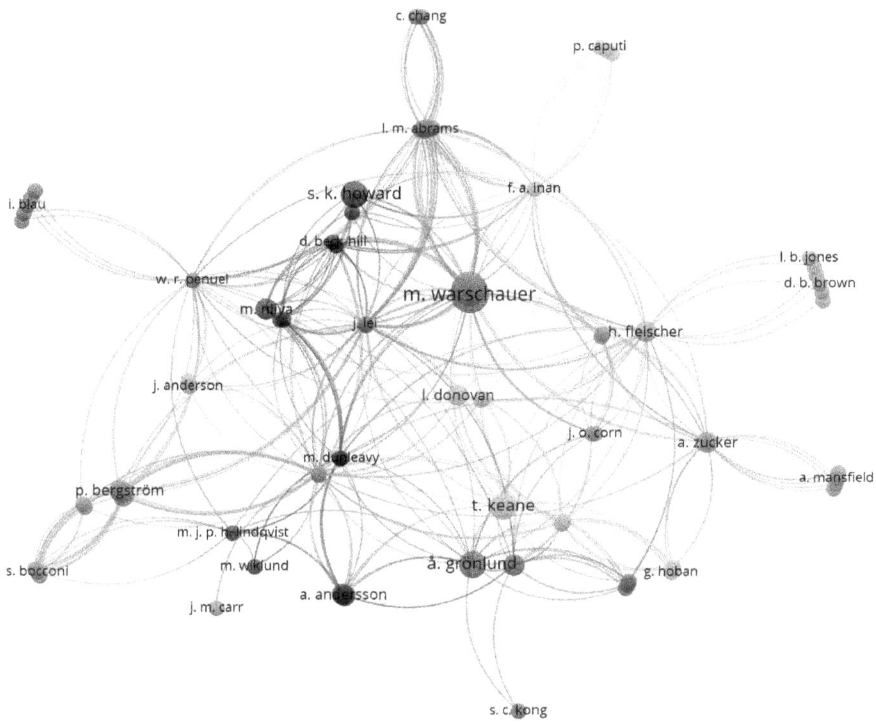

Fig. 4. Network of the citations among the authors of the papers under review depicting the authors that co-cited each other. With the same color, researchers that have co-authored papers. Only the names of the main authors of both the papers under review and the cited papers are visualised. To simplify the graph, authors with less than 15 citations on semanticscholar.org were hidden. (Color figure online)

of them in the Related Work section. Only 5 papers were theoretical framework, or models that guided the implementation of 1:1 initiatives (with yellow), such as the TPACK framework that describes the type of knowledge that teachers need for a successful integration of technology in teaching practices [12]). Several papers focused on the different contexts, the implementation and lessons learned from specific 1:1 initiatives (with red; see for instance [19] for a context involving low-income students). We also identified 10 papers that presented the evaluation of specific 1:1 initiatives (with blue in Fig. 5; see, for instance [5]).

RQ2: The Main Topics Emerging from the Papers

Theme 2.1. Explicit Topics. The network of the co-occurrence of keywords depicted three main clusters referring to the methodology, context and objective of 1:1 initiatives (see Fig. 6). The methodologies used seem to include both qualitative and quantitative approaches. Apart from the main objectives relate to

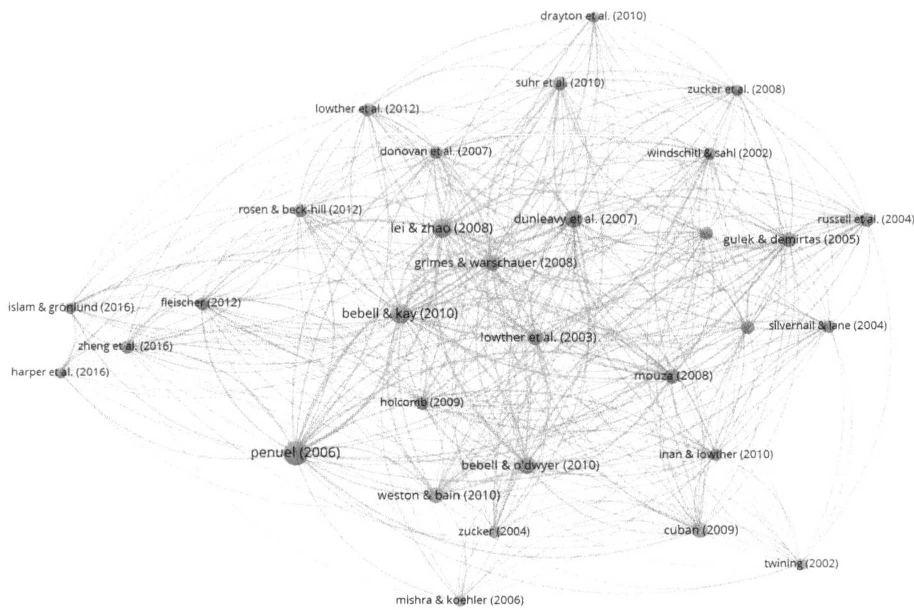

Fig. 5. Network of the literature co-cited by the papers under review, including: reviews about 1:1 computing (green); evaluations of 1:1 initiatives (blue); theoretical models/frameworks relevant to the context (yellow); papers describing the different contexts, strategies and guidelines (red). (Color figure online)

the integration of educational technologies, other ones seem rather related to the two main stakeholders (i.e., teachers, students and their teaching and learning practices), or to the 1:1 initiatives themselves (e.g. their effectiveness, or sustainability). Regarding the context, the emphasis seems to have been rather on the specific technology that was implemented (e.g. laptops, or mobile devices), or on the technical context (e.g., ubiquitous computing). Nevertheless, various pedagogical contexts relevant to TEL are mentioned, such as mobile learning, or computer-supported collaborative learning (cscl).

Theme 2.2. Latent Topics. We grouped topics resulting from the LDA analyses into four main clusters (see Fig. 7). Similar to theme 2.1., we noticed that two topic clusters referred to the methodology and the context of 1:1 initiatives. The context cluster included three topics with similar relevance (as represented by their size) that seem to refer to the pedagogical, sociocultural and technical context. For instance, topic 12 that we named as *technical* context, included keywords such as laptop, computer, mobile, ubiquitous, etc.). Learning and teaching practices (with red in Fig. 7) have been the most relevant topics. For instance, keywords related to teaching practices (apart from obvious keywords such as teacher, or teaching) included planning, management, or guidance. Finally, several topics were related to the evaluation, or outcome of 1:1 computing.

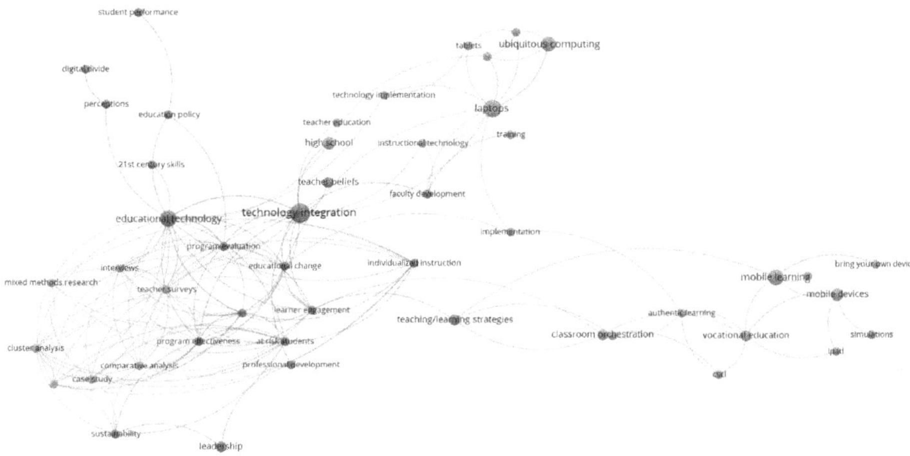

Fig. 6. Network of the co-occurrence of keywords in the papers under review, including keywords related to the methodology (blue), the context (green) and the objectives (red) of 1:1 initiatives. (Color figure online)

5 Discussion

The body of research evaluating the impact of 1:1 initiatives showed little explicit collaboration among the involved research groups, as evidenced by the small number of co-authored papers (theme 1.1). While these results need to be complemented by an in-depth qualitative analyses of the papers, they might suggest that when evaluating the 1:1 initiatives, researchers have focused on the specific sociocultural contexts (e.g. such as [19] in USA). Thus, future work could target comparative studies that consider different contexts (e.g., comparing the impact that 1:1 initiatives in different countries), which would help to identify transferal good practices and produce guidelines that could better guide the implementation of future initiatives.

Only a core number of research groups seems to be aware of each-others' work (theme 1.2), which coincide broadly with both the groups that had co-authored together (see Fig. 4) and the authors of the most cited sources (see Fig. 5). On the short term, the body of literature produced by these core groups could serve as a source of good practices. On the long term, further communication between the different research groups could be raised through transnational co-operations, or workshops on on-to-one computing.

Interestingly, we identified few theoretical approaches used to guide the pedagogical evaluation of 1:1 initiatives (e.g., the TPACK framework [12]). Meanwhile, topic modeling analyses (see RQ2) identified several pedagogical keywords connected to teaching and learning practices (e.g., classroom orchestration, or teaching/learning strategies), suggesting that pedagogical aspects have been part of the evaluation even if there were few specific frameworks that guided the process. For instance, guiding frameworks that might be relevant to the community

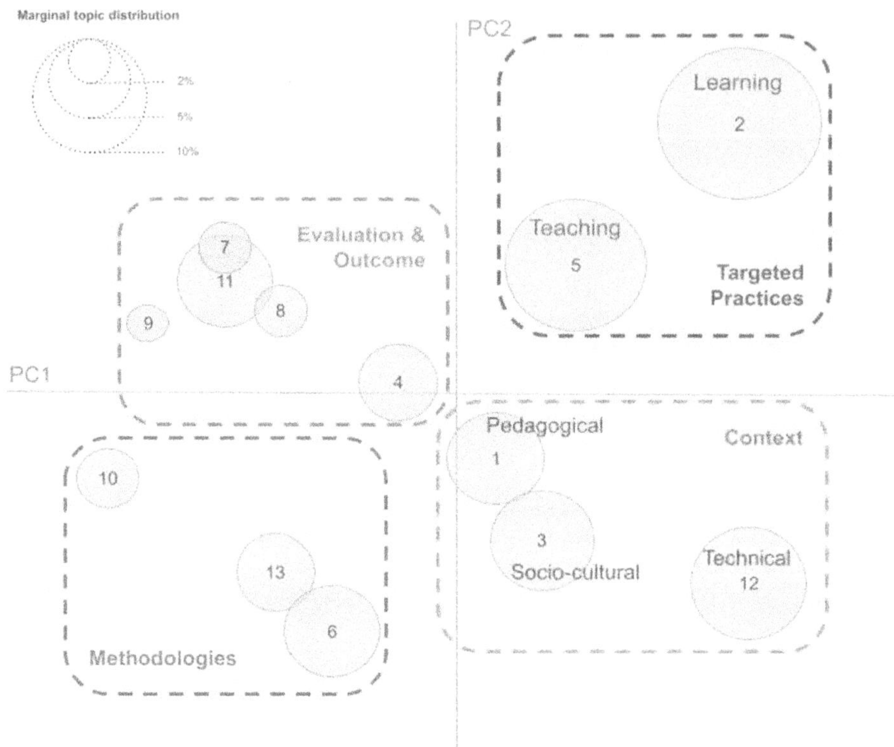

Fig. 7. Two-dimensional PCA of the 13 topics resulting from the LDA, with colors the interpretation of the topics. (Color figure online)

of 1:1 computing include learning design frameworks (e.g., [15] that would enable researchers to understand teachers' design practices and needs in on-to-one initiatives), or mobile learning frameworks (which was identified as an important topic in Fig. 6) such as iPAC [9] that could guide the evaluation of mobile learning scenarios. Future analyses of the papers should investigate the validity of this result, by identifying guiding frameworks used to evaluate 1:1 initiatives, as well as specific teaching and learning practices that the evaluations targeted.

Apart from targeting teachers and students (as seen in RQ2), the evaluation of 1:1 initiatives should also focus on other stakeholders that can contribute to the success 1:1 initiatives and the sustainability of their pedagogical impact, such as managers of the educational institutions, or parents. Future evaluations of 1:1 computing should go beyond assessing the implementation of educational technologies (which was the main keyword), or the impact on specific pedagogical contexts (e.g., mobile and ubiquitous learning). For instance, aspects that could be further explored include: the combined impact that equipping schools with devices and guiding them pedagogically is having on learning practices (e.g., students' self-regulated learning); the learning outcome (e.g., students' performance and engagement, which were topics with a small weight in Fig. 6); or teacher practices (e.g., learning design). Surprisingly, learning analytics, despite its popularity in TEL, did not appear as a topic. While these results should be confirmed by the in-depth analyses of the papers, learning analytics has the potential to inform researchers on the impact that a 1:1 initiative is having on teaching and learning practices. Existing learning analytics frameworks (e.g., [4]) can help researchers to structure the evaluation process and to consider relevant indicators.

Our approach of analysing quantitatively the papers before the in-depth qualitative analyses could help researchers conducting systematic reviews to:

- *Identify core papers and authors.* In our case, these are represented by the different clusters in Figs. 4 and 5. For instance, we checked if the papers evaluating 1:1 initiatives (with blue in Fig. 5) were also found in our pool of 175 papers, to check if our search query needed modifications. Moreover, reading these core papers helped us to define a list of guiding questions for the future in-depth qualitative analyses. We also checked the identified reviews (with green in Fig. 5) to confirm the need for our systematic review on the evaluation of 1:1 initiatives (discussed in the Related Work section).
- *Understand the research community under investigation.* For instance, we identified a fractured research community. Therefore, we defined questions for the future work that will focus on understanding the unique contexts where the 1:1 initiatives have been implemented and evaluated.
- *Have a preliminary view on the most relevant topics.* For example, we identified that the focus has been mainly on teachers and students, while the most important topics included the implementation of educational technologies on specific pedagogical context (e.g., mobile learning). Therefore, in future qualitative analyses we will focus on the stakeholders involved in the implementation and especially in the evaluation of 1:1 initiatives, their evaluated practices and indicators that were used to inform the evaluation.

Limitations of this work include our sole quantitative approach. Complementing them also with qualitative analyses would provide a broader understanding of the body of research under review. Nevertheless, we discussed before that our approach of conducting quantitative exploratory analyses before the qualitative ones has several benefits and this study will be followed by a qualitative analyses of the papers. The query that we used is another limitation, as other keywords (such as analysis, apart from evaluation) might have turned out other related papers. Nevertheless, we experimented with different versions of the query, as discussed in the Methodology section. We applied our query on April 30, 2021, and since then other relevant papers might have been published. Topic modeling and network analysis also include a subjective interpretation, which we tried to diminish by involving two researchers in the interpretation of the results, and by discussing doubtful cases among all the co-authors. We did not manually check the textual content of the 175 papers considered for the analyses, but only filtered the out-of-scope papers based on their title, abstract and keywords (see the Methodology section). Future manual filtering might exclude part of these papers, if they do not describe in detail the evaluation process.

6 Conclusion and Future Work

This paper presented exploratory results from a systematic review on the evaluation of 1:1 initiatives, focusing on topic modeling and bibliographic analyses of the related research community. Results showed a community with little explicit alignment, but that had considered a common pool of literature (provides a pool of good practices for future evaluations) and that had targeted several common learning contexts (such as mobile learning), or practices (e.g., collaborative learning, or classroom orchestration). Thus, research evaluating 1:1 initiatives would benefit from studies comparing different sociocultural contexts where 1:1 initiatives have been evaluated, as well as from the implementation of pedagogical frameworks that can guide the evaluation process (e.g., from Learning Analytics, or Learning Design).

Moreover, our work presents an example on conducting automatic quantitative analyses about the research community being investigated before the in-depth manual analyses of the papers. Our approach enabled us to better understand the community under review and helped us to define a set of core questions that we want to respond through future qualitative analyses. The same approach might be useful for other researchers conducting systematic reviews. Future work will extend this approach with qualitative analyses of the papers under review, focusing among others, on exploring in-depth the contexts where 1:1 initiatives have been evaluated, their objectives, stakeholders involved and their roles, pedagogical approaches used, or the methodology and the maturity of the evaluations (e.g., in terms of participants, time, methods used).

Acknowledgements. This research was supported by the ETAG project PRG1634 and HarNothe, as well as the European Social Fund through the IT Academy Programme and the Estonian Research Council grant PSG728.

References

1. Bethel, E.C.: A systematic review of one-to-one access to laptop computing in K-12 classrooms: an investigation of factors that influence program impact. Ph.D. thesis, Concordia University (2015)
2. Carr, J.M.: Does math achievement h'APP'en when iPads and game-based learning are incorporated into fifth-grade mathematics instruction? J. Inf. Technol. Educ. Res. **11**(1), 269–286 (2012)
3. Decker, A., McGill, M.M.: A topical review of evaluation instruments for computing education. In: Proceedings of the 50th ACM Technical Symposium on Computer Science Education, pp. 558–564 (2019)
4. Greller, W., Drachsler, H.: Translating learning into numbers: a generic framework for learning analytics. J. Educ. Technol. Soc. **15**(3), 42–57 (2012)

5. Grimes, D., Warschauer, M.: Learning with laptops: a multi-method case study. J. Educ. Comput. Res. **38**(3), 305–332 (2008)
6. Holcomb, L.B.: Results & lessons learned from 1:1 laptop initiatives: a collective review. TechTrends **53**(6), 49 (2009)
7. Islam, M.S., Grönlund, Å.: An international literature review of 1:1 computing in schools. J. Educ. Change **17**(2), 191–222 (2016)
8. Kay, R., Schellenberg, D.: Comparing byod and one-to-one laptop programs in secondary school classrooms: a review of the literature. In: Society for Information Technology and Teacher Education International Conference, pp. 1862–1866. Association for the Advancement of Computing in Education (AACE) (2019)
9. Kearney, M., Schuck, S., Burden, K., Aubusson, P.: Viewing mobile learning from a pedagogical perspective. Res. Learn. Technol. **20**(1), n1 (2012)
10. Kitchenham, B., Charters, S.: Guidelines for performing systematic literature reviews in software engineering (2007)
11. Matatall, A.: The impact of 1:1 technology initiatives on new literacy in the secondary ELAR classroom: a metasynthesis (2019)
12. Mishra, P., Koehler, M.J.: Technological pedagogical content knowledge: a framework for teacher knowledge. Teach. Coll. Rec. **108**(6), 1017–1054 (2006)
13. Penuel, W.R.: Implementation and effects of one-to-one computing initiatives: a research synthesis. J. Res. Technol. Educ. **38**(3), 329–348 (2006)
14. Pishtari, G., et al.: Learning design and learning analytics in mobile and ubiquitous learning: a systematic review. Br. J. Educ. Technol. **51**(4), 1078–1100 (2020)
15. Pishtari, G., Rodríguez-Triana, M.J.: An analysis of mobile learning tools in terms of pedagogical affordances and support to the learning activity life cycle. In: Gil, E., Mor, Y., Dimitriadis, Y., Köppe, C. (eds.) Hybrid Learning Spaces. Understanding Teaching-Learning Practice, pp. 167–183. Springer, Cham (2022). https://doi.org/10.1007/978-3-030-88520-5_10
16. Sell, G.R., Cornelius-White, J., Chang, C., McLean, A., Roworth, W.R.: A metasynthesis of research on 1: 1 technology initiatives in k-12 education, pp. 1–57. Ozarks Educational Research Initiative (2012)
17. Tedre, M., Hansson, H., Mozelius, P., Lind, S.: Crucial considerations in one-to-one computing in developing countries. In: 2011 IST-Africa Conference Proceedings, pp. 1–11. IEEE (2011)
18. Zheng, B., Warschauer, M., Lin, C.H., Chang, C.: Learning in one-to-one laptop environments: a meta-analysis and research synthesis. Rev. Educ. Res. **86**(4), 1052–1084 (2016)
19. Zucker, A.A., Hug, S.T.: Teaching and learning physics in a 1:1 laptop school. J. Sci. Educ. Technol. **17**(6), 586–594 (2008)

Designing a Moodle Plugin for Promoting Learners' Self-regulated Learning in Blended Learning

Mar Pérez-Sanagustín[1(✉)], Ronald Pérez-Álvarez[2], Jorge Maldonado-Mahauad[3], Esteban Villalobos[1], and Cédric Sanza[1]

[1] IRIT, Université de Toulouse, CNRS, Toulouse INP, UT3, Toulouse, France
{mar.perez-sanagustin,esteban.villalobos,cedric.sanza}@irit.fr
[2] University of Costa Rica, Sede del Pacífico, Puntarenas, Costa Rica
ronald.perezalvarez@ucr.ac.cr
[3] Department of Computer Science, University of Cuenca, Cuenca, Ecuador
jorge.maldonado@ucuenca.edu.ec

Abstract. After the COVID-19 pandemic, universities moved towards online and Blended Learning (BL) modes to offer greater curricular flexibility. Yet, recent research shows that students have difficulties regulating their learning strategies to adapt to the different learning modes that BL entails, which mixes face-to-face with online activities taking place in different learning contexts and environments. Prior work on Self-Regulated Learning (SRL) has explored the use of dashboard-based scaffolds for supporting students' learning strategies. However, most existing solutions are designed for supporting students in online settings (i.e., MOOCs), disregarding the teachers' role in BL settings and the support they need to monitor and promote students' SRL. This paper presents the design process followed for transforming a tool designed for supporting students' SRL in MOOCs into a Moodle plugin for BL. Following a design-based research methodological approach, we describe all the phases conducted for identifying the most appropriate indicators and visualizations for supporting SRL in BL practices, implementing and evaluating a first prototype. Results of a local evaluation with 114 teachers and a broad evaluation with 311 students shed some light on the type of indicators, dashboards and functionalities that should be considered when designing solutions for supporting SRL in BL settings.

Keywords: Blended learning · Self-regulated learning · Dashboards · Learning analytics · Design-based research

1 Introduction

After the COVID-19 pandemic, Higher Education Institutions (HEIs) are especially interested in fostering students' SRL skills because of the transformation towards a more flexible Blended Learning (BL) models of learning and instruction. BL combines *traditional face-to-face (f2f) with online activities* taking place in different learning

I. Hilliger et al. (Eds.): EC-TEL 2022, LNCS 13450, pp. 324–339, 2022.
https://doi.org/10.1007/978-3-031-16290-9_24

environments and contexts [1] which has been proven an effective method for supporting students' SRL [1, 2]. However, recent research points out that some students show difficulties in regulating their learning strategies in BL, since they must vary their learning strategies depending on the learning mode (online or face-to-face) [2–4].

To support learners in their SRL process, researchers have proposed different approaches [5], being tools based on dashboards the most frequent. These solutions transform trace data into "actionable insights" to foster students' meta-reflection, self-monitoring and produce behavioral changes [6]. So far, most of this prior work have been conducted in online settings in which students have low interaction with teacher, such in Massive Open Online Courses (MOOCs) [7], but very few have been proposed for BL (i.e., [8–10]). These studies suggest that dashboards could be a good approach for supporting SRL strategies, being goal setting, strategic planning, time management and monitoring the SRL processes proved as the more effective for promoting students' motivation, and impact in course performance.

However, these solutions entail two important limitations when applied in BL. First, they are focused mainly in providing students' support disregarding the teachers' role, even when prior literature stresses the essential role they play in BL [11]. Second, only some tools have been designed taking as a basis theoretical models of SRL, which makes it difficult to evaluate their actual impact on learners' behavior when evaluated in actual learning scenarios. Thus, there is a need to expand the diversity of tools for supporting self-regulation in BL, considering not only the students, but also the teachers, offering dashboards that could help them do timely interventions to promote self-regulated behaviors.

1.1 Contribution, Research Questions and Methodology

This paper presents the design process followed for transforming a previous plugin designed for supporting SRL in MOOCs called NoteMyProgress MOOC (NMP MOOC) [12] into a Plugin for Moodle aimed at supporting SRL in BL courses. The NMP MOOC is a web application that complements the Coursera MOOC platform to support students' SRL through interactive visualizations. The result of this transformation is the plugin NMP for Moodle, which includes visualizations for both teachers and students.

For the design of NMP Moodle we followed the Design Based Research (DBR) methodological approach [13]. This approach mixes empirical research on education with theories oriented towards the design of learning environments, from the analysis and design to the implementation and evaluation. To apply the DBR methodological approach, we used the Interactive Learning Design (ILD) framework [14]. The ILD framework organizes the research process into four phases: (1) *Informed exploration*, in which we studied the needs, available theories and audience of the tool; (2) *Enactment*, phase in which the design of a tool is proposed and implemented; (3) *Evaluation of local impact*, which aims at evaluating the impact of the intervention at a local level, focusing on particular research questions for that context; and (4) *Evaluation of broader impact*, which considers the analysis of the technological intervention into a wider audience. Figure 1 shows how the ILD methodology was implemented for the design and evaluation of the new version of NMP Moodle. The following link includes all the collected data and its analysis in the different phases: https://osf.io/w2p83/. Two **research questions** guided the whole process:

- **(RQ1) What are the indicators and visualizations that should be included in a tool for supporting SRL in BL settings?** The objective was to identify the dashboards and indicators in prior work (including NMP MOOC) that could serve as a basis for proposing a tool for BL settings.
- **(RQ2) How a prototype of a tool including the identified indicators is perceived by the end-users in terms of usability and sense making?** The objective was to evaluate the meaningfulness of the dashboards, in terms of usability and sense making, produced for both teachers and students.

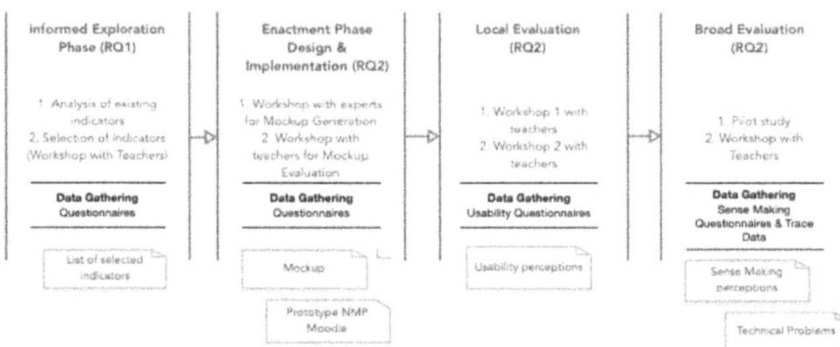

Fig. 1. Cycles of the ILD framework conducted for developing and evaluating NMP Moodle.

2 Informed Exploration Phase

The main objective of the **Informed Exploration phase** was to identify what indicators to include in the dashboards of the NMP Moodle for supporting SRL in a BL course considering both teachers and students (related with RQ1). Specifically, we conducted an analysis of existing indicators used in existing proposals and platforms to identify the indicators to be used in teachers' and students' dashboards. This process was structured into two phases: (1) an analytical phase; and (2) a selection phase.

Phase 1. Analysis of Existing Indicators. In this phase, we conducted an exhaustive analysis of the indicators used in NMP MOOC, in the Coursera dashboards (platform in which NMP MOOC was evaluated), and in existing Moodle plugins designed for supporting teachers in students' monitoring (such as SmartKlass, Dropout Detective dashboard, Plugin Analytics, GISMO, Intelliboard moodle dashboard). The NMP MOOC was included in the analysis for identifying what indicators to be used in students' dashboards, while the analysis of the Coursera dashboards and Moodle plugins were selected for the indicators to be used in teachers' dashboards.

As a result, we obtained a list of indicators organized and classified according to the categories defined in Schwendimann et al. (2017) [15] (i.e., Action-related; Content-related, Results-related, Social-related, Context-related and Learner-related). A total of 135 indicators were identified (See https://osf.io/kez2d/) in this first phase. From these 135 indicators, some of them appeared only in one of the tools, while others appeared in sevarl tools. 61 were used in the Coursera teachers' dashboards and included, among others: students with difficulties, number of events per day, students who did not submit an evaluation, students' progress in the course. 28 were in the Moodle plugins, which included information such as: the number of evaluations performed by the learner per day, individual assessments, number of students with difficulties or average grades. 59 were included in NMP MOOC, which included information for students such as: time spent during the week, numbers of started activities, numbers of completed activities, number of sessions per week, among others.

Phase 2. Selection of Indicators. With the list of indicators obtained in the analysis, we generated an instrument to collect information on teachers' feedback needs in a BL context (See https://osf.io/u8dnz/). The survey included 11 questions to identify what teachers expect from a tool for supporting their BL practices, the functionalities that they consider relevant to include in the tool, and the indicators that they would expect to see in the dashboards of this tool. In addition, we included 11 questions (5 closed and 6 open ended) asking about their experience with BL courses and their expectations of using a tool for supporting them in this type of learning setting. A total of 40 teachers (out of 50) from 20 Latin American universities from 10 countries that belong to the LALA community[1] participated in the survey.

The answers to the questionnaire were analyzed by 3 researchers, but only the answers to close questions Q8, Q9, and Q10 were considered for this study. These questions are related with the expectations of the teachers regarding a tool for supporting SRL in BL, the functionalities they would like to include and the indicators that should be considered. The results (See https://osf.io/tpn5b) indicate that over 70% of the teachers wanted a tool: (1) for monitoring and evaluating learners during the learning process; (2) with visual graphs to display the data; (3) with indicators about students' progress; (4) for identifying students at risk and add indicators about their interaction with the course content to provide them with timely feedback.

[1] LALA SIG: https://www.solaresearch.org/community/sigs/lala-sig/.

Table 1. Summary Table of the selected indicators to be included in the NMP Moodle in relation with the SRL process they support (GS: Goal Setting; SP: Strategic Planning; TM: Time Management; and SE: Self-Evaluation). See the extended list of indicators: https://osf.io/6ux5r/.

#	Indicator	GS	SP	TM	SE
1–3	Planned Time to spend by week/resource/activity	X	X	X	
4–6	Average time spent by students per week/resource/activity			X	X
7–15	Average time spent by high/middle/low performance students by week/resource/activity			X	X
16–18	Time spent per student per week/resource/activity			X	X
19–24	Number of students' interactions per resource/activity per day/week/hour				X
25	Resources with the fewest interactions				X
26	Average attempt by assessment				X
27	Students' grade per evaluation				X
28,29	Percentage of progress of a student per week/ on the course				X

2.1 Results of the Informed Exploration Phase

Three researchers cross-analyzed the results to extract a set of indicators that could support teachers in their BL practices and support students' SRL processes. Specifically, they selected from the list of indicators in Phase 1 those which aligned with the expectations, functionalities and indicators requested by the teachers in the questionnaire (Q8, Q9 and Q10) and related them to the SRL processes that they could support. The result was a list of 29 indicators to be included in the first version of the tool NMP Moodle. Table 1 includes the selected indicators as well as the SRL processes they are associated with for both teachers and students. The indicators for the students were extracted from NMP MOOC tool. The list includes the 29 indicators to support Goal Setting, Strategic Planning, Time management, and Self-evaluation.

3 Design

The main objective of this phase was to extract the design requirements of a NMP Moodle plugin considering the indicators and functionalities identified in the Informed Exploration phase. This phase was structured into two different phases: (1) a workshop with Experts for Mockup generation; and (2) a workshop with teachers for Mockups evaluation. The objective of the workshops was to produce mockups of the dashboards to be implemented in NMP Moodle plugin. For this purpose, both workshops were designed according to the framework for Creative Visualization-Opportunities Workshops proposed by Kerzner et al. (2018) [16], which offers a set of steps for guiding the production of visual dashboard mockups.

Both workshops were structured into three activities. (1) A "workshop opening" to set the stage and engage the participants. In both workshops, the opening was organized to inform the participants about the objective of the workshop, the problem addressed and the relevance of the results. To motivate creativity and make the participants aware of the expectations of the design, they were presented with the list of needs and indicators extracted from the Informed Exploration phase and discussed them to have a full perspective of the problem. (2) A "workshop core" to encourage the participants to explore different visualizations for addressing the requirements discussed in the previous phase and produce mockups to represent them. (3) A "workshop closure" in which the organizers close the session with the main outcomes (See the procedures for the workshops in https://osf.io/vnf6d/).

Six professionals in dashboard development, visualization design and human-computer interaction participated **in the Workshop with Experts for Mockup generation**. In this case, the "workshop core" was structured into three activities. In **Activity 1**, and as a form of elicit visualization opportunities and explore different solutions, participants were provided with a document with a list of numbered visualizations used in Coursera, Moodle and NMP 1.0 that were related with the needs extracted from the Informed Exploration phase. This document was accompanied by two other documents for classifying the visualizations according to both, the identified needs/goals, and the indicators. Individually, participants should indicate which of the proposed visualizations addressed each need and to which indicators they related to. The results of classifying the different visualizations are available in the supplementary Material (https://osf.io/86qd7/). In **Activity 2**, the participants were grouped in pairs to discuss the advantages and disadvantages of each of the analyzed visualizations. Finally, in **Activity 3**, each pair was asked to propose three dashboard mockups with visualization to meet the explored requirements following a co-design process. Participants could design dashboards containing one or more visualizations in the same view, include several indicators in the same visualization and propose functionalities of interactivity with the visualizations to meet the requirements. All the visualizations produced in this activity are provided in the supplementary material https://osf.io/86qd7. With the data collected from this workshop, we proposed a final dashboard capturing the discussed indicators and some of the visualization proposals. See the resulting dashboard proposal at: https://osf.io/t5dcy/. This dashboard mockup was used as a basis for the workshop with teachers.

15 teachers from 6 different universities participated in the **workshop with teachers for Mockups evaluation.** The "workshop core" consisted of analyzing the mockup resulting from the Experts WS. First, each participant individually analyzed the experts' proposal and filled in the same questionnaire used for the Experts WS for indicating whether the proposed dashboard answers the teachers' needs and whether the visualizations included all the required indicators. Then, the participants were distributed in groups of 2–3 people to discuss the advantages and disadvantages of the mockup and propose a new one (See proposals https://osf.io/9vk2r). Finally, each group presented their approach and discussed with the rest.

3.1 Results of the Design Phase

Two researchers analyzed the results of the different dashboards and proposals and defined a list of visualization and functionalities to be included in the tool. For this, all the mockups proposed by the teachers were considered to decide the final views and functionalities to be implemented. The views and associated functionalities were defined in a generic way and considering how to adapt to the Moodle Platform requirements. For the students' perspective, we kept those visualizations and indicators that were proven more useful in the NMP MOOC version as well as some of the suggested indicators proposed by the teachers about students' progress in the course. For selecting the most appropriate visualizations for each indicator, we kept those which were more frequently proposed by the experts and validated by the teachers.

We also considered in the final design two main suggestions proposed by the teachers. First, to use the model red-yellow-green model in the graphs as a form of alert to guide the teachers on identifying those students with problems. This was proposed to address a teacher suggestion: "*There is a lack of display and alarm about what is going wrong, display of information about at-risk students, identification of content and assessments where students are notoriously having learning problems*". The colors were not explicitly evaluated during the design phases, but were chosen using the most standard model employed in occidental cultures to indicate that everything is good (green), there's some risk (yellow) and there are troubles (red). Second, the graphs were designed with interactive properties a suggested by a teacher to: (1) provide more deep information about an indicator in a graph, and (2) send specific and personalized feedback to students.

Table 2 includes the list of requirements for both the teachers' and students' views and the final indicators included in each view. Notice that not all the indicators from the 29 proposed were considered in this first version of the tool.

Table 2. Design requirements of teachers' and students' view. (GS: Goal Setting; SP: Strategic Planning; TM: Time Management; and SE: Self-Evaluation) (T: Teacher; S: Student)

Visualization & functionalities	Description	SRL processes supported & indicators
Week plan (T)	View to allow teachers organize their course resources according to the different weeks. This view should allow teachers to define the planned time per week according to the resources associated to provide a reference point to the students	SRL Proc: GS; TM Indicators: Minutes to be dedicated per week; Content goal

(*continued*)

Table 2. (*continued*)

Visualization & functionalities	Description	SRL processes supported & indicators
General view (T&S)	View including course aggregated indicators about students' progress and time spent on the course	SRL Proc: TM; Indicators: Percentage of progress of a student on the course; Number of students' sessions of different length (less than 30 min, between 30 and 60 min, more than 60 min) per week; Time spent by a student per week and session; Planned time vs student mean time on platform
Study Sessions (T&S)	Views for visualizing students' time management process, showing where and how they allocate the time in the course. The time has to be organized by students' study session. In this case, a study session is defined as the time since the student connects to the platform for the first time and interacts with resources until there is an inactivity period over 30 min	SRL Proc.: TM; Indicators: Average time spent by students per week; Average time spent high/mid/low performance students per week/resource/activity
Assignments (T)	Views for visualizing students' interaction with the course resources. Functionalities to send feedback to students according to their interactions	SRL Proc.: SP; SE Indicators: Number of interactions by resource category/activity by week; Resources with fewer interactions; Tasks on time, late and pending; Course contents accessed
Grades (T)	Views for visualizing the students' grades on the course. Functionality to send feedback to students' according to their performance	SRL Proc.: SP Time spent by a student per week; Grade of student by evaluation; Percentage of progress of a student on the course; Number of interactions by category by week; Questionnaires actions (correct answers, partially right, incorrect, in blank, no graded); Questionnaires rating

(*continued*)

Table 2. (*continued*)

Visualization & functionalities	Description	SRL processes supported & indicators
Assessments (T&S)	Grades and activity with the different assessments of the course	SRL Proc.: SP; SE Number of interactions by category by week; Grade of student by evaluation; Questionnaires actions (correct answers, partially right, incorrect, in blank, no graded); Questionnaires rating
Dropouts/Academic performance (T)	View including course aggregated indicators about the performance of students organized by risk of dropping depending on their progress	SRL Proc.: SE; SP Average time spent by students per week; Number of interactions by category by week; Grade of student by evaluation; Percentage of progress of a student by week; Percentage of progress of a student on the course; Time invested on platform; Number of sessions; Overall grade; Course content accessed overall; Student grades vs course mean

Implementation

The main objective of this phase was to implement a first version of the tool considering the requirements extracted from the design phase. This section presents the NMP Moodle plugin that was implemented as a first prototype.

3.2 Description of the Tool

The NMP Moodle provides teachers and students with dashboards for supporting the following SRL strategies in BL contexts: Goal Setting, Strategic Planning, Time management, Self-evaluation, and Monitoring. All the views and functionalities present in the current version of the tool were defined in the Design phase (Table 2). We describe in what follows the some of its features to exemplify how the design method was incorporated for the purpose of supporting SRL.

For supporting **Time Management**, the teachers count with several functionalities and visualizations. First, there is a functionality for planning the course weekly or thematically. With this functionality, teachers can assign the course content to a week (or section) of the course and allocate a reference dedication time (in hours) for the students to invest. This functionality was generated in order to create the indicators about the students' time management in the course highlighted as relevant in the Informed Exploration

Phase (indicators #1 to 18 in Table 1). Second, NMP includes different visualizations to represent the indicators in Table 1. For example, teachers can see indicators about how much time in average students spend in the course per week compared with what they planned (Fig. 2(a)), when students connected for a learning session (Fig. 2(b)) and the number of study sessions organized by length in minutes (less than 30; more than 30 and less than 60; and more than 60). These visualizations were defined taking into consideration the results of the Design phase, in which experts proposed using hit maps for representing students' sessions and bars to compare the time invested compared with the time expected. Teachers can also access to the same information about a particular student. The same information is provided in the students' view, but personalized for each student. In this case, students could see the indicators and visualizations showing their time management indicators as well as the average indicators of the course as a reference point.

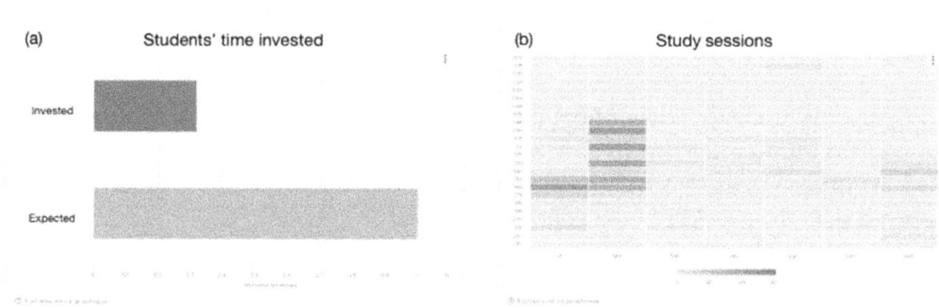

Fig. 2. Teachers' view. Visualizations offered for supporting time management. (a) Time invested by the students in the course (blue) vs. the time expected by the teacher (green). (c) Study sessions in a week. The dark squares represent the timeslots with the highest number of sessions. (Color figure online)

For supporting **Strategic Planning**, teachers' view includes information about the indicators identified in the Informed Exploration Phase (indicators #1 to 3 in Table 1), which are mainly related the students' activity with the course resources and activities. On the one hand, it includes visualizations in the form of bar charts representing which resources students consulted the most (green) and which the least (red). This allows the teacher to have an idea of what the most interesting resources are. A similar visualization is proposed for showing which students submitted the assignments on time (green), late (yellow) or which did not submit (red). Bar charts were selected as the best representation because it was one of the most recurrent proposals in the experts' mockups, and which were later validated by the teachers (see Sect. 3.1). Also, the graphs are interactive and organize students in colors (red, green and yellow) to let teachers click on a particular group and send a personalized e-mail in a form of feedback. Similar graphs are used to represent a summary of the students' grades for the grading activities of the course (Fig. 3a). In this case, bar charts are used to represent the questions that were answered correctly or incorrectly. When selecting one of the grading activities, the teachers see the grade distribution for that activity, as well as the best and worst marks (Fig. 3b). It always takes the latest mark in case the assessment activity can be done several times. As for the time management support, the teachers' view for supporting strategic planning offers this same information about each student individually so as to follow up students with difficulties.

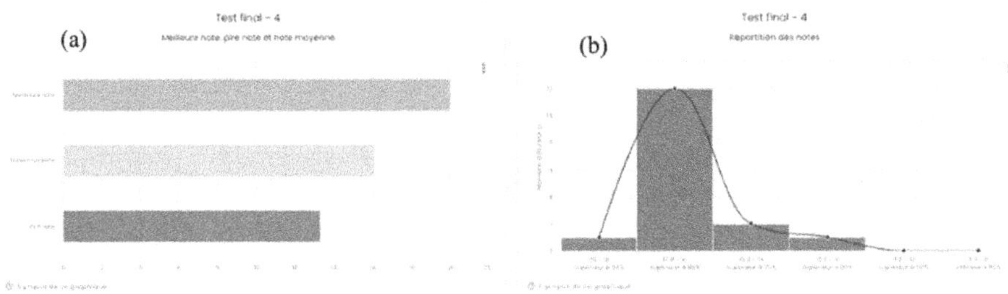

Fig. 3. Grade's view from Teachers' view. Visualizations offered to one of the graded activities in the course.

Finally, the students' view offers the same visualizations but only for the students accessing the information. In this case, students can access the list of completed and completed list of resources (marked in green and red, respectively) and the grades obtained compared with the average of the course.

4 Local Evaluation

A local evaluation was conducted **to understand how teachers perceived the indicators and visualizations used in the prototype NMP Moodle in terms of usability and sense making (related with RQ2)**. For this local evaluation, we organized two workshop rounds with teachers. Some of the results are already available in a previous publication [17].

The first workshop (WS1) was conducted with 78 teachers from different universities from Ecuador. The workshop was framed within a 10-week online diploma in Digital Teaching for Higher Education. The workshop was run in the 4th week. The objective of this week was to learn about the different types of BL Models existing in the literature. It lasted 6 h. As part of the course, the teacher presented the NMP Moodle tool as a tool to support these types of pedagogical models. For one hour, the teachers had the opportunity to explore the tool and explain how its use could be integrated in the Blended Learning course they designed in the first part of the session. After that, teachers were grouped in teams of 6 people and asked to reflect about the different visualizations. A total of 14 visualizations were evaluated related to the different indicators: week plan (1 visualization), general views (3 visualizations), study sessions (3 visualizations), assignments (1 visualization), grades (3 visualizations), and academic performance (3 visualizations). For each visualization, each group was asked to complete a form with 7 questions about the clarity of the information provided (See https://osf.io/v9tdb/).

The second workshop (WS2) was organized into two sessions, one online and one face-to-face. A total of 35 teachers from 4 different French Engineering Schools participated in these sessions. In both sessions (1 h length) the organizers presented the NMP

Moodle tool to the teachers (15 min) and then, asked them to interact with the tool during 45 min for conducting the following tasks: (1) interact with the tool with a test account populated with data and answer a series of questions about what do they observe in each view; and (2) organize their own courses in Moodle so as to use the tool in the following semesters.

At the end of both workshops, teachers were asked to answer the "sense making" questionnaire, obtaining a total of 41 answers. This questionnaire was designed combining questionnaires defined in prior research to evaluate Learning Analytics Dashboards: the Evaluation Framework of Quality Indicators for Learning Analytics (EFLA) [18] and the work by [19], which studies how learners' goals and self-regulated learning skills influence dashboards sense-making as well as the notion of transparency, not included in EFLA. The result was a questionnaire with 17 questions related with: (1) Transparency on the data collection; (2) Transparency of Dashboard Design and Explain ability; (3) Data & Reference frames; (4) Impact for learning/teaching and (5) Support for action. You can see the references considered for each item in the supplementary material https://osf.io/rcjpw/.

4.1 Results Local Evaluation

Two results were extracted from analyzing the questionnaire of WS1 about the different visualizations (See analyzed data https://osf.io/9anhw/). First, **teachers consider that the 14 graphs proposed in NMP Moodle are good for monitoring student's interaction the course resources and their commitment with the course** (Partial Result 1 – **PR1**). Second, the **tool lacks:** (1) **flexibility** for assigning objectives to topics and not weeks, and (2) **visualizations** for **monitoring** students' activity when working in **groups** and activity (**PR2**).

The results of analyzing the sense making questionnaire show that **most of the teachers make sense of the information and dashboards provided (PR3)**, obtaining 3,28 marks over 4 (See analyzed data https://osf.io/3w2ty/). Teachers found that the tool is transparent in term of the data collection and the dashboard design (>95% answers between 3 and 4; mean 3.309/4) and offers a good support for teaching and learning (>92% answers between 3 and 4; mean 3.306/4). The teachers also consider that the dashboards provided can support efficient teaching and help adapting their teaching processes (>92% answers between 3 and 4; mean 3.309/4). It was less clear in the tool who has access to the data, what elements are presented and how they relate to each other (85% with values between 3 and 4; mean 3.189/4).

5 Broad Evaluation

A pilot study was conducted as a broad evaluating **to understand how students perceived the prototype NMP Moodle in terms of usability and sense making (related with RQ2)**. The pilot was run in 2 courses at a Technological University (1) at a second-year course in Databases (Course 1); and a first year of a course in Basics on Informatics (Course 2). A total of 311 students (119 from Course 1 and 192 from Course 2) and 2 teachers participated in this pilot study. The students do not have an expertise in informatics but the two teachers have. Both courses were designed as a Blended Learning course. Students participated in 1,5 h face-to-face lessons once a week and were asked to complete several online activities and projects at home planned for 1–2 h dedication. In both cases, the NMP tool was introduced by the project in the middle of the course in a face-to-face session, presented as a tool to help students organize their activities and tasks in the course. The Course 1 lasted 16 weeks and the Course 2, 12 weeks.

For understanding students' perception about the tool (RQ2), we asked them to answer the sense making questionnaire and analyzed those questions that were evaluated with the highest and lowest values. Also, we analyzed the logfiles collecting information about how students interacted with the NMP Moodle tool to see how they adopted the tool. For the logfile analysis we counted the number of interactions per visualization and the percentage of students that adopted the tool. 86 students out of 90 answered the sense making questionnaire and give its consent to use the collected data.

5.1 Results Broad Evaluation

Regarding the student's use of NMP and their perception about the tool, we found two different results. First, **the information provided with the NMP Moodle tool is not enough for supporting students' actions and helping them support their learning process (PR4)** (See results sense making https://osf.io/f3xy2/). Students' overall evaluation of the sense making was 2,8 over 4. They evaluated better those items related with Transparency on data collection (73% between 2–3), Transparency on LAD Design and explainability (71% between 2–3); and Data Frame & References (74% between 2–3), than those related with Impact for Learning and Support for action (64% between 2–3 for both items). Second, even of the usage of the NMP Moodle tool was not mandatory, **most of the students used it and preferred those visualizations related with Strategic Planning (PR5).** The NMP Moodle log-data registered a total of 91 unique interactions in Course 1 and 150 in Course 2 (76,47% and 78,12% of students, respectively). From these interactions, we observe that, in both courses, most of the interactions are registered on those visualizations related with strategic planning and time management (see Table 3).

Table 3. Counts of the number of students' interactions with NMP (SP: Strategic Planning; TM: Time Management; and SD: Standard Deviation)

Course	Total amount of actions	Mean active days	NMP action	Count	Mean
Course 1	91	91 (SD = 1.13)	SP	91	15.25 (SD = 14.81)
			TM	78	13.27 (SD = 11.15)
Course 2	150	150 (SD = 3.09)	SP	149	17.17 (SD = 14.00)
			TM	137	13.54 (SD = 12.05)

In addition to these results, we also identified some technical and usage problems when scaling up the tool. First, in terms of installation related problems, technicians from 3 different universities agree that, even if NMP is compatible with Moodle versions 3 and 4 **the tool should be implemented according to the requirements proposed by the Moodle community for plugin development.** This will avoid installing an external database for collecting log data (currently it requires MongoDB), and the use of other programming languages apart from PHP for avoiding security holes. In terms of usage, the **tool needs a functionality for viewing/deleting users' data for being fully compliant with the EU General Data Protection Regulation (GDPR) rules and data privacy.**

6 Summary of Results and Future Work

This paper presents the Design Based Research process followed for creating a Plugin for Moodle aimed at supporting SRL in BL courses. From the whole process, we addressed two research questions, which results could serve as an inspiration for those researchers willing to propose solutions for supporting SRL strategies in BL settings. **Regarding RQ1 about the type of indicators and visualizations to be used**, we identified through different workshops with experts and teachers: (1) the types of indicators needed for supporting goal setting, strategic planning, time management and self-evaluation SRL processes; and (2) a set of visualizations for representing them. Based on these indicators and visualizations, we implemented a first prototype of the NMP Moodle tool to be evaluated in actual contexts. Regarding the **RQ2 about the usability and sense making perception of the end users about the tool.** We run a local evaluation with 114 teachers and a broad evaluation with 311 students. Results indicate that teachers valued positively the information provided with the tool as good and clear to monitor students' activity, progress and engagement with the course (PR1, PR3). However, some improvements should be done to improve the tool from both the teacher and student perspective. First, changes should be made for teachers to flexibly adapt their objectives to the topics and modules as well as functionalities to monitor students' activity when working in group (PR2). Second, students used the tool mainly used for Strategic Planning (PR5), visualizations should be improved for helping them to make sense of the data for supporting their learning process (PR4), which they valued lower than the teachers. This last result could be due to the functionalities offered to the students in its current version, which only include self-awareness interactive graphs, but not much information about what actions to improve or what information is relevant to promote behavioral changes. Finally, some changes are required to facilitate its installation and adoption at scale. The tool should be updated to conform with the design structure of a standard Moodle Plugin and with the RGPD directions.

This study has also some limitations that will be addressed in future work. On the one hand, in the Design Phases of the methodology, we have mainly worked with teachers and students were only included for the broad evaluation. This could have caused the lower acceptance of the tool from the students' side. Future work will include focus groups and sessions for better design the students' side. On the other hand, we run the broad evaluation with only two courses for analyzing the usage and usability problems of the tool, but not its effect on students' behavior. To complement this study, we plan to run large-scale and long-term studies for analyzing how students' and teachers use the tool in actual learning context and its impact on their strategies. Finally, we plan to improve the sense making instrument and validate it with users in different contexts.

We believe that the results obtained in this work could benefit other researchers in the community. Firstly, we expect that indicators and visualizations extracted from our empirical study could serve as an inspiration for designing new tools with similar purposes. Second, we think that the instruments and methods employed could also serve other researchers to validate their own solutions and run comparative studies. Finally, we hope that the process described could serve as an example of how to apply the Design Based Research approach to adapt an existing tool to another context.

Acknowledgments. This paper was supported by the ANR LASER (156322) and the Vicerrectorado de Investigación de la Universidad de Cuenca. The authors acknowledge PROF-XXI, which is an Erasmus+ Capacity Building in the Field of Higher Education project funded by the European Commission (609767-EPP-1-2019-1- ES-EPPKA2-CBHE-JP). This publication reflects the views only of the authors and funders cannot be held responsible for any use which may be made of the information contained therein.

References

1. Graham, C.R.: Blended learning systems. Definition, current trends, and future directions. In: Handbook of Blended Learning: Global Perspectives, local designs, pp. 3–21 (2016)
2. Broadbent, J.: Comparing online and blended learner's self-regulated learning strategies and academic performance. Internet High. Educ. **33**, 24–32 (2017)
3. Broadbent, J., Fuller-Tyszkiewicz, M.: Profiles in self-regulated learning and their correlates for online and blended learning students. Educ. Tech. Res. Dev. **66**(6), 1435–1455 (2018). https://doi.org/10.1007/s11423-018-9595-9
4. Wang, F.H.: An exploration of online behaviour engagement and achievement in flippedclassroom supported by learning management system. Comput. Educ. **114**, 79–91 (2017)
5. Devolder, A., van Braak, J., Tondeur, J.: Supporting self-regulated learning in computer-based learning environments: systematic review of effects of scaffolding in the domain of science education. J. Comput. Assist. Learn. **28**(6), 557–573 (2012)
6. Jørnø, R.L., Gynther, K.: What constitutes an 'actionable insight' in learning analytics? J. Learn. Anal. **5**(3), 198–221 (2018)
7. Wong, J., Baars, M., Davis, D., Van Der Zee, T., Houben, G.J., Paas, F.: Supporting self-regulated learning in online learning environments and MOOCs: a systematic review. Int. J. Hum.-Comput. Interact. **35**(4–5), 356–373 (2019)
8. Alario-Hoyos, C., et al.: Redesigning a freshman engineering course to promote active learning by flipping the classroom through the reuse of MOOCs. Int. J. Eng. Educ. **35**(1B), 385–396 (2019)
9. Shyr, W.J., Chen, C.H.: Designing a technology-enhanced flipped learning system to facilitate students' self-regulation and performance. J. Comput. Assist. Learn. **34**(1), 53–62 (2017)
10. Michel, C., et al.: Supporting awareness and self-regulation in project-based learning through personalized dashboards. Int. J. Technol. Enhanc. Learn. (IJTEL) **9**(2/3), 204–226 (2017)
11. Moos, D.C., Ringdal, A.: Self-regulated learning in the classroom: a literature review on the teacher's role. Educ. Res. Int. **12**, 423284 (2012)

12. Pérez-Álvarez, R., Maldonado-Mahauad, J.J., Sapunar-Opazo, D., Pérez-Sanagustín, M.: NoteMyProgress: a tool to support learners' self-regulated learning strategies in MOOC environments. In: Lavoué, É., Drachsler, H., Verbert, K., Broisin, J., Pérez-Sanagustín, M. (eds.) EC-TEL 2017. LNCS, vol. 10474, pp. 460–466. Springer, Cham (2017). https://doi.org/10.1007/978-3-319-66610-5_43
13. Reimann, P.: Design-based research. In: Markauskaite, L., Freebody, P., Irwin, J. (eds.) Methodological Choice and Design. Methodos Series, vol. 9, pp. 37–50. Springer, Dordrecht (2011). https://doi.org/10.1007/978-90-481-8933-5_3
14. Bannan-Ritland, B.: The role of design in research: the integrative learning design framework. Educ. Res. **32**(1), 21–24 (2003)
15. Schwendimann, B.A., et al.: Perceiving learning at a glance: a systematic literature review of learning dashboard research. IEEE Trans. Learn. Technol. **10**, 30–41 (2017)
16. Kerzner, E., Goodwin, S., Dykes, J., Jones, S., Meyer, M.: A framework for creative visualization-opportunities workshops. IEEE Trans. Vis. Comput. Graph. **25**, 748–758 (2018)
17. Maldonado-Mahauad, J., Aguilar, B., Sigua, E.: FlipMyLearning: a tool for monitoring and predicting learner behavior in moodle. In: XVI Latin American Conference on Learning Technologies (LACLO), pp. 16–23 (2021)
18. Scheffel, M., Drachsler, H., Toisoul, C., Ternier, S., Specht, M.: The proof of the pudding: Examining validity and reliability of the evaluation framework for learning analytics. In: Lavoué, É., Drachsler, H., Verbert, K., Broisin, J., Pérez-Sanagustín, M. (eds.) EC-TEL 2017. LNCS, vol. 10474, pp. 194–208. Springer, Cham (2017). https://doi.org/10.1007/978-3-319-66610-5_15
19. Jivet, I., Scheffel, M., Schmitz, M., Robbers, S., Specht, M., Drachsler, H.: From students with love: An empirical study on learner goals, self-regulated learning and sense-making of learning analytics in higher education. Internet High. Educ. **47**, 100758 (2020)

Uncovering Student Temporal Learning Patterns

Daniela Rotelli(✉), Anna Monreale, and Riccardo Guidotti

Computer Science Department, University of Pisa, Pisa, Italy
daniela.rotelli@phd.unipi.it, {anna.monreale,riccardo.guidotti}@unipi.it

Abstract. Because of the flexibility of online learning courses, students organise and manage their own learning time by choosing where, what, how, and for how long they study. Each individual has their unique learning habits that characterise their behaviours and distinguish them from others. Nonetheless, to the best of our knowledge, the temporal dimension of student learning has received little attention on its own. Typically, when modelling trends, a chosen configuration is set to capture various habits, and a cluster analysis is undertaken. However, the selection of variables to observe and the algorithm used to conduct the analysis is a subjective process that reflects the researcher's thoughts and ideas. To explore how students behave over time, we present alternative ways of modelling student temporal behaviour. Our real-world data experiments reveal that the generated clusters may or may not differ based on the selected profile and unveil different student learning patterns.

Keywords: Log data · Temporal student profile · Temporal student segmentation · Time-on-task · Temporal behaviour analysis

1 Introduction

The increased adoption of online learning environments has resulted in the availability of a vast amount of educational log data, which generates questions that could be answered by a thorough and accurate examination of students' behaviours while learning online. Log data provides several dimensions that help to characterise what actions students carried out, when and where (in which course and in which part of the course). Whether or not a set of dimensions should be evaluated depends on the type of phenomenon being studied.

Learning takes place over time and temporal analysis has been demonstrated to be relevant in Learning Analytics research [15]. The flexibility of online learning requires students to organise and plan their own time, or to develop the ability to self-regulate their study by selecting where, what, how, and how long they study [17]. Nonetheless, to the best of our knowledge, the temporal dimension has received little investigation on its own with the purpose of understanding when students usually learn and, in particular, when and how much time they spend in specific tasks, to investigate and model their temporal learning behaviours. In this regard, each individual has their own routines and habits that define their

I. Hilliger et al. (Eds.): EC-TEL 2022, LNCS 13450, pp. 340–353, 2022.
https://doi.org/10.1007/978-3-031-16290-9_25

behaviour and distinguish them from the others. Distinctive student behaviours could be shared? Two students who always study in the morning could share the same temporal learning pattern. Yet, if we consider the weekday window rather than the daytime, their behaviours can be different: the former may study on weekdays, whereas the latter on weekends. Besides, they may share the same time windows but choose different activities (e.g. quizzes vs. video).

The selection of variables to observe reflects the researcher's beliefs and ideas, and it is a subjective process: it is possible that highly selective variables are overlooked, resulting in a partially wrong grouping; on the other hand, the inclusion of variables with a high discriminating capacity but no relevance to the study's purposes can lead to results of little practical significance. This suggests that depending on the selected variables, two learners may exhibit similar or completely dissimilar behaviours. Hence, a question arises. Is this selection affecting potential similarities amongst students?

Given these considerations, in this paper we want to tackle the problem of discovering prototypes of student temporal learning behaviour by using information describing *whether* and *when* students typically work in an online learning environment that uses a logging system (e.g. Moodle), and on *what type* of learning activity they spend their time. To this aim, we propose alternative ways of modelling student temporal behaviour and by examining various configurations and techniques, we observe how students organise their study time.

To investigate the heterogeneous nature of various learning behaviours, we first define distinct profiles tailored to the specific temporal analysis. Then, using real data, we analyse different clustering algorithms to uncover diverse learning behaviours in relation to a given temporal profile. Our results show that students' clusters may or may not differ based on the selected profile. Thus, the temporal learning behaviour of some students is unique, while some others are similar independently form the perspective adopted to model the profile.

2 Background and Related Work

Study skills, also known as *study behaviour* or *learning strategies*, are described as the "*ability to manage time and allocate other resources in accordance with the demands of the academic tasks, ability to organise, summarise, and integrate material*" [4]. In this context, time management is a strategic learning component of the *self-regulation* [21]. In traditional presence-based learning environments the practice of spreading out study activities over time have been shown to boost students' performance [7]. In a study conducted on a blended course by Goda et al. [9], clusters of students who regularly visited the LMS applying diverse learning strategies performed better than students characterised by a very selective usage of the LMS. In this regard, weekly face-to-face lectures, such as those offered in blended courses, may be beneficial to students to distribute online learning tasks over time. However, previous research has mostly focused on learning strategies in voluntary online courses [10] and it is still not evident how students deal with the obstacles of mandatory online courses, where dropout and poor grades might have major consequences [19].

The analysis of the temporal dimension is a relevant aspect in the LA research [5,15]. Nonetheless, the majority of studies in the literature consider the time spent online as one of the independent variables to forecast performance and avoid drop-out [3,13], rather than focusing on the temporal dimension itself to understand how students organise their online study time. Because each student acts according to their own needs depending on various learning styles [8], which can be described by different types of tracking variables (such as number of online sessions, total time spent online, file viewed, assessments started and finished, discussion read) [14], it is usually difficult to develop a complete model describing the overall student behaviour. Although previous works considered the temporal dimension, it is worth noting that the total time spent online or on some resources as independent variables in linear regression, or as one of the features in clustering, does not explain student behaviour with respect to time, nor the presence of typical temporal learning patterns amongst students.

Clustering is typically used to identify groups of students who share patterns reflecting similar learning characteristics. Bovo et al. [2] focused on clustering student activity based on the performance grade by taking into account a number of factors (e.g., login frequency, time spent, number of activities read or created). Beaudoin [1] studied the degree of involvement in a forum to detect learners of lurkers. Hecking et al. [11] investigated bipartite graphs in which students were connected to materials used over a period of time. Sherin [18] clustered students to identify the dynamics of their mental constructs. We are not interested in forecasting success in the current work, but in exploring learning behaviour across time that might help in detecting student temporal regularities.

3 Temporal Learning Profile

In this study we intend to use information about *whether* and *when* students tend to learn online and on *what type* of learning activity they spend their time to uncover student temporal learning patterns. To this aim, we propose first the modelling of a *temporal learning profile* to describe an individual student's temporal learning behaviour; then we extract all of the students' profiles, which we analyse using a clustering based approach to identify prototypes of temporal learning behaviours in relation to a given configuration. Our modelling enables a student segmentation that takes into account the learning activities and allows for exploratory analysis of students from a new perspective.

The analytic process assumes as input a learning activity dataset, i.e., a collection of activity sequences $\mathcal{D} = \{A_1, \ldots, A_m\}$, where each A_x is a sequence of events describing the activities of a student x on an online learning environment.

Definition 1. *(Student Activity Sequence) The activity sequence of a student x is a sequence of pairs $A_x = \langle (a_1, t_1), \ldots, (a_n, t_n) \rangle$, where t_i $\forall i \in [1, \ldots, n]$ denotes a timestamp such that $\forall_{1 \le i \le n} t_i < t_{i+1}$ and a_i, describes the learning activity that the student engages on the platform.*

The *duration* of an activity in a sequence can be calculated as the difference in time between its timestamp and that of the next activity in the sequence.

Definition 2. *(Activity Duration) Given two consecutive activities* (a_i, t_i) *and* (a_j, t_j) *of a student activity sequence* A_x *(with* $t_i \leq t_j$*), the duration* d *of the activity* a_i *is the difference between the timestamps* t_i *and* t_j*, i.e.,* $d_{a_i} = t_j - t_i$*.*

As a consequence, given a student x we can enrich its activity sequence with the duration of each activity, i.e., we can derive $A_x^d = \langle(a_1, t_1, d_1), \ldots, (a_n, t_n, d_n)\rangle$, which we name *duration enriched activity sequence.*

A student can enroll in multiple courses active in a platform. Thus, to investigate the learning habits of a student on specific courses, we need to extract the subsequence of activities related to a certain course, from the *duration enriched activity sequence.* More formally:

Definition 3. *(Subsequence) Let* $A^d = \langle(a_1, t_1, d_1), \ldots, (a_p, t_p, d_p)\rangle$ *be a duration enriched activity sequence.* $S^d = \langle(a'_1, t'_1, d'_1), \ldots, (a'_h, t'_h, d'_h)\rangle$ *is a subsequence of* A^d *(*$S^d \preceq A^d$*) if there exist integers* $1 \leq i_1 < \ldots < i_h \leq p$ *such that* $\forall\ 1 \leq j \leq h\ (a'_j, t'_j, d'_j) = (a_{i_j}, t_{i_j}, d_{i_j})$*.*

Because online courses include a variety of learning modules (e.g., files, videos, quizzes) and students can undertake a variety of activities on each learning module (e.g. view, create, update, etc.), each *learning activity* can be described by the learning module μ_i and the type of action α_i on the course γ_i, i.e. $a_i = (\mu_i, \alpha_i, \gamma_i)$. Now, we can define the *student learning sequence* as follows:

Definition 4. *(Student Learning Sequence) Let* A_x^d *be the duration enriched activity sequence of a student* x*. The learning sequence of* x *is the subsequence* $L_x^\gamma = \langle(\mu_1, \alpha_1, t_1, d_1), \ldots, (\mu_r, \alpha_r, t_r, d_r)\rangle$ *concerning all the activities performed on a course* γ*, i.e.,* $L_x^\gamma \preceq A_x^d$*.*

Frequency and duration measures (e.g., number of clicks and total time spent) are frequently used to predict performance outcomes or prevent drop-outs [14]. However, they are increasingly being used as a qualitative indicator of online student engagement which is "*about students putting time, energy, thought, effort, and, to some extent, feelings into their learning*" [6]. Measuring student engagement is complex and it involves both qualitative (interviews, surveys, discourse analysis, or observation) and quantitative measures, namely *frequency* measures of behaviours (such as the number of assignments completed, of logins, of forum posts, replies, and views, of resources accessed) or *temporal* measures of behaviours (like the time spent to write a post and the amount of time spent online) [12]. In this work we aim to discover prototypes of student temporal learning behaviour by using measures of time spent on each learning module within a well-defined period. Thus, we must first create an aggregation measure for all actions connected with a single learning module across a period of time. For that reason, we pinpoint the concept of *temporal constrained task* as follows:

Definition 5. *(Temporal Constrained Task) Given a learning sequence of a student* x *on a course* γ*, i.e.,* $L_x^\gamma = \langle(\mu_1, \alpha_1, t_1, d_1), \ldots, (\mu_r, \alpha_r, t_r, d_r)\rangle$ *and a time window* $w = [t_l, t_u]$*, a temporal constrained task* T_w^μ *is a subsequence of* L_x^γ *concerning the same learning module* μ *such that* $T_w^\mu \preceq L_x^\gamma$*, where* $\mu = \mu_j = \mu_{j+1} = \ldots = \mu_q$ *and* $t_j, t_{j+1} \ldots t_q \in w$*.*

To make things clearer, given a time window $w = [t_l, t_u]$, where t_l indicates the lower bound and t_u the upper bound, a temporal constrained task T_w^μ is the subsequence of all learning activities α related to a same learning module μ within w. Because our purpose is to create a student model that can aid in the understanding of temporal learning habits and to capture the similarities that characterise students' behaviour, we introduce the notion of *temporal learning profile* of a student that exploits measures of engagement estimations.

Definition 6. *(Temporal Learning Profile) Let* $L_x^\gamma = \langle(\mu_1, \alpha_1, t_1, d_1), \ldots, (\mu_r, \alpha_r, t_r, d_r)\rangle$ *be a learning sequence of a student* x *on a course* γ. *Given a period* τ *of day-intervals, a temporal learning profile of the student* x *is a matrix* $\mathcal{P} \in \mathbb{R}^{|M| \times |F|}$*, where* M *is the set of learning modules* $\mu \in M$*,* F *is a set of temporal aggregations of day-intervals, and* $P_{i,j}$ *estimates the total engagement of the student in the set of temporal constrained tasks related to the learning module* i *and the temporal aggregation* j*, i.e.,* $T_{w_1}^i, \ldots, T_{w_h}^i$*. Here, each* w_k *represents a time window corresponding to the* k*-th day-interval of* τ *involved in the temporal aggregation* j*.*

To clarify, given a period τ, each profile $\mathcal{P}$ represents the activity of students discretised with respect to some identified temporal aggregations of days. As an example, given τ equal to January, F could be equal to the set $\{Monday, Tuesday, Wednesday, Thursday, Friday, Saturday, Sunday\}$, where with *Monday* we intend to aggregate the engagement on the tasks performed on all *Mondays* in January. The engagement $P_{i,j}$ can be expressed by any value related to learning behaviours (frequency or temporal measures).

4 Learning Data

To present our findings, we refer to two datasets of log data describing the interactions of 30 students on two blended courses of a Postgraduate Master's program organised on a Moodle platform that supported lectures and laboratories. The two courses (*Course A* and *Course B* in the following) were taught at the same period and their related Moodle courses, provided with a great number of Resources and Activities[1], have a highly comparable structure.

Course A was organised in 4/6h of theory and laboratory practice per week spread over 4 weeks. The Moodle course has been structured in five sections (plus one for the laboratory). After data consolidation, which we will describe in the following, the number of available logs was 31,095.

Course B was organised in 6/8h of theory and laboratory practice per week spread over 5 weeks. The Moodle course followed the same format as course A: four sections (plus one for the lab.) with the same type of resources and activities, though their content and number differ[2]. Available logs: 59,583.

[1] https://docs.moodle.org/39/en/Managing_a_Moodle_course.

[2] Both courses were structured with *Assignment* (11,4), *Book* (1,1), *Database* (1,1), *Feedback*(1,1), *File*(6,24), *Forum*(7,6), *Glossary*(1,1), *H5P*(6,9), *Lesson*(5,8), *Page*(2,10), *Quiz*(5,10), *Survey*(6,4), *URL*(10,14), *Wiki*(1,1). The numbers represent the quantity of resources/activities available in course A and B.

Data Consolidation. The analytic process we propose assumes as input log data, namely a collection of ordered sequences of records describing the actions of a set of students. Each record is an object with an ID that stores information about a specific user action and is described by the values of its attributes. Since on Moodle some logs are stored at the site level, while some other at the course level, to collect our data, we followed the approach proposed in [16]. Firstly, we extracted the dataset of all logs of the platform, then we extracted the timestamps directly from Moodle database and we added them to the dataset as an additional field. Secondly, for each of the platform's courses, we extracted the logs of the course and every time we added to the dataset an additional field identifying the course; then we merged all course datasets into one. Finally, we joined this latter table to the table extracted at the site level, yielding all logs pertaining to user actions ensuring that the time information was not lost. Then, we converted the timestamp values in a Date&Time standard format to make it more readable. An example of the integrated log record is: **ID**: 402267, **Time**: 1615214006, **Course**: A, **Date&Time**: 2021-03-08T15:33:26, **Username**: USER 37 **Recipient**: -, **Context**: Lesson: Intro, **Component**: Lesson, **Event name**: Course module viewed, **Description**: The user with id '37' viewed the 'lesson' activity with course module id '641', **Origin**: web **IP address**: 109.52.45.53. We refer to the reference paper for data cleaning and preparation [16].

For the purposes of the current work, to extract the temporal constrained task T_w^μ (Definition 5) and the temporal learning profile $\mathcal{P}$ (Definition 6), we have first to extract the learning sequence L_x^γ (Definition 4) by selecting the fields: *Component, Event name, Time* from the integrated log records. In Moodle, the component refers to the learning module, i.e., *Lesson, Quiz, Forum, Assignment, Book, etc.*, whereas the event name represents the actions taken such as *module view, post created, question viewed, question answered, etc.*. Then for each record, the duration d is calculated as the temporal difference (with a granularity per second) between its timestamp t and that of the next record in the sequence.

Most research involving the temporal dimension of educational data found that some learning activities take anomalous durations, as a result of off-task behaviours or inaction, which should be handled before any analysis. To identify and mitigate the effect of outliers we performed an outlier detection analysis of the duration values for each type of action α_i taken on each specific learning module μ_i, separately. Since most of the duration distributions tended to be right-skewed, for each action of each learning module we computed the median value and the median absolute deviation (MAD) and we considered as outliers all the duration values higher than the threshold calculated as the sum of the median and the MAD. Finally, all the identified outliers have been replaced with the median value. The median can be considered a good measure of central tendency and this median based approach works relatively well for skewed distribution and high asymmetry when detecting outliers.

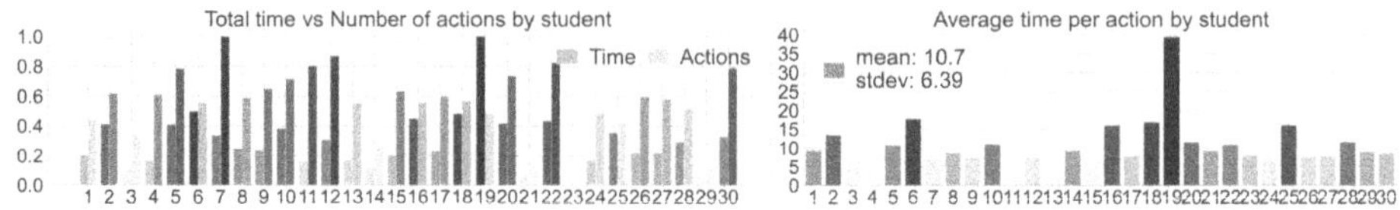

Fig. 1. Course B. *Left:* time spent (reds) vs number of actions (blues). *Right:* average time per action. Xticks are students IDs. Darker colors highlights higher values. (Color figure online)

Given the consolidated data, in the following section we explain in detail how we defined the different profiles tailored to the specific temporal analysis.

5 Temporal Learning Profile Analysis

In the literature, frequency (number of actions carried out) and duration measures (total time spent on a task) are typically used as a qualitative indication of student engagement [6,12]. The total amount of time spent on a task T^μ (called *time-on-task*) is calculated by summing up the duration d of each of its actions α. More formally, given $T^\mu = \langle(\mu_j, \alpha_j, t_j, d_j), (\mu_{j+1}, \alpha_{j+1}, t_{j+1}, d_{j+1}) \ldots, (\mu_q, \alpha_q, t_q, d_q)\rangle$, the time spent is defined as $\sum_{i=j,j+1,\ldots,q} d_i$. While the number of actions in T^μ, named *frequency*, corresponds to the task length q.

However, to the best of our knowledge, previous studies do not consider that two students who spend the same time on a task, or perform the same number of actions, may instead behave very differently. In the following sections, we propose a student temporal learning model that overcomes these issues by using a specific measure of engagement that can be used to derive typical temporal behaviours by a clustering analysis.

5.1 Average Time-On-Task

When using our data to examine overall time spent and number of actions taken by students, we noticed that examining simply one of the two variables at a time does not provide a comprehensive picture of student learning behaviour.

Let us consider Fig. 1. The plot on the left reports, for Course B, the total time spent in seconds with respect to the number of actions and shows a substantial difference amongst students, as also evidenced by the significant standard deviation (5,913.39 for time spent and 336.82 for actions). The students could repeat exercises as often as they wanted, so when comparing the total time to the overall number of actions carried out on the course, we can notice that student *7*, who was in the lower range in terms of total time spent, performed considerably the greater number of actions. The comparison with student *19* who stands out as having spent the most time on the course implies that the actions of student *7* were shorter and demonstrates a completely different behaviour. The average time per action (on the right) enables us to comprehend for instance that students *16* & *25* behave similarly, as well as students *8* & *23* and *14* & *21*.

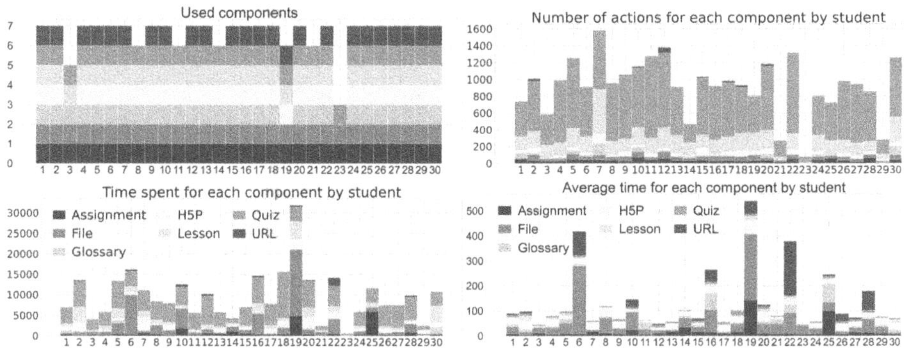

Fig. 2. *Component* use. For all plots, student IDs are reported on the x-axis and the legend is the same.

However, we are not only interested in *whether* and *when*, but also in the *types* of tasks on which students spend their time. Therefore, we would like to capture two distinct behaviours which can be identified in the online environment: *observational* learning (taking in content: reading postings and information, watching videos, etc.) and *application/interactional* learning (producing/demonstrating: writing postings, taking quizzes, writing assignments, etc.) [6]. Thus, we select only those modules directly relevant to 'Quality Learning' defined as *learning in which learners are provided with the ability to effectively learn, and retain skills and knowledge gained* [20]. Specifically, out of all the *components* (learning modules μ) of the courses, we choose: *File*, *Glossary*, and *URL* for observational learning; *Assignment*, *H5P*, and *Quiz* for application/interactional learning; and the *Lesson*, provided with a number of questions, for both types of learning(see footnote 1).

The examination of each component's use in Fig. 2 reveals different individual needs and learning styles [8]. For example, some students never used some components (top left) while student *7* used the *Glossary*, *Lesson* and *H5P* more than the others in terms of number of actions (top right) as did student *12* with the *URL*. A different summary is outlined in the analysis of the time invested in each component (bottom left). Student *19* spent most of their time on the *File* as did student *6*, while student *25* on the *Assignment* for a more or less comparable time than student *19.* Student *30* preferred the *Lesson*, student *18* the *Quiz.* On the contrary, students *14* and *21* hardly used the *Quiz.*

This preliminary analysis of the data shows that certain students may have similar behavioural patterns although limited to the total duration or total frequency of use. We argue that the separate use of neither the total amount of time spent nor the number of actions taken can be enough to describe behaviours. As a result, to investigate learning habits, we propose the adoption of a central tendency measure combining the two factors to better define student behaviour. In particular, we employ the *average time-on-task*, that can be simply calculated as the *time-on-task* divided by its *frequency.* Thanks to the usage of the average time-on-task, we are able to comprehend that, as depicted in Fig. 2 (bottom right), students *7*, *13*, and *17*, exhibit very comparable behaviour, which we would not have been able to observe if we have only looked at the total time or the frequency of actions.

The study presented so far highlights several differences, but also a number of similarities that we would like to capture. Therefore, since time is the focus in our work and we want to explore how students behave over time, we constrained the engagement in time frames (Definition 5). In the next section we present alternative ways of modelling student temporal behaviour.

5.2 Temporal Aggregations

As humans we operate under the cadence of a seven-day week and the week-day alternation drive our lives. Since the flexibility of e-learning requires student self-regulation (time management and self-testing) [9] some questions arise. How do students act at different days of the week? May any time segmentation be representative of their own learning habits? Starting from the above considerations, we examine data from various time frames and we identify three profile configurations: *week*, *days* and *knowledge domain*, that we illustrate below.

Week. Our data represents students that carried out online activities while attending remote face-to-face lectures scheduled on a weekly basis. Could this scheduling generate comparable distributed behaviour while learning online over a week? In order to examine students' weekly engagement, we look at their average time-on-task, distributed over the weeks. Fig. 3 - *left* shows for each student the overall engagement in all tasks week by week. This setting highlights some behaviours that are common to all learners as well as extremely unique habits. For instance, in the first week students *6* and *19* have similar behaviours while student *22* emerges; in the second week, students *6* and *19* still have similar habits; in the fourth week students *16* and *25* behave quite similarly while students *19* emerges. However, when we dig deeper and unpack the engagement with respect to the components of the first week, for students *6* and *19* (Fig. 3 - *right*), we observe a completely different picture. Despite having similar weekly overall engagement, student *6* spent more time than student *19* on File, whereas student *19* engaged on H5P and URL more than student *6*.

Days and Domain Knowledge. A weekly view ignores any variances that might occur on different days. On Mondays, one student may study more than

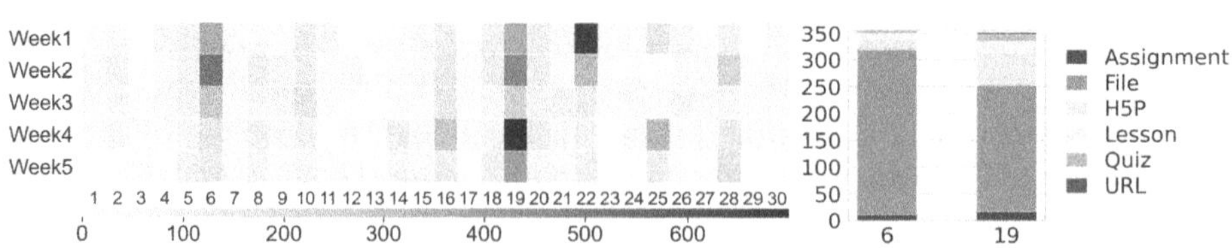

Fig. 3. Overall engagement over the *weeks* & detail by component of the engagement in the first week for students *6* and *19*.

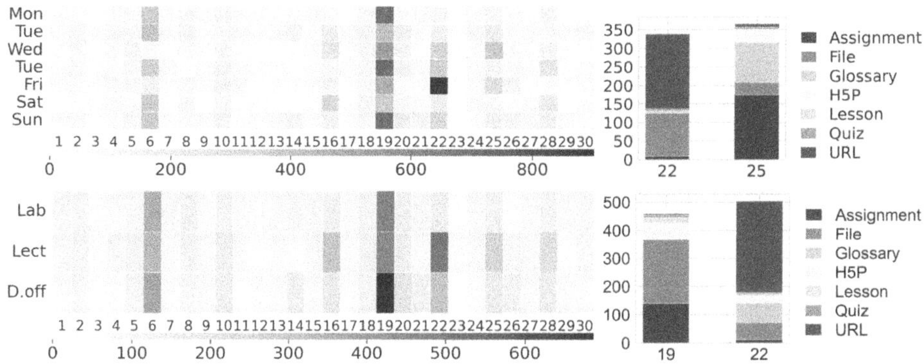

Fig. 4. Overall engagement over the *Days* of the week & over the *Domain Knowledge*

on Sundays despite having the same weekly behaviour as another student. Therefore, we looked at how students behave on a daily basis. In Fig. 4 - *top left*, which represents the overall engagement for all tasks with regard to the *Day* aggregation, we can observe that on Tuesdays, students *6* and *19* still behave similarly, as well as students *22* and *25* on Wed. However, since in our dataset the laboratories took place on some days and the lectures on others, to capture potential different behaviour on the basis of the teaching activity, we also propose a model based on this *Domain Knowledge*, i.e., we aggregate data into three categories: laboratory, lectures, and days off. In Fig. 4 - *bottom left* we now observe a pretty similar level of activity on lecture days for students *19* and *22*.

If we dig deeper into the study, we can see that despite being apparently similar, the learners have radically distinct learning styles. Considering again the case of Wednesday, student *22* is more engaged in File and URL, while student *25* in Assignment and Glossary (Fig. 4 - *top right*). On a domain basis (Fig. 4 - *bottom right*), during lecture days, student *19* is more engaged in Assignment and File than student *22*, who is more engaged in URL.

In the next section, we describe the clustering algorithms that we used to find groups of students having a similar temporal learning behaviour with respect to the proposed profile configurations.

6 Temporal Learning Behaviour Discovering

Our goal is to find groups of students that share temporal regularities, namely, to cluster students with similar temporal profiles whose knowledge is contained in each $P_{i,j}$ describing the engagement of the student in the learning module i and the temporal aggregation j (Definition 6). According to this definition, the temporal aggregation F and the type of engagement value $P_{i,j}$ are set when the framework is instantiated to analyse a real dataset and are dependent on the aim of the study. In this paper, we use the three different temporal aggregations F, presented in Sect. 5.2, as variables to observe and the *average time-on-task* as

Table 1. Comparison of clustering results for profile configurations with different temporal aggregations.

	Course A												Course B											
	K-means				Bisecting				Hierarchical				K-means				Bisecting				Hierarchical			
Profile	K	K_1	SSE	SSH	K	K_1	SSE	SSH	K	K_1	SSE	SSH	K	K_1	SSE	SSH	K	K_1	SSE	SSH	K	K_1	SSE	SSH
Week	15	10	8.6	**0.11**	19	16	11.7	0.01	12	7	12.8	0.105	12	8	14.1	0.06	16	8	15.6	0.04	11	8	15.4	**0.08**
Day	14	11	22.7	**0.10**	19	16	15.2	0.02	12	7	27.3	0.09	12	8	17.7	**0.08**	17	11	14.6	0.06	11	8	19.8	**0.08**
Domain	13	6	6.9	**0.14**	15	5	14.5	0.08	13	6	7.0	0.13	12	8	3.9	**0.20**	14	4	13.1	0.05	12	8	3.9	**0.20**

tracking variable contained in each $P_{i,j}$. Given the difference in terms of temporal aggregation of each student profile configuration, we also have a different size of the matrix $\mathcal{P} \in \mathbb{R}^{|M| \times |F|}$ representing the temporal learning profile, where $|M| = 7$ represents the number of the learning modules μ taken into account. The difference in terms of matrix size is due to the temporal aggregation: $|F| = 4$ for the *Course A* and $|F| = 5$ for the *Course B* in the *week* based configuration; $|F| = 7$ in the *days* of the week, and $|F| = 3$ for the domain knowledge.

We experiment and compare three clustering algorithms: K-means, Bisecting K-means and Ward hierarchical clustering by using the Euclidean distance function[3]. We compare the performance of these three approaches by reporting the sum of squared errors (SSE) measuring the compactness of the clusters, the silhouette score (SSH) that captures both compactness and separation, the number of clusters (K), and the number of singleton clusters (K_1).

6.1 Results and Discussion

The first outcome of our comparative analysis is that in each course, for any combination of profile configuration and clustering algorithm, the clustering analysis discovers a not negligible number of singleton clusters (see K_1 values in Table 1) identifying specific learning behaviours that are *unique*. This is likely due to the fact that in the platform students have the possibility to freely organise their learning activities choosing the learning modules from time to time, how many times to access them, and how much time to spend on them. Comparing the other metrics in Table 1 we can also observe that looking at the silhouette score, most of the time K-means has slightly better performance than the hierarchical and always a better SSE. Bisecting K-means instead has lower performance with respect to the others. Moreover, among the three profile configurations we highlight that the *Domain Knowledge* enables better clustering performance for all the algorithms both in terms of SSE and SSH.

In order to comprehend the characteristics of the extracted prototypes we also analyse the centroids of the clusters. Fig. 5 shows the centroids obtained by

[3] K-means has been implemented in Python with SCIKIT-LEARN, Bisecting K-means with PYCLUSTERING, and Hierarchical clustering with SCIPY. For K-Means we select the number of cluster k analysing the SSE curve. For Bisecting K-Means we vary the parameters controlling the split. For the hierarchical we obtain the clusters by cutting the hierarchy w.r.t. the median value of the distance matrix.

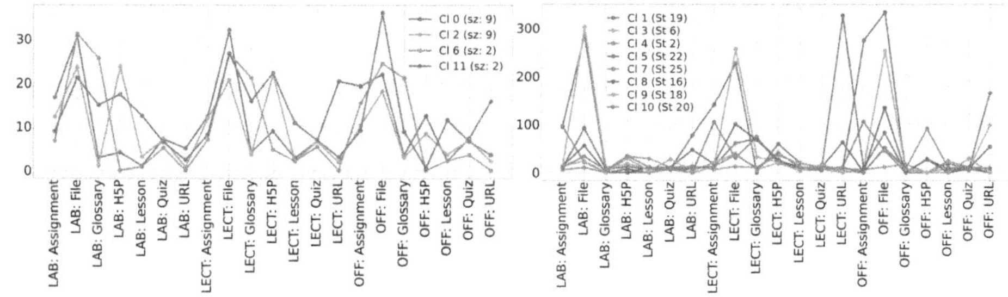

Fig. 5. Centroids of K-means on *Domain Knowledge*: clusters (left), singleton (right).

applying K-means on Course B. In particular, centroids for clusters with at least two students are shown on the left, whereas singleton clusters are shown on the right. These two plots highlight that among the singletons, there are students who have low activity across time frames for most of the components but high peaks for a few specific components. For example, during laboratory and lecture days, student *19* prefers to learn by reading Files and watching videos (URL) but always works on Assignments. Conversely, student *6* prefers to use Files with respect to other activities both in laboratory and in lecture days, although we observe a growth in the use of videos (URL) in days off. Student *22* prefers to watch videos lectures. Some students, such as student *20*, have a low overall activity level but some peaks on the interactive tools (H5P).

In Fig. 5-*left* we notice that all clusters are characterised by a high activity on File. We highlight that *Cluster 0* is more engaged in interactive activities (H5P) on days off, and is the cluster with the highest level of activity in video lectures (URL) in general. *Cluster 2* devotes the majority of its activity to Files and H5P, while the latter are used less frequently during the day off. *Cluster 6* is similar to *Cluster 0* but we note a low level of engagement on days off. *Cluster 11*, on the other hand, uses a lot of File, H5P and Glossary on laboratory and lecture days, whereas reading Files increases on days off.

The selected features for the profile configuration clearly influence the user modelling, providing more or less details, and the clustering result. As a consequence, given the same students as input, the clusters can move depending on the profile configuration and two students may or may not stay in the same cluster. Since we are interested in understanding if there are students who are similar regardless of the profile configuration chosen, we examined how the groupings change, i.e., how students migrate across clusters.

Fig. 6 illustrates the movement of students between clusters. This analysis reveals that some students are constantly alone (students *6, 16, 18, 19, 22, 25*) in comparison to others (such as students *4, 7, 9, 24* and students *3, 15, 23*) who always stay in the same cluster for each configuration. Therefore, regardless of the temporal profile configuration, some students have unique learning behaviours, while others are similar regardless of the perspective used to define similarity or the clustering approach. The uniqueness of the students, which

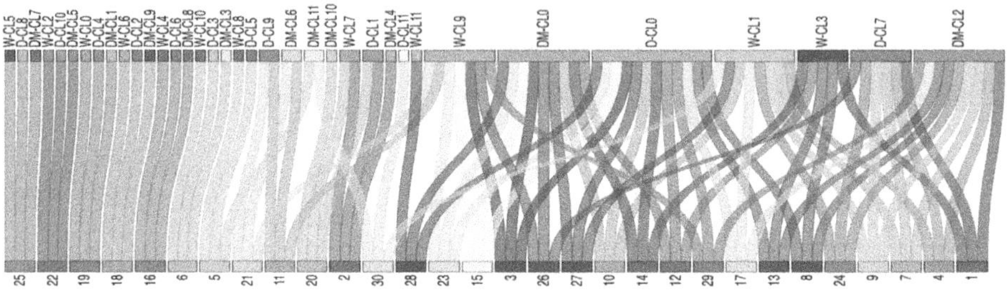

Fig. 6. Clustering for each profile configuration (DM = domain knowledge, W = week, D = days) in Course B with K-means. Students IDS are reported on the bottom.

allows them to remain independent in any configuration, is a result of their selective selection of learning modules. Hence, singletons have significant peaks in their preferred learning modules and very poor engagement in the others in whatever configuration.

We also looked into the habits of students who remain together regardless of the temporal profile configuration, and found that they have peaks in the same learning modules, as expected. For example, students *4, 7, 9, 24* in any time aggregation of each profile configuration are always engaged in File, Glossary, and H5P. Moreover, they are not interested in watching videos (URL) unlike students *3, 15, 23* or student *22*.

The temporal analysis enables us to comprehend the various habits that each student uses when learning online. The uncovered profiles may enable different teaching strategies tailored to each student or customised recommendations for learning time schedule. These traits could also be correlated with information, such as sequence of activities performed, to explore individual learning traits that might positively affect performance, engagement, and success and to be employed for predictive analysis or to improve learning design. Furthermore, knowledge of any associations between any temporal aggregations and the average time-on-task could aid in the implementation of a well-designed and personalised dashboard that extracts and displays real-time data on student engagement.

7 Conclusion

We have presented an analysis aimed at discovering prototypes of student temporal learning behaviour by using information describing *whether* and *when* students typically work in specific learning modules of an online learning environment, and on *what type* of learning activity they are engaged. Three temporal representations of the student profile, as well as distinct clustering algorithms, are used. Using real student learning data from two courses, we discovered that some students have distinct learning behaviours, while others are comparable and always cluster together, regardless of the temporal profile configuration.

Acknowledgments. This work is supported by the EU H2020 Program under the scheme H2020-INFRAIA-2019-1: Research Infrastructure G.A. 871042 *SoBigData++*.

References

1. Beaudoin, M.F.: Learning or lurking?: tracking the "invisible" online student. Internet High. Educ. **5**(2), 147–155 (2002)
2. Bovo, A.: Clustering moodle data as a tool for profiling students. In: ICEEE (2013)
3. Chen, B., Knight, S., Wise, A.: Critical issues in designing and implementing temporal analytics. J. Learn. Anal. (2018)
4. Credé, M., et al.: Study habits, skills, and attitudes: the third pillar supporting collegiate academic performance. Perspect. Psychol. Sci. **3**(6), 425–453 (2008)
5. Dermy, O., Brun, A.: Can we take advantage of time-interval pattern mining to model students activity? In: EDM (2020)
6. Dixson, M.D.: Measuring student engagement in the online course: the online student engagement scale (OSE). Online Learn. **19**(4), n4 (2015)
7. Dunlosky, J., et al.: Improving students' learning with effective learning techniques: promising directions from cognitive and educational psychology. Psychol. Sci. Public Interest **14**(1), 4–58 (2013)
8. Fleming, N.D., Mills, C.: Not another inventory, rather a catalyst for reflection. Improve Acad. **11**(1), 137–155 (1992)
9. Goda, Y., et al.: Procrastination and other learning behavioral types in e-learning and their relationship with learning outcomes. Learn. Indiv. Diff. **37**, 72–80 (2015)
10. Hart, C.: Factors associated with student persistence in an online program of study: a review of the literature. J. Interact. Online Learn. (2012)
11. Hecking, T., Ziebarth, S., Hoppe, H.U.: Analysis of dynamic resource access patterns in a blended learning course. In: LAK (2014)
12. Henrie, C.R., Halverson, L.R., Graham, C.R.: Measuring student engagement in technology-mediated learning: a review. Comput. Educ. **90**, 36–53 (2015)
13. Lee, Y.: Effect of uninterrupted time-on-task on students' success in massive open online courses (MOOCs). Comput. Hum. Behav. **86**, 174–180 (2018)
14. Macfadyen, L.P., Dawson, S.: Mining LMS data to develop an "early warning system" for educators: a proof of concept. Comput. Educ. **54**(2), 588–599 (2010)
15. Riel, J., Lawless, K.A., Brown, S.W.: Timing matters: approaches for measuring and visualizing behaviours of timing and spacing of work in self-paced online teacher professional development courses. JLA **5**(1), 25–40 (2018)
16. Rotelli, D., Monreale, A.: Time-on-task estimation by data-driven outlier detection based on learning activities. In: LAK22 (2022)
17. Schmitz, B., et al.: New perspectives for the evaluation of training sessions in self-regulated learning: time-series analyses of diary data. Contemp. Educ. Psychol. **31**(1), 64–96 (2006)
18. Sherin, B.: Using computational methods to discover student science conceptions in interview data. In: LAK (2012)
19. Theobald, M., et al.: Identifying individual differences using log-file analysis: distributed learning as mediator between conscientiousness and exam grades. Learn. Indiv. Dif. **65**, 112–122 (2018)
20. Thindwa, H.: The role of technology in improving quality of teaching in higher education: an international perspective. Teach. Educ. (2016)
21. Weinstein, C.E., Palmer, D.R., Schultz, A.: Lassi. User's Manual for those administering Learning and Study Strategies Inventory (2002)

The Disciplinary Learning Companion: The Impact of Disciplinary and Topic-Specific Reflection on Students' Metacognitive Abilities and Academic Achievement

Elien Sijmkens[1,2(✉)], Mieke De Cock[1,3], and Tinne De Laet[1,2]

[1] Leuven Engineering and Science Education Center (LESEC), KU Leuven, Leuven, Belgium
{elien.sijmkens,mieke.decock,tinne.delaet}@kuleuven.be
[2] Tutorial Services, Faculty of Engineering Science, KU Leuven, Leuven, Belgium
[3] Department of Physics and Astronomy, KU Leuven, Leuven, Belgium

Abstract. One of the main goals of science and engineering education is to guide students in becoming proficient problem solvers. Metacognitive abilities play an important role here, since they help students to regulate their own solving process. The Disciplinary Learning Companion (DLC) is an online tool that aims at developing these abilities through discipline- and topic-specific reflection on the solving process. In this contribution, we report on the results of the implementation of the DLC in a first-year Newtonian mechanics course. We studied the interplay between students' interaction with the DLC (online learning traces), their metacognitive abilities (pre and post self-reported questionnaire), academic achievement (final exam score and particular exam problem score), and conceptual understanding (coding exam problem). We found no significant relationship between students' interaction with the DLC and their metacognitive abilities as measured by the self-reported questionnaire. The results, however, show that students that used the tool more frequently obtain a higher final exam score and have a better conceptual understanding of the exam problem considered. Moreover, the results suggest that the topic-specificity of the reflection questions plays a role in the improvement in academic achievement.

Keywords: Metacognition · Self-regulation · Reflection · Problem solving · Physics · Newtonian mechanics

1 Introduction

One of the main goals of science and engineering education is to guide students in becoming proficient problem solvers. Metacognitive and self-regulating abilities are needed to become a skilled problem solver in addition to sufficient content

I. Hilliger et al. (Eds.): EC-TEL 2022, LNCS 13450, pp. 354–367, 2022.
https://doi.org/10.1007/978-3-031-16290-9_26

and procedural knowledge in different disciplines [11]. These abilities help students to regulate their solving process and to guide their decisions on which approach to follow when solving a problem [19]. This study investigates whether the development of metacognition can be stimulated through reflection on the solving process. Moreover, we consider whether there are preliminary indications that discipline-specific reflection contributes more strongly to the development of metacognitive abilities than generic reflection. We focus on the use of metacognitive knowledge and skills when solving physics problems, in particular problems in Newtonian mechanics.

1.1 Metacognition

Based on the well-known framework of Flavell [4], metacognition can be described as "students' knowledge about their processes of cognition and the ability to control and monitor those processes as a function of the feedback received via outcomes of learning" [6]. Metacognitive abilities consist of two major components: metacognitive knowledge and metacognitive skills or control [6,7,23,26]. Metacognitive knowledge refers to the knowledge and beliefs students have about their own cognition, the cognitive strategies they use and how these strategies interact with a cognitive task. Moreover, Flavell recognizes three subcategories in metacognitive knowledge: knowledge about persons, tasks, and strategies [4,23,26]. In the context of problem solving, the latter is the most important one: it includes knowledge about when, why, and how certain strategies can be applied to achieve certain goals [4,26]. Metacognitive skills refer to the strategies students use to plan, monitor, control, and evaluate their cognitive activities to ensure effective learning [4,26].

The notion of metacognition is closely related to self-regulated learning. There is an extensive literature on these two notions and the relationship between them. According to Schraw's model metacognition is, besides cognition and motivation, one of the components of self-regulated learning [20]. Since considering students' motivation is not the aim of this study, we look through the lens of metacognition in this contribution.

1.2 Role of Metacognition in Problem Solving

Problem solving is a complex process. Many generic and discipline-specific problem solving models exist. In the context of physics problem solving, the logical problem solving model of the University of Minnesota has been developed to help students improve their understanding of physics problem solving [6].

To become skilled problem solvers students need a solid basis of content and procedural knowledge in different disciplines. Indeed, a profound conceptual understanding of the problem and knowledge of the relevant procedures is a prerequisite to be able to solve a problem [8,11,13]. This knowledge and these skills, however, do not help students to make decisions on which actions to undertake when solving a non-routine problem. Here students' metacognitive abilities play an important role, since they help students to guide their decisions on which approach to follow [19] and to monitor their progress [1,7]. The research of Schoenfeld [19] showed that experienced problem solvers spend relatively more time on metacognitive processes, such as analysing the problem and reflecting on the solution process, than novice problem solvers. Comparatively, novice problem solvers spend most of their time on cognitive processes, such as finding a solution plan and calculating. The research of, e.g., Rozencwajg [18] confirmed that students are more successful in problem solving when they show a higher level of metacognitive abilities.

Berardi-Coletta et al. showed that transfer of learning to new problems is more likely to take place if students acquire information on the solution of a problem via metacognitive processes [1]. Similarly, the study of Kapa showed that training students in metacognition with a focus on the product and the process phase of problem solving (i.e., on the use of metacognitive activities after and during the solving process) is beneficial for near and far transfer (i.e., for transfer to similar and dissimilar problems) [9].

The results above show that fostering students' metacognitive abilities can contribute to the education of successful problem solvers. Ample research has confirmed that metacognitive abilities positively affect learning outcomes, hence, academic achievement [10,22,27].

1.3 Metacognition and Educational Technology

Numerous interventions have been developed to foster students' self-regulating and metacognitive abilities, many of them use some kind of technology and/or learning analytics [24,25]. The majority of studies on mobile-learning showed that mobile-learning can enhance self-regulated learning [15]. The research of Garcia Rodicio et al. showed, however, that only offering a minimal or intermediate support system does not improve students' learning [5]. Students need a broad support, at least if they have to study complex materials with little prior-knowledge on the subject. In the context of our study, we expect students to need a broad support system to improve their conceptual understanding and metacognitive abilities for problem solving as physics and Newtonian mechanics in particular are known to be conceptually challenging.

2 Motivation and Research Questions

As discussed before, many technology-based interventions have been developed to foster students' self-regulating and metacognitive abilities [24]. Tormey et al. [21] combined a learning diary with a learning analytics dashboard in order to stimulate self-regulating abilities in relation to problem solving. The result is an online application called the Learning Companion, which is carefully grounded in theory. The learning diary provides a predefined list of generic reflection questions related to problem solving. Students can reflect on their solution and the solving process by answering these generic questions after solving any problem. Ample research has indicated, however, that it is more effective to teach self-regulating and metacognitive abilities in a discipline-specific context, rather than covered in a discipline-agnostic package [7,19,23]. Therefore, we believe that the concept of the Learning Companion can be augmented by supplementing or replacing the generic reflection questions by discipline-specific, and even topic-specific reflection questions. This forms the motivation to develop the Disciplinary Learning Companion (DLC).

In this contribution, we discuss the concept of the DLC and its implementation in a first-year course on Newtonian mechanics for students in bioscience engineering at KU Leuven (Belgium). The aim of our study is to investigate the possible impact of the DLC on students' metacognitive abilities, academic achievement, and conceptual understanding. The research question are:

RQ1. How is students' interaction with the DLC related to their metacognitive abilities as measured by a validated questionnaire?
RQ2. How is students' interaction with the DLC related to their academic achievement on a final exam?
RQ3. How is students' interaction with a particular physics topic in the DLC related to their performance on the corresponding exam problem and their conceptual understanding of this exam problem?

3 Concept of the Disciplinary Learning Companion

The idea of the Disciplinary Learning Companion (DLC) is to foster students' metacognitive abilities for problem solving by triggering reflection on the solving process. The self-reflection is elicited by discipline-specific or even topic-specific reflection questions and personalized feedback. The DLC consists of reflection modules, where each reflection module discusses one particular problem. In this study, we focus on problems in Newtonian mechanics. The reflection questions are structured according to five problem solving dimensions that can also be linked to the logical problem solving model of the University of Minnesota [6]: (1) strategy plan, focusing on setting up a well-considered and complete strategy plan to tackle the problem; (2) concepts, focusing on identifying the relevant discipline-specific concepts needed to solve the problem; (3) mathematical model, focusing on translating the relevant physical laws and concepts into a set of equations; (4) computations, focusing on the necessary computations to solve the mathematical model obtained; and (5) interpretation, focusing on interpreting and evaluating the answer obtained. Each reflection module counts 10–15 reflection questions, such that we expect students to work on it for about 20–30 min.

The reflection questions are multiple-choice questions[1], where the answer options include answers based on common student difficulties. For each reflection

[1] For some examples, see https://set.kuleuven.be/LESEC/groups/study-career-guidance-of-steam-students/DLC-documents/.

question, students receive feedback based on their answer. The feedback explains why the answer is (in)correct, what reasoning could lead to the correct answer, why particular solving strategies could be more suited or efficient, and suggests specific actions (e.g., "Would you solve the problem differently with this new information. If yes, try to do so."). Once students have gone through all topic-specific reflection questions, they can download a model solution to the problem.

To stimulate transfer of acquired concepts and strategies to future problem solving, the last question of the reflection module instructs students to write down a point of attention, i.e., something they have learned by solving the problem or completing the reflection module and want to take with them to future problem solving. This can be, for example, a concept they did not fully understand yet, a common strategy or how they can write something down. This is an open question such that they are stimulated to reflect on what they have learned themselves. However, as students are not always able to come up with a useful point of attention themselves, a list with suggestions, structured according the five problem solving dimensions described above, is provided afterwards.

4 Methods

This section discusses the participants, course design and the three different data sources in our study.

4.1 Participants and Course Design

Since we believe that the development of metacognitive abilities can help students in the transition from secondary to higher education, we implemented the DLC in an introductory physics course for first year students in bio-engineering science at KU Leuven (Belgium) ($N \sim 350$). This course mainly dealt with Newtonian mechanics and consisted of two 1,5 h weekly lectures and one 2 h problem solving session for each chapter. The professor of the course provided the lectures, while teaching assistants guided the problem solving sessions. For each of the nine Newtonian mechanics topics, we selected an additional problem for which we developed a reflection module. Students were instructed to solve this problem and reflect on their solving process using the reflection module after the problem solving session. The goal of this task was to help students process the concepts and strategies discussed in the problem solving session and to prepare for the next problem solving sessions. The task was not graded nor mandatory, but the students were stimulated by the professor as well as the teaching assistants to engage in the reflection modules as part of the learning activities for the course.

4.2 Students' Interaction with the DLC

To measure students' interaction with the DLC, we checked how many reflection modules they completed and to what extent. In the context of the study, we

Table 1. Overview of the grouping of students for the three research questions and the number of students in each group. For RQ1 and RQ2 students were divided in four groups depending on how many reflection modules of the DLC they completed (interaction groups). For RQ3 the groups were combined two-by-two, but then split depending on whether students did or did not complete the particular reflection module on angular momentum (angular momentum interaction groups).

	RQ1	**RQ2**			**RQ3**
#modules completed	**#students**	**#students**	**#modules completed**		**# students**
0	24	100	0–3	NOT ang momentum	189
1–3	48	94	0–3	ang momentum	(5)
4–6	53	71	4–9	NOT ang momentum	64
7–9	40	51	4–9	ang momentum	58
Total	**165**	**316**			**316**

only wanted to include "valid" participations to the reflection modules. Hence, we only considered participations to the reflection modules that were completed timely (i.e., at the latest 2 weeks after the next problem solving session), almost fully (i.e., ≥80% of topic-specific reflection questions are answered), and carefully (i.e., ≥10 min spent to complete the module).

For RQ1 and RQ2, the students were divided in four "interaction groups" based on the total number of reflection modules completed: 0, 1–3, 4–6, or 7–9 reflection modules. For RQ3, we studied the exam problem on the particular topic of angular momentum in more detail. Therefore, we took into account whether students did or did not complete the reflection module about angular momentum in addition to the total number of reflection modules completed (0–3 or 4–9 modules). In this way, we obtained four "angular momentum interaction groups". In the analysis of students' metacognitive abilities (RQ1), we could only include students that participated in both the pre- and the posttest of the MSLQ ($N = 165$). In the analysis of students' performance on the exam (RQ2 & RQ3), we included all students that participated to the final exam ($N = 316$). Table 1 presents the number of students in each (angular momentum) interaction group. Note that for RQ3 only 5 students were in the second group, which made this group too small to include in this part of the analysis. The performance of these students on the exam problem was very diverse, ranging from a zero score to a score of 8/10, such that no trend could be observed in the data of this small group.

4.3 Metacognitive Abilities

To investigate whether there is a relationship between students' interaction with the DLC and their metacognitive abilities (RQ1), we administered a pretest during the first lecture of the course and a posttest during a lecture at the end of the semester. These tests were based on (the second part of) the Motivated Strategies for Learning Questionnaire (MSLQ) developed by Pintrich and De Groot [16,17]. In this self-reported questionnaire, students have to assess 50 statements about learning strategies on a 7-point Likert scale (coded 1–7). We translated the statements to Dutch, which is the native language at our university, and made them more concrete for the context of the course.[2] The 50 statements are originally categorized into 9 subscales: rehearsal, elaboration, organization, critical thinking, metacognitive self-regulation, time and study environment, effort regulation, peer learning, and help seeking. Using a confirmatory factor analysis, we investigated whether the same subscales applied to our adapted questionnaire as interpreted by the participants to the pre- and posttest. Some adjustments to the categorization of the statements were made (see Footnote 2). Among others, the subscales "time and study environment" and "effort regulation" were merged.

4.4 Academic Achievement and Conceptual Understanding

We studied students' performance on the exam on a quantitative and on a more qualitative level. We considered students' final exam score for the course and studied their solution to one problem of the exam in more detail. For the latter, we defined a concept score assessing students' conceptual understanding of this problem. A coding frame was developed that considers whether students recognized the relevant concepts and whether they applied these concepts correctly. In total, five concepts that should be applied to answer the two subquestions of the problem were identified. Each of these concepts was worth one point if recognized as relevant and worth another point if also applied correctly, resulting in a concept score between 0 and 10. For each relevant concept, some criteria were set up to decide when students did or did not recognize it and did or did not apply it correctly. In total, a sample of 25 student solutions to the exam problem was scored by three independent raters and discussed in two rounds. After refining the criteria another sample of five student solutions was rated. Interrater reliability was tested for the two subquestions and yielded a Cohen's kappa of .88 and .79, respectively, which can be seen as a substantial agreement.

4.5 Data Analysis

Students' data were linked to each other by using student numbers. Students were asked to fill in their student number in the reflection modules, pretest, and posttest. Moreover, students signed an informed consent before voluntarily participating to the pretest. Filling in the student number was not mandatory to be able to use the reflection modules. However, for each reflection module only a small fraction of students ($\leq$8%) did not provide a (valid) student number. The data were pseudonymised after linking them to each other by replacing the student numbers with unique codes.

[2] For some more details, see https://set.kuleuven.be/LESEC/groups/study-career-guidance-of-steam-students/DLC-documents/.

5 Results

This section presents the observed relationships and trends in the data obtained in the study. For the analysis, students were grouped based on their interaction with the DLC as discussed in Sect. 4.2 and shown in Table 1.

5.1 Interaction with DLC vs. Metacognitive Abilities (RQ1)

For each subscale of the MSLQ, the pre- and postscore and the normalized change between both tests were compared for the four interaction groups. *Kruskal-Wallis rank sum tests* showed that there were almost no significant differences between the four interaction groups, except for the postscore on the subscale "time and study environment and effort regulation" ($\chi^2 = 10.90, p = .01, df = 3$). Post-hoc *pairwise Wilcoxon tests* showed which pairs of groups scored significantly different (see Fig. 1). This result indicates that students using the DLC more frequently reported that they spend their studying time more effectively and are more committed to reaching their goals.

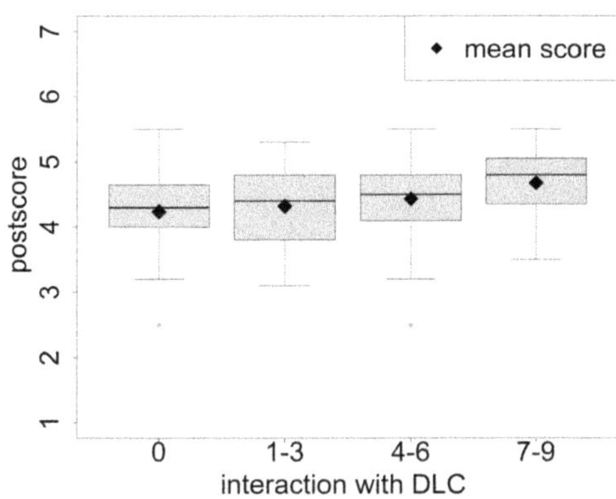

#modules	0	1-3	4-6
1-3	p = .684 r = .048		
4-6	p = 0.541 r = .062	p = .541 r = .061	
7-9	p = .031* r = .214	p = .024* r = .220	p = .294 r = .109

Fig. 1. Relation between interaction with the DLC measured as the number of reflection modules completed and the postscore on "time and study environment and effort regulation". The table shows the results of the post-hoc *pairwise Wilcoxon tests*.

5.2 Interaction with DLC vs. Academic Achievement (RQ2)

We measured students' academic achievement quantitatively by their final exam score. When comparing the final exam score for the four interaction groups, we noted an increasing trend. A *Kruskal-Wallis rank sum test* indicated that there were significant differences between the four groups ($\chi^2 = 48.84, p < .001, df = 3$). Further analysis using *pairwise Wilcoxon tests* showed that there was a significant difference between each pair of groups (see Fig. 2). This result indicates that students using the DLC more frequently obtained a higher final exam score.

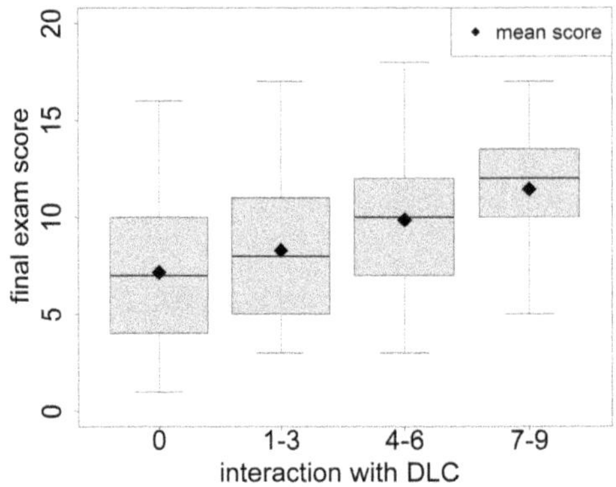

#modules	0	1-3	4-6
1-3	p = .029* r = .156		
4-6	p < .001* r = .303	p = .021* r = .180	
7-9	p < .001* r = .450	p < .001* r = .389	p = .029* r = .197

Fig. 2. Relation between interaction with the DLC measured as the number of reflection modules completed and the final exam score. The table shows the results of the post-hoc *pairwise Wilcoxon tests.*

5.3 Interaction with Module on Angular Momentum vs. Performance and Conceptual Understanding for Corresponding Exam Problem (RQ3)

We further investigated the relationship between students' interaction with the DLC and academic achievement by studying the role of the topic-specificity of the reflection modules in this relationship. To this end, we investigated students' performance on one particular problem of the exam, the problem on angular momentum, and their participation to the corresponding reflection module. The score on the exam problem on angular momentum was compared for the three angular momentum interaction groups. A *Kruskal-Wallis rank sum test* confirmed that there were significant differences between the three groups ($\chi^2 = 15.37, p < .001, df = 2$). Post-hoc *pairwise Wilcoxon tests* showed that there was a significant difference between the group of students that completed 4–9 modules including the module about angular momentum and both groups of students that did not complete the module about angular momentum (Fig. 3). Note that there was no significant difference between the two groups of students that did not complete the module about angular momentum, but that completed a different number of reflection modules in total. These results suggest that the particular topic of the reflection modules plays a role in the relationship between interaction with the DLC and academic achievement.

To measure students' academic achievement on a more qualitative level, we considered students' conceptual understanding of one of the exam problems, again the problem on angular momentum. Students' conceptual understanding was assessed by the concept score as defined in Sect. 4.4. A *Kruskal-Wallis rank sum test* indicated that there were significant differences between the three angular momentum interaction groups ($\chi^2 = 25.39, p < .001, df = 2$). Post-hoc *pairwise Wilcoxon tests* showed that there was a significant difference between the group of students that completed 4–9 modules including the module about

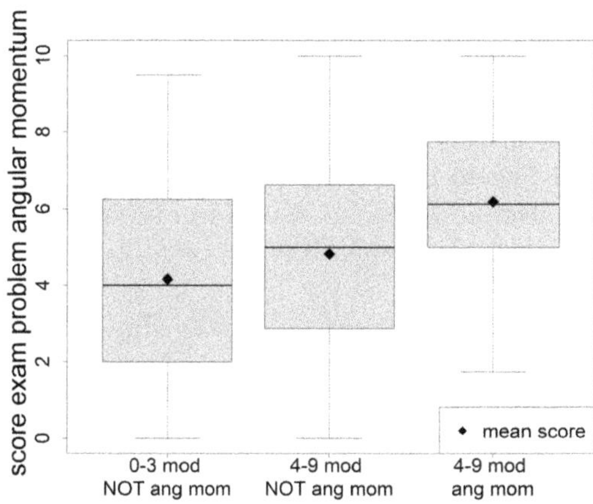

#modules	0-3 NOT ang	4-9 NOT ang
4-9 NOT ang	p = .088 r = .107	
4-9 ang	p < 0,001* r = .429	p = .005* r = .256

Fig. 3. Interaction with DLC and module on angular momentum vs. score exam problem on angular momentum. The table shows the results of the post-hoc *pairwise Wilcoxon tests.*

angular momentum and both groups of students that did not complete the module about angular momentum (Fig. 4). Note that again there was no significant difference between the two groups of students that did not complete the module about angular momentum, but that completed a different number of reflection modules in total. This means that the topic of the reflection modules is important in the development of students' conceptual understanding, as would be expected.

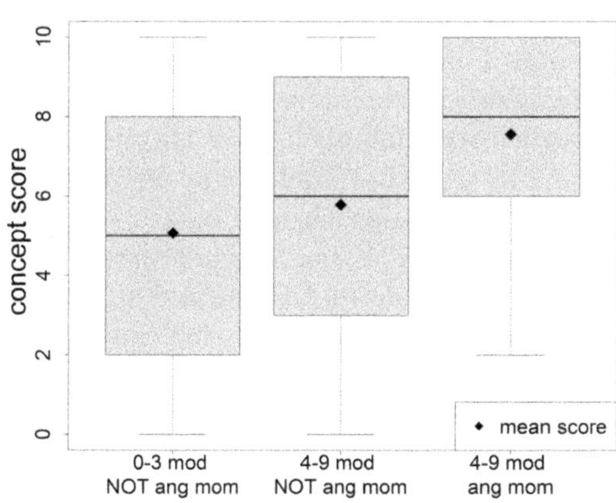

#modules	0-3 NOT ang	4-9 NOT ang
4-9 NOT ang	p = .134 r = .094	
4-9 ang	p < 0,001* r = .419	p = .003* r = .273

Fig. 4. Interaction with DLC and module on angular momentum vs. concept score exam problem on angular momentum. The table shows the results of the post-hoc *pairwise Wilcoxon tests.*

6 Discussion and Future Work

We studied the interplay between students' interaction with the DLC and their metacognitive abilities, academic achievement and conceptual understanding of one of the exam problems. We would like to emphasize that the design of the study did not allow us to draw any causal conclusions. We did not work with a control and experimental group, since this was not feasible in the context of this study due to practical and ethical reasons.

Concerning **RQ1**, the results obtained show almost no relationships between students' interaction with the DLC and their metacognitive abilities as measured by the self-reported questionnaire. This could indicate that the reflection modules are not effective for improving students' metacognitive abilities. However, research [22] already suggested that self-reported questionnaires, such as the MSLQ, are not very accurate measurements of metacognitive abilities. It seems that students are often not able to accurately assess their own use of metacognitive strategies. Moreover, the items in the MSLQ address very general learning strategies, such as how to organize, summarize, and memorize learning materials, how to study for a test, or how to concentrate while studying. By contrast, the DLC focuses specifically on metacognitive strategies for problem solving. Hence, the link between the abilities elicited by the DLC and the items in the questionnaire might be missing or unclear for the students. Therefore, we believe it is still possible that the DLC fosters students' metacognitive abilities for problem solving. Even stronger, if future qualitative research would indicate that the DLC triggers metacognitive activities, then learning traces from the DLC could be valuable microanalytic measures of metacognitive activity. To this end, systematic observations, think-aloud protocols [22], or existing microanalytic measures [2] could be used, which is very challenging in the context of a large-scale administration.

In answer to **RQ2**, the results reveal a positive relationship between students' interaction with the tool and their academic achievement (Sect. 5.2). This corresponds with findings in the literature that metacognitive training results in improved academic achievement [3,14] and that metacognitively oriented ICT-based interventions and mobile-learning enhance learning outcomes [15,24]. However, when interpreting this result, we must take into account that students using the DLC more frequently might also be more motivated and spend more time on studying in general than other students. Therefore, we can not conclude that there is a causal relationship between interaction with the DLC and academic achievement. Moreover, we can wonder whether the improvement in academic achievement can be explained by the fact that students have been reflecting on their solving process or by the additional topic-specific feedback that was offered in the reflection modules.

Concerning **RQ3**, the results indicate that students' performance on a particular exam problem is related to their participation to the corresponding reflection module. As would be expected, also students' conceptual understanding of a problem involving a particular concept depends on the topic of the reflection modules that they completed (Sect. 5.3). From these results, we could conclude that the reflection modules only help students to improve their conceptual understanding of physics concepts and therefore also their academic achievement, but not necessarily their metacognitive abilities. We could, however, also argue that these results indicate that reflection on problem solving strategies should be linked to a certain context, as was suggested in the literature [7,19,23]. Transfer of learned strategies and metacognitive abilities to new contexts might be difficult for students.

This discussion above shows that there is need for **future research**, since we do not completely understand yet how the DLC contributes to students' metacognition and academic achievement. It seems that the improvement in students' academic achievement by using the DLC can be explained by a combination of improvement in metacognitive abilities and conceptual understanding. As suggested by Verschaffel et al. [24], further research is necessary to disentangle the mediating effect of metacognition on learning outcomes from other possible mediating factors, in this case improvement in conceptual understanding. We need to better understand how students interact with the tool and which reflection questions might trigger metacognitive activities. To this end, we will organize think-aloud interviews in the context of the same course. During individual think-aloud interviews, the students will be instructed to solve a new problem and reflect on the solving process using the corresponding reflection module afterwards, while making their thinking process explicit by talking aloud. We will use an observation protocol for metacognitive activities [12] to analyse which metacognitive activities students use to regulate their solving process, and which metacognitive activities are triggered by the reflection questions.

7 Conclusions

In this work, we presented an online tool, the Disciplinary Learning Companion (DLC), for fostering students' metacognitive abilities for problem solving through discipline- and topic-specific reflection on the solving process. We studied the relationship between students' interaction with the DLC and their metacognitive abilities, academic achievement and conceptual understanding. We found no significant relationship between students' interaction with the DLC and their metacognitive abilities as measured by a self-reported questionnaire. Hereby we contribute to the research evidence questioning the validity of such self-reported questionnaires for measuring metacognitive abilities. The results do show that students that used the tool more frequently obtain a higher final exam score and have a better conceptual understanding of the exam problem considered. Moreover, the results suggest that the topic-specificity of the reflection questions plays a role in the improvement in academic achievement. Future research will use qualitative observations to better understand the interplay between metacognitive activities, conceptual understanding, and problem solving strategies and how this is mediated by the reflection activities of the DLC.

Acknowledgements. We would like to thank professor Hans Van Winckel and the teaching assistants for supporting this study in the context of their course. Moreover, we would like to thank all students in the first bachelor of Bioscience Engineering at KU Leuven (Belgium) that participated in the study.

References

1. Berardi-Coletta, B., Buyer, L., Dominowski, R., Rellinger, E.: Metacognition and problem solving: a process-oriented approach. J. Exp. Psychol. Learn. Memory Cogn. **21**(1), 205–223 (1995). https://doi.org/10.1037/0278-7393.21.1.205
2. DiBenedetto, M., Zimmerman, B.: Construct and predictive validity of microanalytic measures of students' self-regulation of science learning. Learn. Individ. Diff. **26**, 30–41 (2013). https://doi.org/10.1016/j.lindif.2013.04.004
3. Dignath, C., Büttner, G.: Components of fostering self-regulated learning among students. A meta-analysis on intervention studies at primary and secondary school level. Metacogn. Learn. **3**(3), 231–264 (2008). https://doi.org/10.1007/s11409-008-9029-x
4. Flavell, J.H.: Metacognition and cognitive monitoring: a new area of cognitive-developmental inquiry. Am. Psychol. **34**(10), 906 (1979). https://doi.org/10.1037/0003-066X.34.10.906
5. García Rodicio, H., Sánchez, E., Acuña, S.R.: Support for self-regulation in learning complex topics from multimedia explanations: do learners need extensive or minimal support? Instr. Sci. **41**(3), 539–553 (2013). https://doi.org/10.1007/s11251-012-9243-4
6. Gok, T.: The general assessment of problem solving processes in physics education. Eurasian J. Phys. Chem. Educ. **2**(2), 110–122 (2010)
7. Hollingworth, R.W., McLoughlin, C.: Developing science students' metacognitive problem solving skills online. Australas. J. Educ. Technol. **17**(1) (2001). https://doi.org/10.14742/ajet.1772
8. Hung, W., Jonassen, D.H.: Conceptual understanding of causal reasoning in physics. Int. J. Sci. Educ. **28**(13), 1601–1621 (2006). https://doi.org/10.1080/09500690600560902
9. Kapa, E.: Transfer from structured to open-ended problem solving in a computerized metacognitive environment. Learn. Instr. **17**(6), 688–707 (2007). https://doi.org/10.1016/j.learninstruc.2007.09.019
10. Kramarski, B., Mevarech, Z.R.: Enhancing mathematical reasoning in the classroom: the effects of cooperative learning and metacognitive training. Am. Educ. Res. J. **40**(1), 281–310 (2003). https://doi.org/10.3102/00028312040001281
11. Lucangeli, D., Tressoldi, P.E., Cendron, M.: Cognitive and metacognitive abilities involved in the solution of mathematical word problems: validation of a comprehensive model. Contemp. Educ. Psychol. **23**(3), 257–275 (1998). https://doi.org/10.1006/ceps.1997.0962
12. Meijer, J., Veenman, M.V.J., van Hout-Wolters, B.H.A.M.: Metacognitive activities in text-studying and problem-solving: development of a taxonomy. Educ. Res. Eval. **12**(3), 209–237 (2006). https://doi.org/10.1080/13803610500479991
13. Mestre, J.P., Docktor, J.L., Strand, N.E., Ross, B.H.: Conceptual problem solving in physics. In: Mestre, J.P., Ross, B.H. (eds.) Psychology of Learning and Motivation, vol. 55, chap. 9, pp. 269–298. Academic Press (2011). https://doi.org/10.1016/B978-0-12-387691-1.00009-0

14. Mevarech, Z., Fridkin, S.: The effects of IMPROVE on mathematical knowledge, mathematical reasoning and meta-cognition. Metacogn. Learn. **1**(1), 85–97 (2006). https://doi.org/10.1007/s11409-006-6584-x
15. Palalas, A., Wark, N.: The relationship between mobile learning and self-regulated learning: a systematic review. Australas. J. Educ. Technol. **36**(4), 151–172 (2020). https://doi.org/10.14742/ajet.5650
16. Pintrich, P., De Groot, E.: Motivational and self-regulated learning components of classroom academic performance. J. Educ. Psychol. **82**(1), 33–40 (1990). https://doi.org/10.1037/0022-0663.82.1.33
17. Pintrich, P., Smith, D., García, T., McKeachie, W.: A manual for the use of the motivated strategies questionnaire (MSLQ). Technical report, University of Michigan, National Center for Research to Improve Postsecondary Teaching and Learning, Ann Arbor, MI (1991). https://doi.org/10.13140/RG.2.1.2547.6968
18. Rozencwajg, P.: Metacognitive factors in scientific problem-solving strategies. Eur. J. Psychol. Educ. **18**(3), 281–294 (2003). https://doi.org/10.1007/BF03173249
19. Schoenfeld, A.: Learning to think mathematically: Problem solving, metacognition, and sense making in mathematics. In: Grouws, D.A. (ed.) Handbook for Research on Mathematics Teaching and Learning, pp. 334–370. Macmillan Publishing Co. Inc., New York (1992)
20. Schraw, G., Crippen, K.J., Hartley, K.: Promoting self-regulation in science education: metacognition as part of a broader perspective on learning. Res. Sci. Educ. **36**(1), 111–139 (2006). https://doi.org/10.1007/s11165-005-3917-8
21. Tormey, R., Hardebolle, C., Pinto, F., Jermann, P.: Designing for impact: a conceptual framework for learning analytics as self-assessment tools. Assess. Eval. High. Educ. **45**(6), 901–911 (2020). https://doi.org/10.1080/02602938.2019.1680952
22. Veenman, M.V.J., van Cleef, D.: Measuring metacognitive skills for mathematics: students' self-reports versus on-line assessment methods. ZDM **51**(4), 691–701 (2018). https://doi.org/10.1007/s11858-018-1006-5
23. Veenman, M.V.J., Van Hout-Wolters, B.H.A.M., Afflerbach, P.: Metacognition and learning: conceptual and methodological considerations. Metacogn. Learn. **1**(1), 3–14 (2006). https://doi.org/10.1007/s11409-006-6893-0
24. Verschaffel, L., Depaepe, F., Mevarech, Z.: Learning mathematics in metacognitively oriented ICT-based learning environments: a systematic review of the literature. Educ. Res. Int. **2019** (2019). https://doi.org/10.1155/2019/3402035
25. Viberg, O., Khalil, M., Baars, M.: Self-regulated learning and learning analytics in online learning environments: a review of empirical research. In: ACM International Conference Proceeding Series, pp. 524–533 (2020). https://doi.org/10.1145/3375462.3375483
26. Zohar, A., Barzilai, S.: A review of research on metacognition in science education: current and future directions. Stud. Sci. Educ. **49**(2), 121–169 (2013). https://doi.org/10.1080/03057267.2013.847261
27. Zohar, A., Peled, B.: The effects of explicit teaching of metastrategic knowledge on low- and high-achieving students. Learn. Instr. **18**(4), 337–353 (2008). https://doi.org/10.1016/j.learninstruc.2007.07.001

Medical Students' Perception of a Serious Game (ECOGAME) of Simulating an OSCE Station: Case of Mohammed VI University of Health Sciences (UM6SS)

Marouane Talaa[1(✉)], Mohammed Chahbouni[2], Mounir Sadiq[1], Mohamed Radid[1], and Ghizlane Chemsi[1]

[1] Laboratory of Information and Educational Sciences and Technologies (LASTIE), Faculty of Sciences Ben M'sick, University Hassan II, Casablanca, Morocco
marouane.talaa-etu@etu.univh2c.ma

[2] International Medical Simulation Center, Mohammed VI University of Health Sciences (UM6SS), Casablanca, Morocco

Abstract. The Objective Structured Clinical Examination (OSCE) is a summative and certifying evaluation modality in the health sciences. It is a determining and crucial step in the student's career, which requires the mobilization of knowledge, know-how and interpersonal skills. This generates problems such as time management and decision making during its passage. It is in this perspective that it seems interesting to design a digital simulation tool to reduce the intensity of these problems. To do this, we have designed a serious game (ECOGAME) based on the student's clinical reasoning, which illustrates the passage from a surgical station in an OSCE. Experimentation was conducted with 116 students in the 7th year of medicine, followed by an evaluation of perception using a multidimensional questionnaire. The results show that the majority of students are satisfied with the usefulness and usability of the ECOGAME, and that the latter helped the students to overcome their difficulties during the passage of the station of surgery in the presential.

Keywords: OSCE (objective structured clinical examination) · Serious game · Medical simulation

1 Context of the Study and Problematic

In Morocco, as soon as the first cases of COVID-19 contamination emerged, the Ministery of Health declared a state of health emergency to limit the spread of the virus. As a result, a series of preventive measures have been adopted by the public administration to deal with the risks of the pandemic, indeed, the Ministry of Education has implemented a national plan to ensure continuity of education while preserving everyone's health and safety.This type of teaching is problematic for professional learners in the health field, especially, the assessment and certification of professional skills. This

I. Hilliger et al. (Eds.): EC-TEL 2022, LNCS 13450, pp. 368–378, 2022.
https://doi.org/10.1007/978-3-031-16290-9_27

evaluation has become very difficult to carry out. According to a joint survey by the International Labor Organization (ILO), the United Nations Educational, Scientific and Cultural Organization (UNESCO) and the World Bank (WB), published in May 2020, on Information and Communication Technology "Technical and Vocational Education and Training (TVET) and Skills Development during the time of the COVID-19".Including 1349 respondents from 126 countries, the results show that 90% of respondents reported the total closure of TVET institutions in their country, for various reasons, among, the lack of distance learning infrastructure in general, and the difficulty of evaluating and examining these practical trainings.[1].

As a valid and reliable instrument in this field over the last few decades, the Objective Structured Clinical Examination (OSCE) has been used to assess the skills, clinical competencies, and knowledge of health science students [2, 3], several researchers have investigated its use with students as a summative and/or formative assessment tool [4, 5, 6]; In the era of the Covid-19, e-assessment has taken the relay, this was well illustrated with the use of an e-OSCE, to assess medical students, that has proven to be useful and effective in assessing clinical competence with the exception of physical examination, and procedural skills [7], Hence, it is highly justified to use new technologies to unblock this situation.

To solve this problem, it seems essential to suggest students use a digital device such as a serious game as a simulation tool, and demonstrate how clinical skills and knowledge are evaluated as they are in an objective structured clinical examination (OSCE).

Thus, our problematic aims to answer the following questions:

- Does the use of the serious game as a simulation tool help 7th year medical students to overcome their difficulties encountered during the passage of a given OSCE station in the presential?
- What are the students' perceptions of the serious game developed?

2 Definitions

2.1 Simulation in Health

Generally, health simulation involves using equipment such as a mannequin, procedural simulator, the virtual reality, or a standardized patient, re-creating scenarios, to teach diagnostic and therapeutic procedures, repeat processes, and medical concepts and make decisions.

2.2 Approaches to Simulation in Health

According to Gilles Chiniara, various approaches of simulations include organic simulations of humans and animals, as well as non-organic simulations made up of basic, medium and/or high-fidelity mannequins, simulations involving the virtuel reality, serious games, computer-assisted simulators, etc. (Fig. 1).

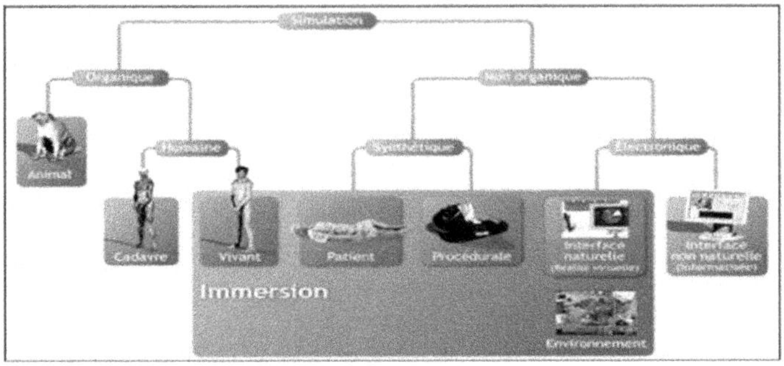

Fig. 1. Approaches to simulation in health according to (G. Chiniara, 2007).

2.3 Serious Games

According to Julian Alvarez a serious game is a computer application, whose initial intention is to combine with coherence both utilitarian aspects (Serious), such as, in a non-exhaustive and non-exclusive way, teaching, learning, communication or even information, with playful springs from the video game [8].

In fact, serious games, are the most commonly popular in the training of health professionals, and their educational effectiveness has been confirmed by several studies [9], through the total immersion they provide by using augmented reality, virtual reality, etc. Pamela B. Andreatta et al.,(2006) indicate, that virtual reality facilitates clinical medicine training in multiple settings [10], Furthermore, the virtual patient, which is a case-based computer program that combines textual information with multimedia elements such as audio, graphics and animation [11], it is increasingly used as a teaching modality by medical educators in various teaching areas, becoming a new method of training health care providers in clinical and communication skills over the past decade [12].

2.4 The Objective Structured Clinical Examination

The concept of the Objective Structured Clinical Examination (OSCE) was first proposed in 1979 by Professor Ronald Harden of the University of Dundee, Scotland, in a document entitled: Assessment of clinical competence using an objective structured clinical examination (OSCE) [13]. It is defined as an approach to the assessment of clinical competence in which the components of competence are assessed in a planned or structured way with attention being paid to the examinations [14], currently considered one of the best modalities, for assessing the clinical competence of medical students [15].

3 Methods

As mentioned before, this research is to design and evaluate students' perceptions of a serious game (ECOGAME), the latter allows to illustrate the passage of a station during an objective structured clinical examination (OSCE). In this section, we present the approach taken, the area of study, the target audience, and the data collection and processing techniques.

3.1 Design and Gameplay

The progression of the scenes of our serious game is based on the clinical reasoning, of the student in front of an acute abdominal pain, according to a pedagogical scenario developed by the pedagogical committee of the Faculty of Medicine of the UM6SS. This, reflects the passage of the surgery station in the presential. The experiment begins by entering the session password, to view the game rules and the clinical case vignette, a time limit of 10 min was set to complete the game (similar duration of time allocated to such a station in reality). The avatar represents a doctor who plays the role of the evaluator in a medical office that receives the evaluated student. The student should follow a clinical reasoning by answering six questions, the answer to the first question of which, will depend on the second and so on (Fig. 2). Each question is followed by a feedback, according to the answer. In case of a correct answer the student receives a reward in the form of points with positive feedback. In case of a wrong answer the student receives an encouraging feedback with negative points (Fig. 3, 4). In the game the avatar helps the student (two times), if he perceives that the student is following good clinical reasoning. At the end of the game, the screen displays to the student the score obtained and the percentage of reasoning of the clinical situation studied. (Fig. 5).

The game was designed using the software Virtual Training Suite (VTS Editor, version 5.0). It is a publisher of simulators and design of pedagogical content such as serious games, e-learning modules, or any other type of digital learning.

Fig. 2. Serious game environment.

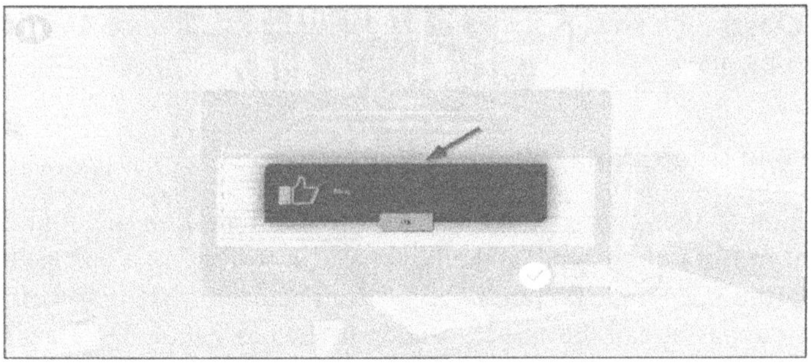

Fig. 3. Feed-back Positive.

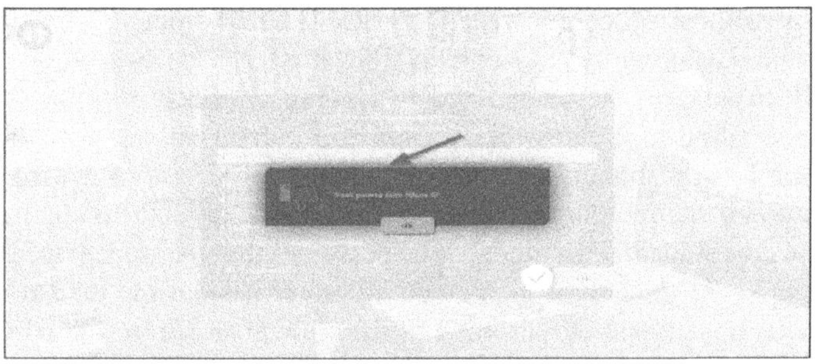

Fig. 4. Feed-back of encouragement.

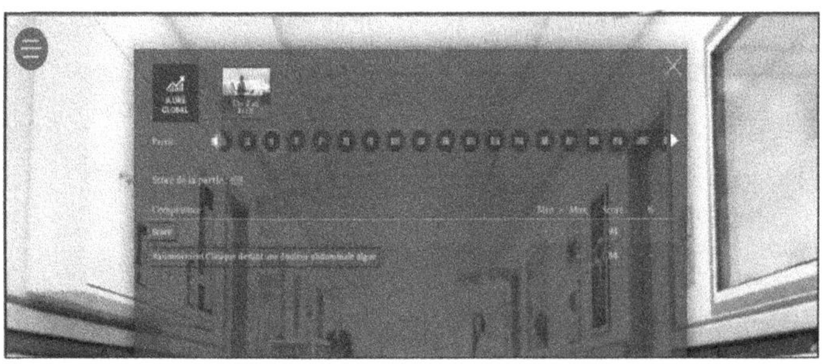

Fig. 5. Score and percentage of clinical reasoning.

3.2 The Area of Study and Sample

This experiment was conducted by 116 students registered in the 7th year of medicine at Mohammed VI University of Health Sciences (UM6SS) in Casablanca, during the 2020–2021 academic year, in the international medical simulation center (IMSC).

3.3 The Measuring Instrument and Data Collection

In order to assess the students' perception of gambling we elaborated a multidimensional questionnaire, four dimensions characterize our questionnaire.

- Use of video games / serious games.
- Facility of use.
- Perceived usefulness.
- Satisfaction with the game

Before the experimentation of the serious game ECOGAME, we asked the student volunteers to test the forecast version of our game. Hege Mari Johnsen et al., (2016) in their study, point to the importance of conducting an evaluation of the usability during the development process of the serious game. The students who voluntarily presented themselves for the pre-test were 11 students. Thus, we have identified the following elements as points of adjustment to the serious game ECOGAME.

- Display the clinical case vignette as a slide, not on a single page.
- Introduce and explain the rules of the game before starting.
- Implementing a reward system for each question.

The respect of ethical aspects is taken into consideration. Participation in this study is voluntary and the informed consent of the students is obtained after explanation of the purpose and interest of the study, as well as the respect of anonymity. The questionnaire was developed with Google Forms, and distributed on March 10, 2021 just after the experimentation of the ECOGAME.

3.4 Presentation and Analysis of Results

Among the 156 registered in the 7th year of medicine at UM6SS for the 2020/2021 academic year, 116 students voluntarily participated in this study with an average age of 24 years, of which 58.6% were girls and 41.4% boys.

1. Using serious games (Figs. 6, 7 and 8):

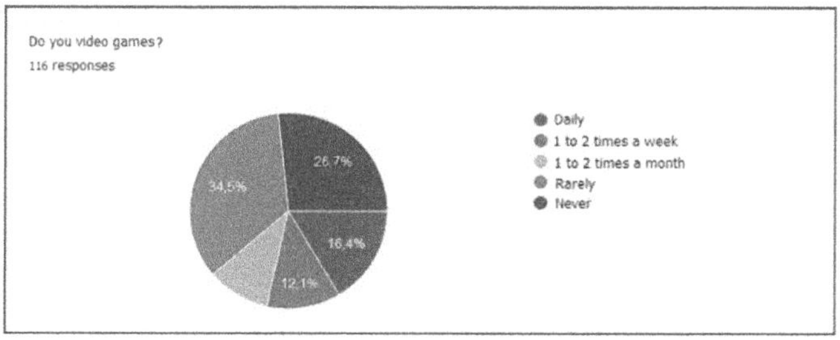

Fig. 6. Cadence of student use of video games.

From the standpoint of cadence of student use of video games, more than half do not playing video games, with only 16.4% and 12% respectively playing daily, once to twice a week.

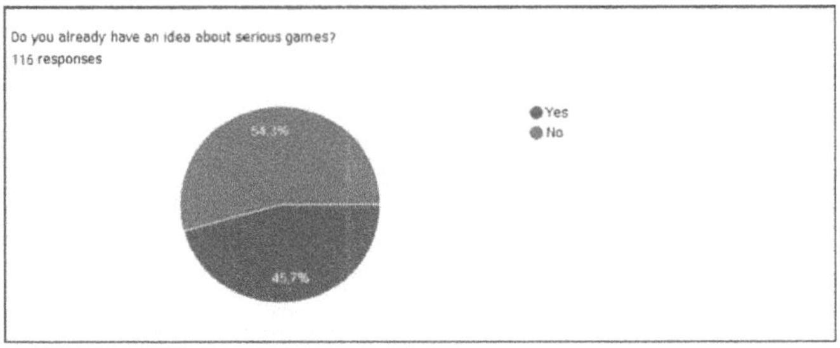

Fig. 7. Degree of student knowledge by-report serious games.

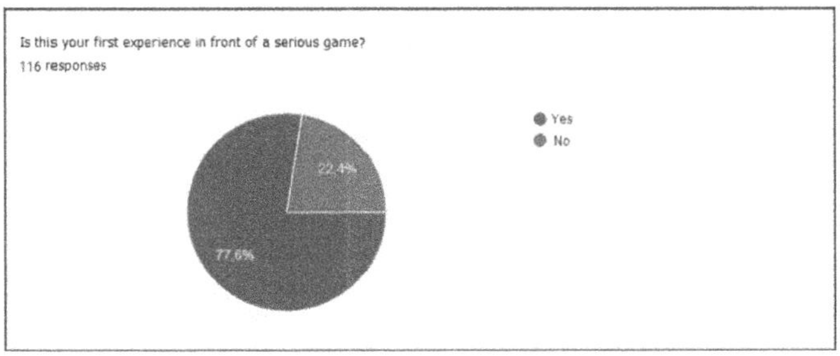

Fig. 8. Degree of student use of serious games.

Only half of students interviewed said they had an idea about serious games, and nearly 80% of students, reported that ECOGAME was their first experience with a serious game.

2. Facility of use (Fig. 9):

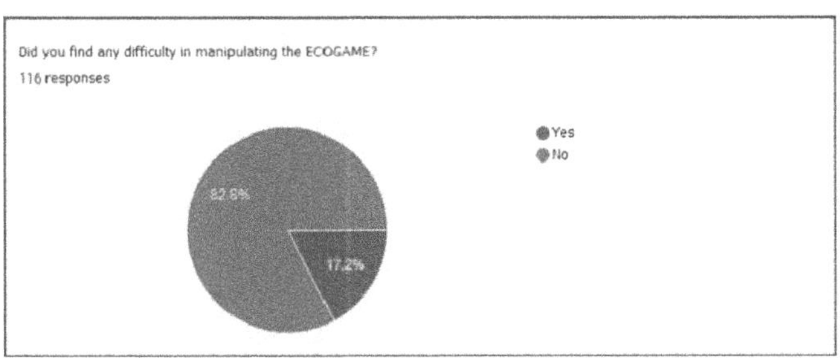

Fig. 9. Degree of difficulty of manipulation the students of the (ECOGAME).

Regarding the facility of use of the game by the students, 82.8% of the students stated that they did not find any difficulties in manipulating the ECOGAME, and only 17.2% who found difficulties (Figs. 10 and 11).

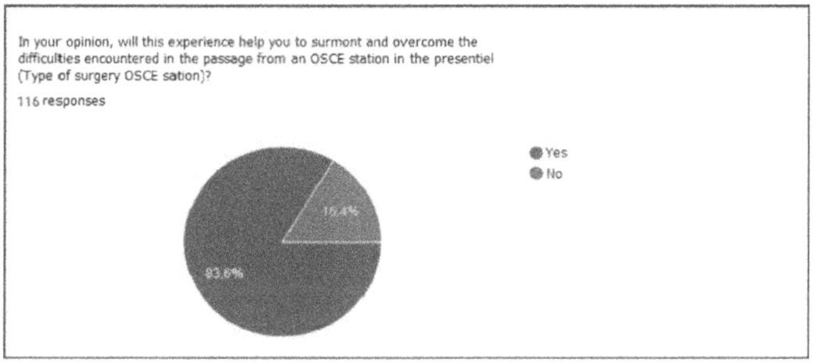

Fig. 10. Effect of the experience with ECOGAME on the presential passageof the OSCE station students.

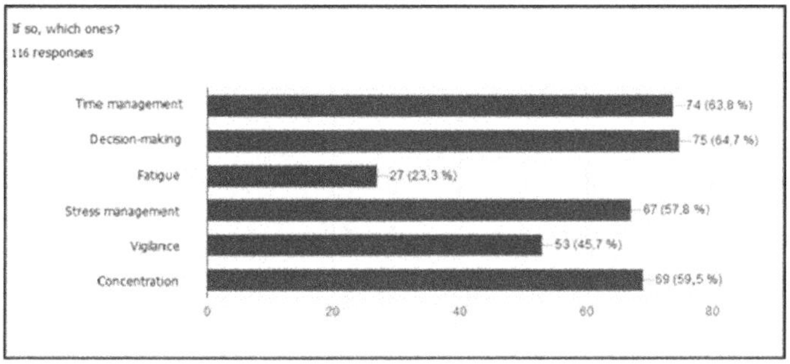

Fig. 11. Percentage of students' difficulties overcome with the ECOGAME experience.

Regarding the perceived usefulness of the ECOGAME. 83.6% of the students, find that their experience with the ECOGAME, help them overcome the difficulties encountered during the passage of an OSCE surgery station in the presential. Thus, the students, declared that the game allowed them to overcome problems, such as, decision making, time management, stress management with a percentage respectively 64.7%, 63.8%, 57.8%.

Also, the students declare that this experience helps to overcome the problems of concentration, vigilance and fatigue with a percentage respectively 59.5%, 45.7%, 23.3%. While 16.4% of the students said that the ECOGAME game not helps to overcome these difficulties.

3.5 Satisfaction with the game.

In this regard, we used the Likert scale to acquire the students' perceptions towards ECOGAME on three elements (Table1), which reflected the environment of passing

Table 1. Student satisfaction according to the Likert scale.

	Not at all satisfied	Not satisfied	Satisfied	Completely satisfied
The game environment	–	–	50%	45,7%
The character	–	–	46,6%	47,7%
The design	–	–	51,7%	44,8%

such OSCE station in the presential, which are: the game environment, the character used, and the design.

- From the table, we see that there is general satisfaction with these three elements.

4 Discussions

This study is conducted at the international medical simulation center (IMSC) at the Mohammed VI University of Health Sciences (UM6SS) in Casablanca, and aims to study students' perceptions of ECOGAME.

Our survey results show that students expressed their satisfaction with the serious game, its relevance and perceived usefulness, these results corroborate previous studies [16] [17], which indicated that students can gain responsibility for decision making by using serious games, as well as the consolidation of knowledge. In addition, the study by Mary EW Dankbaar et al., (2017) demonstrated that a serious game about emergency care had a positive effect on residents' complex cognitive skills, indicating that they may have felt stress in the game, the point that influenced on their final scores of positive way [18]. Moreover, students stated that ECOGAME helps manage the time allocated to the surgical OSCE station by 63.8% of students, as well as concentration, alertness and fatigue of 59.5%, 45.7%, 23.3% respectively. These results appeared very motivating and encouraging having read Alice Germa et al.'s (2020) study demonstrating that a serious game for training in OSCE, capable of improving the time management skills, and anxiety of students in the 4th and 5th years of dental education, related to OSCE, respectively of 65% and 60% [19].

In addition, students expressed satisfaction with the game environment, the design, and the character, as well as the ease of manipulation the game. Similarly, Fonseca et al., (2015) state that students highly appreciated the serious game for its, easy use at any time, its didactic design that gives access to feedback based on their actions, mistakes and its motivational power by encouraging them to be active and autonomous in their learning, in order to improve their skills and build new knowledge [20].

We think that the use of serious games as tools for simulating the passage of OSCE, will have a great acceptance among students in 7th year of medicine.

5 Limitations

The design of the serious game was limited to a single OSCE station; therefore, the results obtained cannot be generalized until the serious game is used in an entire OSCE, despite the overall satisfaction with the game. Also, only motivated students who volunteered to participate in the study, the point that will also can influence on the feedback with ECOGAME.

6 Conclusion

This study, conducted at the international medical simulation center at the Mohammed VI University of Health Sciences in Casablanca, Its aims to design and study the perception of students in 7th year of medicine towards a serious game.

The main results show that the serious game ECOGAME designed was satisfactory, usable and useful. And this simulation tool can help overcome cognitive difficulties encountered during the passage of the OSCE in the presential.

In the continuity of the present research we plan to carry out a study with a fairly large number of participants this time, based on the correlations that existed in the dimensions used previously, and compared to the results of the research with a control group that used virtual patient simulator (VPS), in the clinical reasoning of medical students.

1. References

1. ILO-UNESCO-WBG Joint Survey on Technical and Vocational Education and Training (TVET) and Skills Development during the time of COVID-19
2. Khan, K.Z., et al.: The objective structured clinical examination (OSCE): AMEE guide no 81. Part I: an historical and theoretical perspective. Med. Teach. **35**(9), e1437–e2146 (2013). https://doi.org/10.3109/0142159X.2013.818634
3. Sloan, D.A., Donnelly, M.B., Schwartz, R.W., Strodel, W.E.: The objective structured clinical examination. The new gold standard for evaluating postgraduate clinical performance. Ann. Surg. **222**, 735 (1995). https://doi.org/10.1097/00000658-199512000-00007
4. Townsend, A.H., Mcllvenny, S., Miller, C.J., Dunn, E.V.: The use of an objective structured clinical examination (OSCE) for formative and summative assessment in a general practice clinical attachment and its relationship to final medical school examination performance. Med. Educ. **35**, 841–846 (2001). https://doi.org/10.1046/J.1365-2923.2001.00957.X
5. Lien, H.H., Hsu, S.F., Chen, S.C., Yeh, J.H.: Can teaching hospitals use serial formative OSCEs to improve student performance? BMC Res. Notes. **9**, 1–6 (2016). https://doi.org/10.1186/s13104-016-2266-1
6. Lee, M.H.M., Phua, D.H., Heng, K.W.J.: The use of a formative OSCE to prepare emergency medicine residents for summative OSCEs: a mixed-methods cohort study. Int. J. Emerg. Med. **14**, 1–8 (2021). https://doi.org/10.1186/s12245-021-00383-4
7. Shorbagi, S., et al.: Assessing the utility and efficacy of e-OSCE among undergraduate medical students during the COVID-19 pandemic. BMC Med. Educ. **22**, 156 (2022). https://doi.org/10.1186/S12909-022-03218-9
8. Alvarez, J.: Du jeu vidéo au serious game: approches culturelle, pragmatique et formelle (2007)

9. Graafland, M., Schraagen, J.M., Schijven, M.P.: Systematic review of serious games for medical education and surgical skills training. Br. J. Surg. **99**, 1322–1330 (2012). https://doi.org/10.1002/BJS.8819
10. Andreatta, P.B., et al.: Laparoscopic skills are improved with LapMentor^{TM} training: results of a randomized. Double-Blinded Study. Ann. Surg. **243**, 854 (2006). https://doi.org/10.1097/01.SLA.0000219641.79092.E5
11. Tan, Z.S., Mulhausen, P.L., Smith, S.R., Ruiz, J.G.: Virtual patients in geriatric education. Gerontol. Geriatr Educ. **31**, 163–173 (2010). https://doi.org/10.1080/02701961003795813
12. da Silva, D.T., et al.: Using virtual patient software to improve pharmacy students' knowledge of and attitudes toward geriatric patients. Am. J. Pharm. Educ. **84**, 561–571 (2020). https://doi.org/10.5688/AJPE7230
13. Harden, R.M.G., Downie, W.W., Stevenson, M., Wilson, G.M.: Assessment of clinical competence using objective structured examination. Br Med J. **1**, 447–451 (1975). https://doi.org/10.1136/BMJ.1.5955.447
14. Harden, R.M.: What is an OSCE? Med. Teach. **10**(1), 19–22 (1988). https://doi.org/10.3109/01421598809019321
15. Norcini, J.J., McKinley, D.W.: Assessment methods in medical education. Teach. Teach. Educ. **23**(3), 239–250 (2007). https://doi.org/10.1016/j.tate.2006.12.021
16. Stefan, I.A., Hauge, J.B., Hasse, F., Stefan, A.: Using serious games and simulations for teaching co-operative decision-making. Procedia Comput. Sci. **162**, 745–753 (2019). https://doi.org/10.1016/J.PROCS.2019.12.046
17. Vallefuoco, E., Mele, M., Pepino, A.: A Serious game to support decision making in medical education. In: Cristani, M., Prati, A., Lanz, O., Messelodi, S., Sebe, N. (eds.) ICIAP 2019. LNCS, vol. 11808, pp. 237–243. Springer, Cham (2019). https://doi.org/10.1007/978-3-030-30754-7_24
18. Dankbaar, M.E.W., et al.: Preparing residents effectively in emergency skills training with a serious game. Simul. Healthc. **12**, 9 (2017). https://doi.org/10.1097/SIH.0000000000000194
19. Germa, A., et al.: OSCEGame: a serious game for OSCE training. Eur. J. Dent. Educ. **25**, 657–663 (2021). https://doi.org/10.1111/EJE.12643
20. Fonseca, L.M.M., Aredes, N.D.A., Dias, D.M.V., Scochi, C.G.S., Martins, J.C.A., Rodrigues, M.A.: Serious game e-Baby: nursing students' perception on learning about preterm newborn clinical assessment. Rev. Bras. Enferm. **68**, 13–19 (2015). https://doi.org/10.1590/0034-7167.2015680102P

Integrating Digital Learning Resources in Classroom Teaching: Effects on Teaching Practices and Student Perceptions

Kairit Tammets[1(✉)], Edna Milena Sarmiento-Márquez[1], Manisha Khulbe[1], Mart Laanpere[1], and Tobias Ley[2]

[1] Tallinn University, Tallinn, Estonia
kairit.tammets@tlu.ee
[2] Danube University Krems, Krems an der Donau, Austria

Abstract. During recent decades, technologies have been widely available for educational institutions, being just one step in the long process of adoption and integration. Despite the number of studies focusing on the adoption of technologies in education, they often focus on teachers' perspectives, leaving out students' perceptions. Given that student learning is the cornerstone of technology-enhanced learning, this oversight is a serious drawback in promoting fruitful integration of technology in education. In this paper, we have tracked the use of over 6000 digital learning resources in the authentic setting of secondary schools in Estonia. Using qualitative analysis of open answers by teachers about their teaching practices and a structural equation modelling of school students' reactions to these teaching practices, we uncovered several influencing factors of students' perceived usefulness and experiences of using Digital Learning Resources (DLRs). Results show that similar to teachers, the use of DLRs presents students with new challenges that they need to adapt to in their learning.

Keywords: Digital learning resource · Adoption of technology · Learning design

1 Introduction

Across the world, governments have developed guiding policies to support efficient digital innovation and successful implementation of digital technologies at the school [32]. Investment in teacher training, teachers' digital competence, and access to digital learning resources (DLRs) have increased. It is also already well established that the way technology is blended into teaching and learning practices is crucial for ensuring that its use can lead to better student outcomes [1]. Quite often, increased access to technology does not change teaching and learning fundamentally, and learning gains remain unimpressive [2]. The evidence of the impact of technology-enhanced learning practices on students' learning is ambiguous, reported successes of implementing digital innovation at schools are often small-scale [3], not always sustainable [4] and frequently, learning technologies are used to replicate existing practices in school [5] instead of changing education more fundamentally [6]. OECD results indicate that although students who

I. Hilliger et al. (Eds.): EC-TEL 2022, LNCS 13450, pp. 379–392, 2022.
https://doi.org/10.1007/978-3-031-16290-9_28

use digital technologies at school often have better learning outcomes compared to students who use technologies infrequently, students who use digital learning technologies at school very frequently perform significantly worse at most of the included learning outcome measures [19]. However, these findings do not provide evidence on how learning technologies are integrated into teaching-learning.

It is evident that making technology available for educational institutions is just one from several aspects, as the adoption of such innovation depends on different individual and organisational aspects [7]. Research has shown that students' experiences with new technologies are dependent on the choices teachers make about the technologies, which in turn reflect teachers' skills, pedagogical values, philosophies, and curriculum approaches [8]. It is quite clear that the way teachers are integrating learning technologies and especially DLRs into their pedagogical practice will have an impact on students' learning experiences. Teachers' technology-related teaching skills are closely linked to multifaceted and complex technology-enriched learning activities [33]. There is evidence that teachers, on the other hand, need support and training to create meaningful learning designs (LD) to uncover the potential of learning technologies impacting student learning [9]. This is particularly important if a textbook, which usually gives clear guidance to teachers on how to teach, is replaced by DLRs which are usually more flexible in their application.

There have been studies focusing on the adoption of technologies in the classroom from teachers' perspective, but there is still much we do not fully understand about secondary education students' experiences when introducing new technologies in teaching and learning [11]. Though the students already exhibited some behaviours which can be productive for learning (e.g., easiness using digital tools), it has been argued that teachers fail to provide a technology-rich environment that can foster students' engaging experiences with digital learning technologies [32].

This study is motivated by an understanding of how students experience when teachers introduce new technologies in the learning process. Based on a national-level initiative to launch DLRs we analyse teachers' practices and students' experiences to answer the following research questions: RQ1. How did teachers adopt the DLRs in their pedagogical practices?; RQ2. How did teachers' pedagogical practices impacted students' perceived experience with DLRs in the learning process?

2 Theoretical Underpinnings of DLR Implementation

Learning in a digitally-enhanced environment means that the teacher uses learning technologies to foster students' learning through a variety of (personalised) instructional methods, challenging content, and feedback through formative assessment to ensure all students reach their potential [12]. One of the technologies that has great potential to transform student learning experiences is DLRs (e.g., e-textbooks, interactive materials, digital tasks). DLRs have become an essential part of learning environments where teachers and students work together [13].

There is no universally accepted definition of DLRs, synonyms used to describe the practices of learning with digital content: digital textbooks, e-textbooks, digital learning materials, digital learning resources, open educational resources, digital learning objects, etc. A spectrum of characteristics has been proposed by different authors and initiatives to describe these concepts technically or instructionally. The efficient implementation of DLRs in teaching and learning could be seen from two perspectives: First, it is important to consider how the tasks are designed and whether they activate students' thinking (the instructional design aspect). Second, no matter how tasks are designed, teachers have multiple options in terms of the pedagogical approach the tasks are embedded in (learning design aspect).

Concerning instructional design, DLRs could follow a behaviourist approach - for effective learning one needs appropriately presented material to initiate the desired responses [14]. From the cognitive perspective, instructional design approaches could be followed by emphasising the importance of learning by employing whole problems to avoid fragmentation and encourage the integration of knowledge, skills, and attitudes [15]. From a constructivist perspective, a learning object is a resource to mediate learning activity leading to learning outcomes while students' knowledge is constructed, transformed, and applied through active engagement [16].

The second aspect, how the teacher implements the design, is as important as the design of the task. Currently, teacher-centred lessons dominate and often aim at knowledge transmission and promote mere rote learning, but educational practices should enhance active learning by emphasising the interest, motivation, and engagement of the learners [17]. The way teachers integrate DLRs into practice, by taking into account subject-related aspects, and an understanding of how students learn, can fulfil the potential of DLRs in teaching and learning [18]. Some of the authors have proposed using the ICAP framework [34] as a systematic approach to differentiate the levels of students' cognitive engagement while interacting with digital technologies. Despite the trend for teachers' pedagogical practices to become more diverse, passive learning approaches are fostered more often compared to approaches in which learners are active, constructive, and interactive [35].

Evidence regarding the effects of technology use on student outcomes, however, paints a rather sobering picture. For example, on analysing the relationship between students' access to technology and their results on PISA tests, it was found that students without access to computers in mathematics class achieved better results on both the paper- and computer-based assessments [19]. One reason for this discrepancy between prediction and reality is that the fields of educational technology, educational research, and educational practice have largely remained detached from each other [20]. Teachers, confronted with rapidly changing technology for the classroom, but supplied with very little guidance about its use, and insufficient time to experiment with it, either resist change or adopt technology only to use it in ways they are already accustomed to, treating it as merely a substitute for conventional resources and methods [21]. National-level investments can ensure that teachers have access to high-quality DLRs based on the national curriculum. However, the pedagogical design of the materials and knowledge practices around learning technologies are decisive in deciding whether students benefit from the technology or not. The aim of the present study is therefore to uncover teacher practices around DLRs and to find out how students experience the usage of these resources.

3 Research Design

3.1 Research Context

This study reflects experiences from the national level piloting experience of DLRs in Estonian secondary schools. Estonia is well-known for its educational innovation and widespread implementation of technologies for teaching and learning [10]. The education system of Estonia is decentralised and teachers have autonomy in deciding how to deliver educational content to achieve set learning outcomes. The nationally implemented Digital Turn program was a strategy to provide Estonian schools with DLRs, providing teachers with a variety of ways to enrich the learning process [10].

During the project's lifespan, the team of Estonian researchers, didactics, and practising teachers from different subjects developed nearly 6000 tasks to cover the national curriculum. The instructional design of the DLRs was based on Merrills' task-centred instructional design model [15]. According to this model, DLRs should be designed at different levels which enable students to be engaged in solving real-world problems, and activate existing knowledge as a foundation for new learning, new knowledge is demonstrated to the learner, can be applied by the learner, and is integrated into the learner's world. Based on this model, tasks were developed inspired by four different types of instructional interaction (Tell, Show, Ask and Do). The technical infrastructure for authoring and storing DLRs was built on Drupal Content Management System enhanced with H5P module, allowing easy generation of interactive DLRs from HTML5 templates. It enabled the teachers to use more than 40 different types of interactive resources (e.g. multiple-choice, fill-in-the-blanks, drag-and-drop, interactive video) in line with selected LDs and make the finalised resources available to all interested users through the national repository called eKoolikott.

LD - plans laying out instructional activities and experiences - for implementing the DLRs were created by the project team to foster the effective combination of teacher practices, DLRs, and students' practices. Instead of using DLRs to replace textbooks, teachers were guided to implement Student-Centred Learning (SCL) LDs created by the teachers, researchers, and didactics to fulfil the potential of the developed DLRs. The following scenarios were designed: (a) **Flipped Classroom.** Before the lesson, the student gets familiar with the basic concepts using DLRs suggested, and in class, they apply new knowledge in solving vital problem situations; (b) **Project-based learning.** Students in groups work on different activities, some of which require individual work with the DLRs to produce the collaborative outcome of the project; (c) **Task-based learning.** Students solve increasingly complex tasks while learning a new topic, relying on DLRs. Once the tasks given by the teacher have been solved, the students themselves work in pairs to create new tasks and give them to other students to solve. (d) **Game-based learning.** Students participate in a game with predefined rules the aim of which is to find and apply new knowledge while solving tasks. Some of the tasks are created by the students themselves and most of the tasks require the answer to be provided as a digital artefact. Before the piloting phase, teachers received a short training (4 h) to understand the pedagogical ideas behind the DLRs and innovative learning scenarios, technical aspects of DLR use, and the possibilities of mixing the DLRs and re-designing learning scenarios. Each teacher was asked to pilot the DLRs in their class at least three times during one month.

3.2 Sampling, Data Collection, and Analysis

Teachers were recruited voluntarily to pilot the developed DLRs through an open call for participation among Estonian secondary schools. 21 teachers from 17 schools applied: 8 for mathematics, 7 for science, 4 for social sciences, and 2 for music and art. They piloted the DLRs with their students from grades 10 and 11. Altogether, data was collected from 1200 students in the piloting phase. Once the data quality was checked, we analysed the data of 683 students and 21 teachers. A mixed methods research was carried out:

Teachers' Reflections. To understand how teachers employed DLRs (i.e., using different instructional strategies), we asked them to fill a report after each piloted lesson describing how they designed classroom activities. Teachers' reflections were coded independently through thematic analysis by two of the authors of the paper. A second iteration in the data analysis included two authors discussing the themes and categories until reaching an agreement.

Students' Questionnaire. After the piloting experience, students filled a web-based survey including questions related to (a) demographic information (gender, grade, age); (b) earlier experience with DLRs and other TEL practices; (c) piloting experience (pedagogical approach) with DLRs and perceived usefulness; (d) challenges experienced in the process (open-ended questions).

Open-Ended Questions. A thematic analysis was made to analyse the challenges that students experienced while using the DLRs. Two of the authors read and coded the dataset to identify whether and how students struggled with DLR use. Then both authors reviewed and discussed the codes until reaching agreement.

Likert-Scale Questions. These items required students to rate their agreement with given statements on a scale of 1 to 5 (e.g., I liked the way the teacher organised the testing of DLRs). We used SPSS version 21.0 to extract the underlying factors through an exploratory factor analysis, with Principal Component Analysis and Varimax with Kaiser Normalisation for both sets of items (the first one regarding the context of the use of different technological devices and the second regarding students' attitudes towards the use of technology in the classroom). Missing data were treated through pairwise analysis. The analysis returned a 20-factor solution (12 factors for the first set of items and 8 for the second), explaining 65 and 64% of the variance (respectively). Coherently with our interest to uncover different teacher practices in the use of DLRs, we grouped these factors into teacher-led practices and student-centred ones. In each of these, we also included factors that addressed earlier experiences with these teaching strategies. Moreover, we added two factors related to student experiences (perceived satisfaction and perceived usefulness):

Teacher-led practices (during piloting and earlier):

- **Teacher-instructed piloting experience:** describes students' experience of using DLRs only according to teachers' instructions.
- **Individual DLR piloting practices at school:** describes the usage of DLRs during the piloting by the students individually.
- **Teacher-initiated earlier usage of DLRs:** describes students' earlier experiences of DLR use and information retrieval after teachers' instructions.

Student-centred practices (during piloting and earlier):

- **Collaborative and student-initiated instructional piloting experience:** describes the usage of DLRs during the piloting in groups or pairs, but students' own initiated usage of DLRs at home was also loaded here.
- **Students' earlier experience with TEL practices:** describes students' earlier experience such as searching for information and materials from the web on their own or teachers' initiative and solving e-tests.
- **Students' earlier experiences with DLRs:** describes items regarding students' earlier experience of using DLRs for learning and their habit of searching for relevant DLRs on their initiative.

Effects on the student experience

- **Perceived satisfaction of piloting:** describes the students' satisfaction with the quality of DLRs, level of the difficulty of the DLRs, and the instructional practices implemented by the teacher around the DLRs.
- **Perceived usefulness of DLRs:** describes the students' willingness to use the DLRs in the future, wish that DLRs will be used again in the future by their teacher, and perception that DLRs help them to learn better, organise learning flexibly, and learn new topics faster on their own.

Once we chose the variables for this study, we modelled them through Partial Least Squares (PLS) analysis, in SmartPLS 3.0 software. We used it as a tool for formative measurement of the latent variables due to the exploratory nature of this study [22]. PLS-based Structural Equation Modelling (SEM) is a frequently used technique for estimating path coefficients in structural models [22]. We built a Reflective Model, tested the measurement model (validity and reliability of the measures), and examined the structural model [22, 23]. We tested the significance of the path coefficients, loadings, and hypotheses through a bootstrapping method (10000 resamples) at the 5% significance level [22]. In line with the research questions above, we assumed that the organisation of the instruction would be an important predictor of the students' experience in using DLRs (see structural model in this analysis in Fig. 1). However, no further assumptions were made about specific and differential effects.

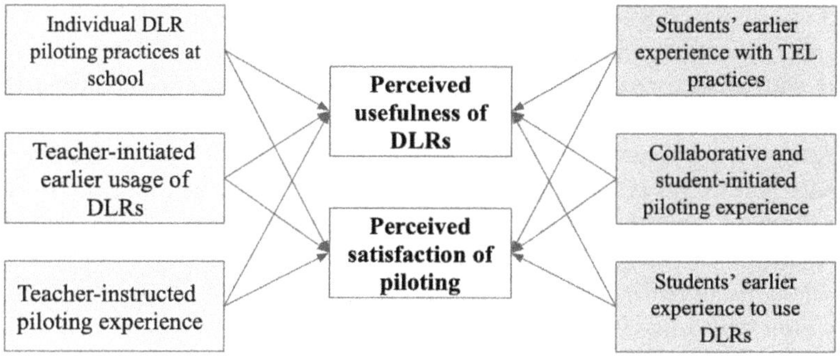

Fig. 1. Hypothetical model.

4 Results

4.1 Adoption of DLRs into Pedagogical Practices

21 teachers piloted the DLRs during two months in 196 lessons in art and music, 60 in history, 41 in natural sciences, and 76 in mathematics. The granularity of these resources varied significantly, covering activities from 10 min (in arts) to 90 min (in maths and science). Analysis of teachers' descriptions of LDs indicated that although they participated in training regarding how to design SCL with the support of DLRs, 90% of the LDs simply replaced textbooks with DLRs, and the potential to activate students through SCL practices remained underused.

For instance, in all the domains (arts and music, natural sciences, mathematics, and social sciences), the majority of teachers used a similar instructional approach: first, they introduced the new topic, after that students interacted with DLRs, and finally, students solved tasks individually or sometimes in pairs (e.g. example from art teacher: "*Initially, I introduced the topic on the basis of my own slides, then I let the students read the DLRs, they performed the tasks and finally they analysed the painting*"). History teachers tended to mainly watch historical resources (videos, film clips), followed by individual work with DLRs to analyse, reflect and make connections with the content of the video material ("*We watched together the material on the screen and discussed it, students read the two materials independently and solved one self-assessment test*"). In itself, it is good practice to guide students to work with historical resources, but behind these materials and LDs also lay the potential to guide students to synthesise knowledge and solve problems. Mathematics teachers especially reported the usage of DLRs for individual solving of tasks in school during the lesson and also, sometimes, at home ("*We had a repetition lesson before the test with the DLRs*"). This may come from the fact that maths, by its very nature, is quite drill and practice-oriented, and much of the material allowed for this pattern of use. A similar trend was also observed in the natural sciences, where the dominant instructional practice was frontal teaching. For instance, the teacher introduced a new topic (often presenting DLRs on the screen), followed by the students' individual work with the DLRs and a joint discussion ("*Individual work in a computer [assisted] class: getting acquainted with a new topic and repeating what has been learned before*").

Next, we analysed in-depth the 10% of the LDs that integrated SCL elements. For instance, one science teacher asked students to work with the DLRs in pairs, debate the strengths and weaknesses of certain aspects of energy resources and come up with a joint poster introducing resources with their benefits and disadvantages. Task-based or problem-based learning scenarios were also designed by some science teachers ((“*Students had to get acquainted with the world's forest types and deforestation as a global problem, and the world's forests and their importance. Each student had to prepare multiple-choice questions on each topic. At the end of the lesson, we answered the questions prepared by the students together*”); (“*At first students got acquainted with the topic and solved the tasks by the river outside, after getting acquainted with the environmental topics, the students went to the school surroundings by the river and answered questions about the environmental topic at a selected point*”)). One history teacher also attempted to engage students in debate, she started the lesson by introducing a new topic, then used DLRs to enhance students' oral argumentation skills by encouraging panel discussions, and at the end of the class students individually repeated what they had learned during the class with the support of DLRs.

It can be concluded that a majority of the 21 teachers mainly perceived DLRs as materials that could support traditional textbooks, which just provides additional advantages such as different types of media (video materials e.g.), level of interaction, and instant feedback for the students. Novel DLRs were used for traditional purposes such as learning new topics, preparing for tests, and repetition and validation. Despite the training and the possibility to redesign and adapt the LDs and DLRs, teachers did not use this opportunity.

4.2 The Impact of Pedagogical Practices on Students' Perceived Experiences

This section reports the test results for the measurement and the structural model.

Measurement Model. We assessed the measurement model through several measures. All factor loadings exceeded the threshold of 0.6 [24]. The Variance Inflation Factor (VIF) statistics (to assess multicollinearity) of the indicators were below five (5) [25]. The Cronbach's alpha and Composite Reliability (CR) were within the accepted range of 0.7–0.95 [22], while the convergent validity of the items, based on the average variance extracted (AVE) measures, was above 0.5. We assessed discriminant validity through the analysis of cross-loadings, the Forner-Lacker criterion, and the heterotrait-monotrait (HTMT) criterion [27]. Regarding cross-loadings, all the items' outer loadings were greater on their respective constructs than their cross-loadings on other constructs [28]. We established discriminant validity through the assessment of the Fornell-Larcker criterion observing that the square root of the AVE of each construct was higher than its correlation with other constructs [28]. The assessment of HTMT shows values lower than 0.90 indicating a satisfactory discriminant validity [27]. All the aforementioned measures and descriptives are available in a live hyperlink[1].

Structural Model Evaluation. To assess the hypothesised relationships we considered the following criteria:

[1] https://bit.ly/MeasurementModel1.

Model Fit. We established a model fit through an acceptable Standardised Root Mean Square Residual (0.085) [29] and confirmed that the original value of d_ULS (i.e., the squared Euclidean distance) and d_G (i.e., the geodesic distance) is smaller than the upper bound of the bootstrap confidence interval [30].

Goodness of Fit (MOdel's Predictive Capabilities). We assessed the coefficient of determination (R^2), beta, corresponding t-values, and statistical significance (p) via bootstrapping procedure. We also assessed the predictive relevance through effect sizes (f^2) [26][2]. Results showed an R^2 value of 0.182 ($p = 0$) for the outcome variable "Perceived usefulness of DLRs", demonstrating a moderate percentage of variance explained by the model (18.2%) and 0.121 for the outcome variable "Perceived satisfaction of piloting", showing a weak percentage of variance explained by the model (12.1%) [31]. We obtained a small but significant contribution of the variables whose hypotheses were confirmed [31]. The bootstrap results are illustrated in Fig. 2 and available online[3].

Path Analysis. According to Fig. 2, the perceived usefulness of DLRs (3.1) was positively (and significantly) impacted by all of the student-centred approach variables (2.1, 2.2, and 2.3), and the individual piloting of DLRs at school (1.1, traditional approach). Yet, the teacher-initiated usage of DLRs (1.2) and teacher-instructed piloting experience (1.3) had a negative but non statistically significant effect on the perceived usefulness.

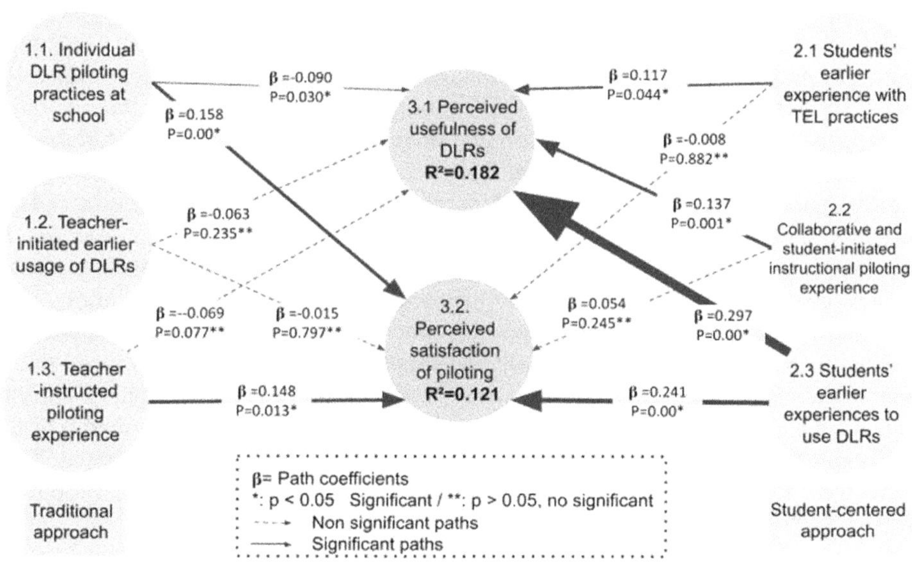

Fig. 2. Structural model with statistics

Moreover, the Students' earlier experiences using DLRs (2.3), Individual DLR piloting practices at school (1.1), and Teacher -instructed piloting experience (1.3) had a

[2] https://bit.ly/StructuralModel.

[3] https://bit.ly/StructuralModel.

positive and statistically significant effect on the perceived satisfaction of piloting (3.2). On the other hand, while the variables Collaborative and student-initiated instructional piloting experience (2.2) and Students' earlier experience with TEL practices (2.1) had a positive but non statistically significant effect on the perceived satisfaction of piloting (3.2), the Teacher-initiated usage of DLRs (1.2) had a negative but non-significant effect on the outcome variable.

4.3 Challenges and Opportunities Perceived by the Students

We identified from students' reflective responses (n = 187) that they mainly faced technical and methodological challenges during the piloting.

Technical Difficulties. A majority of students reported technical difficulties while interacting with the DLRs. The biggest category under this theme was related to small screen size and navigation issues. Next, the lack of possibility to save responses and continue working on the assignment later, the lack of opportunities to zoom in on the content. Students also faced issues with an internet connection, due to which some materials were not accessible, answers were not saved and the overall experience was not satisfactory.

Methodological Aspects and Teaching Practices. Students appreciated video-based and other illustrations next to the text-based materials, which helped them to better understand the content. However, students also felt that there were too many 'Tell'-type questions based on multiple-choice templates and it was not motivating for them ("*I ended up putting answers in arbitrarily to get the work done, but didn't think through any of the tasks or master the topic. Should therefore reduce the number of tasks with multiple answers.*"). Students reported that overall the experience was interesting and positive, but such materials could be used for rehearsal and anchoring the material and not for replacing textbooks and teachers' explanations ("*It was useful more as an introduction and refresher, but not as a deep consolidation of the topic*"). Based on the students' open responses it can be concluded that they did not perceive individual learning with DLRs as an efficient way to learn, especially when it was a new topic that students had to acquire on their own ("*I can say that I understand better when the teacher explains in front of the class. I didn't like learning independently with DLRs*"). About 10% of the students who participated in the pilot pointed out that the pedagogical potential of the DLRs was not clear to them. From the students' responses, it seemed that they felt the DLRs were created to replace textbooks and diminish teachers' roles, which was not the goal of the pilot.

5 Discussion, Implications, and the Conclusion

This study described findings from a national-level initiative, carried out by the Estonian Ministry of Education, during which interactive DLRs were made available for secondary school teachers. It is known that the adoption of innovations needs teachers to scaffold to build a shared understanding of the innovation and create new pedagogical practices that effectively embed technological innovations [9].

First, the aim was to understand from teachers' reflections how they integrated DLRs into their pedagogical practice. Analysis of lesson descriptions demonstrated that most of the learning activities (nearly 90%) focused on teacher-led activities, where novel, pedagogically-meaningful tasks were mostly implemented to replace the textbooks and rarely to activate students in different ways. Despite an introduction to SCL scenarios before the pilot process, teachers found DLR-supported SCL complicated or irrelevant to implement. These results are well aligned with earlier research indicating that teachers tend to use passive learning approaches in technology-enhanced learning environments [35]. This in turn demonstrates once again the importance of supporting teachers in adopting innovations, for instance by providing pedagogical support throughout the implementation of the program, and constantly monitoring and giving feedback [7]. Without such support, it could be that investments are done at the national level, but the full potential of novel technologies remains uncovered and they are only used to replace traditional teaching methods [2].

Second, we aimed to explore students' piloting experience to understand to what extent their earlier experience of TEL practices and different instructional practices during the piloting affected their perceived usefulness of the DLRs and overall satisfaction with the piloting. Results indicate that students' **earlier experience** of searching for and interacting with information resources and DLRs and solving e-tests and quizzes independently outside of the classroom had the largest positive effect on students' perceived usefulness of DLRs, but only if this happened to the students' initiative. When this was encouraged through classroom use under the teachers' guidance, it did not lead to increased perceived usefulness of DLRs and satisfaction with the piloting experience perhaps due to the students' passive role [11].

Prior experience with DLRs and TEL practices and the **experiences during the piloting period** with different pedagogical practices contributed significantly and independently to the students' perception. Both individualised use of DLRs, as well as collaborative and student-initiated use, led to some positive perceptions. Whereas individual practices led to higher student satisfaction, collaborative practices led to higher perceived usefulness. Teacher-initiated use was not related to any student perceptions probably due to the fact that individual interactions with the DLRs are quite straightforward and close to the teaching style students experience in their everyday learning process [2]. In the normal classroom a variety of approaches are used from passive to active learning, constructive and interactive, and all of these approaches are needed depending on the learning goals, but the crucial thing for the teachers to understand is the balance between approaches [32]. We found that students, similar to teachers, need to adapt their learning to a situation where DLRs afford different types of practices. For instance, some students with previous experiences with TEL practices were able to organise their learning differently, or were unsatisfied, in case the teacher was using the resources in a more teacher-directed manner. Students with fewer experience in the use of DLRs may have had more difficulty adapting and were then satisfied with a more traditional use by the teachers. Survey data did not enable us to understand instructional design around the DLRs - we know the DLRs were mainly used individually, but it is not known whether the teacher used the materials for rehearsal, acquiring new content knowledge individually, or as supportive materials in problem-solving tasks and therefore we cannot draw conclusions regarding whether some pedagogical practices lead to higher perceived usefulness and satisfaction of the students.

Even though the teaching practices remained mainly traditional (as reported by the teachers in the previous section), some of the students were satisfied with them. Again, we can assume this is because students have been learning in this manner and are therefore comfortable with it [11]. The students who had been previously guided by teachers to find additional information and resources from the web during the lessons did not perceive the piloted DLRs as useful and did not rate the overall experience as satisfactory. These students have been used to using digital resources, which may not have all been designed for learning, but this experience allowed them to find materials they judged useful. Such results could mean that to some extent some of the students are used to some aspects of SCL practices (finding their resources at their own pace), which hides certain risks if information resources are learning materials. But at the same time it indicates that during the piloting, students may not have experienced SCL practices where they could choose strategies to support their learning. It is important to note that though it is not possible to conclude what kind of piloting experiences lead to a more efficient learning experience, data suggests that variety in teaching practices is needed - to motivate more self-directed learners, but also to scaffold those students who are used to learning traditionally, where technology is merely used for replacing existing resources [11]. A balance between those aspects is needed, hence pedagogical support can aim to train teachers towards a diversity of instructional practices that support student needs [7, 9].

Finally, we aimed to understand students' experiences of the pilot and what kind of challenges and opportunities they perceived. Students faced difficulties with working with small mobile devices and the need to improve the navigation of the DLRs was noted. Students used many different kinds of devices, which must be taken into account when designing the DLR interface. More importantly, students emphasised in their responses that there is a need to think about the pedagogical practices to enhance a deeper learning experience and amplify the teacher's role [2].

Although our study was not very long - about 1,5 months, future national initiatives that promote SCL may introduce the novel DLRs step-by-step and systematically through long-term introductions. External and temporary intervention inviting teachers and students to use new technologies and approaches, without preparing them and creating "ownership" of this innovation, is not welcomed by a relatively large share of students, as it creates extra efforts without perceived benefits to learning (from their perspective) [6, 11]. The results pinpoint the importance of dialogue between teachers, students, researchers, and developers of TEL innovations because, without a shared understanding of the capabilities and role of digital innovations, the potential to transform teaching and learning cannot be reached [21]. Especially now, when we have experienced emergency remote teaching due to the COVID-19 pandemic, the importance of learning technologies and the role of the teacher in their effective use is apparent. To scale up the materials developed under this project, while at the same time ensuring that teachers' use practices are pedagogically sound, there is a need for further awareness-raising among teachers [5]. One way to do this is to follow a teacher's professional development intervention as proposed by Ley et al. [9]. We need to make sure that the practice around learning technologies is student-centred and offers fundamentally new perspectives for students and at the same time enhances the scale of the created DLRs.

Acknowledgments. This research was funded by the ETAG-funded grant PRG1634 and European Union's Horizon 2020 research and innovation program, grant agreement No. 669074.

References

1. OECD: ICT resources in school education: what do we know from OECD work? OECD (2020)
2. Fullan, M., Langworthy, M.: A Rich Seam: How New Pedagogies Find Deep Learning. Pearson, London (2014)
3. Cuban, L.: Why so many structural changes in schools and so little reform in teaching practices. J. Educ. Adm. **51**(2), 109–125 (2013)
4. Toh, Y.: Leading sustainable pedagogical reform with technology for student-centered learning: a complexity perspective. J. Educ. Change **17**, 145–169 (2016). https://doi.org/10.1007/s10833-016-9273-9
5. Glover, I., Hepplestone, S., Parkin, H., Rodger, H., Irwin, B.: Pedagogy first: realising technology enhanced learning by focusing on teaching practice. Br. J. Edu. Technol. **47**(5), 993–1002 (2016)
6. Genlott, A., Grönlund, A.Å., Viberg, O.: Disseminating digital innovation in school – leading second- order educational change. Educ. Inf. Technol. **24**, 3021–3039 (2019)
7. Rolfe, V.E., Alcocer, M., Bentley, E., Milne, D. Meyer-Sahling, J.: Academic staff attitudes towards electronic learning in arts and sciences. Eur. J. Open Dist. Learn. (EURODL) 1–6 (2008)
8. Mohammadi, F., Abrizah, A., Nazari, M., Attaran, M.: What motivates high school teachers to use web-based learning resources for classroom instruction? An exploratory case study in an Iranian smart school. Comput. Hum. Behav. **51**, 373–381 (2015)
9. Ley, T., Tammets, K., Sarmiento-Márquez, E.M., Leoste, J., Hallik, M., Poom-Valickis, K.: Adopting technology in schools: modelling, measuring and supporting knowledge appropriation. Eur. J. Teach. Educ. (2021). https://doi.org/10.1080/02619768.2021.1937113
10. Aru-Chabilan, H.: Tiger Leap for digital turn in the Estonian education. Educ. Media Int. **57**(1), 61–72 (2020). https://doi.org/10.1080/09523987.2020.1744858
11. Beckman, K., Bennett, S., Lockyer, L.: Understanding students' use and value of technology for learning. Learn. Media Technol. **39**(3), 346–367 (2014)
12. Stork, M.G.: Implementing a digital learning initiative: a case study in K-12 classrooms. J. Format. Design Learn. **2**(1), 36–48 (2017). https://doi.org/10.1007/s41686-017-0013-1
13. Pepin, B., Gueudet, G., Yerushalmy, M., Trouche, L., Chazan, D.: E-textbooks in/for teaching and learning mathematics: a disruptive and potentially transformative educational technology. In: English, L., Kirshner, D. (eds.) Handbook of International Research in Mathematics Education, 3rd edn., pp.636–661. Taylor & Francis (2015)
14. Hamel, C.J., Ryan-Jones, D.: Designing instruction with learning objects. Int. J. Educ. Technol. **3**(1), 111–124 (2002)
15. Merrill, M.D.: First principles of instruction. Educ. Tech. Res. Dev. **50**(3), 43–59 (2006)
16. Churchill, D.: Learning object: an interactive representation and a mediating tool in a learning activity. Educ. Media Int. **42**(4), 333–349 (2005)
17. Lonka, K.: Phenomenal Learning from Finland. Edita Publishing (2018)

18. Lafuente, M.: Attuning pedagogies to the context of 'new learners' and technology. In: Understanding Innovative Pedagogies: Key Themes to Analyse New Approaches to Teaching and Learning. OECD Working paper nr 172 (2018)
19. OECD: How computers are related to students' performance. In: Students, Computers and Learning: Making the Connection, pp. 145–164. OECD (2015)
20. Corrin, L., Kennedy, G., Mulder, R.: Enhancing learning analytics by understanding the needs of teachers. In: Proceedings of the Australian Society for Computers in Learning in Tertiary Education 30th Annual Conference (ASCILITE 2013), Sydney, Australia, pp. 201–205 (2013)
21. Taber, K.S.: The role of new educational technology in teaching and learning: A constructivist perspective on digital learning. In: Marcus-Quinn, A., Hourigan, T. (eds.) Handbook on digital learning for K-12 schools, pp. 397–412. Springer, Cham (2017). https://doi.org/10.1007/978-3-319-33808-8_24
22. Hair, J.F., Hult, G.T.M., Ringle, C., Sarstedt, M.: A Primer on Partial Least Squares Structural Equation Modelling (PLS-SEM). Sage Publications (2013)
23. Becker, J.-M., Klein, K., Wetzels, M.: Hierarchical latent variable models in PLS-SEM: guidelines for using reflective-formative type models. Long Range Plan. **45**(5–6), 359–394 (2012)
24. Chin, W.W., Peterson, R.A., Brown, P.S.: Structural equation modelling in marketing: some practical reminders. J. Mark. Theory Pract. **16**(4), 287–298 (2008)
25. Hair, J.F., Sarstedt, M., Matthews, L.M., Ringle, C.M.: Identifying and treating unobserved heterogeneity with FIMIX-PLS: part I—method. Eur. Bus. Rev. **28**(1), 63–76 (2016). https://doi.org/10.1108/EBR-09-2015-0094
26. Ghasemy, M., Teeroovengadum, V., Becker, J.-M., Ringle, C.M.: This fast car can move faster: a review of PLS-SEM application in higher education research. High. Educ. **80**, 1121–1152 (2020)
27. Henseler, J., Ringle, C.M., Sarstedt, M.: A new criterion for assessing discriminant validity in variance-based structural equation modeling. J. Acad. Mark. Sci. **43**(1), 115–135 (2014). https://doi.org/10.1007/s11747-014-0403-8
28. Hair, J.F., Hult, G.T.M., Ringle, C., Sarstedt, M.: A Primer on Partial least Squares Structural Equation Modeling (PLS-SEM). Sage Publications (2017)
29. Hu, L.-T., Bentler, P.M.: Fit Indices in covariance structure modeling: sensitivity to underparameterized model misspecification. Psychol. Methods **3**(4), 424–453 (1998)
30. Dijkstra, T.K., Henseler, J.: Consistent and asymptotically normal PLS estimators for linear structural equations. Comput. Stat. Data Anal. **81**(1), 10–23 (2015)
31. Cohen, J.: Statistical Power Analysis for the Behavioral Sciences, 2nd edn. Psychology Press (1988)
32. Sailer, M., Murböck, J., Fischer, F.: Digital learning in schools: what does it take beyond digital technology? Teach. Teach. Educ. **103**, 103346 (2021)
33. Sailer, M., et al.: Technology-related teaching skills and attitudes: validation of a scenario-based self-assessment instrument for teachers. Comput. Hum. Behav. **115**, 106625 (2021)
34. Chi, M.T., Wylie, R.: The ICAP framework: linking cognitive engagement to active learning outcomes. Educ. Psychol. **49**(4), 219–243 (2014)
35. Fraillon, J., Ainley, J., Schulz, W., Friedman, T., Duckworth, D.: Preparing for Life in a Digital Age. IEA, Amsterdam (2019)

Privacy-Preserving Synthetic Educational Data Generation

Jill-Jênn Vie[1(✉)], Tomas Rigaux[1], and Sein Minn[2]

[1] SODA, Inria Saclay, 1 rue Honoré d'Estienne d'Orves, 91120 Palaiseau, France
{jill-jenn.vie,tomas.rigaux}@inria.fr
[2] CEDAR, Inria Saclay, 1 rue Honoré d'Estienne d'Orves, 91120 Palaiseau, France
sein.minn@inria.fr

Abstract. Institutions collect massive learning traces but they may not disclose it for privacy issues. Synthetic data generation opens new opportunities for research in education. In this paper we present a generative model for educational data that can preserve the privacy of participants, and an evaluation framework for comparing synthetic data generators. We show how naive pseudonymization can lead to re-identification threats and suggest techniques to guarantee privacy. We evaluate our method on existing massive educational open datasets.

Keywords: Generative models · Privacy · Item response theory

1 Introduction

Educational platforms collect massive amounts of data related to human learning. These can be used to personalize education, train AI-assisted learning systems, but using this data may also harm privacy [2,12]. The General Data Protection Regulation (GDPR) protects any information relating to an identified or identifiable natural person. GDPR concerns pseudonymized data, i.e. processing "so that personal data can no longer be attributed to a specific data subject without the use of additional information" (Art. 4[1]) but does not concern anonymized data, i.e. "personal data rendered anonymous in such a manner that the data subject is not or no longer identifiable" (Recital 26[2]).

Privacy risk is hard to quantify, as an open dataset can be archived indefinitely, open datasets can be combined, and technology for re-identification is improving over time. There have been a huge number of privacy issues after the re-identification of pseudonymized data [6,18,25]. When a movie-streaming service organized a 1-million-dollar data challenge, some researchers managed, using solely the movie ratings from the pseudonymized dataset, to match IMDb profiles with the zip code of participants in the pseudonymized dataset [18].

[1] https://gdpr-info.eu/art-4-gdpr/.
[2] https://gdpr-info.eu/recitals/no-26/.

J.-J. Vie and T. Rigaux—Equal contribution.

I. Hilliger et al. (Eds.): EC-TEL 2022, LNCS 13450, pp. 393–406, 2022.
https://doi.org/10.1007/978-3-031-16290-9_29

In this paper, we are interested in generating truly anonymized educational records: data that does not belong to anybody, but still shares some interesting properties than real datasets, in order to power technology-enhanced learning. Our contribution is twofold. We first show how we can generate logs of data using generative models such as Markov chains or neural networks. We also define a way to practically measure re-identification risk and show how naive pseudonymization techniques, such as dropping a set of rows, or renumbering IDs, are not enough to ensure the privacy of participants. One of our methods is easily scalable as it can generate 1 million rows in 3 s while preserving utility and respecting privacy.

This study provides opportunities to open more datasets: instead of just releasing simple statistics, institutions and governments could also provide synthetic datasets so that citizens could provide personalized, innovative solutions for preparing for national examinations. This would benefit research communities such as technology enhanced-learning, educational data mining, and learning analytics, as today it is extremely hard for researchers to have access to student data that is considered too sensitive.

We first review related work, then introduce the task of privacy-preserving synthetic data generation. We then explain our framework for evaluation, the experiments we made on two real educational datasets, and finally discuss our results.

2 Related Work

In order to protect data, mechanisms such as k-anonymity have been considered, i.e., processing the data so that any person is indistinguishable from $k-1$ other ones in a dataset. However, when we consider high dimensional data, such as mobile geolocation data or educational logging data, then few points are enough to make people unique, therefore k-anonymity is no longer feasible: [6] showed that 4 timestamp-location points are needed to uniquely identify 95% of individual trajectories in a dataset of 1.5M rows. The uniqueness of a user in a dataset was defined by [25], which showed that 15 demographic points are enough to re-identify 99.96% of Americans. k-anonymity also has limitations, as sensitive attributes can be inferred either due to a lack of diversity or using external knowledge [17].

Some educational research communities attach importance to synthetic or simulated data; while others are mainly interested in real data. For example, in psychometrics, the science of measurement, the validity of a student response model is usually both shown on simulated and real data. "Pseudo-students" can also be used to test the quality of an instructional design [28,29]. Generative models, recently famous for deep fakes, are mainly encountered in automatic exercise generation [3], simulated response patterns, or student performance prediction, rarely for the generation of a whole dataset. There is a trade-off between generating data that is completely fake, and not very useful; and data that is useful, however easy to re-identify.

A direct identifier is a specific information that references an individual, such as a name, an e-mail address, or an identification number. A quasi-identifier[3] is any piece of information, be it a geographical position at a certain time, or even an opinion on some topic, that could be used, possibly in combination with other quasi-identifiers, with the purpose of re-identifying an individual. In this paper, we are interested to illustrate what can be done using only three simple columns: user ID, item ID and outcome, whether the user got a correct attempt on the item. Our approach can naturally be generalized to several columns, by estimating the conditional probability distributions between variables in order to generate new data that follows those distributions. There are several toolkits to do so, based on Bayesian networks, e.g. sdv.dev [19]; however, in most of them, there is no measurement of re-identification risk.

Item Response Theory: Estimating Outcome Given User and Item Parameters. Response models can be used for estimating both the difficulty of exercises in a questionnaire and the latent abilities of examinees. The Rasch model [24], also called 1-parameter logistic, is the most famous and simplest item response theory model (we will denote it by IRT). It is used in real-world adaptive tests such as GMAT, and can also be used to generate synthetic response data.

$$Pr(R_{ij} = 1) = \sigma(\theta_i - d_j)$$

where R_{ij} is 1 if user i answers item j correctly, $\sigma : x \mapsto 1/(1 + \exp(-x))$ is the sigmoid function, θ_i represents the ability parameter of user i and d_j represents the difficulty of item j.

Privacy-Preserving, One Row per User. Differential privacy [9] (DP) is a theoretical framework for proving that the output of a generative model will be indistinguishable by a parameter $\varepsilon > 0$ had a user be present or absent in the training data. It is hard to know which value of epsilon is needed [15], but it is related to the budget of queries we can make to the generative model. DP usually relies on adding noise to model weights and is useful for performing queries with privacy guarantees such as histograms [1], n-grams statistics [4]. More rarely, DP has been applied to privacy-preserving data generation, usually in settings where there is only one record per user. This is why privacy-preserving Bayesian networks have been proposed such as PrivBayes [31], implemented in the Python package DataSynthesizer [23]. In [8], DataSynthesizer is illustrated on real educational data.

Several Rows per User. In our setting, we have several records per user, and we are dealing with the interaction of two entities, users and exercises, that we don't want to protect equally. We want to protect user data, but we want to be able to precisely estimate exercise difficulty. If we were just adding noise to IRT parameters, we would be blurring the utility of our item bank. Once we move to

[3] https://edps.europa.eu/system/files/2021-04/21-04-27_aepd-edps_anonymisation_en_5.pdf.

high-dimensional scenarios, such as time series, or logging data at irregular time intervals, there are several observations available for each user, and this may arbitrarily increase the risk of re-identification. For example, [16] is collecting typing data in order to predict programming experience. They show that delay between keystrokes is enough to re-identify people, but by rounding or bucketing those values, they can still achieve good prediction for the task at hand while reducing re-identification. If the blur is not big enough, people can still be re-identified [6].

Table 1. Example of minimal tabular dataset.

user ID	action ID	outcome	description
2487	384	1	user 2487 got token "I" correct
2487	242	0	user 2487 got token "ate" incorrect
2487	39	1	user 2487 got token "an" correct
2487	65	1	user 2487 got token "apple" correct

3 Privacy-Preserving Synthetic Data Generation

3.1 Goal

A synthetic dataset should have several properties:

Utility. The fake dataset should bear a strong similarity to the real dataset (histograms, similar results to queries). Also if we conduct a study, e.g. estimating item difficulties using an IRT model, the learned parameters should be similar for both the real and the generated dataset.

Privacy. It should not be easy to re-identify participants in the real dataset from the synthetic dataset.

For example, it is easy to generate random noise, and complete dummy datasets with guaranteed privacy, but it won't be useful if we do not preserve correlation between columns.

For the sake of simplicity, we assume that the data is provided as triplets $(i, j_t, r_t) = (\mathsf{userID}, \mathsf{actionID}, \mathsf{outcome})$ where the $\mathsf{outcome}$ r_t is 1 if user i makes a successful action j_t and 0 otherwise. See Table 1 for an example of such dataset.

We first need a model of sequence prediction, to identify which action comes next. Formally, we need a model of $p(j_{t+1}|j_t, \ldots, j_1)$. Then, we need a response model $p(r_t|i, j_t)$.

3.2 Sequence Generation

Markov Chains. This simple probabilistic graphical model has been used for generating text, music, etc. It relies on a probability transition for jumping from one action to another: $P_{su} = \Pr(j_{t+1} = u | j_t = s)$ is the probability to jump from action s to action u. The Markov chain is trained on existing corpus of actions. Once the P matrix has been estimated, it can be used to sample a random walk from action to action. A Markov chain is said memoryless because the next action only depends on the current action: $p(j_{t+1}|j_t, \dots, j_1) = p(j_{t+1}|j_t)$.

Recurrent Neural Networks. Neural networks are famous for natural language processing, and generation. RNNs have been used in knowledge tracing for predicting student performance [22]. They have many more parameters, so they can remember more than simple Markov chains, but they are way slower to train. Some works have shown that a simple updated IRT model could match the performance of RNN [30] for knowledge tracing. [10] has shown that it depends on how much the dataset contains long sequences and if the sequential aspect of the dataset is prominent. A Gated recurrent unit (GRU) is an example of RNN. In our case, the input is sequence $(j_1, \dots, j_t)$ and the output is sequence $(\widehat{j_2}, \dots, \widehat{j_{t+1}})$ and GRU computes:

$$
\begin{aligned}
s_t &= \sigma\left(W j_t + U h_{t-1} + b\right) \\
z_t &= \sigma\left(W' j_t + U' h_{t-1} + b'\right)
\end{aligned}
\qquad
\begin{aligned}
\hat{h}_t &= \tanh\left(W'' + U''(s_t * h_{t-1}) + b''\right) \\
h_t &= (1 - z_t) * h_{t-1} + z_t * \hat{h}_t \qquad h_0 = 0 \\
\widehat{j_{t+1}} &= \operatorname{argmax}(W''' h_t + b''')
\end{aligned}
$$

where σ is the same sigmoid function as in IRT, $*$ denotes element-wise product, and parts of input and output where shown in red for clarity.

3.3 Response Pattern Generation

Once the sequence of skills has been generated, what is left is to generate outcomes. For this we use the Rasch model:

$$p(r_t = 1 | i, j_t) = \sigma(\theta_i - d_{j_t}).$$

We fit an IRT model on the training dataset to learn the θ_i ability of each user i and the difficulty d_j of each action j. Then, to generate new users, we just need to fit a normal distribution on the histogram of existing θ values and sample from it to generate responses using the IRT model and the estimated action difficulties d_j, see Fig. 1. This is the core of our strategy: as the generated j_t and the sampled θ do not correspond to any particular user anymore, the generated dataset should be anonymous.

4 Evaluation Framework

To compare strategies for educational data generation, our architecture is described in Fig. 2 and explained in this section.

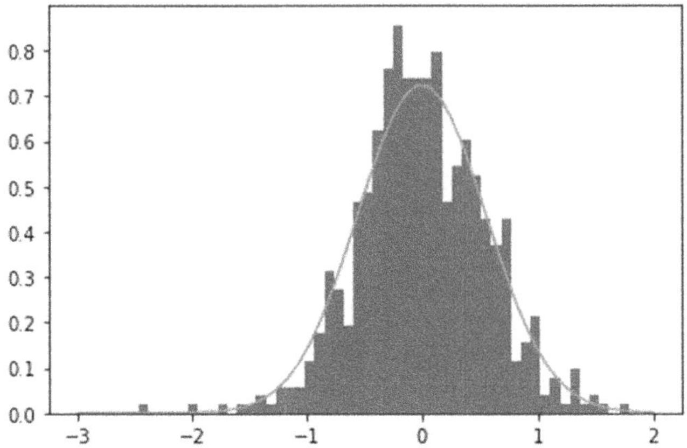

Fig. 1. From the histogram of estimated θ parameters from the training set (blue), it is easy to fit a Gaussian (orange) and sample new users from it. (Color figure online)

4.1 Training Set Sampling and Generation

For each original dataset, we first sample a training set that will be used to train the generators. This training set contains the rows that belong to half of all users. Then our models will generate new, synthetic (or fake) tabular datasets.

4.2 Utility

To compare the real and fake sets, we first compute some histograms for the real and generated sequences: a number of occurrences of each action, sequence lengths, and distribution of repeated skills.

Once the fake dataset has been generated, we want to know whether training an IRT model to estimate the difficulty of actions has similar findings on the real dataset and on the fake dataset. We compute the root mean squared error of action difficulty parameters learned by IRT between the training set and the fake set. The weighted RMSE (denoted $wRMSE$) is given by the following formula:

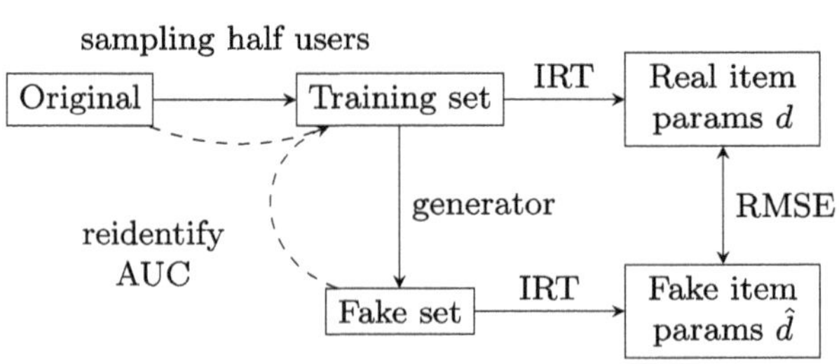

Fig. 2. The architecture of our study

$$wRMSE = \sqrt{\sum_{i=1}^{N} w_i (d_i - \hat{d}_i)^2}$$

The usual RMSE is when all actions are equally weighted, i.e. $w_i = 1/N$ for all i. However some actions are less frequent than others, so it is normal that their parameter is not well estimated. Therefore we also introduce a weighted RMSE where w_i corresponds to the frequency of action i in the training set, i.e. its number of occurrences divided by the size of the training set.

4.3 Reidentification Score

As a measure of how easy it is to re-identify people, we borrow the practical task of membership inference encountered in [13,27]. We assume that an adversary has access to the original dataset (e.g. some auxiliary information about the population from the outside world) and the fake generated dataset, and wants to guess which users were in the training set. This is a classification problem where for each user in the original dataset, we want to guess 1 if it was present in the training set used to generate the fake set, and 0 otherwise. We will now give examples of why membership inference is already an issue: if the dataset used for training the fake set corresponds to some query, i.e. "students with special needs" or "students having a certain socioeconomic status", then membership inference is already something that may harm privacy. More generally, if one person can be re-identified just by a few actions, then using other sources of information (e.g. cookies, other databases), these actions can be used to uniquely describe this user, and re-identify them in other databases. This is exactly the example of the Netflix Prize [18].

Once a classifier is performing membership inference, its performance can be evaluated using the area under the ROC curve (AUC), a number between 0 and 1. Any random guess should have an AUC of 0.5, as half of the original people belong to the training set, as stated in Sect. 4.1.

5 Experiments

5.1 Datasets

Datasets are described below and their statistics are reported in Table 2. Median refers to the median across all users of the median number of repeats for each skill. Max refers to the maximum across all users of the maximum number of repeats for a skill.

Assistments 2009. This dataset contains 279,000 outcomes of 4,163 students attempting math exercises. Each exercise is mapped to one among 112 knowledge components in Mathematics [11]. This dataset is popular in the Educational Data Mining community, notably for knowledge tracing. Here, we consider that a skill corresponds to an action.

Duolingo 2018. This massive dataset contains the outcomes of 1,213 English-speaking people learning French. It contains 1.2M logs of users attempting to type words in the Duolingo app. The actions are the words expected in the correct answer, and the outcomes are at the word level: 1 for a correctly typed word, 0 for a spelling mistake, see again Table 1 for an example. This dataset was part of the Duolingo competition at NAACL-HLT 2018 for a knowledge tracing task [26].

We remove actions where the success rate is either 0% or 100%, as those are either too easy or impossible to get right, and their corresponding IRT parameters are $\pm\infty$. For example, in the Duolingo dataset, the French word « train » had 0% success rate. We were surprised so we looked at the expected sentences and discovered that it was in fact the « en train de » locution, which is the translation of the -ing form in English, which is hard to get right for English people learning French ("She is eating" $\leftrightarrow$ « Elle est en train de manger »).

Table 2. Statistics for the datasets considered in the study.

Dataset	Size	Users	Actions	Repeated actions		Sequence length		
				Med	Max	Min	Med	Max
Assistments 2009	279k	4163	112	3	144	1	20	1021
Duolingo SLAM 2018	1.2M	1213	2416	1	4	90	742	10008

5.2 Generative Models

Baseline Drop. As a baseline, we drop a certain amount of rows from the training set (a ratio $r \in \{0., 0.25, 0.5, 0.75, 0.99, 0.999\}$), then randomize user IDs.

Markov Chain. The Markov chain for generating actions was implemented using the `lea` Python package for discrete probability distributions [7]. As parameters, we define a length limit of 1000 for Assistments and 10000 for Duolingo. Our Markov chain takes 3 s to train and generate the Duolingo dataset.

RNN. Our recurrent neural network is a Gated Recurrent Unit (GRU) implemented in PyTorch. The batch size was 64 for Assistments and 16 for Duolingo. We minimize the cross entropy loss of observed actions using the Adam optimizer [14]. Training takes approximately two hours for the Duolingo dataset. It is trained on smaller sequences first then longer sequences.

IRT. For generating the outcomes from user parameters and actions, we use a Rasch model denoted by IRT, implemented as `LogisticRegression` in the scikit-learn package [21]. We use the default regularization parameter $C = 1$.

5.3 Re-identification Model

We compute, for each original sequence, the longest common subsequence with each fake sequence in the fake dataset. This is performed in $O(\ell\ell')$ time for a pair of sequences of lengths ℓ and ℓ', so $O(MN)$ in total where M is the size of the original dataset and N the size of the fake dataset. Our implementation is written in C++.

Then we take the maximum of those matching scores divided by the length of the fake sequence, i.e. best-normalized percentage of matching. It gives a matching score for each original user, used for the classification task of membership inference. The quality of re-identification is estimated using AUC.

We limit the re-identification to users with enough information. More precisely, we define the cumulative entropy of a user as $\sum_t -p(j_t) \log p(j_t)$, where $(j_t)_t$ is its sequence of actions and $p(j)$ the frequency of action j in the original dataset. We then only try to re-identify users with an entropy larger than $-p \log p$ for p the proportion of users in the training dataset ($p = 0.5$ in our experiments), i.e. the entropy of the information "user as part of the training dataset". In Assistments this induces filtering of 15% of users while in Duolingo it does not change anything, as sequences are already pretty long and diverse, so they contain a lot of information already.

Our experiments can be reproduced using our code which is free and open source software[4].

6 Results and Discussion

6.1 First Look at the Synthetic Datasets

We first compare the histogram of actions in Fig. 3, where Base represents the training set. We see that the Markov chain, a very simple model, approximates the skill histograms better than RNN.

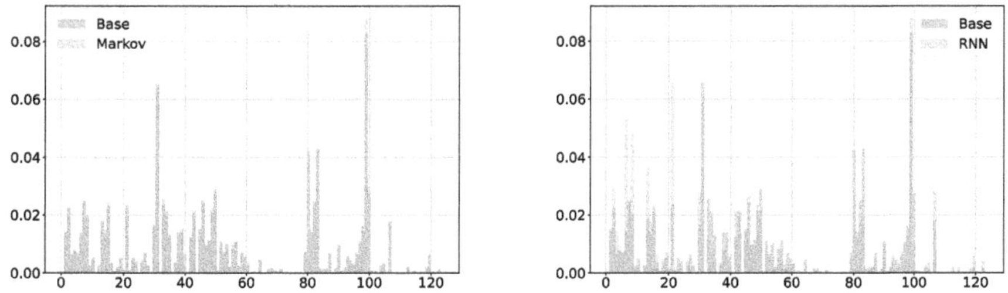

Fig. 3. Histogram of actions for the original and generated datasets by Markov chain and RNN.

We give examples of generated sequences from our approach on the Duolingo dataset in Table 3. For clarity, we do not display the outcomes, only actions which

[4] https://github.com/Akulen/PrivGen.

are French words. Markov chains are simple, but it is a memoryless process that explains why bigrams (consecutive words) are preserved but not whole sentences (e.g. « Il faut du fromage et juin à midi »). RNNs are longer to train but they can preserve longer contexts, such as generating several sentences in the same theme (food for the second sentence, or animals in the third sentence), like in the original dataset. However, it may not preserve bigrams (e.g. « des robe »).

Table 3. Original vs. generated Duolingo sequences.

Original	1. La femme Je suis rouge L' homme Je suis riche Je mange Il est riche Je suis calme
	2. Je suis riche Je suis rouge L' homme Je mange Il est riche Je suis calme...
	3. Je suis rouge Je suis riche L' homme Il est riche Je mange Je suis calme...
	4. ... Les chiens Les chiens Vous êtes grand Je mange des baguettes
Markov generated	1. Le costume La bière est rouge Les filles mangent Cet homme est riche
	2. Aux mois d' accord Tu es grande Je parle Qui suis riche L' éléphant Ma femme
	3. Le tigre Le menu Le sac est un costume Quoi Combien Oui je vais bien
	4. Quatorze enfants C' est violet Ma robe Il faut du fromage et juin à midi Vous avez un animal Vous mangez une secrétaire Sinon je sais Le cheval gagne Ça va Oui je sais Je motive mon chien
RNN generated	1. Nous mangeons Nous apprenons Je parle Il parle Je parle Je sais Il faut J' aime le fromage Je veux veux un poisson
	2. Le bonbon est rouge J' aime boire La carotte J' aime manger Un œuf La confiture Je bois une boisson rouge
	3. Tu es en train de manger Un dauphin Le chat est noir Le éléphant est vert
	4. Il faut du pain Elle pose des chats Les chiennes Il pleut des frites Ces enfants mangent des robe

6.2 Quality and Re-identification Trade-Off

Table 4. Results. RMSE should be low for good utility and Re-identification AUC should be low for good privacy. The best results are shown in bold.

Dataset	Metric	Drop						MC	RNN
		0	0.25	0.5	0.75	0.99	0.999		
ASSISTments 2009	RMSE	**0.000**	**0.093**	**0.147**	0.283	0.719	0.833	**0.245**	**0.213**
	wRMSE	**0.000**	**0.035**	**0.064**	0.105	0.481	0.692	**0.065**	**0.061**
	Re-ID AUC	0.913	0.776	0.680	0.588	**0.497**	**0.497**	**0.495**	**0.508**
Duolingo SLAM 2018	RMSE	**0.000**	**0.208**	**0.308**	0.450	0.730	0.793	**0.369**	0.431
	wRMSE	**0.000**	**0.067**	**0.113**	0.195	0.624	0.985	**0.114**	**0.143**
	Re-ID AUC	1.000	1.000	1.000	1.000	0.554	**0.506**	**0.511**	**0.516**

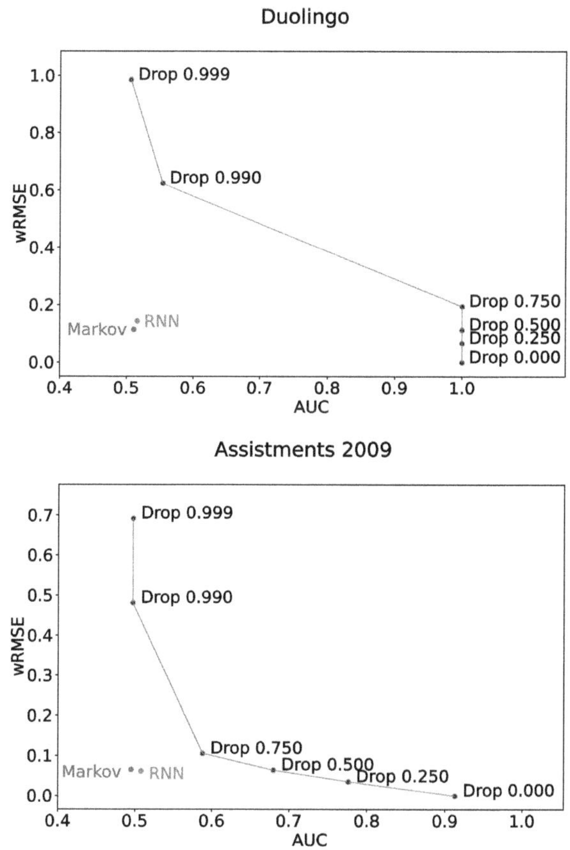

Fig. 4. The trade-off between quality (low weighted RMSE) and privacy (low re-identification AUC) for all models considered. The bottom left is better.

Quantitative results are provided in Table 4 and Fig. 4. Drop baselines with ratios of 0.5 and 0.75 are the worst of possible worlds: loss in estimation quality of the action difficulty parameters, and easy membership inference. What is quite remarkable is that on the Duolingo dataset, even if we drop 75% of rows, it is still possible to exactly recover 100% of the training set. This is probably because there are more tokens and sequences are longer (the minimal length is 90 and the median length is 742), so people are more easily unique.

Markov chain and RNN have comparable quality RMSE scores to the Drop baseline for low ratio. But even Drop 0, which corresponds to keeping all lines and rewriting the user IDs, is very easy to re-identify (AUC 0.913), which shows that simple pseudonymization is not enough. Therefore, the best models are Markov chain and RNN, which is particularly visible in Fig. 4. This means we can freely share the fake dataset: it will follow a similar distribution to the real one, but the underlying "users" do not exist; they cannot be re-identified.

7 Limitations, Impact and Future Work

A limitation is that so far we consider a model of evolution for the skill j, i.e. the question that is assessed at each time, but not for the user ability θ, i.e. a learning model. Natural extensions would be to consider knowledge tracing models such as PFA [20] or more sophisticated ones such as DAS3H [5], to get dynamic models of learning.

In future work, we'd like to test our setting on more sophisticated tabular datasets: users would be even more unique. We notably want to work on timestamps, as the delays between attempts may be unique between participants, therefore may harm privacy. In this paper, we were interested in learning item difficulties, but other applications may have a different objective to optimize. We want to highlight the fact that for the sake of researchers in technology-enhanced learning, item parameters should be as open as possible; while for the sake of students, user parameters should be kept as private as possible.

The example shown in this paper helps raise awareness in what can be done with student data. Our re-identification task of membership inference may seem a bit weak, so here is a more precise example. Let us now assume that for the sake of providing accurate recommendations, a dataset of student logs with a particular condition, say ADHD, is shared. We show that it could be possible, having access to a bigger dataset of students logs, to identify which students have ADHD. Personalized education should be able to provide further help to students with special needs, without letting anyone know which student has what condition.

8 Conclusion

In this paper, we show how we can generate educational data records for research while preserving the privacy of real users. We illustrated that naive pseudonymization or dropping rows from a dataset is not enough, as techniques based on text mining can re-identify who was in the training set. Our approach generates fake users, thus anonymized data that can be freely shared. We advocate for more open datasets to nurture educational research and foster technology-enhanced learning; but privacy-preserving, synthetically generated ones.

References

1. Acs, G., Castelluccia, C., Chen, R.: Differentially private histogram publishing through lossy compression. In: 2012 IEEE 12th International Conference on Data Mining, pp. 1–10. IEEE (2012)
2. Berendt, B., Littlejohn, A., Blakemore, M.: AI in education: learner choice and fundamental rights. Learn. Media Technol. **45**(3), 312–324 (2020)
3. Cablé, B., Guin, N., Lefevre, M.: An authoring tool for semi-automatic generation of self-assessment exercises. In: Lane, H.C., Yacef, K., Mostow, J., Pavlik, P. (eds.) AIED 2013. LNCS (LNAI), vol. 7926, pp. 679–682. Springer, Heidelberg (2013). https://doi.org/10.1007/978-3-642-39112-5_87

4. Chen, R., Acs, G., Castelluccia, C.: Differentially private sequential data publication via variable-length N-grams. In: Proceedings of the 2012 ACM Conference on Computer and Communications Security, pp. 638–649 (2012)
5. Choffin, B., Popineau, F., Bourda, Y., Vie, J.J.: DAS3H: modeling student learning and forgetting for optimally scheduling distributed practice of skills. arXiv preprint arXiv:1905.06873 (2019)
6. De Montjoye, Y.A., Hidalgo, C.A., Verleysen, M., Blondel, V.D.: Unique in the crowd: the privacy bounds of human mobility. Sci. Rep. **3**(1), 1–5 (2013)
7. Denis, P.: Probabilistic inference using generators: the statues algorithm. In: Arai, K., Kapoor, S., Bhatia, R. (eds.) SAI 2020. AISC, vol. 1229, pp. 133–154. Springer, Cham (2020). https://doi.org/10.1007/978-3-030-52246-9_10
8. Dorodchi, M., Al-Hossami, E., Benedict, A., Demeter, E.: Using synthetic data generators to promote open science in higher education learning analytics. In: 2019 IEEE International Conference on Big Data (Big Data), pp. 4672–4675. IEEE (2019)
9. Dwork, C.: Differential privacy: a survey of results. In: Agrawal, M., Du, D., Duan, Z., Li, A. (eds.) TAMC 2008. LNCS, vol. 4978, pp. 1–19. Springer, Heidelberg (2008). https://doi.org/10.1007/978-3-540-79228-4_1
10. Gervet, T., Koedinger, K., Schneider, J., Mitchell, T., et al.: When is deep learning the best approach to knowledge tracing? J. Educ. Data Min. **12**(3), 31–54 (2020)
11. Heffernan, N.T., Heffernan, C.L.: The ASSISTments ecosystem: building a platform that brings scientists and teachers together for minimally invasive research on human learning and teaching. Int. J. Artif. Intell. Educ. **24**(4), 470–497 (2014)
12. Holmes, W., Iniesto, F., Sharples, M., Scanlon, E.: ETHICS in AIED: who cares? An EC-TEL workshop. In: EC-TEL 2019 Fourteenth European Conference on Technology Enhanced Learning (2019). https://oro.open.ac.uk/67263/
13. Jordon, J., et al.: Hide-and-seek privacy challenge. arXiv preprint arXiv:2007.12087 (2020)
14. Kingma, D.P., Ba, J.: Adam: a method for stochastic optimization. arXiv preprint arXiv:1412.6980 (2014)
15. Lee, J., Clifton, C.: How much is enough? Choosing ε for differential privacy. In: Lai, X., Zhou, J., Li, H. (eds.) ISC 2011. LNCS, vol. 7001, pp. 325–340. Springer, Heidelberg (2011). https://doi.org/10.1007/978-3-642-24861-0_22
16. Leinonen, J., Ihantola, P., Hellas, A.: Preventing keystroke based identification in open data sets. In: Proceedings of the Fourth ACM Conference on Learning@Scale, pp. 101–109 (2017)
17. Machanavajjhala, A., Kifer, D., Gehrke, J., Venkitasubramaniam, M.: L-diversity: privacy beyond k-anonymity. ACM Trans. Knowl. Discov. from Data (TKDD) **1**(1), 3-es (2007)
18. Narayanan, A., Shmatikov, V.: Robust de-anonymization of large sparse datasets. In: 2008 IEEE Symposium on Security and Privacy (SP 2008), pp. 111–125. IEEE (2008)
19. Patki, N., Wedge, R., Veeramachaneni, K.: The synthetic data vault. In: 2016 IEEE International Conference on Data Science and Advanced Analytics (DSAA), pp. 399–410 (2016). https://doi.org/10.1109/DSAA.2016.49
20. Pavlik, P.I., Jr., Cen, H., Koedinger, K.R.: Performance factors analysis-a new alternative to knowledge tracing (2009, online submission)
21. Pedregosa, F., et al.: Scikit-learn: machine learning in python. J. Mach. Learn. Res. **12**, 2825–2830 (2011)
22. Piech, C., et al.: Deep knowledge tracing. In: Advances in Neural Information Processing Systems, vol. 28 (2015)

23. Ping, H., Stoyanovich, J., Howe, B.: DataSynthesizer: privacy-preserving synthetic datasets. In: Proceedings of the 29th International Conference on Scientific and Statistical Database Management, pp. 1–5 (2017)
24. Rasch, G.: On general laws and the meaning of measurement in psychology. In: Proceedings of the Fourth Berkeley Symposium on Mathematical Statistics and Probability, Volume 4: Contributions to Biology and Problems of Medicine, pp. 321–333. University of California Press, Berkeley (1961). https://projecteuclid.org/euclid.bsmsp/1200512895
25. Rocher, L., Hendrickx, J.M., De Montjoye, Y.A.: Estimating the success of re-identifications in incomplete datasets using generative models. Nat. Commun. **10**(1), 1–9 (2019)
26. Settles, B., Brust, C., Gustafson, E., Hagiwara, M., Madnani, N.: Second language acquisition modeling. In: Proceedings of the Thirteenth Workshop on Innovative Use of NLP for Building Educational Applications, pp. 56–65 (2018)
27. Shokri, R., Stronati, M., Song, C., Shmatikov, V.: Membership inference attacks against machine learning models. In: 2017 IEEE Symposium on Security and Privacy (SP), pp. 3–18. IEEE (2017)
28. Van Lehn, K.: Two pseudo-students: applications of machine learning to formative evaluation. Technical report, Carnegie-Mellon University, Pittsburgh, PA, Department of Psychology (1990)
29. VanLehn, K., Ohlsson, S., Nason, R.: Applications of simulated students: an exploration. J. Artif. Intell. Educ. **5**, 135 (1994)
30. Wilson, K.H., Karklin, Y., Han, B., Ekanadham, C.: Back to the basics: Bayesian extensions of IRT outperform neural networks for proficiency estimation. In: International Educational Data Mining Society. ERIC (2016)
31. Zhang, J., Cormode, G., Procopiuc, C.M., Srivastava, D., Xiao, X.: PrivBayes: private data release via Bayesian networks. ACM Trans. Database Syst. (TODS) **42**(4), 1–41 (2017)

Supporting Self-regulated Learning in BL: Exploring Learners' Tactics and Strategies

Esteban Villalobos[1(✉)], Mar Pérez-Sanagustin[1], Cédric Sanza[1], André Tricot[2], and Julien Broisin[1]

[1] IRIT, Université de Toulouse, CNRS, Toulouse INP, UT3, Toulouse, France
{esteban.villalobos,mar.perez-sanagustin,cedric.sanza, julien.broisin}@irit.fr

[2] Université Paul-Valéry Montpellier 3, EPSYLON, Montpellier, France
andre.tricot@univ-montp3.fr

Abstract. In the past years, Blended Learning (BL) has gained traction as a methodology in Higher Education Institutions. Despite the positive effects of BL, several studies have shown that students require high levels of self-regulation to succeed in these types of practices. Still, there is little understanding of how students organize their learning in BL authentic contexts. To fill this gap, this paper presents an exploratory study to analyze the learning tactics and strategies of 119 students in a BL course using the Moodle Learning Management System. Specifically, we examined the effects on students' learning behavior before and after an intervention with a dashboard-based plug-in designed to support self-regulated learning (SRL). Using a data-driven approach based on Hidden Markov Models (HMM), we identified the tactics and strategies employed by the students along the course. The results show that students' tactics and strategies changed significantly depending on the course design and the context in which learning occurs (in or beyond the class). Also, we found evidence indicating that the main factor that correlates to the students' learning strategies is their previous knowledge and the students' SRL ability profile.

Keywords: Self-regulated learning · Learning analytics · Blended learning

1 Introduction

In the wake of the COVID-19 pandemic, Blended Learning (BL), which combines online and traditional in-person activities, has gained prominence. While this approach has been shown positive for learning, many students often have problems regulating their learning processes in these contexts [1]. This has raised a great interest in better understanding students' self-regulation and how to support it in BL. This paper aims to shed light on how students' Self-regulated Learning (SRL) manifests in BL when intervening with a dashboard-based solution to support their learning process. The following sections presents prior work

I. Hilliger et al. (Eds.): EC-TEL 2022, LNCS 13450, pp. 407–420, 2022.
https://doi.org/10.1007/978-3-031-16290-9_30

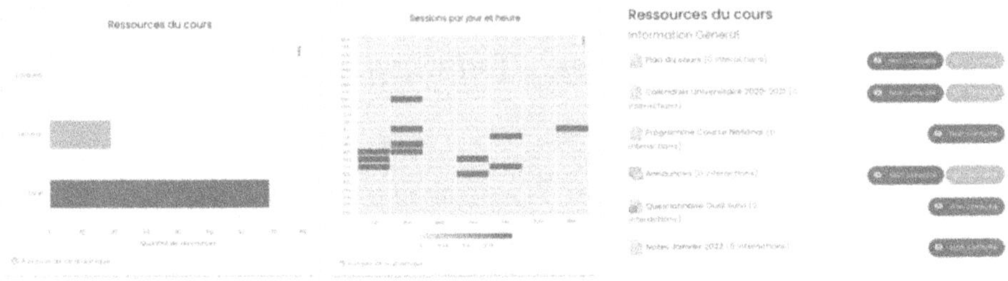

Fig. 1. Examples of visualizations in the NMP plug-in

on SRL and BL, students' trace analysis that supports the research questions of this work and the analytical methods employed.

1.1 Self-regulated Learning and BL

Self-regulated learning (SRL) is defined as a complex process that combines meta-cognitive, motivational, and emotional processes [10]. Recent literature shows that students' SRL ability is a good predictor of their behavior and success in a course [8]. However, most studies on SRL have been conducted in online contexts and little is known about how these processes manifest in BL [1].

Recent works show that students' SRL manifests differently depending on the learning context and course modality [1,2,6,9]. For example, Matcha et al. [9] compared students' strategies in a BL course, in a Flipped Classroom (FC), and in Massive Open Online Courses (MOOCs), showing that students used similar strategies in BL and FC modalities, but these differed from the tactics used in MOOCs. Moreover, Broadbent [1] showed that BL students used SRL strategies less often than online students.

To support students' SRL, researchers propose different mechanisms. One of this mechanisms are tools based on dashboards providing learners with information about their progress. Although most of these tools have been designed and evaluated in online environments with encouraging results [12], only a few works show how students incorporate them into their learning strategies and have an impact on their behavior in BL courses, in which the teacher also supports the SRL [14,16].

In this paper, we used the tool NoteMyProgress (NMP) for intervening a BL course. NMP is a plug-in for Moodle that tracks students' activity on the course and provides them with interactive dashboards for monitoring their actions and performance on the course (see Fig. 1) [13]. This tool was designed to support students' self-regulated learning and offers different visualizations for supporting certain SRL processes: (1) Time management (TM), dashboards showing the number of working sessions performed along the course, showing the dates, hours in which they were performed and their duration; (2) Strategic Planning (SP), showing the resources and activities to be completed by the student each week; and (3) Self-evaluation (SE), dashboards showing students' performance on the course evaluations as well as their average compared with the mean of the course.

1.2 Inferring Tactics and Strategies from Trace Data

The community of Learning Analytics (LA) proposes techniques and methods for studying how SRL manifests in different learning contexts. One of these methods consists of using students' self-reported data about their SRL ability [17] and combine it with approaches for detecting tactics and strategies by using the trace data collected from the course LMS [2–5,9].

To detect tactics and strategies from trace data, most studies have used techniques derived from temporal analysis and sequence mining [3,4]. To make the connection between these techniques and the SRL theory, Fan et al. [3] used a data-driven approach to analyze the underlying SLR processes activated in the learning tactics to help develop interventions. Fincham et al. [4] studied the impact of personalized feedback to support learning strategies using HMM models and hierarchical clustering to detect tactics and strategies in a Flipped Classroom setting. While some of these studies have looked into how to detect strategies in BL courses, little is known about how they manifest across the course. In this study, we build upon the work by [4] as a basis and expand their analysis to a BL context.

1.3 Objective and Research Questions

To extend the knowledge on how SRL manifests and can be supported in BL, this paper presents an exploratory study conducted in a course with 119 students. In this course, students were provided with the NMP plug-in to monitor their study sessions, grades, course planning, and progress through interactive dashboards. The main aim of this exploratory study was to study how learning tactics and strategies manifest in a BL course having the NMP tool as a support for their self-regulatory process and how they integrate its use.

Using the data analysis techniques proposed in Fincham et al. [4], we extracted students' learning tactics and strategies from trace data (actions) and characterized those strategies that are related to performance. Three research questions were derived from the main aim:

RQ1. How do students' learning tactics and strategies manifest along the BL course?

RQ2. Does the NMP tool, designed to support students' SRL, have an effect on their learning tactics and strategies?

RQ3. Is there a relationship between students' learning strategies, course performance and SRL ability profile?

2 Methodology

2.1 Exploratory Study: Context

We conducted an exploratory study in order to address the research questions. We selected this methodological approach as it is recommended for studying a phenomenon when there is insufficient prior research to establish hypotheses.

Table 1. Course description according to modality. Week 6 is excluded from this classification since it was the week of the intervention.

Weeks	Modality	Activities and tasks descriptions	
1–5	Mod. 1	Objective:	To get familiar with the main theoretical concepts of Databases modeling
		Design:	Students had a set of theoretical resources that they need to prepare before in-class sessions. A questionnaire had to be answered before the class, as a form of self-evaluation. In class, students were presented with problems that were worked in an individual manner first, discussed in groups, and presented to the rest of the class
7–11	Mod. 2	Objective:	To work with an actual SQL database and solve several exercises to get familiar with the SQL management and queries with PHPMyAdmin
		Design:	Videos showing how to use PhPMyadmin and solve certain problems that they could see before and after the in-class session. In class, students were provided with a problem to be solved during the class. They had one week to send the results of this exercise.
12–15	Mod. 3	Objective:	To work on a group project (3 per group) for setting up a DB from scratch to manage the books and members of a library
		Design:	The project was presented in class, and students worked autonomously on it during the rest of the sessions and from home. The teacher solved particular problems during the in-class sessions. Students had to send the project at the end of the 12th week

The study was conducted in a Databases course of a Degree in Management of Enterprises. The course counts with 119 students organized into 4 groups (of around 25–30 students) for theoretical sessions and 8 groups with 12–15 students for practical sessions. All students signed a consent form on the first day of the course for participating in the study and all agreed. The course was designed as a BL course using the Moodle Platform as the primary LMS. Students participated in 1.5 h of face-to-face lessons once a week and were asked to complete online activities in Moodle and projects at home planned for 1–2 h of dedication per week. The course lasted 15 weeks and was structured into three parts, each following a different modality of blended learning design. Table 1 shows a summary of the duration and objectives of each modality. In the sixth week of the course, the teacher introduced the NoteMyProgress (NMP) tool in a face-to-face session. Its use was not mandatory but it was presented as a support for organizing their learning in the course that students could use voluntarily whenever they needed.

2.2 Data Gathering Techniques

We used different data gathering techniques that included: (1) students' self-reported data about their SRL ability, (2) students' trace data with the course content and NMP functionalities, and (3) course metadata (see Table 2) Students' SRL was measured using the MSQL questionnaire [11], which they completed in week 6 before the intervention with NMP. The MSQL has 44 questions, scored based on a 7-point Likert scale and provides information on motivation (Intrinsic Value, Self-efficacy, and Text Anxiety) and self-regulated learning (Cognitive Strategy Use and Self-regulation). It was translated into French with a good level of reliability (Cronbach's alpha = 0.93).

Table 2. Description of the data sources used in the study

Source type	Source name	Description
Trace data	Moodle	Records of when students interacted with each element of the course in Moodle
	NMP	Records of when students interacted with elements on the NMP plug-in
Questionnaire	MSQL	Questionnaire by Pintrich and Groot [11] that measures different components of SRL
Metadata	In-Person Class Schedule	Time table of the in person class schedule for each student
	Course Modalities	Information on how each week of the course is organized
	Students' GPA	Average accumulated grades until the start of the course
	Students' Final Grades	Final grade obtained by the students

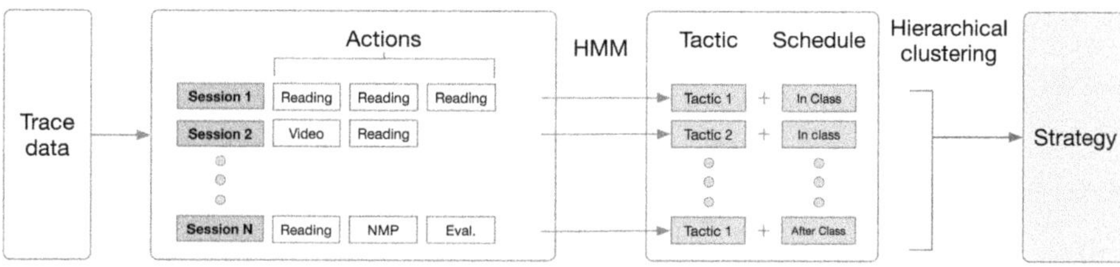

Fig. 2. Diagram of the analytical approach followed in the study.

The trace data was obtained from the log files of Moodle and NMP. The Moodle log files collect information about students' interaction with the course resources: quizzes, assignments, videos, and reading material uploaded by the teacher. The NMP log files collect the students' interaction with the different visualisations and functionalities of the plug-in.

The course metadata includes: the Moodle quizzes counting for the final grade, the student's GPA, the date of the exams, the dates for delivering the practical activities and the project, and the dates of the in-class sessions for each group.

2.3 Analytical Approach

We followed the approach proposed by Fincham et al. [4] that divide the data analysis into four steps: defining actions, detecting tactics, detecting strategies and run statistical comparisons between students' based on the strategies they employed. Before starting, all the data was anonymized, and people who did not give their consent to all parts of the analysis were removed. For replicability purposes, all the scripts used for the analysis are available in the Open Science Framework platform[1]. Figure 2 summarizes the steps we followed for transforming trace data into actions, tactics and strategies.

[1] https://osf.io/s86au/?view_only=455371582ac345809e91eb844f80c5e7.

Table 3. Session classification based on the schedule of the students

Schedule classification	Description
Day Before Class	Session registered 24 h in person class
In-Class	Session registered during class time
Day After Class	Session registered 24 h after in person class
Other Schedule	Sessions performed in all other schedules

Table 4. Library of actions in the LMS

Platform	Action name	Description
Moodle	Class planning	Interactions with the material containing the planning for the semester and the topics addressed in each week
	Evaluation	Interactions with any quiz or assignment in the course
	Hands-on work	Interactions with practical exercises related with the management of databases
	Reading	Interactions with one of the reading materials uploaded in the platform
	Solutions	Interactions with the material containing solutions to the evaluations, both practical and theoretical
	Video	Interactions with the videos uploaded in the platform
NMP	SRL support	Interaction with the visualizations of the NMP plug-in

Detecting Tactics. A tactic is defined as the underlying process that a student is applying in a given period of time Fincham et al. [4]. The period of time is defined as a study session, which corresponds to a sequence of actions not separated by more than 30 min of inactivity. Each session was classified depending on when and where it happened according to the course schedule (see Table 3). The sessions occurring between two schedules were split accordingly.

To detect students' tactics we used a Hidden Markov Model (HMM) as an unsupervised method. The hidden states represent the underlying tactic being applied during a specific session. For that, we computed for each session the proportion of each action being applied. The students' actions are described in Table 4) and are defined as their interactions with Moodle course resources, tagged by their learning purpose (planning, evaluation, hands-on work, readings, solutions or videos), and with NMP functionalities, considered as SRL support.

The number of hidden states of the model was determined using the Bayesian Information Criterion (BIC) and Akaike Information Criterion (AIC) as heuristics. These metrics consider both the complexity of the model (measured in terms of the number of parameters) and the likelihood of model given the data. The HMMs were fitted using the hmmlearn-0.2.7 Python package[2].

To answer RQ1, we analyzed how students applied different tactics over the different modalities of the course (see Sect. 2.1) and between the different schedule classifications (see Table 3). Class sessions dedicated to exams were excluded from the analysis.

[2] https://hmmlearn.readthedocs.io/en/latest/.

To answer RQ2, we analyzed tactics including students' interactions with NMP. We also use the using the Kruskal-Wallis test to compare the final grades and SRL ability profiled of those students using tactics involving NMP interactions and those who did not.

Detecting Strategies. Under the analytical approach proposed by Fincham et al. [4], strategies are defined as sequences of tactics applied by the students. These are extracted by clustering the sequences of tactics of students in the course. In our analysis, we also included the schedule classification in which the session occurred in the clustering process. We added this information to understand better how students adapt to the different BL modalities of the course. Therefore, each session was represented by a token encoding the classification of the session according to the schedule (TokenSchedule) and another token encoding the most probable tactic (TokenTactics). So, each student activity was represented by a sequence of pairs composed of TokenSchedule+TokenTactics for the strategy detection process.

After defining the sequences, we computed the similarities of the sequences using a similarity ratio based on the Levenshtein distance, which is defined as the minimal number of insertions, deletions, and/or state substitutions required to transform one sequence into another. This is then normalized, considering the length of the sequences. The implementation for this similarity measure comes from the python-Levenshtein package[3]. To find the clusters, we performed an agglomerative hierarchical clustering using the scikit-learn-0.22.2 Python package[4]. For selecting the number of clusters, we analyzed the dendrogram of the clustering process and removed for the analysis those clusters containing less than 15 students, treated as outliers.

To answer RQ1, we clustered the sessions in the whole course and separating by course modality. We then analyzed the differences between them. To answer RQ3, we analyzed whether there was a correlation between previous knowledge (GPA) and their SRL ability profile with the strategy applied by the student. In each case, we performed an ANOVA test to see which variables could be significant. Then, we performed a post-hoc analysis using pairwise t-tests between clusters. In order to prevent p-value inflation, we corrected the p-values using Holm's method. Then, we considered the strategies throughout the course without distinguishing per course modality. We then compared the differences in students' final grades using the Kruskal-Wallis. Finally, to see the effect of the overall strategy in the final grade, we performed an ANCOVA using the GPA as a covariate.

3 Results

3.1 RQ1. Manifestations of Learning Tactics and Strategies

We identified that **students use nine study tactics along the course, which differ in the number of actions and duration (Result 1.1)**. A general

[3] https://github.com/ztane/python-Levenshtein.
[4] https://scikit-learn.org/.

Table 5. Description of applied tactics in terms of the mean number of actions performed, number of occurrences during the course and mean duration of the session. F = Focused tactic (mainly 1 action performed), SD = Slightly Diverse tactic (3–4 actions performed), HD = Highly diverse (almost all actions performed). E = Evaluations, H = Hands-on, R = Reading, S = Solutions, V = Video. Wo_NMP = With-out NMP, W_NMP = With NMP.

Tactic name	Mean tactic composition							Num. of occurrences	Mean duration
	Class planning	Evaluation	Hands-on	Reading	Solutions	Video	SRL support		
F_Eval	-	6.47	-	-	-	-	-	613	00:06:59
F_HandsOn	-	-	4.97	-	-	-	-	470	00:07:57
F_Reading	-	-	-	1.38	-	-	-	583	00:03:01
F_NMP	0.04	1.14	0.17	0.22	-	-	15.6	135	00:06:46
SD_EHV	-	3.77	3.07	-	-	1.61	-	485	00:18:36
SD_EHR	0.48	6.24	0.89	1.84	-	-	-	343	00:17:08
SD_HRS	-	-	1.42	1.52	1.15	-	-	500	00:13:00
HD_Wo_NMP	0.24	5.02	2.29	2.8	1.86	0.15	-	177	00:26:06
HD_W_NMP	0.12	5.77	3.62	1.05	0.42	3.1	3.09	102	00:31:46

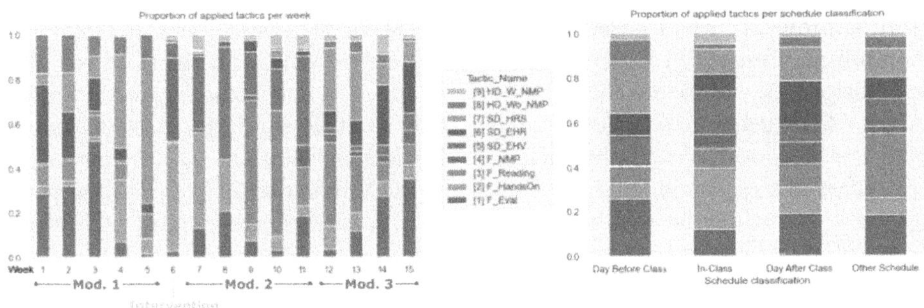

Fig. 3. Evolution of tactics applied during the course. Each vertical bar represents the proportion of tactics applied during a particular week. Below, we indicate the different modalities of the course.

summary of these tactics is provided in Table 5. Those tactics that present a high activity in a particular action were labeled as 'Focused' tactics, since students focus on a particular action (F_Eval; F_HandsOn, F_Reading; F_NMP). Those tactics that present a variety of actions were labeled as 'Slightly Diverse' tactics, with 3 or 4 different actions, or 'Highly Diverse,' with 6 or 7 actions. We also observe that tactics differ in their duration, being the Slightly (mean 13–19 min) and Highly Diverse (mean 26–31 min) longer than the Focused ones (mean of 3–8 min).

We identified that **students deploy three different strategies along the course that differ in the frequency, type of tactics employed and the moment in which they take place (before, after, or during the class) (Result 1.2)**. Table 6 shows a summarized description of the strategies in terms of the frequency of tactic usage and schedule classification. All strategies (SG.1, SG.2, SG.3) involve students' employing all tactics. However, they differ in the frequency in which tactics are deployed. First, in SG.1, the frequency of almost all tactics is higher than in the other strategies. Students using this tactic also performed significantly more sessions in other schedules beyond the in-class, before, or after-class sessions. This suggests that students employing this strategy were more autonomous than students using the other strategies. SG.3 differs from SG.1 mainly in the frequency of tactics, including Reading actions (F_Reading, SD_EHR and SD_HRS). Finally, SG.2 included the least amount of tactics overall, meaning that students who used this strategy also invested less time in the course. They also concentrated on the least varied tactics, mainly using most of their sessions in Focused tactics such as F_Eval and F_HandsOn.

Students apply different tactics and strategies depending on the modality of the course and the characteristics of the course activity (Result 1.3). Figure 3 shows how students' tactics change from week to week and according to the schedule classification. In modality 1, where students were asked to complete activities at home before the class in a more teacher-directed course design, the most frequent tactics are the Slightly and Highly Diverse involving Reading actions, while the Focused tactics involve Evaluation actions. These tactics align with activities students were asked to do in this period: work on theoretical content before the class and do exercises to evaluate their knowledge. In modality 2, in which students were asked to practice with their database without the teacher supervision, the most frequent tactics were the Focused involving reading and hands actions, and the Slightly Diverse involving evaluation actions. Again, the tactics were related with the type of activities to be performed in this phase, in which students were asked to read how to work with a database and then practice with it. Finally, in modality 3, we saw a consistent use of Slightly Diverse tactics involving hands-on, reading, evaluation, and videos. Here, students had to work on a project in groups. At this point, they have to apply all the concepts and materials seen in the course, and they revisit particular resources to review concepts (reading and videos and evaluations) and apply them in their project (hands-on). This result suggest that there is an influence of the course design and the tactics applied by the students. This change is also represented in the overall strategies applied by the students during each modality. For the first modality, students applied two different strategies (S1.1 and S1.2). These two differ in the number of tactics that include Reading actions, again showing the relationship to the activities relevant to the modality. Students applying S1.2 also worked considerably more on schedules far from the class sessions. For the second modality of the course, we found three main strategies applied by the student (S2.1, S2.2, and S2.3). Students from S2.3 used the most tactics overall, followed by S2.1. Finally, in modality 3, we detected three different strategies (S3.1, S3.2, and S3.3). While there are changes in the tactics applied by each strategy, we found that the main differences come from the schedules in which they perform their sessions.

3.2 RQ2. Impact of SRL Support on Students' Learning Strategies

Students incorporate the use of the SRL support tool (NMP plug-in) to reinforce or support their study tactics (Result 2.1). Students incorporate the SRL support in two different ways: (1) within a Highly Diverse

Table 6. Description of strategies detected in the whole course and per course modality with respect to the mean tactic frequency, schedule, and number of students. For each strategy, the two bold entries represent the two tactics most frequently applied. We are excluding from these table the clusters considered outliers (less that 15 students).

	General			Mod. 1		Mod. 2			Mod. 3		
	SG.1	SG.2	SG.3	S1.1	S1.2	S2.1	S2.2	S2.3	S3.1	S3.2	S3.3
F_Eval	**5.55**	**3.87**	**5.20**	**2.38**	**2.72**	1.36	**1.64**	2.00	**3.05**	1.47	**1.60**
F_HandsOn	3.88	**2.65**	2.83	1.30	1.13	1.69	1.16	2.96	1.65	0.46	0.33
F_Reading	**5.62**	2.39	3.37	0.50	1.30	**3.46**	1.30	**3.21**	2.15	**2.02**	1.05
F_NMP	0.82	0.35	0.51	-	-	0.62	0.16	0.62	0.70	0.63	0.43
SD_EHV	4.38	2.39	**4.40**	0.14	0.10	**2.56**	**3.45**	**5.96**	2.00	**2.00**	**1.48**
SD_EHR	3.70	1.61	2.31	0.94	2.03	0.21	0.27	0.33	1.35	1.56	0.36
SD_HRS	5.40	1.43	3.94	**1.38**	**4.20**	0.18	0.11	0.21	**2.25**	1.12	0.40
HD_Wo_NMP	1.72	0.78	1.54	0.64	1.61	0.10	0.07	0.04	0.30	0.25	0.24
HD_W_NMP	1.08	0.52	0.63	0.02	0.04	0.56	0.39	0.67	0.60	0.68	0.17
Day Before Class	6.00	3.96	6.14	3.54	4.25	0.87	1.16	2.38	1.70	1.81	0.83
In Class	7.05	7.04	7.71	1.68	1.48	2.64	3.50	2.96	4.00	4.14	4.12
Day After Class	3.80	1.00	1.86	0.36	1.93	0.90	0.27	1.29	2.15	1.26	0.48
Other Schedule	15.30	4.00	9.03	1.72	5.49	6.33	3.61	9.38	6.20	2.98	0.62
# of students	60	23	35	50	69	39	44	24	20	57	42

tactic (HD_W_NMP), in which the use of NMP is an action combined with others, or (2) within a Focused tactic (F_NMP), in which they only use NMP. Also, these two tactics are employed by students in different moments of the course. The Focus tactic (F_NMP) was mainly deployed during the first week of the intervention in which students' were presented to the tool and had time to explore it, but also during the third modality of the course, in which they had to work on the project. Since the NMP tool provides functionalities for checking which resources of the course have been or not been consulted, its usage in this period was helpful to review previous content. When incorporated with other tactics (HD_W_NMP), its use is distributed more or less equally along the course. We observe, however, that the HD_W_NMP tactics almost substitute the HD_Wo_NMP, suggesting that the use of NMP was incorporated as another action in their Highly Diverse tactics.

Students used NMP mainly in class and in other schedules beyond the class (Result 2.2). If we accumulate the use of NMP from both HD_W_NMP and F_NMP tactics, we observe that the tool was more frequently used in class (47.2%) and other schedules (27.4%) and with a much lower frequency the day after class (15.6%) and the day before class (9.7%). This suggests that students might be using the tool for checking what has to be done.

We observed that **students that had at least one use of the HD_W_NMP had a significantly higher Self-Regulation than those who did not (p-val = 0.001, effect-size = 0.70) (Result 2.3)**. This suggests a relationship between the students SRL ability profile and the adoption of SRL support.

3.3 RQ3. Relationship Between Students' Strategies, Performance and SRL Ability Profile

Students' prior knowledge (GPA) has a relationship with the general strategies they apply, being those with the lowest GPA the ones using the strategy with the least amount of tactics (Result 3.1). We found that students that applied SG.2 (mean = 11.10 out of 20) had a significantly lower GPA compared with students applying SG2.1 (mean = 13.22; p-val = 8e−4) and SG2.3 (mean = 12.86; pvalue = 0.008). Since strategy SG.2 consists of applying tactics with fewer interactions with the Moodle platform than the other two strategies, this suggests that students with lower GPA could also be those less engaged with the course.

The strategy applied by the students is related to their course final grade in the course, but this association disappears when controlling for GPA (Result 3.2). We found that students performing SG.2 had a significantly lower final grade than students performing SG.1 (p-value = 0.022) and those performing SG.3 (p-val = 0.038). However, when controlling for GPA as a covariate, the students' strategy was no longer significantly related to their final grade (p-val = 0.051). This suggests that, while GPA is the most strong predicting factor of the final grade, it is also related to the student's engagement with the course and their applied strategies.

The student's prior knowledge (GPA) has a significant relationship with the strategy chosen in each modality except for modality 2, which is related to the SRL ability profile (Result 3.3). In Modality 1, only GPA was significantly different across strategies. Students applying strategy S1.1 had a significantly lower GPA (mean = 11.9) than students applying S1.2 (mean = 13.2). In Modality 2, in which students are required to perform work in a more autonomous way, we found significant differences across groups for Self-Regulation. Students applying strategy S2.3 had a significantly higher level of Self-regulation than students applying strategies S2.1 (p-val = 0.022, effect-size = −0.86), and S2.2 (p-val = 0.032, effect-size = −0.86). We did not find significant differences in Self-regulation between strategies S2.1 and S2.2. In Modality 3, the only significant difference we found was that students applying S3.2 had a higher GPA (mean = 13.2) than those applying strategy S3.3 (mean = 11.8, p-val = 0.016).

4 Summary of Results and Discussion

Regarding RQ1 about how students' learning tactics and strategies manifest in a BL course, we found that tactics and strategies manifested in different ways depending on the pedagogical design of the course. For example, the tactics and strategies found in this study vary according to the relevant activities (Result 1.1, Result 1.3), scheduling of the study sessions (Result 1.2), and the SRL support available (Result 2.1). Furthermore, tactics and strategies differed in scheduling as well as in frequency of actions (Result 1.1 and Result 1.2). We distinguished between focused and diverse or highly diverse tactics, depending on the number of actions and its frequency. Similar results have been obtained in prior work [9] and [4], where students use tactics involving one action (more focused) or a variety of actions. In any case, it looks like the tactics employed have a relationship with the type of activities the students are asked for, reinforcing prior work which showed that learning tactics are highly dependent on pedagogical decisions [2,9]. This result also aligns with prior work [5,7] indicating that, while some students perform deep approaches to learning during the course, others use surface-level approaches where they look for specific information to pass the course. In our case, strategies SG.3 and SG.1 would be deep strategies, while SG.2 would be surface-level strategies. These results also provide further evidence on how changes in pedagogical decisions may elicit different SRL strategies from students, as shown in previous works [2,9].

Regarding RQ2 about the impact of SRL support on students' learning strategies, we found that even though some students incorporated the SRL support tool into their learning tactics (Result 2.1), the use of the tool was relatively sparse. Students mainly used the tool during face-to-face class sessions or far from the class sessions (Result 2.2). These results suggest that students used NMP functionalities designed to support planning and self-monitoring to check their past performance. Also, we observed that the students with higher SRL self-reported ability were those who use NMP more frequently (Result 2.3). This is consistent with previous work [14], which shows that students' previous abilities influence the adoption of SRL support tools. This suggests that future interventions to support SRL should focus on those with lower SRL abilities and on improving and expanding functionalities related to student planning and self-monitoring.

Regarding RQ3 about the relationship between students' strategies, performance and SRL ability profile. Prior knowledge has been shown as the main factor related to the students' strategy in those modalities including more teacher-directed work and group work as well as in the course as a whole (Result 3.1, Result 3.3). This result is aligned with previous work showing the relationship between learning strategies and prior knowledge [14,15]. The only exception to this is modality 2, where the main differences were in students' Self-Regulation self-reported ability (Result 3.3), in which students were required to conduct a higher amount of independent work. This reinforces the idea that different pedagogical decisions influence the students' strategies and suggests that in those requiring a more independent work the key factor is the students' SRL ability profile. In terms of the final performance, our results suggests that prior achievements are key for explaining students' final grades, although students' strategies also showed correlations with grades (Result 3.2). This suggests that students with prior knowledge are also the ones applying the most effective strategies. This is also consistent with prior work in the study of SRL, which shows a connection between the course design, the students' SRL ability profile, and the strategies applied [2,9].

5 Conclusions, Limitations and Future Work

In this study, we found evidence that the tactics applied by students during a course can change significantly when changing the course modality. We also found evidence indicating that the main factor that correlates to the students' learning strategy is their previous achievements. In fact, even if we found evidence that the students' strategy is related to their final grade, controlling for their prior achievement makes this relationship no longer significant. We found that students had a low level of engagement with the SRL support tool. Nonetheless, when interacting with the tool, they mainly performed highly focused sessions or incorporated this activity into previous highly diverse tactics. We found that students that applied the highly diverse tactic with the tool presented a significantly higher level of self-regulation.

One of the main limitations of this study comes from the data collection of actions performed by the students. As common with BL studies, we analyze the students based on self-reported and trace data. This limits the analysis since we could not capture the actions performed outside the Moodle platform. In particular, we did not include information regarding the interactions with the teachers, something that distinguished BL from other course modalities. Our current findings are also limited to the students of one course. Another limitation comes from the use of unsupervised methods, which makes it challenging to validate the accuracy of the detected tactics and strategies. For example, the use of dendrograms to select the number of clusters introduces a level of subjectivity to the results. Future work could apply the same type of analysis to different courses to see if the current study's findings are generalizable and consider the teacher's interventions in self-regulating students learning strategies using anthropological techniques to complement quantitative data.

Acknowledgements. This paper has been partially funded by the ANR LASER (156322). The authors acknowledge PROF-XXI, which is an Erasmus+ Capacity Building in the Field of Higher Education project funded by the European Commission (609767-EPP-1-2019-1- ES-EPPKA2-CBHE-JP). This publication reflects the views only of the authors and funders cannot be held responsible for any use which may be made of the information contained therein.

References

1. Broadbent, J.: Comparing online and blended learner's self-regulated learning strategies and academic performance. Internet High. Educ. **33**, 24–32 (2017)
2. Fan, Y., Matcha, W., Uzir, N.A., Wang, Q., Gašević, D.: Learning analytics to reveal links between learning design and self-regulated learning. Int. J. Artif. Intell. Educ. **31**(4), 980–1021 (2021)
3. Fan, Y., Saint, J., Singh, S., Jovanovic, J., Gašević, D.: A learning analytic approach to unveiling self-regulatory processes in learning tactics. In: LAK21: 11th International Learning Analytics and Knowledge Conference, Irvine, CA, USA. ACM (2021)

4. Fincham, E., Gašević, D., Jovanović, J., Pardo, A.: From study tactics to learning strategies: an analytical method for extracting interpretable representations. IEEE Trans. Learn. Technol. **12**(1), 59–72 (2019)
5. Gasevic, D., Jovanovic, J., Pardo, A., Dawson, S.: Detecting learning strategies with analytics: links with self-reported measures and academic performance. J. Learn. Anal. **4**(2), 113–128 (2017)
6. Gašević, D., Mirriahi, N., Dawson, S., Joksimović, S.: Effects of instructional conditions and experience on the adoption of a learning tool. Comput. Hum. Behav. **67**, 207–220 (2017)
7. Maldonado-Mahauad, J., Pérez-Sanagustín, M., Kizilcec, R.F., Morales, N., Munoz-Gama, J.: Mining theory-based patterns from Big data: identifying self-regulated learning strategies in Massive Open Online Courses. Comput. Hum. Behav. **80**, 179–196 (2018)
8. Maldonado-Mahauad, J., Pérez-Sanagustín, M., Moreno-Marcos, P.M., Alario-Hoyos, C., Muñoz-Merino, P.J., Delgado-Kloos, C.: Predicting learners' success in a self-paced MOOC through sequence patterns of self-regulated learning. In: Pammer-Schindler, V., Pérez-Sanagustín, M., Drachsler, H., Elferink, R., Scheffel, M. (eds.) EC-TEL 2018. LNCS, vol. 11082, pp. 355–369. Springer, Cham (2018). https://doi.org/10.1007/978-3-319-98572-5_27
9. Matcha, W., et al.: Analytics of learning strategies: role of course design and delivery modality. J. Learn. Anal. **7**(2), 45–71 (2020)
10. Panadero, E.: A review of self-regulated learning: six models and four directions for research. Front. Psychol. **8**, 422 (2017)
11. Pintrich, P.R., Groot, E.V.D.: Motivational and self-regulated learning components of classroom academic performance (1990)
12. Pérez-Álvarez, R., Maldonado, J., Pérez-Sanagustín, M.: Tools to support self-regulated learning in online environments (2018)
13. Pérez-Sanagustín, M., Pérez-Álvarez, R., Maldonado-Mahauad, J., Villalobos, E., Sanza, C.: Designing a moodle plugin for promoting learners' self-regulated learning in blended learning, Toulouse, France (in press)
14. Pérez-Sanagustín, M., et al.: A MOOC-based flipped experience: scaffolding SRL strategies improves learners' time management and engagement. Comput. Appl. Eng. Educ. **29**(4), 750–768 (2021)
15. Taub, M., Azevedo, R., Bouchet, F., Khosravifar, B.: Can the use of cognitive and metacognitive self-regulated learning strategies be predicted by learners' levels of prior knowledge in hypermedia-learning environments? Comput. Hum. Behav. **39**, 356–367 (2014)
16. Yoon, M., Hill, J., Kim, D.: Designing supports for promoting self-regulated learning in the flipped classroom. J. Comput. High. Educ. **33**(2), 398–418 (2021). https://doi.org/10.1007/s12528-021-09269-z
17. Zhou, M., Winne, P.H.: Modeling academic achievement by self-reported versus traced goal orientation. Learn. Instr. **22**(6), 413–419 (2012)

Promoting Universal Design for Learning Through Digital Assistive Tools in GamesHUB

Lionel Alvarez[1,2(✉)], Aous Karoui[2,3], Thierry Geoffre[2], Mireille Rodi[2], and Nathalie Dherbey-Chapuis[2]

[1] University of Fribourg, 1700 Fribourg, Switzerland
lionel.alvarez@unifr.ch
[2] University for Teacher Education, 1700 Fribourg, Switzerland
{aous.karoui,thierry.geoffre,mireille.rodi, nathalie.dherbey}@edufr.ch
[3] University of Grenoble Alpes, 38400 Saint-Martin-d'Hères, France

Abstract. The topic of inclusive education for underrepresented groups in the mainstream education system has long been an issue, mainly because of questions about the modalities and resources used. Today, this matter is much more affordable, thanks to digital technology. Indeed, in an education system that is becoming blended, and in which the computer plays an essential role in the presentation of information, the means are now more varied and the issue of heterogeneity of student profiles can be better addressed. These perspectives relate closely to Universal Design for Learning (UDL).

This article presents a full Web inclusive platform for gamified learning, named GamesHUB. The platform offers special assistance to students with special needs (dyslexic students, L2 speakers, students with language disorders…) through Digital Assistive Tools (DAT) such as text-to-speech, spaced text for dyslexics, high-contrasted display, real-time translation in their native language… The choice of these DAT and their functions will be explained through didactic and psycholinguistic arguments.

GamesHUB platform is developed by the "anonymized laboratory" (Switzerland). It is mainly aimed at primary learning in ordinary classes in the French-speaking part of Switzerland.

Keywords: Universal design for learning · Inclusive learning · Gamification authoring tool · Digital assistive tools

1 Introduction

When schools must deal with the diversity of students and their needs, several approaches exist. After the Salamanca statement [1] that asserted that every child has a basic right to education, integration perspective (pupils are welcome into mainstream education, but must adapt to school) and inclusion perspective (school adapts to students' needs) were promoted. In these approaches, the variety within the school organization and the

I. Hilliger et al. (Eds.): EC-TEL 2022, LNCS 13450, pp. 421–426, 2022.
https://doi.org/10.1007/978-3-031-16290-9_31

teaching practices were driven by perceived or assessed students' needs and, per se, leave the cause of the adjustment effort to the child and his/her special educational needs.

With universal design for learning (UDL), the approach is different [2]. As diversity becomes the norm, variety is a standard. Different means of engagement (why should I learn), of representation (how is the knowledge presented), and of action and expression (what should I do with this knowledge) should be offered by the teacher to move toward an education for all. With the diversity embedded within the school environment, the hope is to facilitate every child learning, whatever her/his needs. However, UDL is not rejecting the inclusive approach where adaptations are made based on students' needs. So, the variety of means should be included from the very beginning of instructional design. That is what is being done with GamesHUB learning platform, thanks to digital technologies that can facilitate diversification of learning experiences.

In this context, we present the online platform for playful learning GamesHUB, developed by the University for Teacher Education Fribourg (HEP-Fr) in partnership with the IT section of the Fribourg Vocational School (EMF). The paper is organized as follows: Firstly, GamesHUB platform and its features are presented. Secondly, the additional features are described, we call them Digital Assistive Tools (DAT), and they are built into GamesHUB from the start to tend toward UDL.

2 GamesHUB

2.1 Purpose

GamesHUB is designed for students aged 6–12 in French-speaking school, using game-based learning and customized learning pathways. Its purpose is to allow every student, including those with special needs, to develop skills if they can interact with the computer. The platform provides learning games related to various learning areas within the framework of the Plan d'Études Romand[1] which is the official competency framework in the context of GamesHUB implementation. It also supports the teacher in the continuous improvement of teaching and learning by recording tracks of students' activities in compliance with the European GDPR (General Data Protection Rules). The data of each learning game is recorded and can then be visualized and analyzed by the teacher to identify the difficulties of students. A variety of additional features were embedded into GamesHUB framework as DAT (see Sect. 2.4).

2.2 Architecture and Hosting

GamesHUB is a client-server platform. It is hosted on the AlpHosting server as shown in Fig. 1. The platform is designed on a three-layer architecture (View, Processing, Data access) that is independent and allows for great flexibility. The View layer is based on a Node.JS server that publishes a lightweight interface used by a web browser. The Processing layer is based on a JavaEE RESTful server on Apache Tomcat. This access method guarantees independent access to the data. The database is hosted on the open-source MariaDB platform. Each component is called through the secure HTTPS protocol.

[1] https://www.plandetudes.ch.

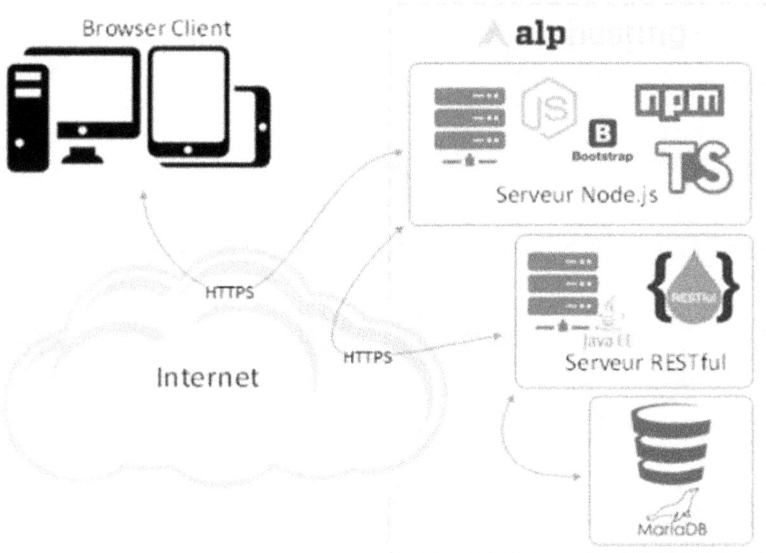

Fig. 1. Internal architecture of the GamesHUB platform

2.3 Features

Currently, the GamesHUB platform provides access to learning games on various themes, mainly learning French as the schooling language. This access is possible in a "self-play" mode and in the "custom pathway" mode. Indeed, the "self-play" mode provides game sessions for exploration, training, evaluation, and content creation each time for a single learning game. These four ways of interacting with each game are already a move toward diversity of experiences, based on four different taxonomy level of learning [3, 4]. Students can easily switch from one taxonomy level to another in the "self-play" mode, so they can choose if they want to explore the knowledge, practice the associated skills, pass tests, and send data to their teachers, or create new game levels to submit to the classroom or the whole community of users.

However, the "custom pathway" mode allows to have specific sequences of different games and/or game levels. The teacher can design a specific pathway based on didactic considerations and assign it to specific students or the whole class. In this mode, the student loses her/his freedom to browse through games, levels or ways of playing (explore, train, evaluate, create), because the choice of games and game levels is made by the teacher. It is then possible to track the overall progression of a student through these pathways and the teacher can access an extensive view of this progression (see Fig. 2) with what has been done, scored, etc.

Whatever the mode engaged ("self-play" or "custom pathway"), the student must be able to access the content and the instructions of the game level. This might require maximizing student's autonomy and facilitating the reading comprehension. That is where the DAT come into the play.

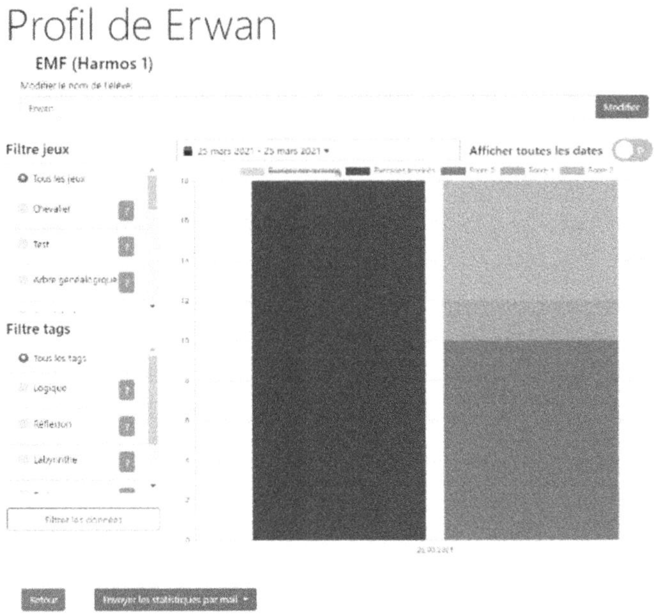

Fig. 2. A screenshot of the dashboard monitoring student activity

2.4 Digital Assistive Tools

Several features are built into GamesHUB so a diversity of students can use it whenever s/he wants to support her/his learning. The features were chosen according to three main criteria: (1) responding to needs often present within the schools where GamesHUB implementation is planned, (2) supported by scientific literature [5], and (3) based on libre/free technologies, as far as possible. Currently, six features (out of eight) are available (see Fig. 3 and 4).

- "Mon Pad" is a free online text editor – based on Etherpad[2] technology – associated to each student (the teacher can read/write its content, too) designed to free up working memory with the help of note taking. To be aligned with state regulations, the notes are completely erased every year, end of July.
- "Pad de classe" is built on the same technology as "Mon Pad" but is integrated in GamesHUB for a whole class (typically 20 to 25 students), where everyone can ask for help and give support. The intent is to enable peer learning and subtle mediations from the teacher that target one need but could be useful for everyone.
- "Dico image" is a simple image search engine based on Wikimedia that is designed to help students that struggle with vocabulary to understand the contents. The intent is to reduce learning barriers for students who speak French as a second language or do not have the cultural background to understand the cultural foundations of a specific assignment.

[2] https://etherpad.org/.

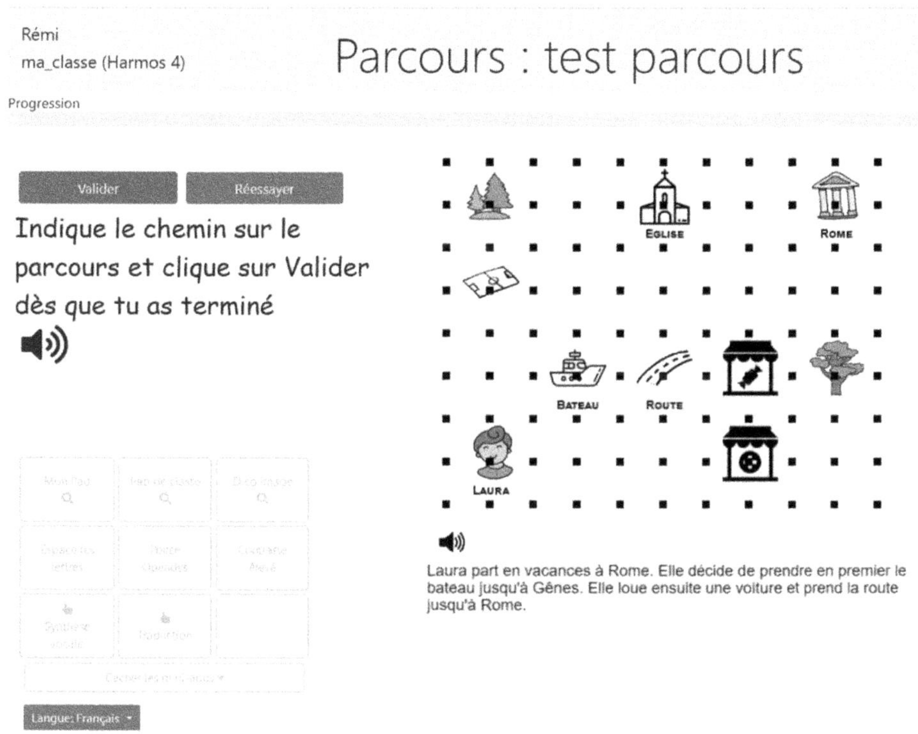

Fig. 3. An overview of the Digital Assistive Tools component integrated to the GamesHUB screen

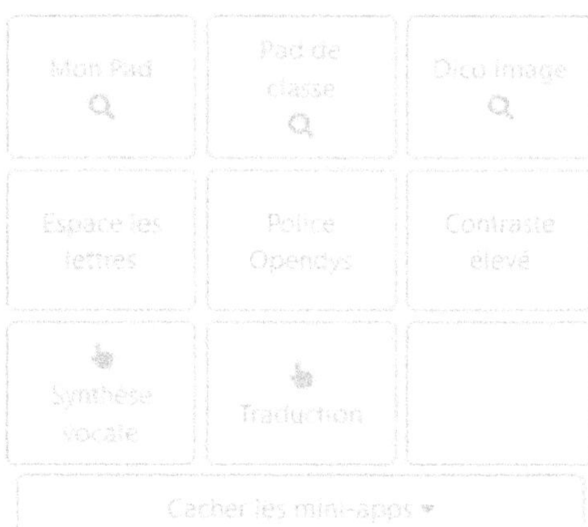

Fig. 4. An overview of the Digital Assistive Tools within GamesHUB

- "Espace les lettres" (add space between letters) and "Police Opensys" (https://opendyslexic.org/) are two text display alternatives to facilitate learning for students with reading disabilities or difficulties.

- "Contraste élevé" (high contrast) is a simple solution that does what it announces. It also helps the game designers to identify if contrast is needed to assess the games and assignments and, in this case, make changes in the development of the game.

Two last features are currently being deployed. "Synthèse vocale" is a text-to-speech solution for struggling readers, and "Traduction" is a translator for students who speak French as a second language. The challenge for these two features development is mainly about finding a solution in French that is efficient and free/open source.

3 Future Work

Currently, experiments have begun in schools in French-speaking Switzerland to verify whether GamesHUB design allows for more inclusive learning. Targeted classrooms are 5–6 Harmos (8- to 10-year-old children), because currently the games developed are based on contents for this degree that are didactically organized. First, GamesHUB usability is tested in two classrooms for layout improvement (for instance, accessibility of feature, clarity of assignments, ease of use). Then, performance improvement in reading and comprehension skills will be systematically assessed thanks to multiple baselines single-case experimental design—DAT introduction is the independent variable—with a variety of pupil profiles to document if GamesHUB is effectively promoting UDL.

4 Conclusion

In this paper, we presented GamesHUB platform designed for inclusive education and intended to ordinary and special needs learners (L2 speakers, dyslexics, students with language impairment…). We introduced the general features of GamesHUB including the self-play and the pathway modes. Then, we presented additional features that we call Digital Assistive Tools (DAT), intended to promote UDL. Our future work consists in experimenting GamesHUB platform with all these features to gather feedback from teachers and students on both DAT and personalized learning pathways.

References

1. UNESCO: Déclaration de Salamanque et cadre d'action pour l'éducation et les besoins spéciaux. Conférence Mondiale sur l'éducation et les besoins éducatifs spéciaux: accès et qualité (1994)
2. CAST: About Universal Design for Learning. https://www.cast.org/impact/universal-design-for-learning-udl. Accessed 21 Apr 2022
3. Anderson, L.W.: A Taxonomy for Learning, Teaching, and Assessing: A Revision of Bloom's. Pearson, London (2013)
4. Alvarez, L., Karoui, A., Ramalho, M., Geoffre, T.: Fondements pédago-didactiques d'un environnement informatique d'apprentissage destiné aux jeunes apprenants de l'école primaire. In: Lefevre, M., Michel, C., Geoffre, T., Rodi, M., Alvarez, L., Karoui, A. (eds.) EIAH2021 (2021). https://blog.hepfr.ch/eiah2021/wp-content/uploads/sites/12/2021/07/actesEIAH2021-VersionPubliee-VersionHAL.pdf
5. Rodi, M., Dherbey Chapuis, N., Geoffre, T., Alvarez, L.: Faciliter l'accès à l'apprentissage du français pour tous au sein de parcours adaptables de jeux éducatifs numériques. ALSIC (2022). (in press)

iTeachApp, A Teaching Analytics Tool for Providing Self-assessment and Recommendations to Teachers

Ibtissem Bennacer(✉), Rémi Venant, and Sébastien Iksal

University of Le Mans, Avenue Olivier Messiaen, 72085 Le Mans, France
{Ibtissem.Bennacer,Remi.Venant,Sebastien.Iksal}@univ-lemans.fr

Abstract. In order to support teachers to engage themselves in a learning process to improve their techno-pedagogical skills, and to relieve instructional designers (IDs) of their workload, we have previously designed a behavioral computer model of teachers that allows their evaluation from a LMS mastery perspective, and paves the way to teaching analytics and recommendations. To instrument this model and provide teachers and IDs with a digital support that best meets their expectations, we present here the user-centered method we followed to (i) evaluate our model to their perceptions, (ii) determine consistent uses relative to their needs, and (iii) develop iTeachApp, an application that provides teachers with a personal analytics dashboard and automatic recommendations, and offer IDs institutional analytics, to detect specific profiles of teachers and get insights of common LMS behaviors at different scales.

Keywords: Teaching analytics · Academic analytics · Learning management system · Teacher evaluation · User-centered approach · Behavioral model · Dashboard

1 Introduction

Learning management systems (LMS) have been widely adopted by higher education institutions around the world for over a decade, with a considerable acceleration during the COVID period [8]. On the other hand, the number of LMS users was not growing as quickly as expected, although they were considered for a long time as a useful tool to facilitate teaching and learning activities [10]. Many teachers face several difficulties in integrating these platforms into their practices. Their main problems seem to be technical and organizational, due to the lack of support and the lack of time dedicated to its learning [5]. Furthermore, many universities hire instructional designers especially for helping teachers to develop, enhance and diversify their pedagogical designs as well as their skills in technology enhanced learning (TEL) tools. However, universities still struggle to carry out their missions with only few instructional designers (IDs) compared to the teacher population (e.g., there are 6 engineers for 630 teachers in our university). They also lack

I. Hilliger et al. (Eds.): EC-TEL 2022, LNCS 13450, pp. 427–433, 2022.
https://doi.org/10.1007/978-3-031-16290-9_32

insight into teachers' competencies, while teachers are not always aware about the features TEL systems such as an LMS offer.

In order to deal with these issues, we aim to support teachers' self-assessment of their own practice on a LMS for them to engage as learners of their TEL environment, and at the same time, to reduce the work pressure of the instructional designers. Hence, we have proposed in a previous work a behavioral model composed of six axes (evaluation, reflection, collaboration, resources, communication, interactivity and gamification), on top of which we have built several teaching analytics (TA) indicators to provide teachers with self and social awareness (usage trends, curiosity and homogeneity scores) [2].

In this paper, we expose the user-centered method we applied to instrument our model and its indicators within a TA application that we describe in detail as well. To reach these goals, we first examine (RQ1) how understandable our model was by teachers and what limitations we could detect with regard to their own perception of their LMS use. Secondly, we attempt to (RQ2) determine how teachers would be willing to engage in an activity of self-assessment and improvement of their LMS skills. In particular, we seek to determine what type of recommendation would best fit teachers' needs and practices (RQ2.1). Since our goal is not to provide an application that would completely substitute for instructional designers but a way to leverage teacher solicitation, we aim to find out (RQ2.2) whether teachers would be willing to help their peers and collaborate with IDs. Finally, we want to identify the kind of visualizations and functionalities that could be interesting for IDs in order to assist them in the decision-making process (RQ3).

2 Related Work

Teacher evaluation has been defined by [1] as the achievements of teachers and what they need to develop or improve in their performance. However, there are few studies that focus on the evaluation of teachers' techno-pedagogical performances in LMS. We suggest then to provide teachers with sufficient material for self-evaluation and learning, a requirement that should be met before attempting to include such skills as part of any institutional evaluation.

To involve end-users in a research project, two types of approaches are commonly followed: a user-centered approach and a participatory approach. They both allow to capture the users' needs and thus to develop, in an iterative way, a quality tool that meets the users' expectations [3]. The user-centered design practice incorporates careful consideration of users' needs, desires, and their limitations throughout the design process, which allows for the assessment of both effectiveness and relevance of the tool [4]. For instance, [3] employed this approach to ensure an explicit understanding of user needs and contexts in order to develop a dynamic learning dashboard generator. On the other hand, participatory approaches belong to the user-centered approaches, but they advocate the active involvement of users, which means performing all the steps of a project in a collaborative and shared way so that the product meets users' needs and is usable

[9]. For example, [6] have developed a method for participative design of learning dashboards, which they call PADDLE (PArticipative Design of Dashboard for Learning in Education). In the context of our work, we aim at developing an application for teachers that does not require teacher involvement in all the design phases. Therefore, we have opted for a non-participative user-centered approach to instrument our behavioral model and its indicators.

3 Methodology

In order to instrument the model and its indicators within an application that would be more easily accepted by teachers and IDs, we elaborated an online questionnaire for teachers, and we also scheduled three interviews with the instructional designers of the university (IDs).

The questionnaire consists of four sections. The first section focuses on general questions to capture contextual factors that characterize the teacher (university site, gender, age, etc.). The second section aims to study teachers' satisfaction of LMS via the SUS questionnaire (system usability scale)[1]. The third section is devoted to validating the range of features our model covers by letting teachers check that their practices could be described through our model. In the last section, we collect the teachers' needs and expectations so that we could anticipate and make possible modifications to our application before the experimentation.

Subsequently, we conducted three non-directive interviews with IDs to gather their feedback given their experience with teachers, in order to define and develop the support tool. We chose this type of interview to ensure that interviewees would be free to develop further hypotheses during the exchanges. During the first interview, we used the statistical results of the questionnaire addressed to teachers as a basis for discussion, together with a first prototype of the application. In the second and third interviews, we proposed a new prototype, taking into account the comments made beforehand.

4 Findings

Questionnaire: we received 76 responses from teachers. With respect to the use of the platform's features, most teachers (63 respondents strongly agree and 11 agree) frequently use the LMS resources. Assessment features are in second place with 20 respondents strongly agreeing and 30 agreeing. In third place, gamification, collaboration, feedback and communication features have similar but low usage compared to the first ones (respectively 4 teachers, 7 teachers, 11 teachers and 18 teachers who use them very frequently). On the other hand, some teachers mentioned using other features: (i) activity reports indicating the number of views for each activity and resource, as well as (ii) the use of "groups" functionality allowing a teacher to form groups of students within a course. With the exception

[1] https://www.usability.gov/how-to-and-tools/methods/system-usability-scale.html.

of these two functionalities, we have not identified any use of the LMS that is not covered by our model. This model will therefore be enriched to integrate a student management dimension and complete the reflection axis with an activity reports functionality.

In the last section, 57 teachers expressed their wish to have a tool for peer recommendations or feedback on their use of the platform, and 14 teachers for self-assessment. We left the question opened to other proposals, so one teacher mentioned that they preferred trainings over several times, two other teachers proposed tutorials for certain functionalities or a guide of good practices and what they can do on the LMS. 7 teachers mentioned their unwillingness to get a tool complementary to the university's LMS, probably because they are satisfied with the platform, so they do not need help. Among teachers seeking help, we received 51 responses, both asking for help from IDs and from a close colleague. Finally, 65 teachers are willing to help their colleagues if they ask. Therefore, these responses assess the need to provide a support tool for teachers as a significant portion are interested in having one and many would like to be able to incorporate recommendations from close colleagues and instructional designers.

Interviews: based on the results of this questionnaire, we developed prototype of our application that was presented during the first interview with IDs, and improved afterwards. The latter provided insights on the need to promote digital trust (e.g., identity protection, document protection) [7]. In our case, this trust implies the need to give the teacher the right to accept or refuse to be recommended to colleagues. On the other hand, they emphasized the importance of presenting teachers with the list of courses studied and the time interval of each course so that they are aware of the origin of their results. In addition, they suggested clarifying some of the terms so that they would be more understandable to teachers; for example, the regularity score becomes homogeneity score, and the subtitle "active" used to refer to the pattern of use of the LMS becomes "intensive use". On the dashboard intended to the instructional designers, they were interested in having a filter by indicator (LMS usage trend, curiosity score and homogeneity score) to better identify teachers in need or those considered as experts by axis. Additionally, they indicated their desire to have a link to see each teacher's dashboard (without having access to their profile page).

5 Application

After we made all the necessary modifications to our tool, we were able to develop a first version of the iTeachApp application, which is now ready to be experimented by teachers and IDs.

Once logged in, teachers can have an overview of their situation. Each axis (**A** in Fig. 1) is detailed in an accordion with a different background color: green for axes where the teacher has a high tendency to use the platform features represented by the axis in question (intensive use), and red color for the opposite case (non-intensive use). For each accordion, the two different curiosity and homogeneity scores are also included as well as a description of the axis and the scores. On **B** in Fig. 1, we provide a radar visualization that summarizes both scores so that the teacher can have a comparative view of the different axes. This allows them to easily visualize the representation of their use of the institutional LMS and to position themselves on their wishes and preferences to improve their mastery. Axis and scores are provided with help message that allow the user to understand its overall signification through a simple vocabulary.

We have also proposed 3 recommender systems aiming at helping teachers to improve their practices in the university LMS. These latter, given for each axis, are shown on part **C**. In this specific case of the axis "Evaluation", the expanded part of the accordion allows to visualize: (i) a set of unused features that might facilitate the teachers' evaluation of their students, (ii) the "Contact an Instructional designer" button which opens an email box to directly contact the IDs with a pre-formatted email indicating the name of the axis and the scores obtained, and finally (iii) the "Solicit a close colleague" button opening a window that displays the top 3 most recommended colleagues who are close physically and thematically. For each teacher, an example of one of their courses selected as relevant for that specific axis is given with a description of the course.

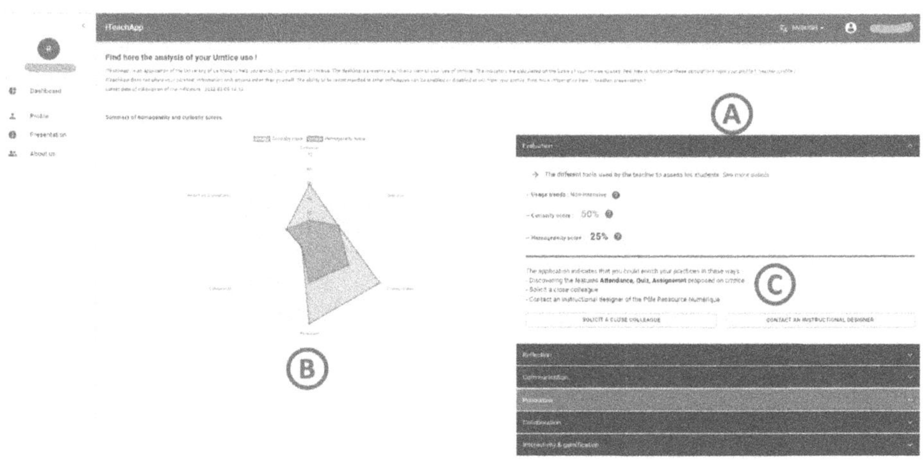

Fig. 1. Teacher's dashboard.

On a page devoted to the teacher's profile, the latter can accept or refuse to be recommended to their colleagues, choose the maximum number of recommendations per month in which they can appear, by default, each teacher can be recommended to a maximum of 3 colleagues per month. Finally, the teacher can consult the list of their courses taken into account in the evaluation and choose to remove those that do not seem relevant.

iTeachApp is also addressed to instructional designers to help them detect cases of interest. The Fig. 2 represents the ID's dashboard. On part **A**, a data table is provided to visualize the list of teachers with their information (name, first name, service and specialty). On section **B**, visualizations provide aggregated evaluation result over the entries of the table (depending of the filter chosen). Individual evaluation dashboard can be displayed by clicking on the "Axis/score" button for a given teacher. At right of section **B**, a radar visualization shows the average of the two scores (curiosity and homogeneity) by axis. On the left, a bar chart summarizes the average number of teachers with intensive/non-intensive use by axis as well. The data in these 3 elements (table, radar, bar chart) depends on the two filters at the top of the page. The first allows IDs to select teachers according to their specialties or departments to which they are assigned, which makes it easier for them to compare specialties and evaluate departments. The second one filters teachers according to their metric values and by axis. For example, the choice of the indicator "LMS trend usage" with the value "intensive use" and the axis "Communication" allows to identify all the teachers of the university who frequently use the communication tools of the institutional LMS.

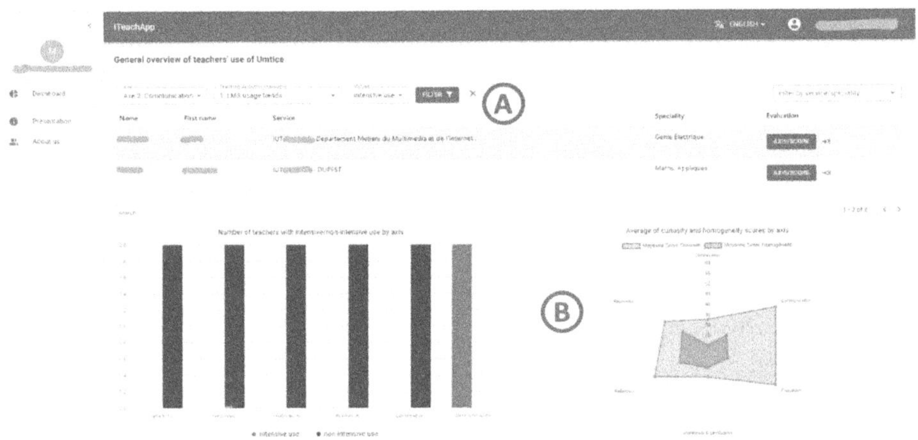

Fig. 2. Instructional designers' dashboard.

The different TA metrics we propose can thereby be used to detect teachers in particular needs for a certain axis, in order to propose them consistent and precise help. On the other hand, expert teachers in particular domains of competencies can also be identified, a wish IDs have as they are also looking for these profiles to obtain precise feedback on their LMS in order to define its functional evolution, and to better organize tutoring for newcomers.

6 Conclusion

On the basis of an explainable machine learning model, we followed here a user-centered method to evaluate our model from the teachers' point of view, and to identify how best we could provide teachers and IDs with suitable Teaching Analytics based on this model to help them improve their LMS skills and support teachers' needs respectively. Given the results we obtained from questionnaire to teachers, we discovered that the behavioral model could be enriched by integrating a dimension concerning student management, while the existing "reflection" axis could be completed with a functionality we did not detect previously. Regarding teachers' expectations, we noticed a great interest on their part to have a support tool that provides recommendations from close colleagues and instructional designers. The majority of them were also open to help each other and to improve their practices on the LMS. With respect to these results together with the interviews of the IDs, we were able to select wise types of visualizations and recommendations to provide to teachers.

With an operational version of iTeachApp, our short-term perspective is to experiment it at a university scale in order to study its usability and appropriation by teachers as well as IDs' interest in it. In the medium term, we intend to improve the behavioral model and our application by considering teachers' and IDs feedback after the experimentation. At long term, we obviously project to study the impact this application could have on teachers' practice.

References

1. Almutairi, T.S., Shraid, N.S.: Teacher evaluation by different internal evaluators: head of departments, teachers themselves, peers and students. Int. J. Eval. Res. Educ. **10**(2), 588–596 (2021)
2. Bennacer, I., Venant, R., Iksal, S.: Towards a self-assessment tool for teachers to improve LMS mastery based on teaching analytics. In: De Laet, T., Klemke, R., Alario-Hoyos, C., Hilliger, I., Ortega-Arranz, A. (eds.) EC-TEL 2021. LNCS, vol. 12884, pp. 320–325. Springer, Cham (2021). https://doi.org/10.1007/978-3-030-86436-1_28
3. Dabbebi, I., Gilliot, J.M., Iksal, S.: User centered approach for learning analytics dashboard generation. In: CSEDU 2019: 11th International Conference on Computer Supported Education, vol. 2, pp. 260–267 (2019)
4. Khaled, M.: Learning styles, personalization, and learning management systems: towards a student-centred LMS approach (2021)
5. Nashed, N.N., Lahoud, C., Abel, M.-H.: Educational resources recommender system for teachers: why and how? In: Troiano, L., et al. (eds.) Advances in Deep Learning, Artificial Intelligence and Robotics. LNNS, vol. 249, pp. 71–80. Springer, Cham (2022). https://doi.org/10.1007/978-3-030-85365-5_7
6. Oliver-Quelennec, K., Bouchet, F., Carron, T., Pinçon, C.: Can a learning analytics dashboard participative design approach be transposed to an online-only context? In: 18th International Conference Cognition and Exploratory Learning in Digital Age (2021)
7. Pietrzak, P., Takala, J.: Digital trust-asystematic literature review. In: Forum Scientiae Oeconomia, vol. 9, pp. 59–71 (2021)
8. Setiawan, A., Munzil, Fitriyah, I.J.: Trend of learning management system (LMS) platforms for science education before-after Covid-19 pandemic. In: AIP Conference Proceedings, vol. 2330, p. 060005. AIP Publishing LLC (2021)
9. Spinuzzi, C.: The methodology of participatory design. Tech. Commun. **52**(2), 163–174 (2005)
10. Wang, W.-T., Wang, C.-C.: An empirical study of instructor adoption of web-based learning systems. Comput. Educ. **53**(3), 761–774 (2009). https://doi.org/10.1016/j.compedu.2009.02.021

Deliberate Practice of Handwriting: Supervision Under the Ghost of an Expert

Olivier Dikken(✉), Bibeg Limbu, and Marcus Specht

Center for Education and Learning, TU Delft, The Netherlands
o.d.f.dikken@student.tudelft.nl

Abstract. It takes considerable time, experience, and direct assistance from teachers to become a skilled writer. Handwriting fluency is one of the predictors of writing quality among students. However, students do not receive enough teacher supervision as a beginner to develop handwriting fluency in a proper manner. The "Calligraphy tutor" presented in this paper, is an application developed to assist teachers to help students learn proper handwriting fluency skills. Calligraphy tutor is designed to support deliberate practice of handwriting, in which teachers play the central role. To reduce workload of teachers, Calligraphy tutor automates repetitive actions such as providing mundane real-time feedback, while also collecting performance data from students, allowing students to practice without the presence of a teacher. The collected performance data is used by teachers to further personalise students' training.

Keywords: Psychomotor · Deliberate practice · Handwriting · Sensors

1 Introduction

Handwriting is an essential complex skill which encapsulates many other sub skills such as attention, perception and fine motor skills [10]. Handwriting impacts children's literacy skills [17]. Functional MRI techniques show that writing activates parts of the brain in children required for reading success [11]. Poor handwriting skills potentially impede the academic development of children well into their adulthood [7]. Handwriting is further advantageous into the adulthood as well. For example, in adolescents, taking notes with handwriting shows better retention and retrieval of information [16]. Therefore, it is fundamental to acquire proficiency in handwriting. However, [5] found that the students' handwriting performance is continuously degrading.

Prolonged repeated practice is required to internalise fine psychomotor skills such as handwriting, especially for children with dysgraphia [9]. Internalisation of any lower-level skills, such as in handwriting, is defined as the acquisition of fluency and automaticity of that particular skill such that no additional cognitive load is incurred during its execution. Internalisation of low-level handwriting skills, such as gestures, lead to lower cognitive demands which increases overall

I. Hilliger et al. (Eds.): EC-TEL 2022, LNCS 13450, pp. 434–440, 2022.
https://doi.org/10.1007/978-3-031-16290-9_33

writing performance [15]. However, incorrectly internalised skills are difficult to rectify and further affect mastery of complex skills [1]. Accordingly, Bonneton-Botte et al. [2] found that teachers felt their presence was especially necessary in the early phases of handwriting learning, namely in gesture recognition. Teachers indicated, the lack of time and resources necessary [14] to supervise children in a personalised manner during gesture recognition, as one of the primary causes of incorrect internalisation of handwriting techniques. They consider it essential to provide enough teacher support to children early on during their discovery phase of learning handwriting. In this paper, we present "Calligraphy Tutor (CaT)", a handwriting teaching/learning sensor-based application which aids teachers to train students while reducing time and resources required of teachers, such that a single teacher can effectively instruct multiple students. CaT explores the following research question

1. How can we use sensors to support teachers to teach handwriting?

2 Deliberate Practice

Deliberate practice (DP) is essential for attainment and maintenance of skills such as handwriting [3]. DP is a teacher/ mentor (simply mentioned as teacher here onward) driven practice with the explicit goal of improving performance [6]. It aids students in internalising handwriting, improving their overall writing performance [15]. DP depends on the teacher's active involvement before, during, and after practice. Ericsson [6] states that expert teachers are vital for supporting the five key conditions for improving performance which lead to DP.

DP1 The teacher must define the task concretely with a clear goal and ensure that the student understands it.
DP2 Task difficulty must be barely above the students expertise level.
DP3 The practice task must be designed and performed in accordance with individualised instruction and guidance of a teacher.
DP4 The teacher should provide immediate informative and actionable feedback on each performance of the practice task which allows students to make appropriate adjustments to improve.
DP5 The students are able to "repeatedly perform the same or similar tasks".

In DP, a teacher is involved from planning a practice task for an individual student, creating it, and providing feedback during and after practice repeatedly. The teacher is also responsible for deciding when the student should progress to more complex tasks [6]. Evidently, teachers are central to the idea of DP. Hence, the CaT intends to support the teacher in classes with many students where it is not possible for him/her to provide sufficient time and resource to each student, such that students may achieve DP. To do this, the CaT implements a multitude of features which facilitate the five key conditions mentioned above. The mapping of these features with conditions (DP 1-5) are presented in Fig. 1. The teacher must create a practice task (Target trace) in the CaT environment

(DP1), and provide meta data in the form of written instructions that indicate the learning goals of the task and a list relevant of features in order of priority (DP3). The teacher then needs to replicate the target trace multiple times which generates the Expert Distribution Model (EDM, see Sect. 3.1). The student loads the created task and receives instructions on how to perform the task (DP3). While practising, live performance data from the student is used to compare his/her performance with the EDM to provide real-time actionable feedback (DP4). We define actionable feedback as simple immediate responses to incorrect actions of the student, which helps the student correct them without demanding high mental effort. To avoid information overload, this feedback is given on the mistakes in dimensions most relevant to the task which is predefined by the teacher (DP3). Feedback is provided via multiple modes (modalities) such as visual (e.g. ink color, width) or audio (e.g. a beep) and should primarily raise awareness about the student's mistakes. The student practices the task repeatedly (DP5). At the end of the session, the student submits the session, after which, writing analytics are generated, with the help of EDM, for the teacher to plan the next practice session.

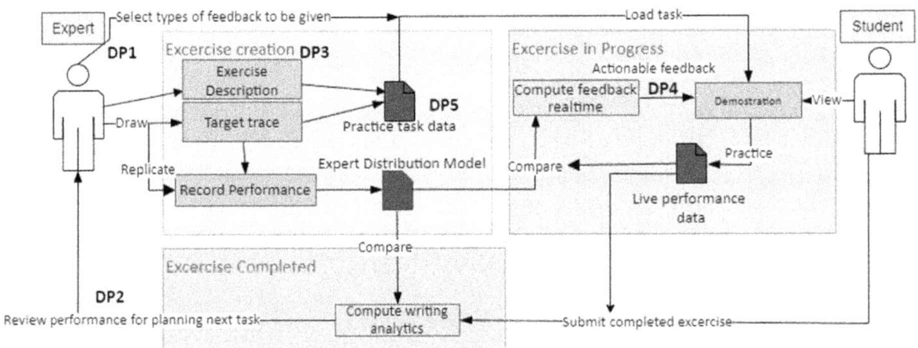

Fig. 1. Handwriting practice loop with CaT

3 Calligraphy Tutor (CaT)

CaT is a Windows application built for any Microsoft Windows™PC or tablet with a digitizer and a pen support using Windows INK API. CaT uses the sensor data from the pen and the digitizer to allow a teacher to create EDMs and practice tasks. Practice task data is recorded in a temporal format. Students can load the practise task and the CaT provides feedback with the help of EDM. Feedback is provided by visual and auditory means using the PC. The CaT software is written in c# using the ASP.Net core 3.1 framework.

The CaT aims to internalise correct low-level psychomotor aspects of handwriting, in contrast to other language learning applications. Such skills are trained in early phases of handwriting learning, such as gesture recognition, where the process is more important than the end product [4]. Therefore, the CaT focuses not on retrieval of alphabets/characters but fluency and automaticity of correct psychomotor skills in the context of handwriting. This is similar to what Limbu et al. [13] pursued. The CaT takes their idea further by implementing, comparatively, more advanced algorithms for generating feedback and additional features such as writing analytics. Below we present some of the key components in the CaT, in contrast to Limbu et al. [13]'s application .

3.1 Expert Distribution Model (EDM)

Limbu et al. [13] relied on a single instance of expert performance data, i.e. their expert model relied only on one specific instance of a written trace/s as the ground truth. We define trace as individual lines that from a character. However, in handwriting, minor variations in certain properties/dimensions of the written trace/s are often acceptable. EDM dynamically accounts for these variations in the target trace/s based on the replication attempts by the teacher(s) (see Fig. 2b). These variations can be scaled to increase the tolerance as needed.

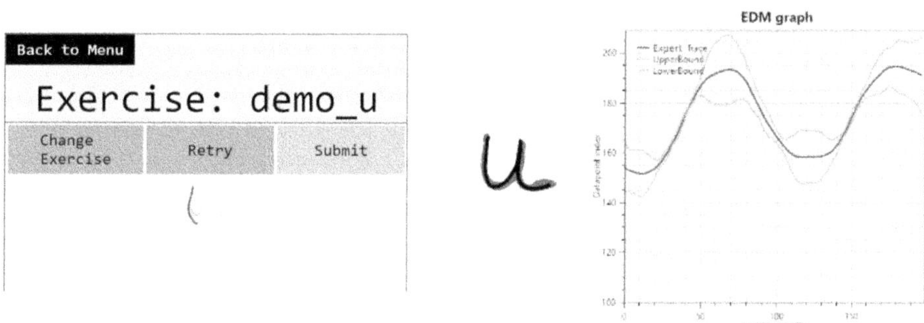

(a) Real-time feedback on features X, Y in CaT

(b) Visualisation of EDM's spatial distribution (green) & it's graph for feature Y

Fig. 2. CaT feedback elements (Color figure online)

The EDM in CaT is used as ground truth for a single exercise, and represents the teachers' performance. The EDM captures data as a list of sequential datapoints each containing several dimensions considered as important feature for handwriting as determined by Shin et al. [18] e.g. *pressure*, *direction*. For each task the EDM is annotated with meta data such as the most important features for feedback selection and specific task instructions. The EDM is used to identify errors by comparing its distribution with the student's performance. Finding errors by comparing with the EDM allows identifying the precise location and amplitude of the errors. This is in contrast to a standard machine learning approach used in [8] which involves a large labelled dataset that need to contain all errors that are to be identified, the EDM requires only a small amount of expert recordings, and can, therefore, be used in more niche contexts where large datasets are not readily available. The teacher creates an exercise by tracing the target trace/s, then recording several attempts at the exercise. The teacher should only add 'acceptable' attempts to the EDM, and in this way, the teacher can control where and which variation is allowed. The EDM is stored as a series of EDMDataPoints, which contain the average and standard deviation for each feature. To determine if the student made an error, the EDM compares each datapoint of the student's trace/s with the corresponding EDMDataPoint(s) using online dynamic time warping (O-DTW) for generating real-time feedback and DTW for batched feedback (see Sects. 3.2 and 3.3).

3.2 O-DTW for Real Time Feedback

To detect the error and measure its amplitude, the student trace/s needs to be compared, both temporally and spatially, with the corresponding part of the target trace/s which involves a form of alignment. Naive alignment methods such as the minimum euclidean distance used by Limbu et al. [13] can fail to align correctly when trace/s differ in scale, aspect ratio, rotation or when the student trace/s contains large errors in the x,y coordinates but is still a serious attempt. Automatically detecting errors in real-time is more intricate than marking the parts of the student trace/s that do not overlap with the target trace/s. Therefore, a more advanced alignment model *Online Dynamic Time Warping* is used to match student trace/s datapoints with their corresponding 'correct attempt' target trace/s datapoints in real-time. Once a student datapoint is matched with the target trace/s, the EDM's corresponding EDMDataPoint values are used to evaluate the student datapoint's accuracy per feature. To provide immediate timely actionable real-time feedback to the student (see Fig. 2a), the student-to-EDM comparison must take place several times per second, therefore the O-DTW algorithm needs to be configured to run efficiently, and uses several techniques to speed up execution, such as resampling the time series at a lower frequency, using bounds on the maximum match distance (known as *warping windows*) [20], and pruning partial paths that will lead to unpromising warping paths [19].

3.3 DTW for Batched Feedback

Batched feedback is presented and stored after an exercise is submitted, allowing the teacher to have an insight into the writing process of a student instead of only the final static output. In CaT, feedback is presented per feature, with interactive graphs that helps to map data to the context by displaying the student trace/s feature values in comparison to the EDM average and thresholds along the trace/s (see Fig. 3). Batched feedback computations do not have to run in real-time and can therefore perform alignment on sequences with higher sample rates using the complete DTW algorithm, which makes the alignment less sensitive to large handwriting mistakes (at the cost of execution time).

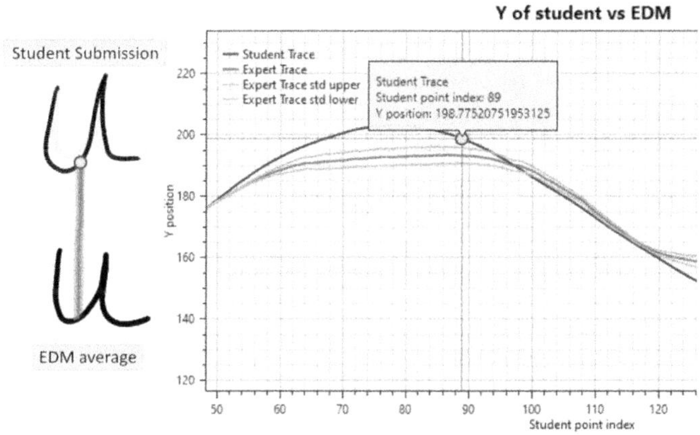

Fig. 3. Writing analytics batched feedback on feature Y in CaT

4 Conclusion and Future Work

The CaT is a teacher oriented tool for DP of handwriting during the early stages of learning. It complements the teacher by automating several aspects of handwriting teaching while still giving the teacher full jurisdiction over students' learning. The future work can include machine learning components to automate additional aspects. Furthermore, the CaT, theoretically, implements DP as originally defined by Ericsson[6]. However, other more concrete and practical frameworks such as ID4AR framework [12] which have adopted DP could potentially be an interesting future endeavour. Currently, we plan to test the current implementation of CaT for its' efficacy as a tool for teaching handwriting.

References

1. Barnes, R.W.: Surgical handicraft: teaching and learning surgical skills. Am. J. Surg. **153**(5), 422–427 (1987). https://doi.org/10.1016/0002-9610(87)90783-5. Papers of the North Pacific Surgical Association
2. Bonneton-Botte, N., et al.: Teaching cursive handwriting: a contribution to the acceptability study of using digital tablets in French classrooms. J. Early Child. Lit. **21**, 259–282 (2019). https://doi.org/10.1177/1468798419838587
3. Cai, L., Chan, J.S., Yan, J.H., Peng, K.: Brain plasticity and motor practice in cognitive aging. Front. Aging Neurosci. **6**, 31 (2014). https://doi.org/10.3389/fnagi.2014.00031
4. Dikken, O., Limbu, B., Specht, M.: Expert distribution similarity model: feedback methodology for non-imitation based handwriting practice, pp. 1–7 (2021). http://ceur-ws.org/Vol-2979/paper6.pdf
5. Doug, R.: Handwriting: developing pupils' identity and cognitive skills. Int. J. Educ. Literacy Stud. **7**(2), 177–188 (2019)

6. Ericsson, K.A.: Given that the detailed original criteria for deliberate practice have not changed, could the understanding of this complex concept have improved over time? A response to Macnamara and Hambrick (2020). Psychol. Res. **85**(3), 1114–1120 (2020). https://doi.org/10.1007/s00426-020-01368-3
7. Feder, K.P., Majnemer, A.: Handwriting development, competency, and intervention. Dev. Med. Child Neurol. **49**, 312–317 (2007). https://doi.org/10.1111/j.1469-8749.2007.00312.x
8. Frenoy, R., et al.: Callismart : an adaptive informed environment for intelligent calligraphy training. hal id : hal-01310792 (2016)
9. Gargot, T., et al.: Acquisition of handwriting in children with and without dysgraphia: a computational approach. PLoS One **15**, 1–22 (2020). https://doi.org/10.1371/journal.pone.0237575
10. Hayes, J.R.: Modeling and remodeling writing. Written Commun. **29**, 369–388 (2012). https://doi.org/10.1177/0741088312451260
11. James, K.H., Engelhardt, L.: The effects of handwriting experience on functional brain development in pre-literate children. Trends Neurosci. Educ. **1**(1), 32–42 (2012). https://doi.org/10.1016/j.tine.2012.08.001
12. Limbu, B.H., Jarodzka, H., Klemke, R., Specht, M.: Using sensors and augmented reality to train apprentices using recorded expert performance: a systematic literature review. Educ. Res. Rev. **25**, 1–22 (2018). https://doi.org/10.1016/j.edurev.2018.07.001
13. Limbu, B.H., Jarodzka, H., Klemke, R., Specht, M.: Can you ink while you blink? assessing mental effort in a sensor-based calligraphy trainer. Sensors **19**(14), 3244 (2019). https://doi.org/10.3390/s19143244
14. Marquardt, C., Meyer, M.D., Schneider, M., Hilgemann, R.: Learning handwriting at school - a teachers' survey on actual problems and future options. Trends Neurosci. Educ. **5**, 82–89 (2016). https://doi.org/10.1016/j.tine.2016.07.001
15. McCarney, D., Peters, L., Jackson, S., Thomas, M., Kirby, A.: Does poor handwriting conceal literacy potential in primary school children? Int. J. Disabil. Dev. Educ. **60**, 105–118 (2013). https://doi.org/10.1080/1034912X.2013.786561
16. Mueller, P.A., Oppenheimer, D.M.: The pen is mightier than the keyboard: advantages of longhand over laptop note taking. Psychol. Sci. **25**(6), 1159–1168 (2014). https://doi.org/10.1177/0956797614524581. pMID: 24760141
17. Ray, K., Dally, K., Rowlandson, L., Tam, K.I., Lane, A.E.: The relationship of handwriting ability and literacy in kindergarten: a systematic review. Read. Writ. **35**, 11191155 (2022). https://doi.org/10.1007/s11145-021-10224-8
18. Shin, J., et al.: Important features selection and classification of adult and child from handwriting using machine learning methods. Appl. Sci. **12**(10), 5256 (2022). https://doi.org/10.3390/app12105256
19. Silva, D.F., Batista, G.E.: Speeding up all-pairwise dynamic time warping matrix calculation. In: Proceedings of the 2016 SIAM International Conference on Data Mining. pp. 837–845. SIAM (2016). https://doi.org/10.1137/1.9781611974348.94
20. Wang, X., Mueen, A., Ding, H., Trajcevski, G., Scheuermann, P., Keogh, E.: Experimental comparison of representation methods and distance measures for time series data. Data Min. Knowl. Disc. **26**(2), 275–309 (2013). https://doi.org/10.1007/s10618-012-0250-5

CHEST: A Linked Open Data-based Application to Annotate and Carry Out Learning Tasks About Cultural Heritage

Pablo García-Zarza(✉), Miguel L. Bote-Lorenzo, Guillermo Vega-Gorgojo, and Juan I. Asensio-Pérez

Group of Intelligent and Cooperative Systems, Universidad de Valladolid, Valladolid, Spain
pablogz@gsic.uva.es, {migbot,guiveg,juaase}@tel.uva.es
https://gsic.uva.es

Abstract. There is a deluge of Cultural Heritage Linked Open Data containing detailed information (e.g., location, architectural styles, etc.). Teachers could use this Open Data to generate meaningful learning tasks. However, most teachers are not using this information. This may be because they are not aware of these information sources or because they have technological difficulties in accessing the information (as they need to know Semantic Web related technologies). To overcome that limitation, this demonstration paper presents Cultural Heritage Educational Semantic Tool (CHEST), a distributed application aimed at supporting teachers in authoring Cultural Heritage learning tasks based on existing Cultural Heritage Linked Open Data. Teacher annotations are published as Linked Open Data, thus facilitating the reuse of such data by other teachers (using CHEST or other applications). This new application also supports students in the completion of the learning tasks created and/or reused by their teachers. CHEST can be used by both teachers and students using a web-based desktop interface or Android/iOS mobile apps.

Keywords: Linked open data · Cultural Heritage · Learning tasks · Semantic annotation

1 Introduction

Organisations and agencies all over the world offer high quality information related to Cultural Heritage (CH) as Open Data. Some information sources such as DBpedia[1] and Wikidata[2] offer data at a global level, but others focus

[1] https://www.dbpedia.org/.
[2] https://www.wikidata.org/.

This work has been partially funded by the European Regional Development Fund and the Spanish National Research Agency under project grant PID2020-112584RB-C32.

I. Hilliger et al. (Eds.): EC-TEL 2022, LNCS 13450, pp. 441–447, 2022.
https://doi.org/10.1007/978-3-031-16290-9_34

on local CH such as Open Data of Castile and Leon[3] or La Palma Open Data[4]. Information from these Open Data sources offers an excellent opportunity to be adapted, to a greater or lesser extent, and used to support learning situations related to CH. This is the case of Casual Learn's dataset which contains learning tasks semi-automatically generated from three of the information sources showed above [5]. Casual Learn educational tasks are geolocated in Castile and Leon (Spain) and were published as Linked Open Data (LOD), a type of Linked Data [1]. Data published as Linked Data must follow a set of rules so that relationships can be established between datasets from different entities.

Educational applications aimed at exploiting datasets such as the above face the challenge of providing educational tasks to students in ways they are familiar with. For example, Casual Learn app [4] is a mobile application that supports ubiquitous learning [2] about CH. Casual Learn app provides students with an interactive map of geolocated learning tasks, obtained from the Casual Learn dataset, thus hiding all the details related to Semantic Web technologies. Another example of the use of LOD is the approach presented in [6], which generates questions to be carried out in Virtual Learning Environments (such as Moodle).

Teachers could generate meaningful educational tasks with the information from the Cultural Heritage related datasets that could complement the automatically generated tasks that already exist in the previous applications. However, most teachers are not using this information. This may be because they are unfamiliar with this information or because they have problems working with the formats in which it is found. In this demonstration paper we present Cultural Heritage Educational Semantic Tool (CHEST) that allow teachers to annotate points of interest (POI) where to add educational tasks for their students leveraging information stored as LOD where possible. According to the teacher's instructions, students will be able to use CHEST to carry out the educational tasks near the POI location or from anywhere (e.g., in classroom). The information annotated by teachers is stored as LOD. This makes it easy to be reused by other teachers or other applications.

2 Sample Scenario

A History teacher is working with her students to help them understand the main characteristics of the Romanesque style and decides to use CHEST for this purpose. First, when she is planning the lesson, the **teacher checks the information already available in CHEST** and notices that there are many POIs with learning tasks created in Valladolid (Fig. 1a), the city where she teaches in a high school, and in other nearby cities. For this reason, the teacher decides to design an educational scenario in two phases. In the first one the teacher will use CHEST to visualise with her students in **class** some of the most representative POIs of Zamora, one of the nearby cities with a large number of buildings of the style studied. In these POIs she will highlight some of the Romanesque features

[3] https://datosabiertos.jcyl.es/web/es/datos-abiertos-castilla-leon.html.

[4] https://www.opendatalapalma.es/.

she considers most important. While this visualisation is taking place, **students will have to carry out with their laptops the educational tasks** that the teacher will indicate to them. To do this, the **teacher will have added some learning tasks** (Fig. 1c) to CHEST and will **reuse some tasks from other teachers**. The tasks that students will have to perform in this phase will be to answer questions textually or choose between multiple options having to look for information in the content offered by CHEST or other external sites indicated by the teacher. This happens in the tasks that she wants to add with Fig. 1c, in which the teacher asks them to answer true or false to a statement associated with the Cathedral of Zamora.

In the second phase of the activity (that the teacher plans before class again), she designs an itinerary of some of the Romanesque-style buildings in Valladolid for her students. They will visit this POIs individually or in small groups. The teacher wants her students to visit, at least, the Church of Saint Mary the Ancient and Church of San Martín where they **will have to carry out in person with their smartphones**. The learning tasks that the students must complete must be carry out quickly, so they can answer them by taking photographs or selecting a textual answer from among multiple options. To this end, she reuses the POIs of this churches that already exist in the CHEST dataset and adds a task to each of these POIs asking them to take photographs of the Romanesque style elements of these buildings. The answers provided by students in these two phases will reach the teacher so that she can assess them.

Tacking advantage of the fact that her students are going on their end-of-studies trip to France, the teacher decides to add an optional phase (without evaluating it, to respect students who do not go to this trip). The teacher searches for POIs in France and notices that the POI of the Basilica of Saint-Sernin (Toulouse) has not yet been created by other teachers. For this annotation, she **selects one of the suggestions provided by CHEST** (Fig. 1b and 1d). Once the POI has been added, she adds two educational tasks where she asks her students to look for similarities and differences with the buildings they visited virtually in Zamora. In this way, students will be able to connect the contents seen in-class with the external world.

3 Linked Open Data and Semantic Annotation

CHEST initially uses the data generated available in Casual Learn triple store in read mode so that teachers and students do not find themselves with an application without any information. This information can be used since it was published[5] as LOD and is accessible through a SPARQL endpoint[6]. CHEST follows a similar philosophy as the data generated by teachers will also be published as LOD, making it easier for data generated by some teachers to be reused by others. For this reason, the ontology used by CHEST is compatible with the ontology used in Casual Learn [3] but has been extended to add new features.

[5] https://github.com/gsic-emic/casual-learn-LOD.

[6] https://casuallearn.gsic.uva.es/sparql.

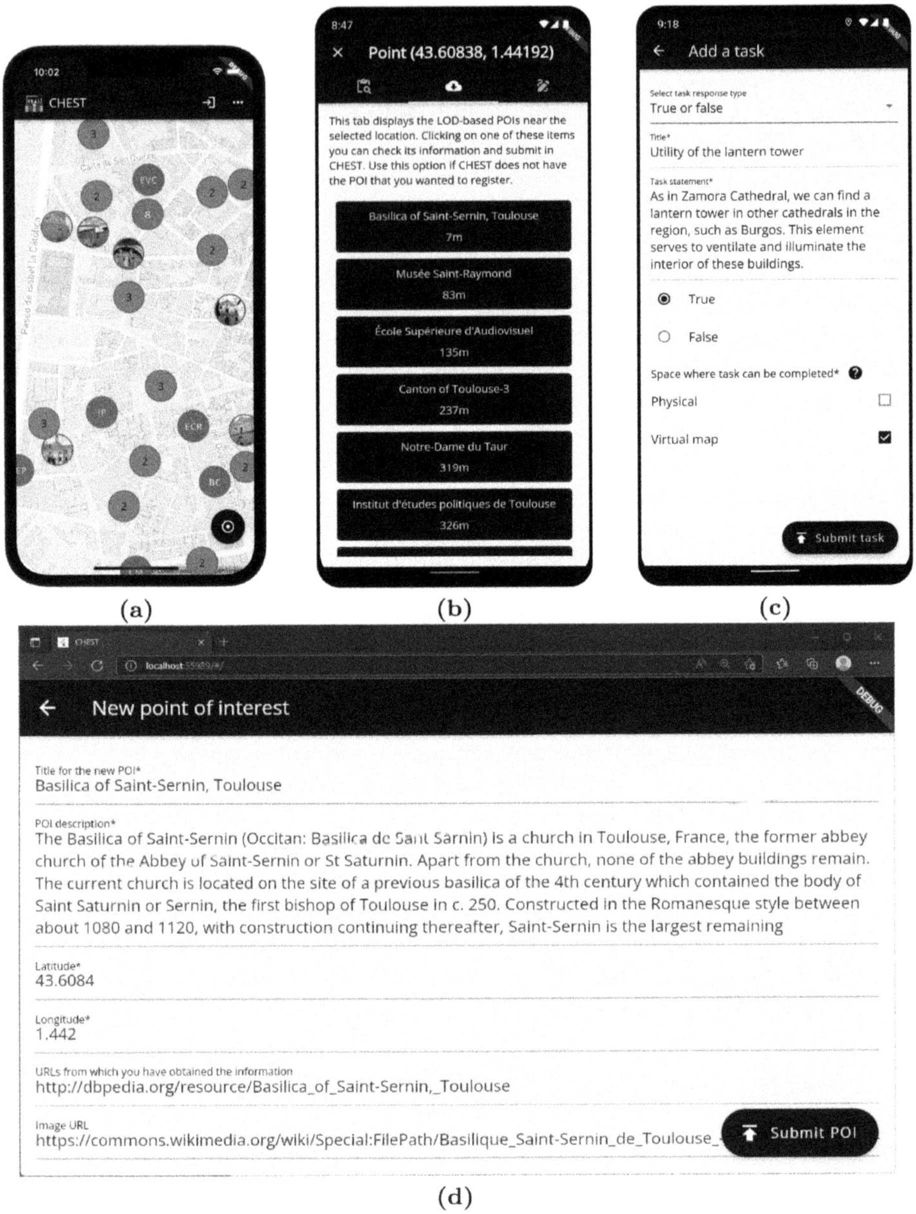

Fig. 1. CHEST Client GUI snapshots of mobile, (a), (b) and (c), and web, (d), applications. (a) Map-based interface with markers indicating the location of POIs (markers with numbers indicate the number of POIs clustered). (b) first step to add a POI showing the suggestions obtained from the LOD. (c) Form to add a task to a POI. (d) POI data obtained through LOD that can be modified by the teacher before submission.

Among the classes it will add are the categories by which information can be classified, the learning space where each learning task can be performed (near the POI location or from anywhere) and the itineraries (task and POI routes defined by teachers so that students know what tasks they have to carry out and, possibly, in what order) requested by teachers when evaluating the performance of a first version of CHEST. Although CHEST and Casual Learn partially use the same dataset, they are different and independent applications.

For the sample scenario, when the teacher views POIs in an area or the associated educational tasks for a particular POI, CHEST retrieves this information form the Casual Learn dataset and the dynamical CHEST dataset. This second dataset is generated from the POIs and learning tasks added by teachers. The Listing 1.1 shows, in partial form, the information that a teacher annotates, through a form (Fig. 1d), when adding the POI of the Basilica of Saint-Sernin. CHEST offers teachers a series of suggestions (Fig. 1b), based on LOD from DBpedia information via CRAFTS [7], to facilitate this annotation. LOD dataset sources are preconfigured to CH and cannot be edited by teachers in this version. If a suggestion is used, as in the case of the Listing 1.1, an attempt is made to retrieve the information in multiple languages so that CHEST can be used by as many people as possible. In 1.1(1) a unique identifier is defined for the resource to be added, in addition to providing a label (1.1[3–5]), a short description (1.1[6–8]), the location (1.1[9–10]) and the POI categories (1.1[11–12]).

Listing 1.1. Example of stored POI data based on DBpedia's information

```
1  cd:Basilica_of_Saint-Sernin,_(Toulouse)
2   a co:POI ;
3   rdfs:label "Basilica of Saint-Sernin, Toulouse"@en ,
4     "Basílica de San Sernín"@es ,
5     "Basilique Saint-Sernin"@fr ;
6   rdfs:comment "The Basilica of Saint-Sernin [...]"@en ,
7     "La basílica de San Sernín (en francés, [...]"@es ,
8     "La basilique Saint-Sernin est le plus [...]"@fr ;
9   geo:lat 43.608398 ;
10  geo:long 1.442000 ;
11  co:hasCategory dbc:Romanesque_architecture_in_France ,
12    dbc:Roman_Catholic_churches_in_Toulouse .
```

Learning tasks added by teachers will also be stored as LOD (Fig. 1c). The Listing 1.2 shows the data that is saved in the triple store when the teacher add a learning task to the POI of Saint-Sernin. Unlike Listing 1.1, in this case the data to be stored will only be available in the language in which the teacher adds it. In 1.2(2) relationship between the LearningTask and the POI is found. Also, in 1.2(6) the type of response the student is expected to provide to the question is indicated and in 1.2(7) where the educational task can be carried out.

Listing 1.2. Example of annotation of stored task information

```
1  cd:abcdef09_87ghijkl-654
2   a co:LearningTask ;
3   co:hasContext cd:Basilica_of_Saint-Sernin,_(Toulouse) ;
```

```
    rdfs:label "Similarities"@en ;
    rdfs:comment "Can you photograph any features that this
        cathedral has in common with buildings in Zamora?
        Indicate building name."@en ;
    co:answerType co:multiplePhotosAndText ;
    co:inSpace co:PhysicalSpace ;
    dct:creator cd:teacherVa .
```

4 CHEST Application

4.1 Architecture

CHEST has been designed following the classic client-server architectural model. The server oversees converting the information annotated by the teachers into LOD following the ontology previously indicated. For this purpose, the server keeps control over which users have the role of students and which have the role of teacher. This is important to determine which users are allowed to annotate. This type of data is stored in a private database to which only the server has access, clearly determining which CHEST data is public and which is not. For example, tasks annotated by teachers are public (being accessible from the same public endpoint as Casual Learn data), but students' answers to these learning tasks are private.

CHEST client provides an interface that is adapted to the device where it is executed. This interface is based on interactive maps with which the user visualises where the educational tasks are located (which will always be linked to a POI). The information of the learning tasks, the POIs and, in the future, the itineraries, is obtained from CHEST server (which will later consult the public repository). Teachers can record the data through a series of forms in an equivalent way to how students complete the proposed tasks.

4.2 Prototype

A preliminary version of CHEST[7] was used by two secondary school teachers to prepare an educational activity. The teachers encountered no technical problems using this version. We interviewed them after they used the system and they proposed some new requirements, such as itineraries (to control the path of their students), which we are going to design and develop for new versions of CHEST. Tasks and POIs were added as LOD to the public repository using SPARQL UPDATE, since an open version of Virtuoso[8] is used in this repository. CHEST server that carries out these inserts (and queries using SPARQL) is being developed using the Node.js[9] JavaScript runtime environment and multiple libraries

[7] https://chest.gsic.uva.es.
[8] https://github.com/openlink/virtuoso-opensource.
[9] https://nodejs.org.

to facilitate its implementation (such as Express[10] to develop the RESTful API that queries the client). Private data is stored in a MongoDB database.

CHEST client (Fig. 1) is being deployed using Flutter[11] so that a single development can be used to create both a web application (like the one used by the teachers) and mobile applications that can be installed on iOS and Android mobiles. This decision has been taken so that users are provided with a solution that is as standard as possible, so that they are comfortable using it. In addition, the mobile applications make it easier to temporarily store POI information and learning tasks on users' devices in case students do not have a data plan that allows them to connect to the Internet from anywhere. It also facilitates the implementation of other functionalities such as being able to send notifications to users based on their location. As with the previous client, different libraries (or packages) are being used to facilitate its implementation. One of the most relevant is `flutter_map`[12], which allows the map interface to be managed in a similar way to Leafleft[13].

References

1. Berners-Lee, T.: Linked data - design issues (2009). https://www.w3.org/DesignIssues/LinkedData.html. Accessed 20 Apr 2022
2. Hwang, G., Tsai, C.: Research trends in mobile and ubiquitous learning: a review of publications in selected journals from 2001 to 2010. Br. J. Educ. Technol. **42**(4), E65–E70 (2011)
3. Ruiz-Calleja, A., et al.: Sleek: an ontology for smart learning in the web of data. In: IEEE 21st International Conference on Advanced Learning Technologies, pp. 365–366. ICALT 2021 (2021). https://doi.org/10.1109/ICALT52272.2021.00117
4. Ruiz-Calleja, A., et al.: Casual learn: a linked data-based mobile application for learning about local cultural heritage. Semant. Web, 1–15 (2021). https://doi.org/10.3233/SW-212907
5. Ruiz-Calleja, A., Vega-Gorgojo, G., Bote-Lorenzo, M.L., Asensio-Pérez, J.I., Dimitriadis, Y., Gómez-Sánchez, E.: Supporting contextualized learning with linked open data. J. Web Semant. **70**, 100657 (2021). https://doi.org/10.1016/j.websem.2021.100657
6. Ruiz-Calleja, A., et al.: Automatic creation of moodle activities out of the web of data to link formal and informal learning contexts. In: Eighth International Conference on Technological Ecosystems for Enhancing Multiculturality, pp. 238–244. TEEM 2020. Association for Computing Machinery, New York, NY, USA (2020). https://doi.org/10.1145/3434780.3436569
7. Vega-Gorgojo, G.: CRAFTS: configurable REST APIs for triple stores. IEEE Access **10**, 32426–32441 (2022). https://doi.org/10.1109/ACCESS.2022.3160610

[10] https://expressjs.com.

[11] https://flutter.dev/.

[12] https://github.com/fleaflet/flutter_map.

[13] https://leafletjs.com/.

Towards an Automated Adaptive Learning Web Platform Through Personalization of Language Learning Pathways

Aous Karoui[1,4](✉), Lionel Alvarez[1,2], Thierry Geoffre[1], Nathalie Guin[3], Marie Lefevre[3], Valentin Lachand-Pascal[3], and Mario Ramalho[5]

[1] University for Teacher Education, 1700 Fribourg, Switzerland
{aous.karoui,thierry.geoffre}@edufr.ch, lionel.alvarez@unifr.ch
[2] University of Fribourg, 1700 Fribourg, Switzerland
[3] Univ Lyon, UCBL, CNRS, INSA Lyon, LIRIS, UMR5205, 69622 Villeurbanne, France
{nathalie.guin,marie.lefevre,valentin.lachand}@univ-lyon1.fr
[4] University of Grenoble Alpes, 38400 Saint-Martin-d'Hères, France
[5] Fribourg Vocational School, 1700 Fribourg, Switzerland
mario.ramalho@edufr.ch

Abstract. Adaptive learning is increasingly gaining ground thanks to the rise of digital tools which are becoming more accessible to teachers. Indeed, the possibilities of adaptive learning are growing and can now vary according to the implemented digital tools and (most importantly) the needs of teachers and the often-heterogeneous profiles of students. This article presents the interactive platform GamesHUB, designed to promote Universal Design Learning (UDL) in Swiss French-speaking classrooms. GamesHUB is a full Web platform that allows the customization of teaching pathways depending on didactic goals and the needs of teachers and students. As part of the European "PEAPL" project, GamesHUB aims to assist teachers in pathways customization through an automation of this process, in partnership with the LIRIS computer science laboratory (France). This automation will be relying on a suggestion system based on the calculation of competency profiles from the learning tracks analytics. The article will describe the current functioning of GamesHUB, namely the adaptable pathways. In a second step, we introduce the principle of automation while mentioning the problem of trust and the need for transparency when it comes to artificial intelligence. Therefore, we present the learner and domain modeling underlying to the profile of competences.

Keywords: Adaptive learning · Inclusive learning · Gamification authoring tool · Learning pathways

1 Introduction

1.1 The Adaptive Issue in Technology Enhanced Learning

The issue of adaptive learning environments has been addressed from different angles and in different educational contexts. It concerns face-to-face or distant learning, academic

I. Hilliger et al. (Eds.): EC-TEL 2022, LNCS 13450, pp. 448–454, 2022.
https://doi.org/10.1007/978-3-031-16290-9_35

or vocational training, and has been implemented in environments as varied as Intelligent Tutors, Serious Games, Adaptive Hypermedia, MOOCs and other online courses [1, 2]. It is aimed at "classical" or special needs learners, at a learner working alone or at learners working in groups, and has multiple pedagogical objectives, including the promotion of autonomy and self-regulation of learning.

In this paper, we address adaptive learning of the schooling language for learners with or without learning disabilities (L2 speakers, dyslexic learners, students with language impairment...) through personalized learning pathways.

Indeed, in order to facilitate the adaptation of technology-enhanced learning (TEL) to the learner, many artificial intelligence techniques have been used [3]. These different techniques make it possible to better identify the learner's characteristics and needs to improve the personalization provided. They can also help to enable learners to carry out a reflective activity on their learning, when it comes to adaptable learning pathways with personalized activities, trying to change the role of the learner from a passive receiver of information to a collaborator in the educational process.

Personalization can be desired by several actors (the learners themselves, the educational teams), and the approaches proposed may vary, leaving the control of personalization sometimes to the learner, sometimes to the educational teams, sometimes to artificial intelligence techniques [4, 5]. Personalization can include contextual recommendation of resources, the use of adapted materials or taking into account the affective and cognitive state of the learners [6].

1.2 Paper's Structure

In the above-described context, we introduce the European Platform for Personalized Language Learning (PEAPL). Project PEAPL is funded by the European Erasmus fund within the online platform GamesHUB, maintained by the University for Teacher Education of Fribourg (HEP) in partnership with the Fribourg Vocational School (EMF).

Therefore, in this paper, we firstly present the GamesHUB platform and its features. Secondly, we describe how the PEAPL project outcomes take place on GamesHUB platform.

2 GamesHUB Platform with Adaptive Learning

2.1 Purpose

GamesHUB[1] is designed for students aged 6–12 in French-speaking Swiss schools, using game-based learning and customized learning pathways. Its purpose is to allow every student, including those with learning disabilites, to develop skills if they can interact with the computer. The platform provides learning games related to various learning areas within the framework of the Plan d'Études Romand[2] (PER) which is the official competency framework in the context of GamesHUB implementation. It also supports the teacher in the continuous improvement of teaching and learning by recording tracks

[1] https://hep3.emf-infopro.ch/

[2] https://www.plandetudes.ch.

of students' activities in compliance with the European GDPR (General Data Protection Rules). The data of each learning game played is recorded and can then be visualized and analyzed by the teacher to identify difficulties of students.

2.2 Features

Customized Pathways. Currently, the GamesHUB platform provides access to learning games on various themes, mainly learning French as the schooling language. This access is possible in a "self-play" mode and in the "custom pathway" mode. Indeed, the "self-play" mode provides game sessions for exploration, training, evaluation, and content creation, each time for a single learning game. However, the "custom pathway" mode allows to have specific sequences of different game levels and to track the overall progression of a student through these pathways.

As mentioned in our related work [7], the concept is to create a learning pathway targeting some specific skills and pieces of knowledge (from the PER, for example). Then, it requires to access all the learning games corresponding to these target pieces of knowledge and skills with different levels of difficulty. The principle also consists in creating mandatory steps in the scenario and optional steps (that we call remediation steps) from these different levels of difficulty (see Fig. 1). The remediation steps will only be triggered when the student has failed certain mandatory steps.

Fig. 1. A pathway being created, combining mandatory and remediation steps

Once the pathway has been created, it can be assigned to one or more students or directly to one or more classes as shown in Fig. 2.

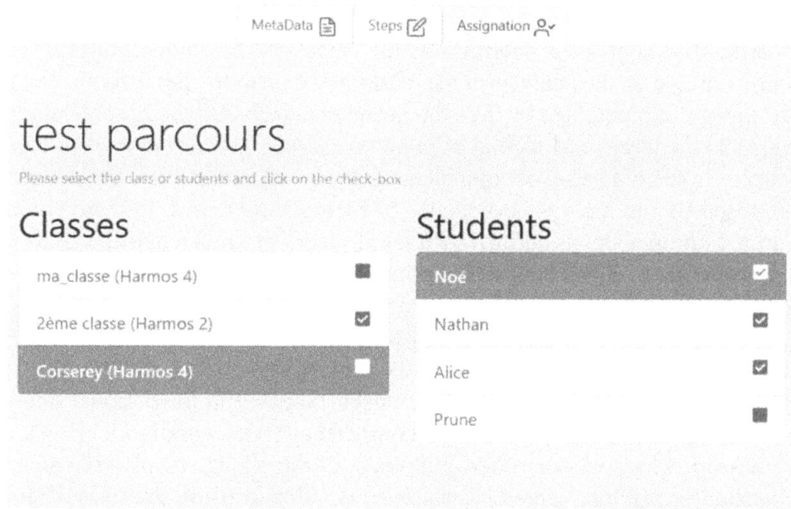

Fig. 2. Assigning a learning pathway to a group of students on GamesHUB

2.3 Automating the Generation of Personalized Pathways

The operations described above certainly allow a better adaptation of each student's path according to his/her needs and to the teacher's estimation. However, this process can be tedious if the teacher must target each task or each pathway to every pupil in the class.

Indeed, when the hand is given to teachers to implement adaptive learning, two approaches are possible: (1) to let teachers describe the sequence of activities and learning sequences provided to learners, by providing them with authoring tools, or (2) to acquire their knowledge as experts and teachers to help them via more automated processes. For example, the PERSUA2 model [8] allows a pedagogical team to express a personalization strategy describing which activity could be proposed to the learner according to the content of his profile. This strategy, expressed in the form of rules, can then be exploited by a process that adapts to each learner.

The aim of the PEAPL project is to use artificial intelligence to assist teachers in this tedious process by generating personalized pathways for students based on an automated calculation of their competency profile. However, we believe that, in these approaches including automatic processes that take decisions in place of human actors, the latter do not have sufficient knowledge of AI techniques to understand and trust the recommendations coming from these systems. Therefore, the acceptability and appropriation of these systems necessarily require more transparent processes, in which the user can understand the knowledge and reasoning implemented by the system, with the aim of obtaining an explanation of the decisions suggested [9]. We explain in the following section the learner modeling principle used to calculate the competency profile.

2.4 Modeling the Domain to Model the Learner

When the aim of personalization is to propose resources or activities on concepts adapted to the learner's pieces of knowledge/skills and the teacher's pedagogical objectives, the competency-based approach makes it possible to model the subject area [10, 11]. Modeling the learner then consists in determining the pieces of knowledge and skills acquired by the learner, based on the analysis of the marks and data of his/her activity. The personalization strategy implemented by the system can then be based on a double modeling of the domain and the learner. Modeling a domain according to the competency-based approach consists in defining a set of competencies for this domain, this set of competencies being proposed by researchers in didactics or by teaching teams. In these competency frameworks, a competency is defined by a set of pieces of knowledge and skills that can be linked altogether by different kinds of relationships (for example, *requires/is required by*), leading to an ontology modeling.

For example, a first competency framework used in GamesHUB is the Plan d'Études Romand (PER) as already stated (Sect. 2.2). It allows to choose the general objective of the pathway through the general competences expected in the national program for French-speaking Switzerland. The second competency framework is the PEAPL competency framework which models skills and pieces of knowledge involved in the reading-comprehension in primary school. It has been developed using the COMPER project meta-model of framework[3]. It is used to guide the teacher in his or her choice of progression and articulation of specific objectives within the pathway. The pedagogical resources (games and levels of games) are associated with skills and/or pieces of knowledge (specific objectives) constituting the target competence (general objective). The PEAPL competency framework[4] has been published[5], as well as an excerpt from the praxeological organization that underpins this framework[6].

Technically speaking, this step relies on sending data from GamesHUB to the external Learning Record System of the LIRIS (Lyon Computer Science Laboratory). The data sent is in xApi format. It mainly contains information about the actor, the activity, the submitted answers, and a score between 0 and 1. The latter defines a percentage of success which will also be used for the calculation of the competence profile.

3 Future Work

As mentioned in Sect. 2.3, teachers must understand AI techniques used by their TEL environments so that they can trust the recommendations coming from these systems. Therefore, our future work will be focused on two main research questions:

(1) How do teachers understand, adapt, and perceive the adaptable pathways based on their knowledge of their students' needs and their use of the platform?

[3] https://comper.fr/en/productions/wp1.
[4] https://traffic.irit.fr/comper/repository/viewframework_public?name=92.
[5] https://zenodo.org/record/4462850#.YmEik9PP2Uk.
[6] https://zenodo.org/record/4001381#.YmEi7NPP2Uk.

(2) How can we implement system-generated explanations that allow teachers to take ownership of the adaptive system and its settings?

Thus, our future work consists in starting a series of experiments with teachers to have elements of answers to the two questions above. In addition, this would be our opportunity to understand how teachers perceive the adaptive features.

For all these assessments, we will use semi-structured interviews, participant observations and the tracks collected on GamesHUB, during gameplay within the learning pathways sessions and during the processes of pathways adaptation.

4 Conclusion

In this paper, we presented the GamesHUB platform designed with adapting learning paradigm, toward a universal design for learning thanks to TEL, and intended to learners with or without learning disabilities. We introduced the manual personalized learning pathways allowing the setup of a personalization adapted to the teachers' different objectives and the students heterogenous profiles. Then, we presented the automation concept of personalized pathways, within the PEAPL project. Our future work consists in experimenting the GamesHUB platform with all these features to gather feedback from teachers and students on both manual and automated personalized learning pathways.

References

1. Auguste, D.: Intelligent tutoring systems. In: Sleeman, D., Brown, J.S. (eds.) Artificial Intelligence, p. 345. Academic Press, New York (1985)
2. Brusilovsky, P., Peylo, C.: Adaptive and intelligent web-based educational systems. Int. J. Artif. Intell. Ed. **13**, 159–172 (2003)
3. Markowska-Kaczmar, U., Kwasnicka, H., Paradowski, M.: Intelligent techniques in personalization of learning in e-Learning systems. In: Xhafa, F., Caballé, S., Abraham, A., Daradoumis, T., Perez, A.A.J. (eds.) Computational Intelligence for Technology Enhanced Learning, pp. 1–23. Springer, Heidelberg (2010). https://doi.org/10.1007/978-3-642-11224-9_1
4. Bull, S., Dimitrova, V., McCalla, G.: Open learner models: research questions. Int. J. Artif. Intell. Educ. **17**, 83–87 (2007)
5. Murray, T.: EON: authoring tools for content, Instructional strategy, student model and interface design. In: Murray, T., Blessing, S.B., Ainsworth, S. (eds.) Authoring Tools for Advanced Technology Learning Environments, pp. 309–339. Springer, Dordrecht (2003). https://doi.org/10.1007/978-94-017-0819-7_11
6. Santos, O.C., Kravcik, M., Boticario, J.G.: Preface to special issue on user modeling to support personalization in enhanced educational settings. Int. J. Artif. Intell. Educ. **26**, 809–820 (2016)
7. Karoui, A., Alvarez, L., Goffre, T., Dherbey Chapuis, N., Rodi, M., Ramalho, M.: Adaptive pathways within the European platform for personalized language learning PEAPL. In: Adjunct Proceedings of the 29th ACM Conference on User Modeling, Adaptation and Personalization, pp. 90–94. Association for Computing Machinery, New York (2021)
8. Lefevre, M., Jean-Daubias, S., Guin, N.: An approach for unified personalization of learning. In: UMAP Workshops (2012)
9. Ye, L.R., Johnson, P.E.: The impact of explanation facilities on user acceptance of expert systems advice. MIS Q. 157–172 (1995)

10. Paquette, G.: A competency-based ontology for learning design repositories. Int. J. Adv. Comput. Sci. Appl. **5**, 55–62 (2014)
11. Johnson, M.D., Bull, S., Kickmeier-Rust, M.: Student competency visualisation for teachers. In: 3rd International Workshop on Teaching Analytics, EC-TEL (2013)

Miranda: A Chatbot for Supporting Self-regulated Learning

Jorge Maldonado-Mahauad[1(✉)], Mar Pérez-Sanagustín[2], Juan Carvallo-Vega[3], Edwin Narvaez[1], and Mauricio Calle[1]

[1] Department of Computer Science, University of Cuenca, Cuenca, Ecuador
{jorge.maldonado,edwin.narvaez,mauricio.calle}@ucuenca.edu.ec
[2] IRIT, Université de Toulouse, CNRS, Toulouse INP, UT3, Toulouse, France
mar.perez-sanagustin@irit.fr
[3] Corporación Ecuatoriana para el Desarrollo de la Investigación y la Academia, Cuenca, Ecuador
jpcarvallo@cedia.org.ec

Abstract. Learning Analytics (LA) aims to understand and optimize the learning process in the environments in which they occur. It also offers opportunities for teachers to understand students' behavior and promote the use of effective strategies that allow them to achieve their goals. Most of current solutions proposed in the literature for supporting students' SRL are based on dashboards. However, if students do not interact with them, it becomes difficult to understand whether they have an impact in their self-regulated behavior. This demonstration, presents Miranda: A Chatbot that acts as a conversational agent to recommend and make suggestions on SRL strategies based on students' the behavior. The first version of Miranda has been developed for Moodle, but it could be adapted to any other Learning Management System.

Keywords: Learning Analytics · Recommender system · Chatbot · Self-regulated learning · Conversational agent

1 Pedagogical Background

Self-regulated learning (SRL) is defined as the ability that students have to initiate metacognitive, cognitive, motivational and behavioral processes in order to take actions to achieve their learning goals and persevere until they succeed [1]. SRL is a crucial skill to adapt to the constant changes inherent to the twenty-first century. This has become specially in the past's years with the COVID-19 pandemic, where teaching-learning modalities have passed from face-to-face to online or hybrid, mediated by technology. This change in modalities has forced both students and teachers to rethink the way they address their teaching and learning experiences and, for students, their ability to self-regulate has become more important than ever.

Different studies have shown the positive relationship that exists between the use of SRL strategies and academic achievement (i.e., Goal Setting; Strategic Planning;

I. Hilliger et al. (Eds.): EC-TEL 2022, LNCS 13450, pp. 455–462, 2022.
https://doi.org/10.1007/978-3-031-16290-9_36

Time Management; Self-evaluation; and Monitoring) [2, 3]. However, this prior work also shows that students face difficulties when planning, executing and monitoring their learning process [4], especially in hybrid and online settings. From the teachers' perspective, monitoring and tracking students in these types of settings is complex and time-consuming, especially in large scale courses. In these contexts, LA solutions could provide them with mechanisms to follow-up and monitor students to better understand how they progress and make timely interventions to help them deploy the adequate SRL strategies.

So far most of the LA solutions proposed for supporting SRL in online and hybrid learning settings are based on the use of dashboards [5, 6]. However, one of the limitations of these proposals is that students should actively access these dashboards to see how they progress, which is not always the case. New solutions, fostering students' more proactive behavior regarding their strategies are required.

To address this challenge, we propose a conversational agent designed taking into consideration SRL theories for recommending students actions to support them along the course. In this paper we present a chatbot implemented as a plugin for Moodle designed to support students' SRL strategies. Through this chatbot, students can get information about their progress in the course and receive personalized notifications and recommendations to improve their learning processes by supporting SRL strategies.

2 Technological Background

Chatbots, also known as conversional agents, are technologies that have a great interest due to advances in Artificial Intelligence and Machine Learning. They are computer applications that simulate conversations with a person for providing, for example, answers to questions automatically [7, 8]. So far, the chatbots proposed use third-party Application Programming Interface (API) such as Facebook, DialogFlow, IBM Watson, or Alexa Lex in order to control and generate the conversational flow of chatbots through technologies such as Natural Language Processing (NLP) [9].

Some researchers have already proposed solutions based on chatbots, however, as far as we know, none of them have focus on supporting SRL strategies, or any other type of message that can improve the students' learning process [10]. In the case of the LMS Moodle, Souali [8] proposed a chatbot developed in PHP language integrated to the platform. However, we didn't find no more information about the integration of this tool with Moodle interface. Moreover, as far as we know, there are not prior studies proposing conversational agents specifically to support SRL strategies. This work will contribute to expand current studies on the use of chatbots in education with two purposes: (1) to explore the use of this technologies in online and hybrid contexts; and (2), to show how these technologies could be used to support SRL.

Specifically, we propose the chatbot named Miranda, in honor of Juana Miranda (1842–1914) who was the first university professor in Ecuador. "Miranda" was developed as a plugin for Moodle. The visualizations proposed as well as the analytics in which their recommendations are based, use as a reference the work in [5], which propose a plugin for Moodle based on dashboards for supporting the SRL processes of Goal Setting, Strategic Planning, Time management, and Self-evaluation.

3 Description of the Prototype

3.1 Chatbot Architecture

The plugin architecture has ***a Backend and a Frontend*** (Fig. 1). Both modules communicate synchronously and bidirectionally, which offers a greater flexibility for interacting with the chatbot. The Backend is responsible for collecting and analyzing the data to provide general information or recommendations. The data sources used in the plugin are the Moodle database. The Frontend is intended to be the point of user interaction with the entire system. The Miranda icon will be displayed on each page of the courses in which the student is enrolled and will allow you to receive and request recommendations, rate resources and display information.

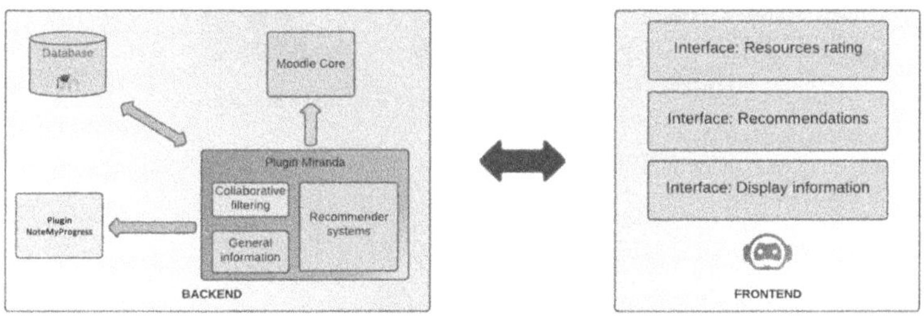

Fig. 1. Miranda plugin architecture

The plugin is divided into 3 sub-modules (see Fig. 1): (1) *recommendation submodule* that is responsible for providing recommendations of session time and student behavior within the course; (2) *collaborative filter submodule* that is responsible for giving recommendations of the resources scored by other students of the course; and (3) *general information submodule* that provides general dashboards for student and course information.

The chatbot integrates a rules-based approach, as this is the one that best adapts to the development environment in Moodle, as well as the one that allows us to deploy a chatbot without the need to have specialized libraries in AI and ML, which are not easily adapted to the language with which Moodle was built (PHP). As for the recommendation system, the chatbot implements a hybrid recommendation system based on the parallel design that mainly uses two algorithms: a proprietary cluster-based comparison algorithm to recommend actions within the platform and slope One [11] to predict resource ratings.

Obtaining the recommendations for students is the result of a process based on the clustering and comparison of groups of students, as shown in Fig. 2. Thus, the first type of recommendations are suggestions of actions within the platform. These recommendations are the result of a process that consist of: (1) identify groups of students, using a set of indicators related to the student's interactions with the platform (i.e., the number of active days, total time on the platform in minutes, the number of sessions, the average time of sessions in minutes, the total number of interactions on the platform) and an average of Moodle LA indicators (i.e., cognitive depth with 5 levels, social breadth with 2 levels). Cognitive Depth is defined as "*the extent to which participants in any particular configuration of a research community are able to construct meaning through sustained communication"* [12]. While Social Breadth is defined as "*the ability of participants to identify with the group or course of study"* [13], among others. (2) Once the students have been grouped, we proceed to categorize them into students who need help and those who do not need help, for this purpose we compare the means of the input characteristics of the K-means algorithm.

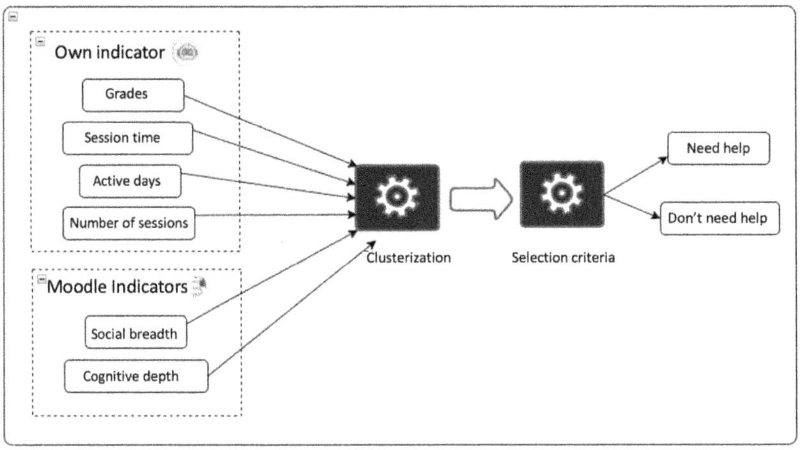

Fig. 2. Clusterization process to recommend to students

If a student classified in the group of those who need help, a comparison of the interactions of this student versus the group of students who do not need help is made. By analyzing the level of cognitive depth and social breadth of an activity, it is possible to generate recommendations, based on the level a student is at and should be according to their similar peers, thus generating recommendations such as: "*There are Forums that your classmates usually check, you should check them"*.

Another types of recommendations can be provided and are related to: (1) resources (employing collaborative filters, which use user ratings on certain items and predict ratings on the remaining items and recommend those with the highest predicted rating); (2) study sessions (the chatbot will analyze the student's participation within the course and defined by the teacher and will recommend both, the time that should be invested and the resources that have not been seen in the current week).

3.2 Message Chatbot Architecture

The plugin has a client server architecture, this leads to each click in the chatbot options sending a request to the server, it returns a message in JSON format with the response to the request adding the reference to a new request, as indicated in Fig. 3. *The message architecture has 4 properties:* (1) Text: the response message of each request; (2) MessageType: type of answer. The MessageTye can be (a) Question: Answer to type question, which requires an extra answer interaction; (b) Text: Plain text response, shows the result; (3) NextMessage: Validation if a response contains more than 2 messages; and (4) Option: Response options if the message is of type Question.

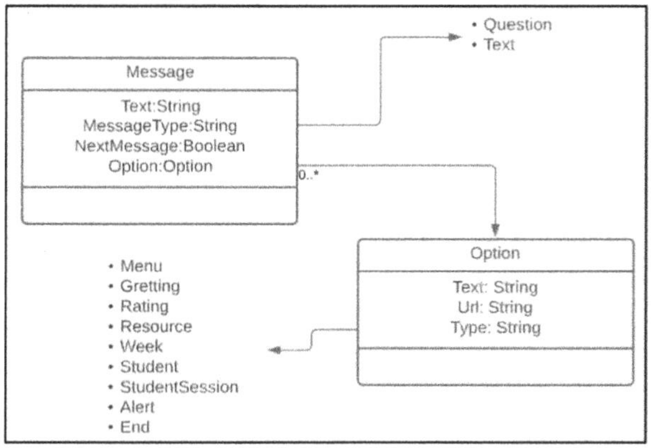

Fig. 3. Architecture to answer the messages sent by the chatbot

The architecture of the options has the following properties: (1) Text: Text of the response to the request; (2) Url: Used in case of redirection to various resources; (3) Type: Type of answer option, this can be (a) Menu: Returns to the menu when pressed; (b) Gretting: Returns to interaction initiation options when pressed; (c) Rating: Returns the options to rank a resource; (d) Resource: Returns options for obtaining recommended resources; (e) Week: Returns options to check weekly recommendations; (f) Student/ StudentSession: Returns display information options; (g) Alert: Returns random recommendation options; and (h) End: Ends interaction with the chatbot.

3.3 Miranda's Characteristics

When interacting with students, Miranda shows a welcome message (Fig. 4a). This message is shown every time the student enters a course, when clicking on it, all the available options of the chatbot will be displayed (Fig. 4b).

Table 1. Mirandas' options menu

Main options	Sub options	Description
Courses and events	View courses	Option that allows you to see the different courses where the student is enrolled
	Upcoming events	Option that allows the student to verify event, tasks close to being solved

(continued)

Table 1. *(continued)*

Main options	Sub options	Description
	New resources	Option that allows the student to verify new resources added to the system that the student has not yet seen
Tasks and recommendations	See recommendations	Options that allow the student to verify the recommendations provided by the system
	Most viewed resources	Option that allows to verify which were the resources most viewed by the other student
	Weekly recommendations	Option that allows the student to check how much time the teacher expects the student to devote time to a course
	Recommended Resources	Option that allows students to receive resource recommendations, using collaborative filters
Show dashboards	General indicators	Show visualizations presented in the NMP plugin to check general student indicators
	Study sessions	Show visualizations presented in the NMP plugin to check study sessions progress

Then when selecting *"Task and Recommendations"* the chatbot shows a recommendation (Fig. 4b). Table 1 shows the message options that can be sent to the student and is presented by the chatbot.

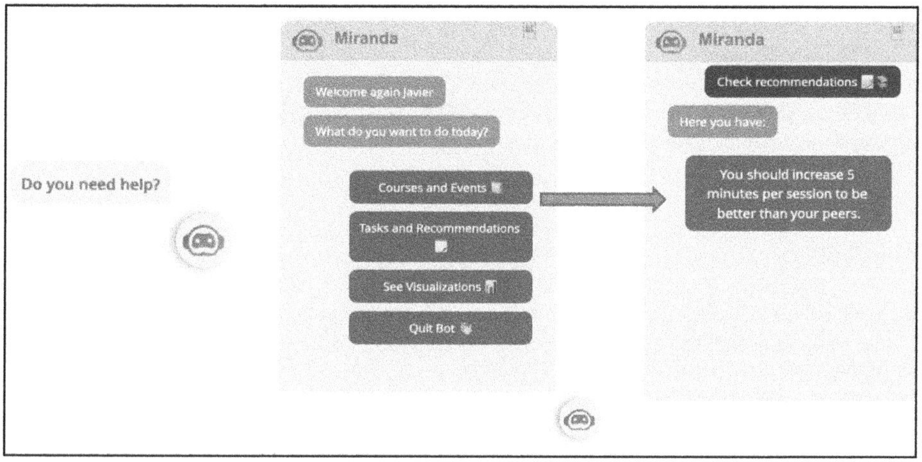

(a) (b)

Fig. 4. (a) Welcome message / (b) Recommendation presented by Miranda

4 Conclusions and Future Work

This work in progress presents the design and implementation of a Miranda, a chatbot implemented for Moodle to support students' self-regulated learning in hybrid and online courses. Miranda recommendations are based on prescriptive learning analytics using the students' logfile data collected and processed by the LMS Moodle. Miranda offers time and session recommendations, the most visited resources of the course, make time suggestions, what missing tasks and resources to check, and provide additional information in form of visualizations.

The main contribution of this work lies not only in the creation of the chatbot, but also in the development of the recommender system behind that. However, the current version of the tool entails several limitations that should be explored in future work. First, some of the recommendations use data from different students for comparison. However, during the first weeks of the course not enough data is available to group students and compare their behavior. Second, in the weekly recommendations, it is necessary for the teacher to allocate a dedication time for each module and week. In case this is not done, recommendations related with time-management SRL processes are limited. And third, resource recommendations are also limited by student ratings, which means that if students do not value resources no recommendations will be provided. Explained the above, finally, as future work it is expected to improve the recommendation system, and we plan to validate the chatbot testing it in an actual learning environment for analyzing students' and teachers' perceptions about these types of tools, as well as their potential effects on their behavior.

Acknowledgments. This paper was supported by Vicerrectorado de Investigación de la Universidad de Cuenca, the ANR JCJC LASER project (ANR-20-CE38–0004) and Corporación

Ecuatoriana para el Desarrollo de la Investigación y la Academia – CEDIA. The authors acknowledge PROF-XXI, which is an Erasmus+ Capacity Building in the Field of Higher Education project funded by the European Commission (609767-EPP-1–2019-1- ES-EPPKA2-CBHE-JP). This publication reflects the views only of the authors and funders cannot be held responsible for any use which may be made of the information.

References

1. Azevedo, R., Cromley, J.G.: Does training on self-regulated learning facilitate students' learning with hypermedia? J. Educ. Psychol. **96**, 523–535 (2004). https://doi.org/10.1037/0022-0663.96.3.523
2. Broadbent, J., Poon, W.L.: Self-regulated learning strategies & academic achievement in online higher education learning environments: a systematic review. Internet High. Educ. **27**, 1–13 (2015). https://doi.org/10.1016/j.iheduc.2015.04.007
3. Richardson, M., Abraham, C., Bond, R.: Psychological correlates of university students' academic performance: a systematic review and meta-analysis. Psychol. Bull. **138**, 353–387 (2012). https://doi.org/10.1037/a0026838
4. Maldonado-Mahauad, J., Pérez-Sanagustín, M., Kizilcec, R.F., Morales, N., Munoz-Gama, J.: Mining theory-based patterns from big data: identifying self-regulated learning strategies in massive open online courses. Comput. Human Behav. **80**, 179–196 (2018). https://doi.org/10.1016/j.chb.2017.11.011
5. Pérez-Álvarez, R., Pérez-Sanagustín, M., Maldonado-Mahauad, J.J.: NoteMyProgress: supporting learners' self-regulated strategies in MOOCs. In: Lavoué, É., Drachsler, H., Verbert, K., Broisin, J., Pérez-Sanagustín, M. (eds.) EC-TEL 2017. LNCS, vol. 10474, pp. 517–520. Springer, Cham (2017). https://doi.org/10.1007/978-3-319-66610-5_53
6. Matcha, W., Gašević, D., Pardo, A.: A systematic review of empirical studies on learning analytics dashboards: a self-regulated learning perspective. IEEE Trans. Learn. Technol. **13**, 226–245 (2019)
7. Shawar, B.A., Atwell, E.: Chatbots: are they really useful?. In: Ldv Forum, pp. 29–49 (2007)
8. Souali, K., Rahmaoui, O., Ouzzif, M., El Haddioui, I.: Recommending moodle resources using chatbots. In: Proceedings of the15th International Conference on Signal Image Technology & Internet Based Systems. SISITS 2019, pp. 677–680 (2019). https://doi.org/10.1109/SITIS.2019.00110
9. Ayanouz, S., Abdelhakim, B.A., Benhmed, M.: A smart chatbot architecture based NLP and machine learning for health care assistance. In: Proceedings of the 3rd International Conference on Networking, Information Systems & Security, pp. 1–6 (2020)
10. Pérez, J.Q., Daradoumis, T., Puig, J.M.M.: Rediscovering the use of chatbots in education: a systematic literature review. Comput. Appl. Eng. Educ. **28**, 1549–1565 (2020)
11. Zhang, R., Liu, Q., Hu, R., Ma, H., Yuan, Y.: Collaborative filtering: user similarity in slope one algorithm. In: JCIS, pp. 10413–10422 (2014)
12. Garrison, D.R., Anderson, T., Archer, W.: Critical thinking, cognitive presence, and computer conferencing in distance education. Am. J. Distance Educ. **15**, 7–23 (2001)
13. Garrison, D.R.: Communities of inquiry in online learning, pp. 352–355. https://doi.org/10.4018/978-1-60566-198-8.CH052, https://services.igi-global.com/resolvedoi/resolve.aspx?doi=10.4018/978-1-60566-198-8.ch052

Superpowers in the Classroom: Hyperchalk is an Online Whiteboard for Learning Analytics Data Collection

Lukas Menzel[1,2], Sebastian Gombert[2(✉)], Daniele Di Mitri[2], and Hendrik Drachsler[1,2]

[1] studiumdigitale, Goethe University, Frankfurt am Main, Germany
menzel@studiumdigitale.uni-frankfurt.de
[2] DIPF: Leibniz Institute for Research and Information in Education, Frankfurt am Main, Germany
{gombert,dimitri,drachsler}@dipf.de
http://studiumdigitale.uni-frankfurt.de, http://www.dipf.de

Abstract. In e-learning, collaborative online whiteboards have become a popular choice for implementing collaborative learning. However, existing solutions fail to deliver data in a way that allows for the application of learning analytics in this field. While the market offers several solutions, most of them cannot be integrated with existing learning management systems and do not provide data that can be used for learning analytics. To overcome this, we implement a digital collaborative whiteboard based on the open source Excalidraw and a custom back-end. The whiteboard can be self-hosted, it collects rich log data appropriate for learning analytics purposes and it integrates with learning management systems – such as Moodle – using the LTI 1.3 Advantage standard.

Keywords: Online whiteboard · Collaborative learning · Learning analytics · Learning tools interoperability

1 Introduction

In schools and universities, blackboards – and later whiteboards – have been used as tools for thinking and teaching for hundreds of years [1] . They are admired for their simplicity and the relative freedom that their users have in laying out what they want to teach and think about [11,18]. But this paper is not meant to be solely an ode to the blackboard. In this digital era, we increasingly shift towards remote and blended learning. Therefore, teaching now relies on a variety of online tools. These tools are ideally as simple and effective as the classic blackboard while they can incorporate the advantages of digitality into educational work.

One such advantage is their potential ability to enable learning analytics (LA). Through collecting rich data about learning processes and deriving indicators from that, students and educators can be provided with meaningful insight into their learning and teaching [5].

I. Hilliger et al. (Eds.): EC-TEL 2022, LNCS 13450, pp. 463–469, 2022.
https://doi.org/10.1007/978-3-031-16290-9_37

Utilizing the open source component Excalidraw [4], we implemented a collaborative online whiteboard to implement collaborative learning tasks. To further support the use of our solution in teaching, it can be integrated with established learning management systems (LMS) via the LTI 1.3 Advantage standard [7]. Furthermore, we discuss how our whiteboard implementation enables data collection in an ethical and privacy-sensitive manner to support research efforts in the field of LA in line with the *Trusted LA Approach* [2].

2 Collaborative Online Whiteboards

Collaborative online whiteboards have already been used to enhance and also—especially during the COVID-19 period—to enable learning through implementing a collaborative drawing environment [12,14]. This section will shed light on the possibilities and constraints on their usage and their enhancement through learning analytics.

2.1 Possibilities

Carefully designed collaborative learning assignments allow students to collectively grasp a topic by building a collective working memory [9]. Online whiteboards are one method to provide an environment in which students can learn collaboratively. As they offer a high degree of freedom of expression, they also allow for numerous possibilities on how to use them in education. They could, for example, be used as a digitally enhanced derivative of classic collaborative learning tasks like the making of posters. Online drawing assignments for single students are possible as well.

Because online whiteboards are digital, they can collect data, which researchers can use to conduct LA. It is important to note that different types of collaborative assignments require different LA indicators [13]. Developing an application for new collaborative tasks thus poses research opportunities to implement known indicators using the application's data and to provide new learning indicators that may be tailored specifically to be used on online whiteboards.

2.2 Constraints

Collaborative whiteboards are a very visual class of tools. They are therefore hardly accessible to people with severe visual impairments, even when they use assistive technology [10]. As for now, if there are visually impaired students included in the classroom, educators should reach for a different set of tools in most cases. These tools should be more text-based and linear so that those students can have a first-class learning experience instead of only being "enabled" as an afterthought [15].

There is usually some loose visual structure to the content created using digital whiteboards when used for learning purposes. Still, digital whiteboards lack structured data about this content, while the information they contain has more structure than is easily derivable from the data. Complex methods like machine learning would have to be employed to retrieve that data. Thus, using such software in education imposes a higher need for qualitative assessment of the students' work and constrains possibilities for quantitative evaluations.

3 Related Work

There are a plethora of collaborative online tools which allow for some form of more or less structured drawing and ordering of items. Especially in the commercial field, many solutions exist which are directed at a more general audience and thus only have minimal support for the needs of LA, if any.

Prototypical solutions in the field, such as Miro – a popular solution with a broad feature set that has already been used in educational scenarios [12] – lack support for data extraction which is crucial for LA. The same goes for Flinga, another popular solution within education, which has LTI support and where the vendor provides guides for its deployment in pedagogical contexts. We also considered other solutions as well. During our search for solutions, it became clear that there was yet no open source solution to support the kind of data collection that is needed to implement LA. Hosted commercial solutions as well as the available commercial on-premise solutions we found also do not enable the degree of hands-on customization that is needed for our LA research. We thus opted to implement a new solution and used Excalidraw as its base component.

Excalidraw is an open source online whiteboard solution which runs in the browser. It has a simple set of operations and tools that allow filling the board with content: within this set are basic shapes like rectangles and ellipses, lines, arrows, a text tool, and a free-hand drawing tool, as well as the ability to add images to the scene. Excalidraw also has a library feature that allows reusing collections of elements as components on different boards than the ones they stem from. These components can also be shared with others, whether as a file or via the public Excalidraw library.

The Excalidraw front-end is available in the form of a React component to supply its functionality to any website. This component supports adding a custom collaboration layer by exposing collaborator-aware APIs to update the scene and to register event handlers for scene updates.

We deem Excalidraw's feature set, usability, aesthetics, and – very importantly – its integration possibilities very fitting for teaching purposes. We thus chose to use Excalidraw as the basis for our application to implement an LTI-compatible, LA-ready collaborative online whiteboard.

4 Hyperchalk

Hyperchalk is constructed to support studying collaborative learning through LA. This is made possible by combining multiple techniques to provide a real-time collaborative experience as well as features and data collection for qualitative and quantitative research about the learning process of Hyperchalk's users (Fig. 1).

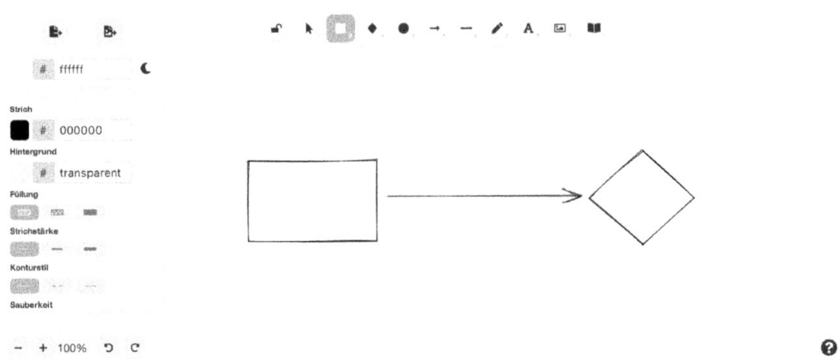

Fig. 1. Screenshot of hyperchalk's excalidraw client

4.1 Assignment Types And Modes

Hyperchalk provides several assignment types. When creating an assignment via an LMS over LTI, a teacher can choose between three assignment types: In "Single Person Assignments", each student is given their own whiteboard. In "Group Assignments", the teacher can create an arbitrary number of whiteboards for groups of students to work on. Finally, for "Classroom Assignments", exactly one whiteboard is created per assignment.

The default mode in which each board will open is the collaboration mode. In this mode, everyone connected to the whiteboard will be able to make changes to it. People connected to the whiteboard will be able to collaborate in real-time. The second mode is the replay mode. Whiteboards opened in replay mode are read-only. Everyone connected to the whiteboard in replay mode will be able to replay all changes made to the whiteboard from its creation to the moment the user presses the play/replay button. The replay can also be paused and resumed later in time.

Use cases for the replay mode are to be expected for both teachers and researchers. Not only does it allow teachers to qualitatively comprehend how students developed their solution to the given assignment. It also allows LA researchers to devise theories about student behavior, leading to the development of better indicators.

4.2 Data Collection And Privacy

The learning progress of a person is by any means personal data. LA is thus a field where secrecy and trusted environments have to play a large role [2]. This also aligns with the findings of Scheffel et al. [16], who found that privacy is one of the highest-rated issues among students using applications that provide LA. Hyperchalk was developed with this in mind, adhering to the Codex for Trusted Learning Analytics for Universities in Hesse [6].

Hyperchalk is a self-hosted application. This gives the institution using the application complete control over the application's stored data. That being said, LA, of course, requires the collection of data to analyze. Hyperchalk tracks collaborators' cursor movements, every change to the elements on the board, as well as information on connections and disconnections. All those data points carry timestamps. It also has a user database, where a user record is automatically created from the information supplied by the LMS when a user logs in via an LTI Deep Link [8]. This record contains a username, the user's real name, the user ID and the LMS instance that the user came from.

However, Hyperchalk does not link its users to the stored actions directly. Instead, it creates a hash from the room ID and the user ID and uses that as the user pseudonym. This pseudonym is then stored in an association table that administrators can delete to restore anonymity. This table is needed to assign users to their pre- and post-tests during learning indicator evaluation (Fig. 2).

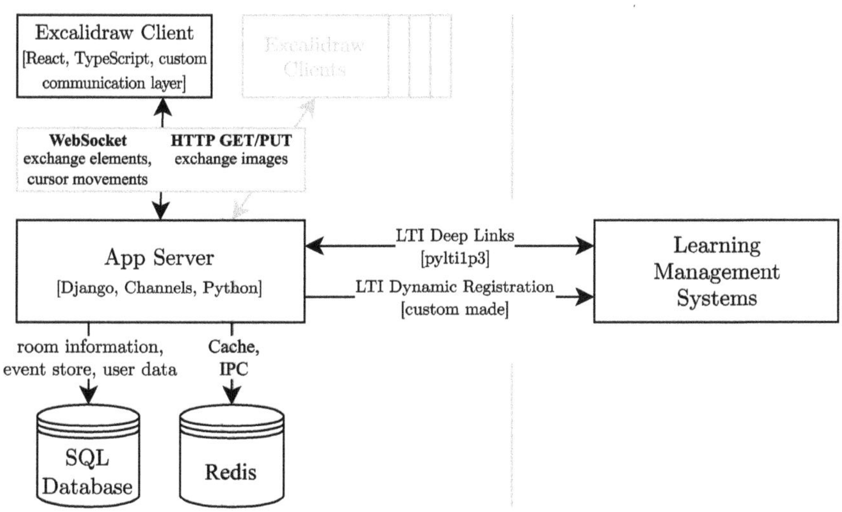

Fig. 2. Structure of the application implementation

5 Conclusion and Outlook

Online whiteboards allow their users to express their thoughts with a high degree of freedom in their structuring and visualization. We see massive potential for utilizing such tools in general and Hyperchalk specifically for allowing learning analytics studies on computer supported collaborative learning. With its various modes and by embracing privacy within learning analytics, we aim to make Hyperchalk a provider of responsibly collected data for researchers in the field, and a tool that both teachers and learners find helpful and enjoyable to support their education.

We plan to deploy Hyperchalk in the future for several scenarios, including, e.g., in chemistry lessons, where students will collaboratively draw structural formulas. As a start, we may search for indicators to assess the quality of the collaboration between students. Such indicators have proven useful in other assignment types before [17] which is why we deem them to be promising as a start. In addition to the assessment of collaboration quality, the indicators we search for shall also help us to assess the sufficiency of the application for assignments, as well as the adequacy of the assignments themselves. In the long term, to evaluate the learning progress of students, we plan to conduct studies combining the data which Hyperchalk delivers with pre- and post-tests.

Moreover, by utilizing the replay mode, we could conduct case studies on student behavior to build further theoretical understanding [3] of how learners approach tasks using Hyperchalk, and what makes them successful at solving those. Enhanced by such methods as thinking-alouds, this theory could then help us to generate LA indicator candidates that are to be tested in larger experiments.

References

1. Comenius, J.A.: XCVII. Schola. In: Orbis Sensualium Pictus, pp. 198–199, Nürnberg (1658)
2. Drachsler, H., and Greller, W.: Privacy and analytics: it's a delicate issue. a checklist for trusted learning analytics. In: Proceedings of the Sixth International Conference on Learning Analytics & Knowledge - LAK 2016, pp. 89–98. ACM Press, Edinburgh, United Kingdom (2016). https://doi.org/10.1145/2883851.2883893
3. Eisenhardt, K.M., Graebner, M.E.: Theory building from cases: opportunities and challenges. AMJ **50**(1), 25–32 (2007). https://doi.org/10.5465/amj.2007.24160888
4. MISC
5. Greller, W., Drachsler, H.: Translating learning into numbers: a generic framework for learning analytics. J. Educ. Technol. Soc. **15**(3), 42–57 (2012)
6. Hansen, J., Rensing, C., Herrmann, O., Drachsler, H.: Verhaltenskodex Für Trusted Learning Analytics. Version 1.0. Entwurf Für Die Hessischen Hochschulen (2020). https://doi.org/10.25657/02:18903
7. IMS Global: Learning Tools Interoperability (LTI) 1.3. Standard 1.3, IMS Global Learning Consortium Inc. (2018)
8. IMS Global: Learning Tools Interoperability (LTI) Deep Linking 2.0. Standard 2.0 (2019)
9. Janssen, J., Kirschner, F., Kirschner, P.A.: The collaboration principle in multimedia learning. In: Mayer, R.E., Fiorella, L. (eds.) The Cambridge Handbook of Multimedia Learning, pp. 304–312. Cambridge University Press (2021). https://doi.org/10.1017/9781108894333.032

10. Kieninger, T.: The "Growing up" of HyperBraille – an office workspace for blind people. In: Proceedings of the 9th Annual ACM Symposium on User Interface Software and Technology - UIST 1096, pp. 67–73. ACM Press, Seattle, Washington, United States (1996). https://doi.org/10.1145/237091.237100
11. Langner-Geißler, T., Lipp, U.: Pinwand. Flipchart und Tafel. Beltz, Weinheim (1994)
12. Ng, B.J.M., et al.: Supporting social and learning presence in the revised community of inquiry framework for hybrid learning. J. Chem. Educ. **99**(2), 708–714 (2022). https://doi.org/10.1021/acs.jchemed.1c00842
13. Praharaj, S., Scheffel, M., Drachsler, H., Specht, M.: Literature review on co-located collaboration modeling using multimodal learning analytics-can we go the whole nine yards? IEEE Trans. Learn. Technol. **14**(3), 367–385 (2021). https://doi.org/10.1109/TLT.2021.3097766
14. Rojanarata, T.: How online whiteboard promotes students' collaborative skills in laboratory learning. In: Proceedings of the 2020 8th International Conference on Information and Education Technology, pp. 68–72. ACM, Okayama Japan (2020). https://doi.org/10.1145/3395245.3396433
15. Savidis, A., Stephanidis, C.: The HOMER UIMS for dual user interface development: fusing visual and non-visual interactions. Interact. Comput. **11**(2), 173–209 (1998). https://doi.org/10.1016/S0953-5438(98)00025-3
16. Scheffel, M., Drachsler, H., Kreijns, K., de Kraker, J., Specht, M.: Widget, widget as you lead, i am performing well indeed!: using results from an exploratory offline study to inform an empirical online study about a learning analytics widget in a collaborative learning environment. In: Proceedings of the Seventh International Learning Analytics & Knowledge Conference, pp. 289–298. ACM, Vancouver British Columbia Canada (2017). https://doi.org/10.1145/3027385.3027428
17. Scheffel, M., Drachsler, H., Stoyanov, S., Specht, M.: Quality indicators for learning analytics. Educ. Technol. Soc. **17**(14), 17 (2014)
18. Shahbazi, Z., Shahbazmohamadi, S.: From black boards to digital boards: students and professors experience challenges and remedies. In: 2013 ASEE Annual Conference & Exposition Proceedings, pp. 23.619.1-23.619.16. ASEE Conferences, Atlanta, Georgia (2013). https://doi.org/10.18260/1-2-19633

An Educational Conversational Agent for GDPR

Behzad Mirzababaei[1(✉)] and Viktoria Pammer-Schindler[1,2]

[1] Know-Center GmbH, Graz, Austria
bmirzababaei@know-center.at
[2] Graz University of Technology, Graz, Austria
viktoria.pammer-schindler@tugraz.at

Abstract. Large-scale learning scenarios as well as the ongoing pandemic situation underline the importance of educational technology in order to support scalability and spatial as well as temporal flexibility in all kinds of learning and teaching settings. Educational conversational agents build on a long research tradition in intelligent tutoring systems and other adaptive learning technologies but build for interaction on the more recent interaction paradigm of conversational interaction. In this paper, we describe a tutorial conversational agent, called GDPRAgent, which teaches a lesson on the European General Data Protection Regulation (GDPR). This regulation governs how personal data must be treated in Europe. Instructionally, the agent's dialogue structure follows a basic GDPR curriculum and uses Bloom's revised taxonomy of learning objectives in order to teach GDPR topics. This overall design of the dialogue structure allows inserting more specific adaptive tutorial strategies. From a learner perspective, the learners experience a completely one-on-one tutorial session in which they receive relevant content (is "being taught") as well as experiences active learning parts such as doing quizzes or summarising content. Our prototype, therefore, illustrates a move away from the dichotomy between content and the activity of teaching/learning in educational technology.

Keywords: Educational conversational agent · Intelligent tutoring · General data protection regulation · Learning by argumentation · Bloom's taxonomy

1 Pedagogical and Technological Background

Lifelong learning is necessary for an individual, organisational and societal success and well-being. At the same time, increasing numbers of students in education or employees in workplaces in parallel to always seemingly too few resources make it challenging to provide a good level of individualised and interactive teaching. This, however, is desirable in order for teaching and learning to be of satisfactory quality [6,13]. Educational technology has long been investigated as a means to address this insight.

I. Hilliger et al. (Eds.): EC-TEL 2022, LNCS 13450, pp. 470–476, 2022.
https://doi.org/10.1007/978-3-031-16290-9_38

In this paper, we are particularly interested in the promise of conversational agents that act as tutors. Conversational agents constitute a human-computer interaction paradigm in which people can interact - so the ideal - in a relatively natural (for humans) way in natural language with technology. Ideally, with conversational agents, a learner can discuss concepts in a learning domain, move from talking about basics toward core complex definitions, do a self-assessment by answering questions, and receive feedback. This is what good educators do, given sufficient resources to interact bilaterally or with small groups of learners.

Much research in artificial intelligence for education has gone into developing computational systems that are able to, at least partially, fulfil some of these functions that (good) human tutors take on. Such systems are typically called intelligent tutoring systems [9,14]. More recently, researchers have investigated tutorial conversational agents, e.g., for question answering [7], helping students to efficiently use a large body of content [3], helping learners in assessing their own abilities [8], and providing administrative services such as answering students' questions on behalf of the academic faculty [10]. Many conversational agents that focus on teaching a topic are of course domain-specific, and by now research efforts span a plethora of subjects such as mathematics [2], medicine [11], computer science [16], physics and chemistry [17]. Typical research questions in these works are about the agents' architecture, how to model learners, different communication methods such as text or voice, or the impact of the appearance of agents on learners. Complementing such works, our research emphasis is on how to systematically design tutorial dialogues - which we propose to do by following Bloom's revised taxonomy of learning objectives [5] - and how to insert different teaching strategies into this overall structure.

This demo paper presents a conversational agent, named GDPRAgent, that carries out a complete tutorial conversation. The agent covers the complete content of a lesson step by step, asks questions after each step and gives feedback on learners' answers, and summarises content at the end of the lesson. GDPRAgent thereby simulates a whole learning session in a one-to-one situation between a teacher and a learner. The learning session is about the General Data Protection Regulation (GDPR), which is the European regulation that governs how personal data must be treated. The GDPR brings some new definitions and structures for data handling and management, as a result, individuals and organisations need to be adapted to the GDPR concepts. Therefore, it is a typical topic of MOOCs as it is relevant, at an introductory level, to a broad range of professions.

2 Description of the Prototype

GDPRAgent conveys the basic knowledge about the GDPR. The conversation contains four parts, which, topic-wise, we created to represent a typical introductory GDPR curriculum. First, it starts with a greeting and shows the agenda (Fig. 1). Second, the agent talks about what is the GDPR and where and when it should be applied. Third, the definition of personal data and sensitive data, and their differences are covered. Finally, the seven data protection principles of the

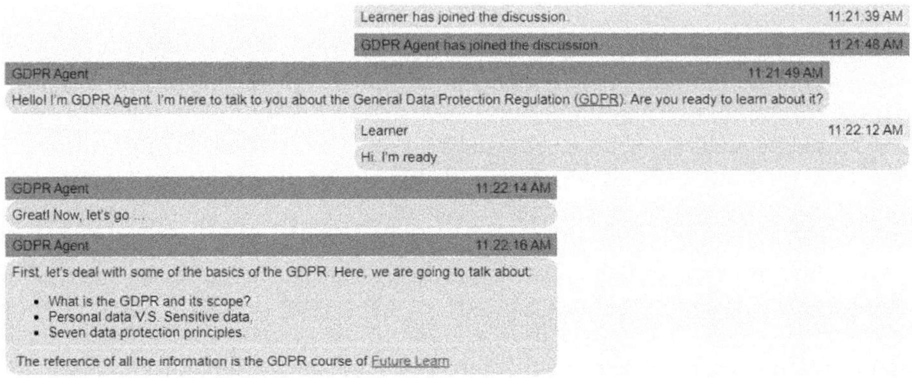

Fig. 1. The responsive web page in which the greeting section of the conversation and the agenda are shown.

Table 1. The flow of the conversation. It includes four subsections: greeting, the GDPR and its scope, personal and sensitive data, and seven data protection principles.

ID	Subsection
1.1	Greeting and agenda
2.1	What is the GDPR?
2.2	Where and when should it be applied?
3.1	What is personal data?
3.2	What is sensitive data?
3.3	What are the differences?
3.4	Asking relevant questions
3.5	Summarising information
4.1	Seven data protection principles
4.2	Asking relevant questions
4.3	Summarising information

GDPR are presented. Table 1 shows the order of the content in the whole dialogue. The GDPR content has been synthesised based on several online resources including the authoritative GDPR information[1]. Especially, we have benefited from FutureLearn[2], based on the open content license for non-commercial purposes, for the question parts of the dialogue, Parts 3.4 and 4.2.

Different teaching strategies are embedded into the conversation. In this prototype agent, we followed the revised Bloom's revised taxonomy of learning objectives [5]. For instance, in the third part of the conversation which is about personal and sensitive data (See Table 1), the agent first covers the "remem-

[1] https://eur-lex.europa.eu/homepage.html.

[2] https://www.futurelearn.com/courses/general-data-protection-regulation.

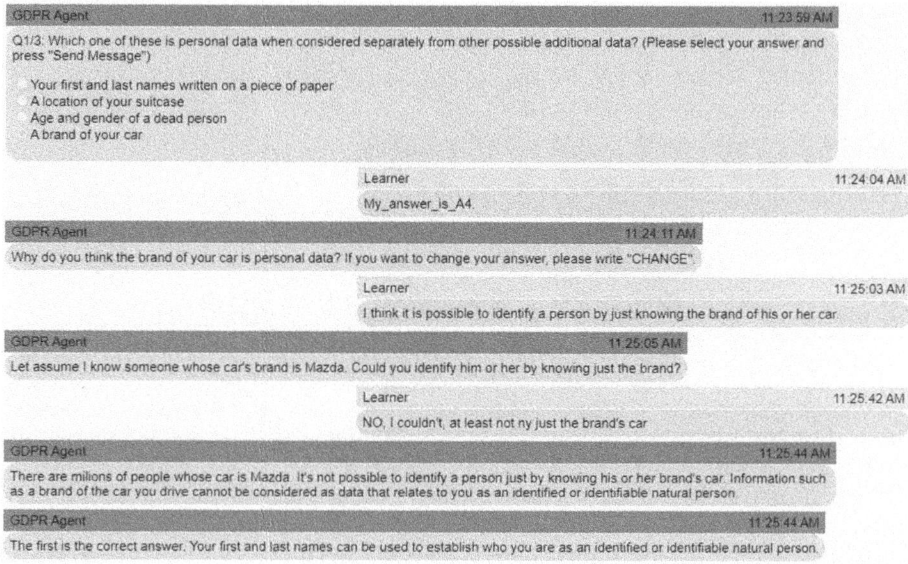

Fig. 2. The agent asks argumentative follow-up questions before showing the answer.

bering" and "understanding" levels of Bloom's taxonomy by talking about the definitions of personal and sensitive data. Second, by focusing on the differences between these two types of data and asking learners some questions in which the learners need to apply the information in various scenarios, the agent covers "applying" and "analysing". Finally, the agent addresses the "evaluating" level by having an argumentative conversation in which the learners are asked to justify their answers. At this point, we therefore also followed the teaching strategy of learning through argumentation [12]. Learning through argumentation guides learners to analyse a problem from various perspectives and also to distinguish what is correct and incorrect. Figure 2 shows how the agent asked follow-up questions in order to guide the learner to find out why the selected option was incorrect. Here the agent asked the user to justify his answer and then the agent explained a situation in which the user's answer is not valid. In general, the agent adapts to learners' responses. Based on each response, the agent asks the learner to think again about their own response and justify it and then, in case of selecting a wrong answer, the agent explains a situation in which the user's argument is not valid anymore. This part of the dialogue uses learning by argumentation.

The example of the "learning through argumentation" teaching strategy above already shows, how an overall instructional design following Bloom's revised taxonomy of learning objectives allows and actually needs the insertion of more specific teaching strategies. Note that from an instructional perspective "teaching strategies" are inserted, whilst this means that from a technical perspective "adaptation mechanisms" need to be inserted. Here, the full spectrum of intelligent tutoring and adaptive teaching systems [4] is available to conversational agent designers.

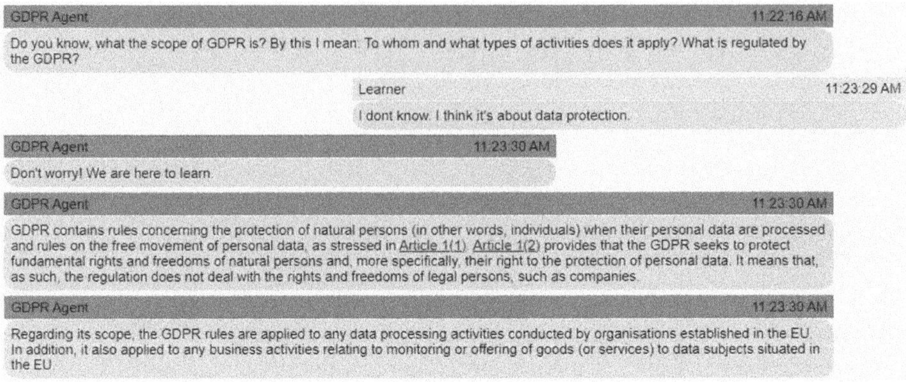

Fig. 3. The agent asks for the learner's idea about the GDPR's scope before teaching it. The agent is also adapted to the learner's responses

In the current prototype, we have inserted two more adaptation strategies. The first is to adapt to learner knowledge (cp. [4]' taxonomy of adaptation strategies), and to exercise what a learner does not know. We did this in Parts 3.4 and 4,2 (See Table 1), such that when the agent asks questions about the different type of data (Part 3.4) and about data protection principles (Part 4.2), the number of questions for each learner depends on the number of his or her correct answers. We defined five different questions for Part 3.4 and six questions for Part 4.2, but the agent first asks three questions. In each part, if a learner answers at least two questions, the agent asks the learner for answering more questions. In case of agreement, the agent asks the rest of the questions. Otherwise, the conversation is continued. The second adaptation strategy could be understood as an adaptation that targets learners' affect. At the beginning of a new topic, the agent asks what the learner already knows about this. In Fig. 3 for instance, the agent asks the learner, about the GDPR's scope before giving the information. The agent is to some extent adaptive to the learner's responses. The agent uses keyword matching in order to understand the learners' responses. For each topic, a set of keywords are defined which helps the agent to have an adaptive reaction. For instance, in Fig. 3, since the user did not know the answer, the agent gave encouraging feedback in order to motivate the learner. In general, if the agent does not understand the user's responses, it will try to keep the conversation coherent and meaningful by giving a proper reply.

Technically, we have implemented GDPRAgent based on the open-source Bazaar framework [1] as back-end[3], and as an HTML/JS responsive web page for the front-end. This framework allows both rule-based and machine-learning-based classifiers to decide between dialogue branches. GDPRAgent is ready to use and publicity available[4].

[3] https://github.com/DANCEcollaborative/.

[4] http://chatbot.know-center.tugraz.at/bazaar/landing_page/chatbot_landing_page.

3 Future Work and Vision

In ongoing work, we are working on assessing the agent's usability, which is an important baseline that educational technology needs to meet. We are further working on investigating what qualities of the learning process and learning outcomes change as the interaction paradigm is more conversational when compared to other interactive digital content formats.

We see the main contribution of our research to existing research on conversational agents in education in the systematic instructional dialogue design, based on Bloom's revised taxonomy of learning objectives. We aim to show that this structure can also be used in other domains than the GDPR. Further, above we have explained already a few teaching (instructional perspective) and adaptation (technical perspective) strategies. A systematic guideline for educational conversational agent developers would be helpful that summarises which teaching strategies can be inserted in a single conversational agent lesson. Finally, we have been working on natural language processing capabilities that allow processing and feedbacking more open-ended questions of a particular argumentative form [15] and think that there is overall still room for improvement in research on being able to accommodate more complex question types and feedbacking them in intelligent tutoring systems.

Overall, we see the promise of such fully conversational intelligent tutoring systems as moving beyond the content/learning dichotomy, that separates the provision of content with the support for active learning activities in computational environments for learning. GDPRAgent can demonstrate what such an educational technology could look like in the future. As a note of caution: We are thereby not supporting the stance that human teachers can or should be replaced. Readers will note that our agent teaches the basics of GDPR. Given the instructional and content design effort that goes into creating a conversational agent such as ours, which ultimately covers just a single tutorial unit, we foresee that such agents will rather replace, or become the norm in, learning content management systems and MOOCs, which already step ahead of very traditional content-focused computational environments for learning.

Acknowledgements. This work was supported by the "DDAI" COMET Module within the COMET-Competence Centers for Excellent Technologies Program, funded by the Austrian Federal Ministry (BMK and BMDW), the Austrian Research Promotion Agency (FFG), the province of Styria (SFG) and partners from industry and academia. The COMET Program is managed by FFG.

References

1. Adamson, D., Dyke, G., Jang, H., Rosé, C.P.: Towards an agile approach to adapting dynamic collaboration support to student needs. Int. J. Artif. Intell. Educ. **24**(1), 92–124 (2014). https://doi.org/10.1007/s40593-013-0012-6
2. Aguiar, E.V.B., Tarouco, L.M.R., Reategui, E.: Supporting problem-solving in Mathematics with a conversational agent capable of representing gifted students'

knowledge. In: 2014 47th Hawaii International Conference on System Sciences, pp. 130–137. IEEE (2014)
3. Akcora, D.E., et al.: Conversational support for education. In: AIED 2018. LNCS (LNAI), vol. 10948, pp. 14–19. Springer, Cham (2018). https://doi.org/10.1007/978-3-319-93846-2_3
4. Aleven, V., McLaughlin, E. A., Glenn, R. A., Koedinger, K.R.: Instruction based on adaptive learning technologies. Technical report (2017)
5. Anderson, L.W., Krathwohl, D.R., Bloom, B.S.: A taxonomy for learning, teaching, and assessing: a revision of Bloom's taxonomy of educational objectives, p. 352 (2001)
6. Brinton, C.G., Rill, R., Ha, S., Chiang, M., Smith, R., Ju, W.: Individualization for education at scale: MIIC design and preliminary evaluation. IEEE Trans. Learn. Technol. **8**(1), 136–148 (2014)
7. Clarizia, F., Colace, F., Lombardi, M., Pascale, F., Santaniello, D.: Chatbot: an education support system for student. In: Castiglione, A., Pop, F., Ficco, M., Palmieri, F. (eds.) CSS 2018. LNCS, vol. 11161, pp. 291–302. Springer, Cham (2018). https://doi.org/10.1007/978-3-030-01689-0_23
8. Durall, E., Kapros, E.: Co-design for a competency self-assessment chatbot and survey in science education. In: Zaphiris, P., Ioannou, A. (eds.) HCII 2020. LNCS, vol. 12206, pp. 13–24. Springer, Cham (2020). https://doi.org/10.1007/978-3-030-50506-6_2
9. Gertner, A.S., VanLehn, K.: Andes: a coached problem solving environment for physics. In: Gauthier, G., Frasson, C., VanLehn, K. (eds.) ITS 2000. LNCS, vol. 1839, pp. 133–142. Springer, Heidelberg (2000). https://doi.org/10.1007/3-540-45108-0_17
10. Hien, H.T., Cuong, P.N., Nam, L.N.H., Nhung, H.L.T.K., Thang, L.D.: Intelligent assistants in higher-education environments: the fit-ebot, a chatbot for administrative and learning support. In: Proceedings of the Ninth International Symposium on Information and Communication Technology, pp. 69–76 (2018)
11. Jagtap, R., Phulare, K., Kurhade, M., Gawande, K.S.: Healthcare conversational chatbot for medical diagnosis. In: Handbook of Research on Engineering, Business, and Healthcare Applications of Data Science and Analytics, pp. 401–415. IGI Global (2021)
12. Jonassen, D.H., Kim, B.: Arguing to learn and learning to argue: design justifications and guidelines. Educ. Tech. Research Dev. **58**(4), 439–457 (2010). https://doi.org/10.1007/s11423-009-9143-8
13. Kim, B.: Social constructivism. Emerg. Perspect. Learn. Teach. Technol. **1**(1), 16 (2001)
14. Koedinger, K.R., Anderson, J.R., Hadley, W.H., Mark, M.A.: Intelligent tutoring goes to school in the big city (1997)
15. Mirzababaei, B., Pammer-Schindler, V.: Developing a conversational agent's capability to identify structural wrongness in arguments based on Toulmin's model of arguments. Front. Artif. Intell. **4** (2021)
16. Mitrovic, A.: An intelligent SQL tutor on the web. Int. J. Artif. Intell. Educ. **13**(2–4), 173–197 (2003)
17. Pérez-Marín, D., Boza, A.: A procedure to create a pedagogic conversational agent in secondary physics and chemistry education. Int. J. Inf. Commun. Technol. Educ. **9**(4), 94–112 (2013)

e-FeeD4Mi: Automating Tailored LA-Informed Feedback in Virtual Learning Environments

Alejandro Ortega-Arranz(✉), Paraskevi Topali, Juan I. Asensio-Pérez, Sara L. Villagrá-Sobrino, Alejandra Martínez-Monés, and Yannis Dimitriadis

GSIC-EMIC Research Group, Universidad de Valladolid, Valladolid, Spain
{alex,evi.topali}@gsic.uva.es

Abstract. The provision of personalized and timely feedback can become challenging when shifting from face-to-face to online learning. Feedback is not only about providing support to students, but also about identifying when and which students need what kind of support. Usually, educators carry out such activities manually. However, the manual identification, personalization and provision of feedback might turn unmanageable, especially in large-scale environments. Previous works proposed the use of data-driven tools to automate the feedback provision with the active involvement of human agents in its design. Nevertheless, to the best of our knowledge, these tools do not guide instructors in the process of feedback design and sense-making of the data-driven information. This paper presents e-FeeD4Mi, a web-based tool developed to support instructors in the design and automatic enactment of feedback in multiple virtual learning environments. We developed e-FeeD4Mi following a Design-Based Research approach and its potential for adoption has been evaluated in two evaluation studies.

Keywords: Feedback · Learning analytics · Learning design · Instructors · Virtual learning environments · e-FeeD4Mi

1 Introduction

Feedback is one of the most important features in learning, influencing positively both the feedback provider and the feedback receiver [2,3,9]. Hattie & Timperley (2007, *p. 8*) [3] define feedback as *"the information provided by an agent (e.g., teacher, peer, book, etc.) regarding aspects of one's performance or understanding"*. Effective feedback interventions involve timeliness and personalization as two core aspects to keep students engaged and to benefit the learning process [3,6,9]. Thus, feedback is not only about providing support, but also about identifying when and which students need what kind of support.

Usually, instructors[1] are responsible for performing all these feedback-related tasks that require additional effort and can become time-consuming.

[1] For simplicity, we refer to *instructors* as any person involved in the design and provision of feedback, including instructional designers, teachers and teaching assistants.

I. Hilliger et al. (Eds.): EC-TEL 2022, LNCS 13450, pp. 477–484, 2022.
https://doi.org/10.1007/978-3-031-16290-9_39

Nevertheless, the manual identification, personalization, and provision of feedback can turn unmanageable when scaling up the learning situation (*e.g.*, many activities, many students). To this end, several tools have been developed to automate the detection of students who need support and to deliver feedback reactions in online environments. For instance, previous works, such as those by Kochmar et al. (2020) [4] and Lafifi et al. (2020) [5] suggested the use of intelligent tutoring systems as an alternative to human tutoring to achieve students' real-time tracking and provide timely and personalized data-driven feedback.

However, literature reports that many of the data-driven tools do not consider the course context (*e.g.*, the difficulty of the activities, the relation among course components) [7,15]. The consideration of the course context could be achieved by involving instructors in the design of feedback strategies [14,18]. To that end, many researchers propose conceptual and technological tools that actively involve the course instructors in fine-tuning the metrics, permitting them to detect learners who would need further support and provide feedback accordingly.

For instance, Pardo (2018) [10] proposed a data-driven feedback model, in which the feedback providers (*e.g.*, instructors, peers) make the associations between the Learning Analytics (LA) and the course context. The author implemented this model into a digital tool, OnTask [11], enabling instructors to select different student cohorts by choosing data-driven metrics, and to deliver personalized feedback through email messages. Similarly, Liu et al., (2017) [7] presented a LA tool named Student Relationship Engagement System (SRES) to promote teacher agency by permitting the decision-making of informative features based on learners' activity and the provision of personalized teacher-led feedback. Also, Reza et al. (2021) [13] developed a framework where course instructors create if-then rules to provide feedback in form of recommendations to MOOC learners based on their course engagement and behavior.

However, to the best of our knowledge, these tools do not guide instructors in the design of feedback (*e.g.*, feedback suggestions based on the learning design or on the expected problems). Indeed, as Mangaroska & Giannakos (2019) [8] reported, course instructors often need further guidance on their sense-making and use of data-driven information to result in actionable feedback (*i.e.*, feedback grounded on the course design and pedagogical theories, and informed by learners' actions). Another significant limitation of existing LA-informed feedback tools is that the connections needed between learning design and learning analytics is limited to specific Learning Management Systems (LMSs), and do not consider analytics from third-party general-purpose tools (*e.g.*, Google Docs, Slack), frequently used in technological-enhanced learning situations. This technological shortcoming reduces the applicability of existing research proposals.

To satisfy the above-mentioned limitations (*i.e.*, lack of human involvement in the provision of personalized feedback, lack of guidance during the feedback design process, and lack of feedback tools connecting LMSs and external tools), we propose e-FeeD4Mi, a web-based tool developed by the authors to support the design and automatic enactment of feedback in multiple virtual learning environments. Thus, the overarching research question guiding this study is:

- *"To what extent does e-FeeD4Mi support instructors in the design and enactment of tailored data-driven feedback?".*

2 e-FeeD4Mi Overview

e-FeeD4Mi is a web-based tool that guides instructors through a five-dimension process to design and automate personalized data-driven feedback in learning management systems (*e.g.*, Canvas, Moodle) and external tools (*e.g.*, Slack, Google Docs). The tool includes a set of catalogues of potential problems, indicators and reactions, and associated recommendations for the configuration of the most appropriate decisions to give feedback to students. e-FeeD4Mi is based on a conceptual framework [16,17] that involves the aforementioned process, catalogues and recommendations. Thus, its implementation in a digital tool enables the configuration of computer-interpretable feedback designs and the automation of the whole feedback procedure (*i.e.*, student identification and feedback provision) during course runtime. The five-dimension process involves:

1. **Import the learning design**. e-FeeD4Mi is able to automatically retrieve learning designs, including title, modules, types of configured activities (*e.g.*, quizzes, discussion forums, peer reviews) and their temporal sequence, from mainstream learning management systems. Instructors just need to provide the LMS type (*e.g.*, Moodle), the location of the course (*i.e.*, URL) and their authentication bearer for external integration (*i.e.*, credentials).
2. **Identify inherent features of the learning design**. This step aims at reflecting about the critical points of the learning design where students can potentially experience learning issues that might require instructor feedback. To this end, e-FeeD4Mi provides instructors with a set of tools (*i.e.*, visual labels and colors) that can be used to tag the resources and activities of the learning design (see Fig. 1 - top). For instance, instructors can tag the difficulty of the quizzes, the connections between resources, course milestones, etc.
3. **Select potential student problems**. In this phase, and considering the reflection from the previous phase, instructors can select from a list of student problems (obtained from the literature and from evaluation studies [16]) which of them can apply to instructors' course in general, or to concrete activities of the learning design (see Fig. 1 - middle).

4–5. **Configure indicators and reactions for the selected problems** (Fig. 1d). For each selected problem, e-FeeD4Mi recommends a set of indicators that can potentially identify students experiencing such problems (see Fig. 1 - bottom). Instructors can choose between monitored indicators within the learning resources (*e.g.*, low score in peer reviews) or self-reported problems. Similarly, e-FeeD4Mi recommends a set of useful feedback reactions for each configured problem, considering the classification

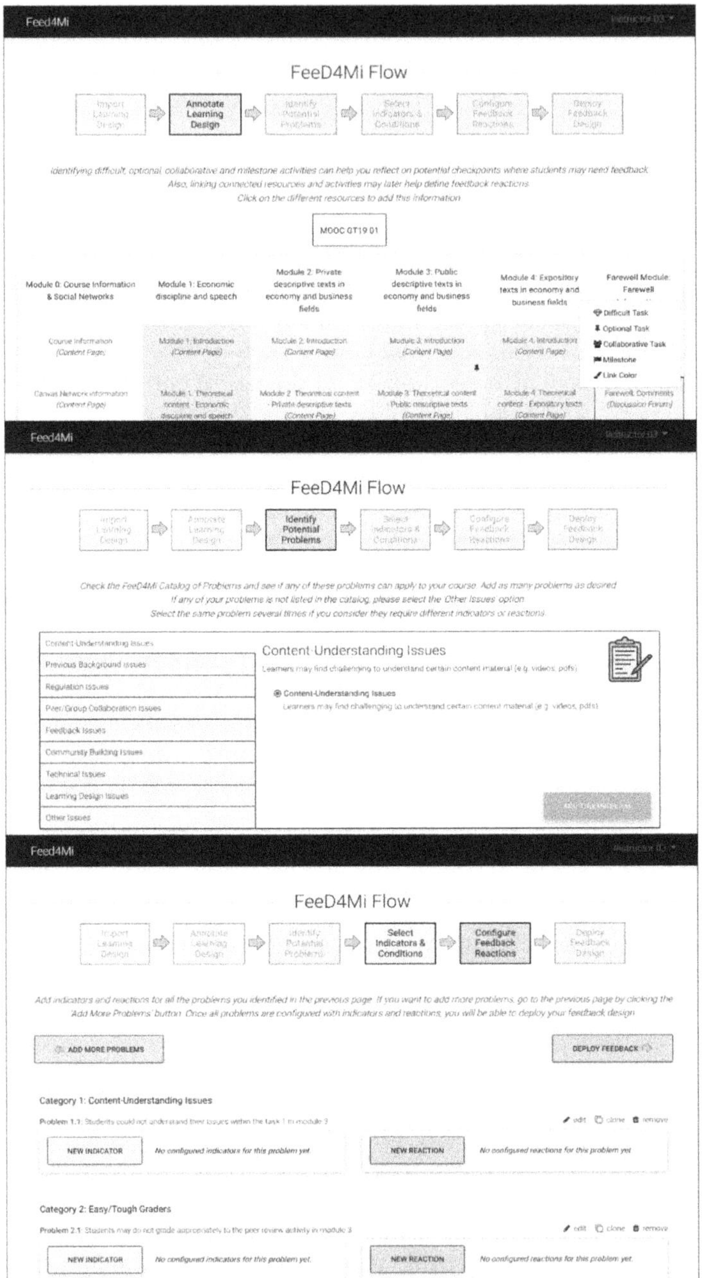

Fig. 1. e-FeeD4Mi interfaces: (top) annotate learning design page; (middle) identify potential problems page, selecting a content-understanding issue; (bottom) feedback overview page where indicators and reactions for each problem can be configured.

made by Hattie & Timperley (2007) [3]: task-related (*e.g.*, predefined message, badges), process-related (*e.g.*, learning design modifications, student mentoring), and self-regulation (*e.g.*, enable learner statistics) feedback.

Finally, instructors may deploy their feedback design by clicking the 'deploy' button. This automatic deployment involves the insertion of a LTI tool page in the course VLE (using the same instructor credentials as used for importing the LD). The LTI standard[2] avoids the need of students to authenticate again in this tool, and distinguishes between instructors and students, so that different interfaces can be provided according to users' role. In the instructor interface, instructors can monitor and manage the configured feedback strategies (*e.g.*, number of students identified with a problem, manual feedback reactions). On the other hand, in the student interface, learners can report those problems that were configured as self-reported and they are also notified with the different feedback reactions applied.

The adapter-based architecture of e-FeeD4Mi enables the connection of the tool with multiple VLE and external tools through pre-established contracts. Such adapters permit the automatic retrieval of learning designs, learners' behavior tracking, and feedback delivery, all of them aiming to decrease the associated workload of the tool installation and to foster its adoption.

3 Preliminary Results

The development of e-FeeD4Mi followed a Design-based Research (DBR) approach [1]. DBR aims to tackle actual problems employing a set of iterative cycles, in a close collaboration between researchers and practitioners [1]. Likewise, we employed two cycles of inquiry for tool development, involving stakeholders in the evaluation of aspects related to the e-FeeD4Mi tool. The first evaluation took place in a 3-hour workshop with MOOC experts (N=11), who designed and implemented feedback strategies for given learning designs with e-FeeD4Mi. The second evaluation targeted instructors with previous experience delivering online courses (N=6). In this evaluation, the instructors designed and implemented feedback strategies for their own courses.

As stated in the Introduction, the underlying goal of e-FeeD4Mi is to support instructors in the design and enactment of tailored data-driven feedback. In this regard, the authors already performed an evaluation to understand the support of e-FeeD4Mi towards such an aim [16]. Nonetheless, we also considered it relevant to measure its potential for adoption, *i.e.*, to understand if it can be used recurrently in real contexts. To measure e-FeeD4Mi potential adoption, we used the Net Promoter Score [12] together with some open-ended questions in both evaluations. The Net Promoter Score is calculated as the percentage of tool promoters (*i.e.*, participants selecting 9 or 10 in the likelihood-to-recommend item) minus the percentage of tool detractors (*i.e.*, participants selecting 0 to 6).

[2] IMS Global. Learning Tools Interoperability (LTI): https://www.imsglobal.org/activity/learning-tools-interoperability, last access: June, 2022.

The score obtained in the first evaluation (which involved a tool version prior to the one presented in this article) was -18. This negative score together with some qualitative self-reported perceptions collected from participants revealed some usability problems that led to one single promoter and three detractors. Most of the improvements pointed out by participants served for enhancing the next version of the tool (*e.g.*, *"I think there should be an adaptive connection between the module type, potential problems and proper solution (feedback)"*).

In the second evaluation, and after applying most usability improvements, the obtained score was 67 (4 promoters, 0 detractors). For comparison, in Reichheld (2003) [12], 400 enterprise tools were evaluated using the same instrument and they obtained a median score of 16. Therefore, the obtained high score together with the fact that e-FeeD4Mi evaluation was carried out with real instructors, suggest that e-FeeD4Mi can potentially be adopted in the regular practice of instructors. Nevertheless, instructors also reported some usability issues and suggested potential improvements, which will help us to enhance the next version of the tool. For instance, regarding the cognitive load, some participants proposed the use of predefined feedback templates that could reduce the temporal load of using e-FeeD4Mi, and some more options to be used as indicators and reactions.

4 Conclusions and Future Work

This paper presents e-FeeD4Mi, a web-based tool developed by the authors to support the design and automatic enactment of feedback strategies in multiple virtual learning environments. Following the DBR research approach we conducted two iterative cycles involving course stakeholders in the design of data-driven feedback, exploring the participants' potential adoption of the tool.

The results obtained in the most recent evaluation of e-FeeD4Mi shows the potential of the tool. However, the performed evaluations came along with several limitations, mainly related to the small number of participants and the short time using the tool. As a future work, we plan to use e-FeeD4Mi for designing and providing feedback in a real course, thus enabling us to study its impact during the whole life-cycle of an online course. This evaluation will help understand, for example, the orchestration workload of feedback strategies during course enactment and the tool perceptions from learners.

Acknowledgements. This research is partially funded by the Spanish State Research Agency (AEI) together with the European Regional Development Fund, under project grant PID2020-112584RB-C32; and by the European Social Fund and Regional Council of Education of Castile and Leon (E-47-2018-0108488).

References

1. Amiel, T., Reeves, T.C.: Design-based research and educational technology: rethinking technology and the research agenda. J. Educ. Technol. Soc. **11**(4), 29–40 (2008)
2. Al-Bashir, M.M., Kabir, M.R., Rahman, I.: The value and effectiveness of feedback in improving students' learning and professionalizing teaching in higher education. J. Educ. Pract. **7**(16), 38–41 (2016)
3. Hattie, J., Timperley, H.: The power of feedback. Rev. Educ. Res. **77**(1), 81–112 (2007)
4. Kochmar, E., Vu, D.D., Belfer, R., Gupta, V., Serban, I.V., Pineau, J.: Automated personalized feedback improves learning gains in an intelligent tutoring system. In: Bittencourt, I.I., Cukurova, M., Muldner, K., Luckin, R., Millán, E. (eds.) AIED 2020. LNCS (LNAI), vol. 12164, pp. 140–146. Springer, Cham (2020). https://doi.org/10.1007/978-3-030-52240-7_26
5. Lafifi, Y., Boudria, A., Lafifi, A., Cheratia, M.: Intelligent tutoring of learners in e-learning systems and massive open online courses (MOOC). In: Who Runs The World: Data, pp. 176–192. Istanbul University Press (2020)
6. Leibold, N., Schwarz, L.M.: The art of giving online feedback. J. Effective Teach. **15**(1), 34–46 (2015)
7. Liu, D.Y.-T., Bartimote-Aufflick, K., Pardo, A., Bridgeman, A.J.: Data-driven personalization of student learning support in higher education. In: Peña-Ayala, A. (ed.) Learning Analytics: Fundaments, Applications, and Trends. SSDC, vol. 94, pp. 143–169. Springer, Cham (2017). https://doi.org/10.1007/978-3-319-52977-6_5
8. Mangaroska, K., Giannakos, M.: Learning analytics for learning design: a systematic literature review of analytics-driven design to enhance learning. IEEE Trans. Learn. Technol. **12**(4), 516–534 (2019)
9. Molloy, E.K., Boud, D.: Feedback models for learning, teaching and performance. In: Spector, J.M., Merrill, M.D., Elen, J., Bishop, M.J. (eds.) Handbook of Research on Educational Communications and Technology, pp. 413–424. Springer, New York (2014). https://doi.org/10.1007/978-1-4614-3185-5_33
10. Pardo, A.: A feedback model for data-rich learning experiences. Assess. Eval. High. Educ. **43**(3), 428–438 (2018)
11. Pardo, A., et al.: OnTask: delivering data-informed, personalized learning support actions. J. Learn. Anal. **5**(3), 235–249 (2018)
12. Reichheld, F.F.: The one number you need to grow. Harv. Bus. Rev. **81**(12), 46–55 (2003)
13. Reza, M., Kim, J., Bhattacharjee, A., Rafferty, A.N., Williams, J.J.: The MOOClet framework: unifying experimentation, dynamic improvement, and personalization in online courses. In: Proceedings of the 8th ACM Conference on Learning @ Scale, pp. 15–26 (2021)
14. Rodríguez-Triana, M.J., Prieto, L.P., Martínez-Monés, A., Asensio-Pérez, J.I., Dimitriadis, Y.: The teacher in the loop: customizing multimodal learning analytics for blended learning. In: Proceedings of the 8th International Conference on Learning Analytics and Knowledge, pp. 417–426 (2018)
15. Shibani, A., Knight, S., Shum, S.B.: Contextualizable learning analytics design: a generic model and writing analytics evaluations. In: ACM International Conference Proceeding Series, pp. 210–219 (2019)
16. Topali, P., et al.: Identifying learner problems framed within MOOC learning designs. In: 29th International Conference on Computers in Education, pp. 297–302 (2021)

17. Topali, P., et al.: Supporting instructors in the design of actionable feedback for MOOCs. In: 2022 IEEE Global Engineering Education Conference, pp. 1881–1888 (2022)
18. Wiley, K.J., Dimitriadis, Y., Bradford, A., Linn, M.C.: From theory to action: developing and evaluating learning analytics for learning design. In: Proceedings of the 10th International Conference on Learning Analytics and Knowledge, pp. 569–578 (2020)

"Digital? Sicher!" – An Educational Game to Build Digital Competences

Kathrin Marie Otrel-Cass[1], Stefan Thalmann[1], Viktoria Pammer-Schindler[2], Michael Fasching[1(✉)], Analia Cicchinelli[2], Eva Griesbacher[1], Christine Malin[1], Julia Mayr[1], Alfred Wertner[2], and Thomas Doppelreiter[3]

[1] University of Graz, Universitätsplatz 3, 8010 Graz, Austria
michael.fasching@uni-graz.at
[2] Know-Center GmbH, Inffeldgasse 13/6, 8010 Graz, Austria
[3] Logo, Karmeliterpl. 2, 8010 Graz, Austria

Abstract. "Digital? Sicher!" is a free educational game designed to build students' digital competences in cybersecurity, privacy, tracking and datafication. The target group are students aged 14–16, although the educational game can be used by younger or older students. The game was co-designed in Austria by an interdisciplinary team together with 18 industry representatives, 157 school students and 11 teachers. To embed the game in teaching practices we also co-designed a pedagogical concept for teachers on how to integrate the game. Our evaluation showed that the game is functional, relevant and in combination with the pedagogical concept ready for implementation in classrooms. The game supports building young people's digital competences to operate safely in the digital spaces. The development of critical digital skills at school is urgently needed which was the aim of the learn-app. Consulting with industry representatives and including relevant examples ensures also the importance of safe cyber skills for a future work life. The storyline of the game includes that players have to make decisions through interactive elements. They playfully experience real-life examples exposing risks and dangers the internet entails. We share design recommendations and an outlook based on evaluation results.

Keywords: Serious gaming · Cybersecurity · Co-creation

1 Introduction

The goal of "Digital? Sicher!" an educational cybersecurity game, is to build the data handling awareness of grade 9–11 students (age group 14–16). The learning game was developed for Austrian secondary school students to work through selected cybersecurity topics. The intention was that the game should prepare them for their future lives where they should avoid ICT security incidents caused by human error. In this regard we also stressed the professional perspective by involving industry representatives in our co-creation efforts. The game follows the concept of serious gaming [1, 15] implying that players are asked to play through scenarios that have learning objectives underpinned

I. Hilliger et al. (Eds.): EC-TEL 2022, LNCS 13450, pp. 485–491, 2022.
https://doi.org/10.1007/978-3-031-16290-9_40

by entertainment principles. The serious gaming aspects include narratives that support players engage with an immersive environment. For this game it means that they have to solve challenges connected to e.g. privacy attacks, the nature of algorithms or safety issues related to social networks, etc.

2 Pedagogical/Technological Background

Serious games typically involve that players immerse themselves in a game world environment where they have to apply domain knowledge to solve complex challenges. This should support players in internalising the subject matter embedded in the game [9]. The topic of cybersecurity should be introduced early on in education, and the literature suggests that data handling concepts should be introduced gradually already during school years so young people are better prepared and operate safely on the internet [9].

While policy makers globally push for digital competency development [7], it has been argued that game-based approaches align with the interests of youth who often play with a variety of online games [14]. However, designing serious games for young people, and making them appealing, engaging *and* educational is a difficult task, compared to the commercial games young people play that are often visually highly attractive and include sophisticated levels of interactivity [2].

In preparation for the development of the educational cybersecurity game, we investigated existing gamified approaches for digital competence development. Our research identified the following formats: quiz-based knowledge building (like the Safer Internet Digital Competence Quiz and the "Surfschein Quiz" of Internet ABC), resource management simulations (like "Data Dealer" from Cracked Labs) and scenario-based interactive games (like CyberCIEGE), as well as roleplay-based games (like the "Cyber Threat Defender"). We reviewed the strengths and weaknesses of these existing approaches for digital competence development and decided to develop a scenario-based game that incorporates effective elements of other approaches like quizzes and roleplays [16].

The aim was to design a game that included the following key components: clearly stated rules; clearly stated goals; timely feedback on performance; interaction (clear distinction between student-to-computer and student-to-student interactions); and clearly stated subject or topic of the game [9].

3 The Co-creation Approach

In participatory design-based approaches it is important to focus on understanding situated practices and change [6]. For that reason, we collaborated with a diverse set of stakeholders early on to design the technology and engaged in collaborative practices together with designers and developers [10]. We applied a co-creation approach in order to ensure that the developed technology and surrounding practices would fit into the larger ecosystems and to create a meaningful game for the target group [5]. This process is presented in Fig. 1.

We started the co-creation with an initial concept developed based on relevant literature as well as a survey involving 219 business and company representatives. Focusing on the storyline in the first cycle, we identified relevant trends in cyber-crime and -safety requirements that enterprises place on their workforce [13]. In our industry workshops we checked for the topics and collected content ideas and examples to highlight relevance and make connections to regional companies and future professional careers. Next, we asked school graduates in online focus group interviews how they evaluate the digital education they received at school and propose potential improvements. Finally, we worked closely with students representing the target group of this learning game. The format we used in this collaboration was that of co-creation, that is, the collaborative and joint work to produce a product that fulfilled the aims of both groups [17]. We collaborated in video recorded workshops. These sessions included practical test runs of the learning app during school time. As a final result of the first design cycle we established the main storyline. The second design cycle focused on the interface of the learning app. Again, we engaged with industry and students in video recorded workshops to co-create a suitable interface. In our third design cycle, we focused on school integration and the development of the pedagogical concept for teaching. In addition to the interaction with students, we engaged with teachers in interviews to ensure a fitting integration into classroom teaching. Finally, we assessed the impact of the learning app through a qualitative inquiry and learning analytics.

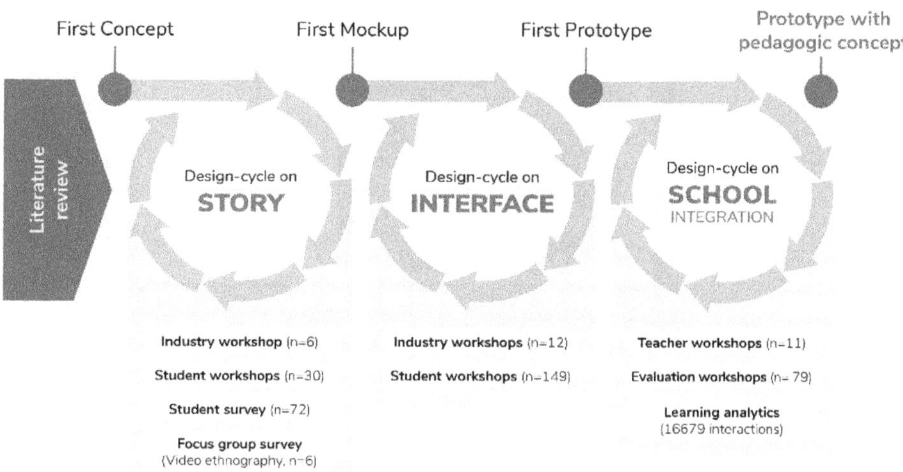

Fig. 1. Summary of co-creation cycles during the project.

The co-creation activities with our stakeholders produced a number of improvements, including: the shortening of text passages, accompanying explanatory videos, the integration of social media and entertaining online content focusing on smartphone use. In the storyline, we strengthened the focus on experiences in real scenarios and examples from young people's everyday online life combined with the focus on digital careers. A specific wish from the students was to make the game visually more appealing by using more colours, images and improving the visual layout. As a result of this input we collaborated with a design class from a local high school, who developed the graphic design for the learning app based on common social media platforms.

4 Description of the Prototype and Use Case

The storyline of the game places the student at the start of a digital career. The student has to choose a digital profession consistent with current trends, such as influencer, blogger, digital designer, or social media manager. An avatar, Goosy the goose, acts as a guide and explains relevant functions in the game. During the course of the story, the players also interact with other characters. The storyline places the player in diverse life-like situations (botched job interviews, public confessions of love or family issues) where they have to make decisions about their digital behaviour. Their decisions affect their popularity showed with followers and the guidance offered by the avatar Goosy.

The game interface is divided into three areas: On the left side are chat conversations with the avatars. In the middle section is the newsfeed with information, tasks and exercises. On the right side is the profile bar with scores and an individual nickname. A screenshot of the game is presented in Fig. 2.

Fig. 2. Screenshot of the game “Digital? Sicher!”.

Guidance through the avatar is designed to make players reflect on what has been learned and how it relates to real-life. The reflection concept was built in the form of prompts after each module, structured in such ways to focus students’ attention on the relevant concepts and on what is important and interesting for them [4]. Two weeks after students piloted the game we invited them to a second reflection session to promote a long-term effect of learning contents. The concept aims to support the transfer of the learning content to the students’ engagement with computer technologies as part of their daily lives.

We used the learning management system Moodle as software platform for the game. Since Moodle is a free, adaptive and easy-to-use platform, it provides for sustainability of the project and can continue to be used after completion of the project. We were able to divide tasks in the project team to create and upload content due to the intuitive operation of Moodle. Another advantage of Moodle includes also that its responsive design allows the application to be operated from a computer, tablet or smartphone. In order to make the learning game as easy to access as possible, we set up a landing page[1], which leads directly to the game on Moodle after logging in. In addition, we set up a project website[2], to provide information for interested stakeholders already during the development phase.

The game was designed to be integrated into classroom activities on the subject of cybersecurity, i.e. it was not developed to be used as a stand-alone game outside an educational context. However, the game is now freely available and could be used in this manner.

The playful approach (through serious gaming) and concrete case studies from the business community were intended to support the development and increase the overall attractiveness of the game [8]. The development and evaluation for the use in schools focused on central guidelines such as EU values, conformity with fundamental rights, consideration of technical and human factors, orientation towards learning goals, gamification, social inclusion and freely accessible software. The "Digital? Sicher!" game is fully functional and openly available online as an open educational resource (OER).

5 Results and Outcomes Achieved

The workshops we conducted in schools showed that students were interested in cybersecurity topics and that they wanted to learn about those at school. However, we found large differences in prior knowledge amongst the 13 to 18-year-olds students we worked with, and therefore we narrowed the band of target age group down to 14 to 16-year-olds to optimally adjust the level of difficulty and topics. Feedback from the students also suggested that they liked the storyline of the game. The degree of difficulty was rated very differently amongst the age groups and depended on prior knowledge.

We conducted quantitative analysis in order to evaluate the game. We compared and analysed the interactions of a subsample of 40 students. This way we examined student activities in regard to the goals of the game and the learning effectiveness of the game. While the game utilises a cyclic structure allowing students to return to previous stages, we found that the number of interactions across the different modules remained stable. Hence, the game appears to have a stable structure. Analysing responses to reflection questions we found that they align with the learning goals in terms of content. The students' reflections seem to confirm that key concepts were learned. We found no noteworthy differences in the interactions between the number of male and female students. It can therefore be assumed that the basic structure of the learning game does not show any gender-specific interaction differences. The analysis also showed no indication that students with non-German language background were disadvantaged, quite the opposite: students identifying themselves with a mother tongue other than German showed particularly high interaction counts. We detected however, that male students seemed to have greater awareness of the need for secure login information, while female students appeared significantly more aware when dealing with potentially threatening content.

[1] https://digital-sicher.at/

[2] https://digitalsicher.uni-graz.at/

6 Future Perspective

Through the co-creation process and the testing of the final game we found that the students played the game because they seemed to be motivated to do so. Their engagement with the game was goal oriented and this means they had to understand the game's functionality and stay enthusiastic to play it [3, 12]. The design recommendations and feedback received from students, teachers, business community and the analysis of our interaction data resulting from the project include: a promotion of the use of the game in the lessons of young people in secondary school (for instance through pre- or in-service training workshops), continuation of the modules with new and more difficult content levels for the age group 16 +, and a possible expansion of the target groups of the prototype also for adults, senior citizens or people with disabilities. Future topic areas could include e.g., disinformation, bullying, sexting/grooming. The game could also expand to topics with more relevance for professionals, alongside training workshops for professionals. Regarding the reflection concept, students mentioned that they are not used to reflecting as part of their learning activities. However, they found the questions useful and helpful for their learning. In the future, we intend to develop a continuous reflection concept and investigate the effect of reflections on retaining learned concepts. Finally, also internationalisation of the game through translations (e.g. European languages) would be a useful expansion for the game in the future.

Our stakeholder groups emphasised the important role teachers play in this process. Future activities will need to look into the successful integration of digital games into different subject settings [11]. The feedback from the teachers in this project was that they appreciated and needed the suggestions provided in the pedagogical guidelines and similar games should include this as part of the game development process. Finally, the co-creation process increased creativity and produced positive dynamics in this project.

Acknowledgements. This work was funded by the Zukunftsfonds Steiermark and within the Austrian COMET Program (Competence Centers for Excellent Technologies) under the auspices of the Austrian Federal Ministry of Transport, Innovation and Technology, the Austrian Federal Ministry of Economy, Family and Youth and by the State of Styria. COMET is managed by the Austrian Research Promotion Agency FFG.

References

1. Abt, C.C.: Serious Games. University Press of America, Lanham (1987)
2. Bellotti, F., Berta, R., De Gloria, A.: Designing effective serious games: opportunities and challenges for research. Int. J. Emerg. Technol. Learn. (iJET) **5**, 22–35 (2010)
3. Bower, M.: Design of Technology-Enhanced Learning: Integrating Research and Practice. Emerald Group Publishing, Bradford (2017)
4. Cicchinelli, A., Pammer-Schindler, V.: What makes volunteer mentors tick? A case study in a preparatory online training course. J. Work. Learn. **34**(3), 256–276 (2022)
5. Dennerlein, S., Pammer-Schindler, V., Ebner, M., Getzinger, G., Ebner, E.: Designing a sandpit- and co-design-informed innovation process for scaling TEL research in higher education. In: 15th International Conference on Wirtschaftsinformatik (WI) (2020)

6. Ehret, C., Hollett, T.: Affective dimensions of participatory design research in informal learning environments: placemaking, belonging, and correspondence. Cogn. Instr. **34**, 250–258 (2016)
7. European Commission, Directorate-General for Education, Youth, Sport and Culture, Key competences for lifelong learning, Publications Office, (2019). https://data.europa.eu/doi/10.2766/291008. Accessed 21 Apr 2022
8. Greitzer, F.L., Kuchar, O.A., Huston, K.: Cognitive science implications for enhancing training effectiveness in a serious gaming context. J. Edu. Resour. Compu. (JERIC), **7**(3), 2-es (2007)
9. Hill, W., Fanuel, M., Yuan, X.: Comparing serious games for cyber security education, (2020)
10. Leinonen, T., Durall-Gazulla, E.: Design thinking and collaborative learning. Comunicar, **21**(42), (2014)
11. Scheiter, K., Gogolin, I.: Editorial: bildung für eine digitale Zukunft. Z. Erzieh. **24**(5), 1033–1037 (2021). https://doi.org/10.1007/s11618-021-01049-w
12. Squire, K.: From content to context: videogames as designed experience. Educ. Res. **35**(8), 19–29 (2006)
13. Thalmann, S., Zeiringer, J., Alic, H.: Bericht über die Erhebung des Cybersecurity-Bewusstseins der Angestellten in steirischen Organisationen in Zeiten von COVID-19. BANDAS-Center, Universität Graz (2021).
14. Turkay, S., Hoffman, D., Kinzer, C.K., Chantes, P., Vicari, C.: Toward understanding the potential of games for learning: learning theory, game design characteristics, and situating video games in classrooms. Comput. Sch. **31**(1–2), 2–22 (2014)
15. Zyda, M.: From visual simulations to virtual reality to games. Computer **38**(9), 25–32 (2005)
16. Sandford, R., Williamson, B.: Futurelab: games and learning (2006)
17. Fladkjaer, H.F., Otrel-Cass, K.: A cogenerative dialogue: reflecting on education for co-creation. In: Co-Creation in Higher Education (pp. 83–98). Brill Sense (2017)

Towards Effective Blended Learning Through the Eyes of Students: A Survey Study in Transition into Face-to-Face Education

Gabriel Astudillo[1](✉), Isabel Hilliger[1], Fernanda Rodríguez[2], and Jorge Baier[1]

[1] Pontificia Universidad Católica de Chile, Santiago, Chile
{gastudillo,ihillige,jabaier}@ing.puc.cl
[2] Universidad Finis Terrae, Santiago, Chile
maria.rodriguez@uft.cl

Abstract. Many researchers consider that blended or hybrid learning implies a meaningful combination of online and face-to-face activities. Before the COVID-19 pandemic, studies had shown promising results of blended learning to improve student performance. However, the design and implementation of effective combinations is far from trivial, considering students' differences regarding their demographics and self-regulatory capacities. This paper presents a survey study developed in an Engineering school of a Latin American university that transitioned from online learning to a hybrid format in mid-2021. Quantitative data was collected throughout an online questionnaire applied to a convenience sample of 1,124 students. Subgroup differences were identified by means of exploratory factor analysis and clustering. Two different subgroups emerged from the data: those who prefer online learning and those who prefer face-to-face activities. This difference is particularly observed in students from different cohorts and regions of origin: students who are closer to graduation preferred online activities, as well as students who come from regions outside the campus location. Students' preferences varied regarding feedback delivery and collaboration with peers, which are usually synchronous activities. Further implications are discussed to inform instructional design of blended and hybrid approaches beyond COVID-19.

Keywords: Blended learning · Hybrid learning · Higher education · Student experience · Survey study

1 Introduction

Since the outbreak of the COVID-19 pandemic, most higher education institutions invested significant efforts to continue its activities throughout different learning modalities. According to the findings of a survey conducted by the International Association of Universities during 2020 [1], 67% of higher education institutions implemented distance learning strategies, particularly in Europe (85%), the Americas (72%), and the Asia-Pacific (60%). Among these regions, the majority implemented 'emergency online education' or 'emergency remote teaching' [2]. This new learning modality implies the

I. Hilliger et al. (Eds.): EC-TEL 2022, LNCS 13450, pp. 492–499, 2022.
https://doi.org/10.1007/978-3-031-16290-9_41

use of different types of synchronous and asynchronous strategies, expanding the ways in which teachers and students can interact [1].

When the spread of COVID-19 seemed under control, many universities rapidly resumed some face-to-face activities. This effort to reincorporate face-to-face components gave rise to different hybrid formats combining physical classrooms with online environments. Unfortunately, the instructional design of these new combinations did not necessarily follow existing learning theories, pedagogical models, or empirical research. Most changes were influenced by administrative decisions concerning practical issues, such as the availability of infrastructure or technical equipment [3]. Consequently, emergency educational practices extended the traditional classroom model through lectures delivered both virtually and face-to-face, without necessarily having designed a blended approach that meaningfully combined synchronous and asynchronous strategies in different formats [3].

Different combinations of face-to-face and online delivery methods had already been documented before the pandemic [4]. A common blended learning approach is the flipped classroom [4, 5], where synchronous work time is freed up for in-depth discussions and feedback, while asynchronous work is reserved for self-paced online activities [6]. Studies have reported mixed preferences towards different blended learning approaches from students' perspectives [7, 8]. For example, some students have perceived face-to-face lectures to be more beneficial for interacting with the lecturer and their peers face-to-face, whereas others might prefer online lessons due to their flexibility [7]. However, the design of these approaches is usually common to all students, so the learning preferences of different student subgroups between the online and face-to-face components has remained unknown.

In order to explore the student's preferences for online and face-to-face components since the outbreak of the pandemic, this work describes a survey study developed in an Engineering school at a Latin American university transitioning from online to hybrid format in mid-2021. During the transition, students could choose whether they could attend online vs. face-to-face. Quantitative data was collected through an online survey completed by a convenience sample of 926 students. Prior research concerning blended learning is used to discuss the emergent combinations that resulted beneficial for specific student subgroups, along with extrapolating implications for future curriculum design and improvement.

2 Methodology

2.1 Research Design and Context

In this work, we addressed the following research question: How do higher education students differ in their preferences for online and face-to-face learning activities since the onset of the COVID-19 pandemic? To answer this question, a survey study was conducted in mid-2021. This study analyzed the experience of undergraduate students in an engineering school founded in 1892, which is part of a non-profit private university that has become one of the flagship higher education institutions at a regional level. Every academic period, this school offers over 300 courses that typically last 18 weeks.

Between March 2020 and June 2021, all undergraduate and graduate courses were carried out through synchronous and asynchronous online activities. In July 2021, the university leadership decided to partially resume face-to-face activities in four different modalities: 1) fully online, 2) online with face-to-face activities, 3) hybrid courses with classes taught simultaneously face-to-face and online, and 4) face-to-face courses. Among these courses, students could choose to attend face-to-face classes or online. In this context, this study focuses on the implementation of different blended and hybrid strategies since August 2021, and student preferences concerning face-to-face and online course components.

2.2 Study Participants and Sample

The school's enrollment is about 5,300 students (4,600 undergraduates and 700 graduates). Its student body is composed of high-achieving students, i.e., who perform outstandingly in pre-university examinations. Each admission cohort consists of 800–850 students of which approximately 35% are female and about 23% come from regions outside the campus location.

The survey was applied in October 2021, and 926 students answered the entire questionnaire. Different student subgroups are represented in this sample, including students from different engineering majors: Operations Research, Software Engineering, Electrical Engineering, Mechanical Engineering, among others. 22% of students come from a region other than that of campus location (22.68%). There is a slight overrepresentation of first year students and students identified as female (39.84%).

2.3 Data Gathering Techniques and Analysis

As aforementioned, the main objective of our survey was to measure students' preferences concerning face-to-face and online componentes. To meet this objective, the survey included two 5-point Likert scales whose creation was based on prior literature about blended learning. The first scale aimed to assess the online learning elements that were implemented since the lockdown in March 2020; while the second scale had the goal of measuring students' perceptions regarding the contribution of the newly incorporated face-to-face elements to their learning. Both scales were revised by an expert in survey development, and cognitive interviews were held with students to improve language usage.

The survey was applied online and survey results were analyzed in R. In order to validate the two Likert scales, an exploratory factor analysis was carried out using the psych R package [9]. Polychoric correlations were calculated following Rdz-Navarro & Asun [10] recommendations for ordinal items. Maximum Likelihood was used as the extraction procedure. Assuming the factors were not independent but correlated with each other, we decided to use a rotation oblimin.

Once the scales were already statistically validated by using the exploratory factor analysis, a cluster analysis was implemented using k-means, aiming to identify two student subgroups who maximized their differences according to their level of agreement or disagreement concerning different statements regarding online and face-to-face learning activities. In order to characterize the resulting clusters, we each cluster in relation to the factors that emerged from the exploratory factor analysis, and we performed Chi-2 tests to assess whether there was an association with sociodemographic variables such as gender, admission cohort, and region of origin.

3 Results

3.1 Student Preferences Regarding Online and Face-to-Face Learning Activities

Table 1 shows statistics for responses to the items about online learning activities. The activities that were better evaluated (4 or higher in the scale) were the use of support resources, the possibility of asking questions in class held through video conference calls, and the possibility of clarifying doubts by watching class recordings.

Table 1. Statistics for responses to items associated with online learning activities

Item	Mean	Sd	1. Qu	3. Qu
Support resources, such as videos or readings, that are available on virtual platforms have contributed to my learning	4.13	0.92	4	5
In classes through videoconferences, I have been able to ask questions when I have not understood something	4.09	0.99	4	5
In the class recordings, I have been able to clarify doubts about concepts or explanations seen during class	4.00	1.04	4	5
In general, I believe that I have been able to learn the most important contents of each course in activities carried out virtually	3.69	1.14	3	5
Classes through video conferences were essential to learn	3.56	1.14	3	4

Table 2 shows statistics for responses to items about face-to-face activities. Scores are slightly lower than those of online learning activities. The items with highest scores were associated with the desirability of having face-to-face activities, the perceived contribution of face-to-face activities to learning, and the possibilities of collaborating with peers (3.5 or higher in 5-point agreement Likert scale).

3.2 Exploratory Factor Analysis

We identified three factors that we named *face-to-face learning*, *online learning,* and *online deepening*. Detailed loadings are shown in Table 3.

3.3 Results of the Cluster Analysis

We found two clusters with systematically heterogeneous patterns between themselves (and entirely homogeneous within themselves): one with favorable attitudes towards face-to-face activities (named pro face-to-face) and another one with favorable towards

Table 2. Statistics concerning students' responses to items associated with face-to-face activities

Item	Mean	Sd	1. Qu	3. Qu
I was pleased to have face-to-face activities again	3.88	1.19	3	5
The face-to-face activities have contributed significantly to my learning	3.59	1.16	3	5
In the face-to-face activities I was able to talk with my peers about the difficulties we have with the content	3.53	1.24	3	5
The face-to-face activities have favored the feedback provided by the teachers	3.40	1.23	3	4

Table 3. Standardized loadings for an exploratory factor analysis [a, b, c]

Item	Face-to-face learning factor	Online learning factor	Online deepening factor
I was pleased to have face-to-face activities again	0.86		
The face-to-face activities have favored the feedback provided by the teachers	0.82		
The face-to-face activities have contributed significantly to my learning	0.81		
In the face-to-face activities I was able to talk with my peers about the difficulties we have with the content	0.74		
Classes through videoconferences were essential to learn		0.83	
In general, I believe that I have been able to learn the most important contents of each course in activities carried out virtually		0.67	
In classes through videoconferences, I have been able to ask questions when I have not understood something		0.34	0.33
In the recorded classes, I have been able to clarify doubts about concepts or explanations seen in classes			0.71

(continued)

Table 3. (*continued*)

Item	Face-to-face learning factor	Online learning factor	Online deepening factor
Support resources that are available on virtual platforms have contributed to my learning			0.65

[a] SS loadings: Face-to face learning = 2.67; Online learning = 1.39; Online deepening = 1.17
[b] Proportion Var: Face-to face learning = .30; Online learning = .15; Online deepening = .13.
[c] Ordinal Alpha: Face-to face learning = .88; Online learning = .77; Online deepening = .67.

online learning activities (named pro online). Both present similar proportions: 48.38% in pro face-to-face (n = 448) and 51.62% in pro online (n = 478).

Both clusters exhibited statistically significant differences for the three latent dimensions of the factorial analysis. Coherently, pro face-to-face showed high factorial scores for the face-to-face learning factor (mean = 0.74), and low scores for online learning (mean = −0.36) and online deepening factors (mean = −0.19). The other cluster exhibited exactly the opposite behavior: low factorial scores in the face-to-face learning factor (mean = −.87), and high factorial scores in online learning (mean = 0.42) and online deepening (mean = 0.22). According to ANOVA analysis, the clusters showed statistically significant differences concerning the three factors (Face-to-face learning factor: F = 1711.90, p-value < 0.01; Online learning factor: F = 225.47, p-value < 0.01; Online deepening factor: F = 68.39; p-value < 0.01).

A Chi-squared test showed a statistically significant association between the clusters and some demographics variables. We found a significant association between clusters and the admission cohort: students closer to graduating (cohorts 2015–2017) seem to prefer online learning (54.84% in cohort 2017 to 71.11% cohort 2015 or earlier), while cohorts who began their studies during confinement or shortly after (cohorts 2019–2021) prefer face-to-face learning activities (65.31% cohort 2019 to 57.37% cohort 2021; Chi-squared = 31.25, p-value < 0.01, Df = 6).

Finally, Chi-squared test revealed an association between clusters and region of origin: 53.71% of students who live in the same region where the university campus is located prefer face-to-face learning, while 67.39% of students who live in a different region prefer online learning activities (Chi-squared = 13.92, p-value < 0.01, Df = 1).

4 Discussion and Limitations

This study shows how students differ in their preferences for online and face-to-face learning activities since the gradual return to face-to-face activities. We identified two different clusters which exhibited statistically significant differences concerning three latent dimensions: face-to-face learning, online learning, and online deepening. Within the face-to-face learning dimension, the most noteworthy items account for different preferences regarding the delivery of synchronous strategies, such as opportunities to interact with peers and to receive feedback from teaching staff. Within the online learning dimension, item differences are also associated with synchronous activities, such as class delivery through video conference calls and other types of activities that could be carried out online. Finally, the online deepening dimension accounts for differences concerning asynchronous learning activities, such as the review of support materials and class recordings.

In the light of prior literature, this study confirms that students have different preferences for face-to-face and online learning components. Previous studies have reported student mixed preferences towards different blended learning approaches [7, 8]. In this context, our findings suggest that not all students perceive those face-to-face synchronous interactions the most beneficial for their learning.

This study contributes to expanding the knowledge about student preferences in blended and hybrid learning settings by revealing the role played by demographics. In this particular context, findings show that students who are closer to their graduation prefer online learning activities. Although we did not collect information concerning student self-regulatory capacities, this result may be partly explained by students' career interests and higher self-regulatory skills. Our findings also show that students who come from regions outside the campus location preferred online learning activities. This result might be associated with socio-affective dimensions of learning as well as cost-benefit factors related to the fact that students who are not from the region must afford a place to live on their own.

This study has some limitations. First, the use of a convenience sampling method could imply biases in student survey responses, limiting the generalization of the findings of this study. Moreover, the sample represents engineering students in a Latin American university. It is not clear to what extent the interaction between the type of content and teaching methods influences the results obtained. Third, there is a lack of empirical research to contrast findings concerning the transition into hybrid and blended learning formats. Finally, there might be limitations concerning the measurements used to assess student perceptions. Self-regulation capacities were not measured, so we cannot evaluate the relationship between student preferences and their self-regulatory skills. Along those lines, future work will focus on understanding preferences for different types of learning environments in the light of self-regulation capacities and student learning results. Further qualitative research will also be used to triangulate quantitative findings.

References

1. Marinoni, G., Van't Land, H., Jensen, T., et al.: The impact of COVID-19 on higher education around the world. IAU Glob. Surv. Rep. **23** (2020)
2. Bao, W.: COVID-19 and online teaching in higher education: a case study of Peking University. Hum. Behav. Emerg. Technol. **2**(2), 113–115 (2020). https://doi.org/10.1002/hbe2.191
3. García-Aretio, L.G.: COVID-19 and digital distance education: pre-confinement, confinement and post-confinement. Ibero-Am. Assoc. Distance High. Educ. **24**(1), 9–32 (2021). https://doi.org/10.5944/ried.24.1.28080
4. Bergmann, J., Sams, A.: Before you flip, consider this. Phi Delta Kappan **94**(2), 25 (2012)

5. Olakanmi, E.E.: The effects of a flipped classroom model of instruction on students' performance and attitudes towards chemistry. J. Sci. Educ. Technol. **26**(1), 127–137 (2017)
6. Kim, M.K., Kim, S.M., Khera, O., Getman, J.: The experience of three flipped classrooms in an urban university: an exploration of design principles. Internet High. Educ. **22**, 37–50 (2014)
7. Wright, B.M.: Blended learnings student perception of face-to-face and online EFL lessons. Indonesian J. Appl. Linguist. **7**(1), 64–71 (2017). https://doi.org/10.17509/ijal.v7i1.6859
8. Keeling, C., Haugestad, A.: Digital student preferences: a study of blended learning in Norwegian higher education. Nord. J. Lang. Teach. Learn. **8**(2), 89–112 (2020)
9. Revelle, W.: psych: procedures for psychological, psychometric, and personality research. (Version 2.2.3) [Computer software], Northwestern University (2022). https://CRAN.R-project.org/package=psych
10. Rdz-Navarro, K., Asun, R.A.: Recent developments in statistics: theoretical and methodological contributions to sociological research. Sociol. Technoscience **1**(6), 1–13 (2016)

Measuring Learners' Self-regulated Learning Skills from Their Digital Traces and Learning Pathways

Marie-Luce Bourguet(✉)

Queen Mary University of London, London, UK
marie-luce.bourguet@qmul.ac.uk

Abstract. Flipping the classroom requires from students some self-regulated learning skills, as they must have engaged in learning activities prior to attending classes. The study we describe in this paper was done in the context of a 15-week flipped course delivered online to a large class of undergraduate students. We collected various time-stamped digital traces generated by the students' engagement in the required weekly learning activities (H5P interactive videos, quizzes and worksheets). The collected data allowed the generation of visual learning pathways, from which several types of learning profiles emerged. A distance measure between the students' learning pathways and the instructor's recommended pathway was found to be negatively correlated with exam performance. The results from a survey collecting students' perceptions of their engagement with the learning activities are also presented.

Keywords: Flipped classroom · Self-regulated learning · Learning analytics · Learning pathways · Distance measure

1 Introduction

Over the past 10 to 15 years, there has been a significant increase in adoption of the flipped classroom model. Flipping the classroom requires from students some self-regulated learning (SRL) skills, as they must have engaged in learning activities prior to attending classes. According to Zimmerman [1], students can be described as self-regulated learners when they are metacognitively, motivationally, and behaviourally active participants in their own learning. The instructor or facilitator may provide initial instructions and expectations, but the self-regulated learners are responsible for planning and timing their learning engagement. Some of the responsibility to learn is thus shifted from an external source (typically a teacher) to the individual learner. Students' SRL skills needed for a successful flipped course delivery primarily include organisation, time management, and effort regulation [2].

More and more educational institutions are turning to asynchronous or hybrid teaching, increasingly relying on students' SRL. These delivery modes are benefiting students with different paces and learning strategies [3], however, students often report difficulties sustaining commitment to their studies. Recently,

I. Hilliger et al. (Eds.): EC-TEL 2022, LNCS 13450, pp. 500–506, 2022.
https://doi.org/10.1007/978-3-031-16290-9_42

researchers have been recognising the potential advantages of learning analytics as a means of capturing and understanding different patterns of students with different SRL profiles [4,5], aiming to provide better support for individual students [6]. In [7] for example, the analysis of weekly logs and digital traces revealed that the profiles of the non self-regulated students were characterised by less study regularity, and their low academic achievement was found to be aligned with empirical evidence reported in prior studies (e.g., [8]) that regularity is one of the strong indicators of academic achievement. In [9] an analysis of MOOC (Massive Open Online Courses) learners' engagement with summative continuous assessment activities and built-in and external social tools served to detect seven learners' profiles, including observers, drop-ins, engaged and non-engaged learners.

In the study described in this paper, we investigate the use of students' "learning pathways" as a measure of the SRL skills needed for flipped learning. We define a learning pathway as a student's chosen route through a range of available learning activities. The central assumption behind the study is that students with learning pathways that match closely the instructor-recommended pathway are demonstrating good SRL and time management skills, which should then be reflected in their course performance. The instructor-recommended pathway is a pathway that shows study regularity and timely engagement with the learning activities required to be completed prior to attending a class.

2 Context of the Study

2.1 Course and Participants

The context of the study is a 15-week flipped course on Multimedia Fundamentals, delivered online during the Autumn 2021 to a rather large class of 234 3rd year undergraduate students on a 4-year UK-China transnational program on Telecommunication Engineering. The students are all Chinese nationals, between 20- and 21-year-old. About 40% of the students are female. For the duration of the course, the students were physically on campus in Beijing, while the instructor was in another country.

The digital learning activities made available on the Learning Management System (LMS) consisted in reading materials, short interactive videos (H5P technology), quizzes and worksheets. A total of 65 digital learning activities were proposed for which time-stamped digital traces could be collected. At the end of the course, the number of completed activities were consolidated into a *completion score (C)*.

In each interactive video, various exercises were embedded, which encouraged active learning and served as formative assessment: multiple choice questions, drag and drop exercises, etc. Each week, further formative assessment was provided in the form of a 5-question quiz, randomly generated from a question bank. Students were encouraged to attempt the quizzes several times to be exposed to a greater variety of questions. Marks gained from the video embedded exercises and the quizzes were aggregated into a total *activity score (S)* at the end of the course.

Each week, prior to attending an online synchronous tutorial, students were asked to have completed all exercises embedded in the interactive videos, attempted the quiz and completed the worksheet covering the topic of the tutorial. The tutorial itself was used to answer students' questions and to discuss the quiz and worksheet exercises. The digital learning activities were released on a weekly basis, the week before the corresponding tutorial. An activity released on the LMS would then remain available until the end of the course and could be attempted as many times as desired until the final examination in week 15. The instructor recommended to engage in learning activities weekly, prior to attending the tutorials. However, the learning was mostly self-regulated as students could choose when to engage in the learning activities, or even not to engage at all. The responsibility given to the students for their own learning led to various strategies.

2.2 Digital Traces

Each week and for each student the following data were collected: date of the latest engagement in each available learning activity, and latest video and quiz scores. The data were then anonymised, only student enrolment numbers were preserved to be able to track a student's level of engagement across the duration of the course. We collected data the day before each weekly tutorial, when the material related to that tutorial had already been available on the LMS for a week. That way, we could capture whether a student had engaged in the learning activities before (as recommended) or after the corresponding tutorial. Data were collected weekly until the date of the final examination in week 15.

3 Analytics Results

3.1 Learning Pathways

Visualisation. Figure 1 shows several examples of learning pathways. On the horizontal axis, the 65 learning activities are plotted in chronological order (i.e., in the order in which they should be completed). The vertical axis shows all the weeks of the semester, including the last 3 weeks dedicated to revisions and leading to the final examination in week 15. The gaps between weeks 3 and 4 and between weeks 5 and 6 correspond to weeks with no scheduled tutorial. The graphs indicate when a learning activity has been completed for the first time. The recommended pathway shows that each learning activity should be completed by the time of the corresponding tutorial. It resembles a step function of varying step length as for each weekly tutorial the preparatory material contains a varying number of activities (from 3 to 7 short videos, 1 quiz and 1 worksheet).

Several patterns emerged. Regular learners are students who followed the lecturer's recommendations. Their pathway is typically just below the recommended one, showing that they have engaged in the learning activities within the week preceding the tutorial. Irregular or selective learners tended to choose the type of activities they engaged in (e.g., some students used only the videos, others only the quizzes) and often did this irrespectively of the timing of the tutorials. Finally, the late learners are students who seldom engaged during the semester and typically used the learning activities at the end of the course to prepare for the final exam (i.e., combining massing and procrastination).

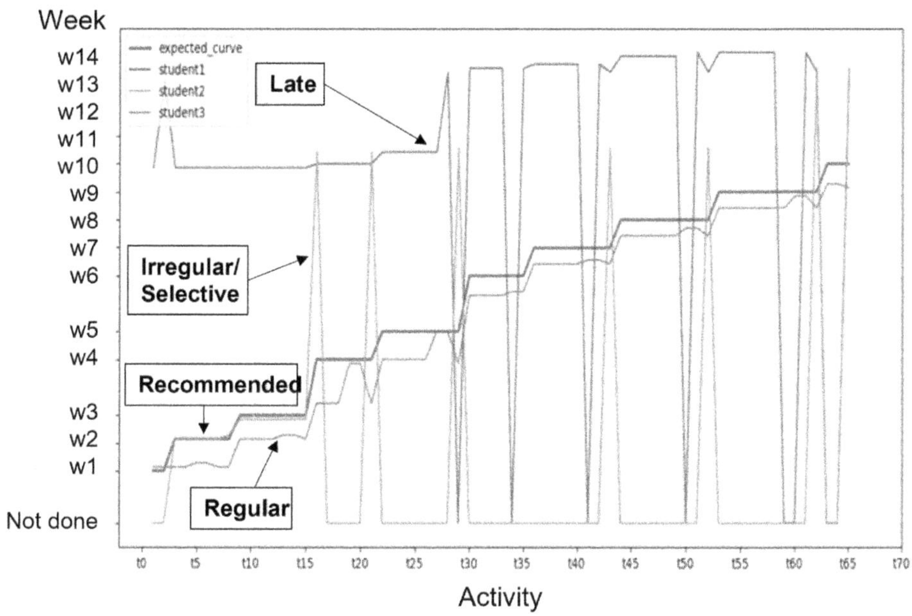

Fig. 1. Various learning pathways.

Distance Measure. We have formulated a distance measure (D) between a student's and the recommended learning pathways. It is calculated by adding together all the differences (in number of days) between when an activity was due and when it has been completed for the first time (see Eq. (1)). When an activity has not been completed, the maximum distance between the expected day and the end of the course (date of the examination in week 15), plus one day, is added to the sum. The sum is then normalised, dividing it by the maximum distance value (corresponding to a student who has not completed any of the activities) and multiplying by 100 (see Eq. (2)). D ranges from 2.38 (minimum distance found) to 96.9 (maximum distance found). The mean value of D is 31.61 (std = 25.95).

$$Distance = \sum_{k=1}^{65} |expectedDay - completedDay| \quad (1)$$

$$D = Distance/(MaxDistance) * 100 \quad (2)$$

Learner Profiles. Using K-means clustering (k = 3), the pathways were then grouped into three clusters.

The first (low distance) cluster represents 20% of the students. These students can be classified as regular learners. The maximum value of D in this cluster is 25.5, which can be used as a threshold value to qualify as a regular learner.

The second (middle distance) and largest cluster represents 55% of the students. The value of D in this cluster ranges between 25.5 and 56.8.

Finally, the third (high distance) cluster represents 25% of the students. In this cluster, the students adopted either a selective or a late learning strategy from the start of the course.

3.2 Correlation with Grade

Learning Pathway. We hypothesised that students would do well in their final exam when their learning pathway is close to the recommended learning pathway, i.e., when the distance measure D is low. We indeed found D to have a moderate but significant negative correlation (r = −0.6087) with the students' final examination marks. The negative correlation between exam performance and the distance to the recommended learning pathway confirms that regular learning is conducive to deeper learning.

Completion Score (C) and Activity Score (S). Although neither C or S reflect study regularity but rather the students' successful engagement with the learning and formative continuous assessment activities by the end of the course, we found both C and S to have a moderate but significant positive correlation (r = 0.5320 for C, and r = 0.5683 for S) with the students' final examination marks.

4 Student Perceptions

We have started to survey student perceptions of their level of engagement in the course, at the same time probing the reasons behind their chosen SRL strategies. Currently, 42 students have responded (18% of the class).

From the 28 respondents stating that they generally engaged in the learning activities before the synchronous tutorials (i.e., the regular learners), the majority **agrees** with the following statements: *I did this because I followed the lecturer's instructions* (82.2%); *Doing the activities in advance helped me understand the tutorials* (89.3%); *Doing the activities in advance allowed me to* *participate more actively in the tutorials* (82.1%); *Doing the activities in advance allowed me to prepare questions for the tutorials* (92.8%).

From the 7 respondents stating that they did most of the learning activities after the synchronous tutorials (i.e., the irregular learners), the majority **agrees** with the following statements: *I preferred doing the activities after the tutorial to check my understanding of it* (100%); *I did the activities after the tutorial because I thought I would get better grades in the videos and quizzes* (71.5%); *I felt I was not able to do the activities correctly before the tutorial* (71.5%). The majority **disagrees** with the following statements: *I was not aware that the lecturer recommended to do the activities before the tutorial* (71.5%); *I didn't think it would help my understanding of the tutorial if I did the activities before* (57.2%). There is no clear agreement or disagreement with the following statement: *I didn't have time to do the activities before the tutorial.*

From the 7 respondents stating that they did most of the learning activities well after the synchronous tutorials (i.e., the late learners), the majority **disagrees** with the following statements: *I was not aware that the lecturer recommended to do the activities regularly and before the tutorials* (71.5%); *I didn't have time to do the activities during the semester* (57.2%); *I didn't think doing the activities would help me understand the course* (85.7%); *I felt I was not able to do the activities correctly during the semester* (57.2%). There is no clear agreement or disagreement with the following statements: *I preferred doing the activities at the end of the course, for my revisions*; *I preferred doing the activities at the end of the course because I thought I would get better grades in the videos and quizzes.*

5 Conclusion

Although the level of responses to the student perceptions survey is still low, it is clear from the responses that the regular learners are aware of the benefits of regularity, and that engaging in the learning activities prior to attending the tutorials was part of their strategy. Concerning the irregular learners, it appears that delaying their engagement in the learning activities was also a strategic decision, but this time to avoid getting low scores in the activities, although these were used for formative assessment only. This demonstrates a need for reassurance about one's abilities. No clear reason for not engaging in the activities during the semester emerge from the responses of the late learners, which appears to be a more heterogeneous group. Lack of time is not recognised as an issue by any of the learners' groups.

Next academic year, we are planning to use the learning pathways combined with the distance measure to raise the students' awareness of their lack of self-regulation skills, and nudge them through regular, timely, and personalised feedback. At course level, we anticipate that the distance measure will be useful to alert the instructor about a worrying students' disengagement trend. A constantly high distance value could be indicative of a flaw in the course design, and a sudden increase of D could be indicative of a particularly challenging topic which causes disengagement from the students. It could also indicate that the students are too busy and forced to make undesirable choices concerning their time and effort allocation.

References

1. Zimmerman, B.J.: A social cognitive view of self-regulated academic learning. J. Educ. Psychol. **81**, 329–339 (1989)
2. Broadbent, J., Poon, W.L.: Self-regulated learning strategies and academic achievement in online higher education learning environments: a systematic review. Internet High. Educ. **27**, 1–13 (2015)
3. Van Rooij, S.W., Zirkle, K.: Balancing pedagogy, student readiness and accessibility: a case study in collaborative online course development. Internet High. Educ. **28**, 1–7 (2016)
4. Srivastava, N., Fan, Y., Rakovic, M., et al.: Effects of internal and external conditions on strategies of self-regulated learning: a learning analytics Study. In: 12th International Learning Analytics and Knowledge Conference (LAK22), pp. 392–403. ACM (2022)
5. Zhang, T., Taub, M., Chen, Z.: A multi-level trace clustering analysis scheme for measuring students' self-regulated learning behavior in a mastery-based online learning environment. In: 12th International Learning Analytics and Knowledge Conference (LAK22), pp. 197–207. ACM (2022)
6. Lahza, H., Khosravi, H., Demartini, G., Gasevic, D.: Effects of technological interventions for self-regulation: a control experiment in learnersourcing. In: 12th International Learning Analytics and Knowledge Conference (LAK22), ACM, pp. 542–548 (2022)
7. Kim, D., Yoon, M., Jo, I., Branch, R.M.: Learning analytics to support self-regulated learning in asynchronous online courses: a case study at a women's university in South Korea. Comput. Educ. **127**, 233–251 (2018)
8. Effeney, G., Carroll, A., Bahr, N.: Self-regulated learning: key strategies and their sources in a sample of adolescent males. Aust. J. Educ. Dev. Psychol. **13**, 58–74 (2013)
9. Alario-Hoyos, C., Pérez-Sanagustín, M., Delgado-Kloos, C., Parada G, H.A., Muñoz-Organero, M.: Delving into participants' profiles and use of social tools in MOOCs. IEEE Trans. Learn. Technol. **7**(3), 260–266 (2014)

Digital Media in Schools During the Covid-19 Lockdown: Teachers' Experiences with Choosing Teaching Strategies

Nadine Esterl[1], Sonja Berger[1], and Nicolae Nistor[1,2(✉)]

[1] Faculty of Psychology and Educational Sciences, Ludwig-Maximilians-Universität, Leopoldstr. 13, 80802 Munich, Germany
esterl.nadine@campus.lmu.de, sonja.berger@psy.lmu.de, nic.nistor@uni-muenchen.de

[2] Richard W. Riley College of Education and Human Sciences, Walden University, 100 Washington Avenue South, Suite 900, Minneapolis, MN 55401, USA

Abstract. The Covid-19 pandemic unexpectedly led school teachers to exclusively using digital technologies. Few insights exist so far on how teachers choose, in such situations, digitally supported teaching strategies to actively engage their students in the learning process. We explored these choices by conducting semi-structured interviews with eight secondary school teachers from a large city in southern Germany during school closures. Relaying on the ICAP framework, we found that, for instance, teachers used websites with hypertexts to engage students actively, playful programming platforms to engage them constructively, or online group discussions to engage them interactively. Teachers' choice had to take technical constrains into account, such as the limits of available mobile data volumes, students' digital literacy, and the purpose for which new material was presented. Our findings suggest that categorizing learning activities according to students' ICAP levels of cognitive engagement can help teachers make decisions about their use of educational technologies.

Keywords: Digital media in schools · Cognitive activation · ICAP framework · Teaching strategies

1 Introduction

Instructional researchers have identified the ubiquitous problem that no guidelines are available on how to engage students in intensive interactions with the learning materials [2, 3]. This instructional design challenge was even bigger during the Covid-19 lockdown, when no face-to-face teaching was possible [6]. Increasingly, research was also concerned with learning loss caused, for example, by school closures [9]. Consequently, the question arose as to how teaching with digital media can be designed to avoid learning loss among students despite the pandemic. In this vein, we explored school teachers' choice of teaching strategies with digital media during lockdown, focusing on various levels of active engagement the teachers aimed at.

I. Hilliger et al. (Eds.): EC-TEL 2022, LNCS 13450, pp. 507–513, 2022.
https://doi.org/10.1007/978-3-031-16290-9_43

The ICAP framework [1, 2] specifies four modes of cognitive engagement in the learning process. In the *passive (P)* mode, students only receive information without performing any other visible learning activities. An example of passive engagement during learning with digital media is watching a PowerPoint presentation [6]. In contrast, students in *active (A)* mode not only receive information, but also manipulate the learning material. This means that they actively engage with the material physically or mentally. For example, highlighting text fragments from online documents that are most relevant for a specific task can be regarded as active engagement [6]. *Constructive (C)* engagement comprises students generating ideas that go beyond the learning material. An assignment may ask students learning with a simulation to generate hypotheses that they would test in a next step [6]. In the *interactive (I)* mode, students interact with peers, parents, or teachers while learning. This can occur, for example, when students create tutorials on a given topic [6].

Research has demonstrated that the mode of engagement impacts both the learning process and the academic achievement. The higher the mode of engagement, ascending from passive to active, constructive, and interactive, the higher the academic achievement [2, 8]. Moreover, the use of digital media has a significant, low to medium positive effect on academic achievement – again increasing from the passive to the interactive mode of engagement [6]. Contextual factors generally influence the actual use of digital media, as Sailer, Schultz-Pernice, and Fischer [6] propose in their C♭ model. Accordingly, teachers are influenced by their qualifications, their media-related competencies (knowledge, skills, attitudes), and by various characteristics of the school where they work. The technological equipment can also have a moderating influence on the use of digital media. Finally, students' knowledge, skills, and attitudes, can influence teachers' choice of teaching strategies by affecting how students engage with learning materials [6]. In this sense, the C♭ model integrates the ICAP framework such that all factors impact the nature of cognitive engagement.

In addition, the stages of instructional models are decisive for the choice of teaching goals and strategies. One way to do this is through Slavin's [7] description of the direct instruction stages. Accordingly, the first stage is *stating learning objectives and orienting students to the lesson.* The teacher describes what the students will be learning and stimulates their interest for the lesson topic. *Review prerequisites* means that the teacher gets an overview of the students' prior knowledge and activates it. In the next step, the teacher *presents new material* to the students in different ways (e.g., links to websites). The stage of *providing independent practice* builds upon the new material of the previous stage and involves students completing tasks related to the content. Finally, the teacher *assesses student performance*, and *provides feedback*. The definition of these stages implicitly specifies teaching goals for the learning activity, which can be, for example, the activation of prior knowledge while prerequisites are reviewed. Findings imply that, during the pandemic, teachers were less likely to use digital media as a learning tool to support student learning and more likely to use it to present information to them [5].

While contextual and individual factors, and the stages of instructional models may determine teaching goals at specific moments of teaching and learning, we still lack an overarching understanding and practical guidelines for the choice of teaching strategies throughout the teaching and learning process [3]. This gap in practice is even deeper when teaching at a distance with digital media, as required during the pandemic lockdown, and when we emphasize the importance of active learning engagement in the sense of ICAP.

2 Research Question

Addressing the gap in practice identified above, we examined the following research question: How did teachers choose teaching strategies to support active, constructive and interactive and therefore a higher level of student engagement during the Covid-19 pandemic?

3 Methods

Eight teachers ($N = 8$, 4 female and 4 male) from different types of secondary schools from a large German city participated in the study. Two of them taught STEM subjects (science, technology, engineering, mathematics) and three of them taught non-STEM subjects, such as German, foreign languages, social sciences, arts, religion, philosophy, and ethics. In addition, three teachers from general secondary schools participated who often taught all subjects. The teachers had varying levels of experience with using digital media in the classroom (2 to 14 years), mostly explained by varying lengths of teaching tenure. Semi-structured interviews were conducted via video chat. The interviews started with a description of the ICAP framework so that it could be addressed in the discussions during the interview. Afterwards, the teachers were asked how they had chosen their teaching strategies for each mode of engagement (active, constructive and interactive) in both face-to-face and online teaching. After teachers described their teaching strategies, the interview was concluded with general closing and organizational questions about the interview topic. The interviews took between 62 min and 112 min. The interview transcriptions were analyzed using thematic content analysis applying Mayring's [4] specifications on content structuring, which enabled assigning the teaching strategies choice criteria at one of the ICAP levels. During the data analysis using deductive category application, inductive categories were formed if the developed categories were not sufficient to explain the material [4]. This resulted in a total number of 19 categories. Data analysis was performed by two researchers. For this purpose, training was conducted with a transcript, then discrepancies were discussed and the description of the category scheme was adjusted. The inter-rater reliability was not calculated because the assigned categories were subsequently discussed for the entire data analysis.

4 Results

4.1 Teaching Strategies to Support *Active* Engagement

The majority of the interviewed teachers used *internet-based apps and websites* to provide independent practice, assess performance and provide feedback. They regarded the available technical equipment as an important criterion for this choice, both in the classroom and online. Further criteria were the usability of the used tools, apps' data protection compliance, and teachers' effort to install the apps before the class. Five teachers used *websites with hypertext and tutorials.* A teacher explained that, due to her design, one computer was sufficient. For bring-your-own-device (BYOD) scenarios, two requirements were described as essential: students' computers needed enough data capacity to display images, and students' research on the internet to appear responsible. To present new material to the students, mainly *video tutorials with follow up tasks* were used, which were available online or created by the teachers themselves. One teacher felt that simple language was important to convey the learning material in an understandable way. Also, students' current knowledge was essential when creating more detailed work assignments. All teachers described the possibility of using videos not only to present new material to the students, but also to state learning objectives and provide students with orientation aids within the lesson. *Online quiz tools* were used in a variety of stages in online as well as in classroom teaching to state learning objectives and support students' orientation within the lesson, to review prerequisites, to provide independent practice, to assess performance, and to provide feedback. It was important that the student's devices had sufficient mobile data limits. Thus, the teacher conducted these at the beginning of a month. Two teachers used *digital dictionaries* (e.g., Latein.me; the iOS app "Lexicon" or "Dictionary" preinstalled on iOS systems) in assignments so that students could look up the meaning of required words. In BYOD scenarios, in the experience of only one of the two teachers, the use was in principle possible for all students due to the small amount of data transferred. Two teachers used *augmented reality apps* (e.g., JigSpace, GeoGebra Augmented Reality) to present new material to the students and for providing independent practice. This allowed students to explore the individual parts of a skeleton projected into a room and how a microphone works, but also to lay out planes in geometry in the classroom.

4.2 Teaching Strategies to Support *Constructive* Engagement

Four teachers indicated that *video tutorials with follow up tasks* created by themselves or available online supported not only active engagement but also constructive engagement through appropriate tasks. This strategy was mainly used to present new material to students so that they could work out differences between two versions of the Macarena song, for example. However, this type of task was also described as suitable for providing independent practice, for example by transferring the knowledge conveyed in the video to answer questions about an interactive city tour. Two teachers indicated *presentation programs* as a way for students to prepare visual content. One teacher stated she used presentation programs and comic apps for providing independent practice, while the second teacher considered this task suitable for iPad classes in which enough iPads were available. Wikis and the design of a book cover with information from a book were each described as further possibilities that could be used for providing independent practice. *Playful programming platforms* (e.g., Scratch) were described as possible tools that introduce students to programming languages, and therefore provide independent practice, as well. According to a teacher, students' diverse cognitive requirements could be addressed using additional tasks for skilled students. Instead of merely playing a quiz with the students, two teachers had the students *create a quiz*. The task to *create videos* could be used to provide independent practice so that students could, for instance, analyze the purchasing behavior of consumers through video interviews in a shopping mall. Students' technical equipment in online classes needed to be available for them so that they were able to create videos. The tasks also needed to be adapted to the technical equipment of the students, some of whom had to use the small display of the smartphone. One teacher mentioned students' *creating podcasts, raps, and songs* as independent practice, such as practicing a foreign language or summarizing learning material. One teacher mentioned that the students need to have the knowledge of how to use these tools.

4.3 Teaching Strategies to Support *Interactive* Engagement

Of the total of five teachers who conducted *group discussions via video chat*, three stated that they used them to provide independent practice so that students could interactively discuss learning content. Partially, it was necessary for the students to have technical equipment at home that allowed them to participate in videoconferences. In addition, in one case, this type of learning was prevented by the limitations of the Microsoft Teams platform used, which did not yet allow breakout sessions at the time of the survey. School conditions played a role as use of Zoom was not supported, hence there were no breakout sessions to use. In particular, students in the lower grades did not yet have the skills necessary to participate in group discussions independently. Four teachers regarded *video creation* was seen as a learning activity that could be done in groups, especially as independent practice. In addition, the technical equipment in the classroom (e.g., presence of a sufficient number of iPads which were used to create the videos) and the students' knowledge of how to use the software must be given. *Collaborative writing tools* (e.g., Etherpad) were used in that students worked together to create a text document related to the lesson content as independent practice. One influencing factor was the school subject, as for example mathematical aspects could not be elaborated well with collaborative writing tools. Possible tasks depended on the cognitive prerequisites of the students, because they primarily needed to be able to handle the application for the learning activity to be successful, but differentiation tasks could also be set.

5 Discussion and Conclusions

In this study we investigated school teachers' choice teaching strategies to support active, constructive and interactive student engagement. Several theories describe influential factors, like media-related competencies (knowledge, skills, attitudes) [6] or the stages of instruction, like providing independent practice or present new material [7]. The teachers we interviewed described some of their strategies to support student engagement in education with digital media.

The use of apps in which tasks could be completed, quizzes could be worked on, or research could be conducted, was a representative example how active student engagement could be generated. Active engagement was used for several stages described by Slavin [7]. Prerequisites, such as the technical equipment availability (including the availability of mobile data) of the students and the teachers required for implementation, played a central role [6]. The interviews showed that, in principle, one device per classroom can be sufficient to implement digital teaching strategies. It can be deduced from this that the teaching strategies can be adapted to the available resources.

As Sailer, Schultz-Pernice, and Fischer [6] explained, digital media can be used well for students' creative work for a constructive mode of engagement. This picture was also evident in the teachers' responses, who mentioned, for example, digital text editing, work with programming platforms, creation of videos or audios by the students for constructive engagement. Constructive engagement was reported by teachers to be used primarily to provide independent practice and to present new material. Similar to active engagement, the technical equipment of the students and teachers, but also the cognitive preconditions, of the students were most often seen as crucial for the planning of the learning activities.

Some learning activities with a constructive mode of engagement can be transferred to the interactive level by creating videos in groups. In addition, already highlighted possibilities in the literature, such as online discussions or collaborative text processing [6], are also used for (online) teaching. In the descriptions on interactive learning, it was noticeable that creative work with media, as for constructive engagement, was mostly used to provide independent practice. But here, too, other factors played a role, such as the school conditions or the school subject, which entails certain restrictions.

In addition to the overview of media-based teaching strategies, it could be concluded from the results that the ICAP framework is suitable as a lesson planning tool for teachers. First, there is a rough idea of a method on one of the ICAP levels. Considering different prerequisites or criteria, this can be concretized by choosing a learning activity and technology. Whether such an approach can be used successfully, will be established in future studies.

The ICAP framework can also be used to classify educational technologies according to the highest possible level of learning activity that can be achieved with a particular technology or in a particular learning environment [1, 2]. For media education purposes, this would provide a more detailed taxonomy – for example more detailed than the C♭ model, where the ICAP framework was included but the functions of media in the classroom were not included [6]. If their model, especially the distinction of the four modes of engagement defined in the ICAP framework, was complemented by functions of media derived from [7], like providing independent practice or present new material it could be a step forward for media didactics (easier and more precise design of media-based instruction and corresponding learning environments. For example, collaborative writing tools could be categorized on a matrix as interactive and as providing independent practice. Instead of a specific guideline such a matrix could be used as an aid in deciding for or against certain digital equipment or teaching strategies.

A limiting factor of the present study is that all the interviewed teachers were unfamiliar with the ICAP framework. The beginning of each interview was a short description of the ICAP framework with the aim of being able to refer to it directly in the interview, but due to the lack of internalization of this knowledge, the teachers could not always refer specifically to the respective level and often jumped between them. This made it difficult to clearly assign the individual activities mentioned to the stages of the

ICAP framework, which is why individual decisions were discussed at length during the evaluation. Further research may be able to directly address the ICAP framework in interviews, when teachers already know about it and used it for their teaching. Because teachers did not refer specifically to the respective level, it appears that the choice of these different types of engagement were not intentional. Rather, it seemed to be the conditional or target factors that influenced the type of digital media used and thus the stage of the ICAP framework. Nevertheless, this work provides some suggestions for future uses of digital media and how high-quality instruction can be conducted with them.

Acknowledgements. This paper was based on first author's bachelor thesis, also submitted in a more extensive version to the German journal *Ludwigsburger Beiträge zur Medienpädagogik*. The paper was facilitated by the DigitUS project (Ludwig-Maximilians-Universität in Munich).

References

1. Chi, M.T.H.: Active-constuctive-interactive: a conceptual framework for differentiating learning activities. Top. Cogn. Sci. **1**(1), 73–105 (2009). https://doi.org/10.1111/j.1756-8765.2008.01005.x
2. Chi, M.T.H., Wylie, R.: The ICAP framework: linking cognitive engagement to active learning outcomes. Educ. Psychol. **49**(4), 219–243 (2014). https://doi.org/10.1080/00461520.2014.965823
3. Fiorella, L., Mayer, R.E.: Eight ways to promote generative learning. Educ. Psychol. Rev. **28**(4), 717–741 (2015). https://doi.org/10.1007/s10648-015-9348-9
4. Mayring, P.: Qualitative content analysis. Forum Qual. Res. **1**(2), 1–10 (2000). https://doi.org/10.17169/fqs-1.2.1089
5. Pozo, J.-I., Pérez Echeverría, M.-P., Cabellos, B., Sánchez, D.L.: Teaching and learning in times of Covid-19: uses of digital technologies during school lockdowns. Front. Psychol. **12**, 1–13 (2021). https://doi.org/10.3389/fpsyg.2021.656776
6. Sailer, M., Schultz-Pernice, F., Fischer, F.: Contextual facilitators for learning activities involving technology in higher education: The C♭-model. Comput. Hum. Behav. **121**, 1–13 (2021). https://doi.org/10.1016/j.chb.2021.106794
7. Slavin, R.E.: Educational Psychology. Theory and Practice, 8th edn. Pearson, Allyn and Bacon, Boston (2006)
8. Wiggins, B.L., Eddy, S.L., Grunspan, D.Z., Crowe, A.J.: The ICAP active learning framework predicts the learning gains observed in intensely active classroom experiences. AERA Open **3**(2), 1–14 (2017). https://doi.org/10.1177/2332858417708567
9. Williamson, B., Macgilchrist, F., Potter, J.: Covid-19 controversies and critical research in digital education. Learn. Media Technol. **46**(2), 117–127 (2021). https://doi.org/10.1080/17439884.2021.1922437

Process and Self-regulation Explainable Feedback for Novice Programmers Appears Ineffectual

Esther Félix[1(✉)], Franck Amadieu[2], Rémi Venant[3], and Julien Broisin[1]

[1] IRIT, Université de Toulouse, CNRS, Toulouse INP, UT3, Toulouse, France
{esther.felix,julien.broisin}@irit.fr

[2] CLLE, Université de Toulouse, CNRS, Toulouse, France
franck.amadieu@univ-tlse2.fr

[3] LIUM, Le Mans Université, Le Mans, France
remi.venant@univ-lemans.fr

Abstract. This paper investigates how to provide novice programmers with feedback about their learning process including hints and explanations to improve their learning. The aim is to improve the feedback effectiveness and perceived utility by making it more meaningful through the use of explanations. Our proposals were implemented in the context of computer science education and an experiment was conducted to evaluate the effect of explainable feedback on changes in learners' strategies, performance and perceptions. The first results of this experiment show no significant effect of process and self-regulation feedback (explained or not) on students' strategies or learning outcomes. Also, we conducted a qualitative analysis that allowed us to propose a series of recommendations for stakeholders exploring feedback explainability.

Keywords: Feedback · Explainability · Computer science education

1 Introduction

Technology-Enhanced Learning (TEL) environments offer the opportunity to provide learners with automated feedback on the basis of the data collected by these environments. However, prior works showed that designing feedback is very complex, as the best type of feedback to provide to students depends on many variables including their age, ability and the learning environment [12]. When addressing computer science education, most of the work studying automated feedback focuses on the task level [8] even if feedback on learning strategies is one of the most effective type of feedback [13]. Moreover, the way in which data is used to design the feedback is not explained to the end-user [5].

In this paper we are interested in the possibility of introducing the notion of explainability into automatically generated feedback. We believe that the models used for feedback generation can be exploited to provide personalised explanations that will promote the acceptability of the virtual environment.

I. Hilliger et al. (Eds.): EC-TEL 2022, LNCS 13450, pp. 514–520, 2022.
https://doi.org/10.1007/978-3-031-16290-9_44

The next section presents a state of the art on feedback in (computer) education, and introduces the notion of explainable feedback. Section 3 and 4 respectively describe and evaluate our proposal for a process and self-regulation feedback enhanced by explanations. We then discuss the results in Sect. 5 before concluding and exposing future directions for explainable feedback.

2 State of the Art

2.1 Feedback in Education and Computer Science Education

In 2007, Hattie and Timperley defined feedback as "information provided by an agent (e.g., teacher, parent, peer) about an individual's performance or understanding" [6, p. 102]. According to their model, the purpose of feedback is to "reduce discrepancies between current understandings and performance and a goal" [6, p. 86]. Thus, they classify feedback into several levels: **Task level** feedback indicates whether a specific task has been well accomplished or understood; **Process level** feedback gives feedback on the resolution strategies that have been used by the learner; **Self-regulation level** feedback focuses on learners' regulation of their strategies; **Self level** feedback consists of feedback on the learner but not on the task itself.

The results of Hattie and Timperley, revised by a meta-analysis in 2020 [13], highlighted that feedback should contain high-level explanations, i.e., why errors were made and how to avoid them, rather than simply stating that errors were made. It is also desirable to provide learners with personalised feedback. TEL environments offer interesting perspectives on this issue, with the possibility to exploit learning analytics to automate and personalise the feedback provided to learners [11]. In 2018, Keuning et al. used a framework by Narciss [10] to propose a literature review on automated feedback for computer science education [7]. This review compared the types of feedback provided by 101 tools supporting novice programmers. The results showed that most of the tools consider the task level (i.e. feedback on "Knowledge about Mistakes"). Out of the 101 tools, only one offered "Knowledge about Meta-Cognition" type feedback.

2.2 Feedback and Explainability

The recent development of artificial intelligence and machine learning raised the need for explainability. The aim of eXplainable Artificial Intelligence (xAI) is to increase the transparency of a system as well as the confidence of users in this system [9]. Research on explainability has until now mostly targeted experts in artificial intelligence, and studies exploring explanations intended for education stakeholders are scarce [5]. Conati et al. offer explanations on suggestions given by an ITS about *how* and *why* the AI reached that suggestion [5]. A recent paper from Afzaal et al. also presented an explainable ML approach for generating explanations [1], using a predictive model for students' academic performance on the basis of some student features collected in a learning management system.

Limitations of Sect. 2.1, combined with the recent advances in the field of explainability, motivate our overall objective to advance the field of explainable feedback for computer science education. The two following research questions will guide the remaining of the document: **RQ1:** How to design explainable process and self-regulation feedback for novice programmers that can be automatically generated? **RQ2:** What is the impact of this type of feedback on students' behaviour, performance, and perception of the feedback?

3 Design of High-Level Explainable Feedback

This section tries to bring an answer to RQ1 by proposing an elaborated feedback in the context of learning programming. Before developing our proposals, we present the learning platform from which the feedback is generated.

Lab4CE. Our proposals are based on a virtual and remote laboratory called Lab4CE [4]. Lab4CE is a web-based environment that uses virtualisation technologies to provide each learner with virtual machines. Students can log into the platform and enter commands via a web terminal to propose solutions to the given problems. As each interaction between learners and the platform is recorded as an xAPI statement, automatic analysis of the tasks performed by learners can be designed to provide them with additional intelligent features.

Proposals for Explainable Feedback. On the basis of the data collected on Lab4CE, we proposed in prior works an unsupervised machine learning approach to automatically classify students into different programming profiles based on features describing their programming activity [3]. The features used by the clustering algorithm include the number of code submissions, the average time between two submissions, the average number of changes within the source code between two submissions and the percentage of submissions with syntactical errors. As a result, learners' behaviours are classified in one of the three clusters identified by the algorithm. The best academic performance are achieved for students in Cluster 3, then Cluster 2, and finally Cluster 1. The objective of our explainable feedback is to provide learners with the diagnosis of the clustering algorithm so that they can be aware of the programming strategies they adopted and guide them towards better learning strategies. To achieve this objective, we focused on the process and self-regulation levels of feedback and combined Afzaal's approach [1] to expose learners to some features of the clustering algorithm, with Conati's approach to provide hints and advice to help improve the exposed features.

Explainable Feedback Content. The personalised explainable feedback is composed of three main parts: a process level diagnosis about how students behaved during past sessions; an explanation on why they were diagnosed with this behaviour; a self-regulation hint to improve the learning strategy. Figure 1 illustrates an example of feedback provided to a student during the experiment.

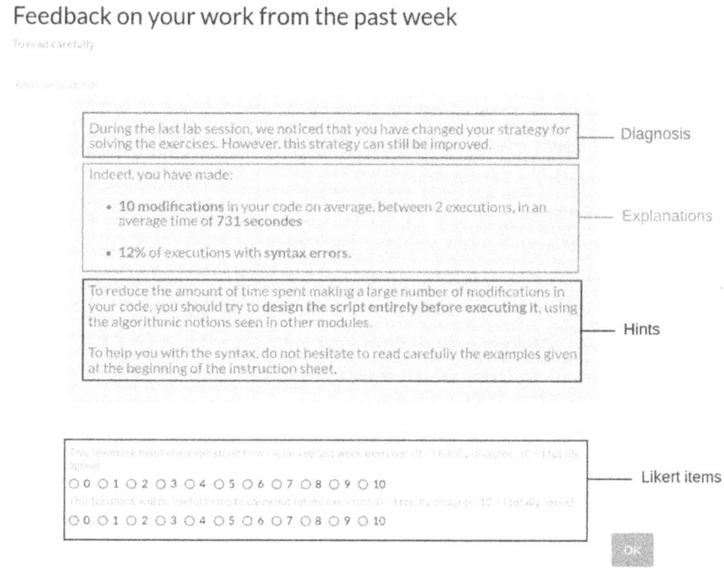

Fig. 1. Example of an explainable feedback provided to a student

4 Methods

We present in this section the experiment we set up to answer RQ2. Especially, the experiment was designed to assess the impact of feedback with explanations about the diagnosis versus feedback without explanations, on students' behaviour, performance, and perception of feedback.

4.1 Tools and Experimental Setting

The experiment took place in higher education for 5 weeks, in a Shell programming course, with 155 first-year students. They had a weekly 90-minutes face-to-face lab session on Lab4CE with one teacher, and the platform was also accessible online throughout the experiment. From the second week onwards, logs from Lab4CE were extracted the day before each lab session so that students were classified in one of the clusters 1, 2 or 3 (see Sect. 3). The profiles were then used to provide students with feedback. To study the impact of explanations, we created three comparable groups of students in terms of programming level. The group with explanations was provided with a feedback comprising the diagnosis, the explanations, and the hints. The group without explanations received the diagnosis and the hints only. The control group was exposed to a short text about the topics studied during the coming lab session.

4.2 Data Analysis

Our second research question is interested in the impact of the feedback on students' behaviour, performance, and perception of the feedback.

The behavioural perspective was assessed using the data from Lab4CE. We studied students' behavioural trajectories over the weeks by analysing their moves from one cluster to another, and we analysed the evolution of the features composing the clusters (see Sect. 3). For each feature (the dependent variable), we applied a mixed ANOVA for each type of feedback (the factor) and repeated the measures each week.

To evaluate the impact of the different types of feedback on students' performance, we collected grades obtained by students at the practical exam after the experiment, and we performed a one-way ANOVA with the grades as the dependent variable, and the type of feedback as the factor.

The perception of the feedback was evaluated with the questionnaire delivered to the students. It consisted of 7-level Likert items and open-ended questions. The items were about the students' satisfaction, understanding and perceived utility of the feedback, and the open-ended question asked students for suggestions or comments regarding the explanations. We collected 138 answers. One-way ANOVA was applied to compare the answers between the three experimental groups. Two months after the experiment, we also set up and recorded a 60-minutes focus group with 10 students involved in the experiment, in order to collect students' opinions and ideas about the form of the feedback and the content of the explanations. The focus group recording was analysed along with the answers to the open-ended question to help interpreting the quantitative data, but also to identify new avenues for feedback improvements in Lab4CE.

5 Results and Discussion

5.1 Results

The analysis were conducted on students who attended all face-to-face lab sessions, as we considered that missing data for a week or more would lead to unreliable results. The data set thus comprises data from 29 students of the control group, 26 students of the group without explanations, and 29 students of the group with explanations.

The statistics about students' changes of behaviour (i.e. evolution of the features composing the clusters) and performance at the final practical exam were not significant as the p-value was greater than .05 for all post-hoc tests. The 3 experimental groups also did not answer significantly differently to the Likert-scale evaluations of feedback and to the questionnaire, for either perceived usefulness or satisfaction with feedback. Regarding students' understanding of the feedback, results showed that the group without explanations reported a greater understanding of feedback ($Mean = 5.17$, $SD = 1.40$) than the group with explanations ($Mean = 4.24$, $SD = 1.71$) and the control group ($Mean = 4.85$, $SD = 1.44$).

The open-ended questions in the questionnaire and the focus group provided interesting insights from the students on different topics. Regarding the feedback design, students were not bothered by the fact that the feedback was in the form of a popup. Inputs from students about the feedback content can be grouped into two main areas: the need for a baseline, and the need for greater precision. They would have liked the statistics to be presented together with a reference to allow them to better make sense of the figures provided. They also felt that the advice given was "too broad" and therefore too difficult to apply. Regarding the timing, students liked the fact that the feedback was given at the beginning of each session, because it "helped to set a goal for the session".

5.2 Discussion and Implications

Discussion. Regarding RQ2, our results show no impact of our high-level feedback on students' programming behaviour and performance. The lower students' perceived understanding of feedback with explanations might be due to the higher cognitive load required by explanations to fully read and understand the whole feedback. This hypothesis is confirmed by the focus group, where some students stated that when the explanations are "too long", they become "tiring to read". Additionally, some students said that receiving statistics of different types was confusing, and were not sure how to interpret the features. For instance, those who did not read carefully the hint thought that they had to decrease the time between submissions.

Implications for Research. Our works allow for recommendations about the process of designing explainable feedback intended for novice programmers. First, explanations should include small pieces of information that are similar in terms of semantics and should not comprise words or sentences with opposite meaning in order to ease their understanding by students. Second, explanations should be provided with other information such as baselines regarding the features from the intelligent mechanism. Third, the diagnosis and hints should be displayed at first sight, whereas the explanations should be hidden but quickly accessible. Fourth, in order to avoid persistent epistemic emotions such as confusion promoting learner frustration or boredom [2], some features should not be presented to learners or they should be presented in a positive fashion. Despite these recommendations, other aspects of explainable feedback still have to be investigated. More empirical studies are required to find a balance between utility and ease of understanding of explanations.

6 Conclusion and Future Directions

The work presented in this paper is, according to our knowledge, one of the first contributions that attempt to provide process and self-regulation feedback to novice programmers. Results do not show a significant positive impact of (explainable) feedback on students' learning behaviour or performance, but do not reveal any negative impact either. The mixed methods we used to assess our proposals, and especially the qualitative analysis, resulted in a series of recommendations for research exploring feedback explainability.

Providing learners with explainable feedback at the resolution strategy level is much more complex than designing task level interventions. The outcomes of the focus group emphasised the need for consideration of inter-individual differences at the cognitive level (e.g., knowledge, skills) when designing explanations. Also, the intra-individual level that influences the subjective cognitive effort [14] could be another avenue for research. These point to the need for further joined research efforts exploring what information can be used to automatically generate explainable feedback that is fully responsive to the needs of learners, and emphasises the call for interdisciplinary research with social sciences already expressed by the research community.

References

1. Afzaal, M., et al.: Generation of automatic data-driven feedback to students using explainable machine learning. In: Roll, I., McNamara, D., Sosnovsky, S., Luckin, R., Dimitrova, V. (eds.) AIED 2021. LNCS (LNAI), vol. 12749, pp. 37–42. Springer, Cham (2021). https://doi.org/10.1007/978-3-030-78270-2_6
2. Arguel, A., Lockyer, L., Kennedy, G., Lodge, J.M., Pachman, M.: Seeking optimal confusion: a review on epistemic emotion management in interactive digital learning environments. Interact. Learn. Environ. (2019)
3. Bey, A., Pérez-Sanagustín, M., Broisin, J.: Unsupervised automatic detection of learners' programming behavior. In: Scheffel, M., Broisin, J., Pammer-Schindler, V., Ioannou, A., Schneider, J. (eds.) EC-TEL 2019. LNCS, vol. 11722, pp. 69–82. Springer, Cham (2019). https://doi.org/10.1007/978-3-030-29736-7_6
4. Broisin, J., Venant, R., Vidal, P.: Lab4CE: a remote laboratory for computer education. Int. J. Artif. Intell. Educ. **27**(1), 154–180 (2015). https://doi.org/10.1007/s40593-015-0079-3
5. Conati, C., Barral, O., Putnam, V., Rieger, L.: Toward personalized XAI: a case study in intelligent tutoring systems. Artif. Intell. **298**, 103503 (2021)
6. Hattie, J., Timperley, H.: The power of feedback. Rev. Educ. Res. (2007)
7. Keuning, H., Jeuring, J., Heeren, B.: A systematic literature review of automated feedback generation for programming exercises. ACM Trans. Comput. Educ. **19**, 1–43 (2018)
8. Kleij, E., Veldkamp, T.: Effects of feedback in a computer-based assessment for learning - ScienceDirect. Comput. Educ. (2012)
9. Kraus, S., et al.: AI for explaining decisions in multi-agent environments. In: Proceedings of the AAAI Conference on Artificial Intelligence. Springer (2020)
10. Narciss, S., Huth, K., Narciss, D.: How to design informative tutoring feedback for multi-media learning. Inst. Des. Multimedia Learn. (2002)
11. Serral, E., De Weerdt, J., Sedrakyan, G., Snoeck, M.: Automating immediate and personalized feedback taking conceptual modelling education to a next level (2016)
12. Timmers, C., Veldkamp, B.: Attention paid to feedback provided by a computer-based assessment for learning on information literacy. Comput. Educ. (2011)
13. Wisniewski, B., Zierer, K., Hattie, J.: The power of feedback revisited: a meta-analysis of educational feedback research. Front. Psychol. (2020)
14. Yeo, G., Neal, A.: Subjective cognitive effort: a model of states, traits, and time. J. Appl. Psychol. **93**, 617 (2008)

Exploring Teacher's Orchestration Actions in Online and In-Class Computer-Supported Collaborative Learning

Lubna Hakami(✉), Ishari Amarasinghe, Eyad Hakami, and Davinia Hernandez-Leo

Universitat Pompeu Fabra, Barcelona, Spain
{lubna.hakami01,eyad.hakami01}@estudiant.upf.edu,
{ishari.amarasinghe,davinia.hernandez-leo}@upf.edu

Abstract. Teacher orchestration of technology-enhanced learning has received increasing attention as a factor for enhancing students' learning gains. However, a limited number of studies have investigated the impact of learning settings on teachers' orchestration actions. In this paper, we considered two different settings of computer-supported collaborative learning (CSCL) activities, namely online and in-class, and studied their influence on teachers' orchestration actions. Data was collected from five sessions for each setting. The findings indicated that during the in-class sessions there were more teacher-individual interactions, announcements, checking participation/responses tabs, and dashboard interventions conducted by the teacher. In the online setting, however, more teacher-class interactions occurred when compared to the in-class setting. The implications of this study and its continuation are related to the consideration of the learning setting in the design, redesign, and evaluation processes of orchestration technologies.

Keywords: Computer-supported collaborative learning · Orchestration · Dashboards · Teacher support tools

1 Introduction

The term "orchestration" has been used in Education to describe the real-time management of multiple classroom activities, various learning processes and involving numerous teaching actions [1]. In technology-enhanced learning, orchestration technologies are the digital tools that support teachers in the orchestration of complex learning activities [2]. Such tools have been especially proposed to support teachers in orchestrating student collaboration across learning flows, in the sense of guiding, the managing and coordinating, activity sequences, group formation, resource distribution, etc. [3]. In alignment with the concept of orchestration technologies, the field of Computer-Supported Collaborative Learning (CSCL) studies the use digital tools to design and deploy collaborative learning activities [4]. In this context, teacher orchestration refers to three dimensions of a distributed CSCL environment: cognitive (e.g., regulating individual, small-group and

I. Hilliger et al. (Eds.): EC-TEL 2022, LNCS 13450, pp. 521–527, 2022.
https://doi.org/10.1007/978-3-031-16290-9_45

class-wide interactions), pedagogical (e.g., real-time adaptation of the designed activities to the classroom needs), and technological (e.g., management of the transactions between software components) [5].

Orchestration technologies are being mostly designed for classroom, with the most salient part of the scenario occurring face-to-face [1]. Thus, the implementation of CSCL activities in fully online environments can be challenging for teachers and students at both levels, educationally and technologically. Several studies have discussed the difficulties the students face when performing online collaborative activities [e.g., 6, 7]. Major challenges include ineffective communication, conflict among group members, and negative behavior toward group work [6]. Less attention has been paid to understand how teachers' orchestration actions differ across different learning settings, e.g., in-class and online setting.

Therefore, in this paper we explore the teacher's orchestration actions in two settings namely in-class and online in the use of PyramidApp [8], a web-based tool that allows teachers to deploy Pyramid collaborative learning flow pattern based scripted collaborative learning activities. PyramidApp consists of an authoring space which facilitates activity authoring, activity enactment space for students and a teacher-facing dashboard that provides orchestration support, e.g., information about students' activity participation as well as functionalities to adapt the flow of script in real-time. The activity flow is as follows: First students require to provide an individual option to a given task. Then they join in small groups and later in larger groups to discuss and improve individual options and to reach a consensus at the end of the activity.

We analyzed data collected from a single teacher across ten sessions, five of which were online and five in-class. We used a mixed-methods approach to answer the following research question: *To what extent do the teacher orchestration actions differ in online sessions when compared to in-class sessions of computer-supported-collaborative-learning activities?*

We posit that the contribution of this study, as a work in progress, to the field of technology-enhanced learning would advance the examination of how different learning settings, i.e., online and in-class, influence teachers' orchestration actions which could also help us to explain better the orchestration load experienced by the teachers in future studies.

The rest of the paper is structured as follows. In Sect. 2, describes the provides methodology followed to answer the research question. In Sect. 3, presents study findings and lastly Sect. 4, discuss the results, limitations, and future work.

2 Method

2.1 Data Collection

A female teacher from a public university in Spain has participated in this study. She had over 17 years of teaching experience and had previous experience in authoring and orchestrating CSCL activities. The main criteria for selecting the participant were the existence of teaching experience, prior knowledge, and experience in using PyramidApp in both online and in-class settings. The teacher conducted ten Pyramid activities five of which were online and the other five were in-class sessions.

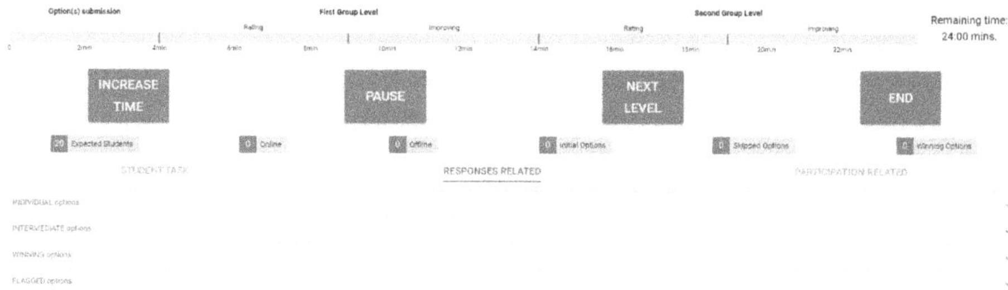

Fig. 1. Teacher-facing dashboard used by the teacher.

Data was collected through capturing audio data from each session, screen- recording the teacher-facing dashboard (see Fig. 1) and taking observation notes while the teacher was orchestrating the activity. Moreover, the log data that indicated the relevant details were extracted from the PyramidApp database (e.g., the number of students participated in the activity, duration of the task, the task given for each session and the actions taken by the teacher in the dashboard). The screen and audio recordings, the observations notes, and the log data were analyzed to explore how teacher's orchestration actions differ in two settings (i.e., Online and In-class) using PyramidApp tool.

The tasks for the five online sessions were the same as those for the five in-class. However, the design of each collaborative learning activity differed depending on the teacher's requirements for conducting CSCL activities in each session. Table 1 presents the tasks given by the teacher and the number of students who participated in each session. In addition, tasks A and B were conducted in an undergraduate class and tasks C and D were conducted in a master class. Task B was used in four sessions (i.e., Online1, In-class1, Online2 and In-class2), while each of the other three tasks were used in two sessions (i.e., Online1 and In-class1). Each activity lasted around 9 to 19 min.

Table 1. A Summary of Collaborative-Learning Activities Conducted".

Task given to students	Sessions by condition and number of students			
	Online1	Online2	In-class1	In-class2
Task A. Identify and explain three errors in the shown servlet, which aims to implement a change in its behavior depending on the web page from which it is linked to:	15	–	8	–
Task B. Analyze a scenario to identify non-functional requirements	15	16	8	11
Task C. Which factors should be considered when considering the implementation of learning analytics?	16	–	14	–
Task D. List differences between a LMS and MOOC platform	15	–	15	–

2.2 Coding Teacher's Orchestration Actions

To be able to answer the research question, we analyzed orchestration actions of the teacher across the ten sessions. Teacher's orchestration actions were coded following a coding scheme defined in [9]. This coding scheme includes six codes as follows: 1) *Teacher-individual interaction* 2) *Teacher class interaction* 3) *Announcements to class* 4) *Check responses tab* 5) *Check participation tab* and 6) *Dashboard interventions.* More details about the codes are presented in Table 2.

Table 2. Codes defined to describe teacher's actions.

Codes	Actions
Teacher-individual interaction	Teacher responds to specific questions asked by individual students
Teacher class interaction	Interactions between teachers and the whole class (i.e., teacher requests information from the class, debriefs the final answers, provides directions to the class about how to use the tool and perform the given task)
Announcements to class	Teacher makes announcements to the class (i.e., time remaining for the activity and phase transitions of the script)
Check responses tab	This code describes actions of the teacher in the dashboard (i.e., scrolling answers received from individual students and the highly rated answers at the group level)
Check participation tab	This code describes actions of the teacher in the dashboard (i.e., checking information related to satisfactory and unsatisfactory voting participation of groups, opening a group box, and scrolling the chat messages posted by the students and the new option formulated)
Dashboard interventions	Summarizes dashboard interventions by the teacher (i.e., use of Next Level, Increase Time, End and Pause buttons in the dashboard)

3 Findings

This section presents the results obtained after the analysis of ten sessions distributed to four collaborative learning tasks. We compare the number of teacher's actions in each task of both settings (i.e., Online and In-class). Figure 2 shows two graphs, one for the actions taken during the online sessions and one for the actions taken during the in-class sessions. Then we present and compare the aggregated actions for all the tasks in different settings. (Table 3).

As shown in Fig. 2, in all tasks there were differences in the *teacher-individual interaction.* The individual students interacted more with the teacher in the in-class sessions when compared to the online sessions. In tasks A and D, the teacher conducted more

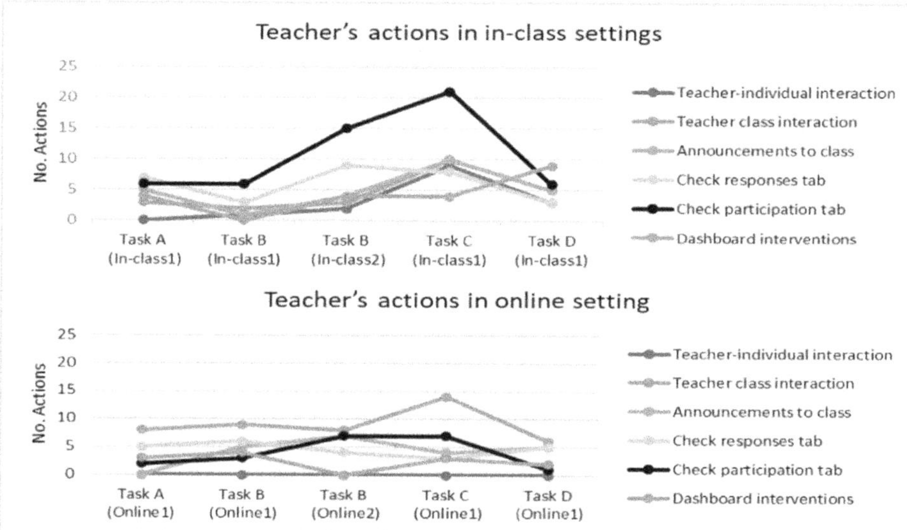

Fig. 2. Teacher's actions in both online and in-class settings.

class interactions in the online sessions. Moreover, actions from *announcements to class*, *check responses tab*, *check participation tab* and *dashboard interventions* occurred more in the in-class sessions than in the online. Task B was used in two different sessions. The first one (i.e., Online1 and In-class1), actions such as *teacher class interaction*, *announcements to class*, *check responses tab* and *dashboard interventions* occurred more in online sessions. However, *check participation tab* actions occur more in in-class sessions. The second session (i.e., Online2 and In-class2), the teachers conducted more *class interactions* and *checked the responses tab* in the online session. The number of announcements to the class were the same in the online and in-class sessions. In addition, the teacher conducted more *dashboard interventions* during in-class sessions when compared to the online sessions. In task C, the teacher interacted with the class and made more announcements in online sessions when compared to the in-class sessions, while actions from *check response/participation tabs* and *dashboard intervention* happened more in in-class sessions.

Table 3 shows the difference between aggregated actions of each code in the two settings. The findings show that during the in-class setting there were more *teacher-individual interactions, announcements, check responses tab, check participation tab* and *dashboard interventions.* In the online setting, however, the teachers conducted more class interactions and fewer individual interactions when compared to the in-class context (Table 3). It is also interesting that the teacher was not using less the monitoring features of the classroom in the In-class condition, but the contrary. Differences in the number of times that the teacher decided to check student participation are substantial.

Table 3. Teacher's actions in all online sessions and all in-class sessions.

Actions	Online	In-class
Teacher-individual interaction	0	15
Teacher class interaction	45	23
Announcements to class	21	25
Check responses tab	22	29
Check participation tab	21	49
Dashboard interventions	12	21
Total	121	162
Average	20	27

4 Discussion and Future Work

Teacher-individual interactions occurred less often in the online sessions, even though there were more participants in this setting (n = 77) than in the in-class sessions (n = 56). The lack of interactions with individual students might indicate less workload to the teacher. This might be due to a communication issue connected to the students' willingness to raise questions during online sessions, which is consistent with the literature suggesting that communication has shown to be the biggest challenge in online collaboration. [6]. Also, we assume that the number of *teacher-class interactions* in the online setting indicates the need for more explanations about how to use the facilitating CSCL tool when compared to the same interactions in the in-class setting. Most of the actions in this category (31 out of 45 in the online setting, and 20 out of 23 in the in-class) were technology-related, i.e., the teacher is giving directions to the students about the use of the facilitating tool. To further investigate such assumptions in the future, we are working on analyzing the students' performance during online and in-class sessions (e.g., the total number of students who completed the task in each session, quality of their outcomes).

The data collected for this study is limited due to the criteria of data collection, and the differences between learning designs across sessions. More data will be collected in the future from other teachers who taught the same course to enable for more in-depth analysis and generalizable findings.

The implications of this study and its continuation are related to the consideration of the learning environment in the design, redesign, and evaluation processes of orchestration technologies, and how they can impact the teacher orchestration load as well as the student learning and collaboration. This ongoing research would also further the investigation of how orchestration tools could facilitate teachers to regulated CSCL activities in different settings. It can be of interest to practitioners who teach in distance, online and hybrid settings and other stakeholders in the wider TEL field.

Acknowledgements. This work has been partially funded by the National Research Agency of the Spanish Ministry (PID2020-112584RB-C33/MICIN/AEI/10.13039/501100011033). D.

Hernández-Leo acknowledges the support by ICREA under the ICREA Academia program. E. Hakami acknowledges the grant by Jazan University, Saudi Arabia.

References

1. Dillenbourg, P., Jermann, P.: Technology for classroom orchestration. In: Khine, M., Saleh, I. (eds.) New Science of Learning, pp. 525–552. Springer, New York (2010). https://doi.org/10.1007/978-1-4419-5716-0_26
2. Wang, P., Tchounikine, P., Quignard, M.: Chao: a framework for the development of orchestration technologies for technology-enhanced learning activities using tablets in classrooms. Int. J. Technol. Enhanc. Learn. **10**(1–2), 1–21 (2018)
3. Prieto, L.P., Holenko Dlab, M., Gutiérrez, I., Abdulwahed, M., Balid, W.: Orchestrating technology enhanced learning: a literature review and a conceptual framework. Int. J. Technol. Enhanc. Learn. **3**(6), 583–598 (2011)
4. Suthers, D.D., Seel, N.M.: Computer-supported collaborative learning. In: Encyclopedia of the Sciences of Learning, pp. 719–722 (2012)
5. Dillenbourg, P., Fischer, F.: Basics of Computer-Supported Collaborative Learning (2010)
6. Thompson, L., Ku, H.: A case study of online collaborative learning. Q. Rev. Distance Educ. **7**(4), 361–375, 448–449 (2006)
7. Curtis, D.D., Lawson, M.J.: Exploring collaborative online learning. J. Asynchron. Learn. Netw. **5**(1), 21–34 (2001)
8. Manathunga, K., Hernández-Leo, D.: Authoring and enactment of mobile pyramid-based collaborative learning activities. Br. J. Educ. Technol. **49**(2), 262–275 (2018). https://doi.org/10.1111/bjet.12588
9. Amarasinghe, I., Hernández-Leo, D., Ulrich Hoppe, H.: Deconstructing orchestration load: comparing teacher support through mirroring and guiding. Int. J. Comput.-Supp. Collab. Learn. **16**(3), 307–338 (2021). https://doi.org/10.1007/s11412-021-09351-9

Using Dialogic Feedback to Create Learning Communities During COVID-19: Lessons for Future Teacher Development

Ana Hibert[1(✉)], Michael Phillips[2], Dragan Gašević[2], Nataša Pantić[1], Justine MacLean[1], and Yi-Shan Tsai[2]

[1] University of Edinburgh, Edinburgh EH8 9YL, UK
ana.hibert@ed.ac.uk

[2] Monash University, Melbourne, VIC, Australia
yi-shan.tsai@monash.edu

Abstract. The COVID-19 pandemic substantively impacted educational processes and posed urgent questions regarding how teachers can adapt their practices to create supportive learning communities in online environments. The purpose of this study was to understand how teachers provided dialogic feedback using technologies to create learning communities despite the unexpected switch to online learning during the COVID-19 lockdowns. Ten pre-service teachers and six in-service teachers were interviewed to understand their experiences using technology-assisted feedback during the COVID-19 lockdowns. Our findings show that the focus of feedback shifted during the pandemic. Over time, both teachers and students became more comfortable navigating online environments, going from self-level feedback that provided little support for learning to using technologies in innovative ways to create opportunities for dialogue around feedback and learning. We provide directions for future research and suggestions on how these findings can inform the creation of teacher training opportunities.

Keywords: Dialogic feedback · Technology-enhanced feedback · Learning communities · COVID-19

1 Introduction

The COVID-19 pandemic disrupted educational activities around the world, forcing educational institutions to adopt online learning and posing urgent questions regarding how teachers can adapt their practice to online environments and support students during this rapid change to teaching and learning. The lockdowns associated with the pandemic forced teachers to re-imagine how they related to students, including how they used feedback to establish dialogue about

Supported by British Academy.

I. Hilliger et al. (Eds.): EC-TEL 2022, LNCS 13450, pp. 528–533, 2022.
https://doi.org/10.1007/978-3-031-16290-9_46

learning with their students and provide them with support to engage with their learning process and adapt to the new online learning environments. One of the ways in which teachers can do this is through dialogic feedback, which helps students develop feedback literacy - the practices, skills and attributes that allow students to understand and use the feedback they receive [8].

This type of literacy needs to be cultivated and developed, which means that teachers need to develop their own feedback literacy to nurture the skills needed to design and manage environments that enable students to develop feedback literacy and create the conditions for dialogue around feedback [3]. They can achieve this by incorporating feedback literacy into their class design and by using dialogue to clarify feedback and set expectations for students [2]. Dialogue also fosters interactions and helps build relationships between students and teachers, and is an essential factor in creating a sense of psychological closeness in online environments, where there are limited opportunities for students and teachers to interact with each other [9]. This is especially important in the context of the COVID-19 lockdowns, when opportunities for in-person interaction were virtually nonexistent.

Research has found that the creative use of technologies also helps develop a sense of closeness between teachers and students and foster relationships between them. Ryan et al. [7], for example, found multimedia feedback much more effective than text-only, with video feedback and screencasts being better than audio feedback because they conveyed richer information and non-verbal cues to help students understand feedback.

However, teacher training has not kept up with the use of new technologies, and teachers are seldom trained in the pedagogy of applying technologies to provide feedback and create learning communities [6]. This became particularly evident during the pandemic, as teachers struggled to move their classes and materials online with little preparation or training [4].

The purpose of this study was therefore to understand in-service and pre-service teachers' experiences with using technology-enhanced feedback to create learning communities and support their students during the COVID-19 lockdowns. This will allow us to draw lessons from practices teachers employed during the pandemic which could help inform future teacher training programs.

2 Methodology

Six in-service teachers were recruited through professional networks and ten pre-service teachers were recruited from universities in Scotland and Australia known for their teacher training programmes. The in-service teachers had an average of 12 years' experience, and the pre-service teachers had their first experiential placement during the lockdowns.

Data was collected through interviews with in-service teachers and focus groups with pre-service teachers. Given the busy schedule of in-service teachers, one to one interviews were chosen for flexibility. Focus groups were chosen for pre-service teachers because this format allowed them to support each other's responses given their shared experiences.

Interview questions focused on how their feedback-giving practices changed during the pandemic, the responses they received from students to the feedback they had provided, their use of technology to provide students with feedback, and the pros and cons of using technology-assisted feedback to connect with students.

The interviews and focus groups were transcribed and coded using thematic analysis. We identified two major themes related to teachers' use of feedback during the pandemic: the purpose of the feedback teachers gave to their students, and the medium through which feedback was delivered.

The purposes of feedback were encouragement, engagement and feedback for learning and revision. In our sample, feedback was delivered through multimedia, written means, or verbally. An elaboration of these codes can be found in Table 1.

Table 1. Coding scheme.

Code	Subcode	Definition
Purpose of feedback	Encouragement	Feedback meant to motivate or encourage students regardless of performance
	Engagement	Feedback meant to elicit engagement with students, not necessarily task-related
	Learning and revisions	Feedback to help students monitor their progress in relation to their goals
Mode of feedback	Multimedia feedback	Using audio, video or other multimedia to deliver feedback
	Written feedback	Feedback given through written means
	Verbal feedback	Feedback given verbally in-person or in synchronous virtual environments

3 Results

Our results showed a shift in the mode and purpose of feedback during the pandemic. At the beginning of the pandemic, several participants reported providing mostly encouraging feedback, which consisted of phrases such as 'good job!', 'well done!' and 'thank you!' because they lacked experience with online teaching and wanted to support student well-being by being encouraging. As one participant put it: "even if it wasn't maybe the best work or they hadn't gotten that much right on the answers, you didn't say oh, try again, you'd just be like thanks for engaging, like have a good weekend". Pre-service teachers mentioned giving this type of feedback more than in-service teachers (40% of their total utterances as opposed to 20% for in-service teachers), and mentioned lacked confidence in their authority to provide feedback as one of the reasons: "I didn't feel confident giving them anything too super formal, but it was a lot of just like, just trying to generally be encouraging".

This 'self-level feedback' gives little or no information about the task [5], and has been found to be detrimental to learning [1] because it takes away attention from the task. Participants reported wanting to learn skills to provide more constructive feedback, pointing out that, despite their best intentions, encouraging feedback did little to help with learning and students rarely participated in online lessons in response to this type of feedback. One teacher specifically mentioned that "there's nothing there for them to respond, there's no expectation. I mean I had to train them to look for the feedback for a start".

As teachers began receiving training in using technologies and got more comfortable with online teaching, they started giving students feedback designed to enhance learning and revision. One initial challenge was that teachers predominantly used comment boxes on the learning management platforms to provide feedback, a medium which has been found to be ineffective in helping students understand and act on feedback [7]. Our participants remarked students did not find these comments helpful and rarely took action based on them. One participant even noted many students were not aware they had received feedback or did not know how to find it on the learning platforms. This seems to indicate students did not have sufficient feedback literacy to seek feedback, did not have enough knowledge of the learning platforms to use them effectively, and/or teachers did not have enough online feedback literacy to create an environment where students would know where to find this feedback and how to use it. Pre-service teachers especially struggled with this, as they received little training and lacked confidence in their skills to experiment.

However, most participants did not limit themselves to giving feedback through text boxes, especially during subsequent lockdowns when they'd had an opportunity to upskill in the use of different technologies through training offered by their institutions and through resource-sharing within their professional networks. Synchronous feedback delivered using videoconferencing software was one of the tools teachers used to get students involved in their own learning. Some teachers set up one-to-one sessions with their students or used breakout rooms to divide their students into smaller groups so feedback could be manageable and personalized. One in-service teacher mentioned that setting one-to-one meetings using videoconferencing software meant that students "felt valued, and I think that helped the engagement as well because they weren't left behind". Another in-service teacher mentioned using the 'share screen' function of the videoconferencing software to annotate and discuss students' work. The participant reported that this method of delivering feedback, also called screencasting, was very well-received by students, who began sharing their screens without being prompted so they could receive feedback.

In-service teachers also turned to multimedia asynchronous feedback, recording audio clips to give students specific feedback on their work. Multimedia feedback tends to be considered more personal and more useful by students, given that it can provide them with more verbal and non-verbal cues than written feedback [7], and reduces the feeling of psychological distance between teachers and students [9]. Our participants reported their students appreciated the verbal and multimedia feedback, and it elicited a higher rate of responses from students than feedback given through comment boxes. One participant mentioned that the students thanked them for providing audio feedback, as "it was very personalised and they were able to work on, like again, how do they improve it". Another participant mentioned that their students specifically requested more video feedback, as "being able to do something like that for their learning, for feedback, especially the personalised ones, they were just really good" because "they could pause, rewind and just go through at their own pace".

It is interesting to note that only in-service teachers mentioned taking advantage of multimedia to provide students with feedback. This might be due to two reasons: first, pre-service teachers mentioned feeling like they did not have the authority to provide students with comprehensive feedback, and so might have been less inclined to experiment with different modes of feedback. Second, their placements lasted only a few weeks, so they did not have the same opportunities as in-service teachers to experiment and upskill.

4 Conclusions

The training teachers received during the pandemic helped them move from feedback that encouraged students without giving them actionable information on their learning, to learning and revision feedback given through comment boxes that did not necessarily encourage them to take action, to more useful multimedia feedback that helped students engage more with their learning.

Three main lessons can be gleaned from these results to aid in teacher training. First, one struggle mentioned by the teachers was that students rarely used the feedback they received and, in some cases, were not even aware they had received feedback. Given that students do not inherently have feedback literacy, teachers need to support them by integrating feedback into their course design [3]. Therefore, teachers should be taught how to integrate feedback loops into their online course design so students are incentivised to find and use feedback. This includes creating opportunities to seek out and apply feedback to their work as part of the class design.

Second, the overwhelming use of comment boxes to provide feedback at the beginning of the pandemic might have been another cause for lack of engagement, given that written feedback has been found to be lacking in guidance and more impersonal when compared to multimedia feedback [7], especially in online contexts where there opportunities for student-teacher interaction are more limited and the lack of face-to-face interactions makes it harder to build relationships [9]. Teachers should be taught different options in multimedia technologies to provide dialogic feedback that can foster learning, such as audio and video feedback, and screencasts, which our participants reported were much more effective.

Third, one of the main struggles our teachers faced was lack of experience in online environments, so providing teachers with experiences teaching online is key in helping teachers bridge the gap between theoretical knowledge about the use of technologies and implementing them in an online classroom setting.

Future research should investigate what specific skills should be developed by teachers to help them promote feedback literacy skills in online environments and create the conditions for dialogue around feedback with their students. Research should also focus on how teacher training and experiential learning can help teachers develop these skills and acquire the experience they need to support students in online or hybrid environments.

References

1. Brooks, C., Carroll, A., Gillies, R.M., Hattie, J.: A matrix of feedback for learning. Aust. J. Teach. Educ. (Online) **44**(4), 14–32 (2019)
2. Carless, D., Boud, D.: The development of student feedback literacy: enabling uptake of feedback. Assess. Eval. High. Educ. **43**(8), 1315–1325 (2018)
3. Carless, D., Winstone, N.: Teacher feedback literacy and its interplay with student feedback literacy. Teach. High. Educ. 1–14 (2020)
4. Carrillo, C., Flores, M.A.: Covid-19 and teacher education: a literature review of online teaching and learning practices. Eur. J. Teach. Educ. **43**(4), 466–487 (2020)
5. Hattie, J., Timperley, H.: The power of feedback. Rev. Educ. Res. **77**(1), 81–112 (2007)
6. Ottenbreit-Leftwich, A., Liao, J.Y.C., Sadik, O., Ertmer, P.: Evolution of teachers' technology integration knowledge, beliefs, and practices: How can we support beginning teachers use of technology? J. Res. Technol. Educ. **50**(4), 282–304 (2018)
7. Ryan, T., Henderson, M., Phillips, M.: Feedback modes matter: comparing student perceptions of digital and non-digital feedback modes in higher education. Br. J. Educ. Technol. **50**(3), 1507–1523 (2019)
8. Sutton, P.: Towards dialogic feedback. Crit. Reflective Practice Educ. **1**(1) (2009)
9. Swan, K.: Building learning communities in online courses: the importance of interaction. Educ. Commun. Inf. **2**(1), 23–49 (2002)

Development of Actionable Insights for Regulating Students' Collaborative Writing of Scientific Texts

Christian Hoffmann[1](✉), Nadine Mandran[1], Cédric d'Ham[1], Sébastien Rebaudo[1], and Mohamed Anis Haddouche[2]

[1] Univ. Grenoble Alpes, CNRS, Grenoble INP, LIG, 38000 Grenoble, France
christian.hoffmann@univ-grenoble-alpes.fr
[2] IMT Atlantique, LABSTICC, 29238 Brest, France

Abstract. We develop indicators for teachers to monitor and regulate students' collaborative writing on a web-based science learning environment. Visualizations of carefully selected indicators are proposed to teachers in order to facilitate the tracking, analysis and management of the students' collaborative work process over time. Our research method is based on a user-centered approach. Via focus groups and interviews, teachers have participated in the design of the indicators and visualizations. This communication presents (a) the mapping from collected data to educational constructs underlying our analytical approach for collaborative writing, (b) indicators and visualizations produced to provide actionable insights to teachers, and (c) lessons learned from our iterative human-centered design process. The results are transferable to other learning environments and design processes.

Keywords: Collaborative learning · Collaborative writing · Learning analytics dashboards · User centered design

1 Introduction and Motivation

Supported by online learning environments (OLE), collaborative writing (CW) of scientific texts is nowadays a frequent task asked to students at high school and university level. The aim of our work, falling within the field of educational collaboration analytics, is to deliver actionable insights [1] to teachers via a learning analytics dashboard (LAD) [2], *i.e.* figures and visualizations that allow tracking and regulating students' group writing in order to improve collaboration and group learning. Many research papers in the field of computer supported collaborative writing (CSCW), *e.g.* [3–5], are situated in the context of well-defined collaboration scripts allowing the collection and combined analysis of various data (data traces, chat messages, in class observations, etc.). By collaboration script we mean here the specification of a sequence of activities structuring the interaction between learners [6]. We address in this paper a more general case: automated characterization of CW based solely on data traces, designated to OLEs that can

I. Hilliger et al. (Eds.): EC-TEL 2022, LNCS 13450, pp. 534–541, 2022.
https://doi.org/10.1007/978-3-031-16290-9_47

support a wide variety of collaboration scripts of which little is known when designing the analytics on the platform.

Starting from the general problematic dealing with how to improve students' CW of scientific documents on OLEs, we investigate in this communication the following research question: how to measure the degree of collaboration and communicate it effectively to teachers in a LAD?

2 Theoretical Framework

Collaborative Writing

Several authors tried to categorize CW establishing taxonomies of writing strategies and student roles [7, 8]. Onrubia *et al.* [4] observed five different strategies, differentiating in particular between *summative text construction, i.e.* each student adds his text without modifying the text of the others, the result being a juxtaposition of the individual contributions and an *integrative text construction, i.e.* one student proposes an initial version and the other students contribute successively making modifications on the existing. This joins the distinction between cooperative and collaborative work organization. The first is characterized by an explicit division of work between the team members, *i.e.* each student writes a part of the text, the second by a co-construction of the text, *i.e.* all team members take responsibility of the whole text aligning their viewpoints. Students do not necessarily follow one well defined strategy but often a mix of them [9].

Collaboration Analytics for LADs

The challenge for designers of LADs is to provide teachers with actionable group insights defined by Jorno & Gynther [1] as "*data that allows a corrective procedure, or feedback loop, established for a set of actions*". Martinez-Maldonado *et al.* [10] elaborated a conceptual model of collaboration analytics where these actionable insights are the main output. They emphasize the role of a clear "*mapping from low-level data to higher-order constructs that are educationally meaningful, and that can be understood by educators and learners*" for the assessment of the validity of collaboration analytics. They proposed a generic five-steps mapping scheme: Data → Derived features → Behavioral markers → Sub-constructs → Higher order constructs.

In order to characterize students' writing strategies (an example of an educational higher order construct), the CSCW literature suggests different concepts. We outline here two of them that we mobilize in our analytics: symmetry of action and territorial functioning. "*Symmetry of action is the extent to which the same range of actions is allowed to each agent*" [11]. This is usually guaranteed in educational OLEs designed for students, but the question remains to what extent users really use their capabilities and are actually symmetric *in* their action. The second construct we mobilize, territorial functioning, that indicates if the authors write in separate document spaces or revisit the text written by others, was discussed in the context of CSCW of academic documents by Larsen-Ledet & Korsgaard [12]. In addition to the chronology of the text's revisions, they paid particular attention to their spatial position in the document. Territorial behaviors of authors have multiple origins, as for example affective and cultural aspects, social norms, but depends also strongly on the particular task design and work organization in the group.

3 Design and Research Method

We work according to the Design Based Research framework following the properties: "*anchored in the field, pragmatic, collaborative, integrative, iterative, flexible, traceability and generalization*" [13]. Indeed, our research is anchored in a real-life context: (i) we develop a web-based learning environment, called LabNbook, designed for supporting learners in the collaborative writing of scientific documents, which is used by more than 3500 students every year [14]; (ii) we work with all the stakeholders for designing the platform and evaluating it. We proceed in an iterative way so that the produced tools evolve throughout the implementation in the platform. The experimental process is fully documented [15].

To construct and evaluate our contributions, we pursue the following research agenda: a) define the indicators and visualizations allowing to characterize CW activities in terms of educational constructs, involving LAD experts and teachers, b) validate the produced artifacts with the users (acceptability, utility, usability) and c) evaluate the impact of the actual use of the artifacts. In this paper, we report results after going through the stages a) and b) several times in an iterative five step process:

Step 1: Construction of indicators and first visualization mockups by the designers of LabNbook who use it themselves in their teaching in experimental sciences.
Step 2: Semi-directive 40 to 60-min interviews with three teachers (two experienced users of LabNbook and one novice). The exchanges covered (i) teachers' concerns when monitoring the collaborative work of their students, (ii) the usability of the indicators and their understanding, and (iii) the potential utility of the mockups.
Step 3: Production of a second version of the indicators and mockups by researchers.
Step 4: Two focus groups with developers of LADs and teachers using LabNbook. The first focus group (8 participants) was centered on the usability of the indicators, the second (4 participants) on the design and utility of the visualizations.
Step 5: New iteration regarding indicators and mockups. We present in Sect. 4 and 5 the resulting versions at this stage.

4 Analyzing Sequential Collaborative Writing of Scientific Texts

The Field Context: A Web-Based Science Learning Environment
On the LabNbook environment, the teacher can structure the workspace shared by a team of learners according to his learning objectives, *e.g.* the writing of lab notebooks or scientific reports during laboratories, problem-based learning sessions or long-term projects. The scientific output produced by the team of learners, called "report", is an ensemble of different documents, following the structure provided by the teacher. LabNbook operates in a "locked co-editing" mode [16], *i.e.* students can work simultaneously

in the shared workspace but each document composing it can be edited only by one student at the time. Teachers can access learners' productions at any time to be informed of their progress and to send them feedback. For facilitating the monitoring of the learners, the environment provides a LAD for each report. The present work aims at enhancing the existing LAD with a visualization that help teachers to situate students' writing strategies, *e.g.* to distinguish summative from integrative text construction [4].

Mapping "From Clicks to Constructs"

In Fig. 1, we present a mapping scheme, inspired from Martinez-Maldonado *et al.* [11], in order to explain our CW analytics on LabNbook. We split the one-dimensional diagram used in [11] into two parts to bring to light two main processes involved in educational collaboration analytics: (i) teachers' diagnosis and (ii) design choices.

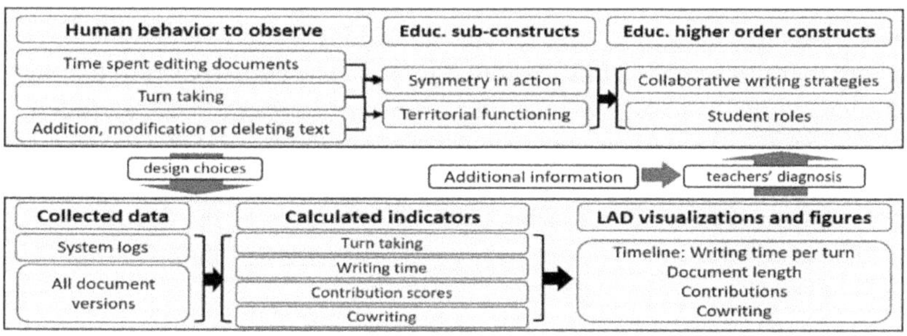

Fig. 1. Mapping of the implemented collaboration analytics

(i) Consistent with the goal of addressing OLEs that support a variety of collaboration scripts, we limit the analysis on LabNbook to the descriptive level and leave the diagnosis to teachers. They can most of the time combine their interpretation of the information given in the LAD with additional information *e.g.* in class observations, exchanges with students, *etc.*, in order to evaluate the ongoing collaboration process in terms of relevant educational constructs. (ii) During the design process, choices are made about which data to collect in order to describe the human behavior, which necessarily leads to an approximate representation.

The lower part of Fig. 1 traces the computer treatment from the collected data via the calculated indicators to the visualizations and figures communicated in the LAD. To capture students' behavior, we collect the following data: who edits a document (authorship), when (timestamp) and a version of the document each time the student validates his contribution.

Indicators to Characterize Collaborative Writing of Scientific Texts

Our analytics are based on the educational sub-constructs described in Sect. 2, symmetry in action and territorial functioning, for which we had to find a translation in terms of computationally calculable indicators.

To evaluate the symmetry in action we construct three indicators, calculated at the level of each document composing a report: (i) turn taking, (ii) writing time and (iii) contribution scores. (i) Turn taking is the number of editor changes. Each time the contributor to the document changes, the indicator is incremented by one. (ii) Writing time is an approximation for the time spent by a student in modifying the document. The system checks for modifications every 30 s, so only 30 s periods when changes are actually made are added up. The writing time is therefore more significative as the usually measured connection time (timespan between login and logout) which contains a larger fraction of inactivity time. (iii) To convert the iterative text modifications in contribution scores for each student, we use the python library 'difflib': the score corresponds to the number of words that the student wrote.

Consistent with automated analytics at a descriptive level, our evaluation of territorial functioning is limited to the observation of the successive authors contributions to the shared document. To this end, we construct a cowriting indicator. The cowriting measures to what extend changes are made by one (or more) author(s) on a text passage produced by another author. The choice of the size of the text passage to consider is not evident. In the actual implementation, we chose to detect cowriting at the level of sentences because we consider them as semantic units where a joint intervention indicates the negotiation of ideas, characteristic of collaboration, in contrast to cooperation. Extending the size of the relevant text passages to paragraphs could be another sound choice. The cowriting score of a document is expressed as a percentage: 0% means that all sentences have been written by a single author; 100% means that all sentences of the document have been written collaboratively.

5 Visualization of the Collaborative Writing Process

Figure 2 shows the visualization that we designed to track the CW on LabNbook. In the example, a team of 3 students produced a report composed of 8 different documents.

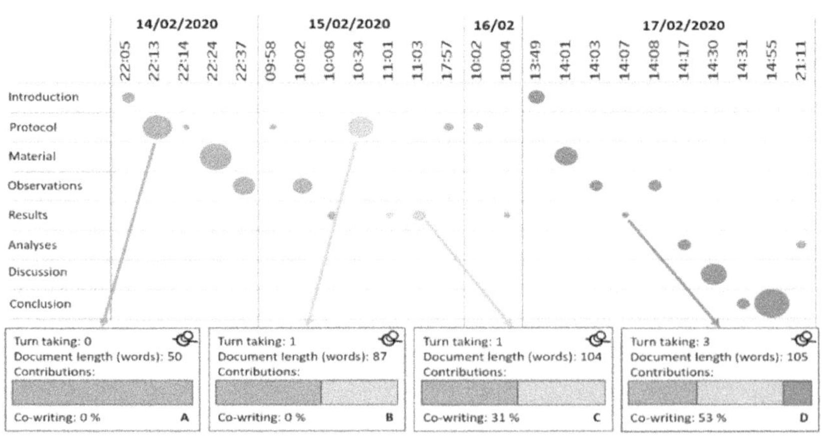

Fig. 2. Mockup for the visualization of CW processes

Each line corresponds to a document with its name in the first column. The x-axis is the timeline and each bubble represents the saving of a new version of the document. We have chosen an equal distance layout (same space between two savings) not a continuous time axis. Three elements of information are given directly in the timeline for each document version: who worked on the document (a different color per student), when it was edited (axis) and the writing time (area of the bubble). With a click on a bubble, the teacher can display additional information in a panel (A to D in Fig. 2) that can be pinned under the timeline: the number of turn takings up to the date, the length of the document (in # of words), the individual contributions (visualized by a stacked bar chart) and the Cowriting score of the document.

Visualization as in Fig. 2 allows a teacher to get a wealth of information about how the report was co-constructed, among others: work duration, work phases, student roles and type of collaboration. We discuss here only the latter, based on the two couples of example panels A/B and C/D. The construction of the "Protocol" (2nd line) is *summative*: student "blue" wrote the beginning (panel A), then student "yellow" added a second part, without revisiting the existing text (Cowriting stays at 0 in panel B). On the contrary, for the "Results" (5th line): student "blue" initiated the document, student "yellow" completed editing some of the existing text (Cowriting at 31% in panel C) and finally student "green" revisited the text, barely adding words (Cowriting increases to 53% in panel D). An *integrative* text construction seems to characterize the writing process of the "Results" document.

6 Lessons Learned

Here we report briefly 4 lessons learned from our human centered design process:

1) **Take time for iterations:** the first mockup was created almost a year ago and 3 major iterations have been necessary so far to stabilize the indicators and visualizations. The design process requires time.
2) **Understanding precedes action:** ensure that teachers understand the indicators so that they can take appropriate action. Our experience suggests that teachers need a brief definition and the properties of each indicator while giving the detailed calculation is not necessary.
3) **Be careful with aggregation:** several complementary indicators describing the situation are more appreciated by the teachers than aggregated indicators, which are more difficult to interpret and may prevent action.
4) **Prefer simple visualizations and options:** the teachers in our interviews and focus groups preferred usual at-a-glance visualizations to more sophisticated representations. They asked for opportunities to obtain additional information on demand.

Lessons 3 and 4 confirm similar observations made by Gibson & Martinez-Maldonado [17] and Michos *et al.* [18].

7 Conclusion and Future Work

We propose indicators and visualizations that allow teachers to diagnose the CW activities of their students, adapted to all OLEs offering collaborative sequential editing of texts. They make it possible to distinguish different strategies, such as the following common examples in higher education: task sharing when writing team reports on a project (summative text construction); co-construction of a scientific argument (integrative text construction). Future research can concern semantic analysis of the produced texts in order to examine what kind of integrative writing is ongoing. We are also working on a LAD designated for students. Students should have access to information about their CW process, to enhance awareness, reflection and self-regulation.

References

1. Jørnø, R.L., Gynther, K.: What constitutes an 'actionable insight' in learning analytics? Learn. Anal. **5** (2018)
2. Sedrakyan, G., Mannens, E., Verbert, K.: Guiding the choice of learning dashboard visualizations: linking dashboard design and data visualization concepts. J. Comput. Lang. **50**, 19–38 (2019)
3. Olson, J.S., Wang, D., Olson, G.M., Zhang, J.: How people write together now: beginning the investigation with advanced undergraduates in a project course. ACM Trans. Comput.-Hum. Interact. **24**, 4:1–4:40 (2017)
4. Onrubia, J., Engel, A.: Strategies for collaborative writing and phases of knowledge construction in CSCL environments. Comput. Educ. **53**, 1256–1265 (2009)
5. Sundgren, M., Jaldemark, J.: Visualizing online collaborative writing strategies in higher education group assignments. IJILT **37**, 351–373 (2020)
6. Kobbe, L., et al.: Specifying computer-supported collaboration scripts. Comput. Supp. Learn. **2**, 211–224 (2007)
7. Posner, I.R., Baecker, R.M.: How people write together (groupware). In: Proceedings of the 25th Hawaii International Conference on System Sciences, pp. 127–138. IEEE (1992)
8. Lowry, P.B., Curtis, A., Lowry, M.R.: Building a taxonomy and nomenclature of collaborative writing to improve interdisciplinary research and practice. J. Bus. Commun. **41**, 66–99 (2004)
9. Limbu, L., Markauskaite, L.: How do learners experience joint writing: university students' conceptions of online collaborative writing tasks and environments. Comput. Educ. **82**, 393–408 (2015)
10. Martinez-Maldonado, R., Gaševic, D., Echeverria, V., Fernandez Nieto, G., Swiecki, Z., Buckingham Shum, S.: What do you mean by collaboration analytics? A conceptual model. J. Learn. Anal. **8**, 126–153 (2021)
11. Dillenbourg, P.: What do you mean by collaborative learning? In: Dillenbourg, P. (éd.) Collaborative-learning: Cognitive and Computational Approaches, pp. 1–19. Elsevier, Oxford (1999)
12. Larsen-Ledet, I., Korsgaard, H.: Territorial functioning in collaborative writing. Comput. Supp. Coop. Work (CSCW) **28**(3–4), 391–433 (2019). https://doi.org/10.1007/s10606-019-09359-8
13. Wang, F., Hannafin, M.J.: Design-based research and technology-enhanced learning environments. ETR&D **53**, 5–23 (2005)
14. d'Ham, C., Wajeman, C., Girault, I., Marzin Janvier, P.: Transposition des démarches expérimentales dans un environnement numérique de support. In: Actes des 11e rencontres scientifiques de l'ARDiST, Bruxelles, Belgique, pp. 705–716 (2020)
15. Mandran, N.: Traceable Human Experiment Design Research. ISTE Ltd./Wiley, Hoboken (2017)

16. Wang, D., Tan, H., Lu, T.: Why users do not want to write together when they are writing together: users' rationales for today's collaborative writing practices. Proc. ACM Hum.-Comput. Interact. **1**, 107:1–107:18 (2017)
17. Gibson, A., Martinez-Maldonado, R.: That dashboard looks nice, but what does it mean?: Towards making meaning explicit in learning analytics design. In: Proceedings of the 29th Australian Conference on CHI, pp. 528–532. ACM, Brisbane (2017)
18. Michos, K., Lang, C., Hernández-Leo, D., Price-Dennis, D.: Involving teachers in learning analytics design: lessons learned from two case studies. In: Proceedings of the Tenth International Conference on Learning Analytics & Knowledge, pp. 94–99. Association for Computing Machinery, New York (2020)

Design a Dashboard for Secondary School Learners to Support Mastery Learning in a Gamified Learning Environment

Xinying Hou[1(✉)], Tomohiro Nagashima[2], and Vincent Aleven[2]

[1] University of Michigan, Ann Arbor, MI 48109, USA
xyhou@umich.edu

[2] Carnegie Mellon University, Forbes Avenue, Pittsburgh 5000, USA

Abstract. Although prior studies have shown the benefits of using learning analytics dashboards (LADs) in non-gamified contexts in higher education, few have focused on pre-college users and gamified learning environments. In this paper, we present the design of *Gwynnette Dashboard*, an interactive student-facing LAD for secondary school learners that aims at promoting mastery learning in a gamified intelligent tutoring system. It contains three main components: a planet chart with two control buttons, a connected skill progress bar with a skill mastery growth line, and an overall mastery progress bar. We also report two user-centered design changes after validating our design with 18 students iteratively. Our preliminary evaluation of a fully-developed version with 2 students revealed that this dashboard with linked representations of skill mastery status and skill growth was easy for learners to understand and motivated learners to use it to regulate learning. Our future work will focus on broader classroom studies to experimentally investigate the effectiveness of this dashboard to foster mastery learning and growth mindset.

Keywords: Learning analytics dashboards · Gamification · Visualization

1 Introduction

Learning analytics dashboards (LADs) are visualization tools that provide learners with information regarding their own learning to help spur and support self-reflection [1]. LADs benefit learners in a variety of areas and domains, and they have been extensively researched in different teaching and learning settings [1]. While LADs for teaching and learning in higher education and non-game contexts have been extensively researched [13], designing LADs for pre-university learner groups in more gamified environments is still under-explored, with the exception of a small number of studies (e.g., [5,7]). One of the earliest studies in this area was carried out by Muldner and colleagues [10], who applied a dashboard as an affective intervention for students in Grade 7. Students could

I. Hilliger et al. (Eds.): EC-TEL 2022, LNCS 13450, pp. 542–549, 2022.
https://doi.org/10.1007/978-3-031-16290-9_48

evaluate their effort, consider mastery level, and decide whether to challenge themselves with more difficult tasks with this dashboard. Results from this study indicated that the dashboard led to improvements in students' attitudes and enthusiasm, but it was less successful in encouraging interest.

In this paper, we present *Gwynnette Dashboard*, a learner-facing LAD that is designed to promote secondary school learners' learning engagement and mastery learning in a gamified intelligent tutoring system. Instead of comparing with others, mastery learning focuses on improving one's own talents and attempting to comprehend learning materials themselves [9]. We also report two main design changes based on design idea validation data. Then we display our preliminary evaluation findings with two students. We conclude the paper by discussing future evaluation plans.

2 Context

The dashboard is meant to be used in conjunction with *Gwynette*, a gamified intelligent tutoring system for secondary school algebra learning [11]. The algebra problems that students practice with *Gwynette* are divided into eight difficulty levels based on the number and difficulty of steps required to solve a problem. *Gwynette* has several playful gamification features, including a space travel theme and an alien character who guides student learning in the system. These features were designed to help students engaged with their learning experience.

The *Gwynnette Dashboard* we designed and built, described in this paper, is used as both the home screen and LAD for *Gwynette* (Fig. 1). Learners can enter the practice environment directly from the dashboard page by clicking the yellow "Practice" button on the screen (F1 in Fig. 1), and exit the practice page to check the information on the dashboard whenever they want. In this design, students can start from any planet (i.e., any level) and it is not required to finish one to move on to the next. The data shown on *Gwynnette Dashboard* are powered by user-generated data logged in *Gwynette* (Fig. 2). As the student works through the algebra problems, the dashboard will update its estimate of the probability that the student masters each skill using Bayesian Knowledge Tracing (BKT) model in real-time [2]. Students' goal is to practice until they master each of the skills in a level.

3 Dashboard Overview

Gwynnette Dashboard, a student-facing interactive learning dashboard, provides three types of information in one screen view: (1) Top area: a planet chart with a progress button and a practice button for each level (F1 in Fig. 1), (2) Middle area: mastery celebration message (F2 in Fig. 1), current skill mastery progress bar (F3 in Fig. 1), and skill mastery growth line (F4 in Fig. 1), and (3) Bottom area: overall mastery progress bar across problem sets (F5 in Fig. 1). A fully-functional version was implemented with Vue and the jQWidgets framework.

Top Area: Planet Chart with Control Buttons. Links to the eight problem sets are placed in the top area of the screen as eight planets (F1 in Fig. 1). Each problem set shares a package of algebra skills and is listed in order, starting from the easiest to the most challenging ("Mercury" to "Neptune," respectively). Students are able to check their detailed progress in different levels by clicking on the progress button under each planet with the level name shown on the left, and can also start the corresponding practice by clicking on the practice button. The charts in the middle area will change based on the specific level they choose. Also, the granularity in planets will "fill up" to show the students' level of mastery of the skills for the particular level. And they will gain the badge as a clear planet when representative skills are mastered.

Middle Area: Skill Mastery Progress Bars and Skill Growth Line Graph. In this section, we use two visual elements to show the probability of skill mastery for each skill students have practiced in each problem set. A celebration message is shown at the top of this area (F2 in Fig. 1). Skill mastery progress bars on the left is displayed to help users keep track of progress and understand how close they are to mastering the skills they are working on. All skills included in the problem set are listed from top to bottom to make up the whole skill mastery progress bar chart (F3 in Fig. 1). The skill growth line graph on the right helps students to see how they performed from the beginning to the current stage in the system (F4 in Fig. 1). With such a sequential visualization, we wanted to encourage students to reflect on how their performance has changed over time. In addition, we implemented a range selector under the line graph, which allows users to change the range of the x-axis (i.e., practice attempts) in the chart.

Bottom Area: Overall Skill Mastery Progress Bar. This progress bar with a rocket (F5 in Fig. 1) generates the overall skill mastery progress that is calculated across all the difficulty levels. The design is similar to individual skill progress bars in the middle area.

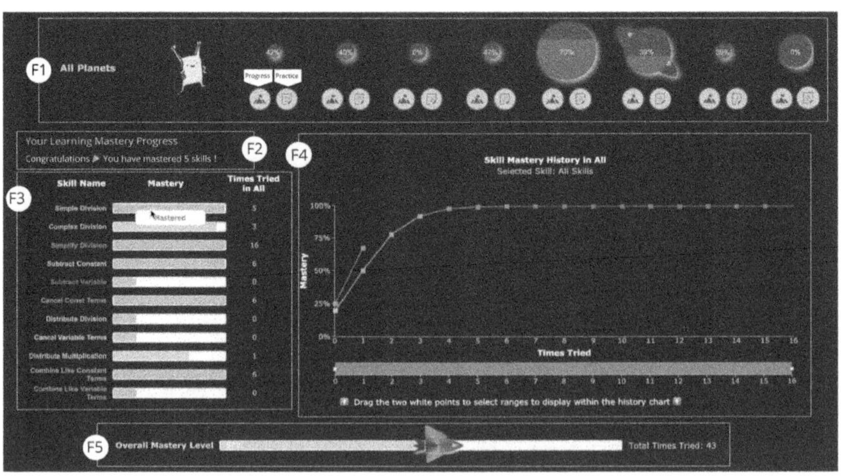

Fig. 1. Dashboard layout with three areas: F1 - Top area; F2 & F3 & F4 - Middle area; F5 - Bottom area

4 Dashboard Design Idea Validation

To create the dashboard, we first engaged secondary school students in a variety of co-design sessions to find the most promising ideas for designing dashboard prototypes (Fig. 3). Based on the insights from these brainstorming sessions, previous work on the gamified design [8], and literature reviews of learner LAD [1], we came up with the initial design. After that, we did two rounds of user testings with 18 secondary school students through interviews, which led to two representative design changes.

Three main visual components were included in the initial design: a spider chart to represent learners' current knowledge level for each of the skills in a level (A1 in Fig. 4); a line chart to show their skill change over time (A2 in Fig. 4); and badges (A3 in Fig. 4). The multi-dimensional spider chart is a typical component in game design to represent character skill structure. We applied it to show students' current skill mastery in this gamified environment. The design motivation behind the line graph was that line graphs were better at showing changes over time, with an expectation that seeing their own growth would be motivating for students. By using this chart, we expected students to develop a good understanding of how their skill has changed over time, which might help them reflect on learning effectively and adjust the way they learn to meet learning goals. As well, it may be motivating for student to be aware that they are gradually becoming better at the new skills. Further, we considered badges as an important component because prior evidence has shown that having badges as a gamification element can promote active use of the system [3].

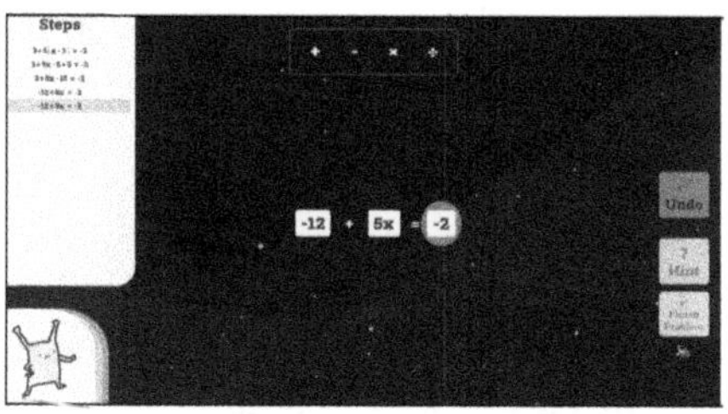

Fig. 2. Screenshot of *Gwynette* practice interface

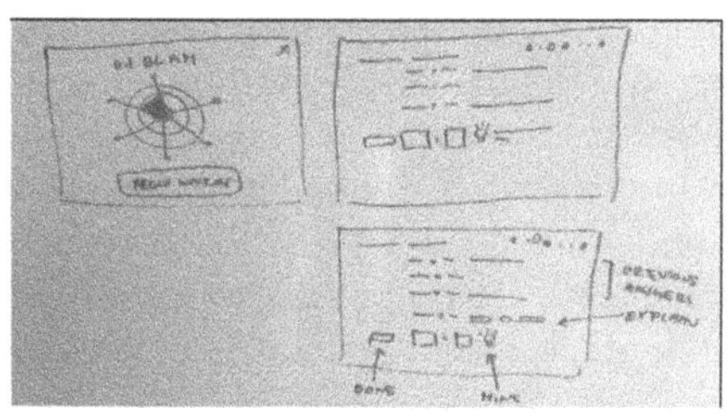

Fig. 3. Screenshot of co-design workshop session with initial brainstorming

We then conducted two rounds of user testing and made design changes based on the feedback we received. In the first round, we tested a medium-fidelity prototype with 10 secondary school learners from five different schools (Grade 5 to Grade 9, all had fundamental algebra knowledge). We let them practice several math problems in the system. Then we showed them the dashboard prototype and asked about their understandings and preferences for visual elements (e.g., "what would this graph tell you?" and "which feature makes more sense?"). In the second round, we evaluated our final dashboard prototype with another eight secondary school students. The same procedure was applied with the high-fidelity prototype.

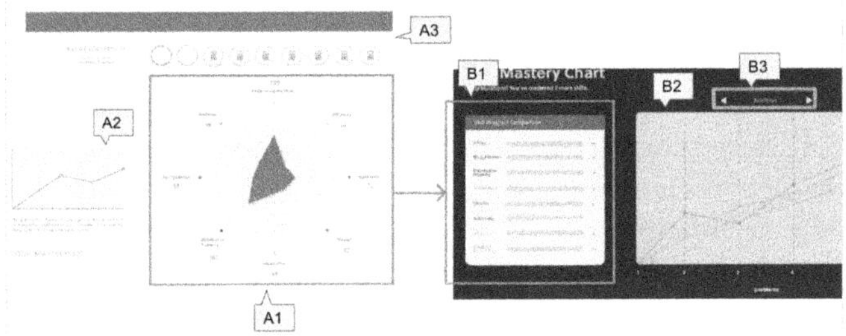

Fig. 4. Screenshots of initial design (left) and design after *Change 1* (right)

Our user studies showed that students expressed a high level of enthusiasm with badges on the screen. They said the badges were "helpful as it tells you what you should work on, or else you might work on the same thing over and over." Students also preferred larger badges since they are more encouraging. As for the line graph to show the skill growth, we found that students generally liked the design of the skill growth graphs and thought it was helpful to see improvements over time, "as long as it's not required to improve every time" (A2 & B2 in Fig. 4). Two design changes are discussed below.

Change 1: Use Easily-Understood Visual Representations (Rules Out Spider Charts for Secondary School Students). We first tested the use of a "spider diagram" (A1 in Fig. 4) or a "progress bar" (B1 in Fig. 4) to show learners' current skill status. Spider diagram was chosen originally as it was a typical visualization in role play game dashboards [4]. However, we realized that students encountered difficulty interpreting spider diagrams as they were confused whether a larger or smaller number in axes indicated better performance. They thought spider diagrams are too complicated, and therefore would not want to use them. For example, one student asked, "will there be an explanation for [the spider chart]? Because I had no idea what it meant at first." To prevent possible misinterpretations, we changed the spider diagram to a set of skill progress bars to show their current skill mastery status, a common visualization in open learner models for students to keep track of learning progress [6].

Change 2: Connect the Representation of Current Skill Status with Growth over Time. We added a connection-making visual cue between the skill progress bar and skill growth line graph as they represent the information about the same bucket of skills. Our hypothesis behind this design is that providing such connection-making scaffold could contribute to a more comprehensive understanding of individual skill learning. Given that we have several skills under one problem set, the old design using left and right buttons to switch highlighted skills in the line graph made those two graphs isolated (B3 in Fig. 4). Therefore, to emphasize these important relations, we added a new visualization cue that shows skill growth and skill status (current probability of mastery) with linked and interactive representations (F3 & F4 in Fig. 1). When users hover on a skill name in the bar, the name of the selected skill will show in the subtitle, and the hovered line will be highlighted with its mastery status percentage on each practice attempt. Also, to create the connection between the same skills that appear both in the bar and the line, the corresponding skill label on the left progress bar would also be highlighted when hovering on the right line and vice versa.

5 Preliminary Evaluation Findings

With *Gwynnette Dashboard*, which had undergone several design and evaluation iterations, we hoped that students could interpret the dashboard components correctly and guide their learning behavior. To evaluate these hypothesized outcomes, we conducted an exploratory user study to investigate how our targeted users would understand and use the current fully-functional dashboard. We recruited two secondary school students for a remote think-aloud/interview session individually. Our results showed that students generally understood the meaning of those visual representations, and were able to use the dashboard to inform strategic next actions (e.g., one student said "[I] probably need to do more" after seeing low mastery percent in the second planet).

To be more specific, when it comes to the skill bar, students understood the meaning of each skill label and bars in general. For example, when being asked about the grey bars, one of them said "[it means] I haven't started". And for the skill history chart, they were able to understand that the line chart showed them "how much you improved each time you tried," and when pointing to a line starts at the bottom left and goes towards the top right reaching nearly 100% mastery, one user interpreted correctly; "[I have] worked on it the whole time, really getting good on it". From a behavioral point of view, when we asked them what they would do next after seeing the skill progress bars (F3 in Fig. 1), one student said, "[I would] work on lessons I haven't started", and "[I would] keep working on mastering lessons" when seeing the overall mastery level bar (F5 in Fig. 1). Future studies with actual behavioral data would help to see whether the dashboard would contribute to strategic behaviors in skill mastery.

6 Future Work and Conclusion

In this early work, we added gamification components to develop a learner-facing learning analytics dashboard in a gamified intelligent tutoring system. Our preliminary results showed that this dashboard design is understandable, easy to interpret, and has the potential to support students' decision-making behaviors in their learning. This dashboard design also enables us to explore the effects of showing skill growth over time, which might be motivating, as well as effects of linking representations of skill growth and current skill mastery.

To further investigate the effectiveness of the *Gwynnette Dashboard*, we are planning to conduct a randomized controlled study in an authentic classroom environment to test how students' learning gain, their attitudes and behavior changes towards mastery learning and growth mindsets will be influenced by the use of the dashboard, following the learning analytics process model [12]. Our results will demonstrate whether the use of the a gamified LAD with linked representations of skill mastery and skill growth over time will provide benefits in guiding users' practice behaviors to achieve higher mastery learning when compared against students without access to the dashboard. Moreover, we will use the log data to gather detailed behavioral traces from user interactions to triangulate research findings.

References

1. Bodily, R., Verbert, K.: Review of research on student-facing learning analytics dashboards and educational recommender systems. IEEE Trans. Learn. Technol. **10**(4), 405–418 (2017)
2. Corbett, A.T., Anderson, J.R.: Knowledge tracing: modeling the acquisition of procedural knowledge. User Model. User-Adap. Inter. **4**(4), 253–278 (1994)
3. Hamari, J.: Do badges increase user activity? A field experiment on the effects of gamification. Comput. Hum. Behav. **71**, 469–478 (2017)
4. Hartwig, K., Reuter, C.: Nudging users towards better security decisions in password creation using whitebox-based multidimensional visualisations. Behav. Inf. Technol. **41**(7), 1357–1380 (2022)
5. Hou, X., Nguyen, H.A., Richey, J.E., McLaren, B.M.: Exploring how gender and enjoyment impact learning in a digital learning game. In: Bittencourt, I.I., Cukurova, M., Muldner, K., Luckin, R., Millán, E. (eds.) AIED 2020. LNCS (LNAI), vol. 12163, pp. 255–268. Springer, Cham (2020). https://doi.org/10.1007/978-3-030-52237-7_21
6. Lane, H.C.: Intelligent tutoring systems: prospects for guided practice and efficient learning (2006)
7. Long, Y., Aleven, V.: Mastery-oriented shared student/system control over problem selection in a linear equation tutor. In: Micarelli, A., Stamper, J., Panourgia, K. (eds.) ITS 2016. LNCS, vol. 9684, pp. 90–100. Springer, Cham (2016). https://doi.org/10.1007/978-3-319-39583-8_9
8. Long, Y., Holstein, K., Aleven, V.: What exactly do students learn when they practice equation solving? Refining knowledge components with the additive factors model. In: Proceedings of the 8th International Conference on Learning Analytics and Knowledge, pp. 399–408 (2018)
9. Meece, J.L., Anderman, E.M., Anderman, L.H.: Classroom goal structure, student motivation, and academic achievement. Annu. Rev. Psychol. **57**, 487–503 (2006)
10. Muldner, K., Wixon, M., Rai, D., Burleson, W., Woolf, B., Arroyo, I.: Exploring the impact of a learning dashboard on student affect. In: Conati, C., Heffernan, N., Mitrovic, A., Verdejo, M.F. (eds.) AIED 2015. LNCS (LNAI), vol. 9112, pp. 307–317. Springer, Cham (2015). https://doi.org/10.1007/978-3-319-19773-9_31

11. Nagashima, T., et al.: Designing playful intelligent tutoring software to support engaging and effective algebra learning. In: Hilliger, I., et al. (eds.) EC-TEL 2022, LNCS 13450, pp. xx–yy. Springer, Cham (2022)
12. Verbert, K., Duval, E., Klerkx, J., Govaerts, S., Santos, J.L.: Learning analytics dashboard applications. Am. Behav. Sci. **57**(10), 1500–1509 (2013)
13. Verbert, K., et al.: Learning dashboards: an overview and future research opportunities. Pers. Ubiquit. Comput. **18**(6), 1499–1514 (2014)

Towards an Authoring Tool to Help Teachers Create Mobile Collaborative Learning Games for Field Trips

Iza Marfisi-Schottman[1(✉)], Aurélie Laine[2], Pierre Laforcade[1], Sébastien George[1], Sebastian Simon[1], Madeth May[1], Moez Zammit[2], and Ludovic Blin[2]

[1] LIUM, Le Mans Université, 72085 Le Mans, Cedex 9, France
iza.marfisi@univ-lemans.fr
[2] CREN, Nantes Université, Nantes, France

Abstract. Pedagogical activities that combine mobility, collaboration and game mechanics present significant advantages to attract students' attention and maintain their engagement in learning. Teachers naturally try to combine mobility and collaboration when they create field trips. Indeed, they identify several Points Of Interest that learners physically need to go to, thus requiring mobility, and they usually group students in teams to encourage collaboration, even if such collaboration is seldom attained. However, using the third element - game mechanics - is harder for teachers because they are not familiar with game models and often not gamers themselves. In this article, we present the MOCOGA Model, a MObile COllaborative learning GAme Model that is designed to adapt to many types of field trips. This model also offers a nested design approach that guides teachers in enriching their field trips iteratively. This model is the first step towards the development of an authoring tool that will enable teachers to create their own smartphone applications.

Keywords: Field trip · Mobile learning · Learning Game · Serious Game · Collaborative Learning · Situated learning · Game mechanics · Authoring tool

1 Introduction

Learning is a complex process that is still not fully understood. However, research has identified several ways of providing conditions that improve learning such as **collaboration**, **mobility** and **game mechanics** [1]. Teachers naturally use collaboration and mobility when they organize educational **field trips**. Indeed, they usually group their students in teams to promote collaboration, and provide them with several Points Of Interest (POIs) they need to find in order to complete activities (*e.g.* answer questions, identify a plant, make field observations). Yet, field trips allow for the integration of another beneficial element for learning: **game mechanics**. Indeed, the concept of Learning Games (Serious Game for education) has shown great potential lately. When used

I. Hilliger et al. (Eds.): EC-TEL 2022, LNCS 13450, pp. 550–557, 2022.
https://doi.org/10.1007/978-3-031-16290-9_49

correctly, game mechanics such as competition, rewards, social recognition or exploration [2] enhance the learners' experience with emotions, which has positive effects on their motivation to start the activity, their engagement throughout the learning process and their memory [3].

In addition, now that almost all teenagers and adults own smartphones and schools are often equipped with tablets, the use of **mobile devices** can offer several advantages. Indeed, the functionalities of mobile devices, such as the GPS location system, can help students find the POIs. The camera and the audio recorder in smartphones can also be very useful for recording field observations. Finally, smartphone applications offer the possibility providing information about a POI when learners are physically in the right place and automatic corrections of the activities. Hence, the use of **digital Mobile Collaborative Learning Games** (MOCOGAs) has great potential for learning during field trips.

In this paper, we first briefly analyze the existing digital Mobile Collaborative Learning Games (MOCOGAs), in addition to a selection of digital and non-digital collaborative games, to extract common game mechanics and elements that are compatible with field trips. Section 2 presents the **digital Mobile Collaborative Learning Games Model** (MOCOGA Model). The third section presents a **step-by-step design process** that helps teachers transform their current field trip progressively into a MOCOGA. The last section presents the ongoing work on the authoring tool that will integrate the MOCOGA Model and upcoming experimentations.

2 Identifying Game Mechanics and Elements for MOCOGAs

The objective of this study is to provide teachers with a simple model and authoring tool that allow them to create mobile collaborative games for their field trips. It is therefore necessary to identify simple game mechanics and elements that **combine mobility and collaboration** and that are **adapted to educational field trips.**

To our knowledge, there are no such models and authoring tools yet. It is, however, possible to find a few authoring tools for solo mobile educational games such as orienteering races [4], city visits [5] and onboarding sessions to help new employees get familiar with office spaces and services [6]. These authoring tools provide several game mechanics that use mobility for learning, but not collaboration. It is also hard to extract game mechanics from existing MOCOGAs because there are very few [7, 8] and their game scenarios are specific to their educational goals and context.

We therefore extend our search for game mechanics and elements to collaborative games which are played outdoors such as *Capture the Flag* and collaborative board games that could be adapted to field trips such as *Pandemic.* Finally, we also identified several collaborative and multiplayer video games for which the game elements could be adapted to field trips. In all, 19 digital and non-digital multiplayer games were analyzed. The identified game elements are summarized in Table 1.

Several other game elements where identified such as hidden role (*Ware wolf, Among US, Spy party, Murder*), slowing the best players down to keep the game more interesting (*Mario Kart*), one against all (*Predator, Battle-royal*) or the means to come back into the game if you lose (*Call of Duty*). However, these game mechanics seemed either too complex to set up or not adapted to educational field trips.

Table 1. Summary of the identified game elements

Game elements	Description	Pedagogical value	Games that use it
Customizable and recognizable teams	Allow players to choose the name and color for their team	Increase the students' sense of belonging to the team and incentive to help each other	*Capture the Flag, chicken-fox-viper, Domination Game*
Team base camp	Safe zone, where players can regenerate their health, rest and discuss privately	Allow students to take time to assimilate knowledge and use it to find and discuss a common strategy	*Capture the Flag, Overwatch, Counter Attack Multiplayer FPS*
Team synchronization	Team members must synchronize (*e.g.* be at the same place at the same time) to do an action	Force collaboration between team members	*Portal 2 Co-Op, It takes two, Tango, We were there, It takes two, Keep talking and nobody explodes* and some *domination games*
Complementary knowledge or roles	Team members must coordinate to make the best use of their complementary knowledge or powers	Encourage collaboration and participation of all team members	MOCOGAs [7, 8], *It takes two, Forbidden Island, Tango, We were there, Pandemic, Unlock, Keep talking and nobody explodes, Overwatch*

3 Mobile Collaborative Learning Game Model

The game mechanics and elements identified above were transformed into the MOCOGA game model presented in Fig. 1, with the help of seven pilot teachers**.** This model is intentionally as simple as possible so that teachers have a clear idea of how the game will unfold and for students to start the activities quickly and not be mentally overloaded [9]. This model (boxes with green stripes) is built on a previous solo Field Trip model [10]. For the sake of clarity, we will describe the key concepts: a *Field Trip* is composed of several *Situated Game Units* that are triggered when the players arrive at a *Point Of Interest*; teachers can provide students with *Information* about the objects of interest in close proximity (*e.g.* tree, lake, stones, building) and ask them to complete several *Activities* such as *Answer a Question*, for which they can win points.

Our contribution - the MOCOGA Model – improves the previous model with new concepts: students are now grouped into ***Teams*** of 2 to 5 players and choose a name and a color. By default, the students team up by themselves but teachers can also compose the groups by choosing students with complementary skills for example. The position of each player is shown on the interactive map with the color of their team. Each team has a ***Base Camp*** from which they will head out to get information and then come back.

The collaborative field trip is composed of several ***Milestones*** (approximately 3 to 5) that are related to one of the skills to be acquired during the field trip. Each milestone contains several *Situated Game Units* (about 4 to 10). Teachers can add a ***time lock*** to the field trip which will encourage team members to coordinate and distribute these game units among themselves in order to win the most points in the allotted time. Students are supposed to use the strengths of each team member (*i.e.* speed and pedagogical skills) to decide who will complete which unit. Once all the game units are completed, all team members need to synchronize to come back to their base camp. This will unlock the ***Milestone Activity***. This activity consists of a broad question requiring team members to analyze all the information and samples collected at the POIs and take time to reflect. This is a key moment of collaboration because the team members will have to share the complementary information they have collected and explain their observations, debate and take decisions in order to answer this question.

Teachers can also **make team scores available to all teams** to make them compete or even encourage to help each other if the common objective of all teams is to reach a minimum score. Students can also indicate that they **need help**, at any time. A notification will be sent to all other students as well as the teacher.

4 Modular, Step-by-Step Design Model

To be adopted by teachers, the MOCOGA Model needs to be integrated into an authoring tool that is easy and fast for them to use. We therefore propose a nested design approach, with several progressive steps, to help them transform their current field trip material into a MOCOGA. Each step reveals new functionalities and game elements that can be added to the initial field trip scenario.

4.1 Step 1: Create a Basic Guide to Find Points of Interests

The information required by the authoring tool is minimal (yellow elements in the model in Fig. 1): the field trip *name*, an *introduction page*, a *conclusion page*, a *map* with at least one POI. For each POI, teachers also need to provide a *name* and *instructions* to help students find this POI. All the other necessary parameters are dealt with automatically. For example, the number of *points* that players win upon arrival at a POI is set to five and the *activation zone* around each POI is triggered by GPS. By default, POIs are done on after the other (called the ***Treasure Hunt*** type of field trip).

If needed, teachers can create several *Itineraries* that can be assigned to a group of students in order to avoid them following each other. They can also decide to configure these itineraries with more or less POIs to adapt them to the learner's level. Teachers also have the possibility of changing the way the POIs are triggered depending on where their field trip takes place. The ***Activity hub*** is particularly well adapted to a field trip in a museum because the POIs are available on the map, from the start of the game, similarly to audio-guides. The ***Interactive Walk*** field trip type is well adapted to field

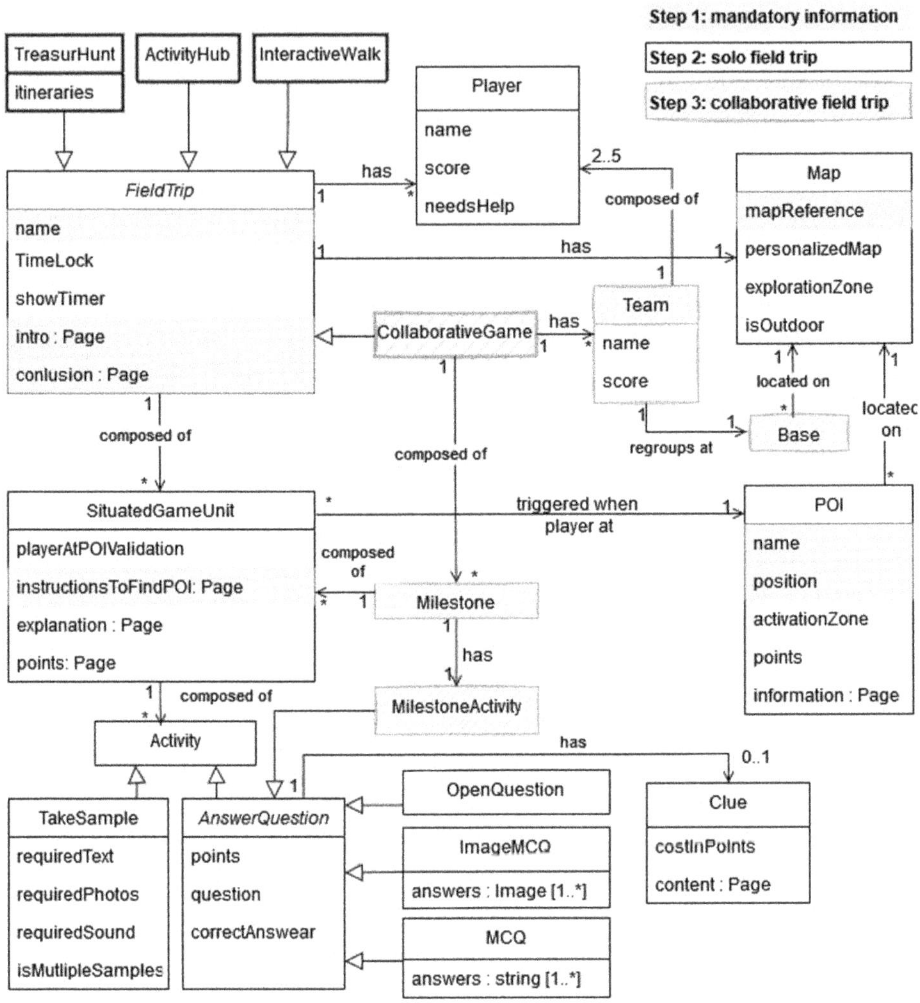

Fig. 1. Mobile Collaborative Learning Game (MOCOGA) model

trips in a city because the phone will send a notification to players when they are in the vicinity of a POI, similarly to tourist office applications.

At this point, teachers can simply use the application as an interactive guide that helps students find all POIs. They can continue using their usual material such as paper quizzes and information sheets.

4.2 Step 2: Set up Situated Game Units on Each POI

After teachers try the first step and feel more confident with the technology, they can easily enhance their field trip by adding complete *Situated Game Units* for each POI. As presented by the white elements in Fig. 1, they can add an ***information page*** about the POI with extra videos and links. They can add several *Activities* that learners will do, once they arrive at the POI, such as ***answering a question*** (i.e. *Open question*, *MCQ* or *image MCQ*). For each question, teachers also have the possibility of adding clues that are revealed in exchange for points. Teachers can also ask their students to ***Take a Sample*** at the POI (take notes, photos or audio recordings). Finally, teachers can add an ***explanation page*** to conclude each *Situated Game Unit* with answers to the questions, for example. In addition, teachers can decide to set a ***Time Lock*** which will displayed the time left on the application and send notifications to alert learners before time is up. Besides, teachers have the possibility of adding a ***timer*** that measures the time learners take to finish activities. This is essential for orienteering races but is an equally interesting game mechanic for other field trips. Finally, teachers have the possibility of adding a personalized map which may display important pedagogical information (*e.g.* type of soil, vegetation, level lines on the map).

At this point, teachers can create more or less complex interactive activities for their field trips. However, the proposed activities still do not contain collaborative elements.

4.3 Step 3: Create a MOCOGA with Collaborative Activities

The third step enables teachers to easily create a MOCOGA by building on the field trip designed in step 2. As shown by the striped elements in the model (Fig. 1), they simply need to create ***Milestones*** by combining the *Situated Game Units* and add a ***Milestone Activity***. Ideally, a *Milestone* corresponds to a particular pedagogical sub-goal. For example, a milestone that has the goal of helping students recognize local tree species could be composed of seven game units on trees. The final milestone activity could be an *Image MCQ* in which learners have to identify the tree that is not local.

Upon completion of this step, teachers have a simple MOCOGA that they should feel comfortable with. In addition, all the functionalities related to creating groups are automatically dealt with by the application. Finally, we suggest teachers ask teams to create their base camps near the starting point. This will enable them to closely monitor teams during key moments of collaboration and provide help if necessary.

4.4 Discussion

The MOCOGA model was presented to seven teachers from various domains and levels of teaching. Those who have less experience with digital applications seem cautious and prefer testing the reliability of the system first. This option is offered by step 1 but can also be accomplished by step 3 if the scenario is kept very minimal. Teachers who are interested in interactivity, especially for children, find the functionalities they need in step 2. Finally, several teachers can imagine going to step 3 but prefer trying step 2 first, in order to assess the reliability of the tool and test the Situated Game Units. The step-by-step design method therefore seems essential for the acceptability of such authoring tools by teachers. Nonetheless, none of the pilot teachers seems ready to test the complete MOCOGA Model. It still seems too distant and "risky" because of all the potential technical problems (connectivity, use of personal phones). The only way to reassure teachers is to provide user-friendly and robust authoring tool and player app.

5 Conclusion

The objective of this study was to enable teachers to create MObile COllaborative learning GAmes (MOCOGAs) for field trips and hence benefit from the pedagogical advantages of collaboration, mobility and game mechanics. In this paper we present the first steps toward this objective: **a MOCOGA Model** that helps teachers design collaborative activities that are adapted to field trips and **a modular step-by-step design model** that is intended to help teachers adopt the MOCOGA model.

The MOCOGA Model is currently being integrated into an authoring tool and will be deployed in a few months. The interface was designed to comply with the three steps of the design model. For example, only the mandatory elements (Step 1 – yellow boxes in Fig. 1) are shown on the interface. This should encourage teachers to create their first field trip and test it out on their smartphone. All the extra are accessible in the option buttons. This tool will need to be particularly user-friendly and robust in order to help teachers embrace the MOCOGA model and use it to its full potential. In addition to this collaborative game model, we are also working on several digital tools that will support collaboration within a group of players [11].

Acknowledgements. The research published in this article was carried out for the SituLearn project, financed by the French *Agence National de la Recherche* (ANR-20-CE38-0012). We would like to thank the students of the IUT de Laval technical school, who participated the initial brainstorming session: Antonin AUBERT, Axel GUERANGER, Ewen GILARD, Maxime GUINOISEAU and Sacha BELLIER-TOULOUZOU. We are also very grateful to Adrien DUPORGE, a game designer, who helped use finalize the MOCOGA Model. Finally, we thank the pilot teachers who of the project: Julie BENOIST, Régis MOURGES, Valerie BODINEAU, Guy THEARD, Ludovic BLIN, Benoit DUCHENNE and Bruno HACQUES.

References

1. Marfisi-Schottman, I., George, S.: Supporting teachers to design and use mobile collaborative learning games. In Proceedings of the International Conference on Mobile Learning, Madrid, Spain, pp. 3–10 (2014)
2. Marczewski, M.A.C.: Even Ninja Monkeys Like to Play: Gamification, Game Thinking and Motivational Design, 1st edn. CreateSpace Independent Publishing Platform, UK (2015)
3. Damasio, A.R.: Descartes' Error: Emotion, Reason, and the Human Brain, 1st edn. Harper Perennial (1995)
4. Maskott: Tactileo (2022). https://support.tactileo.com/tactileo-map/
5. FuretCompany: FuretFactory (2022). https://furetcompany.com/
6. MindfullHouse: Jemos Pro (2022). https://jemos.fr/
7. Pombo L., Marques M. M., Carlos V., Guerra C., Lucas M., Loureiro M.J.: Augmented reality and mobile learning in a smart urban park: pupils' perceptions of the EduPARK game. In: Citizen, Territory and Technologies: Smart Learning Contexts and Practices, Cham, p. 90-100, (2018)
8. Klopfer, E., Squire, K.: Environmental detectives—the development of an augmented reality platform for environmental simulations. Educ. Technol. Res. Dev. **56**(2), 203–228 (2008)
9. Sweller, J.: Cognitive load theory and educational technology. Education Tech. Research Dev. **68**(1), 1–16 (2019). https://doi.org/10.1007/s11423-019-09701-3

10. Marfisi-Schottman, I., Gicquel, P.-Y., Karoui, A., George, S.: From idea to reality: extensive and executable modeling language for mobile learning games. In: Verbert, K., Sharples, M., Klobučar, T. (eds.) EC-TEL 2016. LNCS, vol. 9891, pp. 428–433. Springer, Cham (2016). https://doi.org/10.1007/978-3-319-45153-4_38
11. Simon, S., Marfisi-Schottman, I., George, S.: A conceptual framework for creating mobile collaborative tools. In: Proceedings of the European Conference on Technology Enhanced Learning (EC-TEL), Toulouse, France (2022). In press

Design Pattern for Exploration and Experimentation: Result of Field Study on a Toy-Based Serious Game Design Method

Bertrand Marne(✉)

ICAR UMR 5191, Université Lumière Lyon 2, Parvis René Descartes, Lyon, France
bertrand.marne@ens-lyon.fr

Abstract. In this paper we report how we combined and tested a couple of similar methods to design serious games (SGs) meant to foster learning through exploration and experimentation of the systems of a domain simulation. The main method tested propose basing SG design on toy design set both in the core of the game and the domain to teach. Our experiment on both methods has two objectives: measure the efficiency of both methods and extract new design patterns to help designing serious games based on a toy and thus fostering learning through exploration and experimentation. Our experiment is a longitudinal field study four years long while we contributed and analysed the design of 25 SG prototypes made by 100+ designers. Our results show that the methods are efficient combined and identify some of their issues. Results also provide a field-tested full design pattern to help create new SGs based on a toy.

Keywords: Game-based learning · Serious games · Inquiry learning · Simulation games · Design patterns

1 Introduction

We focus our study on Serious Games (SGs) meant for learning purposes that provide an intrinsic motivation for users rather than using gamification principles. We target SGs beyond increasing motivation, but meant to use interaction to offer a rather constructivist learning thanks to exploration and experimentation. Ryan et al. inspired by the work of Schell [1], describe a design method for such SGs focusing their design on a toy [2]. The work presented in this paper is part of these studies on toy-based SGs design.

We present a longitudinal filed study, consisting of 4 stages intended to experiment on Ryan et al. design methods and to extract Design Patterns (DPs) [3] for a toy-based SGs design.

In the first section, we define "toy-based SG design", as we present the main previous research on the matter. In the second section, we introduce the design-based methodology we adopted. In the third section, we present and discuss the results of this longitudinal study. In conclusion, we summarize our main results.

I. Hilliger et al. (Eds.): EC-TEL 2022, LNCS 13450, pp. 558–565, 2022.
https://doi.org/10.1007/978-3-031-16290-9_50

2 Constructivist SGs Based on a Toy

Bogost et al. and Ryan et al. suggest that SGs can offer in a constructivist fashion, an exploration-based and experimentation-based learning [2, 4].

Ryan et al. base their research on the "*Lens of the Toy*" from Schell [1] that describes the toy as "*A good toy is an object that is fun to play with*" and "*Toys do not have rules.*" Thus, Schell describes a game, based on a toy, as the set of goals and rules to engage the player. Ryan et al. extend Schell's concept of toy: "*A good toy is a complex system with many affordances* [for playful interactions] *that engage cognitive abilities of pattern recognition, strategic reasoning and problem solving.*" Specifically, Ryan et al. describe "*the toy at the heart of an educational game should be a concrete model of the system that governs the learning topic. The student should be invited to play with and explore this system, to learn its patterns and master its control*" [2].

Ryan et al. provide a method with five chronological steps. They are very similar to our previous and older work on the 6 facets of SGs design (however, the facets are not chronological) [2, 5]. The Table 1 compare of the methods. Last column shows whether a step/facet is related to design or use of the toy.

Table 1. Comparison of the 5 steps from Ryan et al. and the 6 facets.

5 Steps from Ryan et al.	6 facets from Marne et al.	Toy
"1. Identify a fine-grained model of the mechanics and dynamics of the real-world system."	"Facet 1: Pedagogical objectives" modelling taught topics, usually with a curriculum, a graph, or an ontology	Design
"2. Present the system to facilitate the recognition of patterns."	"Facet 2: Domain simulation": describing and modelling systems at work. For instance, with an expert rule-based system or equations	
"3. Provide a tool for embodied, playful control."	"Facet 3: Interactions with the Simulation": designing a playful interface to the simulation (described in facet 2) by implementing "basic actions" [1] for players	
"4. Add goals to stage the player's exposure to the system."	"Facet 4: Problems and Progression": designing the challenges given to the players and the progression flow toward them	Use

(*continued*)

Table 1. *(continued)*

5 Steps from Ryan et al.	6 facets from Marne et al.	Toy
"5. Provide support for social sharing of expertise."	"Facet 6: Conditions of Use": Choose the playing conditions (solo/multi? Online? With or without a teacher/trainer? How much time? Which public? etc.)	
	"Facet 5: Decorum": designing the gamification to enhance extrinsic motivation (e.g. sound design, graphic design, narration, specific game mechanics not related to the simulation, etc.)	Unrelated

The comparison shows that the first three steps of Ryan et al. related to toy design, are very close to the first three facets. The next two steps of Ryan et al. related to the use of this toy, are close to the facets 4 and 6. Finally, the fifth facet is not related to toy design, or use, because it is about gamification and extrinsic motivation that are not targeted by Ryan et al. toy-based SG design method.

Unlike the 6 facets, the 5 steps from Ryan et al. were not field-tested [5, 6]. Therefore, we decided to conduct a longitudinal ecological study to test the Ryan et al. method. We had mainly two research questions. First, we wanted to have a better understanding of the 5 steps' efficiency to help designers. And second, we wanted to build some new methods and DPs to enhance both Ryan et al. 5 steps and the 6 facets of SG design.

For the study, we chose a design-based research methodology described in the next section.

3 Methodology: Collaborative Design-Based Research

Usually, DPs extraction is done on SGs that are already developed, because when they are successful, they reify good practices that the DPs are trying to describe [5, 7]. Unfortunately, extracting DPs on already designed SGs do not allow to clearly identify design processes and more importantly design problems. Thus, our first reason for using a design-based research methodology is to identify design issues and what and how solutions emerge.

Hence, we choose the design-driven collaborative research methodology [8] because it allows participants to be closely involved in both the design and the research and to emerge new knowledge from the design processes. We also decided to place our research in an educational context with students learning to design SGs.

Consequently, we identified some bias of our methodology that we considered. First, our participants are not design experts but beginners discovering SG design. Second, the researchers are both involved in teaching of SG design and observing student design for our research.

In a nutshell, our methodology goes beyond the analysis of the finished prototypes designed by our students. We also analysed the prototypes after each iteration. We also conducted direct observations of the design processes and collected several questionnaires and interviews: before the design process, during the design process and after the design process (i.e. after the students' scholar evaluation). This way, we were collecting data about students' preconceptions on design, how and why the design method may have evolved during the design process.

The next section describes and discusses the results of the four stages.

4 Field Study and Results Discussion

The longitudinal study was conducted in four stages over four years: stage Y1, Y2, Y3 and Y4. There was a total of 119 participants from two types of degrees: 58 were students of a master's degree in journalism (Y1 Y2a and Y3), 71 were students of a bachelor's degree in level design (Y2b, Y3, Y4). A total of 25 prototypes were designed.

Table 2 shows the variations in the number of participants and in the methodological and development tools provided to students over the course of the four stages of the whole study. Finally, it indicates whether students were free to choose their own SG topic or whether it was imposed. All students were enrolled in a course about SG design. The course was project-based, with some methodological tools introduced at first. Then each group of students was supervised by a teacher along the agile development of their prototype.

Figure 1 shows, thanks to an alluvial diagram, a synthetic view of the whole results of the four stages of the field study.

In all 25 SGs produced in this study, there are only four means to induce learning, and often in combination: (1) Exploration (discover knowledge and build hypotheses); (2) Experimentation (test hypotheses); (3) Remediation (understand errors); (4) Text to read (learn reading courses). Toy-based SGs target the combination of the first two.

Our first stage is Y1. A variety of authoring tools were provided to the students (e.g. for interactive storytelling, for role-playing games, etc.). They were free to choose both topics, tools, and groups. Six groups produced six prototypes (Table 2).

The most important thing we learned from Y1 is that the students tended to design interactive storytelling SGs (5 out of 6, see Fig. 1). We observed that it was because both of their educational contexts (journalism) and the authoring tools they choose (5/6 choose interactive storytelling tools). Thus 5/6 SGs offer only Manichaean rather than Cornelian choices. As a result, it is remediation: reading content in response to an ill-informed choice. It is not learning based on exploration and experimentation. However, one of the teams managed to introduce systemic content with gauges that gave feedback. Playtests of that SG show that serious players were exploring (assumptions about how to proceed) and experimenting their hypotheses.

Therefore, for the stage Y2(a and b), we focused methodological courses on *gauges* to reify the "*mechanics and dynamics*"[2] of the SG matter. In Y2a, to mitigate influence of tools, we asked students to create a board game first, before digitizing it.

As a result, 2 out of 8 prototypes are still interactive storytelling, but they include a toy, thanks to a gauge system. In total, 6 out of the 8 SGs include a toy according to

Table 2. The 4 stages of the field study.

Stage	Designers involved	SGs made	Methodological tools provided	Development tools provided	SGs topics
Y1	26 journalism students	6	Introduction to SGs + 6 facets [5] + toy-based SGs as a good practice	Interactive storytelling: *Twinery, Klynt*. Role-playing games: *RPG Maker*. Point and click: *eAdventure*. Visual programming: *Construct, Gdevelop*	Free
Y2a	32 journalism students	8	Same as Y1 + concept of gauges as a reification of systemic values	Step 1: papers and scissors (board game) Step 2: same as Y1, but priority on visual programming tools	Free, but systemic
Y2b	23 level design students	5	Work on the "*Lens of the toy*" [1] + 6 facets	*Construct, Gdevelop*	Immune system
Y3	23 level design students + 11 journalism students	3	A detailed methodology based on the 6 facets and the 5 steps [2]	*Construct, Gdevelop Unity 3D*	Imposed topics
Y4	15 level design students + real stakeholders	3	Full DP + additional methodological tools	Same as Y3	Same as Y3

Schell's definition [1]. But only 4 out of the 8, include a toy letting play with *systemic* parameters on the taught matter ("*a fine-grained model of the mechanics and dynamics of the real-world system*") [2]. The 4 toy-based SGs playtests show they allow exploration (make hypotheses) and experimentation (test them) (Fig. 1). Therefore, the work on gauges and the board game constraint helped participants grasp the toy concept, but was not efficient enough to lead all SG to provide exploration and experimentation.

Study Y2b is mostly the same with level design students and assigned authoring tools and topic (Table 2). All SGs developed are *systemic*. Only 2 out 5 SGs playtests show that they provide exploration and match the toy definition of Ryan et al. (Fig. 1).

From Y2a and Y2b we made 3 main findings. We confirm: (1) gauges efficacy to reify *systemic* parameters; (2) the impact of specialized authoring tools on SG type; (3) that systemic topics are easier to design toy-based SGs. Thus, there is a need to find "*mechanics and dynamics*" (i.e. systemic aspect) of some topics. For the latter, we provided participants of stageY3 with some new elements of methodology to find

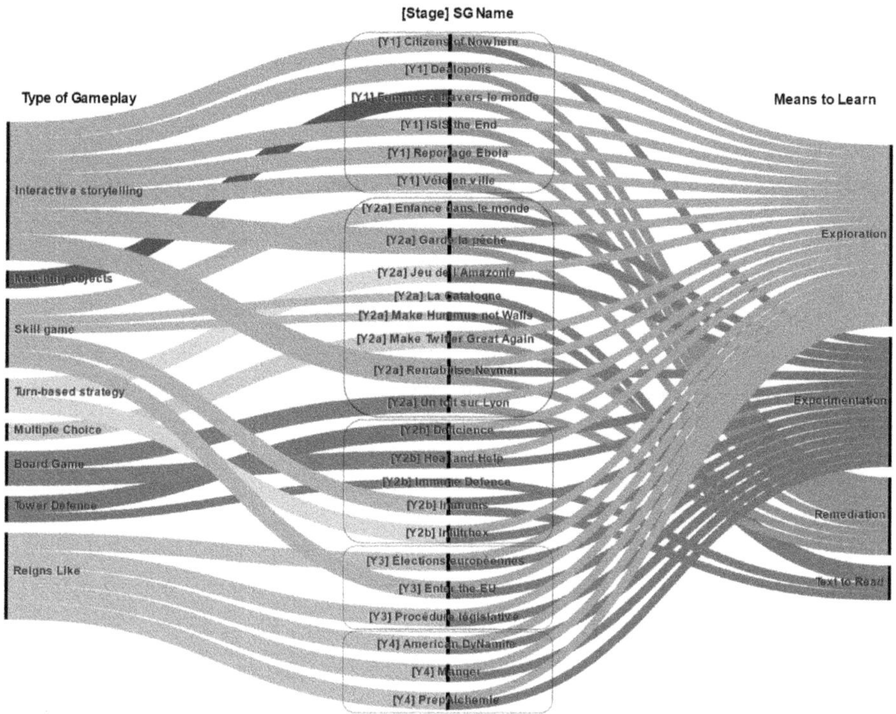

Fig. 1. Alluvial diagram of the SGs designed, the gameplay type and the means to learn.

systemic aspects and build a toy out of them[1]. We also mixed students to mitigate the obstacle of implementation.

Result of Y3 confirms that authoring tools were not obstacles anymore. The main outcome is that all the SGs designed are toy-based. Methodological tools led two of the teams, along different avenues, to design SGs inspired by the videogame *Reigns*.

Reigns describe a situation, then a binary choice is proposed to the player. Depending on it, gauges increase or decrease as feedback. According to the gauges, a new situation and a new choice are presented to the player and so on, step by step.

During playtests of Y3 SGs, we verified that players were exploring and experimenting. Specifically for the two SGs that were inspired by *Reigns*.

Findings of Y3 led us to build a new DP inspired by the lessons learned with *Reigns*. The DP name is "*Mode and Tick Breakdown for Interactions With the Simulation*"[2].

Y4 was close to Y3, but we tested the DP and real stakeholders were involved.

The results are all SGs designed are based on the DP. They look like *Reigns*: at each step several choices can move gauges inducing a new situation. Playtests show that the serious-players are engaged in exploration and experimentation.

The four stages of the study show that Ryan et al. untested method is effective, mixed with the 6 facets, to help designers grasp the concept of toy-based SGs. We also

[1] An outline can be found online: http://6facets.org/d/Methtool.pdf.

[2] The full Design Pattern can be found online: http://6facets.org/d/DP_R.pdf.

learned that there are 3 conditions to be efficient to design toy-based SG. To be able to: (1) identify the systemic aspects (i.e. simulation of parameters, mechanics, dynamics); (2) identify a clear and playful interface to pilot simulation through the toy; (3) master authoring tools to implement simulation and toy-interface.

The stage Y4 of the field study allowed us to experiment a full DP (see footnote 2) designed from Y3 results. It successfully enabled designers (students and their stakeholders) to develop toy-based SG providing exploration and experimentation.

5 Conclusion

To provide Serious Games (SGs) that allow learning through exploration and experimentation using toys [1], we conduct four field studies involving more than a hundred participants and twenty prototypes. Our goals are: (1) to test design method proposed by Ryan et al. [2]; (2) to extract design patterns (DPs) for toy-based SGs.

We have learned that Ryan et al. method for toy-based SG is effective but not efficient enough. Associated with the 6 facets of SG design [5], the first 3 steps of Ryan et al. are helpful to grasp the concept of toy embedding a systemic simulation and to design a toy based-SGs. But they lack (1) support to design simulations about an apparently non-systemic matter, (2) methods to design playful interactions with the simulation, (3) specific authoring tools.

To address the second issue, we extracted and provide a full DP "*Mode and Tick Breakdown for Interactions With the Simulation*" (see footnote 2) based on the game *Reigns*. The DP assessment (3 SGs prototypes made by 15 designers) shows that it supports toy-based SG design that are meant for exploration and experimentation-based learning.

Acknowledgements. The author acknowledges University Lumière Lyon 2 for the APPI 2020 Grant.

References

1. Schell, J.: The Art of Game Design: A Book of Lenses, 2nd edn. A K Peters/CRC Press, Boca Raton (2014)
2. Ryan, M., Costello, B., Stapleton, A.: Deep learning games through the lens of the toy. In: Meaningful Play 2012, pp. 1–29. Michigan State University, East Lansing (2012)
3. Alexander, C., Ishikawa, S., Silverstein, M.: A Pattern Language: Towns, Buildings, Construction. Oxford University Press, Oxford (1977)
4. Bogost, I.: Exploitationware. In: Colby, R., Johnson, M.S.S., Colby, R.S. (eds.) Rhetoric/Composition/Play through Video Games: Reshaping Theory and Practice of Writing, pp. 139–147. Palgrave Macmillan US, New York (2013)
5. Marne, B., Wisdom, J., Huynh-Kim-Bang, B., Labat, J.-M.: The six facets of serious game design: a methodology enhanced by our design pattern library. In: Ravenscroft, A., Lindstaedt, S., Kloos, C.D., Hernández-Leo, D. (eds.) 21st Century Learning for 21st Century Skills, pp. 208–221. Springer, Heidelberg (2012). https://doi.org/10.1007/978-3-642-33263-0_17
6. Marne, B.: Modèles et outils pour la conception de jeux sérieux: une approche meta-design (2014)

7. Marfisi-Schottman, I., Piau-Toffolon, C.: Extraire et réutiliser des patrons de conception à partir de learning games existants. In: Atelier Méthodologies de Conception Collaboratives des EIAH de la Conférence EIAH 2015, 2 June 2015 (2015)
8. Sanchez, É., Monod-Ansaldi, R.: Recherche collaborative orientée par la conception. Un paradigme méthodologique pour prendre en compte la complexité des situations d'enseignement-apprentissage. Educ. Didact. **9**, 73–94 (2015)

The Enablers and Barriers of Using Slack for Computer-Mediated Communication to Support the Learning Journey: A Case Study at a University of Applied Sciences

Tina Papathoma(✉)

Code University of Applied Sciences, Berlin, Germany
Tina.papathoma@code.berlin

Abstract. Slack is a tool originally used for computer-mediated communication within software companies as well as from academics to enable communication and collaboration. Slack is currently used in Higher Education for pedagogical purposes. This paper presents a case study of its application to support the learning journey in a German University of applied sciences. The study identifies enablers and barriers of the use of Slack as they come out from learning experience research with 20 undergraduate student interviews in their first semester as well as from observations of a Slack channel that the students and their educators used. The study identifies enablers with students reporting that Slack is easy to use, the discussions are flowing, the communication with educators is personal and friendly, and they get the opportunity to network and socialize with new fellow students in a less formal environment. However, certain barriers are apparent with students feeling overwhelmed by the information their educators share which often gets lost or dispersed in various other Slack channels and platforms outside slack. The findings indicate that for communication to be effective, teamwork between educators who manage Slack communication is essential and clear objectives of its use need to be timely and clearly defined.

Keyword: Computer-mediated communication student learning teacher support slack

1 Introduction

Teaching and Learning is often facilitated by the use of technological tools that have the potential to enhance communication with the purpose of supporting students' learning journey. Also, since the outbreak of the global COVID-19 pandemic, educational institutions were almost obliged to use various tools to keep students informed about their learning journey. Empirical studies were conducted on the use of various communication tools in different educational environments, Slack being one of them. The current study explores the use of Slack in the context of a university of applied sciences through the student perspective.

I. Hilliger et al. (Eds.): EC-TEL 2022, LNCS 13450, pp. 566–572, 2022.
https://doi.org/10.1007/978-3-031-16290-9_51

2 Background

Slack is a tool originally used for 'computer-mediated communication' within software companies. Currently, Slack is also used in higher education and particularly for 'planning and teaching curriculum to managing student services by over 3,000 higher education institutions, with approximately 1.2 million users, to keep classes and campus affairs running online' [1].

One of the most influential models of tutoring in 'computer mediated' environments has been Gilly Salmon's e-moderating model which was used to train e-moderators across the world to support student learning [2].

According to this model, the e-moderator has an invaluable role to play in the successful implementation of the five-stage model of learning. The stages are presented below:

- Stage 1. Access and Motivation. The e-moderator's role here is to welcome and encourage participants to interact.
- Stage 2. Online Socialisation. The moderator assists in familiarising and providing bridges between cultural, social and learning environments.
- Stage 3. Information Exchange. At this stage the moderator facilitates tasks and supports the use of learning materials.
- Stage 4. Knowledge Construction. The moderator facilitates the process without being involved to a great extent.
- Stage 5. Development. On this last stage the moderator supports and responds to student questions.

Each of these stages enable an e-moderator to assist a student move from access and motivation to online socialisation, to information exchange, to knowledge construction and eventually to development. An e-moderator needs to take technical support for learners, the learning process, and their own role in supporting that learning. This model assists educators in general to understand what teaching online involves and the factors that need to be considered. Additionally, recent research in the context of online learning and, in particular, on Massive Open Online Courses (MOOCs) [3] also uncovers the roles of people who carry out the teaching in the online settings, which demand the technical skills that Salmon proposed along with the subject matter expertise, but also pedagogical decisions about the learning design. Reasons that the learning design and its development are considered important are that it can help educators supporting students online to become more effective in their preparation, in facilitating teaching and learning activities, as well as in exposing educators to new teaching ideas that take them beyond their traditional approaches [4].

The use of Slack for supporting online learning, demands the need for a range of skills for educators using it. Currently, there is some published research on the use of Slack and relates to the support of higher education student peer interactions during Master's thesis seminars [5]. Some other piece of research relates to using slack in education as an alternative communication for groupwork again in graduate level [6]. Some other literature documented the educator experience in managing discussions and involving students in their online learning through active learning exercises in the context of environmental politics courses [7]. Further, researchers previously reflected on lessons learned using Slack in Engineering Education in the context of Innovation Based Learning which had positive impact although sometimes information was getting lost and made recommendations for better practice [8].

The current research study which is in progress aims to shed light in the use of Slack for supporting the learning journey. To the best of the author's knowledge, the use of slack has not been studied in the context of undergraduate studies in applied sciences. Also, this research is unique as it considers online pedagogy and in particular, the five-stage model of learning. The approach that Salmon took was tried-and-tested to online teaching that is currently being used across the world in different contexts is MOOCs in Australia [9] as well as in asynchronous discussions in Malaysia [10].

3 Methodology

The study that this paper introduces is part of a bigger study that relates to the evaluation of learning experience of students in the context of a German University of applied sciences. Due to the global pandemic affecting the face-to-face experience of teaching and learning, teachers and students at the university had to pivot to online learning. One of the main tools the university uses for communication amongst teachers and students even before the pandemic is Slack and is also preferred over email communication. The study therefore asks the following research question: *What are the enablers and barriers in the use of Slack to support the students' learning journey in their first semester of undergraduate studies?* The e-moderator model approach of Salmon is used to identify enablers and barriers in access and motivation, in online socialization and in information exchange.

A case study [11] was conducted to examine the learning experience and specifically to identify enablers and barriers in the use of Slack to support the students' learning journey. Ethical approval for the design and implementation of this case study was received from the university's Research Ethics committee. The method used to collect data was semi-structured online interviews that lasted between 30–40 min. The questions that were asked to students related to all the platforms they used and to Slack in particular during the first semester of their studies. Moreover, they were asked about the support they received through Slack from their educators and the topics they discussed with them. Student participants were also asked about the interaction with other fellow students on Slack and other similar tools.

20 undergraduate students online and, when possible, face-to-face interviews in their first semester were conducted. The reason for choosing students on their first semester was that at that stage, they would be less likely to have used Slack before coming to study at this university, whereas students in more senior semesters would already have experience in using Slack since their first semester. A purposeful sampling approach sought to discover, understand, and gain insights from student participants [12]. In particular, the purposeful sampling aimed at understanding whether various types of learners that were at the same (first) semester, presented profound differences in the use of Slack as a tool used for communication.

In the current sample of the interviews that took place in March 2022, there were five types of participants:

- the ones who came to study at the university right after high school (n = 8)
- the ones who came to study at the university with a degree and work experience from abroad (n = 6)
- the ones who came to study at the university with a degree and work experience from Germany (n = 4)
- the ones who came to study at the university, and had previously studied elsewhere, dropped out and had some work experience (n = 1)
- the ones who come to study at the university, and had previously studied elsewhere, dropped out, do not have work experience or their work experience is unknown to the researcher. (n = 1)

Initial observations of the Slack channel that the students and their educators used during their first semester were also examined. The following section discusses initial findings of the study.

4 Discussion

The study identified initial enablers and barriers in the use of Slack that were thematically analysed [13]. No profound differences between the five types of participants were found in their views about the use of Slack as a tool for communication to support their learning journey therefore the initial analysis is not discerning the different categories of students.

4.1 Enablers

Some students (n = 7) reported that Slack is easy to use as it provided them with the opportunity to go back to the tool and read again discussions with fellow students and announcements of their educators. They also mentioned that they could work collaboratively with their team members (n = 5). Going back to the group discussions assisted students to get an understanding of what they did throughout the semester through the discussions they had which were flowing.

Almost half students (n = 9) also stated that communication with educators through Slack was personal and friendly, something that the experienced students who have studied in more traditional university institutions had not experienced before. Students (n = 4) who were studying from abroad due to the pandemic also mentioned that Slack gave them the opportunity to network and socialize with new fellow students in a less formal environment and make friends, something that email exchange would not allow so easily as they reported. However, certain barriers became apparent and are discussed in the next subsection.

4.2 Barriers

One of the major barriers that many students (n = 12) mentioned was that they felt overwhelmed in the beginning of the semester. Getting onboarded into Slack, as well as on other tools was challenging as they had not used most of the tools before. Also Slack itself had a lot of ‘channels’ to communicate and students (n = 4) indicated that they would get a great number of notifications while being added to different channels from their educators. Slack shows all new messages and interactions in bold fonts (i.e. that means that a message was not yet 'read'). Students (n = 3) also reported that they could not keep track of the plethora of the rest of the tools used and were unsure what is the main channel of communication and through which tool. Other tools involved a Learning Platform as well as Wiki Pages on a platform called Notion.

Furthermore, the fact that all activities were taking place online, was making it stressful and exhausting for some (n = 3) to be sitting in front of a computer and not being able to find the information needed to be prepared for their classes or knowing what the requirements for assessments were.

Some students (n = 3) only found out at the end of the semester that they could actually mute channels, select them and sort them out in different folders from their fellow students. When this happened, they saved themselves a lot of time and they could focus only to the important channels and not miss important information.

Another challenge that students (n = 4) mentioned they faced was that when they did not check Slack regularly, the information would very quickly go out of control. So often students (n = 15) reported that they would turn to tools they were already using in their personal lives such as What's app, Signal and Telegram to ask other fellow learners. The discussions they reported that they had (n = 10) were not only course work related but also for socialising. So, when certain information their educators shared was getting lost or dispersed in various other Slack channels, students (n = 4) mentioned they would attempt to use platforms outside Slack resulting in losing focus from their studies in the plethora of communication tools. It was apparent that there were students who were new to online learning, therefore there is was a need for educators to help them find their way around and to make clear the differences from face to face learning environments.

Although students were given access to the technology environment of Slack as well as to other tools, they did now have access or were not aware of the access they needed to have, or they would not find out the information they needed in a timely manner; this resulted in missing sessions of their courses for some (n = 3). Salmon states that there might be issues in the beginning with access to the tools so students will need human intervention for this. So, the educators or 'e-moderators' as Salmon calls them, need to provide support throughout this scaffold to make sure that students get to the end of it with a productive learning experience whether this is about learning how to work in groups or to online socialization and in information exchange. From the initial slack observations, it seems that the technology changes the context in which learning design takes place, so the educators need to also experiment with what works and what does not work to offer a smooth learning journey to students.

The initial findings indicate that for communication to be effective, teamwork between educators who manage Slack communication is essential and clear objectives of its use need to be timely and clearly defined. The findings are not only relevant to Slack but also to other similar digital tools used to support the learning journey (i.e. Microsoft Teams, What's App, etc.). The role of the educator is to keep the students engaged on a main platform, whether that is Slack or the dedicated Learning Platform of the university, so as not information gets dispersed to so many other communication tools with the risk of students dropping out or failing to register, submit their assessment or receiving feedback.

5 Conclusion

This study which is part of a longer study on learner experience of undergraduate students in a German University of applied sciences, aimed to answer the research question '*What are the enablers and barriers in the use of Slack to support the students' learning journey in their first semester of undergraduate studies?*'. It took a case study approach conducting 20 semi-structured interviews with students who had just started studying their undergraduate degree.

The current study sought to examine the ways students used Slack and is mainly exploratory. For this, it presents certain limitations with regards to its sample and its data sources. It relies in a limited number of interviews. Future research work may include interviews with educators to get a more holistic point of view. Also examine the engagement with the platform through Learning Analytics and look at trends of what students tend to engage more and where they tend to be inactive. This may help in adjusting its use to support a smooth learning journey.

Although the study cannot generalize its findings, it shows that Slack can potentially be used to facilitate communication but there is also a need to guide students on how to use it. It shed lights on what its limitations are with regards to notifications that are getting lost so that students are aware of. The contribution of the initial findings of this study shows that the communication for supporting learning to be effective demands teamwork between educators who manage Slack and clear objectives of its use need to be timely and clearly defined. Working on this direction, continuous professional development for educators on blended teaching tools would be useful. It would be useful for educators to get familiar to models such as the one of e-moderator or to gain a deeper understanding on online learning design activities whether these are to facilitate access and motivate learners or to help them get to know each other and develop group work activities, to exchange information with an end goal to exchange knowledge and develop individual or group projects.

References

1. Slack. https://slack.com/resources/using-slack/your-guide-to-slack-for-higher-education. Accessed 23 Apr 2022
2. Salmon, G.: E-moderating: The Key to Teaching and Learning Online. Taylor & Francis e-Library (2004)
3. Papathoma, T., Littlejohn, A., Ferguson, R.: Enabling Online Learning: Who are the Educators? In: Sharpe, R., Bennett, S., Varga-Atkins, T. (eds.) Handbook of Digital Higher Education, pp. 99–110. Elgar Handbooks in Education, Elgar (2022)
4. Dalziel, J., et al.: The larnaca declaration on learning design. J. Interact. Media Educ. **2016**(1), 7 (2016)
5. Tuhkala, A., Kärkkäinen, T.: Using Slack for computer-mediated communication to support higher education students' peer interactions during Master's thesis seminar. Educ. Inf. Technol. **23**(6), 2379–2397 (2018). https://doi.org/10.1007/s10639-018-9722-6

6. Fulton, L.: Slack in education: a case study of alternative communication for groupwork in graduate level online education. In: Langran, E., Borup, J. (Eds.), Proceedings of Society for Information Technology & Teacher Education International Conference, pp. 1458–1463. Washington, D.C., United States: Association for the Advancement of Computing in Education (2018)
7. Sabin, J., Olive, A.: Slack: adopting social-networking platforms for active learning. PS: Polit. Sci. Polit. **51**(1), 183–189 (2018)
8. Vazquez, E.A., Cortes-Mendez, M., Striker, R., Singelmann, L., Pearson, M., Swartz, E. M.: Lessons learned using slack in engineering education: an innovation-based learning approach. In: 2020 ASEE Virtual Annual Conference Content Access (2020)
9. Salmon, G., Pechenkina, E., Chase, A.M., Ross, B.: Designing massive open online courses to take account of participant motivations and expectations. Br. J. Edu. Technol. **48**(6), 1284–1294 (2017)
10. Ghadirian, H., Ayub, A.F.M., Salehi, K.: Students' perceptions of online discussions participation and e-moderation behaviours in peer-moderated asynchronous online discussions. Technol. Pedagogy Educ. **27**(18), 85–100 (2018)
11. Yin, R. K. Case study research: design and methods 5th edn. (2014)
12. Saldaña, J., Leavy, P., Beretvas, N.: Fundamentals of Qualitative Research. Oxford University Press, Oxford (2014)
13. Braun, V., Clarke, V.: Using thematic analysis in psychology. Qual. Res. Psychol. **3**(2), 77–101 (2006)

Mobile Telepresence Robots in Education: Strengths, Opportunities, Weaknesses, and Challenges

Maria Perifanou[1](✉), Anastasios A. Economides[1], Polina Häfner[2], and Thomas Wernbacher[3]

[1] University of Macedonia, Thessaloniki, Greece
mariaperif@gmail.com, economid@uom.gr
[2] Karlsruhe Institute of Technology, Karlsruhe, Germany
polina.haefner@kit.edu
[3] Danube University Krems, Krems, Austria
thomas.wernbacher@donau-uni.ac.at

Abstract. A mobile telepresence robot (MTR) is a semi-autonomous robot whose movement and interaction with its surrounding environment is controlled by a person from a distance. In education, MTR enable learners or educators to virtually participate in a class from a distance. TRinE: Telepresence Robots in Education is an EU project that aims at providing an interactive toolkit to support educators, learners, and others in order to integrate MTR in education. During January and February 2022, project's partners conducted a qualitative study to collect the experiences and views of educators, learners, and other stakeholders (i.e., administrators, technical support staff, librarians) regarding the use of MTR in education across Austria, Germany, Greece, France, Iceland, Malta, and USA. A total of 19 persons were interviewed and 66 persons participated in 12 focus groups discussions. The findings describe interviewees' experiences with MTR in education as well as the views of interviewees and focus groups' participants with regard to pros, cons, and recommendations of using MTR in education. These findings may help educational policy makers, educational institutes officials, educators, and others to efficiently integrate MTR in education.

Keywords: Distance learning · Distance teaching · Human computer interaction · Telepresence robots

1 Introduction

A mobile telepresence robot (MTR) is a remote-controlled robot with mobility and videoconferencing capabilities. Usually, an MTR is equipped with a screen display, camera, audio speaker, microphone, motor, wheels, and wireless Internet connectivity. The remote operator of the MTR can drive and move it, interact with the people and objects around the MTR, and feel like being present there. Telepresence robots have been used in many areas such as offices, health care, hospitals, and schools [1]. MTR

I. Hilliger et al. (Eds.): EC-TEL 2022, LNCS 13450, pp. 573–579, 2022.
https://doi.org/10.1007/978-3-031-16290-9_52

can be used by persons who cannot be physically present and walk around at a specific location due to being at a distant location, illness, disability, restrictions (e.g., quarantine, restricted access location), bad weather, war, and more.

The advantage of MTR over videoconferencing in education lies in its ability to move around the class and interact with one or more persons. So, the operator of an MTR in a class may experience stronger feelings of social presence [2], belonging and being part of the class.

TRinE is an Erasmus+ project that aims at providing an interactive toolkit to support educators, learners, and other stakeholders in order to integrate MTR in education [3]. With regard to this project, the researchers conducted a qualitative study to collect the experiences and views of educators, learners, and other stakeholders (e.g., administrators, technicians, IT support staff, librarians) regarding the use of MTR in education. This paper describes the results of the study.

2 Previous Studies Regarding Telepresence Robots in Education

Most previous studies use the term telepresence robot (TR) both for static TR and mobile TR. This study focuses exclusively on MTR. Previous studies with regard to TR in education investigated the introduction of TR in various educational settings. When a teacher cannot physically visit the premises of a class due to illness, bad weather, long distance, etc., teacher can deliver teaching using a TR located in the class [4–6]. Similarly, an expert at a distance location (e.g., abroad) or in a limited available time can advise a class via a TR [7–10]. Most previous studies investigated the case of a homebound student (due to illness) participating in a class via a TR [7, 9, 11–16]. Other previous studies investigated the cases of a language learner abroad communicating with a native-speaker via a TR [17–19], two students at a distance discussing a topic and solving a problem using a TR [2], a teacher teaching mathematics [5] or languages [20] to one student as well two classes at a distance (e.g., in different countries) communicating via a TR [21].

Most previous studies investigated a single case of using TR in a specific class. Using interviews, the current study records the experiences of users who have already used TR in various educational settings in Austria, France, Iceland, and USA. In addition, using focus groups, the current study records the perceptions and opinions of both experienced users and inexperienced educators, learners, and other stakeholders (i.e., administrators, technical support staff, librarians) regarding the introduction of TR in education across Austria, Germany, Greece, Iceland, and Malta.

3 Methodology

Using focus groups and interviews, the researchers collected the opinions of interested stakeholders across Austria, Germany, Greece, France, Iceland, Malta, and USA. The proposed research was reviewed and approved by MCAST's Research Ethics Committee. A total of 19 interviews and 12 focus groups with 66 participants were conducted during January and February 2022. A total of 85 persons participated in the interviews and focus groups discussions. The participants included educators, learners, and other stakeholders (e.g., administrators, technical support staff, librarians, MTR manufactures). The duration of a focus group discussion was about 90 min, while an interview lasted about 60 min. The focus groups discussion and the interviews were video recorded (with the consent of the participants). In order to identify patterns and themes related to the participants' views, the videos were transcribed and coded.

4 Results

In this section we briefly present the interviewees' experiences with MTR in education as well as the views of interviewees and focus groups' participants with regard to strengths, opportunities, weaknesses, and challenges of using MTR in education. In addition, participants' recommendations are given with regard to introducing MTR in education. Due to space limitation, only the main results are presented here. Further results are presented in [22, 23].

The interviewees described their experiences with MTR in various settings: 1) Remote educators (at home, office, abroad, ill) teach, advise, and socialize with students; 2) Remote experts, invited professors with disabilities or from overseas give lectures and mentoring; and 3) Remote students (at home, hospital, abroad) attend classes.

Participants in both the focus groups and the interviews mentioned several advantages of using MTR in education across the following themes: 1) Strengths; 2) Pedagogical capabilities; 3) Remote student opportunities; 4) Remote teacher opportunities; 5) General opportunities. The strengths of MTR (such as easy-of-use, mobility, and interactivity) were mentioned 11 times by interviewees and 13 times by focus groups' participants. The pedagogical capabilities of MTR (such as fostering engagement, participation, feel of presence and belonging, and collaboration) were mentioned 30 times by interviewees and 32 times by focus groups' participants. The opportunities given by MTR to remote students (such as enabling ill students or students at abroad to participate in class) were mentioned 10 times by interviewees and 10 times by focus groups' participants. The opportunities given by MTR to remote teachers (such as enabling remote experts to lecture and advise students) were mentioned 8 times by interviewees and 8 times by focus groups' participants. Finally, the opportunities given by MTR to remote students (such as enabling participation in class in case of pandemic and bad weather, or avoiding commuting and long journeys) were mentioned 2 times by interviewees and 7 times by focus groups' participants.

Participants in both the focus groups and the interviews expressed several concerns about using MTR in education across the following themes: 1) Technical weaknesses; 2) Educational and psychological challenges; 3) Environment obstacles; 4) Management and maintenance challenges; 5) Legal and ethical challenges. The technical weaknesses of MTR (such as low quality of audio and video, movement difficulties, and battery limitations) were mentioned 15 times by interviewees and 10 times by focus groups' participants. The educational and psychological challenges (such as fear of using MTR, negative attitudes, human need of being physically present and communicating, and training needs about MTR) were mentioned 17 times by interviewees and 30 times by focus groups' participants. The obstacles of the environment (such as lack of stable high-speed WiFi everywhere and physical obstacles along the MTR's move) were mentioned 27 times by interviewees and 20 times by focus groups' participants. The MTR management and maintenance challenges (such as cost of MTR and needs for assistants to charge, schedule, assign, and collect the MTR) were mentioned 5 times by interviewees and 17 times by focus groups' participants. Finally, legal and ethical challenges of using MTR in education (such as lack of policies and regulations, privacy, security, and illegal recording) were mentioned 25 times by interviewees and 28 times by focus groups' participants.

In total, interviewees mentioned more times weaknesses (89) than advantages (53) of MTR in education. Similarly, focus groups' participants indicated more times weaknesses (105) than advantages (62) of MTR in education.

Participants in both the focus groups and the interviews made several recommendations to facilitate the integration of MTR in education across the following themes: 1) Recommendations for policies; 2) Recommendations for organizational issues; 3) Recommendations for buildings; 4) Recommendations for MTR functionalities. Recommendations for policies (such as policies for the operator of the MTR) were mentioned 3 times by interviewees and 22 times by focus groups' participants. Recommendations for organizational issues (such as funding) were mentioned 2 times by interviewees and 2 times by focus groups' participants. Recommendations for buildings (such as WiFi everywhere and space arrangements) were mentioned 7 times by focus groups' participants. Recommendations for MTR functionalities (such as connectivity, audio, vision, gesturing, movement, and security) were mentioned 20 times by interviewees and 19 times by focus groups' participants.

5 Discussions and Practical Implications

This study provided a list of main themes with regard to strengths, opportunities, weaknesses, challenges, and recommendations for the introduction of MTR in education. Educators, students (and their parents) as the main users of telepresence robots in an educational setting can be inspired by current practices and experiences of respondents and encouraged by the positive feedback from early adopters. Students who face obstacles to physically attend classes can use MTR to participate and being part of the class. In addition, educators and experts can provide teaching and mentoring from a distance using MTR. External experts could participate in class via an MTR to save travel time and costs.

One of the main benefits for students is the feeling of belonging and being part of the class when using such an MTR. The feeling of social presence improves learning and can help the recovery process of sick students. Using a MTR makes it easier for them to return to school.

Despite the advantages that MTR offer compared to other tele-teaching technologies (e.g. Zoom sessions), there are a number of weaknesses that may depend on the technology or other pedagogical, psychological, environmental or administrative aspects. For example, the move of MTR is difficult if there are too many physical obstacles in the building such as stairs, lifts, doors and assistance for the robot is not possible, or if WiFi full coverage requires additional high costs.

Education policy makers and school headmasters can develop strategies and guidelines based on the recommendations. They can use the presented information to select appropriate MTR and take appropriate technological, environmental, and organizational steps. One of the most important tasks here is to issue usage and safety regulations for all users of the MTRs to ensure their smooth utilization.

For the technicians who are to set up the mobile telepresence robots in the facilities of the educational institutions, our results provide a list of recommendations and technical obstacles that should be solved, e.g. high-speed WiFi coverage, possible physical obstacles, positioning of the docking stations, considerations for spare parts, maintenance scheduling and repairing, etc.

Currently, MTR encounter several obstacles for their effective integration in education. However, it is expected that many of these issues (such as high cost, limited WiFi coverage everywhere, lack of policies and support, lack of MTR functionalities) will be soon resolved. For example, the prices of sensors and other hardware components are decreasing, their quality is advancing, and companies are constantly improving software features. Such advances include the management of MTR fleets or the use of artificial intelligence (AI) algorithms for collision detection, pathfinding, simultaneous translation or even facial recognition. In some aspects, MTR shares threats in the area of privacy such as other technologies like augmented reality and self-driving cars, where the sensors deliver real-time data from the environment. Solving these problems in one area will automatically solve the problems in the MTR domain.

Our findings should enable MTR manufacturers to plan their future features based on the given recommendations. What some providers already offer is a developer kit for those users who want to adapt the hardware and software capabilities of their MTR devices to their own requirements. Such modular principles could be further adopted by the community to overcome current limitations. However, some of the technological weaknesses and threats, e.g., in the area of safety and security, could not entirely be solved by technology in the near future or the solution will not be affordable.

6 Conclusions and Future Research

This paper presents concentrated results of a comprehensive study in the field of MTR in education. The study employed interviews and focus groups discussions with the aim of gaining insights into the opinions and attitudes of different target groups. Twelve focus groups and nineteen interviews were conducted with a total of 85 participants across seven countries. The participants had varying degrees of experience with the technology, some of them have been using it for years, others only knew about it recently. The results of this study include opinions and attitudes towards MTR technology as well as recommendations for the use of MTR in educational institutions.

A next step is to create a validated approach for the use of MTR in the classroom. A toolkit will include a knowledge base, a set of guidelines for user-friendly and efficient integration, best practices for educational scenarios from experienced users and much more. The overarching goal is to increase presence, social learning, and inclusion in classrooms and university classes, and to compensate for the lack of mobility or limited travel of students, faculty or other staff. MTR could enhance learning and intercultural exchange and prepare students for the workplace of tomorrow.

Acknowledgments. This publication was partially supported by Erasmus+ project "TRinE: Telepresence Robots in Education". Project Reference: 2020-1-MT01-KA227-SCH-092408. This publication reflects the views only of the authors. The European Commission support for the production of this publication does not constitute an endorsement of the contents which reflects the views only of the authors, and the Commission cannot be held responsible for any use which may be made of the information contained therein.

References

1. Kristoffersson, A., Coradeschi, S., Loutfi, A.: A review of mobile robotic telepresence. Adv. Hum.-Comput. Interact. **3** (2013). https://doi.org/10.1155/2013/902316
2. Schouten, A.P., Portegies, T.C., Withuis, I., Willemsen, L.M., Mazerant-Dubois, K.: Robomorphism: examining the effects of telepresence robots on between-student cooperation. Comput. Hum. Behav. **126** (2022). https://doi.org/10.1016/j.chb.2021.106980
3. Wernbacher, T., et al.: TRinE: telepresence robots in education. In: Proceedings of the 16th Annual International Technology, Education and Development Conference (INTED), pp. 6514–6522. IATED (2021). https://doi.org/10.21125/inted.2022.1653
4. Edwards, A., Edwards, C., Spence, P.R., Harris, C., Gambino, A.: Robots in the classroom: differences in students' perceptions of credibility and learning between "teacher as robot" and "robot as teacher." Comput. Hum. Behav. **65**, 627–634 (2016). https://doi.org/10.1016/j.chb.2016.06.005
5. Lim, M.S., Han, J.H.: Convergence technologies by a long-term case study on telepresence robot-assisted learning. J. Convergence Inf. Technol. **9**(7), 106–113 (2019). https://www.koreascience.or.kr/article/JAKO201921467621155.page
6. Puarungroj, W., Boonsirisumpun, N.: Multiple device controlled design for implementing telepresence robot in schools. In: Cheung, S.K.S., Li, R., Phusavat, K., Paoprasert, N., Kwok, L.-F. (eds.) ICBL 2020. LNCS, vol. 12218, pp. 405–415. Springer, Cham (2020). https://doi.org/10.1007/978-3-030-51968-1_33
7. Cha, E., Chen, S., Mataric, M.J.: Designing telepresence robots for K-12 education. In: 2017 26th IEEE International Symposium on Robot and Human Interactive Communication (RO-MAN), pp. 683–688. IEEE (2017). https://ieeexplore.ieee.org/stamp/stamp.jsp?tp=&arnumber=8172377
8. Shin, K.W.C., Han, J.H.: Qualitative exploration on children's interactions in telepresence robot assisted language learning. J. Korea Convergence Soc. **8**(3), 177–184 (2017). https://www.koreascience.or.kr/article/JAKO201713842135266.page
9. Fischer, A.J., Bloomfield, B.S., Clark, R.R., McClelland, A.L., Erchul, W.P.: Increasing student compliance with teacher instructions using telepresence robot problem-solving teleconsultation. Int. J. Sch. Educ. Psychol. **7**(sup1), 158–172 (2019). https://doi.org/10.1080/21683603.2018.1470948
10. Burbank, M.D., Goldsmith, M.M., Bates, A.J., Spikner, J., Park, K.: Teacher observations using telepresence robots: benefits and challenges for strengthening evaluations. J. Educ. Supervision **4**(1) (2021). https://doi.org/10.31045/jes.4.1.6
11. Ahumeda-Newhart, V.A., Warschauer, M., Sender, L.: Virtual inclusion via telepresence robots in the classroom: an exploratory case study. Int. J. Technol. Learn. **23**(4), 9–25 (2016)
12. Ahumada-Newhart, V., Olson, J.S.: My student is a robot: how schools manage telepresence experiences for students. In: Proceedings of the 2017 CHI Conference on Human Factors in Computing Systems, pp. 342–347. ACM (2017)

13. Ahumada-Newhart, V., Olson, J.S.: Going to school on a robot: robot and user interface design features that matter. ACM Trans. Comput.-Hum. Interact. (TOCHI) **26**(4), 1–28 (2019). https://doi.org/10.1145/3325210
14. Gallon, L., Abénia, A., Dubergey, F., Negui, M.: Using a telepresence robot in an educational context. In: Proceedings of the International Conference on Frontiers in Education: Computer Science and Computer Engineering (FECS), pp. 16–22 (2019)
15. Page, A., Charteris, J., Berman, J.: Telepresence robot use for children with chronic illness in Australian schools: a scoping review and thematic analysis. Int. J. Soc. Robot. **13**(6), 1281–1293 (2020). https://doi.org/10.1007/s12369-020-00714-0
16. Soares, N., Kay, J.C., Craven, G.: Mobile robotic telepresence solutions for the education of hospitalized children. Perspect. Health Inf. Manag. **14** (2017). https://www.ncbi.nlm.nih.gov/pmc/articles/pmc5653953/
17. Liao, J., Lu, X.: Exploring the affordances of telepresence robots in foreign language learning. Lang. Learn. Technol. **22**(3), 20–32 (2018)
18. Liao, J., Lu, X., Masters, K.A., Dudek, J., Zhou, Z.: Telepresence-place-based foreign language learning and its design principles. Comput. Assisted Lang. Learn. 1–26 (2019). https://doi.org/10.1080/09588221.2019.1690527
19. Liao, J., Dudek, J.: Task design in telepresence-place-based foreign language learning. In: Gresalfi, M., Horn, I.S. (eds.) The Interdisciplinarity of the Learning Sciences, 14th International Conference of the Learning Sciences (ICLS) 2020, vol. 3, pp. 1807–1808. International Society of the Learning Sciences, Nashville (2020). https://doi.org/10.22318/icls2020.1807
20. Kwon, O.H., Koo, S.Y., Kim, Y.G., Kwon, D.S.: Telepresence robot system for English tutoring. In: 2010 IEEE Workshop on Advanced Robotics and its Social Impacts, pp. 152–155. IEEE (2010)
21. Tanaka, F., Takahashi, T., Matsuzoe, S., Tazawa, N., Morita, M.: Child-operated telepresence robot: a field trial connecting classrooms between Australia and Japan. In: 2013 IEEE/RSJ International Conference on Intelligent Robots and Systems, pp. 5896–5901. IEEE (2013)
22. Perifanou, M., Häfner, P., Economides, A.: Users' experiences and perceptions about telepresence robots in education. In: Proceedings EDULEARN, 14th Annual International Conference on Education and New Learning Technologies, Palma de Mallorca, Spain, 4–6 July. IATED (2022). https://doi.org/10.21125/edulearn.2022.2379
23. Perifanou, M., Galea, M., Economides, A.A., Wernbacher, T., Häfner, P.: A focus group study on telepresence robots in education. In: Proceedings EDULEARN, 14th Annual International Conference on Education and New Learning Technologies, Palma de Mallorca, Spain, 4–6 July. IATED (2022). https://doi.org/10.21125/edulearn.2022.2397

What Teachers Would Expect from a Pedagogical Agent System Working at a Classroom Level: A Focus Group Study

Eric Roldan Roa[1(✉)], Doris Kristina Raave[1], Irene-Angelica Chounta[2], and Margus Pedaste[1]

[1] University of Tartu, Tartu, Estonia
{eric.roldan.roa,doris.raave,margus.pedaste}@ut.ee
[2] University of Duisburg-Essen, Duisburg, Germany
irene-angelica.chounta@uni-due.de

Abstract. Applications of pedagogical agent (PA) systems incorporating animated characters in school settings have mainly addressed students at an individual level. However, how these systems could be used and designed for supporting teachers while taking advantage of artificial intelligence (AI) technology is an open question. Therefore, we carried out a focus group to understand what teachers would expect and need from such a system at a classroom level. Our focus group protocol sought to discover design and practical considerations in four dimensions. 1) System design considerations, where teachers expect the system to incorporate speech recognition and to "learn" from them while doing their practice. 2) System collaboration, teachers wanted support in their pedagogy by considering students' achievement profiles, and by finding and sorting learning material as needed. 3) PA role in the classroom, we identified the following roles: annotator, scaffolder, peacekeeper, and substitute. 4) PA ethical considerations, teachers perceive PA as a possible replacement threat and controversial opinions on the use and meaning making of this technology. We discuss our findings and present future research directions to develop a PA that could empower teachers with AI pedagogy in the classroom, hence, indirectly supporting learning.

Keywords: Pedagogical agent · Classroom level technology · Artificial intelligence pedagogy · Focus group · Educational technology

1 Introduction

Educational technology that incorporates Artificial Intelligence (AI) is rapidly gaining attention, as it can serve to automate parts of problem-solving processes comparably to how humans will tackle them [1]. For example, pedagogical agent systems are shown to have positive impact on students' learning [2] by playing pedagogical roles (i.e. peer, mentor, tutor, expert) when interacting with learners [3]. However, design and ethical considerations when deploying these systems on a classroom level to support both, teachers' pedagogy and students' learning, are not yet well defined. This paper explores

I. Hilliger et al. (Eds.): EC-TEL 2022, LNCS 13450, pp. 580–586, 2022.
https://doi.org/10.1007/978-3-031-16290-9_53

what teachers would expect from PA systems when deployed on a classroom level in the K-12 context.

PA systems derive from intelligent tutoring system (ITS) and are capable of simulating teachers' personalized help to students. PA systems incorporate digital entities (agents) that can be implemented in multiple multimedia formats (i.e., text, voice, 2D or 3D characters) [4]. Such systems provide timely feedback and support to students based on estimations of continuously updated models of students' interactions and behaviors [5, 6]. Despite reviews reporting on ITSs effectiveness to support students' learning [7], it is not clear how teachers can benefit by integrating it into their pedagogy [8, 9]. Yacef [10] proposed to jointly support students and teachers with ITS and reconceptualized them as "intelligent teachers assistants" (ITAs). Related research suggests that these systems could increase students' learning by leveraging teacher's practice in the classroom [9, 11, 12]. For instance, [11] suggested that ITSs would need to consider leveraging teachers' practice including time management across multiple students, reducing orchestration load, feedback on teachers' own support to students, actionable diagnosis rather than just data visualizations, students' motivation and frustration management, customize the ITS to fit teachers' pedagogy needs, entirely taking control over the ITS, and allow teachers' eyes and ears to be on the classroom instead of metric dashboards. Other studies have taken a broader scope to understand teachers' perception of AI as a tool to support their practice. For instance, [13] found teachers to have limited or basic familiarity with AI. However, teachers suggested that AI could be a means to foster creativity in their practice, automatically forming groups considering students' knowledge state, and sorting learning materials according to the difficulty level. Conversely, teachers perceived AI use in education to hinder human communication, creating passiveness and/or replacing the human factor.

We build on existing work to contribute toward an effective AI pedagogy. Our work differs in that we focus on pedagogical agent (PA) systems [14] incorporating 2D virtual animated characters that have been used with individual students. This is important to address as some authors have report teachers' passiveness in the classroom when students interact with such systems [15]. We carried out a focus group in which teachers engaged in discussions and shared their insights in four broad categories aiming to integrate PA as an effective pedagogical aid: (i) system design considerations, (ii) PA collaboration, (iii) PA role in the classroom, and (iv) PA ethical considerations.

2 Method

2.1 Study Design

A focus group qualitative method was appropriate for this study as it facilitated the researchers to get new insights and understandings about participants [16] in a cooperative manner where participant's interaction will likely yield the best information for the study [17]. The focus group was hosted online in the last week of November 2021. The consent forms were sent via email, and participants granted permission for video and audio recordings for analysis purposes. Our study considered purposive nonprobability sampling [18]. In total, five K-12 STEM subject teachers and one language teacher participated in the focus group (5 female, 1 male). Five participants were active teachers also studying a master's or PhD program in education-related fields (3 = MA, 1 = PhD), and two were solely teaching. STEM-related represented subjects were natural science, mathematics, robotics, informatics, and physics. Four teachers expressed to always use technology in their classroom, one most of the time, and one sometimes. They further explained to use mainly technology like projectors, computers, mobile devices, smart boards, and robots, but no specification was provided software-wise. Only one of the teachers had previous experience with PAs or ITSs.

2.2 Focus Group Protocol and Coding Procedure

We organized our focus group protocol questions into four initial categories: 1) PA design considerations aiming to explore how teachers would like to intervene or inter-act with the system; 2) PA collaboration, aiming to exploring possible co-teaching processes, that teachers would like to be assisted with by the PA; 3) PA role in the Classroom, aiming to identified roles the PA would need to perform when deployed in a classroom; and 4) PA ethical considerations, aiming to understand issues and threats teachers would raise when deploying this technology.

We transcribed the recorded audio file to text, anonymized the data, and all utterances were divided, and organized in a spreadsheet. We followed an inductive approach proposed by Thomas [19] consisting of the following phases: (i) Initial reading and identification phase, where all utterances containing key pieces of information related to our study objectives were marked with bold. (ii) Labeling phase, where an independent parallel coding was carried out in which the first author introduced the initial four categories to the second author. Then, both coders independently labeled key pieces of information to identify specific topics. (iii) Reducing overlapping categories phase, where both researchers discussed the created labels and reduced them to nine different topics in which all utterances were re-coded. To validate coders' concordance and reliability, we used Cohen's Kappa. (iv) Finally, in the creating a model process phase, we further allocate those nine topics (subcategories) into the initial broad categories of our focus group protocol. Our final data consisted of 73 distinguishable utterances.

3 Results

3.1 PA System Design Considerations

Teachers expressed the necessity to interact with the system by using voice commands (speech recognition technology). This was supported by excerpts like "... *Saying a command, that would be amazing because if you have to insert... a code... or touch it [system app]... Takes time and time is very precious in the classroom. If I can just say it [command to the system] then it would be easier... if you make it [PA interaction] time-consuming or difficult, then teachers won't use it*". Another system interaction requirement was linked to the need for monitoring and controlling the students while teachers must go momentarily from the classroom. An example of the latter was "*If I am in the classroom they know that they [students] have to behave, I am usually talking with them [students] and they feel like somebody is there watching them. I think my replacement [referring to the PA] could alert me if there is a problem, sending a SMS or something like that, I could quickly come back.*". Regarding how teachers would like to intervene in the system, one teacher expressed the need for the system to be able to "learn" and re-configure pedagogical aspects. Excerpts of the latter were "*... The scenario that comes to me is... I could use a code word to stop it [the PA system] for a minute, and if it [PA] could be that smart... to learn from me, that would be amazing... Maybe after my lesson, help it [PA] to improve it. I mean, I think that's like artificial intelligence.... If the pedagogical agent can learn... that would be very resourceful for me to use it then... and I would definitely put the time to help it [PA] learn*".

3.2 PA Collaboration

Teachers expressed the need to collaborate with a PA to be able to alternate their attention between individual and classroom needs. This was supported by excerpts like "*For me, the most important part... is that I could give them [students] individual help, but at the same time, think about all the children together. So... the system could probably help me to... give attendance to the students... so... if I have somebody near me... doing a reading exercise, I can give them [students] personal feedback*". Another need for collaboration was custom support depending on students' achievement profiles. One teacher mentioned, "*In Estonia... there is a big problem. We don't have time to help or guide very smart students. It's sometimes too hard [the exercises or activities] for some students... and my smart ones have done all the work. I don't have the time to give them [advanced students] something harder*". Another collaboration request was for the PA to look and show real-life examples where abstract or difficult topics could be applied. One teacher said, "*...some students have a hard time understanding some topics. So... the agent could help me with some... real-life examples so that the students would understand the topics better*". Finally, last request was for managing internet resources while teachers are addressing the classroom, we found this is utterances like "*... I have to always show pictures... so it would be great if like the agent has already all these pictures... I need*", another teacher followed with "*I absolutely agree with this because my students are always [asking] please, show us, show us this picture on Google*".

3.3 PA Roles in the Classroom

We found teachers' requesting the following roles:

The Annotator will have to manage students' turns (forming a cue for the teacher to assist them) and take notes of students' questions. This was supported by utterances like "*For me... it's quite usual that I give the students an experiment to do in pairs and then, I walk around in the classroom and see how they are doing... solving the problems. So, if I could have someone at the front of the classroom to contain them [students] while I am going around, that will help*". The same teacher later added, "*... and the problem... students forget what they wanted to ask or get confused*".
The Scaffolder will need to repeat, keep track, and explain instructions introduced by the teachers to allow students to complete the activities at a different pace. Teachers pointed out this as a strategy to reduce classroom orchestration load and unnecessary

fatigue. The latter was stressed by "*I thought of one example... how it would really help me. I have to give instructions to the ones [doing the activity] fast, and I have to be ready to help those who are behind... I repeat my sayings [instructions] in the class... this pedagogical agent could repeat that for me because I have to do this a thousand times*".
The Substitute would need to be capable of being to momentarily take over the class, or if teachers are not able to go to class, substitute them. For instance, one teacher said, "*The problem that occurs with my students is that during the breaks, I can't go even to the toilet... every time I come back there is some kind of problem.... And the lesson usually begins with me solving like 10 problems*".
The Peacekeeper should be able to mediate students' interactions to avoid conflicts. This was illustrated by the following excerpt, "*Ok, if you could use [PA] in a group that is working together... they [the students] start fighting, so it would be amazing if [the PA] could move them in the right direction. [With some questions] like are you working? What are you talking about?... That's what I would like*".

3.4 PA Ethical Considerations

Teachers expressed their concerns about PA as a threat of possible replacement rather than empowerment. One teacher said "*...important that I am the teacher in the class... not... this agent. I make my rules and it [PA] has to follow them. This is important because maybe schools don't need us anymore. I need my money, but if I don't have money, I can't drink my coffee*". Another important ethical aspect to consider was in relation to personal data and students' psychological wellbeing, this was found in excerpts like "*I was thinking about privacy, maybe some students are not afraid of anything because they are born with computer and mobile phones [digital natives]. But parents might be afraid that this agent is recording something or doing something bad with data, like their [students'] faces or grades.*" One teacher said, "*If education goes more and more to distance learning, then agent games may be more useful and teachers won't be necessary*". Another controversial aspect teachers raised was regarding assessing and grading. The physics teacher mentioned "*When students are doing a test... I would leave the grading to myself because it would create a bad situation when agents follow a different logic in grading. Usually, computers are harsh... but when I grade, I see what they [students] are doing and if they [the students] are going in the right direction, then I am going to give them some points.*" This was discussed by the math teacher with "*But still, these agents could do something [in relation to grading] for us... but the final word is ours, not theirs [referring to PA]*". Another controversial aspect that raised discussion was in relation to a possible modality where the animated character is a virtual puppet, in other words, the PA functioning in a modality where a real human is fully or partially controlling the agent. Teacher 1 mentioned "*I think in the situation where the puppet [animated character] is controlled remotely by another person... then for me... I would rather take the teacher in the remote station with me in the classroom. But if the system doesn't need an extra human resource, then it would be acceptable for me. We have a problem in Estonia... we don't have enough teachers and I think it would be a waste of resources to use another person somewhere else... just to make it fun for the students*" To this argument, another teacher responded, "*But what about teachers that can't teach* *in the class? Maybe they have some kind of'[disability]... They are in a wheelchair, for example... We have teachers at home that can't teach, and they want to teach... and they have so much to give, and they really want to do their job... This agent gives them the opportunity to work*".

4 Conclusion

Our study suggested design and practical considerations for PA systems incorporating an animated character at a classroom level in the following categories: System Interventions and Interactions. Teachers expect to be able to intervene in the system to make the PA learn and reconfigure itself to match the teachers' pedagogy requirements. PA collaboration. Participants expected the PA to allow them to (i) alternate their attention between individual and classroom needs, (ii) offer custom support depending on students' achievement profiles, (iii) and look and show real-life examples where abstract or difficult topics are applied. PA Role in the Classroom. We found four distinctive roles the PA should be able to perform to support teachers meaningfully. (i) The annotator will have to manage students' turns and questions to help teachers with a cue of assistance, as well as keep track of students' doubts to address them. (ii) The scaffolder will need to repeat, keep track of, and explain instructions introduced by the teachers, so students will be able to do the activities and teachers will avoid unnecessary fatigue by repeating instructions. (iii) As the substitute, the agent would need to be capable of momentarily taking control over the class, or if teachers are not able to go to class, substitute them. (iv) Peacekeeper. Teachers expressed the need to have aid when the activity is carried out in small teams. In this case, the PA should be able to mediate students' interactions to avoid conflicts. All teachers shared similar concerns to relevant literature where AI usage in education is perceived as a potential threat to hinder human communication [13], and to be designed to replace them rather than empower them [11]. However, teachers also engaged in controversial discussions that might depict designing flexibility requirements to meet teachers' preferences when incorporating PA technology in their practice, or practical implications in the case the PA system would partially be controlled by a real human from a remote station. We argue that artificial intelligence (AI) pedagogy [1], should empower teachers by leveraging their practice and support their well-being in a holistic meaningful manner.

References

1. Kong, S.C., Ogata, H., Shih, J.L., Biswas, G.: The role of artificial intelligence in STEM education. In: Proceedings of 29th International Conference on Computers in Education Conference, pp. 774–776. Asia-Pacific Society for Computers in Education, Taoyuan City (2021)
2. Schroeder, N.L., Adesope, O.O., Gilbert, R.B.: How effective are pedagogical agents for learning? A meta-analytic review. J. Educ. Comput. Res. **49**(1), 1–39 (2013)
3. Kim, Y., Baylor, A.L.: Research based design of pedagogical agent roles: a review, progress, and recommendations. Int. J. Artif. Intell. Educ. **26**(1), 160–169 (2016)
4. Martha, A.S.D., Santoso, H.B.: The design and impact of the pedagogical agent: a systematic literature review. J. Educat. Online **16**(1), n1 (2019)

5. Xhakaj, F., Aleven, V., McLaren, B.M.: How teachers use data to help students learn: contextual inquiry for the design of a dashboard. In: Verbert, K., Sharples, M., Klobučar, T. (eds.) EC-TEL 2016. LNCS, vol. 9891, pp. 340–354. Springer, Cham (2016). https://doi.org/10.1007/978-3-319-45153-4_26
6. Albacete, P., Jordan, P., Katz, S., Chounta, I.A., McLaren, B.M.: The impact of student model updates on contingent scaffolding in a natural-language tutoring system. In: Isotani, S., Millán, E., Ogan, A., Hastings, P., McLaren, B., Luckin, R. (eds.) AIED 2019. LNCS, vol. 11625, pp. 37–47. Springer, Cham (2019). https://doi.org/10.1007/978-3-030-23204-7_4
7. VanLehn, K.: The relative effectiveness of human tutoring, intelligent tutoring systems, and other tutoring systems. Educ. Psychol. **46**(4), 197–221 (2011)
8. Nye, B.D.: Barriers to ITS adoption: a systematic mapping study. In: Trausan-Matu, S., Boyer, K.E., Crosby, M., Panourgia, K. (eds.) ITS 2014. LNCS, vol. 8474, pp. 583–590. Springer, Cham (2014). https://doi.org/10.1007/978-3-319-07221-0_74
9. Baker, R.S.: Stupid tutoring systems, intelligent humans. Int. J. Artif. Intell. Educ. **26**(2), 600–614 (2016)
10. Yacef, K.: Intelligent teaching assistant systems. In: Proceedings of International Conference on Computers in Education, pp. 136–140. IEEE, Washington (2002)
11. Holstein, K., McLaren, B.M., Aleven, V.: Intelligent tutors as teachers' aides: exploring teacher needs for real-time analytics in blended classrooms. In: Proceedings of 7th International Learning Analytics & Knowledge Conference, pp. 257–266. ACM, New York (2017)
12. Segedy, J., Sulcer, B., Biswas, G.: Are ILEs ready for the classroom? Bringing teachers into the feedback loop. In: Aleven, V., Kay, J., Mostow, J. (eds.) ITS 2010. LNCS, vol. 6095, pp. 405–407. Springer, Berlin (2010). https://doi.org/10.1007/978-3-642-13437-1_85
13. Chounta, I.A., Bardone, E., Raudsep, A., Pedaste, M.: Exploring teachers' perceptions of artificial intelligence as a tool to support their practice in Estonian K-12 education. Int. J. Artif. Intell. Educ. 1–31 (2021)
14. Alfaro, L., Rivera, C., Luna-Urquizo, J., Castañeda, E., Zuñiga-Cueva, J., Rivera-Chavez, M.: New trends in pedagogical agents in education. In: Proceedings of International Conference on Computational Science and Computational Intelligence, pp. 923–928. IEEE, Los Alamitos (2020)
15. Pareto, L., Haake, M., Lindstrõm, P., Sjödén, B., Gulz, A.: A teachable-agent-based game affording collaboration and competition: evaluating math comprehension and motivation. Educ. Tech. Res. Dev. **60**(5), 723–751 (2012)
16. Saldaña, J.: Fundamentals of Qualitative Research. Oxford University Press, Oxford (2011)
17. Creswell, J.W., Poth, C.N.: Qualitative Inquiry and Research Design: Choosing Among Five Approaches, 4th edn. Sage Publications, Thousand Oaks (2016)
18. Lavrakas, P.J.: Encyclopedia of Survey Research Methods. Sage Publications, Thousand Oaks (2008)
19. Thomas, D.R.: A general inductive approach for analyzing qualitative evaluation data. Am. J. Eval. **27**(2), 237–246 (2006)

Designing LADs That Promote Sensemaking: A Participatory Tool

Madjid Sadallah[1(✉)], Jean-Marie Gilliot[1], Sébastien Iksal[2], Katia Quelennec[3], Mathieu Vermeulen[4], Laurent Neyssensas[5], Olivier Aubert[6], and Rémi Venant[2]

[1] IMT Atlantique, Lab-STICC UMR CNRS 6285, 29238 Brest, France
{madjid.sadallah,jm.gilliot}@imt-atlantique.fr

[2] University of Le Mans, Avenue Olivier Messiaen, 72085 Le Mans, France
{sebastien.iksal,remi.venant}@univ-lemans.fr

[3] Sorbonne Université and Univ. Lille, 59000 Lille, France
katia.quelennec@univ-lille.fr

[4] Center for Digital Systems, IMT Nord Europe, Univ. Lille, 59000 Lille, France
mathieu.vermeulen@imt-nord-europe.fr

[5] Ecole de Design Nantes Atlantique, 44306 Nantes, France
l.neyssensas@lecolededesign.com

[6] LS2N - UMR 6004 CNRS, Nantes Université, Nantes, France
olivier.aubert@univ-nantes.fr

Abstract. Learning Analytics Dashboards (LADs) are data visualization tools built to empower teachers and learners to make purposeful decisions that impact the learning process. Due to their relatively recent emergence and the scarcity of studies on their design principles, dashboard design remains a major area of investigation in learning analytics research, and large scale diffusion to their stakeholders remains limited. We promote human-centered approaches for LADs design since their success in terms of acceptance and adoption greatly depends on the level of stakeholder involvement in their design. In this paper, we present a tool to support the participatory design of LADs. First experiments during a pilot study with teachers demonstrate that the proposed tool encourages group work, and in-depth exploration of LADs use.

Keywords: Learning analytics · Dashboards · Participatory design · Sensemaking

1 Introduction

Learning Analytics Dashboards (LADs) are visualization tools designed to enable teachers and learners to make relevant decisions that impact the learning process [10]. Although they have received increasing interest in recent years, large scale diffusion to their stakeholders remains limited. We argue that reasons are multiple: (1) scarcity of studies on their design principles due to the their relative recent emergence [7]; (2) difficulty to design effective LADs without involving stakeholders [5]; (3) lack of relevant expertise and visual literacy among stakeholders [17]; and (4) failure of LADs to turn insights into action as the processes

I. Hilliger et al. (Eds.): EC-TEL 2022, LNCS 13450, pp. 587–593, 2022.
https://doi.org/10.1007/978-3-031-16290-9_54

by which people use these representations for insight seeking and decision-making are still not well understood [19].

According to research, the success of dashboards in terms of acceptance and adoption, and more globally of any LA innovation, greatly depends on the level of stakeholder involvement in the design process [9]. This has motivated the increasing focus of the LA research community on Human-Centered Design (HCD) approaches and the emergence of the Human-Centered Learning Analytics (HCLA) [3].*Participatory design* (or *co-design*) is a popular approach in HCLA. It derived from user-centered design as a particular case of co-creation where designers who are trained in creativity work together with non-designers during the design process. In LA, it is defined as *an approach where learners, educators, institutions, researchers, developers and designers are all included across different stages of the design process, from exploration to actual implementation* [15]. Although LA academics and practitioners are increasingly acknowledging the relevance of HCD methods such as participatory design, their integration into learning analytics has been slow and is still not yet widespread [16], and approaches to achieving this remain unclear [2,6].

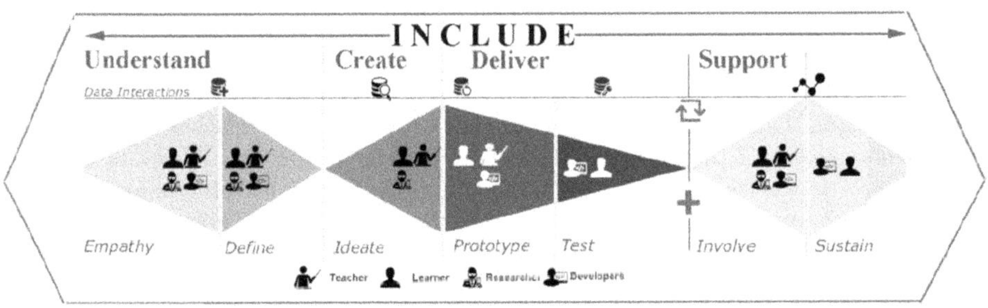

Fig. 1. Interaction co-design process and roles for LA [15]

We aim to instrument more specifically for LADs the co-design process adapted to LA and proposed in [15] (Fig. 1). Its activities are iterated to refine the needs and get closer to the desired solution. In a previous work [4], *Understand* phase was established and has been continuously refined through extensive interaction with different stakeholders. In this paper, we focus more specifically on the *Create* phase. We propose a participatory design tool intended to enable, promote and enhance the accurate and insightful expression of key design elements and requirements (including visualization and idea generation). As recent research on dashboards demonstrates, the sensemaking dimension is pivotal in the construction of relevant dashboards [14]. We thus propose to make this dimension explicit in LAD design.

The remainder of this paper begins with a review of relevant research. It then introduces the proposed participatory design toolkit and briefly describes a case study that illustrates the use of the design tool, before concluding.

2 Background and Related Work

2.1 Participatory Design of LADs

Participatory design promotes consensus building and the convergence of the different stakeholders on the main objective of the dashboard, encourages collective innovation and creativity, and anticipates possible adoption obstacles or usage difficulties. While some examples of successful use for co-design of dashboards are reported in the literature [16], the LA community still lacks tools specific to the needs of LA stakeholders to effectively communicate and understand the design components [2,6]. Popular methods being implemented include workshops and focus groups [1], learning personas [15], and card-based co-design [2]. *Workshops and focus groups* are used to derive design ideas and identify stakeholder opinions. *Learning personas* allow modeling and summarizing essential information about the people who are likely to be involved in the learning ecosystem. *Card-based co-design* provides a common basis for understanding and communication between stakeholders, supports creative combinations of information and ideas, and enhance collaboration and combined creativity [12].

2.2 Supporting Sensemaking with LADs

LADs support and augment human cognition by offering visualizations of learning data [19]. As it is important to know how the user makes sense of the information delivered with LADs, researchers start focusing on how sensemaking occurs with such tools [13]. Proposed models to investigate interaction and sensemaking with LADs tend to break down the process into phases that go from perceiving the dashboard to taking and implementing actions. For instance, the model described in [18] defines four steps: awareness, reflection, sensemaking and action. The steps defined by these models are similar to the levels of situational awareness (SA) investigated by the naturalistic movement to explore human decisions [8]: *perception* of environmental elements in a volume of time and space, *comprehension* of their meaning, and *projection* of their state in the near future. In this paper, we consider sensemaking as the process of constructing situational awareness through which a course of action is developed [11], and interaction as the means by which users draw meaning from LADs.

3 LAD Participatory Design's Support

3.1 Description of the Participatory Design Toolkit

To be effective, a participatory design method needs to be properly instrumented. We therefore designed the PaDLAD (*PArticipatory Design of Learning Analytics Dashboards*)[1] toolkit to support users in better expressing their expectations and needs. Our aim is to foster collaborative workshops. We distinguish three phases

[1] https://padlad.github.io/Participatory-Design-ToolkitV2/en/.

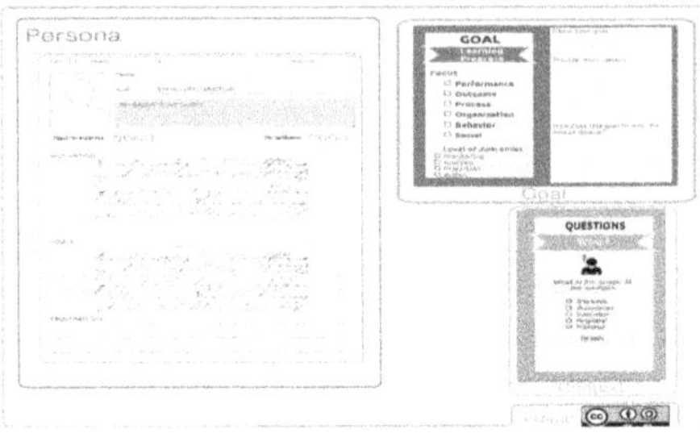

(a) Identification board

(b) DataViz board

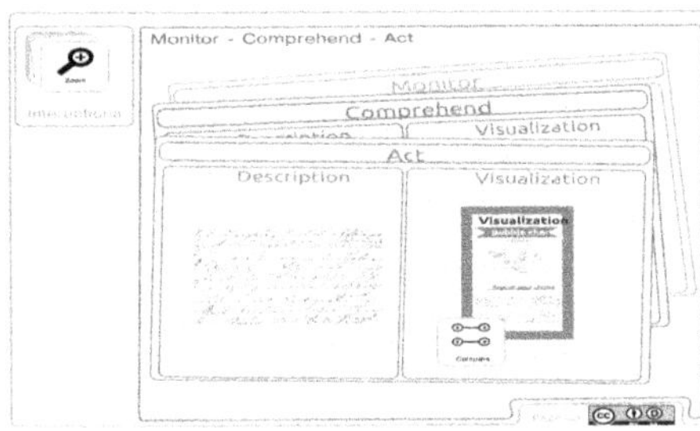

(c) Sensemaking Sketchup board

Fig. 2. Participatory design toolkit

to support the process: (1) *Identification* of the LAD's context and goal; (2) *Data & Visualization* to explore useful data; and (3) *Sensemaking Sketchup* to explore LAD organization and interaction to support sensemaking. These phases are materialized by dedicated boards that group various cards (Fig. 2).

Identification Board. This board is based on the definition of a persona to personify and describe the stakeholders (their expertise, visual literacy, etc.). The goal being essential for ideation, we dedicate a specific domain card to support its expression. Depending on their profiles (learners, teachers, etc.), participants express their goal and relate it to focus and situation awareness level.

Data and Visualization Board. Participants are invited to identify relevant data that are useful to attain their goal. They fill a specific data card for each. They are also invited to associate visualizations they feel relevant. For this, a set of technology cards proposing classical visualizations is provided.

Sensemaking Sketchup Board. The sketching phase supports sensemaking in three ways. First, to foster browsing the Situation Awareness levels, mockups of different colors are used: red for monitoring, blue for analyzing and green for action. Participants have to associate data and visualizations with the different mockups. Second, technology cards are provided to help participants associate interaction options to the LAD. Third, a storyboard form is attached to each mockup to describe the sensemaking process.

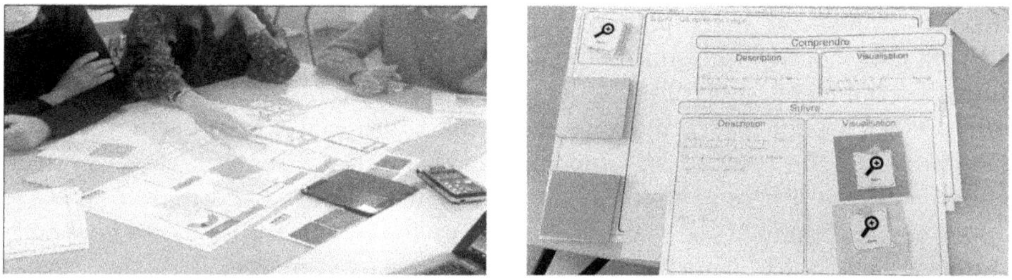

(a) Working in group (b) Example of a produced artifact

Fig. 3. A participatory design workshop using the proposed toolkit

3.2 Ideation Workshop Using the Toolkit

The design session starts with negotiating a goal and setting up the persona (Fig. 3a). Next, participants should work collaboratively to make use of the various boards, cards, and other layouts designed to facilitate the expression of their needs, and to support their creativity. The sequence in which these actions are addressed does not matter, as the participants may have prior ideas (data you want to use, a dashboard you want to use...). Nevertheless, the following order is of interest by default: Who wants to do what, with what data and how to access it to track the achievement of a goal, understand what is happening and act to better fulfill their goal. The more content users can express, the more readily the corresponding dashboard can be created. If they are not inspired by a particular section at a given time, they should not get stuck on it; they can come back to it later. Finally, the session resulted in a potential design represented as filled-in cards arranged in the different boards (Fig. 3b).

3.3 A Use Case

To experiment with the proposed design tool in a real educational setting, we organized a workshop with secondary school teachers. Participants were six teachers (3 male, 3 female), one administrator (male), one instructional designer (female), and three researchers (2 male, 1 female) who played the role of facilitators.

The main challenge encountered during the ideation phase was the negotiation process necessary to establish a persona. This reflects the different and sometimes conflicting personality traits, challenges, needs and aspirations of the participants. Once the description of the persona has been established, the participants moved on to the definition of the pursued goal. They agreed to consider *learning progress*, to focus on the *process* with a *situational awareness level* going from monitoring to planning. Their aim was to adapt their teaching according to the obtained feedback and to develop equality among students.

The participants used the context description cards to express the willingness to consider in-class data of students of each session individually and in combination, and to share the dashboard with the teaching staff. The clear specification of the identification board helped the group in building the target picture using the DataViz board, and simplified the choice of data and visualization to be used. Nevertheless, the different levels of visual literacy have led to debates about which visual representations are most appropriate. The participants felt and expressed the need to be supported in this phase. Finally, the participants constructed the different views of the dashboard following the reasoning stage. Once they had understood the rationale, they found this approach to conceptualizing a dashboard intuitive since it reflects and even materializes the steps of the reasoning and allows them to project themselves into real use scenarios.

4 Conclusion

In this contribution, we proposed PaDLAD, a tool specifically designed to support LAD co-design by promoting a more precise decomposition of the intended goals, including situation awareness level. We combine personas profile to express user needs and ideation card to promote domain needs, and sketching to enable prototyping. A first experiment demonstrated that innovative proposals and LA adoption are possible with teachers, using a participatory approach. Believing that this kind of tools are contextual, we plan to specialize and test the tool in different contexts, with different audiences, and for different purposes. For example, level of situation awareness may be expressed as monitoring, analysis, and decision-making at a governance or institutional level, but will rather be: awareness, reflection and feedback for the student. Adoption of different participatory tools may also vary according to different audiences. To conclude, collecting LAD proposals from users and practitioners may bring out new needs and unveil new intended goals that should be shared with the learning community.

Acknowledgment. This work is supported by the AT41 project funded by the *Digital Education Department* of Ministry of Education (France) and the Orleans-Tours Rectorate.

References

1. Ahn, J., Campos, F., Hays, M., DiGiacomo, D.: Designing in context: reaching beyond usability in learning analytics dashboard design. J. Learn. Anal. **6**(2), 70–85 (2019)
2. Alvarez, C.P., Martinez-Maldonado, R., Shum, S.B.: La-deck: a card-based learning analytics co-design tool. In: Proceedings of the Tenth International Conference on Learning Analytics & Knowledge, pp. 63–72 (2020)
3. Buckingham Shum, S., Ferguson, R., Martinez-Maldonado, R.: Human-centred learning analytics. J. Learn. Anal. **6**(2), 1–9 (2019)
4. Dabbebi, I., Iksal, S., Gilliot, J.M., May, M., Garlatti, S.: Towards adaptive dashboards for learning analytic: an approach for conceptual design and implementation. In: 9th International Conference on Computer Supported Education (CSEDU 2017), pp. 120–131 (2017)

5. Dimitriadis, Y., Martínez-Maldonado, R., Wiley, K.: Human-centered design principles for actionable learning analytics. In: Tsiatsos, T., Demetriadis, S., Mikropoulos, A., Dagdilelis, V. (eds.) Research on E-Learning and ICT in Education, pp. 277–296. Springer, Cham (2021). https://doi.org/10.1007/978-3-030-64363-8_15
6. Dollinger, M., Liu, D., Arthars, N., Lodge, J.M.: Working together in learning analytics towards the co-creation of value. J. Learn. Anal. **6**(2), 10–26 (2019)
7. Echeverria, V., Martinez-Maldonado, R., Granda, R., Chiluiza, K., Conati, C., Shum, S.B.: Driving data storytelling from learning design. In: Proceedings of the 8th International Conference on Learning Analytics & Knowledge, pp. 131–140. ACM (2018)
8. Endsley, M.: Toward a theory of situation awareness in dynamic systems: situation awareness. Hum. Factors **37**(1), 32–64 (1995)
9. Holstein, K., McLaren, B.M., Aleven, V.: Intelligent tutors as teachers' aides: exploring teacher needs for real-time analytics in blended classrooms. In: Proceedings of the 7th International Learning Analytics and Knowledge Conference, pp. 257–266. ACM, New York (2017)
10. Jivet, I., Scheffel, M., Drachsler, H., Specht, M.: Awareness is not enough: pitfalls of learning analytics dashboards in the educational practice. In: Lavoué, É., Drachsler, H., Verbert, K., Broisin, J., Pérez-Sanagustín, M. (eds.) EC-TEL 2017. LNCS, vol. 10474, pp. 82–96. Springer, Cham (2017). https://doi.org/10.1007/978-3-319-66610-5_7
11. Klein, G., Moon, B., Hoffman, R.R.: Making sense of sensemaking 1: alternative perspectives. IEEE Intell. Syst. **21**(4), 70–73 (2006)
12. Lucero, A., Dalsgaard, P., Halskov, K., Buur, J.: Designing with cards. In: Markopoulos, P., Martens, J.-B., Malins, J., Coninx, K., Liapis, A. (eds.) Collaboration in Creative Design, pp. 75–95. Springer, Cham (2016). https://doi.org/10.1007/978-3-319-29155-0_5
13. Nguyen, H., Campos, F., Ahn, J.: Discovering generative uncertainty in learning analytics dashboards. In: Sahin, M., Ifenthaler, D. (eds.) Visualizations and Dashboards for Learning Analytics, pp. 457–475. Springer, Cham (2021). https://doi.org/10.1007/978-3-030-81222-5_21
14. Pozdniakov, S., et al.: The question-driven dashboard: how can we design analytics interfaces aligned to teachers' inquiry? In: Proceedings of the 12th International Learning Analytics and Knowledge Conference, pp. 175–185 (2022)
15. Prieto-Alvarez, C.G., Martinez-Maldonado, R., Anderson, T.D.: Co-designing learning analytics tools with learners. In: Lodge, J.M., Horvath, J.C., Corrin, L. (eds.) Learning Analytics in the Classroom, 1st edn., pp. 93–110. Routledge, Abingdon (2019)
16. Sarmiento, J.P., Wise, A.F.: Participatory and co-design of learning analytics: an initial review of the literature. In: Proceedings of the 12th International Learning Analytics and Knowledge Conference, pp. 535–541 (2022)
17. Schwendimann, B.A., et al.: Perceiving learning at a glance: a systematic literature review of learning dashboard research. IEEE Trans. Learn. Technol. **10**(1), 30–41 (2017)
18. Verbert, K., Duval, E., Klerkx, J., Govaerts, S., Santos, J.L.: Learning analytics dashboard applications. Am. Behav. Sci. **57**, 1500–1509 (2013)
19. Verbert, K., Ochoa, X., De Croon, R., Dourado, R.A., De Laet, T.: Learning analytics dashboards: the past, the present and the future. In: Proceedings of the 10th International Conference on Learning Analytics & Knowledge, pp. 35–40 (2020)

Instant or Distant: A Temporal Network Tale of Two Interaction Platforms and Their Influence on Collaboration

Mohammed Saqr[1,2(✉)] and Sonsoles López-Pernas[1,2]

[1] University of Eastern Finland, Joensuu, Finland
mohammed.saqr@uef.fi
[2] Universidad Politécnica de Madrid, Madrid, Spain

Abstract. This study compared two iterations of the same course where students had the same assignments. In the first iteration, the students had to use the typical discussion forums offered by the popular Moodle learning management system. In the second iteration, students had to use Discord, the popular gaming chat application. Students' interactions were retrieved from both platforms and cleaned. Two social networks were constructed using the same methods to evaluate the differences in patterns of interaction between the two platforms, the group interactivity, the reciprocity, and the quality of interactions. The aim is to study how far an instant messenger facilitates or otherwise constrains collaboration. We use temporal network methods to further understand the pace, rhythm, and temporality of interactions.

Keywords: Social network analysis · Temporal network analysis · CSCL · Learning analytics

1 Introduction

The emergence of big data analysis has kindled the quest to explore its applications in learning. The premise was that studying learners' data may lead to a better understanding of learning [1]. The initial applications have succeeded in modeling and profiling students' performance using trails of their online behavior [2]. Recently, efforts have been directed to using learners' data to understand learning as a dynamic and complex process, i.e., understanding the temporal nature of learning that includes changes, phases, and sequences as well as the complex interactions between learners, learning resources and environments [3, 4]. Such an approach has emerged to address one of the shortcomings of using the data in "aggregate", i.e., static discrete events with no connection to time or temporality [5].

To account for the relational nature of learning, researchers have harnessed the power of network analysis. Networks offer a framework that harnesses the relational dimensions of data. Using networks, researchers have charted the relations, mapped the connections, discovered the interacting communities, and studied the relation between network measures and achievement to mention a few [6–9]. Network mathematical analysis enabled

I. Hilliger et al. (Eds.): EC-TEL 2022, LNCS 13450, pp. 594–600, 2022.
https://doi.org/10.1007/978-3-031-16290-9_55

researchers to quantify interactions, find important actors, study students' roles as well as group interactivity. Yet, researchers have rarely combined the two aspects of learning mentioned (the dynamic and relational aspects) in an analytics framework [8].

Understanding the temporal aspects of interactions or collaborative processes has not received much attention. Most of the existing literature uses aggregate networks where the time dimension has been ignored [7, 8]. Considering how important the timing and order of collaboration events is in learning processes, it is critical that our analysis lens is not time-blind. Taking advantage of time-dynamics allow us to fully understand, e.g., the evolution and devolution of learning communities, the sequence of co-construction of knowledge, the flow of information, and the building of social capital. In this study, we take advantage of the latest advances in temporal networks to reveal the different dynamics of collaborative learning in two different platforms that were used to facilitate collaborative learning [7]. Temporal networks are not just an extension of traditional social networks. In temporal networks, edges form and dissolve, paths are unidirectional (follow the time direction) and vary by time [10].

Different forms of Computer-supported Collaborative Learning (CSCL) have been used; however, asynchronous seems to be the most prevailing type. Asynchronous CSCL comes in many forms: the most common are the forums, bulletin boards or discussion boards and, therefore, almost all LMSs have built-in forums. Forums offer a rich platform where students can interact, collaborate, and manage group projects and assignments. The fact that forum interactions are asynchronous allows students to work at their pace without the pressure of just-in-time replies. However, today's generations are more accustomed to instant messaging services that offer easier, faster replies, notify students with contributions from colleagues and are more mobile friendly [11]. Prior research has shown that instant messaging could help facilitate collaboration and engage students and teachers in productive interactions [12]. However, some studies have also shown that instant messaging platforms may be a distraction [11, 13].

1.1 Motivation for this Study

During the implementation of a computer science course at University of Eastern Finland, where students had to work on a project in small groups and interact together online, students expressed their dissatisfaction with Moodle's asynchronous forum discussions. The dissatisfaction was almost unanimous, where students cited the delay in responses, the lack of notifications and the difficulty in responding to Moodle threads. For instance, a student expressed the lag in response as: *"Chatting in Moodle was also quite hard because of the different timings. If you sent a message, it was possible that you received an answer a week later"*. A move was necessary to an instant messaging platform to accommodate students' needs, and therefore, Discord was chosen as it is open source, works on all platforms and can be accessed from the browser with full function.

This study aims at comparing the two groups: a group that used Moodle forums, and another that used Discord instant messaging. We take advantage of temporal networks analysis as well as statistical analysis. The research question of the study is: *Given the same course, same task, and same teacher: what are the differences in dynamics between Moodle and Discord and how they influence students' interaction patterns?*

2 Methods

2.1 Context

Two iterations of a computer science course where students work collaborative in small groups (5–9 members) for a full month. The two iterations of the course had the same exact task, same group distributions, same teacher and same instructions for the project, while only differed in the interaction platform (Moodle and Discord).

2.2 Data Analysis

Four networks were constructed: two aggregated post-reply networks using the methods of [5, 7] to compare the general patterns of interactions, as well as two temporal networks to compare the dynamics of interactions between the two platforms. Network properties were calculated (Table 1) to compare the patterns across courses (node count, edge count, density, reciprocity, centralization, and transitivity). Temporal graph properties were calculated at each time point. On the individual level, we calculated degree measures which reflect students' participation, interactivity, and reply-worthiness. All network analysis, network measures and computations followed the exact methods described in detail in [5, 7].

3 Results

A comparison between the two networks is presented in Table 1 and Fig. 1. There were 51 active students in the Discord network and 47 in the Moodle network. The interactions

Table 1. Comparison of the two networks

Variable	Description	Discord	Moodle
Node count	Number of students	51	47
Edge count (weighted)	Number of interactions	1750	820
Edge count (unique)	Number of unique interactions (between the same pairs of nodes)	169	106
Network density	Sum of edges divided by the maximum possible edges	0.07	0.05
Mean weighted degree	Mean number of interactions per student	68.63	34.89
Mean degree	Mean number of unique interactions per student	6.63	4.51
Centralization indegree	Distribution of in-degree (received replies) centrality among students	0.08	0.42
Transitivity	Probability that students' contacts are also connected to each other	0.58	0.45

were higher in the Discord network (1750 vs. 820), and so were the measures of density, mean degree, mean weighted degree and transitivity, pointing to a greater cohesion and distribution of interactions and participation among students. The Moodle network was more centralized, i.e., dominated by few students who receive interactions.

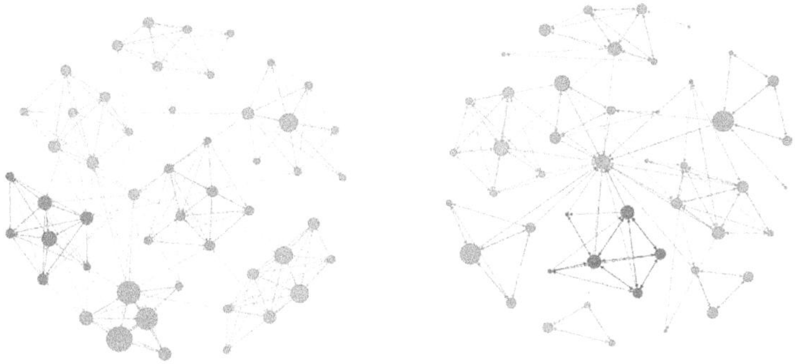

Fig. 1. Left side: Moodle groups with lower number of nodes involved and fewer interactions among them. Right side: Discord networks showing more nodes in each group, and more interactions among students.

Unique Collaborators: At the individual student level, there was no statistical difference in outdegree between both groups (students directed their interactions toward a comparable number of students). However, students in the Discord group had higher indegree (i.e., more students received replies from different collaborators) compared to the Moodle network. A Wilcoxon signed-rank test indicated that the difference was statistically significant p < .01, with a medium effect size. That is, Discord interactions were more participatory. See Fig. 2 for indegree and outdegree distributions and statistical tests.

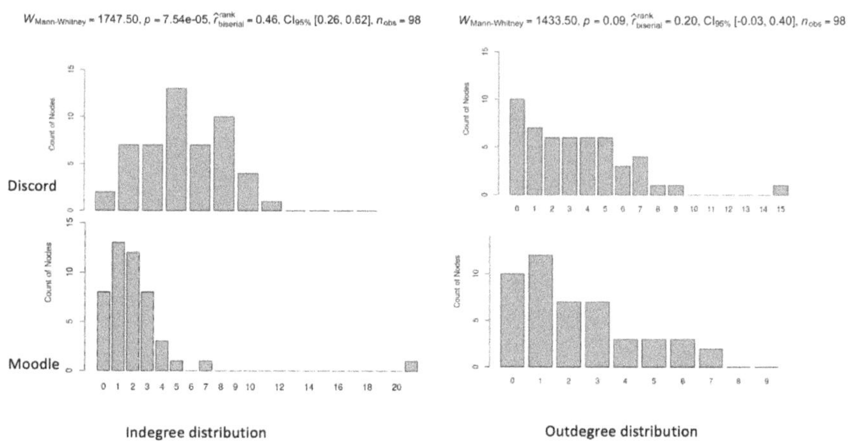

Fig. 2. Comparison between the indegree (unique replies) of two networks.

Interactions: As shown in Fig. 3, students in the Discord group were more likely to post more, with a median of 23 posts as opposed to 9 in the Moodle group. This difference was significant (p < .01) with a small to medium effect size. Students in the Discord group were more likely to receive a reply (latency) within a remarkably short time (median 2.4 vs 63.8 h in Moodle, p < 0.01). However, the number of characters in each post was significantly lower (median of 44 vs. 237.5, p < .01), with a large effect size.

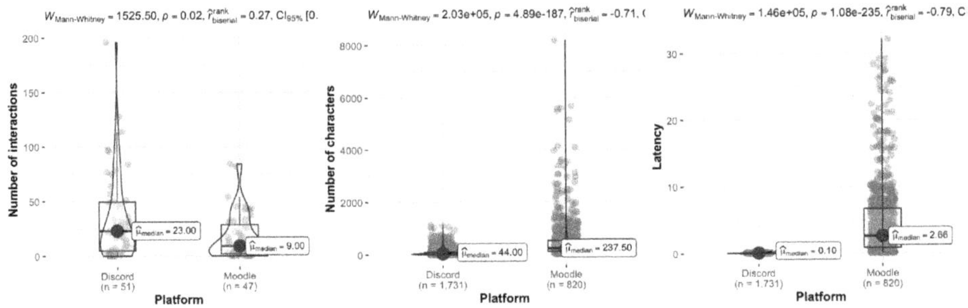

Fig. 3. Comparison between number of interactions (left), length of message (middle), and latency (right) between the two networks.

Temporal Network Dynamics: In contrast with the aggregate network—that gives a single estimate for the density, which was 0.07 in Discord network and 0.05 in the

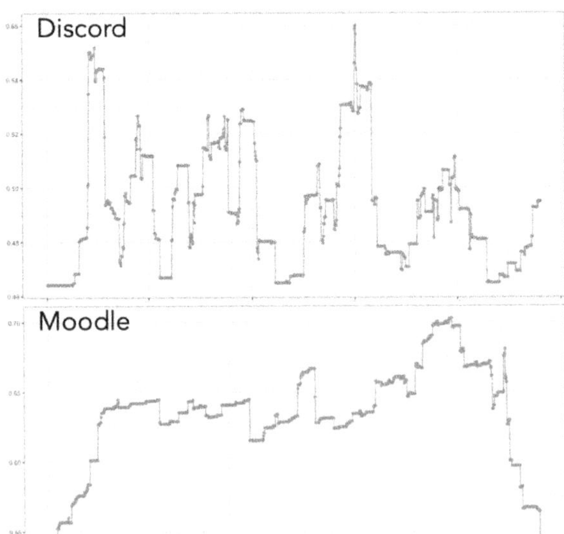

Fig. 4. The Discord temporal density plot (top), compared to Moodle's (bottom). The Discord network shows a bursty nature.

Moodle network—the temporal density is calculated at each time point as a time series, which enables to chart and track the density of network across time. As such, a temporal density plot gives us a more realistic view of the interactivity within the group. Figure 4 shows that the Discord network was more bursty (with frequent peaks) compared to the Moodle network which showed fewer peaks and was therefore "slower", showing less reactivity, which the students complained about (see Sect. 1.1).

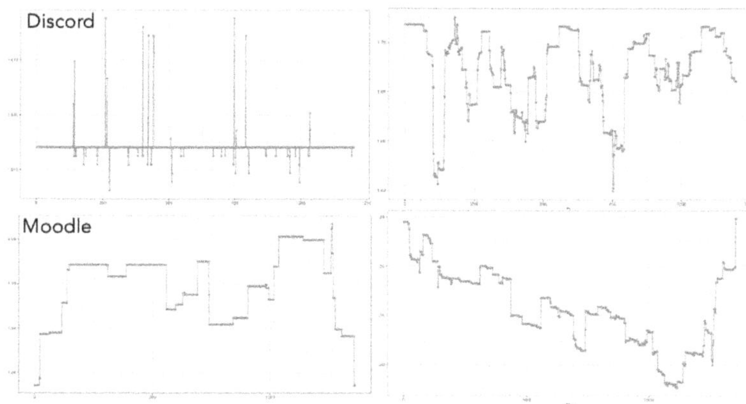

Fig. 5. Discord's temporal reciprocity (top left), compared to Moodle (bottom left). The chart shows the almost instantaneous replies in Discord network. Degree centralization in Discord network (top right), compared to Moodle network (bottom right) shows more variability, while the Moodle network which shows a decreasing trend at the end of the course.

The reciprocity plot (Fig. 5 - left) shows spiky and almost instantaneous reciprocal interactions in the Discord network compared to a flatter and less responsive dynamics in the Moodle network. Degree centralization (a parameter of dominance and lack of distribution of interactions) in the Discord network (Fig. 5 - right) shows a more variable centralization chart. In the Moodle network, centralization showed a decreasing trend at the end of the course.

4 Discussion and Future Directions

The study shows that instant messaging platforms—Discord in our case—may be associated with more participatory contributions both in volume and distribution among collaborators. Our results also suggest that such interactions are more reciprocated, in a relatively shorter time, and are more likely to be discussed or interacted with. The study has also shown the instant messaging is associated with less dominant behavior (low centralization indegree) and therefore highlights the possibility that participation may be easier in instant messaging apps. However, the study suggests that messages are short and, perhaps,—and that needs to be confirmed—lack the depth required. Qualitative analysis of the content using a well-established framework could help verify or refute this hypothesis. Our study has also shown that interactions within instant messages have a higher pace and are more vibrant but also short-lived.

As a future direction, content analysis—which is not addressed by the current study—of the interactions could offer more depth to the analysis. We aim also to use exponential random graph modelling to compare why certain interactions happen and why students choose to respond to certain interactions, harnessing the temporal nature of graph properties and centrality measures using time-series methods to compare the temporal features of interactions.

Acknowledgement. This study is partially funded by the Erasmus+ program of the European Union within the project ENVISION_2027 (grant number 2020-1-FI01-KA226-HE-092653), and by the Academy of Finland (grant number 350560).

References

1. Siemens, G.: Learning analytics: the emergence of a discipline. Am. Behav. Sci. **57**, 1380–1400 (2013)
2. Wong, B.T.M.: Learning analytics in higher education: an analysis of case studies. Asian Assoc. Open Univ. J. **12**, 21–40 (2017)
3. Malmberg, J., Saqr, M., Järvenoja, H., Järvelä, S.: How the monitoring events of individual students are associated with phases of regulation. J. Learn. Anal. **9**, 77–92 (2022)
4. Törmänen, T., Järvenoja, H., Saqr, M., Malmberg, J.: A person-centered approach to study students' socio-emotional interaction profiles and regulation of collaborative learning. Front. Educ. (2022)
5. Saqr, M., Peeters, W.: Temporal networks in collaborative learning: a case study. Br. J. Educ. Technol. (2022). https://doi.org/10.1111/bjet.13187
6. Vu, D., Pattison, P., Robins, G.: Relational event models for social learning in MOOCs. Soc. Netw. **43**, 121–135 (2015)
7. Saqr, M., Nouri, J.: High resolution temporal network analysis to understand and improve collaborative learning. In: Proceedings of the Tenth International Conference on Learning Analytics and Knowledge, pp. 314–319. Association for Computing Machinery, New York (2020)
8. Saqr, M., Poquet, O., Lopez-Pernas, S.: Networks in education: a travelogue through five decades. IEEE Access **10**, 32361–32380 (2022)
9. Saqr, M., López-Pernas, S.: The curious case of centrality measures: a large-scale empirical investigation. J. Learn. Anal. **9**, 13–31 (2022)
10. Holme, P., Saramäki, J.: Temporal networks as a modeling framework. In: Holme, P., Saramäki, J. (eds.) Temporal Networks, pp. 1–14. Springer, Heidelberg (2013). https://doi.org/10.1007/978-3-642-36461-7_1
11. Conde, M.Á., Rodríguez-Sedano, F.J., Hernández-García, Á., Gutiérrez-Fernández, A., Guerrero-Higueras, Á.M.: Your teammate just sent you a new message! The effects of using telegram on individual acquisition of teamwork competence. Int. J. Interact. Multimedia **6**, 225 (2021)
12. Lents, N.H., Cifuentes, O.E.: Increasing student-teacher interactions at an urban commuter campus through instant messaging and online office hours (2010)
13. Fox, A.B., Rosen, J., Crawford, M.: Distractions, distractions: does instant messaging affect college students' performance on a concurrent reading comprehension task? Cyberpsychol. Behav. **12**, 51–53 (2009)

A Conceptual Framework for Creating Mobile Collaboration Tools

Sebastian Simon(✉), Iza Marfisi-Schottman, and Sébastien George

LIUM, Le Mans Université, 72085 Le Mans, Cedex 9, France
sebastian.simon@univ-lemans.fr

Abstract. Field trips combine a number of favourable conditions for collaborative and situated learning. Research has shown that collaboration can be improved by the use of digital tools, such as interactive tables. However, existing tools are heavy and thus unfit for field trips. This article introduces a conceptual framework for the design of collaborative tools in a mobile context. This framework is based on three features: a shared mobile interactive display, a modular tool to support collaboration and scriptable tools to design collaborative educational scenarios. The overall objective is to provide teachers with solutions for designing field-based learning activities and to support learners' collaboration.

Keywords: Computer supported collaborative learning · Field trip · Map · Augmented reality

1 Introduction

Learning is a process that, to this day, is still not fully understood by the scientific community. Models of how learning works have changed significantly over the last 30 years [1]. Two recent theories, collaborative learning [2] and situated learning [3], are being explored in the *SituLearn* project. The aim of this project is to provide digital mobile tools to enhance field trips, such as botanical outings, visits of archaeological sites or museums and event orienteering races. These field trips are part of the school curricula, from kindergarten to college.

Research has shown how digital tools may improve collaborative learning [4]. Having access to a **shared interactive space** is a key element that facilitates collaborative learning [5]. Such shared interactive spaces are most commonly found in interactive tables: a large touch display, horizontally embedded in a table. Those devices have to be plugged into a power outlet, are heavy and cost around 3000€. They are therefore not affordable to public schools and are incompatible with field trips. The work presented in this article addresses the issue of mobility in the current collaboration tools.

Firstly, we briefly introduce the foundations and concepts of our work. Secondly, we present the state of art of current solutions. In the third section, we introduce our contribution in the form of a conceptual framework for the creation of collaborative mobile tools. Finally, the current state of work is presented.

I. Hilliger et al. (Eds.): EC-TEL 2022, LNCS 13450, pp. 601–607, 2022.
https://doi.org/10.1007/978-3-031-16290-9_56

2 Situated and Collaborative Learning

Learning may prove difficult within an education system designed to teach ever more students with fewer teachers [6]. School dropouts are still significant and current educational systems cannot suit everyone. A recent study shows that, in the European Union in 2020 alone, on average 9.9% of all 18–24 year olds do not have any qualifications above lower secondary education levels [7]. Learning means the acquisition and integration of knowledge (or knowhow) in a representation of reality that individuals build throughout a lifetime by interacting with their environment [8]. This representation is intraconnected [9].

Collaboration is therefore very suitable for learning [10], since it requires a group to build a shared representation of the scenario (or the given problem) [11]. The process of creating a shared representation can be considered *auto corrective*: the multidirectional nature of communication in groups allows each participant to get direct feedback to his/her verbal statements, and consequently to adjust his/her own mental representation. Social interactions within the group also are advantageous for the overall learning process [12].

Situated learning also has many advantages. It offers the possibility to learn within a rich and authentic context [3] that may take place outside the classroom (*e.g.* forest, castle ruins etc.). In this case, physical activities and added sensorial input also lead to better memorisation by activating different types of memory [13].

The educational advantages of collaboration and situated learning can be naturally combined in **field trips**. However, traditional tools (*e.g.* maps, scratch books) only allow for static information and limited interaction.

Yet, displaying dynamic information, such as the participants' locations, has proven valuable for enhancing collaboration [5]. A mobile tool allowing for such an interactive shared space would thus be of great benefit for situated collaborative learning in field trips.

3 State of the Art

Current solutions, such as interactive tables, have shown a variety of benefits for collaboration. However, these solutions are not suited for field trips. Thus, this chapter is a state of the art of existing work. The objective is to **exhibit the key principles** a mobile solution should implement, in order to profit from the benefits of non-mobile solutions. Those key principles, noted R1 to R8, will lead to our proposition in the following chapter.

The benefits of interactive tables compared to traditional tools have been thoroughly analyzed in the works of Mateescu *et al.* [5] taking into account 41 studies. The authors established five categories of collaborative processes: *Participation*, *Workspace Awareness, Verbal and gestural communication, Coordination flow, Artefact interaction* and *Level of reasoning*. These five categories will be a guideline for the design of conceptual components of a potential tool (**R1**). The study also provides evidence for disadvantages in the use of interactive tables as collaborative tools. Indeed, large furniture (such as interactive tables) can effectively block important aspects of non-verbal communication such as gestures, hindering important interactions [14] (**R2**).

Hoppe and Ploetzner [15] found that, in groups where members had knowledge on different parts of the topic, collaboration was higher than in control groups where members had the same level of knowledge (**R3**). Members of the same group had to communicate their knowledge and learn about aspects they previously were not aware of. Dillenbourg [16] describes this as one of the ways to increase the probability for collaboration: enforce some kind of collaboration treaty (*e.g.* roles) (**R4**). He also provides three other ways to increase collaboration: an appropriate setup (*e.g.* group size), scaffold interactions (by encouraging or restraining certain types of interactions) and finally, regulating those interactions (**R5**).

Nevertheless, designing and creating collaborative tools is a complex task since it requires resources and skills in multiple disciplines **(R6):** in her thesis, Tong provides a state of the art of 30 digital tools aiming at improving collaboration [17]. Around 40% of the cited studies do not exceed the level of a pre-study. The design and creation of the tool alone seems to use up an important amount of available resources and time.

Among Tong's state of the art figures the study of Sugimoto *et al.* [18]. The authors built *Caretta*, a tool consisting of a **large shared and interactive display** (interactive table) and individual handheld displays (PDAs). This setup has two benefits. Firstly, users decide when to collaborate or to cooperate[1] (**R7**). Secondly, having individual displays allows users to take time to think and reflect, a process hard to do during collaboration, due to its synchronous nature (requiring all participants' constant attention). Sugimoto *et al.* also noticed that participants preferred cooperation with individual displays over collaboration on a shared space. Mechanisms to enforce collaboration had to be put into place (**R8**), such as a voting mechanism that had to be used, at specific times, to progress within the scenario. Another alternative is to restrict functionality on individual displays to foster collaboration on the shared display [18].

4 Conceptual Framework

To our knowledge, there is no mobile tool that covers the above key functionalities R1 to R8. We therefore propose, in the following subsections, a conceptual framework with three main principles.

4.1 A Shared Mobile Interactive Display and Individual Displays

Using a shared display (interactive table) and individual displays (PDAs or smartphones) has proven to be effective (R7). However, the fact that large and bulky hardware can hinder non-verbal communication (R2) and the environment of the field trip require a light and mobile solution. To obtain the benefits of a shared display in a mobile context, the « ***dynamic peephole*** » interaction seems promising: a device is moved on a static surface with respect to an external frame of reference. The device displays an additional layer of information on top of the surface [19]. This allows to augment any surface (*e.g.*

[1] In this article, cooperation is considered as an activity during which each individual works on a part of the problem with few interactions with fellow team members. Collaboration, in contrast, is understood as an activity on which all team members work simultaneously following the same goal.

a map) with functionalities and information. The displayed information can be static (*e.g.* additional pedagogical information about the environment) or dynamic (*e.g.* data collected by participants, participant's position). Having developed a first prototype, we can demonstrate the feasibility of this approach[2]. This shared space can also be combined with individual devices (students' smartphones, see Fig. 1). Collaboration tools can therefore be distributed on shared and individual displays.

Fig. 1. Use of multiple individual displays and a central shared display using a peephole interaction

4.2 A Modular Tool to Support Collaboration

As presented in the state of the art, Mateescu *et al.* have identified five categories of collaborative processes and provided a set of mechanics that can be used to support them (R1). However, we cannot foresee how these different mechanisms (and their technical implementations) impact collaboration, especially due to the complexity of their development (R6). Hence, we propose a number of **individual conceptual modules,** allowing for individual testing (and testing of module combinations). For example, the collaborative process category *Participation* can be supported by the module M1 showing the number of contributions by members to encourage autoregulation. Another module M2 could provide functionality to take decisions in a group by the means of a voting mechanism, increasing performance in the collaborative process categories *Participation* and *Coordination flow*. We strive to provide modules that can be combined and configured depending on end user needs and the context of the field trip.

Those conceptual modules will be implemented through **software modules.** The notion of software modules can be compared to the modularity within software in general, making it easy for other developers to reuse some features without using the entire program. Conceptual modules, on the other hand, might be seen as entire programs (composed of software modules) inspired by the UNIX philosophy[3]. The previously

[2] Currently, we cannot give technical details due to a patent pending.

[3] Software design for reusability and collaboration between software.

mentioned combinations of conceptual modules can be compared (to some extent) to customized UNIX systems in embedded systems. The latter are systems that are highly adapted to their environment, as what is required in the context of field trips and collaborative learning with a variety of conditions and different end users.

4.3 Scriptable Tools

The importance of mechanisms that can coerce participants into collaboration has been shown in R8. It may either be enacted through the absence of functionality on individual devices or by the presence of a mechanism, like a voting mechanism, which has to be used by all participants in order to progress. Therefore, creating such situations through triggering events seems an interesting approach. Such *scripting*[4] abilities would also allow controlling the available functionality and information to each participant at any given moment (R3, R5). Implementing role-play during a scenario would also become possible (R4) [4]. Expanding on the previous example, module M1, that shows the participation of each student in a team, could appear automatically, on a group's displays, if participation appears to be unbalanced or manually, if educators feel the need for it, based on their observations (R5).

The proposed framework therefore allows for the creation of mobile, modularized and scriptable collaboration tools, addressing needs and observations (R1 to R8) identified in our state of art (Table 1).

5 Perspectives and Experiments

Validation of our framework is complex: the number of possible combinations of conceptual modules is a major challenge to the limited resources and experiments that are available to this project. Additionally, the planned configuration both on the conceptual and software level will considerably add to the difficulty of evaluation. The ability to trigger different modules dynamically has the potential to remedy part of this problem by testing multiple modules in a single experimentation. In the medium term, data and results from the scientific community using this framework for further experiments will validate modules and combinations that cannot be tested during this project and provide insights to enhance the interaction model that our experimentations will yield.

Feedback will equally help address the research question related to which combination of modules and under which conditions such a combination maximizes benefits for collaborative learning during field trips.

The modular aspect of the framework is also geared to attract researchers to use it for their own tool creation and to contribute to ongoing development of modules in an attempt to share efforts for complex tool design.

To further encourage use of this framework, design will be technology agnostic and display size independent. Thus, the framework will not be limited to mobile devices. The framework should be able to function on existing interactive tables, as well as tablets or smartphones.

[4] Specific instructions, help or functionality to "guide" participants during collaboration.

In order to test and validate the shared mobile display technology and the first conceptual module combinations, three experimentations are planned for 2022, in diverse contexts: a field trip in geography with master students, an orienteering race with disabled students in secondary school and a history-geography field trip with novice primary school teachers are planned. The design of learning activities will be based on the MoCoGa model developed by Marfisi-Schottman et al. [20].

Multiple prototypes are currently under development to implement the peephole interaction on an A3 sized map. Use cases are not limited to maps exclusively but will enable any surface to be augmented with information and tools depending on context (museums, meetings etc.). The planned experimentations will (or will not) validate the hypothesis that the peephole approach recreates conditions for collaboration in a mobile context and provide the benefits described in studies on interactive tables but with a low-cost and mobile technology, usable during field trips.

Acknowledgements. The research published in this article was carried out for the SituLearn project, financed by the *French Agence National de la Recherche* (ANR-20-CE38–0012).

References

1. Stahl, G., Koschmann, T., Suthers, D.: Computer-supported collaborative learning: an historical perspective. In: Cambridge Handbook of the Learning Sciences, vol. 20 (2006)
2. Lave, J., Wenger, E.: Situated Learning: Legitimate Peripheral Participation. Cambridge University Press, Cambridge (1991)
3. Herrington, J., Oliver, R.: Critical characteristics of situated learning: implications for the instructional design of multimedia. In: ASCILITE 1995, Melbourne, pp. 253–262 (1995)
4. Hmelo-Silver, C., Chinn, C., Chan, C., O'Donnell, A. (eds.): The International Handbook of Collaborative Learning. Routledge, New York (2013)
5. Mateescu, M., Pimmer, C., Zahn, C., Klinkhammer, D., Reiterer, H.: Collaboration on large interactive displays: a systematic review. Hum.-Comput. Interact. **36**, 1–35 (2019)
6. Collins, A., Halverson, R.: Rethinking Education in the Age of Technology: The Digital Revolution and Schooling in America. Teachers College Press, New York (2009)
7. Eurostat: Early leavers from education and training. https://ec.europa.eu/eurostat/statistics-explained/index.php?title=Early_leavers_from_education_and_training. Accessed 19 Dec 2021
8. Wadsworth, B.J.: Piaget's Theory of Cognitive and Affective Development: Foundations of Constructivism. Longman Publishing, White Plains (1996)
9. Adorno, T.W., Hullot-Kentor, B., Will, F.: The Essay as Form. New German Critique **32**, 151–171 (1984)
10. Roschelle, J., Teasley, S.D.: The construction of shared knowledge in collaborative problem solving. In: O'Malley, C. (ed.) Computer Supported Collaborative Learning, pp. 69–97. Springer Berlin Heidelberg, Berlin, Heidelberg (1995). https://doi.org/10.1007/978-3-642-85098-1_5
11. Lajoie, S.P., Derry, S.J.: Computers As Cognitive Tools. Routledge, Milton Park (2013)
12. Lavoué, É., Ju, Q., Hallifax, S., Serna, A.: Analyzing the relationships between learners' motivation and observable engaged behaviors in a gamified learning environment. Int. J. Hum. Comput. Stud. **154**, 102670 (2021)
13. Kennedy, M.: The benefit of field trips. Honors College Theses (2014)

14. Scott, S., Grant, K., Mandryk, R.: System guidelines for co-located, collaborative work on a tabletop display. In: Proceedings of the Eighth European Conference on Computer Supported Cooperative Work, pp. 159–178. ACM, New York (2003)
15. Hoppe, H.U., Ploetzner, R.: Can analytic models support learning in groups? In: Collaborative-Learning: Cognitive and Computational Approaches, pp. 103–121 (1999)
16. Dillenbourg, P.: Collaborative Learning: Cognitive and Computational Approaches. Advances in Learning and Instruction Series. Elsevier Science Inc., Amsterdam (1999)
17. Tong, L.: Designing and analyzing collaborative activities in multi-surface environments. Ph.D. thesis INSA Lyon (2017)
18. Mandryk, R., Maranan, D.S., Inkpen, K.: False prophets: exploring hybrid board/video games. In: CHI'02 Extended Abstracts on Human Factors in Computing Systems, pp. 640–641. ACM, New York (2002)
19. Lucero, A., Keränen, J., Korhonen, H.: Collaborative use of mobile phones for brainstorming. In: Proceedings of the 12th International Conference on Human Computer Interaction with Mobile Devices and Services, pp. 337–340. ACM, New York (2010)
20. Marfisi-Schottman, I., Laine A., Laforcarde, P.: Towards an authoring tool to help teachers create mobile collaborative learning games for field trips. In: Proceedings of EC-TEL (2022). In press

Does Deliberately Failing Improve Learning in Introductory Computer Science?

Sverrir Thorgeirsson(✉), Tanmay Sinha, Felix Friedrich, and Zhendong Su

ETH Zürich, Zürich, Switzerland
{sverrir.thorgeirsson,felix.friedrich,zhendong.su}@inf.ethz.ch,
tanmay.sinha@gess.ethz.ch

Abstract. We report our experience with technology-enhanced Productive Failure (PF) in an introductory computer science course. First, we sought to assess whether the use of algorithm visualization tools during the PF problem-solving phase enhanced learning. Second, we used an experimental study to measure learning effects of administering failure-driven scaffolding (FDS) during the PF sessions, that is, explicitly nudging generation with suboptimal representations deliberately designed to lead to failures. Results from surveys and log data indicated that our visualization tools helped students explore the problem space and performance data signaled that FDS improved students' constructive reasoning (Cohen's d 0.194, BF_{01} 2.55) and did not harm posttest scores (BF_{01} 3.17) relative to no explicit scaffolding during problem-solving prior to instruction. Further, similar levels of induced frustration (BF_{01} 3.29) and curiosity (BF_{01} 3.27) were observed across the conditions.

Keywords: Active learning · Failure · Problem-solving · Scaffolding

1 Introduction

Pedagogical activities inspired by active learning approaches are both expected and well-received by computer science undergraduates [1], and have a positive effect on their learning outcomes [3]. Within that family, a constructivist learning design called *productive failure* (PF) has received significant attention in the literature [5]. PF sessions consist of a (i) *problem-solving phase*, where students are given challenging problems that they are not expected to solve successfully, followed by an (ii) *instruction phase*, where an instructor illustrates the correct solution. Meta-analyses (e.g., [9]) show strong evidence in favor of PF and more generally, learning designs where problem-solving precedes instruction.

PF was initially described as a learning design with no explicit scaffolding. However, there has been recent interest in similar designs that incorporate *failure-driven scaffolding* (FDS), where students' self-generation activity in the problem-solving phase is complemented with prompts that nudge them to generate and reason with additional suboptimal numerical and graphical representations resulting in problem-solving failure by design. Comparative studies in

I. Hilliger et al. (Eds.): EC-TEL 2022, LNCS 13450, pp. 608–614, 2022.
https://doi.org/10.1007/978-3-031-16290-9_57

tertiary data science education have shown that students receiving FDS demonstrate higher quality of constructive reasoning [8,10], that is, provide meaningful elaborations going beyond what was presented. By challenging understanding, FDS may help students activate relevant prior knowledge, reveal knowledge gaps, and aid recognition of deep domain features. However, despite holding promise, this learning design has not yet been explored in computer science.

Here, we report application of PF and FDS in a CS2 course, *Computer Science II*, with just over a hundred enrolled students. This course introduces algorithms and data structures to non-CS majors in the engineering departments of ETH Zürich. Throughout the course, we conducted technology-enhanced PF sessions which incorporated (i) online programming environment with an integrated testing and debugging suite, which was also used for homework assignments, and (ii) custom, interactive algorithm visualization (AV) environments designed to support an alternative and a more inclusive form of domain exploration. We focused on following three research questions (RQs) in our work.

RQ1 How does the provision of FDS during PF sessions impact learning outcomes of conceptual understanding and constructive reasoning for CS2 students?
- **H1** Students receiving FDS during PF sessions will demonstrate better learning outcomes of conceptual understanding and constructive reasoning (compared to students who do not receive FDS).

RQ2 What is the impact of providing interactive AV environment to CS2 students during the problem-solving phase of PF sessions (with or without FDS)?
- **H2** Students working with the interactive AV environment will have positive perceptions about its usefulness in facilitating problem-solving.

RQ3 How do affective factors differentially facilitate learning from FDS in the PF sessions for CS2 students?
- **H3** Students receiving FDS within PF will demonstrate higher frustration and discomfort as well as higher curiosity to know more about the topic.

2 Method

2.1 Study Design

After ethics approval and informed consent, we ran an experimental study on three PF sessions in an introductory computer science course in 2021 ($N = 64$, $n = 28$ female). All sessions were run remotely. In the problem-solving phase of each session, students were asked to devise their own algorithm to solve a problem that they had not encountered before in class. The problems involved (i) sorting numbers by size, (ii) finding shortest paths in a graph, and (iii) solving the cluster assignment problem. We chose these problems for two reasons. First, their discovery implies or requires insight into the key concepts covered in the course. Second, they follow design principles described by Kapur and Bielaczyc [5], namely that they have multiple solution paths and are sufficiently rich to allow "explanation and elaboration" and "compare and contrast" activities during the instruction phase between the canonical solution and student solutions.

In contrast to previous pilot PF sessions, we placed special emphasis on the *PF design fidelity* [9]. For example, we constructed interactive, visual environments (see Fig. 1) for each problem that students could use to explore the problem space and generate multiple solutions, despite lacking coding proficiency. For the session on sorting algorithms, a custom visualization based on the visual programming environment *Algot* [11] was used, which allowed students to demonstrate algorithms under the programming-by-demonstration paradigm. The remaining AVs can be viewed at http://sverrir.helonia.com/pfvis. By introducing AVs, we also hoped to make use of the dual coding framework emphasizing that AVs can be effective when presented together with code as they provide an additional, non-verbal model of the target knowledge [4], thereby offering learners a deeper domain understanding. Our aim was for these AVs to rank well on the AV engagement taxonomy introduced by Naps et al. [7]. To improve *PF design fidelity* further, we introduced failure-driven scaffolds during the problem-solving phase and measured how deliberately designed failure affected learning. Finally, we designed an appropriate social surround emphasizing that the PF sessions were an opportunity to learn and arriving at a correct solution was not the goal, and spent greater instruction time on explaining how the correct solution relates to student-generated solutions.

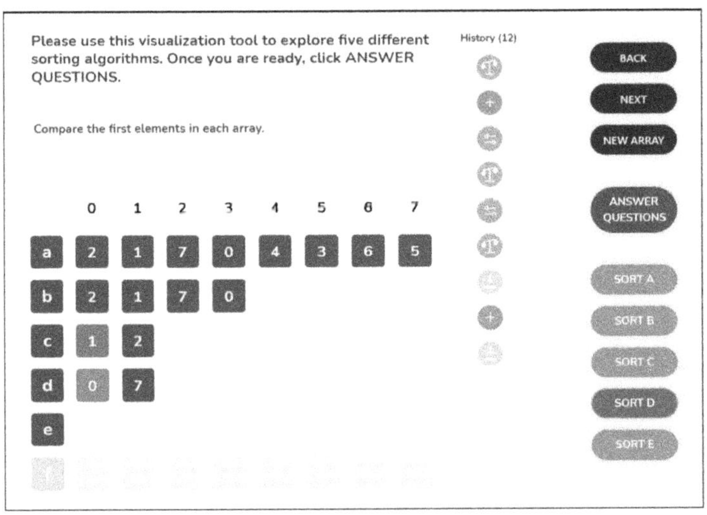

Fig. 1. The visualization environment introduced in the first PF session on sorting algorithms, which is based on the visual programming environment Algot [11].

To measure the effects of FDS, we set up an in-vivo experiment in which some students were randomly assigned FDS during the problem-solving phase, while others were given no explicit scaffolds at all and therefore engaged only in free generation prior to instruction. For example, during the second session on the shortest path problem, all students were given a Python implementation of a graph, preliminary code, and some test cases. However, students in the FDS group were suggested to model their solution based on an implementation of a relatively suboptimal solution (depth-first search), thus making it more challenging to reach the canonical solution when compared to, for example, breadth-first search. Similarly, during the third session on the clustering problem, all students were also given some cues with Python functions that they could use to reach a solution. Students in the FDS group were however given additional functions that they were prompted to use (e.g., `nearest_neighbor_class`), which is not used in the k-means clustering algorithm, and therefore, by design, would likely lead to a suboptimal solution. Taken together, randomly assigning instructional treatments during the problem-solving phase (for high internal validity) as they occur in live classrooms (for high ecological validity), is a strength of our work.

The follow-up instruction phase was identical for both conditions. Posttest questions focused on conceptual understanding of the targeted topics and constructive reasoning. For example, one posttest question introduced the *widest path problem* and the *longest path problem* and asked whether and how Dijkstra's algorithm, which had meanwhile been taught during the lecture, could be modified to solve them. Similarly, another posttest question included a version of the anti-clustering problem, which has a similar conceptual relationship to the clustering problem as the longest path problem has to the shortest path problem. All students were invited to use interactive visualization environments. Here, students could run visualizations of unlabeled sorting algorithms and test them on different inputs, construct paths from a given source node to a sink node on an undirected, weighted graph, as well as assign classes to randomly generated color-coded coordinates on a plane. We measured how students interacted with the visualization environment by administering surveys that focused on perceptions of induced frustration and curiosity to learn more.

2.2 Analysis Plan

To answer RQ1, we graded constructive reasoning and conceptual understanding outcomes on a 5-point scale, in the former case by identifying meaningful elaborations beyond what we presented in class, and in the latter case by identifying correct answers to our questions. Since our sample sizes were small, we used Bayesian analyses to compare the learning outcomes between our conditions. Specifically, we carried out a Bayesian Mann-Whitney U-test with 1000 samples and computed Bayes Factor BF_{01} to test the null hypothesis that administering FDS would have no effect on conceptual understanding and constructive reasoning. To answer RQ2, we conducted a content analysis of answers to analyze student perceptions of the usefulness of visualization modules. We then used the log data to find the frequency of students' interaction with the modules and calculated correlation between the quality of solutions and the use of the visualization. Interaction events, included, for example, actions such as the addition or removal of nodes in the graph. To answer RQ3, we quantitatively and qualitatively analyzed student responses from relevant surveys [8].

3 Results

3.1 Learning Outcomes (RQ1)

Results for one of the topics (shortest path) showed that students who received FDS scored similarly ($M = 2.5$, $SD = 1.07$) on the conceptual understanding posttest as students who did not receive FDS ($M = 2.61$, $SD = 1.26$). Although this difference was not statistically significant ($p = 0.32$) and we failed to reject the null hypothesis, this comparison had a BF_{01} of 3.17, indicating positive or substantial odds favoring the null. The effect size for this comparison was small (Cohen's d −0.095). For constructive reasoning, students receiving FDS scored descriptively higher ($M = 1.55$, $SD = 1.65$) relative to students not receiving FDS ($M = 1.21$, $SD = 1.87$), with a moderate effect size (Cohen's d 0.194), despite non-significance of results ($p = 0.39$). This comparison had a BF_{01} of 2.55, indicating only weak or anecdotal odds favoring the null. Taken together, these results partially support hypothesis H1 of students in the FDS condition scoring higher on the conceptual understanding posttest and constructive reasoning, however only for the latter.

3.2 Use of the Visualization Module (RQ2)

Of the 64 students who participated in the second PF session on shortest path algorithms, all answered a question about the visualization module in a survey provided immediately after the end of the problem-solving phase. 54 students (84%) responded affirmatively when asked if they found the visualization module useful, 6 (9%) responded with a "no" or "not really," and 4 (6%) had mixed reactions such as "a little." No student reported that they did not use it. Of those who explained why the module was helpful, responses focused on reasons such as it "made me realize that my algorithm is crap," helped to "generate an idea," and "just saves time." Of those who had critical comments, one student claimed that while it was better than nothing, it did not help with developing code as it did not support "call stacks and such." One student said that they preferred to work out the solution on pen and paper.

The responses to the survey for the clustering algorithms topic, which was administered online (and outside of class time) a few days after the lecture, showed that 15/25 (60%) students found the visualization module useful, 5 (20%) did not, 4 (16%) had mixed responses such as "a little bit", and one student (4%) claimed not to have looked at it. Two students left technical suggestions about ways to improve the module. In terms of logged data, we saw a fairly high level of engagement, evidenced by the frequency of interaction events per student (average of 14). The frequency of interactions, however did not correlate with learning outcomes ($\rho = 0.075$), suggesting the need to quantify the quality of student problem-solving actions in future work. Taken together, these results support hypothesis H2 of students perceiving the interactive AV environment to be useful in facilitating their problem-solving (with or without FDS).

3.3 Underlying Affective Factors (RQ3)

Results from student reactions collected indicated that 27/62 (43.5%) students responded affirmatively to whether they wanted to learn more about the topic, 12 had reserved responses such as "kind of" or "a little bit," and 23 responded negatively. Overall, there was no difference in reported curiosity ($M = 0.47$, $SD = 0.51$ for FDS versus $M = 0.41$, $SD = 0.5$ for control, $BF_{01} = 3.27$, Cohen's d 0.121). Some students further elaborated on their answers. Of those who responded affirmatively, some wrote that "you get curious because you failed," "I have a lot to learn," and that their failure to solve the exercise prompted them to find and study Dijkstra's algorithm. Of those who had reserved responses, one wrote that they would have preferred to discuss the exercise in small groups. Of other students who submitted negative responses, one wrote that the topic itself was "super interesting" but the exercise itself made them feel frustrated.

We asked students directly about frustration in the same post-experiment survey and also found it to be similar across our conditions ($M = 0.73$, $SD = 0.45$ for FDS versus $M = 0.79$, $SD = 0.41$ for control, $BF_{01} = 3.29$, Cohen's d 0.141). Of the 64 students who responded, 49 reported that the exercise was frustrating to solve. Many of those students added qualifying statements such as "code always frustrates me", "there's always some kind of frustration with coding for me", "on the other hand I am glad that I did find a part of a solution", and "I feel very lost in [the course] in general." Taken together, these results do not support hypothesis H3 of relevant affective factors differentially impacting how students perceive and learn from PF and FDS.

4 Discussion and Conclusion

Our first research question (RQ1) focused on whether students who received additionally received FDS within PF sessions would demonstrate improved learning outcomes. We expected our results to align with prior work in data science education [8,10]. Despite the non-significance of results (owing to our small sample size of 41 students), evidence from Bayesian analyses suggests that students exposed to FDS had conceptual understanding posttest scores similar to (not worse than) students who did not receive FDS. We further found an effect size ($d = 0.194$) favoring FDS for students' constructive reasoning. A contextual interpretation of this effect size, drawing on empirical research from the highest-quality field research on factors affecting objective educational outcomes [6], suggests that our effects are large and correspond to the effects of having a very high-quality teacher (versus an average teacher) for one year [2]. Simply put, our effect size estimate of $d = 0.194$ translates to a 55.5% chance that a person picked at random from the FDS group will have a higher quality of constructive reasoning than a person picked at random from a control group not receiving FDS.

Our second research question (RQ2) focused on the effects of the interactive visualization module and the extent to which it helped students during the problem-solving phase. The survey responses to this question ($N = 99$ in total) were very positive, suggesting high perceptions of usefulness among students. We could not find direct evidence that using the module improved learning outcomes, but a possible explanation is that high-performing students may not have needed the visualization module as much to explore the problem space.

Our third research question (RQ3) focused on the role that affective factors may play in facilitating learning from FDS in generative problem-solving. When working with algorithmic representations deliberately designed to lead to failures, we posit that students would naturally experience frustration and discomfort. However, because this discomfort fuels task progress via problem-space exploration in the presence of FDS, students have a chance to explore relevant problem parameters and develop intuition for what (does not) work. With improved awareness of knowledge gaps, students are better poised to be interested in and learn from the canonical solution. Results showed that not only are FDS students similarly curious, but they also do not experience more frustration.

Acknowledgments. We thank Gustav Hammarhjelm and Dr. Tracy Ewen for valuable feedback on an earlier version of the paper and Dr. Ralf Sasse for helping organize the study.

References

1. Caceffo, R., Gama, G., Azevedo, R.: Exploring active learning approaches to computer science classes. In: Proceedings of the 49th ACM Technical Symposium on Computer Science Education (2018)
2. Hanushek, E.A.: Valuing teachers: how much is a good teacher worth. Educ. Next **11**(3), 40–45 (2011)
3. Hao, Q., Barnes, B., Wright, E., Kim, E.: Effects of active learning environments and instructional methods in computer science education. In: Proceedings of the 49th ACM Technical Symposium on Computer Science Education, pp. 934–939 (2018)
4. Hundhausen, C.D., Douglas, S.A., Stasko, J.T.: A meta-study of algorithm visualization effectiveness. J. Vis. Lang. Comput. **13**(3), 259–290 (2002)
5. Kapur, M., Bielaczyc, K.: Designing for productive failure. J. Learn. Sci. **21**(1), 45–83 (2012)
6. Kraft, M.A.: Interpreting effect sizes of education interventions. Educ. Res. **49**(4), 241–253 (2020)
7. Naps, T.L., et al.: Exploring the role of visualization and engagement in computer science education. In: Working Group Reports from ITiCSE on Innovation and Technology in Computer Science Education, pp. 131–152 (2002)
8. Sinha, T., Kapur, M.: Robust effects of the efficacy of explicit failure-driven scaffolding in problem-solving prior to instruction: a replication and extension. Learn. Instr. **75**, 101488 (2021)
9. Sinha, T., Kapur, M.: When problem solving followed by instruction works: evidence for productive failure. Rev. Educ. Res. **91**(5), 761–798 (2021)
10. Sinha, T., Kapur, M., West, R., Catasta, M., Hauswirth, M., Trninic, D.: Differential benefits of explicit failure-driven and success-driven scaffolding in problem-solving prior to instruction. J. Educ. Psychol. **113**(3), 530 (2021)
11. Thorgeirsson, S., Su, Z.: Algot: an educational programming language with human-intuitive visual syntax. In: 2021 IEEE Symposium on Visual Languages and Human-Centric Computing, pp. 1–5. IEEE (2021)

CLP: A Platform for Competitive Learning

Arpita Vats[1], Gheorghi Guzun[2], and David C. Anastasiu[1(✉)]

[1] Santa Clara University, Santa Clara, CA, USA
{avats,danastasiu}@scu.edu
[2] San Jose State University, San Jose, CA, USA
gheorghi.guzun@sjsu.edu

Abstract. We introduce the Competitive Learning Platform (CLP), an online continuous improvement tool that provides automatic partial performance feedback to students or groups of students on individual or collaborative assignments. CLP motivates students to do their best and come up with new solutions that can lead to improved assignment results before the assignment deadline. In this work, we describe the CLP system and present the results of a comprehensive set of analyses aimed at gauging the impact of utilizing this platform on student motivation, engagement, and performance. The analyses are based on a rich dataset containing CLP submission, student outcome, and student feedback data obtained from a variety of undergraduate and graduate classes using the tool at two universities over a period of five years. The sample includes 18 courses, 606 students, and 15782 CLP submissions. Results indicate that CLP is beneficial in this setting, leading to active student participation and improved motivation.

Keywords: Interactive learning · Competitive learning · Continuous improvement · Immediate feedback

1 Introduction

In the classic lecture-based educational environment, the professor introduces basic concepts during class and students are required to complete homework assignments to strengthen the knowledge they acquired in class. In general, there are few opportunities to compare solutions with those of peers. This traditional way to educate is especially good for those cases where there is a defined set of right answers and where the focus is on correct results, rather than the approach used to achieve them. While this approach has been successful over the years, it does not greatly encourage creative thinking or stimulate enthusiasm in students.

In this work, we introduce the *Competitive Learning Platform* (CLP), an online tool that provides automatic partial performance feedback to students on continuous improvement problems/tasks, motivating them to do their best and come up with new solutions that can lead to further performance improvements. Student submissions for homework problems are evaluated in real-time

I. Hilliger et al. (Eds.): EC-TEL 2022, LNCS 13450, pp. 615–622, 2022.
https://doi.org/10.1007/978-3-031-16290-9_58

and anonymously shared with peers as a motivating factor for subsequent solution refinement. In this paper, we describe the CLP system and present the results of a set of analyses aimed at gauging its impact on student motivation, engagement, and performance. An early analysis of the usefulness of the CLP system, based on only 5 courses, was presented in [6].

2 Competitive Learning Platform

We developed a Competitive Learning Platform (CLP) system that engages students in active learning through peer contests. CLP was developed with the aim to motivate students and promote student engagement in a course, and, unlike systems such as Kaggle[1], is not limited to solving machine learning problems. Students are assigned a (homework) problem they must solve to the best of their ability. Then they submit their assignment results in the CLP on-line portal and, in real time, are given an evaluation score on their submission.

For a particular student, a general CLP dashboard displays a leaderboard with the top three current scorers in the class plus their best score and rank, a graph displaying the class score distribution, a graph displaying the trend of personal submissions, and a table containing all the submissions of the student and corresponding scores. To avoid discouraging students from participating in CLP, only the top 3 scores and the student's own score and rank are displayed. To reduce the potential stress such a competitive environment can pose on some students, CLP provides an option to not display the competition leaderboard.

The CLP system remains open for submission for the duration of the assignment, in most cases 2–3 weeks, and students are allowed a finite number of submissions a day. Students may choose any of their submissions to be counted as their final submission used for grading.

3 Method

The purpose of this study is to gauge the effectiveness of CLP at improving student engagement and learning. To achieve this goal, we have gathered a comprehensive set of data from 18 courses, 606 students, and 15782 CLP submissions at 2 universities. In this section, we will describe these data and the analyses we performed using them.

3.1 Sample

The CLP system has been in use as an active learning tool in more than 20 Computer Science and Engineering classes at San Jose State University and Santa Clara University over the past six years, taught by 3 different faculty. Of these, 3 undergraduate and 15 graduate courses were included in this study. Table 1 lists the number of students in each course and the classification of those students (G/U).

[1] https://www.kaggle.com/competitions.

Table 1. Classes and Student Distribution

Class	Subject	Session	Students	G/U	Survey	Engagement
1	Data Mining	Sp 17	29	G	Y	N
2	Data Mining	Fa 17	40	G	Y	N
3	Data Mining	Fa 17	29	U	Y	N
4	Data Mining	Sp 18	46	G	Y	Y
5	Data Mining	Sp 18	42	G	Y	Y
6	Large-Scale Analytics	Sp 18	46	G	N	N
7	Data Mining	Fa 18	47	G	Y	N
8	Data Mining	Fa 18	25	U	N	Y
9	Data Mining	Fa 18	42	G	N	Y
10	Large Scale Analytics	Sp 19	50	G	N	Y
11	Data Mining	Sp 19	45	G	N	Y
12	Data Mining	Wi 20	31	G	Y	Y
13	Machine Learning	Sp 20	28	G	Y	Y
14	Machine Learning	Fa 20	30	U	Y	Y
15	Data Mining	Wi 21	21	G	Y	Y
16	Deep Learning	Sp 21	31	G	Y	Y
17	Data mining	Sp 21	46	G	Y	Y
18	Data mining	Sp 21	41	G	Y	Y

3.2 Instruments

CLP Submissions and Survey: CLP keeps track of all student profiles and their submissions and partial and full scores for those submissions. For most classes using CLP, we administered a survey at the end of the course to get feedback on the CLP system from the students in the course. In order to reduce bias, the survey consisted of both negative and positive questions, which spurred students to carefully read the survey questions and choose appropriate answers. The survey contains ten closed-ended questions and four open-ended questions. Some of the closed-ended questions were a modified version of the system usability scale [2]. Answers were coded 1–5 in the following order: *Strongly Disagree*, *Somewhat Disagree*, *Neither Agree Nor Disagree*, *Somewhat Agree*, and *Strongly Agree*. Table 2 presents the questions asked in the survey and their polarity (positive or negative). Moreover, Table 1 (*Survey* column) shows which of the classes used the survey instrument.

Table 2. Survey Questions

ID	Question	(+)/(-)
1	I would prefer to use a competitive learning platform for my homework assignments	+
2	I found that the leader board function in CLP discouraged me from trying to improve	–
3	I thought the CLP system was easy to use	+
4	I hope I never have to compete in a homework assignment again	–
5	The leader board function in the CLP motivated me to try my best.	+
6	I found the CLP system unnecessarily complex	–
7	I would imagine that most people would learn to use the submission system in the CLP quickly	+
8	I found the information provided by the CLP was insufficient	–
9	The personal submissions table and graph summary were helpful to gauge my progress	+
10	I found the personal submissions graph for a given assignment unhelpful.	–
11	What were the most useful features of the CLP? Why?	+
12	What were the downsides of using the CLP system? Why?	–
13	How, if at all, did you approach solving a CLP homework assignment in a different way than you would have approached a normal homework assignment?	+/–
14	Did you choose to display leaderboards before submission deadlines? If you could go back to the beginning of the semester and change you choice, would you? Why or why not?	+/–

Learning Management System Data: Courses at both universities use the same learning management system (LMS), which provides both student outcome and engagement data. For each class using CLP, we retrieved student assignment grades for all CLP assignments. Additionally, the LMS provides, for each student, two engagement scores, namely the number of page views and a participation score. We used assignment grades and these scores to gauge the correlation between CLP engagement and course engagement and success. While grades data were available for all but one course, LMS engagement data were only available for more recent courses, as this feature was only recently introduced in the LMS system. Table 1 (*Engagement* column) shows for which of the classes we obtained student engagement scores.

4 Results

As a means to understand the usefulness of the CLP system toward improving student motivation and engagement, we are interested in answering the following research questions:

A. Do Students Believe CLP is a Helpful Tool in Their Learning in the Classes that Use It? After being introduced to the CLP system at the start of each course, even though they are given the option to treat assignments as they do in other classes, the overwhelming majority of students choose to compete in CLP assignments. Figure 1 shows the percentage of students that opted in to the competition for each class. On average, 96.16% of graduate students opted in, while only 88.07% of the undergraduate students did. However, when asked at the end of the course whether they were happy with their opt-in choice or they would have changed it (Q14 of our survey, see Table 2), out of 606 students, only 6 that opted in (0.99%), and 4 that opted out (0.66%), would have chosen otherwise.

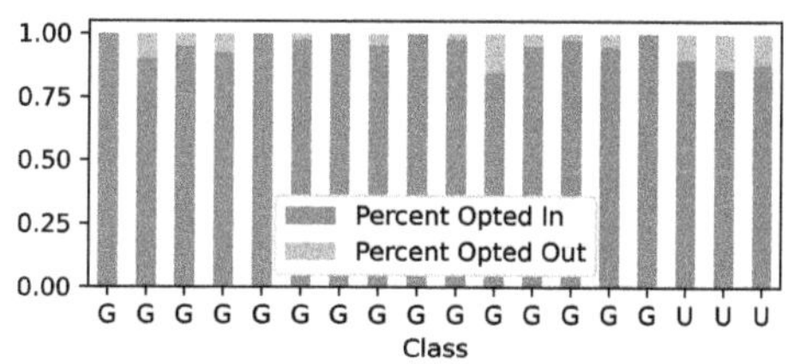

Fig. 1. Competition opt-in distribution for each class in the study.

Figure 2 shows aggregate results for the survey closed-ended questions, after first inverting the negative questions. An overwhelming majority of the students gave 4 or 5 responses, indicating a strong positive perception toward CLP. This means they agreed with all 5 positive questions and disagreed with all 5 negative questions in the CLP survey. While the agreement was more definite for graduate students, with 80.7% of the answers ≥ 4, 70.2% of the undergraduate student answers were also positive (code ≥ 4).

Figure 3 shows the results of our sentiment analysis on the open-ended survey questions. While Q11 and Q12 were positive and negative questions, they show a slightly positive and neutral sentiment polarity from respondents, respectively. Q13 and Q14 are designed as neutral questions that could be answered either positively or negatively. Their sentiment polarity is decisively positive (0.40 mean and 0.14 standard deviation), indicating students enjoyed the platform.

B. Does Using CLP Encourage Students to Try Different Solutions That They May Have Not Previously Considered? One of the major purposes of CLP is to encourage students to approach the homework assignment differently, try multiple solutions, and come up with solutions they did not previously think of. To analyze whether CLP promotes trying a different approach, we studied the sentiments of students in responses to Q13. This question focuses on student attitude towards solving a CLP homework assignment and its comparison with a normal homework assignment. Our analysis shows that sentiments for this question are predominately positive, with a mean of 0.28 and a standard deviation of 0.14. Undergraduate students in Class ID 3, which had the lowest sentiment score of -0.02, complained that the class was structured

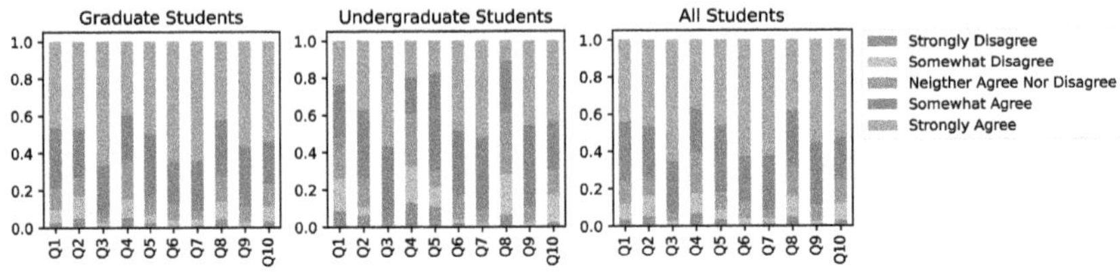

Fig. 2. Response distributions for the closed-ended survey questions.

more like a graduate course and had too many assignments (besides the CLP assignments), which may have affected the sentiment score for this class.

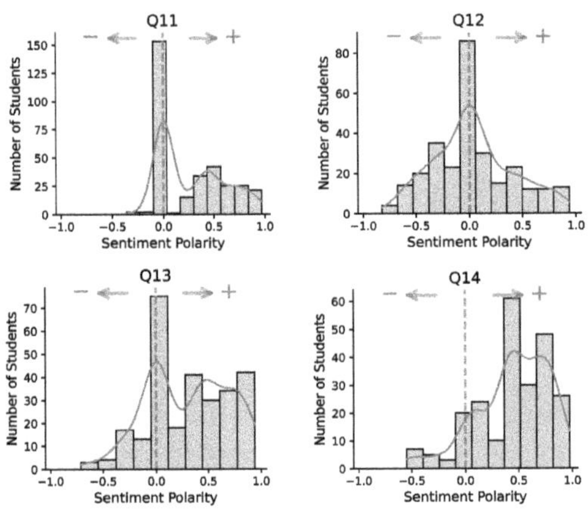

Fig. 3. Sentiment polarity for open-ended survey questions.

Figure 4 shows the distribution of the number of submissions by students in each assignment of each class. The number of CLP submissions can be thought of as an indicator of how willing students are to modify their solution and try to improve their score. As the figure shows, the vast majority of students try more than 5 solutions for each assignment, with some students trying as many as 50 solutions. The average number of submissions for most classes, represented in the figure by the horizontal dotted line, is above 10 for most classes.

C. What is the Impact of Using CLP on Student Performance? The CLP system is expected to aid student performance by encouraging them to engage more in class. Our hypothesis is that, when students engage more in the class, they perform better. To gauge whether student performance is affected by the level of engagement, we studied the relationship between assignment grades and the number of submissions. Results indicate that the students with the best assignment grades have, in general, more submissions than other students with average or low grades, both at the undergraduate and graduate levels. The Pearson correlation scores between class engagement and number of submissions are mostly positive, indicating that students who engage more in CLP will also likely engage more with other class materials.

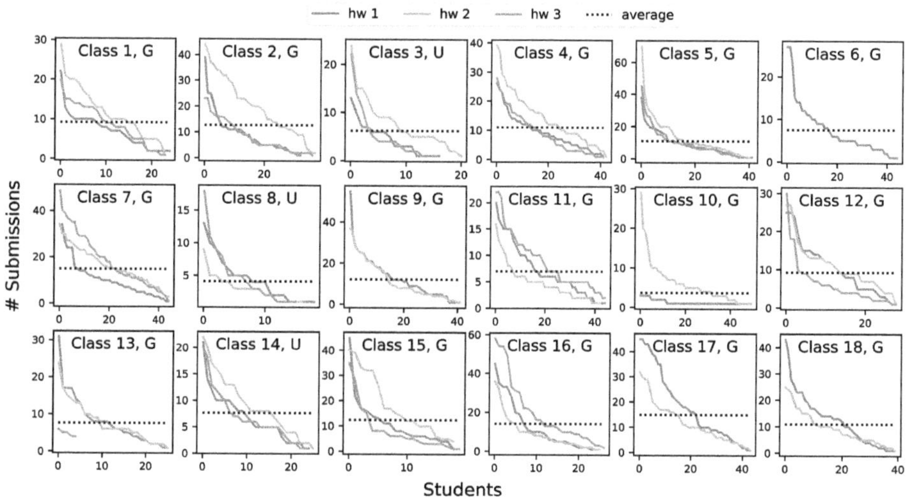

Fig. 4. Competition assignment submission count distribution for each class in the study.

5 Related Work

CLP aims to improve student learning by combining real-time feedback and competitive learning. In this section, we review the body of literature related to this study, including benefits of feedback and competition for student learning in institutions of higher education.

Feedback in Education: Feedback is an integral part of the educational process. It provides learners with a comparison of their performance to educational goals with the aim of helping them achieve or exceed their goals [8]. Studies show that, in general, feedback is a key catalyst for learning [1].

Researchers found that, for tasks such as programming and mathematics, immediate feedback benefits learners [3]. Guthrie and Carlin found that students were generally positive about systems with instant feedback and preferred to take courses that used them. The student response rate approached 100% in class sessions where PRS was used due in part to anonymity, ease of use, and the ability to see how many others answered in the same way [5].

Learning and Competition: Many research studies have focused on utilizing active learning techniques, including collaboration and competition, to enhance student success.

If carefully designed, competitions motivate students and encourage them to do their best [4]. Competitions can enhance student motivation, self-esteem, and learning outcomes. Regueras et al. used competitive and collaborative active learning approaches to motivate students by creating an environment where students collaborate within their group to submit questions to their classmates and compete by answering questions posed by other groups [7].

6 Discussion and Conclusions

In this study, we describe the features of a Competitive Learning Platform (CLP) and evaluate their effectiveness on improving student engagement and learning. We present analysis results based on data collected from the usage of the CLP system over 5 years across 18 courses and 2 universities. Based on end-of-term survey results, the overwhelming majority of students found CLP helpful in their learning (Fig. 1), and only 6 out of 606 students would have opted-out of the competition style learning instead of opting-in. The undergraduate opt-in rate was slightly lower when compared to the graduate rate: 88.07% vs 96.16%. We found that CLP encourages students to try different approaches on our problem solving assignments. Figure 4 shows that students submitted, on average, 10 or more solution submissions, while some students tried up to 50 solutions per assignment. The student CLP activity is correlated with improvements in the assignment objective scores and the assignment grades. In 75% of courses, the CLP activity is also correlated with higher overall engagement in general course activities, as measured by the learning management system. Overall, the rich usage data we collected shows that CLP is effective at encouraging students to try different solutions for their assignments, with significant improvements, while achieving a high user satisfaction as measured by the end of term surveys.

References

1. Black, P., Wiliam, D.: Assessment and classroom learning. Assess. Educ.: Principles Policy Pract. **5**(1), 7–74 (1998)
2. Brooke, J., et al.: SUS-A quick and dirty usability scale. Usability Eval. Ind. **189**(194), 4–7 (1996)
3. Corbett, A.T., Anderson, J.R.: Locus of feedback control in computer-based tutoring: impact on learning rate, achievement and attitudes. In: Proceedings of the SIGCHI Conference on Human Factors in Computing Systems, pp. 245–252. ACM (2001)
4. Fasli, M., Michalakopoulos, M.: Supporting active learning through game-like exercises. In: Fifth IEEE International Conference on Advanced Learning Technologies, ICALT 2005, pp. 730–734. IEEE (2005)
5. Guthrie, R., Carlin, A.: Waking the dead: using interactive technology to engage passive listeners in the classroom, AMCIS 2004 Proceedings, p. 358 (2004)
6. Kapoor, M., Hua, S., Anastasiu, D.C.: Improving student motivation through competitive active learning. In: 2018 IEEE Frontiers in Education Conference (FIE), pp. 1–5. FIE 2018, IEEE (2018)
7. Regueras, L.M., Verdu, E., Verdu, M.J., de Castro, J.P.: Design of a competitive and collaborative learning strategy in a communication networks course. IEEE Trans. Educ. **54**(2), 302–307 (2011)
8. Schartel, S.A.: Giving feedback-an integral part of education. Best Pract. Res. Clin. Anaesthesiol. **26**(1), 77–87 (2012)

Studying Cohort Influence on Student Performance Prediction in Multi-cohort University Courses

Pavani Vemuri[1](✉), Stephan Poelmans[1], Hershal Pandya[2], and Monique Snoeck[1]

[1] KU Leuven, 3000 Leuven, Belgium
{pavani.vemuri,stephan.poelmans,monique.snoeck}@kuleuven.be
[2] Vrije Universiteit Brussel, Ixelles, Belgium
hershal.pandya@vub.be

Abstract. Advances in educational data mining and learning analytics techniques allow instructors and institutions to analyze log data generated from learning management systems to inform themselves about student learning and success. Over the years, several machine learning techniques have been developed, used, and researched to provide more accurate predictions of students' performance in courses. These techniques commonly need and are focused on large sample sizes and low dimensionality which is not the case for university courses in blended contexts. In some studies, student cohorts across years and programs are merged together to increase sample sizes and achieve better prediction accuracies. While there have been other recent studies experimenting with lower samples and fewer dimensions, they do not focus on cohort influences on prediction. There is a need to study this area of analysis and prediction in multi-cohort university courses both to inform (a) instructors, of key course features, prediction insights, and student study behavior to offer relevant interventions to specific cohorts and (b) curriculum designers, who can gain insights into improving program designs. In this study, we look for empirical evidence if performance metrics and key features in prediction are influenced by cohorts in multi-cohort university courses.

Keywords: Predictive learning analytics · Higher education · Multi-cohort university courses

1 Introduction and Related Work

Over the past decade, researchers, instructors, and institutions have been looking for insights from learning analytics (LA) and education data mining (EDM) to inform themselves about student learning and success [3,4,6]. With the increased use of learning management systems (LMS) in higher education (HE) institutions, and capturing data from several sources, the field has extended to several course contexts including MOOCs, online, and blended courses. In most Predictive LA (PLA) studies in HE, data is aggregated over several runs of the course,

I. Hilliger et al. (Eds.): EC-TEL 2022, LNCS 13450, pp. 623–630, 2022.
https://doi.org/10.1007/978-3-031-16290-9_59

and/or including students from different cohorts [2,15,20] to increase the sample size. As some basic courses are sometimes offered across multiple programs in the same discipline, the group of students following a single course may be composed of multiple cohorts of students following different programs. Such multi-cohort courses provide unique opportunities to investigate the impact of cohort/program on outcome prediction. While first-year attrition and student success are common challenges for most HE institutions that look for PLA insights, the effects of the program-cohort (students belonging to a particular program) on predicting success have been rarely considered. We argue the importance of considering program-related features, as some program-cohorts may have different skills than others. For example, for the 4 bachelor programs included in this study, there are simple differences in pre-requisites for the number of Math credits the applicants should have completed in high school. Variables such as pre-university grades have already been used as predictors before, but may not always be available in the data sets at hand. This raises the question of to what extent merging data from different cohorts without keeping the cohort as a variable is a good practice.

The current study is grounded in the constructivist model of self-regulated learning (SRL) by Winne and Hadwin [18,19], which considers learners as active agents who process raw information to create learning artifacts to progress towards their learning objectives. SRL is influenced by internal conditions like motivation, prior knowledge, affective states, and external conditions of the instructional setting like course requirements, the teacher's role and availability, quality of feedback, etc. Featurization in this study is based on SRL as its relevance in online and blended contexts has been well-established [17] for both internal engagement and external instructional design (ID) features. Furthermore, PLA studies that study more than a single course have looked to building portable models, in diverse contexts such as homogeneous courses [4], with the same ID and discipline [12], or those that differ in ID and subject matter [8]; courses across disciplines [7]; courses across disciplines and institutions with different course designs [11,13]. These studies found that predictors and their power changes across different courses, and behavioral indicators are different across disciplines, often with inconsistent or conflicting findings. The current research aligns with these approaches by applying ML algorithms to examine if: (1) program-cohort influences predicting success (2) program-cohort influences (if any) hold across multiple courses and (3) how the influence compares to other features across courses.

2 Dataset and Research Method

2.1 Data Sources and Context

The Business and Economics faculty at a leading European university, offers 4 bachelor's programs Economics (Econ), Business Economics (BEcon), Business Engineering (BE), and Business Information Systems engineering (BISE) in one of its locations. The absence of entrance exams and low tuition fees result in easy access to university education. This promotes an attitude of "trying" university education at the cost of high failure rates in the first year of bachelor's programs. The multi-cohort courses included in this study are the 2020–2021 runs of Global Economy (GE), Markets and Prices (MnP), and Accountancy (ACCT), having each approximately 700+ first-year students from these 4 programs. The primary datasets were extracted from the foundation technologies [9] of the HE institution: log data was extracted from the LMS which was the common platform for all the multi-cohort courses and enrollment and summative scores were sourced from the student information systems (SIS). The datasets across the systems were mapped and pseudonymized by the university guidelines on data management, privacy, and ethics. The course's didactic team had autonomy over how a course is designed, and taught, the use of pedagogy and tools, etc. The teaching duration in a semester for each course was 13 weeks, a 2-week study period, and a 3-week exam period. Quizzes were the only formative evaluations used, and the final grade was based on a written exam that may contain multiple-choice and/or open-ended questions.

2.2 Data Mapping and Preprocessing

The trace data contains granular, low-level click information as events, formative tests as attempts, and forum interactions as posts. Information on errors and missing data was presented to an LMS domain expert, and a curriculum expert, and questions were posed to instructors or SIS experts to better interpret the data and missing values.

Features Construction. Features were constructed from granular log data as indicators of students' online learning behavior based on SRL. To capture the regularity of studying, events (clicks) are aggregated into a number of events per week. As ID is considered an external factor, and each course had a specific design containing documents, videos, forums, etc., this interaction with course design was captured as a cumulative number of events per content type, and, specific to engagement, how much content was accessed by students as a percentage of opened content items. The quiz information in the data was captured as 'Attempts'. Each quiz can have multiple attempts, the average score and highest scores for all attempts per quiz, and (together for) all quizzes were captured as features. Another engagement measure was procrastination - the delay in accessing an item was calculated in days, aggregated as Mean and Median. Specific to this study, to look for program effects on prediction, we utilize one categorical program variable.

2.3 Prediction and Key Feature Extraction

Many or One - Choosing the Right Algorithms. Recent literature reviews [1,5,10] compare extant PLA studies, their methods, featurization, and results. Overall, Random Forest seems the most suitable technique for this data with its two-fold advantages. 1) It is a stable and generalizable algorithm for predicting outcomes on small sample sizes. 2) It allows for key features (KFs) to be identified and reused to reduce high dimensionality. For baseline, we run a Logistic Regression (LR) model as it is a well-established, classical multivariate statistical procedure to predict categorical outcomes and a dummy model that randomly predicts outcomes based on class frequency.

Implementation of Predictive Model. RF and the two baseline models were implemented using the Scikit-learn pipelines [16] in Python. The following explains the model steps for the RF pipeline: (1) A randomized grid search with 10-fold cross-validation is set up via the scikit-learn pipeline. This ensures that no data leakage occurs between train and test samples, (2) the numerical values are scaled after removing features with constant values implementing a variance threshold of zero and the categorical variables are transformed using one-hot encoding, (3) all the features are fed to the Isolation Forest algorithm for outlier removal and the contamination rate of 0%, 2.5%, and 5% were included in the grid search. ANOVA F-score for classification is used to select K best features, (4) Synthetic Minority Oversampling Technique (SMOTE) [14] is used to address the imbalance by oversampling the minority class, and (5) RF classifier is trained. Keeping the sample sizes in mind, we opt for binary classification as SMOTE and k-fold cross-validation do not work well when the minority class population is too low. The final classifier was applied to each course in weekly windows. The ML results were analyzed to construct feature importance tables and week-wise prediction plots.

Classifier Performance Metrics. Accuracy has been the most popular performance metric in research so far but it is not suitable when dealing with imbalanced datasets. The F1-weighted score is a better metric as it optimizes both precision as well as recall while including class imbalances in the metric calculation. The mean and standard deviation of the scoring metric is calculated based on 10 folds of the cross-validation.

3 Results

RF applied to each of the courses on the 18 weekly periods datasets, with grid search and 10-fold classification yielded predictive metrics for each of the 18 weeks. Both LR and RF perform much better than the Dummy classifier as expected. For the courses *GE*, and *ACCT* there was a clear trend of the score increasing from the earlier weeks of the course. In *MnP* however, the first few weeks, the model performs badly, and after the quiz (only one) is introduced by week 6 in the course, both test and train RF scores peak to higher than 0.7 and plateau after week 12. The test score for RF is almost comparable with those of LR for *GE* and *MnP* but RF performs slightly better for the *ACCT* course. Table 1 gives an overview of the top KFs (MeanFI >=0.08) per course and the corresponding importance in other courses is also captured up to the top 15 features. The KFs are calculated using impurity-based feature importances returned by the scikit-learn RF implementation. A Mean Feature Importance (MeanFI) Score for each KF is extracted from the RF algorithm output. Note that the numeric value of significance in Mean FI (with the best feature ranked 1) is specific to each course only and cannot be generalized across courses.

Program Variable KF 10: The one-hot encoded variable *Prog_code_2* is highly significant for the course *MnP* with a MeanFI = 0.085 and Rank 5 and in *ACCT* Rank 15 . *Prog_code_0* (not seen here) holds the 15th rank in the course *MnP*.

Common KFs Across Courses: Table 1 displays three KFs common across the three courses and four common across two courses. If a course contains at least one quiz as in *GE* & *MnP*, the mean score of the highest attempts and average of all attempts were most significant. Percentage of opened content items is a KF across the 3 courses but it is most significant for *ACCT* which does not have any quizzes. Count of clicks on video content (hosted on the Kaltura platform) and the number of events during the teaching weeks (BoC_2_EoC) are key predictors across all 3 courses.

Table 1. Course-wise feature importance

Course abbreviations	GE	GE	MnP	MnP	ACCT	ACCT
Feature*	MeanFI	Rank	MeanFI	Rank	MeanFI	Rank
1. Avg_ScaledScore_AllQuizes _HighestAttempt	0.108	1	0.162	2		
2. Avg_ScaledScore_AllQuizes _AllAttempts	0.09	3	0.168	1		
3. %OpenedUniqContent	0.081	5	0.042	8	0.236	1
4. Mean_Rel_Procr_Opened_Items[a]					0.135	2
5. NEvents_W11[b]	0.099	2			0.036	9
6. ct_kaltura[c]	0.082	4	0.035	12	0.087	3
7. Highest_ScaledScore_Quiz0			0.159	3		
8. BoC_2_EoC	0.043	10	0.04	9	0.083	4
9. Avg_ScaledScore_Quiz0			0.156	4		
10. **Prog_code_2**			0.085	**5**	0.017	15
11. Median_Rel_Procr_Opened_Items[1]					0.077	5

[a] _Rel_Proc - Relative procrastination measure to open content items
[b] N - preceding a feature can be read as Number of (Events, open items, etc.)
[c] ct = Count of clicks on specific content type
* Only limited features are listed in this table with the highest MeanFI

Course Specific KFs: In *ACCT* which has no quizzes, the procrastination scores are KFs. For the course *GE* which contains 11 quizzes, the features, number and percentage of completing quizzes, and the number of clicks on the Quiz link were found to be important (these KFs are not listed in the table due to limited space).

4 Discussion

From the results, we can conclude that the *Program* variable is a KF in some courses (*MnP* & *ACCT*) with varying levels of predictive power across courses. The possible reasons for this result may be: (1) an effect of ID - e.g., the more the quizzes in the course, the attempts variables have higher prediction powers, (2) some courses don't depend on specific skill sets while other do, (3) students can self regulate better in some course than others, (4) some programs are more intensive with a higher workload than others, and (5) some teachers of certain courses are able to smooth out the difference in backgrounds inherent in programs. Further research is needed, using both qualitative and quantitative data collection methods.

Comparing the predictive power of the *Program* variable to other KFs, there is a distinct parity in feature importance related to course contents and design. In courses that have quizzes, the attempts features are the most significant predictors even if the course has only one quiz. While features describing student engagement (representing internal conditions, SRL theory) such as %OpenedUniqContent in Table 1 are common across all courses, they have higher predictive power in courses with no quizzes. With this information, the instructors as domain experts in their own courses can delve into what is happening in their courses during these weeks. Studying trajectories of engagement of successful students in different cohorts during these important weeks could shed more light on what is happening in those specific weeks.

If historical data is not present for courses, the performance metric F1-weighted score reaches an acceptable score by mid-semester leaving enough time for interventions as needed. Nevertheless, the authors note that there is scope for improving on these ML models in this study. The features considered only originated from the event and attempt data. In alignment with SRL, several other features can be explored as demonstrated by [12]. Taking lessons from the predictive power of RF in comparison with LR, it might be worthwhile to explore other simpler algorithms like support vector machines. Additionally, key feature extraction is algorithm-dependent, comparing key features from other algorithms and expanding the number of multi-cohort courses may also solidify the results. In refining results, we can also dive deeper into student trajectories over the weeks. If they are consistent over all the weeks, then having an intervention on this basis would be stronger/more valid. Given that the program may have an impact on prediction, when merging data to obtain a larger sample in PLA studies, it is important to include *Program* as a feature.

In future PLA studies, including the program variable when studying multi-cohort university courses is necessary to inform (a) instructors, who can offer relevant interventions to cohorts at higher risk or those equipped without lower pre-course skill sets, and (b) curriculum designers, who can gain insights on cohort influences into improving program designs and (c) LA researchers to decide on the impact of merging data from different programs/cohorts to obtain larger samples.

5 Conclusion

The reported study examined if a variable specifying the program-cohort a student belongs to in multi-cohort courses is a good predictor for student success; if significance holds across courses (portability) and how its predictive power compares with other key features. The study was based on a sample of 3 multi-cohort courses, with students from different programs, that were homogeneous in terms of institutional setting, discipline, and course size. Along with a comprehensive set of features covering aspects of student activity level, interaction with course content, and engagement, the categorical variable *Program* resulted in models with acceptable performance metrics. The *Program* variable has predictive power for student success and could bring program effects into predicting multi-cohort courses. This has rarely been seen in studies before and this is the novelty the current study brings to the literature. With these results, it is clear that future research is required to further investigate using qualitative and quantitative techniques.

References

1. Al-Tameemi, G., Xue, J., Ajit, S., Kanakis, T., Hadi, I.: Predictive learning analytics in higher education: factors, methods and challenges (2020)
2. Anagnostopoulos, T., Kytagias, C., Xanthopoulos, T., Georgakopoulos, I., Salmon, I., Psaromiligkos, Y.: Intelligent predictive analytics for identifying students at risk of failure in Moodle courses. In: Kumar, V., Troussas, C. (eds.) ITS 2020. LNCS, vol. 12149, pp. 152–162. Springer, Cham (2020). https://doi.org/10.1007/978-3-030-49663-0_19
3. Brooks, C., Thompson, C.: Predictive modelling in teaching and learning. Handb. Learn. Analytics, pp. 61–68 (2017)
4. Conijn, R., Snijders, C., Kleingeld, A., Matzat, U.: Predicting student performance from LMS data: a comparison of 17 blended courses using Moodle LMS. IEEE Trans. Learn. Technol. **10**(1), 17–29 (2016)
5. Cui, Y., Chen, F., Shiri, A., Fan, Y.: Predictive analytic models of student success in higher education: a review of methodology. Inf. Learn. Sci. **120**(3–4), 208–227 (2019)
6. Du, X., Yang, J., Shelton, B.E., Hung, J.L., Zhang, M.: A systematic meta-review and analysis of learning analytics research. Behav. Inf. Technol. **40**(1), 49–62 (2021)
7. Finnegan, C., Morris, L.V., Lee, K.: Differences by course discipline on student behavior, persistence, and achievement in online courses of undergraduate general education. J. Coll. Stud. Retent. Res. Theor. Pract. **10**(1), 39–54 (2008)
8. Gašević, D., Dawson, S., Rogers, T., Gasevic, D.: Learning analytics should not promote one size fits all: the effects of instructional conditions in predicting academic success. Internet High. Educ. **28**, 68–84 (2016)
9. Gasevic, D., Tsai, Y.S., Dawson, S., Pardo, A.: How do we start? an approach to learning analytics adoption in higher education. Int. J. Inf. Learn. Technol. **36**(4), 342–353 (2019)
10. Hu, X., Cheong, C., Ding, W., Woo, M.: A systematic review of studies on predicting student learning outcomes using learning analytics, pp. 528–529 (2017)

11. Jayaprakash, S.M., Moody, E.W., Lauría, E.J., Regan, J.R., Baron, J.D.: Early alert of academically at-risk students: an open source analytics initiative. J. Learn. Analytics **1**(1), 6–47 (2014)
12. Jovanović, J., Saqr, M., Joksimović, S., Gašević, D.: Students matter the most in learning analytics: the effects of internal and instructional conditions in predicting academic success. Comput. Educ. **172**, 104251 (2021)
13. Lauría, E.J., Moody, E.W., Jayaprakash, S.M., Jonnalagadda, N., Baron, J.D.: Open academic analytics initiative: initial research findings. In: Proceedings of the Third International Conference on Learning Analytics and Knowledge, pp. 150–154 (2013)
14. Lemaître, G., Nogueira, F., Aridas, C.K.: Imbalanced-learn: a python toolbox to tackle the curse of imbalanced datasets in machine learning. J. Mach. Learn. Res. **18**(17), 1–5 (2017)
15. Nguyen, V.A., Nguyen, Q.B., Nguyen, V.T.: A Model to Forecast Learning Outcomes for Students in Blended Learning Courses Based on Learning Analytics. Association for Computing Machinery, New York, NY, USA (2018)
16. Pedregosa, F., et al.: Scikit-learn: machine learning in python. J. Mach. Learn. Res. **12**, 2825–2830 (2011)
17. Rasheed, R.A., Kamsin, A., Abdullah, N.A.: Challenges in the online component of blended learning: a systematic review. Comput. Educ. **144**, 103701 (2020)
18. Winne, P.H.: A metacognitive view of individual differences in self-regulated learning. Learn. Individ. Differ. **8**(4), 327–353 (1996)
19. Winne, P.H., Hadwin, A.F.: Studying as self-regulated learning. In: Metacognition in Educational Theory and Practice. The Educational Psychology Series, pp. 277–304. Lawrence Erlbaum Associates Publishers, Mahwah, NJ, US (1998)
20. Zacharis, N.: A multivariate approach to predicting student outcomes in web-enabled blended learning courses. Internet High. Educ. **27**, 44–53 (2015)

What Kind and How Many?: Exploring Feedback in Remote Training of Procedural Skills in Physiotherapy

Ignacio Villagrán[1,2], Rocío Hernández[2], Javiera Fuentes[1,3], Gustavo Torres[1], Diego Silva[1], Nicolás Araya[1], Mauricio Delgado[1], Constanza Miranda[4], Andrés Neyem[2], Julián Varas[5], and Isabel Hilliger[2](✉)

[1] Health Science Department, Pontificia Universidad Católica de Chile, Santiago, Chile
[2] School of Engineering, Pontificia Universidad Católica de Chile, Santiago, Chile
ihillige@ing.puc.cl
[3] School of Health Professions Education, Maastricht University, Maastricht, The Netherlands
[4] Faculty Biomedical Engineering Department, Baltimore, USA
[5] Department of Digestive Surgery, Pontificia Universidad Católica de Chile, Santiago, Chile

Abstract. Practical learning in physiotherapy education became challenging during the pandemic. Socio-sanitary constraints limited hands-on scenarios and instructors' opportunities to provide timely feedback to their students. Asynchronous remote training through a feedback-oriented platform is an alternative with potential benefits beyond emergency distance learning. This preliminary quantitative study analyzes the results of the implementation of an asynchronous remote strategy for teaching manual techniques to Physiotherapy undergraduate students. Sixty-one students reviewed a procedure video, recorded their execution of the procedure, and uploaded it to an online platform. An instructor assessed the video through an observation scale, providing students with different feedback inputs. Students repeated the process if they did not meet the cut-off score. In the development of two procedural skills, the results showed that students with lower performance received more feedback, especially in the form of "common mistakes videos". Finally, instructors showed significant differences in the number of feedback inputs assigned to students with the same performance. This strategy allowed students to train in practical skills remotely, receiving feedback in a specific and unique way. While feedback in different formats was valued, we believe that further research is needed on feedback content and its impact on learning beyond just quantity and format.

Keywords: Remote learning · Health science education · Practical skills · Feedback

1 Introduction

Since the outbreak of the COVID-19 pandemic, many universities and colleges have implemented what researchers call 'remote emergency teaching' or 'emergency online

I. Hilliger et al. (Eds.): EC-TEL 2022, LNCS 13450, pp. 631–637, 2022.
https://doi.org/10.1007/978-3-031-16290-9_60

education' to prevent the spread of the virus among their students [1]. This often implies faculty members teaching in front of computer screens [2], while students attend video lectures from home [1]. In many cases, this involved giving continuity to the study plans in the best way possible. In particular cases, the rapid transition to remote learning restricted skill development and learning outcome attainment. In fact, the transition to distance education affected many programs with a highly practical nature, particularly in health science education [3]. For example, degrees such as Physiotherapy required the development of several practical skills for their professional exercise [4]. Unfortunately, socio-sanitary restrictions limited hands-on scenarios to assess students' capacity to perform procedural tasks, limiting in turn the opportunities to give them timely and quality feedback [3]. Although the global impact of COVID-19 on procedural skills and manual therapy education has not been fully studied [5], studies have already revealed that procedural program trainees had exhibited less educational preparedness compared to their peers in non-procedural degrees [3]. In this context, the teachers have migrated their training processes to a remote format, which led to a series of educational innovations to continue developing clinical skills [6, 7]. In this regard, the literature in health sciences education describes different strategies based on technological resources, such as the use of online tutorials [6] and video assessments [7], tele-simulation [8], virtual demonstrations [9], etc. Regardless of these efforts, students usually report mixed results in the implementation of remote teaching and digital resources, especially for the development of practical skills [10, 11]. This might be partly since feedback delivery has not been necessarily optimized in these new ways of procedural skill training.

This work is part of a larger study to explore technology-based feedback for the development of procedural skills in health science degrees. So far, previous studies have been published concerning experiences in Medicine and Healthcare Professionals [12, 13]. Specifically, asynchronous remote training strategies have been delivered throughout a platform that provide instructors with the possibility of giving feedback in different formats (oral, written, drawn, videos, etc.). Previous results suggest that this functionality to provide timely feedback has benefits for the training of any practical skill beyond remote learning. In this paper, we present preliminary results from an observational study conducted in a physiotherapy program at a Latin American university, aiming to explore how the type and amount of feedback throughout a platform relates to the process of remote acquisition of procedural skills in physiotherapy students. Further details concerning methods and findings are presented in the sections below.

2 Methods

2.1 Design and Context

This Work-In-Progress is part of an observational study conducted in a Latin American university under approval of its ethical committee. This study is a preliminary exercise to illustrate the different forms of feedback that the platform used allows and the implications for student performance and teacher preferences. In this work, we addressed the following research question: (1) How does the type and amount of feedback in a digital environment relate to the process of acquiring procedural skills remotely and asynchronously? Participants were 61 physiotherapy undergraduates enrolled in the

"Movement Analysis" course during the second half of 2021: a core course in the fourth semester of a 10-semester study plan. Throughout formative training, students developed skills concerning upper limb manual therapy techniques, so that they understand how the shoulder, elbow, wrist, and finger joints move from a therapeutic point of view. Participants had an average age of 20 years old and 65.6% were identified as female, and 34.4% were identified as male. In addition, 98% of the students declared to have resources available for recording the requested videos at home, and 100% declared to have a permanent device to watch the video tutorials (e.g., notebook or tablet). Regarding the instructors, 4 higher level students were selected. All the trainees were randomly assigned to the instructors, two reviewed 19 students, and two reviewed 20 students.

2.2 Instruments and Procedures

A feedback-oriented platform was used to develop procedural skills remotely. To develop the skills, students had to watch online video tutorials on this platform and then record themselves at home applying the techniques shown in the video on a simulated patient (usually friends or family). They uploaded their videos to the platform for a trained instructor to review, who can provide a score and type of feedback throughout the same platform. The training consisted of a preliminary theoretical stage and three procedural stages (Fig. 1), ending with a survey about the students' experience. In the theoretical stage, relevant concepts for understanding the techniques to be performed in the next stage were explained. Then, they consecutively advanced to the procedural stages, which consisted of recording the techniques and receiving feedback. If the students reached the minimum expected score, they advanced to the next stage; if not, they had the opportunity to upload a revised video within a maximum period of 4 days until the minimum score was reached so they could move forward.

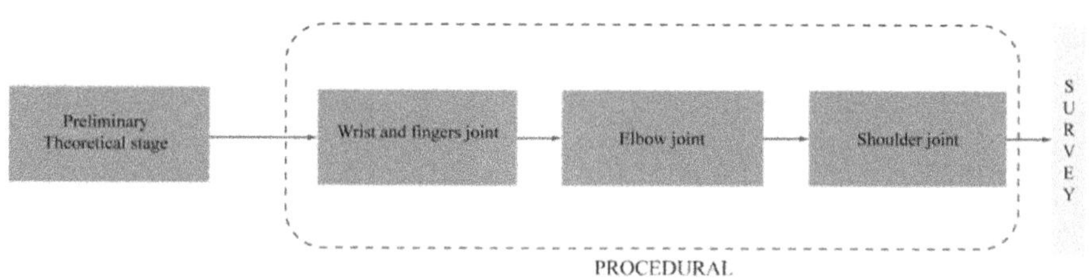

Fig. 1. Diagram of procedural skills training process.

Once students uploaded a video, instructors could deliver feedback through different formats: (1) Audios, where the instructors record their voice delivering narrative information; (2) Texts, where the instructor writes down the information; (3) Videos of common mistakes: were the instructor adds pre-recorded videos showing how to correct a detected error that is common to students; and (4) Drawings, where the instructor mark on the video screen with different colors and shapes. These types of feedback were selected based on teaching needs for procedural assessment and previous experience in other procedures [13].

For each technique, a marking rubric of procedures was used for assessing students. The instruments were validated by expert judgment using the Delphi method [14]. At the same time, the threshold or minimum required score that students had to achieve in each procedure to pass was defined using the Angoff method [15]. The instructors were selected from a group of volunteer upper-level students. As part of their training, each instructor had to assess two dummy videos that were also reviewed by one expert. Then, the instructors' differences with the expert in terms of the score, amount, and type of feedback input were discussed.

3 Statistical Analysis

In this study, a descriptive analysis was conducted on data collected through the use of the feedback-oriented platform. Specifically, we analyzed the scores by each study participant in each one of the stages, students' preferences regarding the feedback format received, the amount of feedback given by instructors, and type of feedback provided. We also performed a Pearson correlation to analyse the relationship between student performance at each procedural stage and the number of feedback inputs per format for each of these stages. Finally, we performed multiple regressions to analyse the effect of instructors on the number of feedbacks given in each procedural stage (controlled by student performance).

4 Results

4.1 Descriptive Analysis

The average performance of the students is shown in Table 1, where the average total score obtained in each delivery is observed. According to the final survey (see Fig. 1), audio was the format of feedback input with the highest preference among students, (55%), followed by video of common mistakes (25%), text (10%) and drawing (10%).

Table 1. Students' academic performance by procedural stage

Stage	Attempt	n	Average score	SD	Median score	Q1	Q3
Wrist/fingers joint	1	61	17.16	2.5	18	15	19
	2	19	19.58	1.43	20	19	20.75
Elbow joint	1	61	19.02	1.72	19	18	20
	2	7	19.86	0.69	20	19.5	20
Shoulder joint	1	61	18.34	2	19	18	20
	2	3	19.4	0.97	20	19	20

Note: Score varies between 0 and 21.

4.2 Number and Type of Feedback According to Students' Performance

A correlation analysis was used to analyze the relationship between student performance and number of feedback inputs per format, treating each procedural stage as a separate event (Table 2). For the wrist and finger joint stage, there are no significant correlations for any of the feedback formats. For the elbow joint stage, there is a negative and significant correlation between students' performance and the number of audios, videos of common mistakes, and drawings, with the highest magnitude and significance for common mistakes. For the shoulder joint stage, there is a negative and significant correlation between students' performance and the number of audios, videos of common mistakes, and drawings, repeating the previous pattern concerning magnitude and significance.

Table 2. Correlation matrix between student performance in each technique and the number of feedback inputs per format for the same stage.

Stage	*Texts*	*Audios*	*C. mistakes*	*Drawings*
Wrist/fingers joint	0.05	−0.01	−0.13	0.03
Elbow joint	0.05	−0.29*	−0.43***	−0.37**
Shoulder joint	−0.35**	−0.29*	−0.60***	−0.38**

* p < ,05 ** p < ,01 *** p < ,001

4.3 Instructors' Effect on the Number of Feedback Inputs

A multiple linear regression analysis was used to compare the instructors' influence on the number of feedback inputs delivered on each video, controlling for student performance at each stage. For this, several analyses were performed to contrast each of the instructors with each other. First, for the wrist and fingers stage, a significant difference is shown between instructors 1 and 3 ($\beta = 2{,}57$, $p < 0.01$), 1 and 4 ($\beta = -3{,}08$, $p < 0.01$), 2 and 3 ($\beta = 4.58$, $p < 0.001$) and 3 and 4 ($\beta = -5.65$, $p < 0.001$). For the elbow stage, there are significant differences between instructor 1 and 2 ($\beta = -3{,}08$, $p < 0.001$), 1 and 3 ($\beta = 3{,}38$, $p < 0.001$), 1 and 4 ($\beta = -0{,}91$, $p < 0.05$), 2 and 3 ($\beta = 6.45$, $p < 0.001$) and 2 and 4 ($\beta = 2.16$, $p < 0.001$). Finally, for the shoulder stage, there are significant differences between instructors 1 and 2 ($\beta = -3{,}08$, $p < 0.001$), 1 and 4 ($\beta = -3{,}04$, $p < 0.001$), 2 and 3 ($\beta = 3.22$, $p < 0.001$), and 3 and 4 ($\beta = -3.19$, $p < 0.001$). These results reflect that some instructors deliver significantly different numbers of inputs at each stage to students with the same performance. For example, for each score given to the same student performance for the wrist and fingers stage, instructor 3 gave 2.57 more feedback, while instructor 4 gave 3.08 feedback less than instructor 1.

5 Discussion

These preliminary results reveal two major findings. On the one hand, there is a correlation between students' performance and the amount and format of feedback inputs provided to each student. In the development of two procedural skills, students with lower performance received more feedback, particularly in the form of "audios", "drawings" and specially "common mistakes videos". On the other hand, multiple linear regressions show that the instructor profile is a predictor of the amount and format of feedback inputs provided. These findings inform further research and practice concerning the use of technology-based feedback in the development of procedural skills.

First, there were differences concerning students' preferences for a format of feedback and what they received concerning their performance. On the one hand, students declared to prefer audio inputs. According to previous studies [16, 17], audio feedback can be perceived closer to students due to the intonation of the instructor in this type of format. On the other hand, videos of common mistakes seemed to have a special relevance to improve student performance of procedural skills remotely. Concerning this, it is worth noting that the format in which feedback is provided can facilitate feedback processes from an interpersonal perspective [16], and audio-visual recordings of performance feedback can also be very effective for learning and help strengthen the relationship between students and teachers [18]. In these lines, this study suggests that the use of different types of technology-based feedback may vary concerning student performance, particularly concerning the development of procedural skills. Thus, design choices might not only follow student preferences, but also pedagogical features concerning what might be more suitable for specific learning outcomes. Second, there is a significant difference in the number inputs assigned by the instructors to students with the same performance. This illustrates that each instructor has personal preferences that make this process variable despite initial training. While this might lead us to believe that the initial training was inefficient, this could relate to the fact that feedback processes require teaching competences for delivering feedback that are variable to respond to the individual needs of learners [19]. It is important to note that this study does not analyze the content of the feedback inputs, which is a limitation since it may impact on the results and preferences obtained. This is particularly relevant, since students must have helpful information to allow them to improve their performances [20] and provide comments that have insights into how students can improve performance, using feedback inputs in a practical way and avoiding general criticisms or generic comments [21]. In this regard, future work must look in depth at how instructors' decisions, student feedback literacy, and the content of feedback inputs influence the incorporation of feedback for procedural skill mastery, along with evaluating new features or nudges that could be included feedback-oriented platforms to promote self-regulated learning.

References

1. IESALC, UNESCO: COVID-19 and higher education: from the immediate effects to the day after (2020)
2. Bao, W.: COVID -19 and online teaching in higher education: a case study of Peking University. Hum. Behav. Emerg. Technol. **2**(2), 113–115 (2020)
3. Enujioke, S.C., McBrayer, K., Soe, K.C., Imburgia, T.M., Robbins, C.: Impact of COVID-19 on post graduate medical education and training. BMC Med. Educ. **21**(1), 1–6 (2021)
4. World Physiotherapy: physiotherapist education framework. World Physiotherapy, London, UK (2021)

5. da Silva, J.B., Abreu, R.: Physical therapy postgraduate education during COVID-19 pandemic: a Brazilian perspective. Eur. J. Physiotherapy **24**(3), 191–194 (2021)
6. Magowan, S., Stewart, M.: A mixed methods study to evaluate physiotherapy student preferences in digital teaching for achieving effective learning of practical skills. Physiotherapy **114**(1), 73–74 (2021)
7. MacDonald, C.W., Lonnemann, E., Petersen, S.M., Rivett, D.A., Osmotherly, P.G., Brismée, J.M.: COVID 19 and manual therapy: international lessons and perspectives on current and future clinical practice and education. J. Man. Manip. Ther. **28**(3), 134–145 (2020)
8. Mercado, E., Morales, J., Lugo, G., Quintos, A., Esperón, R.: Telesimulación: una estrategia para desarrollar habilidades clínicas en estudiantes de medicina. Investigación en Educación Médica **10**(40), 19–28 (2021)
9. Chao, T., et al.: Creation of an interactive virtual surgical rotation for undergraduate medical education during the COVID-19 pandemic. J. Surg. Educ. **78**(1), 346–350 (2021)
10. Ranji, K., Phadke, D., Tilak, P.: Perception of e-learning among physiotherapy students. Int. J. Sci. Healthc. Res. **7**(1), 12–16 (2022)
11. Ray, J., et al.: Virtual telesimulation for medical students during the COVID-19 pandemic. Acad. Med. **96**(10), 1431–1435 (2021)
12. Vera, M., et al.: Implementation of distance-based simulation training programs for healthcare professionals: breaking barriers during COVID-19 pandemic. Simul. Healthc. **16**(6), 401–406 (2021)
13. Quezada, J., et al.: Minimally invasive tele-mentoring opportunity-the mito project. Surg. Endosc. **34**(6), 2585–2592 (2020). https://doi.org/10.1007/s00464-019-07024-1
14. Reguant, M., Torrado, M.: El mètode Delphi. REIRE Revista d'Innovació i Recerca en Educació **9**(1), 87–102 (2016)
15. De Champlain, A.F.: Standard setting methods in medical education. Underst. Med. Educ. 347–359 (2018)
16. Carless, D., Winstone, N.: Teacher feedback literacy and its interplay with student feedback literacy. Teach. High. Educ. 1–14 (2020)
17. Hennessy, C., Forrester, G.: Developing a framework for effective audio feedback: a case study. Assess. Eval. High. Educ. **39**(7), 777–789 (2014)
18. Boud, D., Dawson, P.: What feedback literate teachers do: an empirically-derived competency framework. Assess. Eval. High. Educ. 1–14 (2021)
19. Dawson, P., et al.: Technology and feedback design. In: Spector, M., Lockee, B., Childress, M. (eds.) Learning, Design, and Technology, pp. 1–45. Springer, Cham. (2018). https://doi.org/10.1007/978-3-319-17727-4_124-1
20. Henderson, M., Ajjawi, R., Boud, D., Molloy, E.: Identifying feedback that has impact. In: Henderson, M., Ajjawi, R., Boud, D., Molloy, E. (eds.) The Impact of Feedback in Higher Education, pp. 15–34. Springer, Cham (2019). https://doi.org/10.1007/978-3-030-25112-3_2
21. Henderson, H., et al.: Conditions that enable effective feedback. High. Educ. Res. Dev. **38**(7), 1401–1416 (2019)

Personalizing the Sequencing of Learning Activities by Using the Q-Learning and the Bayesian Knowledge Tracing

Amel Yessad(✉)

Sorbonne Université, CNRS, LIP6, 75005 Paris, France
amel.yessad@lip6.fr

Abstract. In this paper, we present an approach for personalizing the sequencing of learning activities that relies on the Q-learning. The Q-learning learns a sequencing policy to select learning activities that aims to maximize the learning gain of students.

On the one hand, the core of this approach is the use of the Bayesian knowledge tracing (BKT) to model the student knowledge state and to define the Q-Learning reward function. On the other hand, we defined with experts rules to generate simulated students. These simulated data were used to initialize the Q-table of the Q-Learning and answer its"cold start" problem.

We present empirical results showing that the sequencing policy learned from the expert-based initialization of the Q-table provides the system with an efficient strategy to improve the students' knowledge states in comparaison with the Q-table randomly initialized. We further show that Q-Learning approach based on the knowledge states of the students inferred by the BKT are promising way for adaptive instruction in intelligent tutoring systems.

Keywords: Adaptive instruction · Q-Learning · Bayesian knowledge tracing

1 Introduction

In intelligent tutoring systems (ITS), Curriculum Sequencing has been widely studied and consists on the planned sequence of learning activities (definitions, examples, questions, problems, etc.) that are most suitable according to the student caracteristics [1].

Several research [2,4,5] have shown the interest of reinforcement learning (RL) for instructional policies, as RL models can learn complex and latent relationships between instructional tasks, students actions, and knowledge outcomes. In particular, the problem of sequencing the learning activities in ITS according to the student caracteristics fits well a RL problem [2].

ANR PROJECT IECARE

I. Hilliger et al. (Eds.): EC-TEL 2022, LNCS 13450, pp. 638–644, 2022.
https://doi.org/10.1007/978-3-031-16290-9_61

In this paper, we tackle the issue of the personalized sequencing of learning activities. To do this, we propose an approach that relies on the Q-Learning [6], a RL algorithm. The sequencing policy learned in the Q-Learning is guided by the student knowledge state that is inferred by the bayesian knowledge tracing (BKT) [3].

We first formalise the problem of sequencing of learning activities by defining the main elements of the Q-Learning: the Q-table and the reward function. Then, we propose to initialize the Q-table with experts in order to answer the"cold start" problem of the Q-Learning, to fast its convergence and maximize the student learning gain.

To evaluate our approach, we carried out a first empirical study. The obtained results show that the sequencing policy learned from the expert-based initialization of the Q-table provides the system with an efficient strategy to improve the students' learning gains in comparison with the Q-table randomly initialized. We further show that Q-Learning approach based on the knowledge states of the students inferred by the BKT are promising way for adaptive instruction in ITS.

We will use the term Knowledge component (KC) in this paper, others refer to the KC as a skill, a concept or even a competency.

The paper is organized as follows: first, the principle of the Q-Learning and the BKT model are presented. The proposed approach and our contributions are summarized in Sect. 4. Then, the learning process and the experimental study are described in Sect. 6. Finally, the main conclusions are given in Sect. 7.

2 Q-Learning: Q-table and Q-function

Q-Learning is a RL algorithm where an agent learns the make decisions (actions) in different situations (states) through trial and error. It is relies on (1) a table, named Q-table that associates observed states s with actions a and (2) a function, named Q-function that maximizes a "value function" $Q(s, a)$ of an action a for a state s.

In our case, the Q-table is the data structure used to calculate the maximum expected future rewards for each learning activity at each student knowledge state. This table will guide the Q-Learning agent to select the "best" learning activity for each student to maximize her learning gain. Each value of the Q-table is first initialized randomly and then learned via the following Q-function (or the Bellman equation):

$$\underbrace{\text{New}Q(s,a)}_{\text{New Q-Value}} = Q(s,a) + \underbrace{\alpha}_{\text{learning rate}} [\underbrace{R(s,a)}_{\text{Immediate reward}} + \underbrace{\gamma}_{\text{Discount rate}} \overbrace{\max Q'(s',a')}^{\text{Maximum predicted reward, given new state s' and all its possible actions a'}} - Q(s,a)]$$

where $R(s, a)$ is the immediate reward received when selecting the action a in the state s, α is the learning rate ($0 < \alpha \leq 1$) and γ is the discount rate ($0 < \gamma \leq 1$), reflecting the importance of the immediate reward comparing to the future rewards.

The reward function $R(s, a)$ is detailled in the Sect. 5.2.

3 BKT Model

The BKT model [3] is a two state hidden Markov model that is used to infer students' mastery of a knowledge component (KC) and at every practice opportunity, a student who has not mastered the KC has some probability of attaining mastery (the parameter T). If a student has mastered a KC, they will answer a question correctly unless they"slip" with some probability (the parameter S), and if the student has not mastered the KC, they can only guess correctly with some probability (the parameter G). In BKT, each KC is modeled separately without considering any relationships between KCs. Other work on individualized BKT models [7] describes different approaches for defining and learning student-specific parameters but we focus our approach only on the original BKT model.

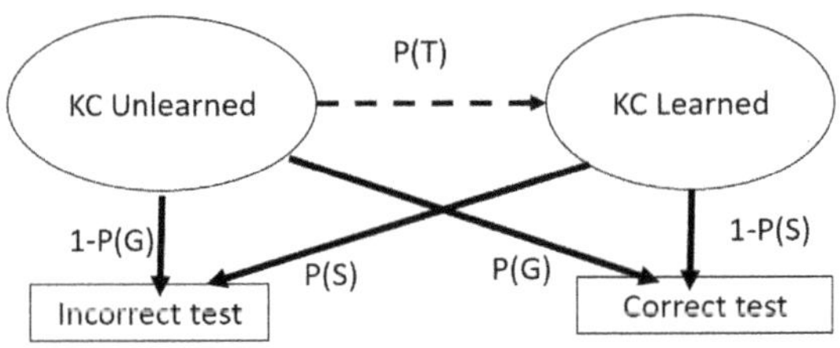

Fig. 1. The BKT model and its parameters L, S and G

4 Our Approach and Contributions

We propose an approach that learns how to assign learning activities to students in order to maximize their learning gains. This approach is based on connecting the Q-Learning to the BKT. Our contributions are:

1. We formulate the problem of sequencing of learning activities in order to maximize the student learning gain,
2. We propose a method based on simulated students to initialize the Q-table with "acceptable" values and answer the"cold start" problem of the Q-Learning algorithm. The simulated students were defined with experts.
3. We carried out a first experiment in order to evaluate the performance of the implemented system

5 Problem Formulation

In this section, we formalize the problem of learning a sequencing policy for maximizing the student learning gain. It implies to define the mains components of the Q-Learning algorithm : the states and the actions of the Q-table and the reward function that maximizes the student learning gain.

5.1 Student Knowledge State and Learning Activities

In accordance with the BKT model, each knowledge component (KC) is either in the learning state or in the unlearned state. Thus, we consider a knowledge state of a student as a vector of the mastering of each KC by the student (1 if the KC is learned by the student, 0 otherwise). The size of the vector is the number of the KC considered in the system. Thus, if we consider N KCs then we have 2^N possible knowledge states.

In Q-Learning, the Q-table is used to associate actions to states. In our case, we consider each student knowledge state as a state of the Q-table and each action as a learning activity (definition, example, demonstration, etc.). Each time a learning activity is proposed to the student, an associated testing activity is also proposed. The testing activity is mandatory and the student has to perform it before passing to new learning activity. That is serves us for updating the mastery of the KCs in the BKT model of the student.

5.2 Reward Function

In each step for each student, the Q-Leaning selects a learning activity to present to the student, based on the Q-table and the ϵ-greedy exploration/exploitation strategy. Once, the student performs the testing activity associated to the selected learning activity, the BKT model infers the new mastery of the KCs worked on the learning activity. After converting the mastery probabilities to a binary values, the binary knowledge state is communicated to the Q-Learning agent for determining the next state in the Q-table. Finaly, the agent recieves the immediate reward corresponding to the move from the knowledge state s to the knowledge state s' and updates the Q table entry according to the Bellman equation (cf. 2).

The reward function is defined as the following:
$R(s,a) = \sum_{i=1}^{N}(s'_i - s_i) \quad \text{if } s'_i > s_i$
where s' is the new knowledge state of the student inferred by the BKT model after selecting the learning activity a and N the number of KCs in the learning plateform. The underlying idea of this reward function is that the more new KCs are mastered, the greater the reward. The cumulatives rewards quantify the learning gains of the students.

6 Learning Process and Experiment

In education, it is quite critical to initialize the Q-table randomly because the RL agent, before learning enough a good sequencing policy, can recommand activities that are not well adapted to the students who may thus have to complete more activities than later students, may spend more time to improve their knowledge state and may be demotivated to use the learning plateform. In order to address this concern—known as the"cold start" problem— we initialize the sequencing policy using simulated students. We focus this paper on this issue and aim to verify that the learning of the RL policy can be speeded up if the Q-table is initialized with data similar to the target data.

Thus, we have implemented a three-step process:

1. An initializing step: it consists on initializing the Q-table with simulated students. Rules were defined with experts to generate simulated students (cf. 6.1). These simulated data were used to train for the first time the sequencing policy and initialize the Q-table.
2. A training step: in this step, the RL agent interacts with real students either by exploiting optimal decisions or by exploring other activities and updating the Q-table based on the expectation of the future rewards. These successive updates would allow the RL agent to converge to a good sequencing policy that maximize efficiently the students' learning gains.
3. A using step: when the RL agent has converged to a good sequencing strategy, it is time to use it to teach other students. These students will achieve their knowledge goals in the best way the RL agent has learned.

6.1 Simulated Students

We model three student classes (strong, medium or weak) based on information provided by human experts about the number of attempts to answer correctly a testing activity and the prerequisite links between KC worked on in the learning plateform. Two rules were defined:

- R1 : a student cannot answer correctly a testing activity on a KC without having first mastered all its prerequisite KC.
- R2 : the probability that a student in the strong class answers correctly a testing activity is much higher than that of a student in the medium class and that of the latter is much higher than that of a student in the weak class.

These two rules were used to generate simulated data (500 simulated students in each class). These simulated students were used to learn a first sequencing policy in order to initialize the Q-table. We notice that these rules are only used to generate simulated data and not to learn to select learning activities.

6.2 Experimental Study

We carried out a first experiment with fifty students who interacted with a programming learning plateform, all of them are high school students starting to learn programming with python. The knowledge domain is composed of the following KCs: "variable","sequential execution", "conditional structure"and "repetition structure". To evaluate the performance of connecting the Q-Learning to the BKT model, we compared our method against a random method of sequencing of learning activities. In the random method, we asked the students to complete learning activities in an order prescribed randomly. We randomly assigned 40 of participants to the Q-Learning sequencing condition (QS), and 10 to the random sequencing condition (RS). The objective of this first study is to answer the following two questions:

1. Is the initialization of the Q-table with simulated students allows real students to achieve efficiently the mastering of all the KC in comparison with the Q-table randomly initialized?
2. Is the time spent by the students interacting with learning plateform in QS condition is less than the time they spent in the RS condition, before mastering all the KCs?

For the first question, we compared the convergence of two sequencing policies: the first policy learned with simulated students from a random-initialized Q-table and the second one learned with real data from the Q-table obtained after the first policy. In addition, we simplified the measure of efficiency as the average of the number of the learning activities proposed to the students. The time having no meaning for the simulated data.

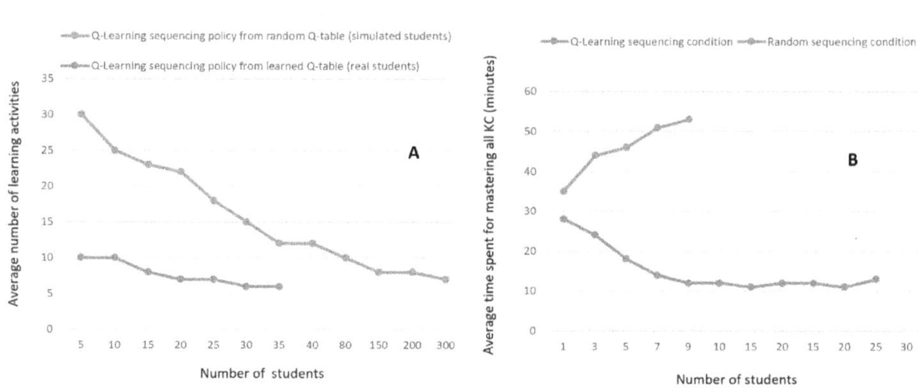

Fig. 2. (A) Average number of learning activities displayed to the students in the case of sequencing policy learned from the Q-table initialized with simulated students and in the case of the sequencing policy learned from the Q-table initialized randomly (B) Average time spent by students interacting with the plateform in the case of random sequencing condition and the case of Q-Learning sequencing condition

6.3 Results

On one hand, Fig. 2A shows the number of learning activities required by the students to master the content. The x axis shows the number of students that have interacted with the plateform. Initially, the Q-Learning needs around 30 learning activities to allow the simulated students to master all KCs. After the first 300 simulated students, the sequencing policy is tuned, obtaining a performance of less than 10 learning activities. However, once the Q-table is initialized thanks to the simulated students, the sequencing policy allows the real students to master all KCs with less than 10 learning activities.

On the other hand, in Fig. 2B we can observe how the students interacting with the Q-Learning sequencing policy spent less time to acquire all KCs than the students of the random condition, even when the Q-Learning is still tuning the sequencing policy. This result shows that the Q-Learning sequencing policy is useful for the students.

7 Conclusion

Personalized sequencing of learning activities is crucial for improving students' learning gains.

This paper establishes connections between the Q-learning and the BKT and show that this mixed approach provides a potential solution.

The obtained preliminary results need to be further tested with other experiments by controlling variables such as the initial level of the students and even by using other individualized BKT models. There are several research directions for future work to provide evidence about the scaling-up of the approach.

References

1. Aleven, V., McLaughlin, E.A., Glenn, R.A., Koedinger, K.R.: Instruction based on adaptive learning technologies. Handb. Res. Learn. Instr. 522–560 (2016)
2. Bassen, J., et al.: Reinforcement learning for the adaptive scheduling of educational activities. In: Proceedings of the 2020 CHI Conference on Human Factors in Computing Systems, pp. 1–12 (2020)
3. Corbett, A.T., Anderson, J.R.: Knowledge tracing: modeling the acquisition of procedural knowledge. User Model. User-Adap. Inter. **4**(4), 253–278 (1994). https://doi.org/10.1007/BF01099821
4. Doroudi, S., Aleven, V., Brunskill, E.: Where's the reward? Int. J. Artif. Intell. Educ. **29**(4), 568–620 (2019). https://doi.org/10.1007/s40593-019-00187-x
5. Efremov, A., Ghosh, A., Singla, A.: Zero-shot learning of hint policy via reinforcement learning and program synthesis. In: EDM (2020)
6. Watkins, C.J.C.H.: Learning from delayed rewards (1989)
7. Yudelson, M.V., Koedinger, K.R., Gordon, G.J.: Individualized Bayesian knowledge tracing models. In: Lane, H.C., Yacef, K., Mostow, J., Pavlik, P. (eds.) AIED 2013. LNCS (LNAI), vol. 7926, pp. 171–180. Springer, Heidelberg (2013). https://doi.org/10.1007/978-3-642-39112-5_18

Author Index

www.ingramconten
Ingram Content Gr
Pitfield, Milton K
UKHW02100505
462611UK0